Southern Africa

Other Travellers' Wildlife Guides

Alaska
Australia: The East
Belize and Northern Guatemala
Brazil: Amazon and Pantanal
Costa Rica
Ecuador and the Galápagos Islands
Hawaii
Peru
Southern Mexico

TRAVELLERS' WILDLIFE GUIDES

Southern Africa

South Africa, Namibia, Botswana, Zimbabwe, Swaziland, Lesotho, and Southern Mozambique

by Bill Branch, Chris Stuart, Tilde Stuart, and Warwick Tarboton

Series Editor: Les Beletsky

Illustrated by:
Randy Babb (Plates 1–20)
Priscilla Barrett (Plates 85–105)
Brian Small (birds)
John Gale (birds)
Norman Arlott (birds)

Photographs by:
Bill Branch (habitats)
Chris and Tilde Stuart (parks, habitats)

DOUBLE STOREY
a juta company

Published 2007 in southern Africa by

DOUBLE STOREY BOOKS
A division of Juta & Co., Ltd
Mercury Crescent, Wetton, Cape Town

Originally published in the United States by Interlink Books, an imprint of Interlink Publishing Group, Ltd., 2007

ISBN-10: 1 919930 67 1
ISBN-13: 978 1 919930 67 1

Cover image: Lioness (*Panthera leo*) © Jeremy Woodhouse, Digital Vision/Getty Images

Printed and bound in China

CONTENTS

PREFACE

This book is aimed at environmentally conscious travellers for whom some of the best parts of any trip are glimpses of wildlife in natural settings; at people who, when speaking of a journey, often remember days and locations by the wildlife they saw: "That was where we watched the elephants," and "That was the day we saw the eagle catch a snake." The purpose of this book is to heighten enjoyment of a trip and enrich wildlife sightings by providing you with information to identify several hundred of the most frequently encountered animals of southern Africa, along with up-to-date information on their natural history, behavior, and conservation. Your skills at recognizing many of the species you see on your travels through the region will be greatly enhanced with this book's color illustrations of 99 species of amphibians and reptiles, 312 birds, and 103 mammals.

The idea to write this book grew out of our own travel experiences and frustrations. First and foremost, we found that we could not find a single book to take along on a trip that would help identify all the types of animals and plants that interested us. There are field guides to individual groups of animals, such as birds or mammals, but their number and weight quickly accumulate until you need an extra suitcase just to carry them all. Thus, the idea: create a single guidebook that travellers could carry to help them identify and learn about the different kinds of animals they are most likely to see. Also, in our experience with guided tours, we've found that guides vary tremendously in their knowledge of nature and wildlife. Many, of course, are fantastic sources of information on animal ecology and behavior. Some, however, know only about certain kinds of animals, such as birds, for instance. Many others, we found, knew precious little about animals, and what information they did tell their groups was often incorrect.

Last, like most ecotravellers, we are concerned about the threats to many species as their natural habitats are damaged or destroyed by people; when we travelled, we wanted current information on the conservation statuses of species we encountered. This book provides the traveller with conservation information on many of the species pictured or discussed in the book.

A few administrative notes: because this book has an international audience, we present measurements in both metric and English system units. The scientific classification of common species by now, you might think, would be pretty much established and unchanging; but you would be wrong. These days, what with molecular methods to compare species, classifications of various groups that were first worked out during the 1800s and early 1900s are undergoing radical changes. Many bird groups, for instance, are being reclassified after comparative studies of their DNA. The research is so new that many biologists are still arguing about the results. We cannot guarantee that all the classifications that we use in the book are absolutely the last word on the subject, or that we have been wholly consistent in the classifications we used. However, for most users of this book, such minor transgressions are probably too esoteric to be of much significance.

We need to acknowledge the help of a number of people in producing this book. First, much of the information we use is gleaned from published sources, and we owe the authors of these books and scientific papers a great deal of credit. Many of their names and titles of their publications are listed in the References and Additional Reading section on page 234. Many of the bird illustrations in this book are reproduced from *Field Guide to the Birds of East Africa*, by Terry Stevenson and John Fanshawe, and published by Christopher Helm, an imprint of A&C Black Publishers; we thank Nigel Redman and Sara Doctors for permission to use these illustrations. Bill Branch would like to thank Aaron Bauer, Don Broadley, and Alan Channing for answering queries readily and helpfully, and Randy Babb, whose love of amphibians and reptiles allowed him to prepare excellent color plates. We wish also to thank the artists who produced the wonderful illustrations: Priscilla Barrett (mammals), Randy Babb (amphibians and reptiles), and Brian Small, John Gale, and Norman Arlott (birds).

Chapter 1

WILDLIFE VIEWING, ECOTOURISM, AND SOUTHERN AFRICA

- *Wildlife Viewing and Ecotourism*
- *How Ecotourism Helps*
- *Ecotourism Ethics*
- *Ecotourism and Southern Africa*

Wildlife Viewing and Ecotourism

People have always travelled. Historical reasons for travelling are many and varied: to find food; to avoid seasonally harsh conditions; to emigrate to new regions in search of more or better farming or hunting lands; to explore; and even, with the advent of leisure time, just for the heck of it (travel for leisure's sake is the definition of tourism). For many people, travelling fulfills some deep need. There's something irreplaceably satisfying about journeying to a new place: the sense of being in completely novel situations and surroundings, seeing things never before encountered, engaging in new and different activities.

During the 1970s and 1980s, however, there arose a new reason to travel, perhaps the first wholly new reason in hundreds of years: with a certain urgency, to see natural habitats and their harbored wildlife before they vanish from the surface of the earth. *Ecotourism*, or ecotravel, is travel to destinations specifically to admire and enjoy wildlife and undeveloped, relatively undisturbed natural areas, as well as indigenous cultures. If you are journeying in southern Africa primarily to view wildlife, consider yourself an ecotourist. The development and increasing popularity of ecotourism is a clear outgrowth of escalating concern for conservation of the world's natural resources and biodiversity (the different types of animals, plants, and other life forms found within a region). Animal species, plant species, and wild habitats are disappearing or deteriorating at an alarming rate, due mainly to the actions of people. Because of the increasing emphasis on the importance of the natural environment by schools at all levels and the media's continuing exposure of environmental issues, people have an enhanced appreciation of the natural world and increased awareness of global environmental problems. They also have the very human desire to want to see undisturbed habitats and wild animals before they are gone, and those with the time and resources are increasingly doing so.

But that's not the entire story. The purpose of ecotourism is actually twofold. Yes, people want to undertake exciting, challenging, educational trips to exotic locales—wet tropical forests, wind-blown deserts, high mountain passes, mid-ocean coral reefs—to enjoy the scenery, the animals, the nearby local cultures. But the second major goal of ecotourism is just as important: The travellers want to help conserve the very places—habitats and wildlife—that they visit. That is, through a portion of their tour cost and spending into the local economy of destination countries—paying for park admissions, engaging local guides, staying at local hotels, eating at local restaurants, using local transportation services, etc.—ecotourists help to preserve natural areas. Ecotourism helps because local people benefit economically by preserving habitats and wildlife for continued use by ecotourists as much or more than they could by "harvesting" the habitats for short-term gain. Put another way, local people can sustain themselves better economically by participating in ecotourism than by, for instance, cutting down rainforests for lumber or hunting animals for meat or the illicit exotic pet trade.

Preservation of some of the world's remaining wild areas is important for a host of reasons. Aside from moral arguments—the acknowledgment that we share the earth with millions of other species and have some obligation not to be the continuing agent of their decline and extinction—increasingly we understand that conservation is in our own best interests. The example most often cited is that botanists and pharmaceutical researchers each year discover another wonder drug or two whose base chemicals come from plants that live, for instance, only in tropical rainforests. Fully one-fourth of all drugs sold in the US come from natural sources—plants and animals. About 50 important drugs now manufactured come from flowering plants found in rainforests, and, based on the number of plants that have yet to be cataloged and screened for their drug potential, researchers estimate that at least 300 more major drugs remain to be discovered. The implication is that if the globe's rainforests are soon destroyed, we will never discover these future wonder drugs, and so will never enjoy their benefits. Also, the developing concept of *biophilia*, if true, dictates that we need to preserve some of the wildness that remains in the world for our own mental health. Biophilia, the word recently coined by Harvard biologist E. O. Wilson, suggests that because people evolved amid rich and constant interactions with other species and in natural habitats, we have deeply ingrained, innate tendencies to affiliate with other species and an actual physical need to experience, at some level, natural habitats. This instinctive, emotional attachment to wildness means that if we eliminate species and habitats, we will harm ourselves because we will lose things essential to our mental well-being.

How Ecotourism Helps

To the traveller, the benefits of ecotourism are substantial (exciting, adventurous trips to stunning wild areas; viewing never-before-seen wildlife); the disadvantages are minor (sometimes less-than-deluxe transportation and accommodations that, to many ecotourists, are actually an essential part of the experience). But what are the real benefits of ecotourism to local economies and to helping preserve habitats and wildlife? In theory, the pluses of ecotourism are considerable:

1. Ecotourism benefits visited sites in a number of ways. Most importantly from the visitor's point of view, ecotourism generates money locally through park admission fees, guide fees, etc., that can be used directly to manage and protect wild areas. Ecotourism allows local people to earn livings from areas they live in or near that have been set aside for ecological protection. Providing jobs and encouraging local participation is essential because people will not want to protect the sites, and may even be hostile toward them, if they formerly used the now protected site (for farming or hunting, for instance) to support themselves but are no longer allowed such use. Finally, most ecotourism destinations are in rural areas, regions that ordinarily would not warrant much attention, much less development money, from central governments for services such as road building and maintenance. But all governments realize that a popular tourist site is a valuable commodity, one that it is smart to cater to and protect.
2. Ecotourism benefits education and research. As both local and foreign people visit wild areas, they learn more about the sites—from books, from guides, from exhibits, and from their own observations. They come away with an enhanced appreciation of nature and ecology, an increased understanding of the need for preservation, and perhaps a greater likelihood to support conservation measures. Also, a percentage of ecotourist dollars are usually funneled into research in ecology and conservation, work that will lead to more and better conservation solutions in the future.
3. Ecotourism can also be an attractive development option for developing countries. Investment costs to develop small, relatively rustic ecotourist facilities are minor compared with the costs involved in trying to develop traditional tourist facilities, such as modern beach resorts. Also, it has been estimated that, at least in some regions, ecotourists spend more per person in the destination countries than any other kind of tourist.

Ecotourism Ethics

A conscientious ecotourist can take several steps to maximize his or her positive impact on visited areas. First and foremost, if travelling with a tour group, is to select an ecologically committed tour company. Basic guidelines for ecotourism have been established by various international conservation organizations. These are a set of ethics that tour operators should follow if they are truly concerned with conservation. Before committing to a tour, travellers wishing to adhere to ecotour ethics should ascertain whether tour operators conform to the guidelines (or at least to some of them) and choose a company accordingly. Some tour operators conspicuously trumpet their ecotour credentials and commitments in their brochures and sales pitches. A large, glossy brochure that fails to mention how a company fulfills some of the ecotour ethics may indicate that an operator is not especially environmentally concerned. Resorts, lodges, and travel agencies that specialize in ecotourism likewise can be evaluated for their dedication to eco-ethics. Some travel guide books that list tour companies provide such ratings. The International Ecotourism Society, an organization of ecotourism professionals, may also provide helpful information (US tel: 202-347-9203; e-mail: ecomail@ecotourism.org; www.ecotourism.org).

Basic ecotour guidelines, as put forth by the United Nations Environmental Programme (UNEP), the International Union for Conservation of Nature (IUCN), and the World Resources Institute (WRI), are that tours and tour operators should:

1 Provide significant benefits for local residents and involve local communities in tour planning and implementation.
2 Contribute to the sustainable management of natural resources.
3 Incorporate environmental education for tourists and residents.
4 Manage tours to minimize negative impacts on the environment and local culture.

For example, tour companies could:

1 Make contributions to the parks or areas visited; support or sponsor small, local environmental projects.
2 Provide employment to local residents as tour assistants, local guides, or local naturalists.
3 Whenever possible, use local products, transportation, food, and locally owned lodging and other services.
4 Keep tour groups small to minimize negative impacts on visited sites; educate ecotourists about local cultures as well as habitats and wildlife.
5 When possible, cooperate with researchers. For instance, Costa Rican researchers are now making good use of the elevated forest canopy walkways in tropical forests that several ecotourism facility operators have erected on their properties for the enjoyment and education of their guests.

Committed ecotourists can also adhere to the ecotourism ethic by patronizing lodges and tours operated by local people, by disturbing habitats and wildlife as little as possible, by staying on trails, by being informed about the historical and present conservation concerns of destination countries, by respecting local cultures and rules, by declining to buy souvenirs made from threatened plants or animals, and even by actions as simple as picking up litter on trails.

Ecotourism and Southern Africa

"Rainbow Nation" is the advertising slogan for the multitude of cultures, peoples, and sights that comprise southern Africa. Despite the hype, it is surprisingly accurate; the biological diversity, cultural richness, and historical complexity of the region all combine to make it a special holiday destination. Since the stunning resolution of political strife in the region, ecotourism in southern Africa has grown in leaps and bounds. In South Africa alone, the tourist industry is expected to generate US$30 billion by 2010 and in the process create 500,000 new jobs. Even if these levels are only partly acheived, ecotourism will play an immense role in protecting wildlife in this region while also improving the lives of many tribal people.

As political normality has returned, the South African government has strengthened its relationships with neighboring countries and with international conservation organizations. One aspect has been the declaration of the first transfrontier conservation area (TFCA) in the subcontinent. The 38,000 sq km (14,700 sq mi) Kgalagadi Transfrontier Park (p. 24) consolidates the management of two adjacent national parks—Gemsbok National Park in Botswana and Kalahari Gemsbok National Park in South Africa—into a single ecological unit. A number of other TFCAs are in development, the most exciting of which is the proposed Gaza/Kruger/Gona-re-zhou TFCA. Mozambique, South Africa, and Zimbabwe have agreed to support the establishment of this unit, which will be one of the largest conservation areas in the world, covering an area of over 95,000 sq km (36,700 sq mi). It has the potential to become one of Africa's premier ecotourism destinations.

South Africa has a number of recently proclaimed UNESCO World Heritage Sites (WHS). The Sterkfontein, Swartkrans and Environs WHS may be unfamiliar by name, but nearly half of the world's hominid fossil remains have been recovered from its sinkholes and dolomite caves. Along with Olduvai Gorge in the East African Rift Valley, it is one of the most important archaeological sites for the study of early human evolution. It is also the most accessible, only an easy 40-minute drive from Johannesburg. Of interest for its more recent human history, Robben Island in Table Bay is another recently proclaimed WHS. Finally, the Greater St. Lucia Wetland Park is a WHS that consolidates a number of protected areas in Maputaland (the northeastern corner of Kwazulu-Natal), bordered in the north by Mozambique and in the west by Swaziland. At its center is St. Lucia, the biggest natural estuarine system in Africa and also a Ramsar Site (a Wetland of International Importance). It also protects Africa's southernmost coral reefs, where a small population of coelacanths, "living fossil" fish, have recently been discovered.

Southern Africa, as covered in this book, encompasses a number of countries: South Africa, the gateway to the region, and three countries to its north: Namibia, Botswana, and Zimbabwe. It also includes the smaller kingdoms of Lesotho and Swaziland (which are all or mostly enclosed within South Africa) and the southern half of Mozambique. (Mozambique is not emphasized in the book's text, but the wildlife described and illustrated in the book ranges into this country.) The region includes extensive areas of temperate forests, arid woodlands, moist savannahs, higher-elevation grasslands, floodplains, and deserts (see Chapter 2). Currently, some of the main wildlife viewing destinations for ecotourists are (described in detail in Chapter 3):

> In South Africa: Kruger National Park and adjacent Kwazulu-Natal Province, with its many wildlife-filled parks, such as Hluhluwe-Umfolozi Park; Western Cape Province, with Table Mountain and the adjacent mountains around Cape Town and its strongly promoted "Garden Route" along the country's southern shoreline; and the Namaqualand region in the northwest corner of Northern Cape Province, adjacent to Namibia and Botswana, with its remote Kalahari Gemsbok National Park.
>
> In Botswana: The Okavango Delta ("Okavango Swamp"), a large wetland area teeming with wildlife in the country's north; Chobe National Park, a huge, accessible, game-rich reserve in the country's north; and the Kalahari Desert in southwestern Botswana, with its game reserves and national parks.
>
> In Namibia: Etosha National Park, with grasslands and woodlands, for wildlife viewing and bush-walking; Sousos Vlei, with the world's highest

desert dunes; and Namib-Naukluft Park, with vast expanses of desert and semi-desert.

In Zimbabwe: Wonderful scenery at Victoria Falls and fantastic wildlife viewing at such reserves as Hwange National Park.

Vertebrate biodiversity in southern Africa includes about 150 amphibian species (all frogs), more than 500 reptiles (including about 300 lizards and 150 snakes), 900 birds, and about 340 mammals.

Now with some information on ecotourism in hand, we can move on to discuss in detail the region under consideration, including its habitats and parks, in the next two chapters.

Chapter 2

SOUTHERN AFRICA: CLIMATE, GEOGRAPHY, HABITATS

by Bill Branch

- *Introduction*
- *Climate*
- *Geography*
- *Habitats*
  - *Evergreen Forest*
  - *Deciduous Woodland and Savannah*
  - *Shrubland*
  - *Grassland*
  - *Desert and Near-desert*
  - *Wetlands*
  - *Marine*

Introduction

The southern African subcontinent is large, more than 3.5 million sq km (1.35 million sq mi) in extent and ten times larger than Germany. It is bounded to the north by the Cunene and Zambezi Rivers and includes the countries of South Africa, Lesotho, Swaziland, Botswana, Namibia, Zimbabwe, and the southern part of Mozambique (Map 1, p. 9). Covering less than 1.7% of the world's land surface, it has more than its fair share of plant and animal life. About 2.7% of the world's amphibian species, 5.1% of the snakes, 6.8% of the lizards, 34.1% of the land tortoises, 9.6% of the birds, and 7.1% of the mammals occur in the subcontinent. This glorious faunal extravagance is overshadowed, however, by the botanical wonder of the southern and western Cape (the "Cape" refers to the southernmost part of the subcontinent). One of only six Botanical Kingdoms in the world, the Cape Floral Kingdom crams more plant diversity into only 90,000 sq km (35,000 sq mi) than the whole of the northern Boreal Forest Kingdom of Eurasia and North America, which covers nearly 50 million sq km (19.3 million sq mi). Although the Cape Floral Kingdom comprises only 0.3% of Africa, it contains nearly 25% of all African plants (and that includes the riches of the Central African rainforests). More than 8,600 plant species are found in the region, of which 5,800 (67%) are endemic. A visit to the Cape Peninsula National Park puts these dry figures into context. This unique park stretches from Table Mountain 60 km (95 mi) south to Cape Point and combines a network of conserved areas with urban sprawl. It is home to 2,285 plant species, more than the whole of the British Isles. Ninety of these are endemic just to the park.

The biological exuberance of southern Africa is a reflection of the diverse habitats present, and these are best understood in terms of the climate and geography of the region. The structure of plant communities is determined by climate and soil characteristics. Some animals, particularly birds and reptiles, are confined to habitats that are defined by their physical characteristics, such as rock outcrops and water bodies. The distribution of most animals, however, is mainly determined by vegetation. For some species, particularly insects, their association with a specific plant is fundamental; that is, they live in association with a particular plant species and only that species. Most other species, though, are adapted to a vegetation type, e.g., forest or grassland, regardless of the particular plant species that compose it. Past climate, through its influence on vegetation and animal distributions, has played an important role in the evolution of biodiversity in the subcontinent. Global climatic fluctuations during the Ice Age caused mass extinctions in Europe and North America as ice fields expanded and retreated. However, these same climatic cycles in southern Africa did not reduce biodiversity, but rather promoted it. Here the climatic effects were less catastrophic, and habitats in the subcontinent were either fragmented or displaced during alternating wet and dry periods. These cyclic changes promoted the isolation of populations, which is an important phase in the evolution of new species.

Climate

Southern Africa has a temperate to subtropical climate, with wide regional and seasonal contrasts in rainfall and temperature. The rainfall is strongly influenced by the cold Atlantic Ocean (Benguela) and warm Indian Ocean (Agulhas) currents that sweep up and down the west and east coasts, respectively. The annual rainfall increases considerably in the north and east, whereas the western coast and adjacent regions are drier. Rainfall is largely dependent on the prevailing winds, which in summer sweep counterclockwise across the continent, carrying moist air from the Indian Ocean, in the form of thunderstorms, across the eastern regions. Because of the high altitude of the interior, little rain remains to fall in the west. In winter the winds bring rain to the western coast, and the rest of the country is dry. The Cape of Good Hope (at the southern tip of Africa) sits at latitude 34°S, equivalent in latitude to the North African coast in the Northern Hemisphere, and the hot, dry summers and wet, cold winters of the southern Cape give this region a Mediterranean climate.

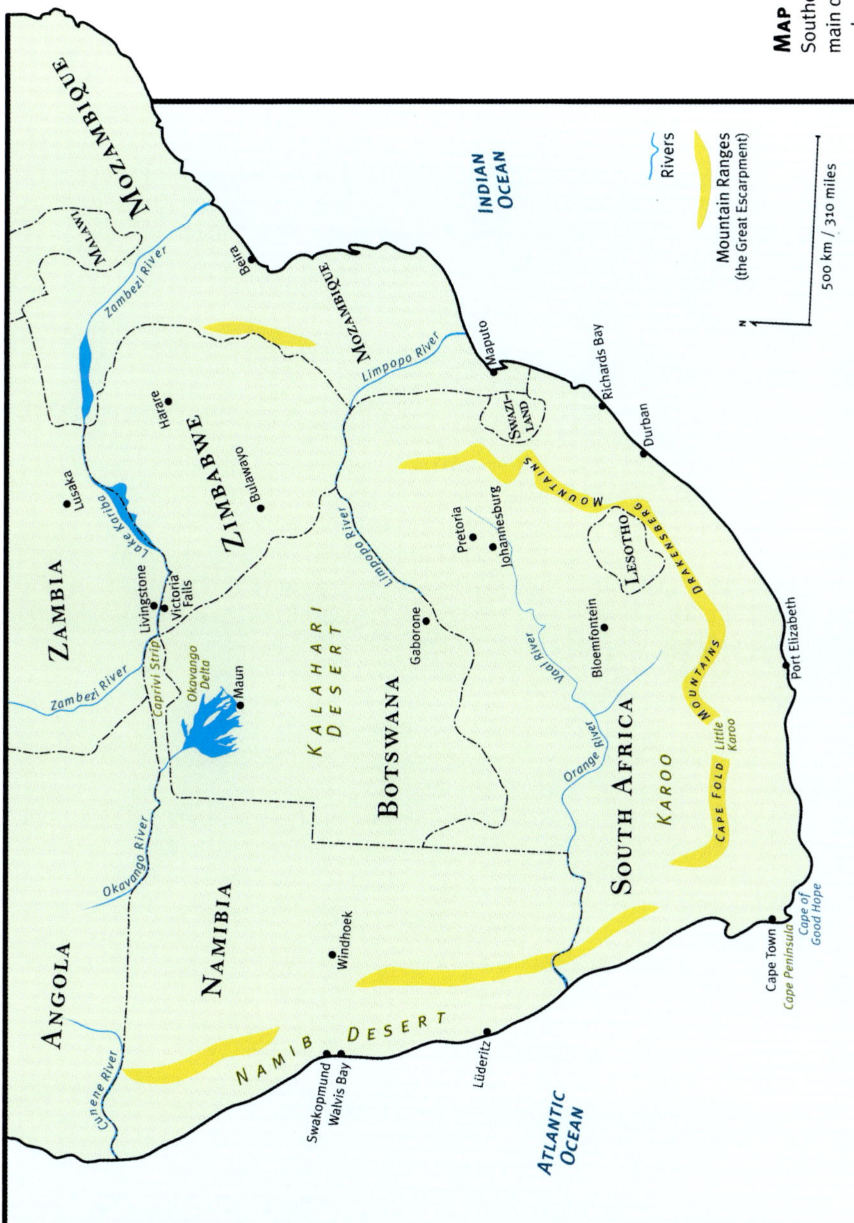

Map 1. Southern Africa, showing main cities, towns, rivers, and mountain ranges.

Southern African temperatures are affected by both the latitudinal position (between 17°S and nearly 35°S) of the region and the high altitude (1,000 to 2,000 m, 3,300 to 6,600 ft) of much of its interior. The cold Benguela Current sweeping up the western coast keeps the air temperatures cool and causes local fogs that sweep inland. Summer temperatures are highest in the central Kalahari and surrounding regions, becoming less intense with altitude on the Highveld (highland areas of the Central Plateau; see below) of the northern provinces and Free State, and the Zimbabwean and Namibian plateaus. The coolest areas at this time are the high mountains of the eastern escarpment and the southwestern Cape. Winters are mild along the eastern coast (the Mozambique Plain and adjacent lowveld of Mpumalanga, and the Limpopo and Zambezi River valleys). The coldest winter regions are the Highveld and the mountains of the Great Escarpment, which regularly have night frosts and where (with the exception of the Namibian escarpment) heavy snowfalls are frequent. The rest of the region has warm, sometimes pleasantly sunny, winter days with cool, occasionally cold, nights.

Geography

The topography of southern Africa can be likened to an upside-down soup bowl, with a shallow depression occupying the center of the subcontinent and the sides falling away steeply to a low-lying coastal margin of variable width. The bowl is tilted so that the eastern edge is slightly higher than in the west. The interior forms the Central Plateau, which ranges in height from 900 m (2,950 ft) in the Kalahari depression to more than 3,482 m (11,420 ft) in the Lesotho mountains. It is bounded by the Great Escarpment, which is composed of a number of distinct and imposing mountain ranges. As the Drakensberg range of Kwazulu-Natal and Mpumalanga, it forms a sheer and continuous edge, but elsewhere it is broken into a horseshoe of isolated highlands. To the north, it extends as the Zimbabwe Eastern Highlands, including Inyanga and the Chimanimani Mountains. In the Cape, it forms the isolated mountains of the Amatolas, Sneeuberg, Nuweveldberg, and Roggeveldberg, and in Namibia it exists as the Aus highlands. In the east, it receives high rainfall.

The Cape Fold Mountains form a parallel series of metamorphosed sandstone peaks running east–west from Port Elizabeth to Cape Town. Deformed and folded during a period of mountain-building nearly 300 million years ago, the sandstone has subsequently weathered to form rugged gorges and spectacular rock forms. They are responsible for the Cape's high winter rainfall as well as its scenic grandeur. Due to their altitude (to 2,325 m, 7,625 ft, elevation), bisected topography, and Mediterranean climate (cold, wet winters and hot, dry summers) they contain a mosaic of habitats. The southern slopes and summits receive higher rainfall and have characteristic fauna and flora that are often strikingly different from that inhabiting the intervening, semi-dry valleys. The typical vegetation, generally termed *fynbos* (although there are a number of subdivisions), consists of a low, fire-adapted scrub that generally lacks trees (except on the well-watered southern slopes) and is tolerant of the nutrient-poor, acidic soils. Due to the high rainfall, the mountains were frequently used as a refuge for hunting Bushmen, whose paintings can still be found in the numerous caves and rock shelters.

The Kalahari Basin lies in the middle of the Central Plateau. It is a huge inland drainage basin covered with deep, old sand. It extended much further north and east in past dry periods. This "place of great dryness," as it is known in the Hottentot language, is sometimes called a desert, but no part of the Kalahari receives less than 100 mm (4 in) of rain a year. The southern region is dry and cold in winter. The southern part, including the Kgalagadi Transfrontier Park (p. 27), is very dry and consists of ancient, long sand dunes. The central Kalahari is flat and has a number of shallow basins that may periodically flood, including the extensive pans of the Etosha and Makarikari depressions. Between these pans run the Okavango and Chobe Rivers, which bring water south from the Angolan highlands. This water never reaches the sea; it drains into the deep sands, forming the lush, seasonal wetlands of the Okavango Swamp and the Savuti and Linyanti floodplains.

A true desert, the Namib, runs along the whole coast of Namibia. It rarely extends more than 120 km (75 mi) inland. Shifting sands are restricted to the coastal region, with two main dune fields lying north and south of Swakopmund. Much of the inner Namib consists of hard gravel plains broken by rugged, barren mountains. The Namib is an ancient desert, perhaps the oldest in the world. Its true age is the subject of some controversy. Some models claim it extends back to the end of the Cretaceous period, 65 million years ago. Recent studies suggested cyclic dry phases interrupted by semi-dry conditions. The formation of the modern Namib Desert started in the Late Miocene, 10 to 7 million years ago, with the establishment of the Benguela Current. This cold-water upwelling holds the key to the Namib's diversity. On more than 100 days a year it generates advective fog that, depending upon local topography and conditions, may travel up to 100 km (60 mi) inland. There the fog condenses, bringing regular and life-sustaining moisture on which so many of the unique Namib fauna and flora depend.

The Great Karoo forms the southern section of the Central Plateau. It is an area of low rainfall, although flash floods can occur with devastating effect. The soils are poor, shallow, and stony, with a stunted, woody, scrub vegetation. Erosion has exposed old rocks, in which plentiful fossils of early reptiles, the ancestors of mammals and dinosaurs, are found. Most of the Karoo lies above the Great Escarpment, but the southern plain falls below it, in the rain shadow of the Cape Fold Mountains, within which the Little Karoo lies as an isolated pocket. The Little Karoo is famous for the unique succulent plants that nestle in large numbers among the quartzite pebbles in the valley bottom. Much of its eastern region is now more famous for its large ostrich farms.

Along its western edge the Karoo merges into Namaqualand, which straddles the lower Orange River. The region includes the Richtersveld, a small area of rugged, mineral-rich mountains that nestles between Great and Little Namaqualand (which sit north and south of the Orange River, respectively). It is dry, sometimes devastatingly so, but if good rains fall in February and March, followed by sustaining showers in June–July, then great stretches of the land burst into life in a blaze of bright flowers. For a few weeks from August to September Namaqualand hosts a brief floral extravaganza that is unequaled anywhere else in the world.

The eastern part of the Central Plateau, lying inland from the highest part of the Great Escarpment, is an area of high-altitude grassland on deep soil. It forms the Highveld of the Free State and Gauteng, and experiences irregular, often violent summer rains and cold, dry winters. There has been extensive agricultural and urban development in this region. North of Johannesburg the land gradually decreases in height and becomes progressively more wooded as it drops into the lowveld of the Limpopo River valley. Granite intrusions form characteristic isolated smooth mountains or hills ("inselbergs") among scattered low rock outcrops ("koppies"). To the east, the Limpopo River runs through the Mozambique Plain to the Indian Ocean. The flat plain is extensively covered with sand carried from the Kalahari by the Limpopo River and its tributaries. The mighty Zambezi River forms the northern boundary of the subcontinent. Along with the Okavango River, it was once a mere northern tributary of the Limpopo River. Geological uplift of land along the northern edge of the Central Plateau separated the Zambezi from the Limpopo, and it now makes its own way to the Indian Ocean. No such route was found by the Okavango River, which drains into the landlocked delta of the Okavango Swamp. The vegetation of the Mozambique Plain is varied, with dry woodland occurring in areas of seasonal rainfall and good drainage. In the low-lying coastal strip, swamp and mangrove forests occur. Despite relatively temperate latitudes, the eastern coastal regions have a subtropical flavor. This is due to the ameliorating effect of the warm Aghulas Current, which originates between Madagascar and the African mainland and sweeps down the eastern coast of Mozambique to the Cape. The distribution of many tropical trees, birds, reptiles, amphibians, and other organisms in this area shows a characteristic southern extension into the subcontinent.

Habitats

The varied landforms of the subcontinent are covered in a complex mosaic of habitats. These result from the interplay of climate, topography, and soils. Detailed studies reveal 70 different vegetation types, but these may be simplified into a number of major categories, called *biomes*, that have numerous subdivisions. The complexity of landforms and vegetation types is best explored in the Eastern Cape, where components of many of these biomes clash in glorious faunal and floral diversity.

Evergreen Forest

Forest vegetation is restricted to high rainfall regions and constitutes less than 1% of southern Africa. True tropical rainforest does not occur in the region. There are, however, several other types of natural forest. They only develop in frost-free areas and where they are protected from fire. *Afromontane forest* is found in isolated pockets along the southern and eastern mountain chains. It consists of tall, thick, cool forest, with the dominant trees including Yellowwood (*Podocarpus* sp.) and Stinkwood (*Ocotea bullata*), and with tree ferns (*Alsophila* spp.) in the open understory. Epiphytes (plants that grow on other plants, such as orchids) may be abundant, but lianas (vines) are rare. This forest type grows down to sea level in the southern Cape (for example, at Tsitsikamma National Park). To the north, it exists as a scattered archipelago of isolated forests associated with moist gorges along the Great Escarpment (for instance, Woodbush Forest, east of Pietersburg; Habitat Photo 1). These isolated pockets were more extensive and contiguous during cooler glacial periods but have contracted over the last 16,000 years as the climate has warmed. They have suffered further in the last 200 years as many remnants have been felled for timber and replaced with pine and eucalyptus plantations. *Coastal forest* (Habitat Photo 3) grows on dunes or lowlands along the Indian Ocean coastal belt (e.g., Dukuduku Forest in Maputaland). It has a low (20 to 35 m, 65 to 115 ft) closed canopy with a fairly dense understory of shrubs and lianas. Epiphytes are present, but not abundant. The False White Ash (*Pseudobersama mossambicensis*) is a characteristic tree, and the banana-like Natal Strelitzia (*Strelitzia nicola*) may form dense stands on the edges of coastal forest in the Eastern Cape and Kwazulu-Natal. True coastal and dune forest is now heavily fragmented due to years of human settlement. However, large tracts are preserved in many of the Natal game reserves, which form a refuge for large mammals, particularly the White Rhino. *Riparian forest* (Habitat Photo 2) grows in patches along the eastern river valleys and along drainage lines in the Mozambique Plain. It has a more varied tree composition, lacking an extensive closed canopy. The linear forest strips serve as refugia and migratory routes for forest species.

Deciduous Woodland and Savannah

Wooded vegetation types cover most of the northern and eastern parts of the subcontinent. It is the dominant vegetation type of northern Namibia and Botswana, all of Zimbabwe and southern Mozambique, and of northern and east coastal South Africa. Tree density varies from sparse (savannah) to relatively dense (woodland), but does not form the closed canopy of forest. The northern savannahs are more or less continuous with those of East Africa, and many animals are common to both regions. Two principal savannah woodland divisions occur, both with numerous subdivisions. The distributions of both are complex, often forming mosaics that are dependent upon local conditions of soil quality and drainage.

Arid savannahs usually occur on richer, heavier, alluvial soils in the hotter, drier valleys and lowlands, particularly in the drier western regions that receive less than 650 mm (26 in) of rain a year (Habitat Photos 4, 6). The nutritive value of arid savannah is high, and in protected areas it supports large concentrations of ungulates. There are a number of subdivisions: *Knobthorn* (*Acacia nigrescens*) *woodland* (also called *bushveld*) occurs on basalt soils in the eastern regions. *Open acacia woodland* (also called *sandveld*) is dominated by a variety of thorny Acacias and covers the Kalahari sands of southern and central Botswana, extending into northern Namibia. Extensive *mopane woodland* (Habitat Photo 5) occurs in the Limpopo, Zambezi, and Cunene valleys. Mopane woodland is dominated by *Colophosperum mopane*, a broad-leaved tree that is deciduous in winter. It may form tall, open woodland. Mopane leaves hang down, and during the day the leaflets move closer together. The tree thus casts little shade and the understory is hot with few grasses. The bizarre "upside-down" Baobab tree (*Adansonia digitata*) is common in mopane woodland. The term *thornveld* is used for arid savannah consisting of small trees with thorny canopies, dominated by Acacias, that often grow in sandy soils with sparse grass cover.

Moist savannahs (Habitat Photo 7) occur typically on the higher plateaus of northern Namibia, Botswana, Zimbabwe, Mozambique, and the North-West Province of South Africa, with rainfall of 500 to 1,100 mm (20 to 43 in) per year. The soils are usually poor in nutrients and occasionally waterlogged during the extended rainy season. There are numerous subdivisions: As *miombo woodland* it is dominated by broad-leaved *Brachystegia* sp. and extends in a wide belt across the sandy soils of the Mozambique Plain, with a secondary belt of more open woodland covering much of Zimbabwe, the Caprivi Strip, and northern Botswana. Miombo is relatively tall and dense, and may approach a closed canopy. However, it is impacted by past and present slash-and-burn agriculture and is now largely replaced with secondary wooded grassland and cultivation. It is nutrient poor, supporting relatively few ungulates, and fire from early summer lightning is a regular phenomenon. In the east, where moist savannah is known as the East Coast Littoral, it forms a mosaic of woodland with coastal grasslands, mangroves, swamps, and dune forests that extends in various forms along the coast as far south as East London. On the sandy soils of the Mozambique Plain and Okavango Delta it is mixed with coastal grasslands and hyphene palms to form an open *palm savannah* (Habitat Photo 8). From Kwazulu-Natal southwards, the terrain is more rugged and the belt may narrow to as little as 8 km (5 mi). Complex soil types occur. Rainfall is moderately high and falls mainly in summer, but there is no obvious dry season. At the extreme southern end, moist savannah is replaced with *mesic succulent thicket* (Habitat Photo 9), a succulent, moist thicket that is usually dense and impenetrable but is of high nutritive value. It is dominated with thorny shrubs, trees, succulents, and creepers, mainly in hot, dry valleys. Large succulent-leaved euphorbias and aloes are conspicuous. In protected areas, such as the Addo Elephant National Park, it may support populations of large mammals. Game ranching, particularly of Kudu, is extensive.

Shrubland

Low rainfall areas in the southern and western parts of the subcontinent are covered with short, shrubby vegetation in which trees and grasses are rare or localized. Two groups occur, both with subdivisions.

Fynbos is a local name (fijnbosch, meaning "fine-leaved") for an evergreen heathland that is common in Mediterranean climates throughout the world (Habitat Photos 10, 11). It is similar to chaparral in California, maquis and garrigue in the Mediterranean region, matorral in Chile, and kwongan in western Australia. It is a low, woody shrubland that grows on poor, acidic, rocky soils. It occurs in a narrow strip along the southwestern and southern Cape from Port Elizabeth to the Cedarberg. Three plant families characterize fynbos, but bulbs (geophytes) of lilies and orchids are abundant in the wetter parts. The Ericaceae include the few heather species of European moorlands and more than 600 species in South Africa. They are low shrubs with hard, small leaves and large clumps of colorful, tubular flowers that are rich in nectar. The Proteaceae include the tallest shrubs in fynbos. They are mostly 1 to 3 m (3 to 10 ft) in height and have large, leathery leaves and large, spectacular flowers that are harvested for the dried or cut flower trade. The grass-like Restionaceae include more than 300 species, some of which grow tall and form dense clumps. They are harvested for thatch.

The climate of fynbos is variable. Rainfall ranges from about 300 to 3,000 mm (12 to 120 in) per year and falls mainly in winter in the west, but peaks in the east with spring and autumn. Summer temperatures may exceed 38°C (100°F), but frosts are rare except in high mountain valleys. Snow falls frequently on the high mountains but rarely persists. The vegetation has a tough texture, low nutritive content, and is rich in tannins and other components that make it unpalatable. It therefore supports few large mammals, but fynbos does have distinctive bird fauna and numerous endemic frogs. Subdivisions include *mountain fynbos* (Habitat Photo 12) on quartzitic and leached granitic soils and *coastal fynbos* on recent coastal deposits. Each is adapted to local conditions, and fynbos communities in the east may also become grassy. Closely related to fynbos is *renosterveld*, in which the restiod (plants of family Restionaceae) component of fynbos has been replaced by grass. It also has fewer proteas and grows on more fertile, clay-rich soils. It takes its name from the renosterbos, a shrubby member of the daisy family (Asteraceae). "Renoster" is the Afrikaans name for rhinoceros, but why it should be applied to this small shrub is a mystery. Less than 1% of renosterveld remains, the rest having been ploughed under for wheat and vineyards.

The *Karoo* is a semi-desert shrubland that covers the central and western Cape, extending into southern Namibia (Habitat Photos 13, 14). The word "karoo" is derived from a Khoi-khoi word meaning "dry." Rain falls in summer and rarely exceeds 250 mm (10 in). The soils are poor, shallow, and rocky, and support only a sparse, dwarf, woody shrubland that forms the *Nama Karoo* biome. The plants are hardy, drought-resistant, and fine-leaved. Succulents are small, usually inconspicuous, and localized. Trees, such as *Acacia karroo*, are mainly restricted to watercourses. Such trees can form extensive stands in southeastern Karoo and along the Orange River. Grass becomes taller and more common from west to east and can be extensive following good seasonal rains, particularly on the summits of the escarpment mountains and in the north, where it merges into the dry savannah of the Kalahari. The climate is extreme. Severe frost and snow on the higher mountains is common in winter, and contrasts with high air and soil temperatures and high levels of sunshine in the summer. Wide rocky plains, with scattered flat-topped "koppies," dominate the topography of the central and southern regions. The northern region is a featureless rolling plain covered by gravel and sand. However, the general monotony of the Karoo landscape hides a rich biodiversity and ecological complexity. The grasses and shrubs are often palatable and highly nutritious, and the Karoo once supported large numbers of migratory ungulates. It is now extensively grazed for sheep farming, but severe erosion and overgrazing have reduced its ability to support livestock.

In the winter rainfall western regions, the Nama Karoo is replaced by the Succulent Karoo (Habitat Photos 16, 17, 18). It occurs on the sandy coastal plain of Namaqualand, extending in the rain shadow valleys behind the Cedarberg (the Tanquwa Karoo) and within the Cape Fold Mountains (the Little Karoo; Habitat Photo 15). Succulent plants are common and are adapted to the hot, dry summers. Indeed, 38% of the world's succulent flora occurs in South Africa, most of this in Namaqualand and the Karoo. "Vygies" are particularly common. They belong to family Mesembryanthemaceae, a group of leaf-succulents comprising more than 2,000 species. Numerous other succulents, including crassulas (Crassulaceae), euphorbias (Euphorbiaceae), stapeliads (Asclepiadaceae), aloes, and haworthias (Asphodelaceae) occur. Many of these have very restricted distributions and more than 1,000 species are classified as rare or endangered. Other botanical highlights are the rich bulb flora and the spectacular displays of spring annuals, particularly Namaqualand daisies. Desert grasses, especially *Stipagrostris* species, predominate in the northern regions and support low level sheep and goat farming.

Grassland

Grassland is defined as areas where woody plants are rare or absent and where the vegetation is dominated by grasses (Poaecae) or plants of grassy appearance, such as sedges (Cyperaceae) and rushes (Juncaceae). They are maintained largely by a combination of relatively high summer rainfall, frequent fires, frost, and grazing, which preclude the development of shrubs and trees. Much of the region's grassland has been transformed by crop farming (particularly maize), afforestation, and dense human settlement (Habitat Photo 24). Various forms of grassland occur in southern Africa. The most extensive occurs on the flat to gently rolling upland plateau, from 1,200 to 2,100 m (3,900 to 6,900 ft), that covers the Highveld of Gauteng, Free State and the northeastern Cape. Rainfall ranges from 250 to 500 mm (10 to 20 in) per year and occurs mainly in summer. Fire is a recurrent event caused by lightning every two to four years. Montane grassland (Habitat Photos 22, 23) occurs at altitudes above 1,850 m (6,050 ft), mainly in Lesotho and the Eastern Cape. Although rainfall is high, this is partially negated by the severe frosts that may occur, even during the summer months. Coastal grasslands, interspersed with bush clumps and dune thicket, are common on exposed ancient dunes along the eastern coast. Large areas of thicket and moist savannah along the eastern coastal regions have been extensively cleared for cattle pasture. In traditional tribal areas, including the Transkei and the Natal Midlands, grassland is common on hilltops and slopes. Much has been generated by a long history of human settlement, with frequent fire, overgrazing, and bush clearance. Large swathes of mesic succulent thicket in the Port Elizabeth–Grahamstown region has been mechanically cleared within the last 50 years to form artificial pasture, often maintained by irrigation, for high-intensity dairy farming.

Desert and Near-desert

True *desert* occurs as a narrow strip along the western coast. The Namib is an ancient desert composed of shifting sand dunes along the coastal strip and hard gravel plains inland. Plant cover is sparse, with scattered grass and specialized succulent plants on the sand and gravel plains, including the unique *Welwitschia mirabilis* (Habitat Photos 19, 20). Stunted acacia trees (Habitat Photo 21) are mainly restricted to the dry river courses. It is unusual for more than 100 mm (4 in) of rain to fall in a year, and droughts lasting 4 to 5 years may occur. Following good rains, however, extensive fields of annual desert grasses and herbs appear. The offshore Benguela Current is responsible for the cold, moisture-laden fogs that may extend up to 100 km (60 mi) inland. These are essential for the survival of many of the Namib Desert's unique fauna and also support a thick, succulent flora on the summits of the isolated rocky mountains. Dense and diverse lichen fields may occur in the coastal fog belt. Areas adjacent to the Namib Desert may also experience protracted droughts. In Damaraland and the Kaokoveld, inland of the Namib's northern dunefield, near-desert conditions prevail. The same occurs in the Richtersveld, which lies in a bight of the lower Orange River in northwestern Namaqualand. It comprises chiseled peaks, steep gorges, and shiny quartzitic plains, and in places is the only true desert in South Africa.

Wetlands

Southern Africa is largely arid and *wetlands* form only a small proportion of the area. They do, however, occur in a wide variety of types. Few major rivers drain to the Atlantic Ocean from the western dry regions of the subcontinent. They include only the Cunene (Habitat Photo 26) and Orange Rivers, which border Namibia to the north and south, respectively. The waters of the latter arise in the grasslands of the Highveld and the mountains of Lesotho, 1,950 km (1,200 mi) to the east. There are no other permanent rivers along the rest of the Atlantic coast of Namibia. The east is wetter and numerous small rivers drain the escarpment mountains. Most flow directly to the sea and have small catchments. In dry periods they may separate into a series of pools. The two major eastern rivers are Rudyard Kipling's "great, grey-green, greasy Limpopo" and Livingstone's mighty Zambezi, which bracket Zimbabwe to the south and north.

The interior of southern Africa is almost devoid of natural freshwater lakes; the few examples include Lake Funduzi in the far northeast of South Africa, Lake Oponono in northern Namibia, and Lake Liambezi in the eastern Caprivi Strip. All other large, static water bodies are either pans or man-made impoundments (Habitat Photo 27). Most freshwater lakes occur in coastal regions. *Pans* have closed drainage systems. Water flows in from a small catchment to a natural hollow and then evaporates, forming brackish water or a salt crust. Water depth is shallow (less than 3 m, 10 ft) and usually ephemeral. They are very flat and can be extensive. Due to their isolation and size, the pans of Etosha (Namibia) and Makgadigadi (eastern Botswana) form critically important breeding sites for the Greater and Lesser Flamingo. The *panveld* of southern Africa occurs on the Central Plateau, especially in the northern Nama-Karoo and southern Kalahari. Pans can be found elsewhere, particularly on the poorly drained "black cotton" soils of mopane woodland in the northern Kalahari. In high rainfall regions, pans can become almost semi-permanent and approach lakes in their ecological functioning.

Swamps, marshes, floodplains, vleis, and dambos form a series of wetlands characterized by static or slow-flowing water, and are extensively covered with tall, emergent aquatic plants, particularly rushes and sedges. Floodplains are typically associated with the lower reaches of larger rivers, and are restricted mainly to the Limpopo and Zambezi Rivers. Following tectonic uplifts in the interior, floodplains may occur, for example, in the Okavango Delta, Linyanti and Chobe floodplains in northern Botswana, and the Nylsveli floodplains in South Africa. The terms "vlei" and "dambo" are used in South Africa and Zimbabwe, respectively, to describe small marshy depressions. They are mostly ephemeral and rarely more than a few square kilometers in extent. The Okavango Delta (Habitat Photo 25), with an area of 16,000 sq km (6,200 sq mi), is probably the single most important wetland in southern Africa. The attractive, yellow-barked Fever Tree (*Acacia xanthophloea*) likes seasonally waterlogged soils. The swampy places it favors harbor malaria, hence the association made by early settlers of fever and the presence of this tree.

Marine

The coastline of southern Africa is one of the most varied and beautiful in the world. It stretches for more than 5,500 km (3,400 mi) from Angola in the west to the Zambezi Delta in the east. Habitats within this immense distance range from the inhospitable, desert-backed Skeleton Coast in northern Namibia to the tropical coral reefs and offshore islands of the Bazaruto Archipelago of Mozambique. West of Cape Aghulas, the southernmost tip of Africa, the warm Aghulas Current, sweeping down from the Mozambique Channel, mixes with the cold Benguela Current sweeping up from Antarctic waters. It causes local upwelling that brings nutrient-rich waters to the surface, supporting good fishing grounds. These attract numerous predators, including whales, dolphins, seals, sharks, and game fish. Seabirds are also common, especially in winter, when numerous Antarctic seabirds, including albatrosses, shearwaters, and petrels, are carried north by storm fronts.

More than 50 species of whales and dolphins have been recorded from the coastal waters, although few occur year-round or are commonly observed.

Various coastal landforms occur. Most of the Namibian coastline consists of sandy beaches derived from the adjacent Namib Desert. There are no sea cliffs and few rock platforms. Rivers with permanent mouths form only the northern and southern international boundaries. The coastline is therefore devoid of estuaries, although sand from the Kuiseb River forms an offshore spit protecting Walvis Bay and Sandwich Harbour. Both are Wetlands of International Importance (Ramsar sites), and the latter may be home to more than 200,000 wading birds in summer. Shorebird densities may reach 7,000 birds per sq km (18,000 per sq mi), the highest recorded in the world. The western Cape coast is also sandy, but with rock platforms. In addition to the Orange River Mouth, other important estuaries occur at the mouths of the Olifants and Berg Rivers. An extensive tidal lagoon at Langebaan forms the center of West Coast National Park. The emergence of resistant sandstones and granites in the southwestern Cape allows the appearance of rocky offshore islands (such as Robben Island and Dassen Island), which are used extensively by breeding Cape Fur Seals and numerous seabirds, including penguins, cormorants, and gannets. High sea cliffs also produce a rugged shoreline, with sheltered bays suitable for harbors and calving whales.

The eastern coast is more varied, with sandy beaches and dunefields interspersed with occasional rocky outcrops (Habitat Photo 29). Numerous small estuaries occur, but many rivers have small catchments and the estuaries become closed by sandbars in periods of low rain. Often the mouths of the rivers are shifted by the migration of dunes, mainly from west to east. This is most notable at the Gamtoos and Sundays River mouths in the Eastern Cape. In the Wilderness area (a well-known tourist area on the "Garden Route" along the southern Cape coast, about midway between Cape Town and Port Elizabeth) of the southern Cape, the vegetated coastal dunes cut off the estuaries from the sea, and a number of coastal lakes have formed (Habitat Photo 28). These are mostly saline, except when completely isolated, like Groenvlei. A similar series of coastal lagoons occurs in northern Maputaland, in the St. Lucia and Kosi Bay systems. Mangroves are rare in South African estuaries south of Durban but are more extensive further north, particularly in the large estuaries and most notably the Zambezi River delta. Isolated coral reefs extend as far south as Sodwana in northern Maputaland.

Chapter 3

PARKS, RESERVES, AND GETTING AROUND

by Chris and Tilde Stuart

- *Introduction*
- *South Africa*
    - *Eastern Cape Province (EC)*
    - *KwaZulu-Natal Province, Lesotho, Swaziland (KZN)*
    - *Northern Cape Province (NC)*
    - *Limpopo and North-West Provinces (LNW)*
    - *Western Cape Province (WC)*
- *Namibia (NAM)*
- *Botswana (BOT)*
- *Zimbabwe (ZIM)*

Introduction

Before the arrival of Europeans in southern Africa, the plains of the interior were teeming with mainly migratory game herds. Within 300 years of the arrival of these foreign settlers, however, the dust that had been raised by those millions of hoofs had settled. These migratory herds were a phenomenon of the past. Toward the end of the 19th century, the realization that the wildlife resources were rapidly diminishing resulted in the setting aside of Africa's first conservation areas. These forerunners, all in South Africa, were the now-world-famous Kruger National Park and several others located in KwaZulu-Natal Province. Today there are more than 500 conservation areas located within this book's coverage area. Therefore, we were highly selective in choosing which sites to discuss. We compiled a list based on which parks/reserves had the most to offer the visitor and those which are relatively easy to access. All of the parks and reserves we describe can be reached on paved or fairly good gravel roads with an ordinary sedan. Internal mobility requires a 4x4 vehicle only in the two Botswana parks we mention. Although the parks presented here are all suited to the self-drive option, those of you without African travel experience may prefer to link up with one of the many safari operators. Park locations are shown in Map 2, p. 22–23; numbers following park names below refer to their assigned numbers on the map.

Important contact details for information on, and visits to, the parks and conservation areas are given below:

South Africa

- (US): South African Tourism Board, 747 Third Avenue, 20th Floor, New York, NY 10017; tel: 212-838-8841.
- National Parks, P.O. Box 787, Pretoria 0001; tel: +27-12-343-1991; fax: +27-12-343-0905 (e-mail: reservations@parks-sa.co.za).
- KwaZulu-Natal Conservation Service, P.O. Box 662, Pietermaritz-burg 3200; tel: +27-33-347-1961 for information or +27-33-347-1981 for reservations; fax: +27-33-347-3137 for information or +27-33-347-1980 for reservations.

Namibia

- Ministry of Environment and Tourism, Private Bag 13346, Windhoek; tel: +264-61-2842111; fax: +264-61-284-2364 (e-mail: tourism@iwwn.com.na).

Botswana

- (US): Botswana Tourist Board, tel: 1-800-BOTSWANA; fax: 212-268-8299 (e-mail: kainyc@worldnet.att.net).
- Department of Wildlife and National Parks, P.O. Box 131, Gaborone; tel: +267-371405.

Zimbabwe

- (US): Zimbabwe Tourist Office, Rockefeller Center, Suite 1905, 1270 Avenue of the Americas, New York, NY 10020; tel: 212-307-6565 or 212-307-6568.
- Department of National Parks and Wildlife Management, P.O. Box 8151, Causeway, Harare; tel: +263-4-706-077 for reservations, or +263-4-707-624 for general inquiries.

South Africa

Eastern Cape Province (EC)

Great Fish River Conservation Area (8)

This protected area is one of the most interesting in the province, yet it sees relatively few visitors. It is less than one hour's drive from the university city of Grahamstown, most of which is on a good paved road. It is an amalgamation of what were originally three separate nature reserves, Double Drift, Sam Knott, and Andries Vosloo Kudu. The main physical feature of the reserve is the Great Fish River. However, do not expect a major waterway, because it is not! This river was the colonial boundary separating the Boer and British settler communities from the African tribes to the east. The area is steeped in history, mainly revolving around a series of wars that extended over more than 100 years. There are several British forts and settler homesteads in and around the conservation area. The terrain ranges from rugged valleys and gorges to open grassy plains. Vegetation here is classified as Fish River Valley Bushveld, which is characterized by dense, semi-succulent, thorny scrub that averages 2 m (6.5 ft) in height. Having worked in the area we can testify to the variety and vicious nature of the thorns. One can feel for the soldiers and warriors that once had to fight in this thicket country. Fortunately, as a visitor, you will move around only on the game-viewing roads and trails and not get tangled up among the thorns. The internal gravel roads are usually in fair condition, except after heavy rain. As with much of South Africa, this is a summer rainfall area (less than 500 mm, 20 in) and summer temperatures can be uncomfortably high at times. The endangered Hook-lipped (Black) Rhinoceros has been re-introduced, as have African Buffalo. A third member of the "Big Five," the Leopard, occurs naturally but in small numbers. Hippopotamuses have been released along the Great Fish River. Most frequently seen are Warthog, Eland, Greater Kudu, Bushbuck, Blesbok, and Vervet Monkey. The most commonly seen and heard predator is the Black-backed Jackal. Some 200 species of birds have been recorded here, including several different eagles. An interesting array of waterbirds are associated with the river and the dams scattered through the area. There are many different species of reptile, but those you are most likely to see are the large Leopard Tortoise and the White-throated Monitor Lizard. There is some self-catering accommodation (tel: 040-635-2115) in the conservation area, which we prefer, but most visitors overnight in Grahamstown. (Area: 45,000 ha, 111,150 ac. Habitats: thorny scrub woodland; grassland; river.)

Greater Addo Elephant National Park (9)

Greater Addo Elephant National Park was proclaimed in 1931 to protect remnant populations of free-ranging elephants and buffalo. Under protection, the elephants have done so well that recently they were becoming too numerous and culling was considered. However, a recent and ongoing land purchasing program has given the surplus pachyderms a reprieve. This park is located about one hour's drive, on paved roads, from the cities of Grahamstown and Port Elizabeth. Although all internal park roads are graded gravel, they are usually in good condition. The dense nature of the vegetation in the park can make game-viewing frustrating. This is what we like to call a "waterhole" park: you select a drinking point (an animal drinking point, that is!) and wait for the animals to come to you. There are several such locations scattered throughout the park, including one adjacent to the main camp that is floodlit at night. It is at the camp waterhole at night that you have the best chance of viewing Buffalo and the Hook-lipped (Black) Rhinoceros. Addo lies in gently undulating country, with the largest portion of its area being covered by low and very dense bush. The elephants, buffalo, and rhinos have created a network of paths and tunnels through this otherwise impenetrable thicket. There are smaller areas of open grassland and low scrub cover. Recent additions to the park include the greater part of the Suurberg Mountain Range, which is dominated by Cape heathland. Also to be incorporated is a large area of coastal sand dunes. In all, 50 species of mammal occur, including Eland, Greater Kudu, Red Hartebeest, and Common Duiker. The largest common predator is the Black-backed Jackal (although lions and other large predators will soon be re-introduced), usually seen in the early morning hours.

SOUTH AFRICA

1 Kruger National Park and bordering private parks
2 Pilanesberg National Park
3 Madikwe Game Reserve
4 Greater St. Lucia Wetland Park
5 Mkuzi Game Reserve
6 Hluhluwe-Umfolozi Park
7 Drakensberg Park
8 Great Fish River Conservation Area
9 Addo Elephant National Park
10 Mountain Zebra National Park

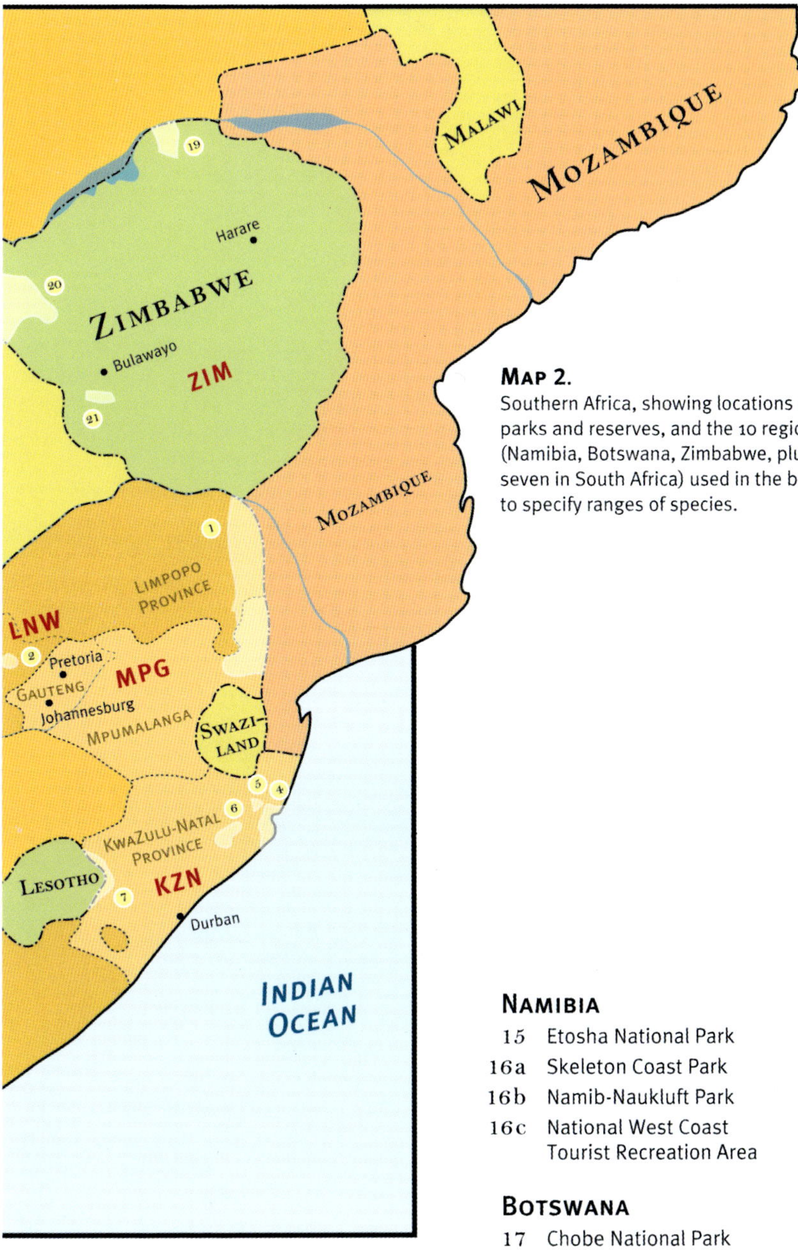

Map 2.
Southern Africa, showing locations of parks and reserves, and the 10 regions (Namibia, Botswana, Zimbabwe, plus seven in South Africa) used in the book to specify ranges of species.

11 Bontebok National Park
12 Karoo National Park
13 Kgalagadi Transfrontier Park (formerly called Kalahari Gemsbok National Park)
14 Cape Peninsula National Park

Namibia

15 Etosha National Park
16a Skeleton Coast Park
16b Namib-Naukluft Park
16c National West Coast Tourist Recreation Area

Botswana

17 Chobe National Park
18 Okavango Delta and Moremi Wildlife Reserve

Zimbabwe

19 Mana Pools National Park
20 Hwange National Park
21 Matobo National Park

Although about 160 bird species occur here, watching them in the dense bush is not easy. An hour or two spent wandering the campgrounds can be rewarding. We have spent as much as a full day in camp, combining bird-watching with observing wildlife visiting the waterhole. In camp there are comfortable self-catering huts and bungalows that are booked through the national parks head office. (Area: 104,000 ha, 257,000 ac, and expanding. Habitats: dense bush and thicket; open grassland and scrub.)

Mountain Zebra National Park (10)

Mountain Zebra National Park was established to protect one of the last remaining populations of the Cape Mountain Zebra (see p. 222). It is set in a magnificent natural amphitheater on the north-facing slopes of the Bankberg range, which rise to the 1,957 m (6,420 ft) high Bakenkop. The park is due north of the city of Port Elizabeth, and the closest town is Cradock, to the east. From Port Elizabeth to the park is approximately a 3-hour drive, most of which is on a paved road. The game-viewing roads in the park are graded gravel and they are usually kept in reasonable condition. Much of the park is situated on mountain and hill slopes, with extensive flat, open plateaus, deep ravines, and the lightly wooded course of the Wilgerboom River. The vegetation is a merging of low, semi-arid scrub and sweet grassland. The common tree here is the Sweet Thorn, or Karoo Acacia. Its v.i.p. inhabitant, the Mountain Zebra, until recently maintained a population of 200 individuals; the ongoing acquisition of land will allow this number to increase. Most zebra foals are born between October and March. Of the 58 mammal species present, apart from the zebra, you have a good chance of seeing Eland, Red Hartebeest, Black Wildebeest, and Blesbok. This is the best park for observing the Mountain Reedbuck. The small Rock Hyrax is common around the camp and easy to approach. More than 200 bird and 45 reptile species have been recorded. This park experiences climatic extremes, with scorching heat in summer and heavy frosts and snow in winter. There are several fully equipped cottages for hire and bookings should be made through the national parks reservations office in Pretoria. There is also a small campground with washing facilities. If you are a keen hiker, there is a very rewarding three-day trail. (Area: more than 7,000 ha, 17,290 ac, and expanding. Habitats: rocky gorges and outcrops; open grassland and low scrub.)

KwaZulu-Natal Province, Lesotho, Swaziland (KZN)

Greater St. Lucia Wetland Park (4)

This wetland park (National Park Photo 3) incorporates several different conservation areas. The park is centered on Lake St. Lucia, which is actually a vast estuarine complex covering almost 37,000 ha (91,390 ac). Although St. Lucia town and Cape Vidal are mainly visited by tourists and fishermen, much of the area is set aside for conservation purposes. Most parts of the park can be reached on good paved roads; most internal roads are graded, all-weather gravel. In the east the park fronts along the warm Indian Ocean, with most of the coastal waters falling within a marine sanctuary. Much of the park fringing the lake and ocean consists of flat to gently undulating sand dune country. There are areas of lowland forest (Dukuduku), dry sand dune forest, marshland, and extensive areas of open grassland. Although game-viewing is not particularly easy over much of the area, it is nevertheless species-rich. More than 600 Hippopotamuses live in the lake, which they share with a very large population of Nile Crocodiles. Close to the St. Lucia village there is an informative crocodile-breeding center. It is probably the best area in Africa to observe the Common, or Southern, Reedbuck. The grasslands in the park are home to the highest known density of these handsome antelope across their wide range. Elephants, Hook-lipped (Black) Rhinoceroses, Buffalo, and Cheetahs have been reintroduced to the area. Difficult to observe elsewhere, Red Duiker are commonly seen. If your interests lean toward primates, Cape Vidal usually offers a very good chance of observing habituated Sykes', or Samango, Monkeys. Bird diversity is rich, with more than 350 species on record. Water-related species are particularly well represented. Although the internal gravel road network is limited, it allows good access to the most interesting areas. Several self-guided and guided walking trails can be tackled by the more energetic visitor. These range from hour-long strolls to up to five-day excursions. To make bookings for the range of cottages, cabins, and camping sites, as well as the guided trails, you need to contact the KwaZulu-Natal Conservation Service in Pietermaritzburg. You should be aware that during the summer months (November to March) temperatures and humidity levels can be uncomfortably high. This is also a high-risk malaria area and taking precautions is essential. (Area: more than 80,000 ha, 197,600 ac. Habitats: Dry sand dune forest; lowland evergreen coastal forest; mixed woodland; open grassland and reedbeds.)

Mkuzi Game Reserve (5)

Mkuzi (National Park Photos 4, 5) is one of our favorite African conservation areas. It is approximately a 3- to 4-hour drive (depending on traffic levels) northeast of the port city of Durban. With the exception of the last 25 km (16 mi), which is gravel, the road is paved. All 84 km (52 mi) of the internal game-viewing roads are graded gravel, but note that during the rains some sections may be closed for short periods. Established in 1912, this is one of Africa's oldest conservation areas. Much of the reserve lies in flat to gently undulating country, with the large freshwater body known as Nsumu Pan being a prominent feature. There are many different habitats, including wooded savannah grassland that is dotted with the distinctive flat-topped Umbrella Thorn Trees. Extensive areas of forest and woodland are dominated by Fever Trees, or Yellow-barked Acacias, and giant Sycamore Fig Trees. The lake (Nsumu) is fringed in parts by dense reedbeds, and large areas of the water surface are covered by water lilies—a very picturesque scene for the avid photographers among us. The lake is home to healthy populations of Hippopotamuses and Nile Crocodiles. Both African rhinoceros species occur here, as do Elephant, Plains Zebra, Giraffe, and Warthog, among others. Among the antelope, it is the very attractive Nyala that is probably most frequently sighted. In fact this is one of the best locations within their limited range to observe this antelope. Substantial numbers of Impala, Greater Kudu, Bushbuck, Blue Wildebeest, Waterbuck, Red Duiker, and Common Duiker occur. One of the major attractions of this reserve is the series of observation hides located at waterholes and Nsumu Pan. Not only are they good for mammal watching, especially from June to October, but they are also superb birding venues. Spending a day in one of these hides is usually very productive. In case you are worried, each hide has a toilet! At the last count, 430 bird species had been recorded in the reserve, as well as 64 different reptiles. There is a variety of accommodation options, including self-contained cottages, units sharing washing and cooking facilities, furnished tents, and a campground. Because this is a popular destination it is essential that you make reservations well in advance through the KwaZulu-Natal Conservation Service office in Pietermaritzburg. As with most of the north of the province, this reserve lies in a malaria area and prophylaxis is essential. (Area: 38,000 ha, 93,860 ac. Habitats: Riparian forest along the Mkuzi River; dry sand forest; wooded and open grassland; reedbeds, pans.)

Hluhluwe-Umfolozi Park (6)

Previously managed as two separate parks and divided by what was known as the Corridor, Hluhluwe-Umfolozi (National Park Photo 6) has now been linked and operates as a single unit. This park is generally credited as being the province's premier game-viewing destination. Hluhluwe and Umfolozi were proclaimed as conservation areas in 1897, making them among the oldest in the world. The Umfolozi section of the park once served as the hunting domain of the Zulu royal family, and was later used by European elephant hunters. Even after the proclamation of the parks, many thousands of game animals were slaughtered in the area in a futile attempt to control the dreaded nagana. This disease, spread by tsetse flies, had a devastating impact on domestic cattle. It was only in the early 1960s that the parks' conservation integrity was assured. Umfolozi is perhaps best known for its role in saving the Square-lipped (White) Rhinoceros from certain extinction. The Hluhluwe section is mainly well-watered, steep hill country, and this, with extensive areas of woodland, means game-viewing can be difficult. Although Umfolozi is also quite hilly, it has extensive open grassland areas, making for easier wildlife spotting. This is also aided by reserve staff who clear and burn brush, making the area more "grazer friendly." The main topographical features in this section are the Black and White Mfolozi Rivers. The rivers were once lined by riverine forest, much of which was swept away during a cyclone that struck the area in the 1980s. Since then it has been slowly recovering. Apart from the Square-lipped (White) Rhinoceros, there are substantial numbers of the endangered Hook-lipped (Black) Rhinoceros. Other species to watch out for are Buffalo, Elephant, Plains Zebra, Giraffe, Nyala, Greater Kudu, Waterbuck, Impala, and Blue Wildebeest. There are also re-introduced populations of the Lion, Cheetah, and Wild Dog. Other predators include the Spotted Hyena, Leopard, African Civet, and several mongoose species. In all, 84 different mammals are known to occur in this complex. This is a prime birding area, with 425 species on record, many of which are residents or regular migrants. There are about 200 km (125 mi) of internal gravel roads that are usually in good condition. A guided wilderness hiking trek (booked through the Pietermaritzburg office), that operates from March to November, offers an excellent opportunity to experience the African bush. Accommodation options in both sectors of the park are diverse. These range from luxury cottages to bush camps, standard huts, and campgrounds. There are restaurants, and each has a small shop and fuel station. Summer days in this area are often hot and humid. Precautions against contracting malaria are essential. (Area: 70,820 ha, 174,925 ac, excluding the Corridor. Habitats: steep wooded hills; grass-covered slopes; riverine woodland; savannah grassed woodland, thicket.)

Drakensberg Park (7)

One of South Africa's major tourist destinations, this park (National Park Photo 7) is a complex of game and nature reserves and wilderness areas. These include Mzimkulwana, Mzimkulu, Mkhomazi, Mlambonja, Mdedelelo, Loteni, Kamberg, Highmoor, and Giant's Castle. All fall under the management of the KwaZulu-

Natal Conservation Service. All lie on the slopes and foothills of the Drakensberg Mountains, the highest range in southern Africa. This is an area to visit if you like dramatic scenery and enjoy walking. The landscape is dominated by the impressive cliffs and peaks of the range. The highest are Injasuti Dome, at 3,409 m (11,185 ft) and the slightly lower Giant's Castle. For hundreds and possibly thousands of years this was the domain of the San people. Drakensberg Park protects some of the country's finest examples of San rock art. Apart from the high basaltic cliffs, there are rolling hills, rocky ridges, deep wooded gorges, and numerous streams. Much of the area is covered by open grassland, with areas of heathland (fynbos) and isolated patches of woodland and forest. This is not an area to visit if you want to see great herds of game! However, Common Eland, Black Wildebeest, Blesbok, Oribi, and Klipspringer populations do occur. The largest carnivore here is the Black-backed Jackal. About 180 species of bird occur in the Drakensberg, including such rarities as the Southern Bald Ibis and the Bearded Vulture. There are few roads within the park but the walking options range from mild rambles to serious hiking. There is a great variety of accommodation options in and fringing the park. These range from upscale hotels, self-contained cottages, and campgrounds to caves! This area is subject to sudden weather changes. Bookings for accommodation within the park fall under the control of the KwaZulu-Natal Conservation Service. (Area: just over 1,800 sq km, 695 sq mi. Habitats: Sheer cliffs; grass-covered slopes and foothills; heathland (fynbos); isolated woodland and forest patches.)

Northern Cape Province (NC)

Kgalagadi Transfrontier Park (13)

Kgalagadi Transfrontier Park (National Park Photos 8, 9) previously consisted of two parts, Kalahari Gemsbok National Park in South Africa and Gemsbok National Park in Botswana. Kgalagadi is the first of its kind in Africa, and because it spans an international boundary, is sometimes referred to as a "peace park." It is a long drive from the major South African cities; allow two days from Cape Town or Johannesburg. The nearest town is Upington, on a mainly paved road of 280 km (174 mi). The last 60 km (37 mi) is on graded gravel. A recent increase in visitor levels has caused deterioration of the extensive network of game-viewing roads. This is now one of Africa's largest conservation areas. The principal topographical features are the usually dry beds of the Auob and Nossob Rivers. The rivers' confluence is at the main camp, Twee Rivieren, in the extreme south end of the park. Much of the park is covered by low sand ridges. After good rains, vast tracks of this semi-desert are covered by seemingly endless "meadows" of grass. Along the riverbeds there are trees and bushes such as Camel Thorn, Black Thorn, and Raisin Bush. At the onset of the usually meager summer rains, a great variety of annuals come into flower. The park lacks permanent surface water but the park's authorities maintain a network of artificial waterholes. These attract a great diversity of game and birdlife and, especially during the dry season, waiting patiently at a waterhole is nearly always rewarding. This is largely a land of nomadic antelope, such as the Common Eland, Southern Oryx, Red Hartebeest, Blue Wildebeest, and Springbok. In most years the best months for game-viewing are from February into May. Africa's three big cats occur here, as do Spotted and Brown Hyenas. Among the most visible of the smaller diurnal mammals are colonial Southern Ground Squirrels and Suricates. Although only 215 species of birds have been recorded, this is quite high for such a dry area. The site is well known for its great diversity of birds of prey, ranging in size from the Pygmy Falcon to the Lappet-faced Vulture. The massive communal nests of the Sociable Weaver are clearly evident. On the South African side of the park there are three rest camps, offering a variety of accommodations, as well as campgrounds. Only Twee Rivieren has a restaurant and it is the most upscale of the three camps. These days it is essential to book in advance, even for camping, at the park's head office in Pretoria. The park's authorities and private enterprises are planning to enlarge facilities and establish new ones. (Area: 45,000 sq km, 17,384 sq mi. Habitats: Sparsely treed river beds; grassed sand dunes; seasonal shallow pans.)

Limpopo and North-West Provinces (LNW)

Kruger National Park (1)

Kruger (National Park Photos 1, 2) is one of Africa's premier and most developed game-viewing destinations. It falls within two of South Africa's nine provinces, Mpumalanga in the south and Limpopo Province. To the east it borders on Mozambique and in the extreme north, Zimbabwe. In the west-central area, within South Africa, it is bordered by several major, upscale, privately owned game parks, such as Mala Mala, Sabi Sand, and Londolozi. The removal of boundary fences has allowed free movement of game in what has become known as "Greater Kruger." As there are eight entrance gates, it is difficult to give an indication of travel time. The average driving time to the gate due east of Johannesburg is approximately five hours, all on good to fair paved roads. The first area of what is today Kruger, the Sabie Game Reserve, was established in 1898. It takes its name from Paul Kruger, then president of the Zuid-Afrikaansche Republiek (South African Republic), who was the main instigator for the park's establishment. This is South Africa's largest conservation area (350 km, 218 mi, long; average 60 km, 37 mi wide) and it has a great diversity of landscapes and habitats. There are extensive flat plains, the low Lebombo Hill range along the eastern border, and rocky outcrops scattered throughout. It is also traversed by several major rivers that flow across the park from west to east. These include, from north to south, the Limpopo, Shingwedzi, Letaba, Olifants, Timbavati, and Crocodile. To the north of the Olifants River the vegetation is dominated by mopane scrub and woodland; in the far north the most prominent tree is the Baobab. To the south of the Olifants there are extensive open grassed plains and mixed woodlands dominated by acacia and bushwillow species. More than 330 tree species have been recorded in the park. The main game concentrations are in the central and southern areas of Kruger. Elephant, Hippopotamus, and Buffalo are common, and there are internationally important populations of both the Hook-lipped (Black) and Square-lipped (White) Rhinoceros. Antelope diversity is great and includes the Common Eland, Greater Kudu, Nyala, Blue Wildebeest, Tsessebe, Roan, Sable, and Impala. It is one of the best parks for observing Lion and Spotted Hyena. Also present are good populations of Cheetah, Leopard, and Wild Dog. With more than 500 bird species, some of them at the southern extreme of their range, it is a birdwatcher's paradise. Game-viewing is at its best during the dry winter months when animals concentrate near rivers, dams, and waterholes. Summer is the time when many mammals are bearing their young and migratory birds are present in considerable numbers. The park has 24 rest camps that offer a wide range of accommodation options, from self-contained cottages to camping sites. The camps offer a range of facilities, including fuel stations, shops, and restaurants. The main road running from north to south in the park is paved, but the majority of roads are graded gravel. Also offered are several guided walks, as well as multi-day hikes and night game-viewing by spotlight. As this is Africa's most frequently visited large park, booking is essential through the Pretoria office. For the private parks, booking is best done through your travel agent. This is a malaria area and prophylaxis is essential. (Area: 19,455 sq km, 7515 sq mi. Habitats: Open grassland; mixed and mopane woodland; low hill country; isolated rocky outcrops; riverine woodland.)

Pilanesberg National Park (2)

Established in 1979, this has become one of southern Africa's most visited parks. In part this can be attributed to its proximity to Johannesburg and Pretoria, and the vast hotel complex (Sun City, Lost City) on its southern boundary. A huge volcanic caldera, with walls rising to 600 m (2,000 ft) above the surrounding plain, is the dominant landscape feature. There are open plains and valleys, and hill-country landscapes. Pilanesberg lies at a point where two distinct vegetation zones meet: semi-arid Kalahari thorntree/grassland mix and more moist eastern woodlands. At the time of the establishment of the park, virtually no game occurred in the area, but an ambitious restocking program changed this. Today there are populations of Elephant, both African rhinoceros species, Hippopotamus, Plains Zebra, Giraffe, and many antelopes. The three African big cats roam here, as does the Brown Hyena. More than 300 bird species have been recorded, of which some 10% are raptors. Close to the Manyane Gate there is a "vulture restaurant," which offers excellent views of several species of "garbage disposal" specialists. The park is northwest of Johannesburg and Pretoria and is reached on good paved roads. Accommodation options range from luxury hotels to campgrounds. Within the park there are also permanent tented camps and chalets available at several locations. Booking in advance is essential (tel: 011-4655437, fax: 011-4651228). For the two hotels, book through a travel agent. (Area: 50,000 ha, 123,500 ac. Habitats: Thorntree/acacia thickets and woodland; mixed woodland; open grassland; river courses; dams.)

Madikwe Game Reserve (3)

Madikwe is one of South Africa's newest game reserves and its Operation Phoenix resulted in what is claimed to have been the largest game restocking in history. (Operation Phoenix was a massive program of game animal translocation from other areas of southern Africa to Madikwe.) The reserve is northwest of Johannesburg and shares its northern border with Botswana. The nearest town, Zeerust, is 70 km (44 mi) to the south. The landscape is principally flat, open plains with rocky outcrops scattered across the area. It is situated on the eastern fringe of the Kalahari Desert. All of the "Big Five" occur, as do many antelope species, the Cheetah, and the Spotted and Brown Hyena. The birdlife is diverse and arid area species are well represented. Apart from getting to the reserve by road, visitors often fly to the two upscale lodges. The Tau and Madikwe River lodges have thatched chalets and are privately owned. At this time there are no other accommodation options. The lodges offer night and day game-viewing drives, hot-air balloon "safaris," and guided walks. (Area: 75,000 ha, 185,250 ac. Habitats: Grassed plains; acacia dominated woodland; rocky outcrops.)

Western Cape Province (WC)

Bontebok National Park (11)

In 1931 only 22 Bontebok existed—all the antelope that you see today descend from that small founder stock! The original area in which they were protected became too small and 84 animals were moved to the present park in 1960. Over the years the population has increased to such an extent that many have been translocated to form satellite herds in other reserves. The park is located just 6 km (4 mi) to the southeast of the historic town of Swellendam. The park lies in a shallow, flat to undulating basin, with the Breede River forming part of its southern boundary. The coastal mountain chain to the east forms a magnificent backdrop. Unfortunately, the park is almost encircled by wheat fields and pastures. More than 470 plants grow in the park, many of which are heathland (fynbos) species. Many of these are shorter than 1 m (3.3 ft) in height. Along the river there are several tree species. Apart from the Bontebok, there is a small population of the very rare Cape Mountain Zebra (see p. 222). The open nature of this small park makes game-viewing easy. Other species that may be seen include Gray Rhebok, Cape Grysbok, and Common Duiker. The carnivores you are most likely to see are the Small Gray and Yellow Mongooses. The bird list tops 200 species, and the park is home to 28 reptiles and 10 frogs and toads. This is a winter rainfall area. We believe that the reserve and its vegetation is at its best from September to November. There is a campground, but most visitors stay in one of the hotels or bed and breakfast establishments in Swellendam. (Area: 2,786 ha, 6,881 ac. Habitat: Heathland (fynbos); river and associated woodland; low, broken ridges.)

Karoo National Park (12)

This is a park of dramatic scenery and diverse wildlife. Established in 1979, the park is dominated by sheer-cliffed plateaus and mesas of the Nuweveld range. The authorities are in the process of buying more land to add to the park. Extensive flat to gently sloping gravel plains spread to the south and west. Impressive riverbeds cut through the mountain rock but in this arid area they carry water only a few times each decade. Vegetation is mainly comprised of dwarf shrubs (known as "Karoo bushes"), succulents, and tree cover along major water courses. The dominant tree here is the fiercely armed Sweet Thorn. Of the "Big Five," only the Hook-lipped (Black) Rhinoceros and Leopard occur, but there is a large population of the rare Cape Mountain Zebra (see p. 222). Antelope include the Red Hartebeest, Black Wildebeest, Greater Kudu, Southern Oryx, Springbok Gray Rhebok, and Klipspringer. One of the most commonly seen mammals is the Rock Hyrax. There is a good selection of small carnivores. Some 190 bird species have been recorded, including several pairs of the cliff-nesting Verreaux's Eagle. The game-viewing road network extends over 90 km (60 mi) and there are several hiking trails in the park. Hot summer days make hiking unpleasant, so this is best tackled from April to November. The park borders on the "capital" of the lower Karoo, Beaufort West. This town lies on the main road linking Kimberley and Johannesburg with Cape Town. There is a pleasantly situated rest camp with fully equipped chalets and a campground with washing facilities. In camp there is a restaurant, small shop, and information center. (Area: 50,000 ha, 123,500 ac—this park is in the process of expansion. Habitats: Sheer cliffs; steep, sparsely vegetated hillsides; low scrub-covered plains; limited river woodland; montane grassland.)

Cape Peninsula National Park (14)

This is one of South Africa's newest, and in some ways most complex, parks. It is located at the southwestern tip of Africa and incorporates parts of the city of Cape Town. It is by far the most popular tourist destination in the country. It is flanked on both sides of the Cape Peninsula by the Atlantic Ocean and in the east by False Bay. Table Mountain and its associated range are incorporated, with their sheer cliffs and rugged slopes. This is primarily a scenic park with one of the richest floral assemblages in the world, which falls within the Cape Floral Kingdom. In fact, many more species of flowering plant grow here than in the whole of the United Kingdom. The only game populations are located in the south of the park, with introduced populations of the Cape Mountain Zebra, Bontebok, and Common Eland. Several small antelope, such as Cape Grysbok, Gray Rhebok, Steenbok, and Klipspringer, occur naturally. There is also a healthy population of the chacma race of the Savannah Baboon. As is the case throughout the Cape heathland, bird diversity is not great, with approximately 220 species on record. However, there are a few heathland endemics, such as the Cape Sugarbird, Victorin's Warbler, and Orange-breasted Sunbird. Cape Town has a great number of accommodation options ranging from five-star hotels to backpackers' lodges. (Area: Most of the Cape Peninsula. Habitats: Rocky and sandy coast; rugged mountains with heathland; open sedge "meadows"; exotic plantations; dams and short perennial rivers.)

Namibia (NAM)

Etosha National Park (15)

Once extending over almost 100,000 sq km (38,630 sq mi), in 1967 this park was reduced to 22,270 sq km (8,603 sq mi) at the stroke of a politician's pen. Despite this dismembering, it is still one of Africa's largest and finest conservation areas (National Park Photo 10). This park takes its name from the Etosha Pan, which covers more than a quarter of its land surface. It was once a great inland lake, but is now a mineral-rich saline desert. No vegetation grows on it and only occasionally does it partly fill with water. With the exception of some rocky outcrops in the south and west, much of the park consists of flatland. The area around the pan is dominated by short grassland. Large areas are covered by mopane woodland, but in the east, especially in the vicinity of Namutoni, this gives way to mixed woodland. Etosha has large game populations with a great diversity of species. These include the Elephant, both African rhinoceros species, Plains Zebra, Giraffe, Southern Oryx, Greater Kudu, Blue Wildebeest, and Springbok. In the east of the park, watch for the dainty Kirk's Dik-dik, one of Africa's smallest antelope, in the mixed woodlands. This is also the best area for observing the Black-faced Impala (a race, or subspecies, of Impala), and in fact the only park in which they naturally occur. Lions are usually easy to observe but Leopard and Cheetah tend to be more elusive. There are floodlit waterholes at Okaukuejo and Halali camps and these make for excellent day and night viewing. Artificial waterholes are scattered throughout the park, and our favorites from the photographic point of view are Klein Okevi, Chudob, and Kalkheuwel in the east and Gemsbokvlakte in the west. Although the area around Halali camp is densely wooded, it is a first-class birding venue. At the last count, 325 bird species had been recorded in the park. For both bird and game-viewing we strongly recommend spending time in and around the three camps and at selected waterholes. Etosha lies between four and five hours to the north of Windhoek on good paved roads. Internal roads are good to fair graded gravel. Some sections may be closed after heavy rain. The three camps have a wide range of accommodations offered, from self-contained cottages to camping. Each camp also has a licensed restaurant. Booking in advance through the Windhoek office is essential because this park is very popular. This is a malaria area, so remember to take your tablets. (Area: 22,270 sq km, 8603 sq mi. Habitats: dry saline desert; short, open grassland; mixed and mopane woodland; isolated granite outcrops.)

Namib-Naukluft Park and Skeleton Coast Park (16)

These are favorite destinations of ours, and we strongly recommend these parks if you are fond of desert landscapes (National Park Photo 11). The size of these two parks combined is almost 66,000 sq km (25,500 sq mi), making them among the largest conservation areas in the world. Although managed as two separate entities, they have many similarities and both are situated in the Namib Desert. This is one of the oldest and most species-rich deserts in the world. Here you will find vast "oceans" of sand dunes, open gravel plains, mountains, and rocky outcrops. Two major river courses, the Kuiseb and Swakop, and many lesser drainage lines cut from the inland escarpment through the desert to the cold waters of the Atlantic Ocean. However, these are usually dry sand rivers, flowing with water just a few times per century. The Skeleton Coast takes its name from the many ships that have foundered on this dangerous shore and the sailors that perished with them. However, this is also a bounteous ocean, with the cold Benguela Current providing the conditions to support vast quantities of life. The great planktonic pastures feed fish shoals, which in turn support fish-eating birds and hundreds of thousands of Cape Fur Seals. On the mainland at Cape Cross is a rookery of more than 100,000 of these eared seals. This easy to visit place is a dramatic blend of noise, smells, and activity. Regular fogs that roll inland from the ocean are the secret behind the great terrestrial animal and plant life in this region. There are many endemic plants, including a primitive ground-hugging conifer that often lives to more than a thousand years. The coastline, sand dunes, and the western plains are sparsely vegetated, but as one moves eastwards, the river courses are lined by a variety of large trees. Following rare rainfalls, the parched earth comes to life. On the central plains, years may pass before decent rain falls. When they do, perhaps once in 10 years, grass seed germinates in abundance and the plains are transformed. Do not expect great game herds; there are none. You have a good chance of seeing Oryx, Springbok, and Hartmann's Mountain Zebra (see p. 222), but although Leopard, Cheetah, and Spotted and Brown Hyena are present, they are rarely seen. On the coast, the Cape Fur Seal colony at Cape Cross is well worth a visit. Bird life is rich, and there are several desert endemics. These include Rüppell's Korhaan, Herero Chat, Monteiro's Hornbill, and the Dune Lark. The great flocks of Cape Cormorants are constantly on the move between the coastal roosts and offshore feeding grounds.

Within the Namib-Naukluft Park there are several artificial water points that attract game and birds. Both parks lie to the west and northwest of the capital, Windhoek. Access to the coastal towns of Swakopmund and Walvis Bay is on a good paved road. There are also two routes that link the interior to the coast by graded gravel roads. You have limited access to the Skeleton Coast Park unless you book a safari with one of the concession holders. It is expensive because you have to fly in, but it is considered to be one of Africa's finest safari experiences. In the Namib-Naukluft your only option is to camp at one of 11 locations. Although Sesriem in the south has washing facilities (often over-utilized!), elsewhere there are only pit toilets and no water. There are several private upscale lodges on the fringes of the Namib-Naukluft, and Swakopmund and Walvis Bay have a wide selection of hotels. A number of operators offer day trips to several interesting locations in the parks. (Area, Namib-Naukluft: 66,000 sq km, 25,500 sq mi. Habitats: Sand dune "seas"; open gravel plains; wooded, usually dry watercourses; mountain ranges and isolated inselbergs (isolated hills that lie on open gravel or sandy plains); beaches and coastline.)

Botswana (BOT)

Chobe National Park (17)

Chobe National Park is named after the river that forms the park's northern boundary. This large conservation area (National Park Photo 12) is for the most part flat and featureless, with low hills only in the southwest. Although there are several natural waterholes, these are dry for much of the year. During the dry season much of the game, especially the vast numbers of Elephants, are concentrated near the only permanent waters. These are the Chobe and Linyanti Rivers in the north and the northwest. Artificial water points in the park are often dry because of minimal equipment maintenance. Much of the park is covered by mopane and mixed woodland. Dominant species in the latter include a number of valuable timber trees such as Kiaat and Zimbabwe Teak. Interspersed between these woodlands are extensive areas of grassland. Although the Chobe and Linyanti Rivers are fringed by forest, much of this has been modified and destroyed by an increasing Elephant population. If you enjoy watching elephants, in the dry season this is one of the best places in Africa to indulge your interest. This is also a good location for seeing Buffalo, Sable Antelope, Red Lechwe, Tsessebe, and Waterbuck. It is the only place in southern Africa where you will see that short-grassland-loving antelope, the Puku. All of the large African predators are present, including the endangered Wild Dog. But also spare a moment for the no-less-interesting smaller animals such as the troops of Banded Mongooses, Tree Squirrels, and the solitary Slender Mongoose. If you are a birder, a visit to Chobe is a dream come true. More than 400 species of bird have been recorded, including the stately Saddle-billed Stork, Long-toed Plover, African Skimmer, Bradfield's Hornbill, and Sousa's Shrike. The northern rivers have very healthy populations of Nile Crocodile, so it is wise to be careful when walking their banks. To watch a sunset across the Chobe River, with scops owls calling and the Lion roaring to proclaim his dominance, is a special moment in one's life! Apart from the extreme north of the park, mobility requires a 4x4 vehicle. Accommodation in the park is limited to private, upscale lodges and camps. If you are on a private camping safari, you are limited to four locations. All are overworked and often crowded, and at most you can expect problems with baboons! (Area: 12,000 sq km, 4,635 sq mi. Habitat: Flat grass and woodland savannah; mopane woodland; riverine woodland; low rock ridges; floodplain.)

Okavango Delta and Moremi Wildlife Reserve (18)

The Okavango Delta (National Park Photos 13, 14), at 15,000 sq km (5,800 sq mi), is the largest inland river delta in the world. Although only one area has been proclaimed for conservation—Moremi Wildlife Reserve—almost the entire delta has large wildlife populations. The area is flat and traversed by numerous clear waterways. The vegetation is predominantly grass-covered floodplains, vast reed and papyrus beds, and wooded islands. There are also extensive mopane woodlands in the east. The richness and diversity of the Okavango is best appreciated when travelling by boat. Only Moremi is accessible by vehicle and this must be a 4x4. During the summer rainy season even 4x4 vehicles won't help you. The Hippopotamus is common, as is the Elephant, and it is these two keystone species that have a major impact on the vegetation of the delta. It is estimated that as many as 50,000 elephants roam the area. Two swamp- and marsh-area-adapted antelope, the Sitatunga and Red Lechwe, are commonly seen. Large herds of Buffalo roam the delta, as do Tsessebe, Greater Kudu, Roan Antelope, Southern Reedbuck, and Waterbuck. A brightly colored race of the Bushbuck is quite frequently seen in this area. There are healthy populations of the Lion, Leopard, and the endangered Wild Dog. Moremi is one of the best locations in Africa for observing this blotched canid. There are also many other smaller, mainly nocturnal carnivores. Crocodiles are abundant in the waterways and although the cool, crystal clear waters may invite a dip, we advise against it. Although many visitors come to see the game, as many again come to view its more than 400 bird species. The best time for birdwatching is between October and February. A number of rarities occur, such as Wattled Crane, Pel's Fishing Owl, Slaty Egret, and Hartlaub's Babbler. It is also a sought-after destination by anglers, especially those in search of Africa's greatest fighter, the Tiger Fish. The vast majority of visitors to the delta fly in to the frontier town of Maun, and then on again by light aircraft to the large number of camps and lodges. Some of these camps can only be accessed by boat, very few by vehicle. Maun itself can be reached on a paved road from Gaborone. This is a long and tiring drive and one has to be alert for cattle and game crossing the roads. Although to many visitors this is still a wilderness area, the rapid growth of tourism, in our view, detracts from this. The accommodation offered is mostly upscale, in other words not cheap, and ranges from tented camps to thatch and wood structures. (Area: Okavango Delta, about 15,000 sq km, 5,800 sq mi; Moremi Wildlife Reserve, 3,900 sq km, 1,500 sq mi. Habitats: floodplain grassland; reed and papyrus beds; wooded islands; mopane woodland.)

Zimbabwe (ZIM)

As this book goes to press, the US State Department has a Travel Warning issued for Zimbabwe due to "continuing political, economic and humanitarian instability" in that country. Travel to Zimbabwe is not currently recommended. Check the US State Department travel website (www.travel.state.gov/travel), or other travel websites, for updates.

Mana Pools National Park (19)

Considered by many to be Zimbabwe's finest national park, Mana Pools has much to offer. It lies 346 km (215 mi) to the northwest of Harare. The road is paved except for the last 30 km (19 mi) to the park entrance. Within the park there is a limited road network that becomes impassable during the summer rains. The park is unique in that the visitor is allowed to walk unaccompanied in the presence of several potentially dangerous species. Mana Pools refers to a number of water bodies that lie on the floodplain of the mighty Zambezi River. The dominant features are the river in the north and, to the south, the rugged Zambezi Plateau. On the opposite bank of the river, in Zambia, is the Lower Zambezi National Park. There are large open areas of grassland, mixed woodland, and extensive stands of mopane trees. Some that stand out are the Winter Thorns, Sycamore Figs, and Sausage Trees. The greatest concentration of game is during the dry winter months. Many species are drawn by the permanent waters of the Zambezi at this time. Hippopotamus, Elephant, and Buffalo are common, as are Waterbuck, Greater Kudu, and Bushbuck. Several large predators occur, including Lion, Leopard, Wild Dog, and Spotted Hyena. Birdlife is also rich, with many species associated with the river and woodlands. This is a malaria area and you should take precautions. Should you wish to walk on your own, avoid high grassland and dense thickets. Never approach wild animals too closely. If you have no experience walking in the African bush, ensure you are accompanied by a guide. You should be aware that summer temperatures and humidity levels can be uncomfortably high. There are several upscale lodges and permanent tented camps located along the bank of the Zambezi. The park authorities operate several camping locations with very basic washing facilities. There are no shops in the park and no fuel is available. Booking for camping should be done through the Harare office. The private camps and lodges are best booked through a travel agent. (Area: 2196 sq km, 848 sq mi. Habitats: Open short grassland; floodplain; riverine woodland; mopane and acacia-dominated woodland.)

Hwange National Park (20)

Hwange (National Park Photos 15, 16) takes its name from a sub-chief of the Rozvi tribe who lived in the area during the 19th century. This is the most visited of all Zimbabwe's major national parks. Although only the northern sector of the park can be explored, this is more than adequate. Hwange has a great diversity of species as well as one of Africa's highest wildlife densities. Much of the park consists of flat, open plains and large pans that hold water only during the summer rains. There are granite outcrops in the north. Large areas of the park are dominated by grass-covered plains and scattered mixed tree and bush thickets. The north is dominated by mopane woodland. During the summer months game-viewing is made more difficult because of the abundance of food and water—several species disperse then over a large area. In the dry season, game is concentrated around the permanent artificial water points. It is at this time that large numbers of Elephants and Buffalo, no fewer than 26,000 of the former, concentrate. Sadly, its once abundant rhinoceros populations were decimated by poachers. Today, it is estimated that only 45 of the Hook-lipped (Black) species survive. There are 16 antelope species in Hwange, including Sable, Roan, Southern Oryx, and Common Eland. Substantial populations of Plains Zebra and Giraffe can also be seen. Twenty-five carnivores occur, ranging from the diminutive Dwarf Mongoose to Lion. Particularly during the dry season, Hwange is what we refer to as a waterhole park. Several hours of patient waiting at a waterhole on a dry winter's day is always rewarding. At several waterholes there are raised, thatch-roofed hides. More than 400 species of bird have been recorded in

Hwange and time spent in the camps is usually rewarding. The park is situated to the northwest of the city of Bulawayo and involves a drive of about 290 km (180 mi) to Main Camp on a paved road. The three principal camps, Main, Sinamatella, and Robins, offer huts and bungalows, as well as campgrounds. There are several small camps, as well as a growing number of mainly upscale, privately run lodges and tented camps. The Hwange Safari Lodge, a conventional hotel, is located a short distance from Main Camp. Booking is advisable for both the park and private camps, the former through the Harare office, the latter through a travel agent. Guided walking trails, a great way of experiencing the African bush, are also offered. Remember that this is a malaria area. (Area: 14,651 sq km, 5660 sq mi. Habitats: Flat, grassed plains; bush thickets; mixed and mopane woodland; rock outcrops in the north.)

Matobo National Park (21)

Matobo is a small but fascinating park. It lies just 54 km (34 mi) to the south of the city of Bulawayo on a paved road. The name Matobo means "the bald heads," a reference to the great round-capped granitic hills, or "dwalas," that dominate the landscape. Matobo was once the domain of the great Ndebele warrior chief Mzilikazi, and long before him, the diminutive San hunter-gatherers. Evidence of their presence remains only in the form of numerous rock paintings. It is also the burial site of that great arch-imperialist, Cecil John Rhodes. The main vegetation type is the so-called miombo woodland, dominated by msasa and munondo trees. There are also areas of open grassland, particularly favored by such species as the Square-lipped (White) Rhinoceros and Plains Zebra. Other game includes Sable Antelope, Impala, Waterbuck, and Klipspringer. The only large predator is the Leopard but here it occurs at one of the highest densities known. Unfortunately, this is a secretive predator and it is seldom sighted, although pugmarks (footprints) and droppings are often seen. This is another park where one is free to wander at will. More than 300 bird species have been recorded at Matobo, but it is particularly well-known for its raptors. There is a very dense population of Verreaux's Eagles, mainly because of the high density of hyraxes, their principal prey, and numerous suitable breeding cliffs. As with all parts of Zimbabwe, you should take malaria prophylaxis. The park's authority operates a camp with lodges and chalets as well as campgrounds. Several upscale lodges operate on the fringes of the park. Park accommodations, as well as those operated by the private sector, should be booked in advance, the former through Harare. (Area: 43,200 ha, 106,700 ac. Habitats: Broken ridges, valleys; rounded, granitic hills; miombo woodland; dams (ponds).)

Chapter 4

ENVIRONMENTAL THREATS AND CONSERVATION

by Warwick Tarboton

The region covered by this guide is home to about 53 million people; it extends across the boundaries of six countries (including Lesotho and Swaziland), stretches over 3 million sq km (1.2 million sq mi), and embraces a remarkable diversity of landscapes and climatic regions. Generalizing about the state of environmental conservation in so large an area, and reflecting on the threats that this diverse environment faces, invites superficiality. Add to this the ever-present specter of political instability in the region and such generalizations are not only assured to be superficial, but are also likely to soon become outdated.

As indicated, southern Africa is a region of remarkable *biodiversity* (the different types of animals, plants, and other life forms found within a region). In fact, South Africa, which is the largest single country in the region, ranks third in the world on a general biodiversity index, trailing behind only Brazil and Indonesia in this regard. The added biodiversity that the five neighboring countries bring to this—the arid landscapes of Namibia and their associated fauna and flora, the remarkable wetlands and associated aquatic biota found in Botswana, and the tropical savannah ecosystems of Zimbabwe—greatly extend this already rich heritage. A considerable proportion of this diverse fauna and flora is endemic to the region; 16,000 of South Africa's 24,000 plant species, for example, are endemic to the country, and about 140 of the 930 bird species found in southern Africa are regional endemics. So the region has a rich heritage of nature in all its forms to be nurtured, enjoyed, and safeguarded.

The preservation of biodiversity provides a common conservation theme in the different southern African countries, and it ranks high on the agendas of the different conservation agencies. Each country, though, is faced with its own dilemmas and challenges in achieving this common goal, and each varies from the next in both the political will needed to conserve the biota and in the resources that they allocate to achieve this. The nature of the threats facing the environment also varies from country to country. For example, in the region's most densely populated country, the mountain kingdom of Lesotho (with 46 people per sq km, or 119 per sq mi), soil erosion and the associated loss of natural plant communities is probably the country's most serious environmental issue; it results from the intense pressure on the land from agricultural and pastoral activities associated with a high rural human population. Soil erosion, on the other hand, doesn't feature as a conservation issue in the region's least-populated country, Botswana (with a population density of fewer than 2 people per sq km, or 5 per sq mi), although pastoral farming here is also having a considerable impact on the country's semi-arid environment. Cattle farming is one of this country's largest sources of revenue, and this extensive and growing pastoral activity has led to thousands of kilometers of veterinary fences being erected to control the movements of migratory game, and to thousands of hectares being sprayed with insecticides alongside sensitive wetlands to eradicate tsetse flies.

Underlying the theme of preserving biodiversity is the need to maintain representative natural habitats in sufficient amounts so that their associated fauna and flora, and the ecological processes and systems that they support, are safeguarded. None of the natural regions or natural communities of southern Africa have escaped the impact of people, from the pelagic fish communities that live offshore in the Indian and Atlantic Oceans, to the wetlands, shrublands, forests, grasslands, savannah, and desert that spread across the interior of the subcontinent. The loss or degradation of natural habitat takes various forms. At one level there is an insidious erosion of biodiversity that accompanies the growing populations of impoverished rural people who survive by making use of natural resources beyond sustainable levels. At another level, there is the climactic transformation of a natural habitat to a *monoculture* (entire plantations or agricultural districts devoted to a single crop plant) of maize, wheat, cotton, timber, or some other commercially grown crop—land-uses which, in many areas, have replaced what were once exceedingly rich and diverse plant communities.

Generally, the least-transformed habitats in the region have been those in the semi-arid and arid regions. These cover much of the western half of the subcontinent—the Karoo and the Kalahari and Namib Deserts, for example—and here the climate, with its low and erratic rainfall, has effectively precluded the growing of crops, thus sparing the natural habitat from the transformation brought about by agriculture. Degradation and loss of biodiversity in such areas is much less visible, at least to the untrained eye, than it is in the more *mesic* (wet, or humid) parts of southern Africa, where the transformation from natural plant communities to croplands is far more obvious. These semi-arid regions have, however, also felt the impact of unsustainable farming practices. Over-stocking is one, where once-diverse plant communities have become impoverished as a result of the sustained heavy pressure by domestic stock; in many districts, too, many of the naturally occurring mammals have been eliminated because they compete with, or prey on, domestic stock.

In the more mesic, eastern parts of southern Africa the transformation of natural habitats is much more visible. In South Africa, for example, which is the most industrialized and commercially developed country in the region and which has the longest history of European settlement, more than half of the savannah (51%) and grassland (58%), the two *biomes* (entire ecological communities) that cover much of the country, have been wholly transformed. Former natural habitats in these biomes have been replaced by one or another crop monoculture, by commercial afforestation, by urbanization, or by some other human activity. This country's unique "fynbos" biome, which is home to 7,300 plant species, has fared a little better, with 26% of it having been transformed to croplands, while an estimated 55% of the country's indigenous evergreen forests, once heavily exploited for timber, remain intact. These proportions probably reflect the level of transformation that has occurred to natural habitats in other mesic environments (Zimbabwe, northern Namibia, and northern Botswana) in the region.

A traditional governmental role in conserving the environment has been to set aside land for wildlife, either designating it as a national park (which offers such land both international recognition and the best security in terms of tenure) or as some other form of wildlife or nature preserve. A number of large, well-known national parks are found in South Africa, Zimbabwe, Botswana, and Namibia; examples of these are Kruger National Park, Hwange National Park, Chobe National Park, and Etosha National Park. In addition to national parks, of which there are about 50 in the region, many smaller tracts of land have been set aside for nature conservation purposes under provincial or regional ordinances; in South Africa, for example, there are about 600 such state-owned nature reserves that fall under the jurisdiction of provincial governments rather than the national government. Overall, the amount of state-owned land designated for wildlife comprises about 10% of the region. Botswana heads the list with about 17% of its land set aside for wildlife; Zimbabwe and Namibia follow with about 12% set aside; South Africa has set aside about 8%, and the tiny states of Swaziland (4%) and Lesotho (less than 1%) come in below this; together, this state-owned wildlife land covers about 330,000 sq km (128,000 sq mi).

But not all of southern Africa's natural regions share proportionately in this land allocation. The grassland region of South Africa, for example, which is home to a host of endemic species, has only 2% of it set aside for conservation purposes, whereas the savannah biome (and especially the more arid parts with the lowest agricultural potential)—home to Lions, Elephants, and the other very marketable members of the "Big Five"—claims a disproportionately large share of the land zoned for conservation. A further negative is that some of the designated conservation areas exist in name only, and the resources and manpower once allocated to their management no longer exist; such areas invite invasion by the landless and their domestic stock. As human populations in rural areas burgeon, the demand for more land for grazing and crop-growing increases. The crisis precipitated in 1999 by the illegal land invasions onto commercial farms in Zimbabwe was a manifestation of this, and the pressure on all the governments in the region to turn over more of the state-owned land "to the people" increases annually. Several of South Africa's national parks have land claims registered against them, and recently 20,000 ha (50,000 ac) in the northern section of Kruger National Park were handed over to a neighboring tribal community.

A way forward in these developments has been to develop the concept of "contractual parks," in which neighboring communities share in a park's management and in the revenue generated from it. The most compelling arguments for maintaining wildlife areas in southern Africa are the jobs they produce and the income they generate from tourism. It is widely claimed that every eight visitors to a country creates one new job, and in a region with rampant unemployment, such statistics have great political appeal. As an example of this, a 75,000 ha (187,000 ac) tract of farmland in northwestern South Africa was purchased in the late 1980s and developed into a wildlife area, now known as the Madikwe Game Reserve; the area now provides employment for 1,200 people, whereas previously the same land had provided jobs for only 80 farm workers. Similarly, in a large, multiple-ownership wildlife area in southeastern Zimbabwe (known as the Save Conservancy) there are 1,200 people working in the wildlife/tourism industry, whereas, when farmed for cattle, only 300 people were employed in the same area. It is also estimated that the changed land use here has increased the economic yield per hectare tenfold.

Recently, an initiative to establish parks that cross national boundaries got underway in southern Africa. The "Peace Parks Foundation" was established in

1997 to undertake this, and six "transfrontier" parks are currently at the planning stage. A seventh, the "Kgalagadi Transfrontier Park" ("kgalagadi" is a tswana name meaning "great thirst"), became a reality in 1999 when it was officially opened by the presidents of Botswana and South Africa—it combined 38,000 sq km (15,000 sq mi) of land along either side of the adjoining borders of these countries to form a single international park. The more that these and other similar initiatives can bring economic opportunities to impoverished rural communities, the more likely it is that the natural habitats in the region will continue to support their rich caches of biodiversity.

Ecotourism is often seen as a panacea for both the unemployment crisis in southern Africa and the salvation of the region's biodiversity. Attracting a share of the estimated 400 million tourists who go globe-trotting every year is important, and in some cases vital, for the economies of many African countries, and southern Africa is increasingly seeing its share of this market. But many of the images that come out of Africa, of war—disease-ravaged people, child-soldiers carrying automatic weapons, lawless land invasions going unchecked by the authorities, and bombs exploding in popular tourist cities like Cape Town—are immeasurably damaging to the tourism industry and hence to the economies of these countries. It often seems that every step forward in developing the tourism market in the region is matched by a step back.

The environmental dilemma facing countries in the region is one of maintaining a balance between satisfying an array of conflicting demands: grow the economy to provide more jobs, yet prevent such developments from impacting on the region's ultimate sustainable resource base (i.e., its natural environment); provide more land for the landless, yet ensure that land use is productive and self-sustaining; maintain the biodiversity (the "golden goose" of a potentially vast ecotourism industry), yet satisfy the more immediate demands for resources by a burgeoning population. Within these bigger issues dwell a host of conflicting lesser issues: how to bring the unsustainable exploitation of wood being used by wood-carvers, or "perlemoen" (abalone), or Cape Lobster, or the diversity of medicinal plants that are exploited in the grasslands and forests, to a situation in which the harvesting rate allows for natural replenishment; how to resolve the moral dilemmas of elephant culling (and the sales of the resulting products), or seal culling (and the sale of their penises as aphrodisiacs in the Orient), or the trapping of wild birds for sale in the vast global market for caged birds.

While it is depressing that governmental spending on dealing with these innumerable environmental issues is diminishing, it is invigorating that so many non-governmental organizations across the region are taking up the challenges and applying creative and innovative ideas to solving seemingly intractable problems. Future generations will judge how well they succeed.

Chapter 5

HOW TO USE THIS BOOK: ECOLOGY AND NATURAL HISTORY

- *What is Natural History?*
- *What is Ecology and What are Ecological Interactions?*
- *How to Use This Book*
    - *Information in the Family Profiles*
    - *Information in the Color Plate Sections*

What is Natural History?

The purpose of this book is to provide ecotourists with sufficient information to identify many common animal species and to learn about them and the families to which they belong. Information on the lives of animals is known generally as *natural history*. More specifically, we can define natural history as the study of animals' natural habits, including especially their ecology, distribution, classification, and behavior. This kind of information is important for a variety of reasons: Researchers need to know natural history as background on the species they study, and wildlife managers and conservationists need natural history information because their decisions about managing animal populations must be partially based on it. More relevant for the ecotourist, natural history is simply interesting. People who appreciate animals typically like to watch them, touch them when appropriate, and know as much about them as they can.

What is Ecology and What Are Ecological Interactions?

Ecology is the branch of the biological sciences that studies the interactions between living things (animals and plants) and their physical environment and with each other. Broadly interpreted, these interactions take into account most everything we find fascinating about plants and animals—what nutrients they need and how they get them, how and when they breed, how they survive the rigors of extreme climates, why they are large or small, or dully or brightly colored, and many other facets of their lives.

A plant or animal's life, in some ways, is the sum of its interactions with other plants and animals—members of its own species and others—and with its environment. Of particular interest are the numerous and diverse ecological interactions that occur between different species. Most can be placed into one of several general categories based on how two species affect each other when they interact; they can have positive, negative, or neutral (that is, no) effects on each other. The relationship terms below are used in the book to describe the natural history of various animals.

Competition is an ecological relationship in which neither of the interacting species benefits. Competition occurs when individuals of the same or different species use the same resource—a certain type of food, nesting holes in trees, etc.—and that resource is in insufficient supply to meet all their needs. As a result, both species are less successful than they could be in the absence of the interaction (that is, if the other were not present).

Predation is an ecological interaction in which one species, the *predator*, benefits, and the other species, the *prey*, is harmed. Most people think of predation as something like a Lion eating an Impala, and they are correct; but predation also includes such things as a wasp killing a caterpillar or an insect eating a seed.

Parasitism, like predation, is a relationship between two species in which one benefits and one is harmed. The difference is that in a predatory relationship, one animal kills and eats the other, but in a parasitic one, the parasite feeds slowly on the *host* species and usually does not kill it. There are internal parasites, like protozoans and many kinds of worms, and external parasites, such as leeches, ticks, and mosquitos. Even an antelope munching on the leaves of a bush can be considered a type of parasitism.

Mutualisms are some of the most intriguing ecological relationships—interactions in which both participants benefit. Plants and their pollinators engage in mutualistic interactions. A bee species, for instance, obtains a food resource, nectar or pollen, from a plant's flower; the plant it visits benefits because it is able to complete its reproductive cycle when the bee transports pollen to another plant. In Central America, a famous case of mutualism involves several species of acacia plants and the ants that live in them: the ants obtain food (the acacias produce nectar for them) and shelter from the acacias, and in return the ants defend the plants from plant-eating insects. Sometimes the species have interacted so long that they now cannot live without each other; theirs is an *obligate* mutualism. For instance, termites cannot by themselves digest wood. Rather, it is the single-celled animals, protozoans, that live in their gut that produce the digestive enzymes that digest wood. At this point in their evolutionary histories, neither the termites nor their internal helpers can live alone.

Commensalism is a relationship in which one species benefits but the other is not affected in any obvious way. For example, epiphytes (p. 12), such as orchids and bromeliads, which grow on tree trunks and branches, obtain from trees some shelf space to grow on, but neither hurt nor help the trees. A classic example of a commensal animal is the Remora, a fish that attaches itself with a suction cup on its head to a shark, then feeds on scraps of food the shark leaves behind. Remora are *commensals*, not parasites—they neither harm nor help sharks, but they benefit greatly by associating with sharks. Cattle Egrets (Plate 25) are commensals—these birds follow cattle, eating insects and other small animals that flush from cover as the cattle move about their pastures; the cattle, as far as we know, couldn't care one way or the other (unless they are concerned about that certain loss of dignity that occurs when the egrets perch not only near them, but on them as well).

A term many people know that covers some of these ecological interactions is *symbiosis*, which means living together. Usually this term suggests that the two interacting species do not harm one another; therefore, mutualisms and commensalisms are the symbiotic relationships discussed here.

How to Use This Book

The information here on animals is divided into two sections: the *plates*, which include artists' color renderings of various species together with brief identifying and location information; and the *family profiles*, with natural history information on the families to which the pictured animals belong. The best way to identify and learn about southern Africa's animals may be to scan the illustrations before a trip to become familiar with the kinds of animals you are likely to encounter. Then when you spot an animal, you may recognize its general type or family, and can find the appropriate pictures and profiles quickly. In other words, it is more efficient, upon spotting a bird, to be thinking, "Gee, that looks like a roller," and be able to flip to that part of the book, than to be thinking, "Gee, that bird is partly blue" and then, to identify it, flipping through all the animal pictures, searching for blue birds.

Information in the Family Profiles

Classification, Distribution, Morphology

The first paragraphs of each profile generally provide information on the family's classification (or *taxonomy*), geographic distribution, and *morphology* (shape, size, and coloring). Classification information is provided because it is how scientists separate plants and animals into related groups, and often it enhances our appreciation of various species to know these relationships. You may have been exposed to classification levels sometime during your education, but if you are a bit rusty, a quick review may help: *Kingdom* Animalia: all the animal species detailed in the book are members of the animal kingdom. *Phylum* Chordata, *Subphylum* Vertebrata: all the species in the book, which have backbones and an internal skeleton, are vertebrates. *Class:* the book covers several vertebrate classes: Amphibia (amphibians), Reptilia (reptiles), Aves (birds), and Mammalia (mammals). *Order:* each class is divided into several orders, the members of each order sharing many characteristics. For example, one of the mammal orders is Carnivora, the carnivores, which includes mammals with teeth specialized for meat-eating—dogs, cats, bears, raccoons, otters and weasels, civets, and mongooses. *Family:* Families of animals are subdivisions of each order that contain closely related species that are very similar in form, ecology, and behavior. The family Canidae, for instance, contains all the dog-like mammals—wolves, foxes, jackals, and wild and domestic dogs. Animal family names end in *-dae*; subfamilies, subdivisions of families, end in *-nae*. *Genus:* Further subdivisions; within each genus are grouped species that are very closely related—they are all considered to have evolved from a common ancestor. *Species:* the lowest classification level; all members of a species are similar enough to be able to breed and produce living, fertile offspring.

Example:	Classification of the Southern Yellow-billed Hornbill (Plate 48):
Kingdom:	Animalia, with more than a million species
Phylum:	Chordata, Subphylum Vertebrata, with about 40,000 species
Class:	Aves (birds), with about 9,700 species
Order:	Coraciiformes, with about 205 species; includes kingfishers, bee-eaters, rollers, motmots, wood-hoopoes, and hornbills
Family:	Bucerotidae, with about 60 species; all the hornbills
Genus:	*Tockus*, with 15 species; one group of hornbills
Species:	*Tockus leucomelas*, known to its friends as Southern Yellow-billed Hornbill

Some of the family profiles in the book cover animal orders, while others describe families or subfamilies.

Species' distributions vary tremendously. Some species are found only in very limited areas, whereas others range over several continents. Distributions can be described in a number of ways. An animal can be said to be *Old World* or *New World*; the former refers to the regions of the globe that Europeans knew of before Columbus—Europe, Asia, Africa; and the latter refers to the Western Hemisphere—North, Central, and South America. Southern Africa falls within the part of the world called the *African region* by biogeographers—scientists who study the geographic distributions of living things. The terms *tropical, temperate,* and *arctic* refer to climate regions of the Earth; the boundaries of these zones are determined by lines of latitude (and ultimately, by the position of the sun with respect to the Earth's surface). The tropics, always warm, are the regions of the world that fall within the belt from 23.5° North latitude (the Tropic of Cancer) to 23.5° South latitude (the Tropic of Capricorn). The world's temperate zones, with more seasonal climates, extend from 23.5° North and South latitude to the Arctic and Antarctic Circles, at 66.5° North and South. Arctic regions, more or less always cold, extend from 66.5° North and South to the poles. The position of southern Africa with respect to these zones is shown in Map 3.

Several terms help define a species' distribution and describe how it attained its distribution:

Range. The particular geographic area occupied by a species.

Native or indigenous. Occurring naturally in a particular place.

Introduced. Occurring in a particular place owing to peoples' intentional or unintentional assistance with transportation, usually from one continent to another; the opposite of native. For instance, pheasants were initially brought to North America from Europe/Asia for hunting, Europeans brought rabbits and foxes to Australia for sport, the British brought European Starlings and House Sparrows to South Africa and North America (among other places), and settlers from India brought Indian Mynas to South Africa.

Endemic. A species, a genus, an entire family, etc., that is found in a particular place and nowhere else. A small lizard species, for instance, may be endemic to the continent of Africa, to a certain region, such as East Africa, or even to a small area, such as the Bazaruto Islands off Mozambique's coast. Galápagos Finches are

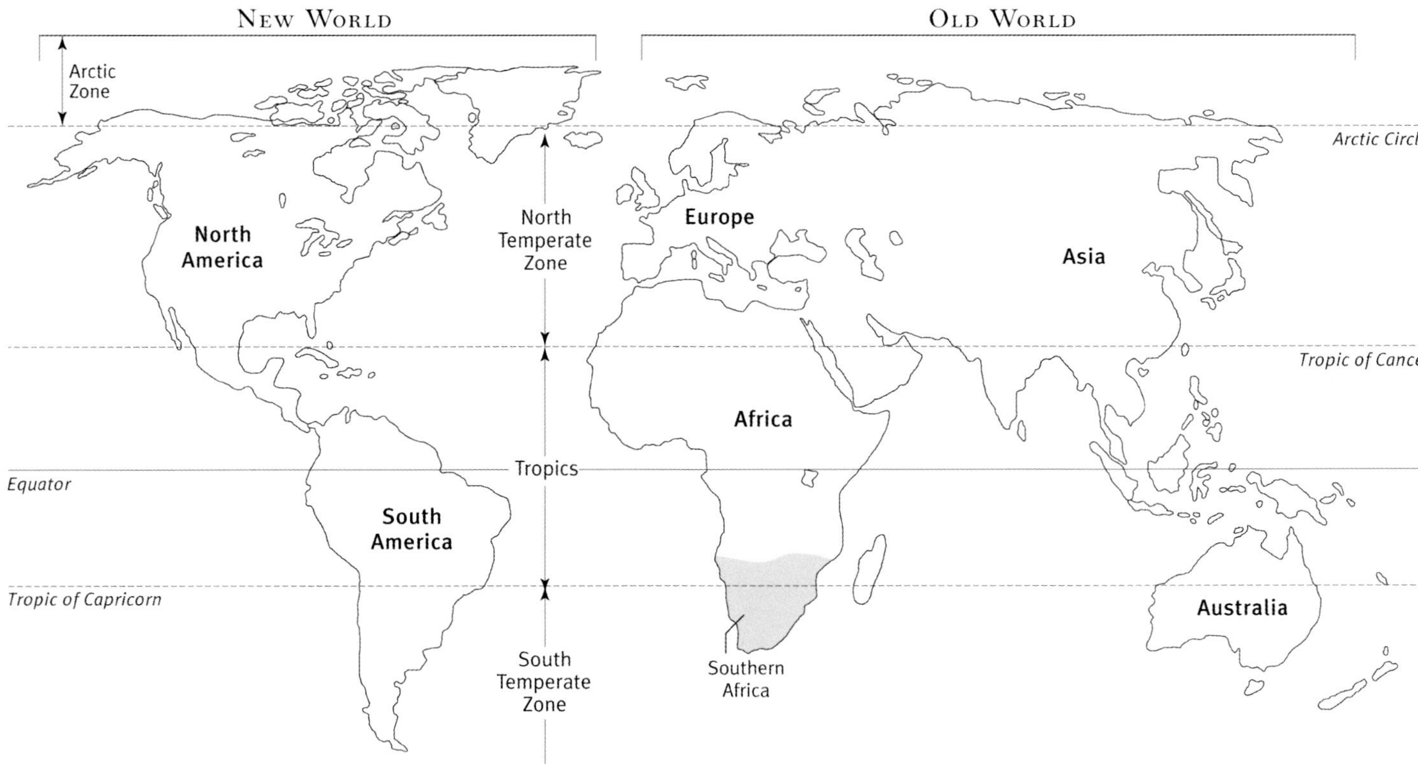

Map 3.
Map of the Earth showing the position of southern Africa; Old World and New World zones; and tropical, temperate, and arctic regions.

endemic to the Galápagos Islands; nearly all the reptile and mammal species of Madagascar are endemics; all species are endemic to Earth (as far as we know).

Cosmopolitan. A species that is widely distributed throughout the world.

Ecology and Behavior

In these sections, we describe some of what is known about the basic activities pursued by each group. Much of the information relates to when and where animals are usually active, what they eat, and how they forage.

Activity location—*Terrestrial* animals pursue life and food on the ground. *Arboreal* animals pursue life and food in trees or shrubs. Many arboreal animals have *prehensile* tails, long and muscular, which they can wrap around tree branches to support themselves as they hang to feed or move about more efficiently. *Cursorial* refers to animals that are adapted for running along the ground. *Fossorial* means living and moving underground.

Activity time—*Nocturnal* means active at night. *Diurnal* means active during the day. *Crepuscular* refers to animals that are active at dusk and/or dawn.

Food preferences—Although animal species can usually be assigned to one of the feeding categories below, most eat more than one type of food. Most frugivorous birds, for instance, also nibble on the occasional insect, and carnivorous mammals occasionally eat plant materials.

Herbivores are predators that prey on plants.
Carnivores are predators that prey on animals.
Insectivores eat insects.
Granivores eat seeds.
Frugivores eat fruit.
Nectarivores eat nectar.
Piscivores eat fish.
Omnivores eat a variety of things.
Carrionivores, such as vultures, eat dead animals.

Breeding

In these sections, we present basics on each group's breeding particulars, including type of mating system, special breeding behaviors, durations of egg incubation or gestation (pregnancy), as well as information on nests, eggs, and young.

Mating systems—A *monogamous* mating system is one in which one male and one female establish a pair-bond and contribute fairly evenly to each breeding effort. In *polygamous* systems, individuals of one of the sexes have more than one mate (that is, they have harems): in *polygynous* systems, one male mates with several females, and in *polyandrous* systems, one female mates with several males.

Condition of young at birth—*Altricial* young are born in a relatively undeveloped state, usually naked of fur or feathers, eyes closed, and unable to feed themselves, walk, or run from predators. *Precocial* young are born in a more developed state, eyes open, and soon able to walk and perhaps feed themselves.

Notes

These sections provide interesting bits and pieces of information that do not fit elsewhere in the account, including associated folklore.

Status

These sections comment on the conservation status of each group, including information on relative rarity or abundance, factors contributing to population declines, and special conservation measures that have been implemented. Because this book concentrates on animals that ecotourists are most likely to see—that is, on more common ones—few of the profiled species are immediately threatened with extinction. The definitions of the terms that we use to describe degrees of threat to various species are these: *Endangered* species are known to be in imminent danger of extinction throughout their range and are highly unlikely to survive unless strong conservation measures are taken. Populations of endangered species generally are very small, so they are rarely seen. *Threatened* species are known to be undergoing rapid declines in the sizes of their populations; unless conservation measures are enacted, and the causes of the population declines are identified and halted, these species are likely to move to endangered status in the near future. *Vulnerable to threat*, or *near-threatened*, are species that, owing to their habitat requirements or limited distributions and based on known patterns of habitat destruction, are highly likely to be threatened in the near future. Several organizations publish lists of threatened and endangered species, but agreement among the lists is not absolute.

Where appropriate, we also include threat classifications from the Convention on International Trade in Endangered Species (CITES). CITES is a global cooperative agreement to protect threatened species on a worldwide scale by regulating international trade in wild animals and plants among the 130 or so participating countries. Regulated species are listed in CITES Appendices, with trade in those species being strictly regulated by required licenses and documents. CITES Appendix I lists endangered species; all trade in them is prohibited. Appendix II lists threatened/vulnerable species, those that are not yet endangered but may soon be; trade in them is strictly regulated. Appendix III lists species that are protected by laws of individual countries that have signed the CITES agreements. The International Union for Conservation of Nature (IUCN) maintains a "Red List" of threatened and endangered species that often is more broad-based and inclusive than these other lists, and we refer to the Red List, or South African Red Data Book, in some of the accounts.

Information in the Color Plate Sections

Pictures. Among amphibians, reptiles, and mammals, males and females of a species usually look alike, although often there are size differences. For many species of birds, however, the sexes differ in color pattern and even anatomical features. If only one individual is pictured, you may assume that the male and female of that species look exactly or almost alike; when there are major sex differences, both the male and the female are depicted. The animals shown on an individual plate, in most cases, have been drawn to the correct scale relative to each other.

Name. We provide a common English name for each profiled species and the scientific or Latin name. Often in southern Africa the local name for a given species varies regionally.

ID. Here we provide brief descriptive information that, together with the pictures, will enable you to identify most of the animals you see. The lengths of amphibians given in this book are usually their *snout-vent lengths* (SVLs), unless we mention that the tail is included. The vent is the opening on amphibian and reptile bellies, approximately where the rear limbs join the body, and through which sex occurs and wastes exit. Therefore, frogs' long legs are not included in their reported length measurements. Unless otherwise indicated, reptile body lengths are given as total lengths (tail included). For the lizards, however, lengths reported are SVLs. For mammals, size measures given are generally the lengths of the head and body, but do not include tails. Birds are measured from the tip of the bill to the end of the tail. For birds commonly seen flying, such as seabirds and hawks, we provide wingspan (wingtip to wingtip) measurements if known. For most birds, we describe their sizes in terms of their overall body length: *very large* (more than 1 m, 3.3 ft); *large* (49 cm to 1 m, 1.6 to 3.3 ft); *medium-sized* (20 to 48 cm, 8 in to 1.5 ft); *small* (10 to 19 cm, 3.5 to 7 in); and *tiny* (less than 10 cm, 3.5 in).

Habitat/Regions. In these sections we list the regions (see Map 2, p. 22–23) and habitat types in which each species occurs and provide symbols for the habitat types each species prefers.

Explanation of habitat symbols (see Chapter 2 for some definitions):

 = Evergreen forest (includes coastal, river-associated, and higher elevation evergreen forests).

 = Deciduous woodland and savannah (includes all non-forest woodland types such as miombo, thornveld, mopane, and Kalahari sandveld).

 = Shrubland (includes fynbos and both karoo types).

 = Grassland (includes natural grasslands and agricultural lands such as pastures).

 = Desert and near-desert.

 = Inland wetlands (includes rivers, marshes, lakes, pans, estuaries, floodplains, impoundments).

 = Marine (includes ocean beaches, intertidal zone and open sea).

Regions (see Map 2, p. 22–23):

EC = Eastern Cape Province
FS = Free State
KZN = KwaZulu-Natal Province, Lesotho, Swaziland
MPG = Mpumalanga and Gauteng
NC = Northern Cape Province
LNW = Limpopo and North-West Provinces
WC = Western Cape Province
NAM = Namibia
BOT = Botswana
ZIM = Zimbabwe

Example:

Plate 48d

Southern Yellow-billed Hornbill
Tockus leucomelas

ID: Medium-sized; long-tailed with large yellow bill and bare red skin around eyes and below bill; upperparts black, extensively speckled and spotted with white; underparts white; solitary or in pairs; to 54 cm (21 in).

HABITAT: Woodland and savannah.

REGIONS: FS, KZN, MPG, NC, LNW, NAM, BOT, ZIM

Chapter 6

AMPHIBIANS

by Bill Branch

- *General Characteristics and Natural History*
- *Seeing Amphibians in Southern Africa*
- *Family Profiles*
    1. *Burrowing Frogs*
    2. *Platannas (African Clawed Frogs)*
    3. *Toads*
    4. *Reed Frogs and Tree Frogs*
    5. *Little Terrestrial Frogs*
    6. *Bullfrogs and Sand Frogs*
    7. *River, Stream, and Grass Frogs*
    8. *Ghost Frogs*

General Characteristics and Natural History

About 400 million years ago, during the mid-Paleozoic Era, amphibians were the first vertebrates to crawl ashore from the early seas. Their common name derives from a Greek word (amphibios) that means to live on both land and water. Life ashore required lots of changes from the anatomy present in their fishy ancestors. Rudimentary lungs breathing air were already present in some fish, but other innovations were needed. They included a movable tongue to help swallow dry food, blinking eyelids and tear glands to keep the exposed eyes moist in dry air, and true ears with external eardrums to detect airborne sounds. Then, presumably after they had learned to hear, the first vocal apparatus (larynx) appeared and frogs began to sing. Later, reptiles, birds, and mammals appeared and refined the adaptations required for a fully terrestrial life. Amphibians, however, retain one characteristic feature that immediately distinguishes them from their terrestrial descendants and which still betrays their aquatic origin. It is the presence of a larval stage, the *tadpole*, or *pollywog*. This is always present, although in some advanced amphibians, such as *squeakers* (p. 61) and *rain frogs* (p. 53), the tadpole undergoes *direct development*—the larval stage is passed within the egg and a full-formed froglet emerges from the soil.

Living amphibians are now found on all major continents and islands except Antarctica, whose frozen wastes exclude most life. Due to their thin, permeable skin, amphibians are unable to maintain salt balance in marine habitats and are therefore absent from most oceanic islands. Exceptions occur where islands were previously connected to the mainland. For instance, the few frogs on Robben Island, near Cape Town, were isolated when sea levels rose again after the last ice age, 9,000 years ago. Currently nearly 5,000 species of living amphibians have been described, of which nearly half occur in the Neotropics (South and Central America). Africa is less blessed, with only 790 species occurring south of the Sahara. Including the frogs of North Africa, which are mainly from European-centered frog groups, just over 800 frog species occur in the continent. As could be expected, the greatest diversity occurs in the wet, warm tropics, particularly in Cameroon and the Congo River basin. These are not areas that have been well surveyed, and many new species probably still await discovery. However, ongoing political turmoil in the region makes scientific exploration difficult. Fortunately for the "frogophile," the subcontinent has a diverse frog fauna. Even the temperate Cape region has 30 species and, moreover, more than 70% of the species are endemic.

Of the three major groups of living amphibians, only *frogs* and *toads* (order Anura, "without tails") occur in southern Africa. *Salamanders* and *newts* (order Caudata, "tailed") are mainly restricted to the Northern Hemisphere, while the strange, legless *caecilians* (sih-SIL-ians; order Gymnophinia) are restricted mainly to tropical swamps. Visitors from more temperate northern climates may be surprised by the diversity of African amphibians. This species richness not only makes identification difficult, it forces us to seek additional, alternative names to the simple "frog" or "toad"; strange and wondrous new labels are needed—such as *cacos*, *chirpers*, *shovel-snouts*, and squeakers.

Seeing Amphibians in Southern Africa

Unfortunately, frogs do not hang around to be enjoyed; too many predators find them tasty. Usually you glimpse only their arching leap from bankside vegetation as they plop into sheltering water. Some *tree frogs* and *reed frogs* do bask on reeds or branches during the day, but they huddle down to escape being seen and to minimize their surface area to prevent water loss. To enjoy the beauty of frogs you need to forego the pleasures of "sundowners" and conversation around the campfire, take a torch, and search the water margins. Most frogs are seasonal breeders, and their breeding activity is linked to the rainy seasons. The western and southern Cape are in a winter rainfall region, so most frogs breed on cold, rainy nights (May to September). Viewing frogs in the northern and eastern summer rainfall region is much more pleasant, as they breed on warm, wet nights between October and March.

Some species are *explosive breeders*. That is not to mean that they pop like dehiscent seedpods, scattering their eggs to the wind. Rather, the frogs emerge *en masse* from their wetland homes and shelters and quickly migrate to their breeding ponds, where, in a brief frenzy that may last only a few days, they mate, lay their eggs, and depart. This usually occurs after the first heavy rains, after which they retreat exhausted to their burrows or reedbeds, to replenish their reserves. Most other species have a more extended breeding season that lasts several months (*extended breeders*). Others, particularly in the western arid regions where rainfall is unpredictable, breed opportunistically whenever rainfall comes to fill the temporary ponds.

Be warned, frogging at night around summer ponds is not without its dangers. Although no South African frog has the dangerous skin toxins of neotropical *poison arrow frogs*, many toads and rain frogs do have distasteful, sticky skin secretions that can cause pain and inflammation if they are accidentally rubbed into wounds or the eyes. In northern and eastern regions, crocodiles are also active at night and kill more people in the region than big cats or elephants. Also keep a lookout for hippos and buffalo; they are bad-tempered company and best admired at distance. These dangers are rare but real, and can add unwanted spice to an otherwise peaceful evening. Mosquitos are a more obvious and more important threat and can ruin frogging even when parasite transmission is not involved. Malaria is present in most of the northern and eastern lowland regions, but the Cape provinces are unaffected. To dissuade the attentions of mosquitos, wear long-sleeved shirts and trousers and wrap a scarf soaked in insect-repellent around your forehead or neck. If you abhor modern insecticides, use citronella oil or some comparable herbal potion. Wear waterproof boots for marshy areas, but if you must wade in deeper water, do get checked regularly for bilharzia. This snail-borne disease occurs in warm, tropical waters, and the fluke-infestation can ruin your plumbing. Finally, for added safety it is also best to search in a group and on private land with permission of the owners.

Site	**Habitat type**	**Best time of year**	**Total no. of species present**
Okavango Delta	Swamp and arid savannah	October–February	30
Victoria Falls	Arid savannah	October–February	30
Kruger National Park	Arid and moist savannah	October–February	34
Zululand reserves	Moist savannah	October–February	46
Addo Elephant National Park	Moist thicket	October–February	16
South Western Cape	Fynbos	August–November	25

Table 1. Amphibian diversity in southern Africa: Where to see the most species.

Family Profiles

1. Burrowing Frogs

Burrows and tunnels form safe, moist habitats, so many frogs, including toads, bullfrogs, dainty frogs, and pyxies, shelter underground, emerging only at night to breed and feed. A few frogs are highly specialized for digging underground and only rarely emerge. They are discussed here, although they are not closely related. They belong to two different frog families, with *rain frogs* and *rubber frogs* belonging to Microhylidae and snout-burrowing frogs, or *snout-burrowers*, to Hemisotidae. The latter is endemic to Africa while the former inhabit mainly the southern continents.

Few frogs are more comical than small, fat rain frogs. Many frogs appear after rain so the common name is not very informative. However, their other names are more apt, as the genus name *Breviceps* means "short head," while the common Afrikaans term *blaasop* ("blow-up") alludes to their amusing habit of inflating their bodies into a round ball. These features easily distinguish them, as do their short limbs and unwebbed feet. The dozen or so species occur in diverse habitats. The BUSHVELD RAIN FROG (Plate 1) is most likely to be encountered in the northern savannahs while the GIANT RAIN FROG may be seen around Cape Town. Rubber frogs are brightly colored, smooth skinned, and have a small mouth that lacks teeth. They swim easily, although their feet are not webbed. They don't hop very well, but can manage a fast, wobbly run. They live mainly in savannahs, and the RED BANDED RUBBER FROG (Plate 1) is widespread in the east and north. Snout-burrowing frogs are also smooth skinned burrowers in savannahs and forests throughout tropical and subtropical Africa. The head is small and pointed and the hind feet are only slightly webbed. The MARBLED SNOUT-BURROWER (Plate 1) is a small, widespread species, with a back marbled in brown and dirty yellow.

Natural History

Ecology and Behavior

Rain frogs are rarely seen except during heavy rain, when they may emerge, like biblical plagues, to breed and feed. They cannot hop, but move quite fast in a waddling walk. In water they inflate and float, but can easily drown if unable to reach firm ground. They feed on small insects, particularly flying termites. If held, their body inflates to a ball, and they may deflate with a curious kitten-like "miaow" sound; their skin also exudes a sticky, distasteful, milky fluid. Despite this, they are eaten by many predators, including monitor lizards, some snakes, and even Bushpigs. Rubber frogs emerge only at night to feed on ants and termites and are agile climbers when in search of food. Unlike the other burrowers, snout-burrowers dig head first, pushing into damp soil with their hardened, pig-like snouts. The soft soil around flooded pans becomes riddled with their tunnels as they search for grubs and worms. If disturbed on the surface, they move in short, quick hops.

Breeding

On foggy days and warm, wet nights, the plaintive whistling sounds of rain frogs can be heard. The males move about the ground looking for females, stopping occasionally to call. Males are aggressive to each other and fight, pushing against each other like dwarf sumo wrestlers. They are much smaller than females and have darker throats. A female attracted by the male's call is quickly grasped around the hips. This is difficult, given the male's small arms and her ample girth. However, after minimal introductions, the male becomes glued to her rump in a comical adhesive embrace. It is impossible to tear them apart without causing damage. The pair burrow backwards into moist soil for 30 to 45 cm (12 to 18 in) and in a small round chamber a clutch of 20 to 60 large, yolky eggs are laid. The male detaches and departs after 3 days, but the female may continue to protect the eggs. These take about 5 to 7 weeks to develop directly into small froglets. Rubber frogs are opportunistic, explosive breeders and lay their eggs in temporary ponds or rock pools. The large tadpoles are transparent and filter food from midwater. The Red-banded Rubber Frog breeds in summer in temporary ponds, where the female lays about 600 eggs, entangling her spawn among submerged aquatic vegetation. The male call is a high pitched trill, rather like one of the more pleasant cell-phone tones. Snout-burrowers lay a small clutch of large yolky eggs in a cavity excavated in damp soil beside a flooded pan. The female may protect her egg mass. The tadpoles usually leave the nest when it floods after rain, wiggling to the nearby pond. They may follow the female across the wet mud, or she may carry them, even uphill, on her back. The tadpole is easy to distinguish by its dark-tipped tail. The male's mating call is an incessant buzz.

Ecological Interactions

Burrowing and giant leaps are incompatible. Digging needs short, powerful feet with specialized "spades" for pushing soil aside. Delicate webbing between long toes, so useful for swimming, gets torn and broken during digging, and long, muscular hind limbs also get in the way. So burrowing frogs have stocky, muscular legs and are therefore poor swimmers; at best they manage only small hops on land. This limits their ability to escape from predators such as snakes, mongooses, etc. For protection, many burrowing frogs produce sticky or toxic skin secretions that make them unpalatable. However, if they are poisonous it is best that predators know it. They could learn by trial and error, but then injury or even death could occur while teaching the lesson. It's better to warn predators at a distance. The bright red-and-black color of rubber frogs (*aposematic coloration*) cautions predators that they are poisonous and best left alone. Although the skin toxins are very toxic to small predators and even other frogs, they are harmless to people, although distasteful and painful if they enter the eye.

Notes

Rain frogs often start calling before the start of rain and emerge in large numbers after heavy storms. Some people therefore consider them prophets and harbingers of good luck. They are held in great respect by tribal people and given the name "inkosazana" (princess). Should one be accidentally unearthed when hoeing fields, it is carefully replaced and a few mealie (maize) grains are placed in its burrow. Many frogs survive long droughts underground. Some, such as bullfrogs, become dormant and lie protected in a cocoon of shed skin. Others search out damp retreats. I was once amazed to be surrounded by calling frogs while standing on bone-dry ground in a depression in coastal grassland. The frogs were all calling underground from flooded rodent burrows in which they had sheltered during the dry season. I have also found other frogs escaping the harsh Highveld winter huddled at the end of lizard tunnels in the dry grassland.

Status

Because they are not dependent on water for breeding, rain frogs adapt well to suburban life and agricultural landscapes. However, three species are vulnerable (South African Red Data Book). Much of the former range of the Giant Rain Frog in the southwestern Cape is now covered with urban homes, vineyards, or wheat fields, while the habitat of the DESERT RAIN FROG is extensively disturbed by alluvial diamond mining in the coastal dunes of Namaqualand and southern Namibia. The FOREST RAIN FROG, which lives in forest patches along the northern escarpment, is threatened by deforestation and exotic pine plantations.

Profiles

Bushveld Rain Frog, *Breviceps adspersus*, Plate 1b
Cape Rain Frog, *Breviceps gibbosus*, Plate 1c
Red-Banded Rubber Frog, *Phrynomantis bifasciatus*, Plate 1d
Marbled Snout-burrower, *Hemisus marmoratus*, Plate 1e

2. Platannas (African Clawed Frogs)

Although most frogs live near water, very few are completely aquatic. Among these are *African clawed frogs* (family Pipidae), locally called *platannas* ("flat hand"). They have many unique features. The hind limbs bear prominent claws on three toes (the scientific name, *Xenopus*, in fact means "strange foot"); they lack a tongue, eardrums, and eyelids; and have a flattened head and body without obvious neck. Their skin is smooth with a series of stitch-like sense organs along the flanks. These are similar to the lateral line system of fish, and detect the vibrations of predators and prey. The COMMON PLATANNA (Plate 2) is found throughout most of the region, even in the Namib Desert, where it survives in rock pools and in underground seepages. The TROPICAL PLATANNA occurs in lowland regions in the northeast and is common in pans and vleis (low-lying ground that is often marshy or flooded) in Kruger National Park and KwaZulu-Natal northern reserves. It has a long tentacle beneath the eye, the belly is usually blotched, and the underside of the thighs is dark yellow.

Natural History

Ecology and Behavior

Platannas like still water and live in ponds, swamps, and slower stretches of gentle rivers. They leave the water only in times of drought or on rainy nights, when they may migrate to other waters. On land they move in ungainly leaps. They can stay submerged for long intervals, but their skin has a poor blood supply and they need to return regularly to the surface to gulp fresh air. Their skin is slimy, which may make them distasteful to some fish, and certainly makes them difficult to hold. Their food ranges from mosquito larvae to fish almost as large as themselves. Food is seized in the mouth and, if small enough, swallowed whole. Larger prey is shredded first with acrobatic overhead sweeps of the large clawed hind feet.

Breeding

Platannas breed at night after the start of summer rains. The males call underwater with a continuous soft metallic rattling that can be heard at surprisingly long distances. The females lay up to 15,000 eggs, which are scattered among vegetation and debris at the bottom of the pond. The unusual, fish-like tadpoles are transparent and have two long tentacles on the snout and a long whip-like tail. They are gregarious and swim head down, filtering plankton (microscopic plants and animals) from the water. Although some South American pipid frogs, such as the Surinam Toad, have maternal care, this is unknown in African platannas.

Ecological Interactions

Platannas are voracious predators that can colonize temporary ponds that fish cannot reach. They may become serious pests in fish hatcheries, eating both eggs and fry. They are also infamous cannibals. Their lifestyle is so specialized that most platanna species are mutually exclusive; they rarely occur together as they would compete for the same resources.

Notes

Platannas are primitive frogs that have swum virtually unchanged in the swamps and marshes of Africa since the time of the dinosaurs. Their closest living relatives are found in South America, the explanation being that millions of years ago Africa and South America were connected. In fact, a fossil platanna collected in northern Brazil can be distinguished only with difficulty from a living West African species. Nearly 250,000 Common Platanna are exported each year from the Western Cape to Europe and the US. Most are now used as fishing bait or in medical research. They were once used in pregnancy tests, after it was discovered in South Africa in 1931 that a virgin platanna laid eggs after injection with urine from a pregnant woman. The frog usually survives the test, but in one celebrated case all the frogs died after being injected. It was discovered that the woman had eaten spicy food at a Mexican restaurant the evening before her test.

Status

GILL'S PLATANNA, considered endangered (South African Red Data Book), is adapted to acidic ponds in the Cape Flats, where it is threatened both by habitat destruction and hybridization with the Common Platanna. The latter dislikes acidic water and does not normally occur in the region. However, crushed limestone used in road construction has reduced the acidity of the shallow ponds, allowing the Common Platanna to move in.

Profiles

Common Platanna, *Xenopus laevis*, Plate 2a

3. Toads

Toads (family Bufonidae) could be called the ugly cousins of frogs. Their body is stout, fat in some species, and usually cryptically colored in brown, rust-red, and cream. They lack teeth and have a long tongue for lapping up prey. The fat hind limbs have at most a small amount of fleshy webbing between the toes. They may grow to a large size and, with the exception of bullfrogs, are among the largest amphibians. They are cosmopolitan and found throughout Africa, Eurasia, and the New World. Toads are not always easy to identify, as most have similar coloration and body shape. Moreover, many also hybridize readily. All have a rough, dry skin that has numerous *tubercles* (bumps) on the back. Typical toads, closely related to those of the Northern Hemisphere, have two prominent, enlarged, bean shaped *parotid glands* on the neck, one behind each eye. These produce a defensive white, sticky, toxic secretion. The GUTTURAL TOAD and RAUCOUS TOAD (both Plate 2) inhabit the central grasslands and savannahs. The red inner surface of the thigh in the former is the easiest way to distinguish between them. *Pygmy toads*, such as the SOUTHERN PYGMY TOAD (Plate 2), are found in scattered populations throughout the northern savannahs, extending south into the central Karoo. They have inconspicuous parotid glands and usually a white spot between the shoulders. Unlike other African toads, the RED TOAD (Plate 2) lacks parotid glands. Instead, it has a granular ridge that runs along both sides of the body from behind the eye to mid-body. It is a colorful species with a rust-red back.

Natural History

Ecology and Behavior

The heavy, dry skin of toads partially protects them from water loss, but it is not completely waterproof. They therefore avoid the sun and are mainly nocturnal, although they do move around on overcast days. Toads are poor swimmers and are also not famed for their jumping abilities. At most, they can manage a short, labored hop. They eat almost anything that moves and that can be swallowed whole. Prey is caught on the sticky, elongate tongue, which is attached at the front of the mouth. In the mouth, prey is not chewed, but simply forced backward, wiggling and squirming, into the gullet. The tongue is not used in this transfer; it is achieved by the bulging eyes, which are forced downwards in a pained blink. Worms and slugs longer than the toad may be grabbed, although they may take 10 to 15 minutes of protracted struggle to swallow.

Breeding

Toads may be extended or explosive breeders. The LEOPARD TOAD is one of the latter, and as usual in such reproductive strategies, male selection occurs. In this, the larger males dominate mating, physically displacing smaller males that may be mating with females. In species such as the Raucous Toad, which breeds over an extended two- to three-month period, female selection occurs in which fussy females choose to mate only with attractive males. But what is "attractive" in a world of slug-eating and puddle-hopping? Bigger toads have deeper voices, and females use this feature to assess whether their suitors have good genes for growth or survival. For whatever reason, a resonant snore or guttural "quarck" is the way to a female toad's heart. Breeding toads gather at favored ponds or slow-moving streams to mate and lay their eggs. They may travel several miles during these breeding migrations, and with the completion of their annual nuptials they return to their same home. The eggs have a dark upper half and are usually laid in characteristic long strings. The larger species may lay up to 20,000 eggs. The small, black tadpoles have plump bodies and bluntly rounded tails, and in many species are gregarious, forming dense, swirling masses. This association may help avoid predation and also serves to generate local currents that oxygenate the water and keep food in suspension. The tadpoles metamorphose quickly in 5 to 6 weeks. Baby toads are very small, and may emerge *en masse* so that it is impossible to walk without treading on them. When food is plentiful they grow quickly, but mortality is high and very few grow into adults. They take 1 to 2 years to reach maturity, and adults are relatively long-lived.

Ecological Interactions

Most large toad species in southern Africa, including the Gutteral Toad and Raucous Toad, have adapted well to urban gardens. They take up residence in holes near dripping taps or under flowerpots and emerge at night to hunt food. In lieu of rent they feed on slugs and crickets. Footpath and outside lights are favorite haunts, as they attract a constant supply of moths and flying ants. Some toads learn to eat dog or cat food left overnight in the pet's bowl. In dry spells they also regularly sit in the dog's water bowl, absorbing water through their skin. The water does not become toxic from the toad's skin glands, so it remains safe to drink. However, toads also regularly defecate while bathing, and a surprisingly large, unwelcome present may be left.

Notes

Toads figure widely in folklore. One common belief, based on their rough, knobbly skin, is that they cause warts. It is a fallacy, although as noted earlier, toad skin secretions are toxic, especially those of the parotid glands. There are tales of frogs encased in stone, but these are probably based on toads that crawled into rock cracks and grew too fat to escape. There, imprisoned in rock, they may survive many years, still growing on the insects that fall in with them. Fat and frustrated, they sit entombed, unless freed by an astonished builder.

Status

Few toads are endangered, although a number have very restricted distributions. Many of the breeding ponds of the WESTERN LEOPARD TOAD (endangered; South African Red Data Book) have been drained or polluted by urban development in the Cape Flats. ROSE'S DWARF TOAD (vulnerable; South African Red Data Book) lives in mountain fynbos and is restricted to Table Mountain and the Cape Peninsula. It is threatened by fires and urban development. Another threatened species is the AMATOLA TOAD (endangered; South African Red Data Book), which is restricted to the grassland summits of the Amatola Mountains in the Eastern Cape.

Profiles

Guttural Toad, *Bufo gutturalis*, Plate 2b
Raucous Toad, *Bufo rangeri*, Plate 2c
Southern Pygmy Toad, *Bufo vertebralis*, Plate 2d
Red Toad, *Schismaderma carens*, Plate 2e

4. Reed Frogs and Tree Frogs

Frogs from various families cling to reeds or clamber in trees. To aid climbing, the fingers and toes bear sticky terminal pads. Most belong to the Hyperoliidae, a family restricted to Africa and Madagascar. These are small, colorful frogs that usually inhabit marginal vegetation and reedbeds, although some also live in trees. They also include a few oddities, including burrowing tree frogs and terrestrial running frogs! Beautiful but disturbing is a good description of the small, agile *reed frogs*. Few can deny their beauty, for they are brightly colored, elegantly proportioned amphibians. However, they disturb in two ways. They are a source of great scientific confusion, as many have very varied coloration, which differs regionally and among males, females, and juveniles. Species boundaries are poorly defined and the classification of many species is chaotic. In addition, the deafening noise of reed frog breeding aggregations can also disturb. Many tired people have spent a restless summer night cursing these tiny songsters as they celebrate their nuptials in a nearby pond.

The PAINTED REED FROG (Plate 3) is common and widespread in wetlands in the east and north. It occurs in a bewildering variety of color patterns. In the north it is boldly striped in black and yellow, with red thighs and feet. Farther south, the pattern becomes more blotched. To confuse matters, juveniles and some adult males are plain tan, while during the day all color forms "bleach" to a creamy white. The color of the LONG REED FROG (Plate 3) is more consistent. It is a tiny green gem, usually with a fine white lateral stripe, that lives in inundated coastal grasslands.

Leaf-folding frogs are easy to confuse with reed frogs; however, their skin is usually spiny, particularly in males. The large GREATER LEAF-FOLDING FROG (Plate 3) has a milky white back that fades when the frog is active at night. *Running frogs* are terrestrial cousins of reed frogs. They are small to medium-sized, "bug eyed" frogs that have elongate, flattened bodies and slender feet. The skin is relatively smooth, except for the granular belly. They are colorful, often boldly striped frogs that are distributed throughout the African savannahs. The BUBBLING KASSINA (Plate 4) is boldly striped, with a continuous stripe along the backbone. It spends its life underground in rodent burrows and under rotting logs.

Two families of tree-living frogs occur in Africa. The most diverse (also family Hyperoliidae) are related to reed frogs and are found throughout the tropical forests of Africa. They have plump bodies and large bulging eyes. When young, one of these frogs, the BROWN-BACKED TREE FROG (Plate 3) is plain green, but with age it usually develops a tan colored horseshoe shape on the back. During the breeding season it is arboreal, but afterward it descends and burrows deep underground to pass the dry winter months. It is found in savannah woodlands from northern Natal to Malawi. The FOAM NEST FROG (Plate 3) belongs to the Rhacophoridae, a family found mainly in Southeast Asia. It is an attractive tree frog, easily distinguished by its large size, cream-colored, sticky skin, and large toe pads.

Natural History

Ecology and Behavior

Reed and leaf-folding frogs are common among the reed fringes of still waters and gentle streams. Many species spend the day in relatively open positions, sheltering in leaf axils or on reed stalks. A favored retreat of the Greater Leaf-folding Frog is inside the long rolled tube of a new banana leaf. When sitting exposed during the day, reed frogs and Foam Nest Frogs turn a creamy white. This aids thermoregulation, as the sun's rays are reflected rather than absorbed. They also sit in a tight, huddled position, reducing their surface area to reduce water loss. Their skin is "water proofed" to prevent dehydration. Small frogs are always in danger of predation, especially if they sit in exposed positions. When seized by a snake or other predator, the Foam Nest Frog gives a prolonged distress scream that may startle its captor, causing it to let go. Although most of these frogs feed on small insects, the Greater Leaf-folding Frog preys on the eggs and tadpoles of other frogs.

Breeding

The breeding habits of reed and tree frogs are among the most unusual of African frogs. The spawn of reed frogs sticks in small clumps to submerged vegetation. Some species have refined this strategy. The TINKER REED FROG lays its eggs in a stiff jelly mass on vegetation just above water level, while the WATER LILY REED FROG lays them between overlapping lily pads that are glued together by the female's sticky secretions. The tadpoles feed on bottom debris and have long tails and well developed fins. Depending on the amount of rainfall, the females often lay more than once during the summer breeding season. In all, 200 to 600 eggs are laid in several small clutches. Leaf-folding frogs also lay their eggs in small clumps glued within a folded leaf, either just below or at the water's surface. This protects the early tadpoles, which are elongate and have a low fin that tapers to a fine point. It allows them to wiggle down wet vegetation into the water below. Leaf-folding frog calls are usually a high pitched buzz or whizz, although that of the Greater Leaf-folding Frog is not unlike a minute machine gun.

The call of the Bubbling Kassina is an explosive "quoip," similar to the celebratory note of a champagne cork. Males call alternately, creating a rippling "peal" of sound around a pond. About 400 eggs are scattered among aquatic vegetation and hatch after about 5 days. The tadpole is distinctive, having a broad head and very wide tail fins, and hangs head-up in the water. Metamorphosis takes over 3 months and the large tadpoles can grow to 8 cm (3 in) in length. The tadpole of a close relative, the VLEI FROG, may reach 13 cm (5 in) and is the largest tadpole of any South African frog. FOREST TREE FROGS also protect their large eggs, which are laid among damp, dead leaves often up to 1 m (3.3 ft) from the water's edge. After about two weeks of development, when the tadpoles are about 1 cm (0.4 in) long, they wriggle in a mass towards the water to complete metamorphosis. The mating call is usually an irregular, harsh quack given from branches above the water.

In summer, Foam Nest Frogs build their nests around muddy waterholes. A female and several males cling together on a branch overhanging the water, and as the eggs are extruded, they use their hind legs to beat the oviduct secretions into a large froth. Within these hanging "meringues" the fertilized eggs hatch and the tadpoles begin their development. About 200 eggs are laid, and within this lofty home they escape predation during their most vulnerable stage. After five days or so, when the tadpoles are about 1 cm (0.4 in) long, the base of the foam nest liquefies and the tadpoles drop into the water below to complete their development.

Ecological Interactions

Free-swimming tadpoles, or *pollywogs*, live in another world, relative to adult frogs. They have to cope with different environments and predators and they also eat different things. Tadpoles' different lives are most obviously reflected in their body forms. A typical tadpole has a round head-body and an eel-like tail, which has a continuous thin fin on both the upper and lower surfaces. The mouth is armed with a variety of remarkable and complex structures, consisting of soft papillae, rows of horny denticles, and a hard, serrated beak. The rasping action of the denticles scrapes off algae from rocks and other surfaces, which is then pumped into the mouth and strained from the water. A few tadpoles, such as those of platannas, lack these denticles and filter plankton (microscopic plants and animals) directly from open water. They shoal together and orient themselves in the same direction. Their swimming movements generate strong water currents that ensure a constant stream of plankton. Stream-dwelling tadpoles need to avoid being swept downstream. They have strong tails and flattened heads, often with enlarged, underslung mouths. The sucker-like mouth is used to graze algal films from rocks in the streambed, but it can also be used to cling to rocks so they are not swept away by the strong currents.

The length of tadpole life depends on the species and also on the environment. Both low temperatures and food scarcity retard growth and hence the length of the tadpole period. Bullfrog tadpoles complete development in only 30 days, while those of the Common River Frog may take from 9 months to over 2 years. Metamorphosis for a tadpole is a period of drastic shape change. Organs are lost, including gills, tail, fin folds, and the larval mouth. They are replaced with a suite of new structures, including limbs, lungs, eardrums, a tongue, and a more robust skin. Kidneys must cope with increased ammonia as the diet switches from herbivory to the carnivorous diet of a frog. Even the hemoglobin in the blood changes to suit the different oxygen tension between air and water. If these drastic events were not enough, gonads and hormones also appear. In concert, they initiate the behavioral and form changes that accompany the one new challenge never faced by tadpoles, that of sex.

Notes

An East African reed frog was once found to undergo sex reversal, breeding first as a female before transforming into a male. Scientifically this is called *sequential hermaphroditism*. It's common in fish but is unknown in amphibians, including other reed frogs. Theoretically it is not obvious why it is rare, as it would seem to have obvious benefits for frogs. Male toads occasionally display characteristics of both sexes, so perhaps sex change can occur as a rare response to certain environmental conditions. The gender sequence is important, and depends on the advantage either sex may gain at a particular size. Normally it is best to be a female when large, as eggs are bulky. Larger females can therefore produce more eggs. However, when male reed frogs fight for females the battles are usually won by the bigger males. The best option for a reed frog is therefore to have a couple of clutches of eggs as a small female (males will mate with any female, irrespective of her size), and then change when larger into a male and fight for additional matings. In this way an individual frog can potentially produce the maximum number of offspring.

Status

A few reed frog and tree frog species have very restricted distributions and are considered endangered. Urbanization and the building of coastal holiday homes threatens PICKERSGILL'S REED in the Durban coastal region, while forestry, agriculture, and fire threaten the LONG-TOED TREE FROG in the foothills of the southern Drakensberg Mountains.

Profiles

Foam Nest Frog, *Chiromantis xerampelina*, Plate 3a
Brown-backed Tree Frog, *Leptopelis mossambicus*, Plate 3b
Painted Reed Frog, *Hyperolius marmoratus*, Plate 3c
Long Reed Frog, *Hyperolius acuticeps*, Plate 3d
Greater Leaf-folding Frog, *Afrixalus fornasinii*, Plate 3e
Bubbling Kassina, *Kassina senegalensis*, Plate 4a

5. Little Terrestrial Frogs

A number of small frogs spend their lives among leaf litter on the forest floor, among the tussocks of mountains and grasslands, or sheltering in rodent burrows. They are not closely related, but have similar lives and so are grouped together in this discussion. *Squeakers* live in rainforests and belong in an endemic African family, Arthroleptidae. They are small, squat frogs with short legs and long, unwebbed toes. Cryptically colored in drab browns, they usually have a dark "hourglass" pattern on their back and dark brown cheeks. People living near forests in the northern coastal region will have heard the incessant summer buzz of squeakers, although they may never have seen the small singers. The SHOVEL-

FOOTED SQUEAKER (Plate 1), as its name implies, has a massive spade-like tubercle on the sole of the foot for digging. It inhabits the sandy coastal plain just entering northern Kwazulu-Natal and Kruger National Park. *Moss frogs* are minute frogs, with only one species exceeding 3 cm (1.2 in) from snout to vent and most others being half this size. Although very similar to squeakers, moss frogs are only distantly related and the two do not occur together. Along with the other remaining small terrestrial frogs we will discuss, moss frogs belong to family Ranidae (*ranids*). They are easily confused with cacos, but their prominent hips give them a distinctive angled back. LIGHTFOOT'S MOSS FROG (Plate 4) is restricted to Table Mountain and the adjacent Cape Peninsula. Four other species live in the seepages and wooded gorges of the adjacent Cape mountains. All are minute, light brown to black frogs that can hardly be differentiated from one another except by the different breeding calls. They are more likely to be heard than seen by hikers in these majestic mountains. *Cacos* (a diminutive of their scientific name) are, perhaps, more descriptively called "dainty frogs." They are small, flattened, elongate frogs with slender limbs that lack webbing between the fingers and toes. The COMMON CACO (Plate 4) is the most widespread. It prefers open grassland or mixed savannah and is found throughout most of southern Africa. It occurs in a wide range of color forms, including bright green, brown, and orange striped. *Puddle frogs*, also called *cricket frogs*, are small to minute ranids. Their common names aptly describe where they may be found and what they sound like. They are squat little frogs with short, narrow heads and rough skin. The hind feet are slightly webbed and have distinctive ankle tubercles. The SNORING PUDDLE FROG (Plate 4) is the commonest widespread species; it prefers open grassland and savannah but does enter coastal bush.

Natural History

Ecology and Behavior

All these small frogs eat tiny invertebrates that creep and crawl in thick vegetation. The forest-living squeakers are active even during the day, while cacos and puddle frogs live around marshes and are mainly nocturnal. All are agile and alert; they quickly clamber through vegetation and are therefore difficult to catch. Most swim easily in shallow water but cannot dive very deep. During the dry season or periods of drought the adults shelter underground, beneath stones, in cracks, or even in rat or lizard burrows.

Breeding

Squeakers breed in summer, when the males form large congregations after rain. At this time their high-pitched, insect-like call buzzes through the forest. Small clutches of about 11 to 30 large, yolky eggs are laid among moist leaf litter, where they develop without a free-swimming tadpole stage. A thick jelly coat around each egg prevents it from drying out. After about four weeks a miniature replica of the adult breaks free from the remnants of the egg capsule and hops away to forage on the forest floor. Moss frogs also lay small clumps of large eggs in seepage spots, behind moss beds, or in clayey soil, and these develop directly into minute frogs. Cacos are opportunistic breeders, and following rain they emerge in great numbers to breed in shallow, temporary pans and marshes. Males call continuously through the day and night. Despite its small size, the metallic clicking call of the Common Caco travels great distances. It sounds much like a thumb being rubbed along the teeth of a comb. The spawn is laid in small clusters of 8 to 25 eggs attached to submerged vegetation. Growth is very rapid and may take only 12–15 days. Puddle frogs are very noisy for such small frogs, and in the summer they keep up an incessant buzz, night and day, for weeks on end. They breed in shallow pans and marshes, laying their eggs among the flooded vegetation.

Ecological Interactions

The life of a small frog is a constant battle to avoid being eaten by predators as diverse as spiders, dragonfly larvae, other frogs, herons, egrets, snakes, and fish. To avoid this, they forage among thick vegetation and are cryptically colored in greens and browns. Despite these precautions, mortality is high. As small frogs cannot produce large numbers of eggs, they must try other reproductive strategies. All grow very quickly, and many may breed more than once a year. For some, such as cacos, the tadpoles metamorphose into froglets that are almost fully grown. They can breed within six months and are therefore perfectly adapted to take advantage of irregular rains. Paradoxically, unlike many bigger frogs, they can survive in very arid regions where rainfall is low and unpredictable. Terrestrial breeding also reduces the risk of predation, but without a free-living tadpole the egg has to be provisioned with enough food to complete development. The eggs of squeakers and moss frogs are therefore big and yolky and the female can only produce a few (usually from 10 to 30). They must be well hidden to avoid predation, and in some species the females remain with the eggs to protect them.

Notes

In the Richtersveld a charming Nama-Khoi myth relates how the NAMAQUA CACO is created by water from the life-giving mists and rare rains as it filters through the deep gorges. It is based on the sudden appearance of these small frogs following rain.

Status

Because they live in forests or in other localized habitats, many of these small frogs are endangered. The MIST BELT CHIRPING FROG lives in a few isolated grassland seepages surrounded by exotic pine plantations. It has the most restricted distribution of any southern African frog, and is critically endangered. The MICRO FROG is also critically endangered, while the CAPE CACO is vulnerable (South African Red Data Book). Both live in scattered lowland marshes in the Cape Flats. Their habitat is threatened by suburbs and motorways built for the Cape's burgeoning human population. Lightfoot's Moss Frog is found only on Table Mountain and the Cape Peninsula, while several closely related species and the MONTANE MARSH FROG live on adjacent mountains. These and the HOGSBACK FROG are all considered near-threatened (South African Red Data Book). POYNTON'S CACO was first described in 1988 from a single specimen collected near Pietermaritzburg in Kwazulu-Natal. Some scientists consider it simply a large, anomalous specimen of the Common Caco. If it was a valid separate species then it is the only extinct southern African frog, as no other specimens have been found and the pond in which it lived has been drained to make way for suburban housing.

Profiles

Shovel-footed Squeaker, *Arthroleptis stenodactylus*, Plate 1a
Lightfoot's Moss Frog, *Arthroleptella lightfooti*, Plate 4b
Common Caco, *Cacosternum boettgeri*, Plate 4c
Snoring Puddle Frog, *Phrynobatrachus natalensis*, Plate 4d

6. Bullfrogs and Sand Frogs

Bullfrogs (family Ranidae) are fat, impressive, burrowing frogs (and not closely related to bullfrogs of the Americas). For many years only a single species was thought to occur in the region. Recently, however, a dwarf species living in the eastern coastal regions has been recognized. The GIANT BULLFROG (Plate 5) lives in the grasslands and savannahs of southern and eastern Africa. Its common name alludes not only to its massive size, but also to the breeding call, which sounds like a bellowing bull. It could have also been called "mega-mouth," because the front of a bullfrog is all mouth. There are also two large "teeth" (bony cones) in the lower jaw, so they can inflict a painful bite. The DWARF BULLFROG appears stunted compared with its giant cousin but is still a relatively large southern African frog. It is mainly restricted to the sandy eastern coastal regions, extending north to Kenya.

Sand frogs (also in family Ranidae) rarely exceed 6 cm (2.4 in) in length and are common in the subcontinent. However, the species are difficult to tell apart and can only safely be distinguished by their characteristic calls. All are attractively mottled in gray and brown, and a light blotch behind the head is often present. Superficially they resemble toads, but they have larger eyes, lack the large parotid glands of toads, and have shiny, wet skin roughened by small, round warts. The belly is usually white and smooth. The TREMOLO SAND FROG (Plate 5) is the commonest, most widespread species in savannah and semi-arid regions.

Natural History

Ecology and Behavior

Like many burrowing frogs, bullfrogs feed and breed during the wet season and then spend the rest of the year inactive underground. When the first summer rain falls, bullfrogs emerge to feed avidly in preparation for breeding. With an appetite that matches their size, they have been aptly described as "walking stomachs." Anything small enough to swallow is eaten, including insects, lizards, and mice. Even snakes are taken, and a large Giant Bullfrog once ate 17 newborn spitting cobras! In southern Mozambique I once found Dwarf Bullfrogs eating dead Guttural Toads killed by passing cars. The bullfrogs were only slightly larger than the toads. As winter approaches and the ground dries, bullfrogs shuffle backwards into damp soil. There, up to 1 m (3.3 ft) underground, a thin cocoon is formed from layers of shed skin. Within this protective bag the frog *aestivates* (sleeps until conditions improve), waiting for the returning rains. During long droughts the frog's blood becomes thicker and nearly half the body water may be lost. When the rains return, perhaps only after two or three years in arid regions, thin, thirsty frogs emerge to feed ravenously and continue their lives. Captive specimens have lived for nearly 20 years.

The fat body and short legs of a sand frog limit its movements to short but lively hops. If threatened it blows itself up like a rain frog. Sand frogs live in sandy regions, and shuffle backwards into the loose soil using a prominent tubercle on the hind foot that aids in digging. During the day they remain buried deep underground, emerging at night to feed on termites and other insects.

Breeding

Parental care is rare in amphibians, but male Giant Bullfrogs are attentive guardians and have a unique breeding behavior. The males gather after the first heavy summer rains in shallow temporary pans. They bellow their charms, even during the day. Dominant males fight and may even kill one another with powerful bites. The much smaller female enters the male arena by swimming underwater. On emergence she is subdued in shallow water, where she arches her back to raise her vent above water so that the emerging eggs are coated in concentrated sperm. Males are so demanding that they may even drown the much smaller females, and larger males will physically try to displace smaller males in *amplexus* (the mating clasp). Egg masses, containing 3,000–4,000 eggs, are laid in freshly flooded pans where fish predators are absent. The males guard the breeding grounds and may attack waterbirds and other animals that come too close to the young. A bullfrog was once filmed attacking young lions coming to drink. (In this case, however, aggression was ill-advised and the frog was eaten!) In the shallow, warm waters the tadpoles grow rapidly and metamorphose in only 30 days. Males have been observed digging channels between pools in drying pans and leading the tadpoles to deeper water. In rainy years successful breeding can lead to the emergence of thousands of baby bullfrogs. Sand frogs also congregate in shallow pans, where the males form deafening choruses. Their high pitched, tinkling calls carry long distances but are only given in short explosive bursts. Afterward the frogs seem to fall into exhausted, albeit temporary, silence. The male Tremolo Sand Frog calls from an exposed position on a mud bank or at the water's edge. About 2,000 to 3,000 eggs are scattered singly in shallow water and hatch in 2 to 3 days. During the day the squat, heart-shaped tadpoles shelter in the muddy bottom, emerging with more confidence at night to feed on detritus. They take about 5 weeks to complete development.

Ecological Interactions

Breeding in temporary ponds has many advantages. Aquatic predators such as fish, many waterbirds, and dragonfly larvae are absent. There is also less competition for food, and the shallow water warms quickly and speeds development. However, there are also many disadvantages. The water evaporates quickly and tadpole growth is a race against time before the pond dries completely. The absence of aquatic plants limits the amount of detritus available to feed the tadpoles. To meet these challenges, bullfrog tadpoles and juveniles are cannibalistic. Food chains in biological communities transfer energy from prey to predator. A food chain is usually composed of different species at different levels. However, bullfrogs fill all these different levels. The small tadpoles feed on detritus and algae blooms that occur soon after the pond has flooded. They are equivalent at this life stage to antelope grazing in the African veld. As the tadpoles grow in size, some become cannibals, eating their siblings. On this protein-rich diet they grow more quickly. This drastic yet logical strategy ensures that at least some of the froglets complete their development before the pan dries. Further cannibalism occurs among the froglets, which helps the larger specimens continue to grow at a phenomenal rate. Again, this is necessary; at the end of the rainy season the survivors need substantial food reserves to allow them to survive the long dry period.

Notes

The Giant Bullfrog is easily the largest amphibian in southern Africa. Giant males may reach 24 cm (9.5 in) from snout to vent and weigh nearly 1 kg (2.2 lb). However, even the biggest female is less than half this size. Despite its impressive dimensions, this bullfrog is only the second largest frog in Africa. It is easily surpassed by the GOLIATH FROG of Cameroon mountain streams, which can reach

37.5 cm (15 in) from snout to vent. In coastal Mozambique, the Dwarf Bullfrog is eaten by local people; hence its scientific name, *P. edulis* ("edulis" from the Latin "edibilis," meaning "eatable").

Status

The Giant Bullfrog is increasingly threatened by urban development (near-threatened; South African Red Data Book). Many of the temporary pans it uses for breeding have been filled in, while the adults in some regions are increasingly killed for food. It takes little effort to collect the adults when they gather at their breeding sites, and many populations have already been wiped out.

Profiles

Tremolo Sand Frog, *Tomopterna cryptotis*, Plate 5a
Giant Bullfrog, *Pyxicephalus adspersus*, Plate 5b

7. River, Stream, and Grass Frogs

These diverse frogs, which could be termed "typical frogs," belong to family Ranidae. These *ranids* have wet skin, large hindlimbs usually with webbed toes, bulging eyes, and are strong leapers. *River frogs* are mainly restricted to the major rivers draining the eastern regions. They are close relatives of the common frogs of Europe and North America. The COMMON RIVER FROG (Plate 5) inhabits the eastern regions from Tsitsikama to Ethiopia. A close relative, the CAPE RIVER FROG, lives mainly in the rivers draining the Cape Fold Mountains. Both are large species, the latter growing to over 12 cm (4.7 in). Within the streams and marshes of the eastern regions live *stream frogs*. They are slim, graceful frogs with long legs that have little webbing. They prefer cool habitats, particularly montane grassland or fynbos. The CLICKING STREAM FROG (Plate 4) is a widespread species, extending in a broad band through the Cape Fold Mountains and Drakensberg escarpment. It is also found in scattered populations in the wetter areas of the Karoo. The body color is very variable, often with a broad stripe down the back. *Grass frogs* prefer permanent water in open grassland (hence their common name), although a few tropical species enter forests. They are sometimes called ridged frogs owing to the characteristic skin ridges on the back. The SHARP-NOSED GRASS FROG (Plate 5) is the largest local species (to 8.5 cm, 3.3 in) and has extensive webbing on the hind toes. It prefers pans in the eastern savannahs and coastal grasslands.

Natural History

Ecology and Behavior

River frogs live alongside permanent water, on the banks of permanent rivers and large dams. During the day they shelter among vegetation, emerging at night to forage along the water's edge. They have a characteristic two part call that is given during both the day and night. It is composed of an initial rattle followed by a sharp grunt. Insects form the main prey, although other frogs may also be eaten. Grass and stream frogs forage in wet and flooded grasslands. When disturbed, some species dive into the water, sheltering among sunken leaves and logs, while others leap away and hide among the bankside vegetation. Sharp-nosed and long-legged, they are built for speed. The larger grass frogs can leap prodigious distances, and a Sharp-nosed Grass Frog holds the world record for frog jumping. It cleared more than 10 m (33 ft) in only three leaps, which is equivalent to three 100 m (330 ft) leaps by you or me!

Breeding

River frogs mate throughout much of the year, although most breeding occurs in spring and autumn. The small eggs are laid in still backwaters. They are surrounded by a large jelly coat to which dirt and debris sticks, camouflaging them. The number of eggs laid varies; the Common River Frog can lay up to several thousand. They take about 7 days to hatch, and the tadpoles develop slowly—they may take 1 to 2 years before they metamorphose. Stream frog eggs are laid in a variety of situations, depending upon the species. Generally they are laid in quiet, shallow backwaters or flooded marshes, although the Clicking Stream Frog lays its eggs just out of the water in bankside vegetation. If eggs remain damp they can survive for more than a month. This semi-terrestrial breeding is an adaptation to prevent the eggs from being washed away in floods or eaten by fish. However, they are still not completely safe and water birds, and even crabs, may eat them. The spawn contains about 200 to 300 eggs and may be laid in a number of small clumps. The small tadpoles are relatively inactive, lying quietly on the bottom and feeding on detritus. Metamorphosis takes from 3 to 6 months, depending upon water temperature. Grass frogs breed in open pans and floodplains and scatter their eggs in small numbers in open water or among flooded vegetation. Calling occurs from long grass and the males form small choruses. About 300 to 400 eggs are laid in shallow water, and they may float for a short time before sinking. Development is relatively rapid, and froglets emerge in about 2 months.

Ecological Interactions

Frog vocalization is more than a lot of wind and hormones. Frogs produce amazingly loud calls for their small size. Depending upon the species they may keep it up for hours each night over a 3- to 4-month breeding season. They can do this owing to a couple of neat tricks. First, they can inflate their lungs to a greater capacity than during normal breathing. Then the air is rapidly expelled into the mouth, causing the vocal cords to vibrate. So far this is no different from the mechanics of opera singing. The clever bit is that frogs do this with their mouths shut! The expelled air has to go somewhere, and it is used to inflate thin-walled vocal sacs. These differ in size and location among frog families. In most, including toads and reed frogs, the floor of the throat balloons out, while in grass frogs the sacs are paired and inflate on each side of the neck. The air is stored in the vocal sacs under tension, and like a balloon collapsing, the elastic energy is used to shunt the air back into the lungs, where it can be reused to produce subsequent calls. This saves considerable energy. However, it is not the whole story, as the vocal sacs do more than just store the air; they also resonate and intensify the sound.

A variety of different calls are made depending upon the circumstances. The most obvious is the *advertisement call,* which males use to attract females. Attracting a mate is not without danger, because snakes, owls, and even bats "home in" on singing suitors. To reduce this danger, male frogs congregate and call in concert. Being in a chorus spreads out the risk, but the resulting cacophony could make it difficult for females to select the best males. To solve this, the males call *antiphonally* (alternately) and different species also have unique calls. To space themselves out and to reduce fighting over prime spots, males also have an aggression call. If this doesn't deter competitors, physical combat can follow. In thick vegetation and in dense choruses, things can become frenetic. In the thick grass at the calling site it is difficult for enthusiastic males to identify the sex of incoming frogs. It is better to clasp first and try to mate, and ask questions later!

Confusion is thus bound to occur, and when one male clasps another, the offended partner gives a *release call*. It is usually a series of short sounds that informs the clasper that his ardor is misplaced. Finally, many frogs give a *distress call* when grabbed by a predator. It is scream-like and sounds similar in all frogs. The intention is to startle the predator so that it releases its prey. It may also warn other frogs in the vicinity of danger.

Notes

Most frogs, especially river frogs, are tasty, and in many African countries large ranids are regularly eaten by people. However, few other mammals eat frogs. This is not only because they are alert and difficult to catch, but because they are also distasteful. Their skin contains proteins called bradykinins, which slow down the heartbeat of mammalian predators and makes them feel nauseous. They sensibly then learn to avoid eating frogs.

Status

Most of these ranids have relatively wide distributions and are common in suitable habitat. None are currently considered threatened, although the AQUATIC RIVER FROG is restricted to the cold waters of the Drakensberg summit and may be threatened by ongoing global warming. It also shares its home with introduced predatory trout.

Profiles

Clicking Stream Frog, *Strongylopus grayii*, Plate 4e
Sharp-nosed Grass Frog, *Ptychadena oxyrhynchus*, Plate 5c
Common River Frog, *Afrana angolensis*, Plate 5d

8. Ghost Frogs

Unique to southern Africa, *ghost frogs* (family Heleophrynidae) are unlike any other African amphibians. They are primitive frogs, isolated in Africa after the break up of continents about 100 million years ago. Their nearest relatives occur in Australia and South America. The adults grow to about 5 to 7 cm (2 to 2.75 in) in body size, and have prominent eyes, smooth bodies, and long legs with broad adhesive toe-pads. The hind limbs are strongly webbed. They inhabit the upper reaches of swiftly flowing rivers draining the Cape Fold Mountains and the eastern escarpment of Kwazulu-Natal and Mpumulanga. There are only five species and most have restricted distributions. The NATAL GHOST FROG (Plate 5) lives in the upper reaches of numerous streams draining from the Kwazulu-Natal Drakensberg and eastern escarpment mountains of Mpumulanga.

Natural History

Ecology and Behavior

Ghost frogs are seldom seen because they live among the jumbled boulders of cascades and waterfalls of mountain torrents. They hide in rock cracks and beneath moss-draped walls, and their large, expanded toe pads allow them to clamber safely on the slippery rocks. They are also good swimmers and shelter beneath partially submerged rocks in the streams. Females are usually larger than males. They feed on land on spiders, crickets, and other insects. The unusual tadpoles have large heads with oral suckers so that they can grip slippery boulders. They feed at night, grazing on algae-covered rocks, and may even climb up wet rock faces. Only during the wet season do the young, newly metamorphosed frogs disperse. Then they may be found some way from the normal specialized habitats of the adults.

Breeding

During the breeding season males develop spiny skin, particularly along the lower jaw, on the fingers, and in the armpits. The call is a soft, high pitched bell-like "ting" that is repeated slowly and is given while the male shelters in cover. Just prior to being laid, the 100–200 large, yolky eggs can be easily seen through the female's almost transparent belly skin. They are laid beneath stones in shallow pools to avoid being swept away in the fast flowing waters. The Cape species breed in summer. This ensures, in a winter rainfall region, that the streams are perennial and do not dry up in the dry season. This is important, as the tadpoles may take one to two years to complete development. Summer breeding also avoids the heavy winter floods that would otherwise wash away the eggs and small tadpoles. The Natal Ghost Frog breeds in late summer, when flash floods are unlikely.

Ecological Interactions

Few other frogs inhabit the fast-flowing torrents in which ghost frogs live. There is little detritus for tadpoles to eat, and the waters are shaded and usually cold. As there is little food available for the tadpoles, development is slow and may take 10 to 18 months. It is probable that ghost frogs are long-lived, because the females lay few eggs each season. Adults have few predators, except for water snakes and otters.

Notes

Why these unusual frogs should have such an unusual common name is not really known. Admittedly they look strange, but they are hardly wraith-like. Perhaps the name alludes to the steep, shady, overgrown mountain kloofs (gorges) in which they live. These can be scary places to look for frogs at night.

Status

The TABLE MOUNTAIN GHOST FROG lives only in a few perennial streams on Table Mountain above Cape Town. Similarly, HEWITT'S GHOST FROG is restricted to four small streams that drain from the VanStadensberg, a small range of hills near Port Elizabeth. Both are critically endangered species (South African Red Data Book) because they have very restricted distributions and face various threats. The few mountain streams in which they live are threatened by small dams in the catchments and loss of water owing to the encroachment of invasive trees and alien pine plantations.

Profiles

Natal Ghost Frog, *Heleophryne natalensis*, Plate 5e

Chapter 6

REPTILES

by Bill Branch

- *General Characteristics and Natural History*
- *Seeing Reptiles in Southern Africa*
- *Family Profiles*
    1. *Terrapins, Sea Turtles, and Tortoises*
    2. *Wormy Reptiles and Primitive Snakes (Including Pythons)*
    3. *Colubrids: Harmless Snakes, the Silent Majority*
    4. *More Colubrids: Back-fangs—Sheep Stabbers and Toad Prickers*
    5. *Dangerous Snakes: A Venomous Few*
    6. *Geckos—Reptilian Acrobats*
    7. *Agamas and Chameleons*
    8. *Skinks and Lacertids*
    9. *Plated and Girdled Lizards*
    10. *Monitor Lizards*
    11. *Crocodiles*

General Characteristics and Natural History

More than 350 million year ago, soon after amphibians took their first faltering steps ashore, some developed a tough skin to retard water loss. In later evolutionary changes, the amphibian egg was supplied with rich food reserves and a waterproof shell. Within the egg, complex membranes surrounded the embryo and maintained it in its own aquatic environment. Within this special "pond," the *amniote embryo* (named after the *amnion*, one of the fetal membranes) avoided the vagaries of feeding and predation faced by free-living tadpoles. Emancipated from living in water, these early reptiles evolved into the rich vertebrate diversity that has dominated the continents for the last 300 million years.

There are four major groups of living reptiles. The smallest group is represented by only two species of *tuatara*, which are lizard-like and now barely survive on small rat-free islands off New Zealand. The three others groups include *chelonians* (tortoises, turtles), *crocodilians* (crocodiles, caimans, alligators), and *squamates* (snakes, lizards). (Incredible as it seems, and based on recent fossil discoveries, modern taxonomic opinion includes birds as a fifth reptile group!) These groups diverged from each other at least 150 to 250 million years ago, and all were distinct groups at the time of the dinosaurs. Perhaps surprisingly, chelonians are more closely related to mammals, and crocodiles more closely to birds, than either are to snakes and lizards. The few living crocodilians and chelonians are survivors of ancient groups. Lizards and snakes are relative newcomers, surviving and diversifying splendidly—or, at least they were, until people arrived on the scene.

Most reptiles, including all crocodiles and chelonians, are *oviparous* (egg-laying). They lay clutches of 5 to 20 eggs, although large sea turtles may lay up to 1,000 eggs in a season, and geckos lay only one or two eggs at a time. With few exceptions, parental care in reptiles ends when the eggs are laid and the nest hole covered. (Exceptions include one southern African python species and the Nile Crocodile, both of which brood their eggs until they hatch.) Many snakes and lizards are *viviparous*, retaining their eggs within the body and giving birth to live young. This is often associated with life in cool climates.

Reptiles usually have a body temperature higher than that of most mammals. They are *ectotherms* ("cold-blooded"), and rely on external heat sources to warm their bodies. To do this they either bask directly in the sun or in contact with sun-warmed surfaces. This contrasts with warm blooded birds and mammals, which maintain constant body temperatures by metabolizing food or fat reserves. Reptiles, along with fish and amphibians, are sometimes classified as *lower vertebrates*, as if the *higher vertebrates* (mammals and birds) were somehow more "meaningful" in the panorama of life. Such a view belittles the importance of reptiles and amphibians, for the truth is that they simply live a different life.

Seeing Reptiles in Southern Africa

Southern Africa has the richest reptile diversity in Africa. With more than 500 species, this diversity exceeds that of North America and Western Europe combined. More than 250 lizard species occur in South Africa, more than in any other African country. Over 75% of these are endemic to the region. The information in this chapter cannot possibly hope to cover such a glorious variety, but it does discuss all the larger groups. It emphasizes the common and colorful species that are likely to be encountered at major tourist destinations. Some species profiled in this book, however, are likely to be encountered only by the enthusiast. They are included to reflect the variety and beauty of what is a unique, but sadly neglected, part of southern Africa's biodiversity.

Unlike amphibians, in which the greatest numbers and diversity occur in the wetter eastern regions of the covered area, reptiles can be seen everywhere. However, the different groups do show regional differences. *Land tortoises* occur in greatest numbers and variety in the Cape, while *terrapins* are commoner in the north and east. Breeding sea turtles can only be seen in Coastal Zululand. Lizards are ubiquitous, but do prefer rocky, dry habitats. They are best seen in the western arid regions. In general, lizards can be considered habitat-linked and snakes, food-linked. This is reflected in their common names. Snakes include *egg-eaters, centipede-eaters*, and *slug-eaters*, while among lizards there are *desert lizards, rock lizards*, and *water monitors*. In practice, this means that lizards often have small ranges within which they inhabit specific habitats, particularly rock-living forms. Snakes, in contrast, usually range over larger areas and occur in different habitats, but search for specific prey. They are therefore commonest where there is suitable prey; and lizard-eating snakes predominate in the west and frog-eaters in the east. The rock and forest habitats of the eastern escarpment and adjacent lowland supports the greatest variety of snakes.

Bird-spotting is enjoyed by millions worldwide—but there is no reason why reptile-spotting cannot be equally enjoyable. Unlike birds, however, which are highly visible, most reptiles are small, secretive, and shy. To find or observe them requires patience and careful searching. The first requirement for such fieldwork is to wear suitable clothing. It should be subdued in color and robust enough to survive thorns and sharp rocks. Compact binoculars, ideally focusing down to 2 to 3 m (6 to 10 ft), are a must, as is a pocket-sized notebook to record observations. Walk slowly and quietly, scanning the ground or rock outcrops ahead. Reptiles usual bask in the sun to keep warm, and on cool days or in winter they are rarely active. Being small, they quickly warm in the sun, and then retreat to shade to avoid overheating and to hide from predators. On hot days, reptiles are best observed in the early morning and late afternoon. On overcast days they may be active all day. Observing need not be limited to daytime. Most geckos are nocturnal and some gather at lights to catch the moths that are attracted. During early evening, nocturnal snakes and some lizards crawl on to paved roads to absorb residual heat from the sun-warmed surfaces. Chameleons can be found at

Site	Habitat type	Best time of year	Total no. of species present
Okavango Delta	Swamp and arid savannah	October–February	65
Victoria Falls	Arid savannah	October–February	65
Kruger National Park	Arid and moist savannah	October–February	110
Zululand reserves	Moist savannah	October–February	130
Addo Elephant National Park	Moist thicket	October–February	55
South Western Cape	Fynbos	August–November	64

Table 2. Reptile diversity in southern Africa: Where to see the most species.

night with a torch as they turn pale and sit in exposed positions. Many lizards and tortoises have small territories in which they spend all their lives. The "fright distance" (the closest approach they will allow before retreating to shelter) is usually small and within easy viewing range of binoculars. Moreover, after several visits, they become habituated to an observer and behave normally. You can then easily watch interesting territorial and mating behaviors.

Family Profiles

1. Terrapins, Sea Turtles, and Tortoises

Common names can be confusing. *Tortoise, turtle,* and *terrapin* have no scientific meaning; the names simply differentiate species that live on land, in the sea, and in fresh water, respectively. *Chelonians* (the correct scientific name for the entire group) have a protective shell, which is divided into an upper *carapace* and lower *plastron*. It may be soft, leathery, hard, flat, knobbed, or hinged, but it is unlike anything else. The shell is a complex structure, with an outer horny layer covering a bony case that is fused to the rib cage. To walk and yet still be protected within the armored shell, a chelonian's shoulder blades and hips are placed inside its rib cage. This body plan evolved more than 200 million years ago. The bones of tortoises found intermingled with dinosaur bones are almost identical to those living today. Some early tortoises had teeth, but these are absent in all living forms, which instead have a horny beak that is similar in appearance and function to that of a parrot.

African terrapins with hard shells are primitive chelonians. One indication of this is that they still withdraw the head sideways into the shell (instead of straight back, as in more advanced groups). The MARSH TERRAPIN (Plate 6) is widespread and occurs in ponds and slow rivers throughout the subcontinent. It has a flattened, thin shell, usually covered in mud and algae. This affords little protection and this species is absent where crocodiles occur. Nostrils placed high on the head on a long neck allow it to breathe air while almost fully submerged. The SERRATED HINGED TERRAPIN (Plate 6) lives in the northern rivers and has a thicker shell that is knobbed along the back. The front of the plastron is also hinged and can be shut to protect the head and forelimbs. The hind feet of terrapins are webbed.

Sea turtles are entirely marine, although the GREEN SEA TURTLE enters estuaries to feed on sea grasses. The forelimbs are large, oar-like flippers for rowing through water. The large head cannot be withdrawn into the shell. Three species are common in the warmer waters of the eastern coast, while the cold-adapted LEATHERBACK SEA TURTLE (Plate 6) swims in all seas. It grows to immense size and has a black, rubbery shell with prominent ridges. The LOGGERHEAD SEA TURTLE (Plate 6) lives around coral reefs and uses its powerful jaws to crush seashells such as conches. The HAWKSBILL SEA TURTLE is relatively small and feeds on sponges, urchins, and soft corals using its hooked beak. It is often killed for its shell, which is brightly polished and carved into tortoiseshell jewelry.

The Cape is justly famous for its wines, scenery, and tortoises. It has the richest diversity of tortoises in the world (25% of all known species) and most are endemic. Some are the prettiest and smallest known tortoises. All land tortoises withdraw the head by a vertical, S-shaped flexure of the neck. The front legs are then pulled together so that the head is completely hidden and protected. The ANGULATE TORTOISE (Plate 7) is the commonest species in the Cape coastal region. It is similar in appearance and behavior to tortoises of the Mediterranean region. The most attractive species are the *tent tortoises* (such as the GEOMETRIC TORTOISE and KAROO TENT TORTOISE, Plate 7), which are named for the raised, tented *scutes* (plates) on the back (these scutes are locally called "knoppies"). The shell usually has a radiating geometric pattern of yellow and black bands. This is most dramatic in the Geometric Tortoise, the most famous and rarest tortoise in the region. The Karoo Tent Tortoise lives in the semi-arid scrublands of the Karoo and Namaqualand. Among other tortoise types in the region, the PARROT-BEAKED TORTOISE (Plate 7) is one of the world's smallest and rarely exceeds 14 cm (5.5 in) in length. Unusually for a tortoise, the Parrot-beaked sexes are different colors. Breeding males have orange-centered dorsal scutes and a bright orange nose, whereas females are green and black. A close relative, the GREATER PADLOPER (padloper is Afrikaans for "road walker"), lives in the central grasslands. Four species of *hingeback tortoises*, such as SPEK'S HINGEBACK TORTOISE (Plate 7), inhabit the northern savannahs. The rear of the carapace in these species develops a hinge in adults that can be closed to protect the hind limbs. The LEOPARD TORTOISE (Plate 7) is the largest tortoise in the subcontinent and the second largest in Africa. A large female can weigh over 60 kg (130 lb). It is found throughout the subcontinent but grows largest in the Eastern Cape, living among the feet of elephants in Addo National Park.

Natural History

Ecology and Behavior

The weight of the chelonian's protective shell limits locomotion and they are not famed for speed. Most tortoises are exclusively herbivorous, although hingebacks will also eat millipedes and animal feces. Terrapins are generally omnivorous. They mainly eat invertebrates, but the lighter shell of the Marsh Terrapin allows it to ambush frogs and even play "crocodile," catching small birds that come to drink at the water's edge. Sea turtles specialize on different foods, such as sponges, mollusks, and shrimps. It is a bit perverse that the Leatherback, the world's largest sea turtle, survives solely on a diet of jellyfish. Although often seen basking on dead logs, or even the backs of sleeping hippos, terrapins are shy and hard to approach. It is just as well, for they are bad-tempered, bite readily, and smell like skunks. Tortoises are very common in the southern Cape region, and populations of over 50 per ha (20 per ac) can occur. Tortoises easily overheat and in summer are only active in the early morning and evening. Local tortoises do not hibernate, although many become inactive during winter. Then they rarely feed but often bask at the entrance to their retreat on a sunny day. When its pond dries, a Marsh Terrapin burrows into soft mud and spends the dry season underground.

Breeding

All chelonians lay eggs, which are usually soft-shelled in sea turtles and side-necked terrapins but hard-shelled in tortoises. The female takes great care to find a suitable moist yet sunny spot in which to lay her eggs. A small vertical pit is dug with the hind legs, and after the eggs are laid, they are covered and left to incubate. This is the extent of maternal care. The eggs and hatchlings must fend for themselves. The time from laying to hatching can vary from 4 to 15 months. In part it is dependent on the season, as eggs laid in autumn undergo very little development during winter and do not hatch much earlier than those laid the following spring. Clutch size varies with the species. Some lay only a single egg and others up to 10 to 20 eggs. Much greater numbers are laid by sea turtles. A female Leatherback may come ashore 4 or 5 times during the breeding season, and lay 100 to 200 eggs each time. The sex of the embryo of many chelonians depends on the temperature at which the egg is incubated. At high temperatures (31 to 34°C) females are formed; males hatch from eggs incubated at lower temperatures. Nests in sunny positions produce more females than those laid in the shade.

Ecological Interactions

The Angulate Tortoise has a dubious distinction; it is the world's most truculent tortoise. Mature males have an enlarged, "spade-like" plate at the front of the plastron. It juts beneath the head and is used in fierce battles as breeding males try to flip one another over. To make this difficult, males develop a low, peanut-shaped shell, which flares at the front and back. This lowers their center of gravity and makes them difficult to overturn. Dominant males do not defend exclusive territories; they simply hog all mating with females. Access to females depends upon victory in combat, and this is related to male size. As a result, males are larger than females, while in most other tortoises it is the opposite. Another unusual feature is that females lay only a single egg and have a protracted breeding season. It is difficult to explain these odd behaviors, but they are probably linked. Tortoises suffer high nest predation, as mongooses and jackals dig up many nests and also eat hatchlings. To limit this impact, perhaps females do not "put all their eggs in one basket," but lay single eggs at frequent intervals. Females thus have a protracted breeding season and are receptive to mating for longer periods. Males that are bigger and more aggressive dominate these mating opportunities. It seems a nice example of the ecological interplay between predation and reproductive behavior. Of course I could be wrong; male tortoises, like humans, could just be aggressive and over-sexed!

Notes

In legend, the Greek tragic poet Aeschylus died in old age 2,500 years ago when an eagle dropped a tortoise on his head. It is unlikely that the unfortunate accident resulted from avian aggression directed at a poor poem. Rather, the eagle was trying to get a small meal. Tortoises are armored and a "hard nut to crack." However, some birds have learned to break open the shell by dropping tortoises onto rocks. Smashed tortoise shells have been found beneath Black Eagle nests in the Karoo, while Kelp Gulls on Dassen Island on the Cape west coast kill hundreds of small Angulate Tortoises. I measured more than 120 broken shells that littered the granite bedrock of the island. The largest was a juvenile of about 10 cm (4 in) in length and 200 g (7 oz) in weight. This appears to be the upper limit that the gull can lift. Above that, in the third or fourth year of life, an Angulate Tortoise is safe from such abuse. Angulate Tortoises on Dassen Island are larger than those on the Cape mainland. Giant tortoises occur on the Galápagos Islands in the Pacific and the Aldabra Atoll in the Indian Ocean. Perhaps these giants, at least in part, are also a response to greedy gulls.

Status

Although many tortoises are endemic to South Africa, only the Geometric Tortoise is currently considered endangered. The species occurs in low densities

(2 to 3 tortoises per ha, 1 per ac) in small pockets of coastal renosterveld. This low-lying scrub habitat previously carpeted the lowlands between Table Mountain and the inland mountains. Only 5% of this habitat remains; the rest has been turned into wheat fields, vineyards, and urban sprawl. Only about 4,000 individuals survive, and the largest population occurs in a private nature reserve. Throughout the world, sea turtle populations are endangered (and all seven species are CITES Appendix I listed). Most are killed for meat as they come ashore to nest. Others are drowned in shrimp nets or choke on swallowed plastic. On the coast of northern Zululand near Kosi Bay, however, hundreds of Leatherback and Loggerhead Sea Turtles haul ashore every spring to breed. In an exception to the sorry decline of sea turtles elsewhere in the world, their numbers are increasing yearly.

Profiles

Serrated Hinged Terrapin, *Pelusios sinuatus*, Plate 6a
Marsh Terrapin, *Pelomedusa subrufa*, Plate 6b
Loggerhead Sea Turtle, *Caretta caretta*, Plate 6c
Leatherback Sea Turtle, *Dermochelys coriacea*, Plate 6d
Parrot-beaked Tortoise, *Homopus areolatus*, Plate 7a
Angulate Tortoise, *Chersina angulata*, Plate 7b
Leopard Tortoise, *Stigmochelys pardalis*, Plate 7c
Karoo Tent Tortoise, *Psammobates tentorius*, Plate 7d
Spek's Hingeback Tortoise, *Kinixys spekii*, Plate 7e

2. Wormy Reptiles and Primitive Snakes (Including Pythons)

The earliest scaled reptiles (*squamates*) were lizards. Evolved from these are snakes and a few bizarre creatures called *amphisbaenians*. They were once called *worm lizards*, but this is misleading because they are neither worms nor lizards. Admittedly they are like worms, pink, segmented, blind, and living underground. They were once thought to be lizards, but like snakes they are now thought to have evolved from an unknown group of burrowing lizards. The blunt head of the amphisbaenian known as the CAPE SPADE-SNOUTED WORM LIZARD (Plate 8) is tipped with a large "thumbnail" shield that is used in digging. The tail is rounded, and in some species it is waved in defense to deflect attacks away from the vulnerable head. The tail is the basis for their scientific name, which derives from the Greek "amphisbaena," meaning "two headed."

Two families of primitive burrowing snakes are common in Africa. They have little need of sight, so their eyes are reduced to two black spots beneath the head scales. The body scales are smoothly polished and not enlarged on the belly. The tail is of similar size to the head and may end in a sharp spine. *Blind snakes* (family Typhlopidae) only have teeth in the upper jaw. SCHLEGEL'S GIANT BLIND SNAKE (Plate 8) is the world's largest member of the family, reaching almost 1 m (3.3 ft) in length. *Thread snakes* (family Leptotyphlopidae) are minute, exceptionally thin, blind burrowers. Their head is blunt, sometimes with a hooked profile, and they have no teeth in the upper jaw. Internally they still retain vestiges of limbs. They are the smallest snakes in the world, and even the largest local species, the WESTERN THREAD SNAKE (Plate 8), does not exceed 30 cm (12 in) in length. Some, such as the FOREST THREAD SNAKE, grow to just over 10 cm (4 in) long and are as thin as a grass stem.

Pythons (family Boidae) are among the largest snakes in the world and kill their prey by constriction. They are primitive snakes that still retain small claws beside the *vent* (the opening on their bellies through which sex occurs and wastes exit). These are vestiges of the hind limbs of their lizard ancestors. They have some sophisticated features, however. Heat-sensitive pits on the lips allow a python to "see" warm-blooded prey in the dark. These sense organs, equivalent to the modern military "infrared sniper scope," have been used by pythons for millions of years. Two of four African python species occur in southern Africa. The SOUTHERN AFRICAN PYTHON (Plate 8) is one of the world's great snakes and can exceed 6 m (18 ft) in length. It is surpassed in size only by the Amazon Anaconda (also in family Boidae), and a few other pythons. A smaller cousin, the ANGOLAN DWARF PYTHON (Plate 8), which rarely exceeds 2 m (6.6 ft), is browner in color and restricted to the rocky scrub of northern Namibia.

Natural History

Ecology and Behavior

Snakes are essentially thin lizards that have no legs, no eyelids, no eardrums, one lung, and, sometimes, big teeth. They are carnivores and potential food must be detected, seized, and subdued. When caught, prey cannot be chewed into small pieces, so it must be swallowed whole. To understand this different lifestyle, it helps to think like a snake. Get on your belly, forget your limbs and cutlery, and wonder how you're going to catch and eat your next meal. The ancestors of snakes were blind, burrowing lizards that ate small, easily swallowed prey. Like their lizard ancestors, worm lizards and blind burrowing snakes still feed on large numbers of invertebrates. Worm lizards burrow in search of beetle larvae and worms, which they detect by scent and vibration. They crush them in their strong jaws or tear large prey to bits by pressing the victim's body against the burrow wall. Blind snakes and thread snakes both feed almost exclusively on the eggs and larvae of ants. Once inside the brood chamber of an ant nest, they consume prodigious amounts of highly nutritious food. Blind snakes are "binge feeders" and can withstand long fasts between meals. Their thick, overlapping, polished scales provide effective armor against the jaws of soldier ants. Thread snakes eat smaller meals, using the long teeth of the lower jaws to rake food into the mouth. They are small and appear defenseless, but can avoid attacks from soldier ants by a scent that is similar to the pheromones ants use to recognize each other. Despite the size and shape of thread snakes, soldier ants treat them as if they were just another ant.

As snakes evolved, they developed ways to feed on active prey such as rats, lizards, fish, and frogs. Overcoming and swallowing large prey without limbs is a hard battle and needs special adaptations. One is to use the elongate body to encircle and immobilize the victim. Constricted prey is not crushed to death, but suffocated. Pythons were among the first snakes to constrict prey and then swallow it whole. Special elastic joints in the skull and jaws allow them to engulf prey much larger than their own heads. The windpipe has been strengthened with cartilaginous rings and the opening (epiglottis) moved to the front of the mouth. This allows them to breathe during the lengthy swallowing process. Pythons live in well-wooded savannah and forest, often among rock outcrops and river-associated scrub. They may submerge in bankside vegetation, waiting in ambush for prey that comes to drink. Although non-venomous, they have a mouth full of sharp teeth and can give a very painful bite. They eat small antelope, monkeys, rabbits, and birds. Even fish, monitor lizards, and crocodiles may be eaten. Stored food reserves allow pythons to fast for more than a year between meals in some cases.

Breeding

Many primitive snakes have sophisticated features. Most worm lizards and blind burrowing snakes lay eggs, but some species give birth to fully formed babies (viviparity). The Cape Spade-snouted Worm Lizard gives birth to 1–3 babies in late summer, and although most blind snakes lay soft-shelled eggs, these may contain advanced embryos that hatch in a few days. The FLOWER POT SNAKE is an alien blind snake unwittingly introduced to the Cape with exotic vegetation transplanted to Kirstenbosch Botanical Garden. It has also colonized Durban, Beira in Mozambique, as well as Florida, Israel, and numerous other places. Its success as a colonizer is due to a bizarre ability—it is the only all-female, self fertilizing (*parthenogenetic*) snake in the world. All thread snakes lay a few elongate eggs, joined together like a string of tiny sausages. Python eggs are similar in size and shape to oranges. The Southern African Python lays 30 to 50 eggs in a secluded spot, such as a hollow tree or disused Aardvark hole. Very large females may lay more than 60 eggs. The female coils around her eggs, protecting them from predators such as mongooses or monitor lizards. They hatch in 60 to 80 days.

Ecological Interactions

Although worm lizards, blind snakes, and thread snakes live underground, they burrow in different ways. The head and body of a worm lizard move within its loose skin, and it burrows into soil with a ramming motion. Spade-snouted Worm Lizards use the "thumbnail" on their head to scrape soil from the front of the burrow. They are capable of driving permanent burrows through hard, compacted soils. Blind snakes, in contrast, have thick, muscular bodies but can only force their way through loose sand or along ant tunnels. Thread snakes have no special adaptations to burrowing, except for being very thin. They wriggle through small tunnels into the brood chambers of ant nests.

Notes

Man-eaters or myth? A 5 m (16 ft) African python in Uganda once swallowed a 60 kg (130 lb) Kob antelope. This is the largest documented meal for any giant snake, although greater feats of gluttony have probably gone unrecorded. Pythons should always be treated with caution; they are capable of attacking and killing people. In 1979, a young Tswana herdboy in the Northern Province was driving his cattle home at dusk. He was seized and constricted by a python 4.7 m (15.4 ft) in length. The snake was disturbed before it could finish swallowing the dead boy. This was a very rare and unfortunate incident, but it emphasizes the respect these giant snakes deserve.

Status

In West and Central Africa, more than 150,000 pythons are killed each year to be turned into shoes and handbags for people who should know better. Fortunately most countries protect pythons, as they help control many pests. But law enforcement is poor in many regions and their numbers continue to decline. Many others are killed for traditional medicine. Python fat is claimed to have great healing powers. It is prized "muti" for many witch doctors. All species of family Boidae (pythons, boas) are CITES Appendix II listed, considered vulnerable or threatened (primarily because they are sought by the international illicit pet trade).

Profiles

Cape Spade-snouted Worm Lizard, *Monopeltis capensis*, Plate 8a
Schlegel's Giant Blind Snake, *Rhinotyphlops schlegelii*, Plate 8b

Western Thread Snake, *Leptotyphlops occidentalis*, Plate 8c
Southern African Python, *Python natalensis*, Plate 8d
Angolan Dwarf Python, *Python anchietae*, Plate 8e

3. Colubrids: Harmless Snakes, the Silent Majority

Snakes are now at their evolutionary peak and are found almost worldwide. The vast majority are harmless and terrestrial, while others live in trees, rock outcrops, or around water. Very few, however, are marine. Most harmless snakes are placed for convenience in the family Colubridae, which contains more than 1,500 species. It is an unwieldy assemblage. Few African *colubrids* are closely related to the common snakes of the New World or Europe, even though some share identical common names. African *water, grass,* and *green snakes* are only distantly related to similarly named snakes from the Northern Hemisphere. Others, such as *house, wolf,* and *file snakes,* and *egg-, slug-,* and *centipede-eaters,* form the common groups that are unique to Africa. The diversity is best understood in terms of their lifestyles (see below). Most colubrids lack fangs (enlarged, grooved teeth), but some groups have fangs at the back of the mouth (see p. 81).

Natural History

Ecology and Behavior

Many snakes specialize on different types of prey. In places where a number of different snakes feed on the same type of prey, they may catch them in different habitats or catch them at different times of the day. Most kill by constriction, although some search out defenseless prey and simply swallow it alive. Perhaps the most ubiquitous local snake is the SOUTHERN BROWN HOUSE SNAKE (Plate 9). It is common in gardens and backyards, where it is attracted by the plentiful supply of mice and rats. Like their prey, house snakes are nocturnal and terrestrial. They creep into tunnels and rubbish piles and ambush passing rodents. Although nocturnal, the CAPE WOLF SNAKE (Plate 9) eats mainly day-active lizards, which are caught as they sleep in their shelters. Long teeth in the front of the snake's mouth (from which it gets its common name) help it grip and pull lizards from their crevices. The unusual name of the CAPE FILE SNAKE (Plate 9) comes from its triangular body and rough scales, which occur particularly along the backbone. It is a fearless predator of other snakes, even venomous species. A large file snake was once opened and found to contain four snakes, including a python, a water snake, a sand snake, and a spitting cobra. The SOUTHERN SLUG-EATING SNAKE (Plate 9) is a little stout-bodied snake. It is mainly nocturnal, although it may move around on mild, overcast days. It prefers damp habitats and can be found among grass roots and rotting timber. It feeds exclusively on snails and slugs. These are detected by their slime trails, which the snake follows to its source. No attempt is made to subdue the prey; it is simply swallowed whole. However, snails sometimes prove a danger. Slug-eaters have died after their heads became jammed when the intended victim withdrew into its shell. The MOLE SNAKE (Plate 9) is a giant cousin of the small slug-eaters. It is a thick-bodied, powerful constrictor that may grow to nearly 2.5 m (9 ft) long. Large mole rats form the main diet, although adults eat other rodents and juveniles also eat lizards. Some adults also eat bird eggs, which they swallow whole. SUNDEVALL'S SHOVEL-SNOUTED SNAKE (Plate 10) is easy to recognize by the angular "shovel" on its snout. It feeds almost exclusively on reptile eggs, which it finds by burrowing in loose soil beneath boulders and dead logs. Bladed teeth slit the eggs before they are swallowed. The COMMON EGG-EATING SNAKE (Plate 10) also feeds on eggs, but only those of birds; it eats nothing else. Numerous adaptations allow it to perform this feat. The mouth is almost toothless, while the skin of the neck and lower jaw stretches dramatically. The lower jaws disarticulate from the skull and are connected at the front by an elastic ligament. The egg, which may be three times the diameter of the snake's head, is pushed against the side of the nest, forcing it into the mouth. Once in the throat, it is moved backwards and forwards against the backbone. Enlarged spines on the vertebrae penetrate the gullet and "saw" through the shell. The liquid contents are then swallowed, and the collapsed eggshell is regurgitated—the process is a rather bizarre achievement.

Breeding

The males of most non-venomous snakes do not fight for mates. One exception is the Mole Snake, the males of which fight with each other in the breeding season. They bite readily, inflicting deep gashes on one another. Most colubrids lay small, soft-shelled eggs. They are hidden in sun-warmed soil beneath a stone or dead log. No maternal care occurs, apart from the selection of the egg-laying site. The hatchling escapes from the egg by cutting a slit with a sharp egg-tooth on the tip of its snout. This falls off soon after hatching. Mole snakes and slug-eaters give birth to live babies, the former having large litters of up to 95, while slug-eaters have only 5 to 15 young. All are born in late summer. Most juveniles look like adults, except for young Mole Snakes, which are boldly spotted, unlike the plain brown or black adults.

Ecological Interactions

Africa has plenty of predators that eat snakes, including mongooses, genets, honey badgers, jackals, secretary birds, several species of snake eagle, large shrikes, ground hornbills, and many kingfishers. To avoid predation, most small snakes are nocturnal and cryptically colored. Others writhe when touched or handled and may void a foul-smelling liquid from the vent. Some harmless snakes even mimic venomous snakes. The toothless Common Egg-eating Snake has keeled and serrated lateral body scales. When threatened, the egg-eater assumes a coiled posture, like a set of nested horseshoes. As the coils move, the rough scales rub against one another, creating a "hissing" sound. The snake also strikes readily with a gaping, black-lined mouth, which creates a dramatic effect. The effect is further enhanced by the blotched color pattern and inverted V-shape on the neck, which is very similar to that of some adders. To the knowledgeable this is a toothless, comical performance. For natural predators, however, the harmless egg-eater looks, sounds, and behaves like a small, deadly viper.

Notes

Most people simply lump snakes into venomous or non-venomous, and believe that "the only good snake is a dead snake." This stigmatization of snakes, and their evil stereotypes, are simply not justified. Admittedly, a few snakes have killed people, but these deaths are no more evil or distressing than those caused by lions, elephants, buffalo, hippos, crocodiles, and even ostriches. Snakebite causes few human deaths—perhaps 10 to 20 in southern Africa each year. These numbers are insignificant compared with car crash victims or smoking and diet-related deaths. Of 131 snake species in southern Africa, less than 25% are dangerous. Of these, the bites of only 14 have caused death, while a further 18 have venom that may cause symptoms. Despite the dangerous minority, most snakes are important predators in ecosystems, where they control many of the animals we view as pests.

Status

Few of these snakes are endangered, although some are very rare or have restricted distributions. During the last 90 years, fewer than a dozen specimens of FISK'S HOUSE SNAKE have been caught from widely scattered localities within the Karoo and Namaqualand. The CREAM-SPOTTED MOUNTAIN SNAKE is known from only three specimens collected in mountain seepages high in the Drakensberg Mountains.

Profiles

Southern Brown House Snake, *Lamprophis capensis*, Plate 9a
Cape Wolf Snake, *Lycophidion capense*, Plate 9b
Cape File Snake, *Mehelya capensis*, Plate 9c
Southern Slug-eating Snake, *Duberria lutrix*, Plate 9d
Mole Snake, *Pseudaspis cana*, Plate 9e
Sundevall's Shovel-snouted Snake, *Prosymna sundevallii*, Plate 10a
Common Egg-eating Snake, *Dasypeltis scabra*, Plate 10e

4. More Colubrids: Back-fangs—Sheep Stabbers and Toad Prickers

Reptile fangs are emotive things. They conjure up visions of deadly snakes and agonizing death. However, although more than a third of snakes have enlarged teeth at the back of the mouth, only a small fraction of these species are dangerous. They may have fangs but lack a potent venom, or produce venom in such small amounts that it is not dangerous to people. *Back-fangs* (fangs at the back of the mouth) are an important innovation for snakes, and they have evolved many times and for various uses. Although most back-fanged snakes are placed along with many harmless species in the family Colubridae (as are all the species profiled here, with the exception of the CAPE CENTIPEDE-EATER, Plate 10), they are not necessarily closely related to one another. Early classifications based on teeth alone do not reflect evolutionary relationships. Instead of worrying about unresolved issues of ancestry, for our purposes here it is more useful to ask why snakes have fangs and venom. What functions do they serve?

Snakes face a number of problems when swallowing large prey. The first is getting food into the stomach, via the gullet. Snakes do this in a strange way. The prey is first manipulated so that it can be swallowed head-first (this helps because the prey's limbs then fold easily along its body, and so do not "jam" the swallowing process). Many of the teeth-carrying bones in the snake's upper jaw are loosely connected to the skull. The bones on one side of the head are lifted, unhooking the teeth from the prey. The bones are then rocked forward and the teeth hooked back into the prey. This cycle is then repeated on alternate sides, and the snake's head is "walked" over the food. For this process, it is best to have larger teeth at the back of the mouth, as they can maintain a stronger hold. These enlarged teeth are *proto-fangs*, although at this stage in evolution they do not transport venom. Some amphibians, especially toads, inflate themselves when grabbed by snakes, making themselves difficult to swallow. To combat this, the enlarged back teeth of the frog-eating RED-LIPPED SNAKE (Plate 12) have cutting edges. They are used to puncture toads so that they deflate and are easier to swallow.

Large meals are difficult to digest because stomach enzymes can act only on the surface of prey swallowed whole. It may take a long time to digest large prey. This is inefficient as well as dangerous because snakes hindered by fat stomachs cannot flee predators very well. Moreover, the food may rot in the center before it is fully digested. Shredding food into smaller pieces helps speed digestion—this is why mammals chew their food. Snakes cannot chew their food, but instead introduce digestive enzymes into the food via their teeth. The enlarged back teeth puncture the prey's body to allow the entry of enzymes. Glands close to these teeth produce strong digestive juices. To make the system more efficient, the enlarged teeth developed grooves to channel the juices into the teeth punctures. These grooved, enlarged teeth are now called *fangs*.

Natural History

Ecology and Behavior

Like the harmless members of their family (p. 79), back-fanged snakes have varied lives that are best understood in terms of the prey they hunt. The WESTERN KEELED SNAKE (Plate 10) is an interesting nocturnal oddity of the rocky plains of the Namib Desert. Females grow much larger than the males and feed on mice, while juveniles and males catch sleeping lizards. They have a weak venom that can kill lizards, but mice are constricted. The BICOLORED QUILL-SNOUTED SNAKE (Plate 10) is a thin African burrower with a quill-shaped head and underslung mouth that helps it to breathe in loose sand. It burrows in sandy savannahs and feeds exclusively on amphisbaenians (p. 76), which are caught, killed, and consumed underground. Centipedes have sharp jaws and powerful venom, and are well able to defend themselves, but they do not deter the small Cape Centipede-eater, which feeds exclusively on centipedes. It hunts them among loose rubble, rotting logs, and old termite nests. Prey is grabbed and chewed until the snake's venom takes effect, often after a violent and lengthy confrontation.

Sand and *grass snakes* are common, active, diurnal African snakes. They have thin bodies but do not constrict prey. Some are reputed to have toxic venom, but it is produced in minute amounts and is rarely a danger to humans. The common, part Afrikaans, name of the SPOTTED SKAAPSTEKKER (Plate 11) translates as "spotted sheep stabber." This is a gross exaggeration, as the snake's venom is incapable of killing even a rabbit. The STRIPE-BELLIED SAND SNAKE (Plate 11) is a graceful inhabitant of northern savannahs, distinguished by its bright yellow, black-edged belly. It chases small lizards and climbs into low bushes to take fledgling birds. Two related snakes live in loose, sandy habitats and have hooked snouts that aid in burrowing. The small, slender DWARF BEAKED SNAKE (Plate 11) shelters at the base of grass tussocks or among stones and ambushes small lizards. The BEAKED SNAKE (Plate 11) is a larger, stouter snake. Slow-moving and diurnal, it searches in mammal burrows and old termite mounds for rodents, lizards, and snakes.

Arboreal snakes rarely constrict prey; they tend to fall out of trees when they try to do so. Most small arboreal snakes are therefore back-fanged and use venom to kill small vertebrates such as birds, lizards, and tree frogs. The BARK SNAKE (Plate 11), as its name implies, shelters beneath loose bark. It feeds on day geckos, small skinks, and tree frogs. These are seized, held until subdued by venom, and then swallowed as the snake hangs head down in the foliage. The TIGER SNAKE's (Plate 12) large cat-like eyes with vertical pupils mean it could only be nocturnal. It hunts lizards, sleeping birds, and even bats in hollow trees, rock outcrops, or caves. The SPOTTED BUSH SNAKE (Plate 12) hunts in open savannah, actively chasing small lizards such as day geckos and chameleons and occasionally catching small mice and tree frogs.

Breeding

Although many back-fanged snakes are unrelated and have varied lives, they share a dull conservatism in their breeding. The vast majority lay a small clutch of soft-shelled eggs in spring, like most other local snakes. There are a few exceptions, however. The Spotted Skaapstekker lays up to 30 eggs in a hole scooped beneath a sun-warmed stone. Unlike other snakes, the female coils around her eggs and stays with them during early incubation. The eggs already have well-developed embryos when laid, and hatch in only 35 to 45 days. Snakes do not form pair-bonds. Females may mate with numerous males and can store sperm to fertilize eggs in later years. DNA testing has also shown that a single clutch of eggs may have been fathered by a number of males.

Ecological Interactions

Sand snakes are common in the western arid regions and are active during the day. Few other snakes are active in the desert during this time. Two features may allow them to survive in this hostile environment. Some species have a nasal gland that gives the snout a somewhat "Roman" appearance. These snakes groom themselves, rubbing the side of the head backwards and forwards across the body. In doing this, they appear to spread the secretion from the nasal glands evenly over their bodies. The composition has not been studied in detail, but it may reduce water loss or be used in territorial marking. There are few places to hide in open desert, so these snakes have an escape mechanism and other defenses. When captured by the tail, these snakes spin wildly and the tail tip is shed (unlike the tail of a lizard, it is not regenerated). Presumably, this allows some captured snakes to escape from predators. The larger species readily bite. The venom is usually harmless to humans, but bites from some species have caused pain, swelling, and in one case mild bleeding.

Notes

In general, snakes are sadly neglected, even vilified. It is not just a modern attitude, and cannot be due simply to the small, venomous minority. Even the famous Swedish naturalist Carolus Linnaeus, who formalized the system of naming species in the mid-1700s, dismissed them as "foul and loathsome creatures." In fact, he went even further and dismissed all reptiles and amphibians—"they are abhorrent because of their cold body, cartilaginous skeleton, filthy skin, fierce aspect, calculating eye, offensive smell, harsh voice, squalid habitation, and terrible venom; wherefore their Creator has not exerted his powers to make many of them." They still have an image problem, and must look with envy at emotive posters urging "Save the Whale" or "Help the Rhino." Too often our awareness of wildlife includes only the warm and cuddly. It is doubtful that pleas to "Save the Puff Adder" or "Protect the Python" would succeed. We will begin to take responsibility for the Earth only when we look with sympathy and understanding on all wildlife, including reptiles and amphibians.

Status

None of these varied and interesting snakes is endangered. The CAPE SAND SNAKE is restricted to the coastal fynbos habitats in the southwestern Cape. Much of this habitat has been lost and the snake is vulnerable to further declines.

Profiles

Western Keeled Snake, *Pythonodipsas carinata*, Plate 10b
Bicolored Quill-snouted Snake, *Xenocalamus bicolor*, Plate 10c
Cape Centipede-eater, *Aparallactus capensis*, Plate 10d
Spotted Skaapstekker, *Psammophylax rhombeatus*, Plate 11a
Stripe-bellied Sand Snake, *Psammophis subtaeniatus*, Plate 11b
Dwarf Beaked Snake, *Dipsina multimaculata*, Plate 11c
Beaked Snake, *Rhamphiophis rostratus*, Plate 11d
Bark Snake, *Hemirhagerrhis nototaenia*, Plate 11e
Red-lipped Snake, *Crotaphopeltis hotamboeia*, Plate 12a
Tiger Snake, *Telescopus semiannulatus*, Plate 12b
Spotted Bush Snake, *Philothamnus semivariegatus*, Plate 12c

5. Dangerous Snakes—A Venomous Few

Snakes are fragile, with thin-boned skulls. Holding struggling prey can cause substantial damage. It is safer to use potent saliva not just to digest prey, but also to kill it. Such salivas are called *venom*. Venom has proved so useful that it has evolved independently in three local snake groups—*adders, burrowing asps,* and *cobras*. These snakes all have very different venom glands and fang mechanisms. In all, the fangs have moved to the front of the mouth and are hollow, so large amounts of venom can be injected in a quick stab. The struggling prey need not be held, thus avoiding potential injury. Like the arrow and dart poisons used by African Bushmen and Amazonian Indians, snake venom may be slow- or fast-acting. Which option is needed depends on the environment or the abilities of the hunter. Slow-acting poisons require efficient prey-tracking behavior. Killing the prey is no use if it cannot be relocated. Bushmen may spend 24 hours following poisoned game, but they are excellent trackers and the prey is unlikely to be lost in open habitats. Adders strike large prey, but do not hold on. They use smell and heat-sensing abilities to track down the dying prey. The arrow poisons of Amazonian Indians and the venom of cobras and mambas work differently. They are *neurotoxic*, blocking nerve impulses and causing rapid paralysis, immobilizing the prey and preventing it from being lost. This explains the apparent paradox of why mambas and some other snakes have venom so powerful that a single drop can kill thousands of rats or up to a dozen people. Such overkill results from the necessity to kill prey within seconds before it escapes and dies unfound. The venom must kill quickly; the numbers it can kill are irrelevant. When viewed from the perspective of evolution and ecology, snake venom becomes an elegant and efficient adjunct to predation. It is no more horrendous or evil than a lion's fangs or an eagle's talons.

Tree Snakes. Few *back-fanged* snakes (p. 81) have venom that can kill humans. Two, however, are found in southern Africa (both are members of family Colubridae). The BOOMSLANG ("tree snake" in Afrikaans; Plate 12) is found wherever trees are common. Its coloration is very variable, with different patterns for juveniles, females, and males. The TWIG SNAKE (Plate 12) is twig-colored and vine-like in body shape. It is restricted to northern savannahs. The lance-like head has large eyes. Both of these snakes have unusual venom that prevents blood clotting. Death can follow within 2 to 3 days, but bites are very rare. In fact, there are no records of bites to "innocent" people; only careless or ignorant snake-handlers get bitten.

Cobras. Cobras and their relatives (*coral snakes, mambas*) belong to family Elapidae. The fangs are short and not hinged. Most are active, alert hunters that flee quickly from people. Bites are therefore rare. The CORAL SNAKE (Plate 13) has a large "bulldozer" shield on its snout to aid burrowing. Cobras are famed for their threat display, in which the forebody rears and a wide *neck hood* is spread. The CAPE COBRA (Plate 13) is not the largest cobra, but it is a "top predator," comparable to the more famed big cats or eagles. Alert or at rest, Cape Cobras exude subtle confidence and supple danger. A number of cobras, including the RINKHALS (Plate 13), have modified fangs to allow them to spit venom in defense. Unlike other cobras, the Rinkhals has keeled scales and a large white throat band. Large, agile, and diurnal, mambas are formidable snakes. They are best left well alone. They have flat sided, "coffin shaped" heads with large eyes, slender bodies, and long tails. The BLACK MAMBA (Plate 13) is poorly named because it is really a dirty gray olive color. It does, however, have a blackish mouth lining and a temperament to match its name. It is the longest poisonous snake in Africa and may exceed 4 m (13 ft) in length.

Adders. These fat-bodied, large-headed snakes, have long, hinged fangs. They belong to family Viperidae (the group that includes most of the New World's venomous snakes, such as rattlesnakes). Most are small snakes, mainly adapted to desert or mountain habitats. One group, the *night adders*, inhabit the moister eastern region. One species, the PUFF ADDER (Plate 14), is widespread and common throughout southern Africa.

Burrowing asps. These elongate, burrowing snakes of family Atractaspididae, are unique to Africa. They were once thought to be primitive adders and called "mole vipers," but are probably more closely related to cobras. The SOUTHERN BURROWING ASP (Plate 14) is easily confused with harmless black snakes, and many people have mistakenly picked it up. The bite is always painful, but not life-threatening. The colorful SPOTTED HARLEQUIN SNAKE (Plate 13) burrows in loose sand and is rarely seen.

Natural History

Ecology and Behavior

Tree Snakes. Hunting by day, these arboreal snakes use their excellent vision to see, pursue, and seize their prey. Chameleons form the main diet of the Boomslang, supplemented with nestling birds. The Twig Snake eats more varied fare, including frogs and other snakes. Much of its prey is terrestrial and ambushed from above, where the snake lies cryptically hidden among the foliage.

Cobras. Cobras are generalists, feeding on a wide variety of prey. Very large cobras often eat other snakes, particularly the Puff Adder. The Black Mamba pursues its prey, stabbing it repeatedly until it succumbs to the potent venom. It is an active, nervous snake that has a favored retreat, such as a hollow tree, rock cave, or old termite nest, that an individual may inhabit for many years.

Adders. The COMMON NIGHT ADDER (Plate 14) is nocturnal, hunting toads and frogs in the moist eastern regions. It has mild venom that rarely causes serious symptoms in people. The HORNED ADDER (Plate 14) lives in the western deserts, ambushing small lizards and rodents. The horn above each eye breaks the outline of the head as the snake waits for prey to come within range. There is little cover in the drifting dunes of the Namib Desert, so PERINGUEY'S SIDE-WINDING ADDER (Plate 14) hides by shuffling down into the sand, leaving only the eyes on top of its head and its black-tipped tail exposed. The tail is wiggled slowly to lure lizards closer. Both small adders "side-wind" in loose sand, a complex, looping movement that reduces the amount of body in contact with the hot sand.

Burrowing asps. These thin, black snakes, have an unusual fang mechanism that is adapted for feeding within the confines of a tunnel. A fang can be partially erected on one side by depressing the lip, and the mouth need not fully open. A single long, straight fang is stabbed backwards into prey. Other common names for these snakes, such as *stiletto snake* or *side-stabber,* allude to this striking ability. Harlequin snakes feed only on other burrowing reptiles, including blind snakes and legless lizards.

Breeding

Tree snakes, burrowing asps, and all cobras, with the exception of the Rinkhals, lay eggs. These are laid in spring (September to November) and take about 60 days to undergo development. The Rinkhals gives birth to up to 60 live young in late summer (February to March). Night adders are primitive adders that still lay eggs. All other adders give birth to live young. The number varies from 2 to 6 in the minute Peringuey's Side-winding Adder to between 20 and 50 in Puff Adders. A gigantic Kenyan Puff Adder once gave birth to 157 babies, the largest number of young produced by any snake in the world.

In the breeding season, pairs of mambas are often observed moving together with their heads and forebodies held high. Most people assume that this is mating, but in most it is male combat. Many large snakes, including mambas, cobras, and the larger adders, perform these ritualized contests. The males move in parallel with their heads raised. As they move they intertwine like rope coils. Periodically they violently stiffen their bodies, and it may cause a weaker opponent to be "thrown." Such combat may last for several hours, even in the absence of watching females. It is assumed that the winner claims the right to mate with females, but this has not been proven. Mating, in many snakes, is similar but less violent. Mates move slowly together, with the male moving in loops on top of the female, not entwined around her. The bodies are also held close together near the vent, often with the female's tail lifted to allow copulation.

Ecological Interactions

Many venomous snakes give *threat displays.* Active daytime hunters give visual warnings. Cobras and mambas rear the forebody and spread hoods using elongated ribs in the neck region. This may be accompanied by an open-mouthed threat that is emphasized in the mamba by the black mouth lining. It is a warning unheeded by only the foolish. The Boomslang and Twig Snake also inflate their neck regions, displaying vivid, brightly colored skin between the scales. Harlequin snakes are gaudily patterned in yellow, black, and red, similar to many coral snakes of the New World. The bright colors are warning coloration, signalling to possible predators that they are venomous. Nocturnal ambush predators, like adders and rattlesnakes, may go unnoticed by large, grazing ungulates. To avoid being trodden on, these snakes give a noisy warning: Puff Adders puff and rattlesnakes rattle. They use very different mechanisms to give similar warnings. All these warnings, audible and visual, are given to avoid confrontation. Should you have such an encounter, show respect, step back slowly, and both you and the snake will go in peace.

Notes

Spitting is an efficient and sophisticated defense—if you're a cobra! A number of Asian and African cobras have developed this unpleasant behavior, which is purely defensive, and not used to capture prey. Strictly speaking, cobras do not spit, rather the venom is squirted from the venom glands. "Squirting cobra" as a name, however, is unlikely to catch on. Spitting is very accurate and cobras can hit an intruder's face at 2 to 3 m (6 to 10 ft). This requires a number of important evolutionary modifications to the fangs and venom. The fangs become straighter and stouter than those of non-spitters. The hole from which the venom emerges is also smaller, "tear-drop" in shape, and opens on the front of the fang, some distance from the tip. It allows the venom to be shot forward, not downward. The width of the venom canal also enlarges to ease the flow of venom. These modifications are only part of the story, as pressing the button on an aerosol will illustrate: Liquid atomizes when emerging from a fine hole under pressure. The droplets get smaller and the spray widens into a mist. To avoid this, a long ridge within the fang's venom canal is angled and imparts a rotation to the venom stream. It thus remains as a cohesive jet for some distance before breaking into a spray. There remains one final and important modification involving the composition and viscosity of the venom. Non-spitting cobras and mambas have syrupy venom due to the high levels of neurotoxins it contains. The venom of spitters, however, is diluted and has a lower viscosity. It also changes in composition. The venom of a spitter causes immediate ulceration and pain in the intruder's eyes. This is also reflected in the swelling, necrosis, and blood abnormalities that occur in bites from most spitting cobras (the Rinkhals is an exception). Although this elegant suite of adaptations to both fangs and venom give spitting cobras an effective defense, a price has to be paid. The diluted venom is less efficient in quickly killing active prey; thus, most spitting cobras are nocturnal and feed on easier prey, such as toads.

Status

Few venomous snakes are endangered, although many are declining in number or have become locally extinct. Three small adders in the covered region do have very localized distributions and are endangered. One, the ALBANY ADDER, lives in the Eastern Cape near Port Elizabeth. Only 12 specimens have ever been found, and the habitat of the only known population is threatened by limestone mining.

Profiles

Twig Snake, *Thelotornis capensis*, Plate 12d
Boomslang, *Dispholidus typus*, Plate 12e
Spotted Harlequin Snake, *Homoroselaps lacteus*, Plate 13a
Coral Snake, *Aspidelaps lubricus*, Plate 13b
Rinkhals, *Hemachatus haemachatus*, Plate 13c
Cape Cobra, *Naja nivea*, Plate 13d
Black Mamba, *Dendroaspis polylepis*, Plate 13e
Common Night Adder, *Causus rhombeatus*, Plate 14a
Puff Adder, *Bitis arietans*, Plate 14b
Horned Adder, *Bitis caudalis*, Plate 14c
Peringuey's Side-winding Adder, *Bitis peringueyi*, Plate 14d
Southern Burrowing Asp, *Atractaspis bibronii*, Plate 14e

6. Geckos—Reptilian Acrobats

Undervalued gems, lizards are the commonest reptiles in southern Africa. South Africa has the greatest diversity of lizards in Africa, and among these, *geckos* are the most varied. In fact, there are more gecko species (more than 100) in southern Africa than there are all kinds of lizards in the entire Congo region. Geckos abound throughout southern Africa. They can be found nearly everywhere, sheltering under debris at the high tide line, hiding in burrows in Kalahari and Namib sand dunes, and under rock flakes on the rocky ramparts of the Cape Fold Mountains and Drakensberg escarpment. A few species live in association with people; that is, they are *commensal*, occupying homes and outhouses. Most local geckos have unblinking eyes. They keep them clean with a lick of their large, fleshy tongues. Their skin is often delicate and finely scaled.

The most common and widespread is TURNER'S THICK-TOED GECKO (Plate 15). It is big-jawed, pugnacious, relatively gregarious, and can form dense colonies in suitable rocky areas. In contrast, the beautiful and unusual WEB-FOOTED GECKO (Plate 15) is a hidden jewel of the Namib Desert. Its unusual webbed toes allow it to dig in the windblown sands. The TROPICAL HOUSE GECKO (Plate 15) is commensal and thrives in urban areas. Night lights and outside water heaters are the key to its success, attracting moths and flies that serve as gecko food and giving off heat to protect the geckos from cool winter nights. Forty years ago this species occurred only in the eastern semitropical regions. Since then it has rapidly expanded inland and south into urban areas. Some are transported accidentally in crates between harbors and warehouses, others via caravans.

Natural History

Ecology and Behavior

Most geckos are nocturnal, although a few, such as the COMMON NAMIB DAY GECKO (Plate 15), forage like other lizards in the warmth of the sun. Most geckos have large, prominent eyes to see well at night. The size and shape of the pupil may vary considerably: It opens wide at night to admit more light, and contracts during the day to the size of a few pinholes. Geckos have a greater tolerance to low temperatures than other lizards. They are therefore common in cold environments, such as mountains and, paradoxically, deserts—most deserts have great temperature fluctuations, and although they get very hot during the day, at night they may also get very cold. Vocalization is unusual in reptiles but very common in geckos. When handled, most species utter a series of distress "clicks." The repertoire of the COMMON BARKING GECKO (Plate 15) is very impressive. The male sits at the entrance to his burrow and emits a series of short, sharp clicks—a familiar sound at sunset in the Kalahari. The sounds attract females and warn other males to stay away from the caller's territory.

Breeding

Except for a few New Zealand species, all geckos lay eggs. Most species lay hard-shelled eggs (unique among lizards and snakes), and large amounts of calciumin their diets are therefore necessary. Most is obtained from their food, but geckos also eat old eggshells. The calcium is stored in special neck glands (*endolymphatic sacs*), which are easily visible in females. Clutches consist of only two eggs, but many species lay several clutches during a breeding season. The eggs are relatively large and can easily be seen through the belly wall just prior to being laid. They are laid in holes in the sand or under bark or rock flakes. Some species are communal nesters, and a suitable crack may contain dozens of fresh eggs from many females as well as the remains of old eggshells from previous seasons.

Ecological Interactions

Geckos are famous for their feet. Many have special pads beneath the tips of all their toes that allow them to walk on vertical, overhanging, and smooth surfaces. Millions of minute "hairs" cover the toe pads. These microscopic *setae* (hair is a mammalian invention) are arranged in rows, the shape and number of which vary between species. In general, the terrestrial species have smaller toe pads while species that defy gravity, inhabiting vertical rock faces, tree bark, or the walls and ceilings of houses, have larger pads. The pads are not sticky and do not rely on suction. It was once thought that support was achieved when the small setae hooked on to tiny irregularities on the surfaces they walk on, but it is now known that this wouldn't work. Instead, scientists have shown that the hairs are so fine and numerous that minute physical forces at the atomic level (van der Waal forces) generate sufficient attraction to support the gecko. Many large geckos also have accessory retractile claws on the toes, which can be hooked down to give the toes greater grip. Toe pads are easily soiled and have to be constantly groomed. Some terrestrial species have special muscles that pull the toe pads up and away from loose soil when "adhesion" isn't required.

Notes

It is a common fallacy that geckos are poisonous. Certainly the larger species can give a painful bite, but none have venom. They avoid predators by hiding in rock cracks, under debris, etc. If caught, all species can shed their tails. These are quickly regenerated, and some adults may grow two or three new tails during their lives. The new tail is always thicker and duller than the original. Some species can shed their skin as well as their fragile tails. When seized they spin rapidly, tearing the delicate skin. The flayed gecko can wriggle to safety, and quickly grows new skin.

Status

Many geckos in the region have very restricted distributions and face various threats. METHUEN'S DWARF DAY GECKO is restricted to a few rock outcrops on the Mpumalanga Escarpment that are not overgrown by exotic pine plantations. The PONDO FLAT GECKO is becoming increasingly rare as it is excluded from its habitat by an invasion of Tropical House Geckos.

Profiles

Tropical House Gecko, *Hemidactylus mabouia*, Plate 15a
Common Barking Gecko, *Ptenopus garrulus*, Plate 15b
Web-footed Gecko, *Pachydactylus rangei*, Plate 15c
Turner's Thick-toed Gecko, *Chondrodactylus turneri*, Plate 15d
Common Namib Day Gecko, *Rhoptropus afer*, Plate 15e

7. Agamas and Chameleons

Agamas and *chameleons* are among the most primitive of living lizards. They share many characteristics, including a similar arrangement of teeth, an inability to shed or regenerate their tails, and small scales on the tops of their heads. Family Agamidae is a large and ancient group found throughout Africa, although the greatest diversity occurs in Asia and Australia. African agamas are plump, squat lizards with rough scales and triangular heads that have a dimpled scale on the crown. This covers the *pineal organ*, or "third eye," which detects seasonal changes in day length. Chameleons (family Chamaeleonidae) are mainly restricted to

Africa and Madagascar, but with one species in Europe and a few found as far away as India and Sri Lanka. The FLAP-NECKED CHAMELEON (Plate 16) is the only species in the northern savannah. It has large fleshy flaps at the back of the head and a continuous crest of small white scales on the throat and belly. *Dwarf chameleons* lack the ventral crest and are restricted to the eastern and southern forests and fynbos. The CAPE DWARF CHAMELEON (Plate 16) is very common in Cape Town gardens and adjacent towns.

Natural History

Ecology and Behavior

Active and diurnal, agamas feed predominantly on ants and termites but will also take other insects. Many live in colonies, with well defined social hierarchies. Dominant males command and defend the best retreats, food sources, and mates. These individuals develop vivid breeding colors and display from the highest points in their realms, advertising their status by bobbing their bright blue heads. Juveniles and females remain drab to match their surroundings. Rock-dwelling species have long legs and toes with sharp claws, and run effortlessly over vertical and overhanging rock faces. The SOUTHERN ROCK AGAMA (Plate 16) is common on the rock outcrops of the Cape, from coastal cliffs to mountain summits. The ETOSHA GROUND AGAMA (Plate 16), as can be guessed from its name, lives on the burnished calcrete flats of Etosha Pan in northern Namibia. Perched on a small boulder, it feeds on passing termites and tiny beetles. For concealment, and to escape the midday heat, it may shuffle into loose sand. It has a peculiar "eye popping" behavior that clears sand from the eyelids and helps shed old skin. Visitors to the lowveld regions, particularly in Kruger National Park, will be familiar with the TREE AGAMA (Plate 16). The colorful head of a big male is a blue jewel against the lichen-covered bark. It is the largest agama; adults can reach nearly 40 cm (16 in) long. When disturbed, they circle around a tree trunk, always keeping it between them and danger.

The oddness of chameleons is best understood in terms of their lifestyle. Life aloft requires numerous adaptations. Walking in the treetops is difficult and the opposable toes, bound in uneven bundles, help grasp swaying vegetation. The long prehensile tail acts as a fifth limb. These lizards are *cryptically colored*, although their claimed ability to match the color of their surroundings is exaggerated. A chameleon's world is visual, so it is not surprising that they are strictly diurnal. Their large turreted eyes constantly scan for food or predators. Each eye moves independently, but when prey is spotted, both eyes focus together for stereoscopic range-finding. Flies and other insects form the diet. They are plucked at a distance by the wet tip of the telescopic tongue. This amazing structure, unique to chameleons, works by muscular contraction. The thick tongue explosively elongates and may become longer than the lizard's length. At rest it is concertinaed on an internal bony spike (the *hyoid*). Like agamas, chameleons have bright breeding colors, but these develop during territorial and mating displays and fade at other times. Bright colors presumably attract the unwanted attention of predators if displayed continuously.

Breeding

Agamas lay large clutches of soft-shelled eggs in a hole dug in warm soil. Australian agamids and one African species have temperature-dependent sex determination (TSD). Well known in crocodiles and some turtles, TSD is rare in lizards. It does not mean that mating is dependent upon warmth, but rather that the sex of the embryo is determined by the egg's incubation temperature. In agamids, higher temperatures produce males.

The only time that chameleons voluntarily come down to the ground is to lay eggs. The female selects a suitable nest site and laboriously digs a deep hole in soft soil. More than 50 eggs may be laid, taking over 6 months to develop. Dwarf chameleons give birth to live babies and may have several broods of 8 to 16 babies each year. Babies are born among the foliage, where their sticky fetal membranes adhere to thin twigs. From these the young wiggle free and, like all lizards, fend for themselves immediately. Growth is rapid and sexual maturity may be reached in a year. This, in association with the ability to produce large numbers of young during each breeding attempt, can lead to local population explosions.

Ecological Interactions

Agamas and chameleons show *sexual dimorphism*, with the sexes differing in color and form. This is usually related to courtship or territorial displays. However, in Flap-necked Chameleons it also reflects a difference in ecology between the sexes. Males have orange throat skin while the female's is white. In some regions males are also usually orange brown in color, unlike the bright green females. This color difference is linked to different behaviors of the sexes. During the dry season, males live high in open, leafless, deciduous bushes, while females are more secretive, sheltering low in evergreen bushes. Both sexes are therefore colored to suit their preferred habitat. Although the males get more food because they can see over a broader area, they are also more conspicuous and so are eaten more often by predators. The difference in the ecology of males and females presumably is an effective strategy for the species because males are more expendable (relatively few males can mate with many females).

Notes

Chameleons can neither run away quickly nor defend themselves, and prefer to remain hidden. If detected, however, they try to appear ferocious. The body puffs up, the head crests become erect, and the mouth is opened wide. Agamas put on a similar display. With strong jaws and sharp teeth, many bite readily and painfully. Most tribal people think chameleons and agamas are deadly and kill them on sight. It is a tragic mistake because they are harmless.

Status

Some chameleons have very localized distributions and are endangered by habitat destruction. The increasing number of fires started by careless people also threatens small fynbos-inhabiting species, such as SMITH'S DWARF CHAMELEON.

Profiles

Southern Rock Agama, *Agama atra*, Plate 16a
Etosha Ground Agama, *Agama etoshae*, Plate 16b
Tree Agama, *Acanthocercus atricollis*, Plate 16c
Flap-necked Chameleon, *Chamaeleo dilepis*, Plate 16d
Cape Dwarf Chameleon, *Bradypodion pumilum*, Plate 16e

8. Skinks and Lacertids

Skinks (family Scincidae) have overlapping scales that are usually smooth and shiny, creating a bright iridescence. Small bony plates (osteoderms) underlie the scales and form a flexible but rigid coat. This shiny armor is ideal for burrowing or living in rock cracks. The family is cosmopolitan and contains more than 600 species. Apart from geckos, they are the most diverse of southern African lizards. The STRIPED SKINK (Plate 17) is probably the most familiar and typical skink. It is common in gardens and around houses in the eastern region. SUNDEVALL'S WRITHING SKINK (Plate 17) is also common in the eastern and northern savannahs, where it burrows in loose, sandy soil hunting termites. It retains small legs that allow it to climb onto dead logs to bask. WAHLBERG'S SNAKE-EYED SKINK (Plate 17) also has small limbs and lacks eyelids, so it has an unblinking stare. *Lacertids* (family Lacertidae) are restricted to the Old World and are the common and familiar lizards of Europe. They are also well represented in Africa, where they occur in great diversity in deserts and semi-arid regions. They are small- to medium-sized lizards with slender bodies, long tails, and well-developed limbs. The back scales are small and granular, although some species have rough, overlapping scales. Most are terrestrial. Some species, such as the SPOTTED DESERT LIZARD (Plate 18), are active, diurnal lizards that hunt insects in open situations, usually capturing them with a quick dash from cover. All can run very quickly.

Natural History

Ecology and Behavior

Limb-loss has evolved in many groups of skinks and is usually associated with burrowing. Some groups, such as *dwarf burrowing skinks*, show a progressive loss of toes and limb bones as the species becomes more specialized for burrowing. The LOWVELD DWARF BURROWING SKINK (Plate 17) forages among leaf litter and in disused termite nests. It still retains small limbs for balance and movement through surface debris. The tail aids in rapid wiggling movements. Fully specialized for burrowing, the GIANT LEGLESS SKINK (Plate 17) lives in moist soils in the lowveld and eastern coastal forests. It is the largest local skink and may reach 55 cm (22 in) in length. It feeds mainly on earthworms and beetle grubs, but its strong jaws are capable of killing and tearing apart small vertebrates such as frogs. Many skinks and lacertids are brightly colored, with the dominant males developing bright breeding coloration. The NAMAQUA SAND LIZARD (Plate 18) has a long rust-colored tail and hunts in sparsely vegetated scrub. To thermoregulate in the baking desert, it rests in the shade of a small bush. When forced to walk in the open, it often pauses to raise alternate feet from the hot sand. The WESTERN SANDVELD LIZARD (Plate 18) is an atypical lacertid. Instead of making a quick dash to grab insects, it excavates scorpions from their burrows. Predators may approach unnoticed as the lizard digs, so its long, bright red tail attracts sudden attacks away from the vulnerable head. The expendable tail, if grabbed by a predator and broken off, is regenerated later.

Breeding

Most skinks lay a small clutch of 3 to 7 eggs, usually in sun-warmed soil beneath a stone or dead tree. A number of typical skinks are viviparous, retaining the yolked eggs and giving birth to live babies in late summer. The CAPE SKINK may have litters of up to 18 babies, but has also on a few occasions laid a clutch of soft-shelled eggs. This "bimodal" reproductive ability is very unusual and needs further scientific study. All burrowing skinks give birth to live young. The small, thin dwarf burrowing skinks have only a single baby, while the Giant Legless Skink gives birth to relatively large litters of up to 14. All lacertids are oviparous and lay a small clutch of soft-shelled eggs in a chamber in moist soil.

Ecological Interactions
Some lacertids are called "annual lizards," which hints at their unusual lives. Over much of the northern savannahs, the CAPE ROUGH-SCALED LIZARD and COMMON ROUGH-SCALED LIZARD (Plate 18) live together. It is a general rule in ecology that two species cannot inhabit the same niche because they would compete for the same resources. Eventually one species would dominate and then replace the other. Adult and juvenile lizards do not usually compete for the same food, and even if they eat the same species, they take different size classes. The two rough-scaled lizards grow to maturity, mate and lay their eggs within a year, and after reproducing, die. Incubation of the eggs takes about 2 months. During the half of the year that the adults of one species mate, lay eggs and die, the eggs of the other species hatch and grow to adults. There is no competition for food between the adults of one species and the hatchlings of the other. In the next half of the year, the roles of the two species are reversed. The two "annual" rough-scaled lizards have therefore evolved an elegant rotating solution that minimizes competition between them.

Notes
Hatchling lizards have numerous predators. Most lacertid hatchlings depend on their speed or *cryptic coloration* to escape predation. The adult BUSHVELD LIZARD (Plate 18) behaves similarly, and is cryptically colored in brown and cream. The juvenile, in contrast, has a jet-black body broken with bold yellow-white stripes. It also walks with a peculiar, stiff legged gait, which seems to invite attention. It can afford to do this is because it mimics an "oogpister" (Afrikaans for "eye-squirter"), a large beetle that squirts a pungent, acidic fluid. Many small predators, such as birds and mongooses, learn to avoid these distasteful beetles. The looka-like hatchling lizards are also left alone.

Status
Few of these common, widespread lizards are endangered, especially because most live in mountains or deserts, where people are scarce. A small colony (200–300) of BOUTON'S SKINKs lives on Black Rock, near Kosi Bay on the northern Zululand coast. The species is widespread in the Indo-Pacific, but only one colony is known in South Africa.

Profiles
Giant Legless Skink, *Acontias plumbeus*, Plate 17a
Lowveld Dwarf Burrowing Skink, *Scelotes bidigittatus*, Plate 17b
Sundevall's Writhing Skink, *Lygosoma sundevallii*, Plate 17c
Wahlberg's Snake-eyed Skink, *Panaspis wahlbergii*, Plate 17d
Striped Skink, *Trachylepis striata*, Plate 17e
Spotted Desert Lizard, *Meroles suborbitalis*, 18a
Bushveld Lizard, *Heliobolus lugubris*, Plate 18b
Common Rough-scaled Lizard, *Ichnotropis squamulosa*, Plate 18c
Western Sandveld Lizard, *Nucras tessellata*, Plate 18d
Namaqua Sand Lizard, *Pedioplanis namaquensis*, Plate 18e

9. Plated and Girdled Lizards

Named after their body scales, *plated lizards* and *girdled lizards* comprise two closely related families. Both types have a prominent lateral body fold that runs on each flank just above the belly. It gives the body a box-like cross-section and allows abdominal expansion. The body scales of plated lizards (family Gerrhosauridae) are plate-like, squarish in outline, and tend to abut rather than overlap. Plated lizards are found throughout most of sub-Saharan Africa and Madagascar. The GIANT PLATED LIZARD (Plate 20) grows to 70 cm (28 in), a size surpassed only by monitors. At the other extreme is the beautiful DWARF PLATED LIZARD (Plate 20), which rarely exceeds 15 cm (6 in) in length. It has a prominently striped back and a brilliant bright blue tail. It is very shy, so a flash of the blue tail is usually your first and last glimpse. Girdles of overlapping, spiny body scales encircle girdled lizards (Family Cordylidae), while the tail has whorls of very spiny scales. The family is endemic to sub-Saharan Africa, reaching its greatest diversity in South Africa. The BLACK GIRDLED LIZARD (Plate 19) is conspicuous as it basks on the summit rocks of Table Mountain in Cape Town. A close relative, the CAPE CRAG LIZARD (Plate 19) lives on the same rock crags; the largest lizard in the Cape Mountains, it is shy and difficult to approach. *Platys*, or *flat lizards*, are bizarre relatives. They have unmistakable, very flat, almost crushed, bodies. They live on smooth granite domes in the northern savannahs and along the lower Orange River. *Grass lizards*, owing to their elongate bodies, very long tails, and minute limbs, are very unusual cordylids. They "swim" through long grass, moving with the speed and agility of snakes (although the scientific name means "creeping lizard"). The body of the CAPE GRASS LIZARD (Plate 19) is cryptically colored in light brown and cream, and the scales are rough and strongly keeled. Although the tail may be shed, it is regenerated rapidly.

Natural History

Ecology and Behavior

The larger plated lizards are omnivorous, eating plant material as well as insects and small vertebrates. They live in burrows at the base of a bush or under a boulder. The long, fragile tail is easily lost but quickly regenerated. When foraging for food, these lizards move slowly, scraping away loose soil or leaf litter, looking for hidden prey. They may slowly toboggan down gentle slopes on their flat, smooth bellies. Close relatives, the *seps*, or *plated snake lizards*, have lost much of their limbs and "swim" through thick vegetation hunting grasshoppers. Girdled and crag lizards eat large, hard-bodied insects, which they crush with their powerful jaws. Most species are rock-dwelling and form diffuse colonies. Dominant males may fight among themselves. Male display and coloration is most fully developed in flat lizards. BROADLEY'S FLAT LIZARD (Plate 19) lives in dense colonies on the vertical granite cliffs of Augrabies Falls on the lower Orange River. Dominant males develop bright breeding colors, which are most intense on the flanks and belly. There the color is less visible to predators but can be "flashed" in territorial "push-up" displays. Females and juveniles have duller, black backs with three pale stripes.

Breeding

All plated lizards lay a few large, oval eggs in moist soil. The thin-bodied AFRICAN LONG-TAILED SEPS lays 3 or 4 eggs in a live ant nest. They complete development undisturbed by the biting soldier ants. Several females may use the same nest site. Unlike other cordylids (girdled lizards), flat lizards still lay eggs. Between November and December two egg clutches are laid among damp leaf mould in a deep rock crack. Numerous females may use the same crack. All other cordylids give birth to a few live young in late summer. Some girdled lizards may perform a simple form of maternal care; the newborn young often share the female's retreat for their first year.

Ecological Interactions

Girdled lizards have very powerful jaws and can give a painful bite. However, the bulging jaw muscles are also used in an unusual defense. The top of the head is rough and protected with thick, bony scales. The skull also has a hinge that allows it to flex, making the head larger. When threatened, crag and girdled lizards retreat into a narrow rock crack and wrap their spiny tails around them. This protects the head and more delicate body. If grasped by a limb, however, the lizard grits its jaws together, flexing the hinge in the skull to thicken the head and jam it tightly against the rock walls. The rough, tough head scales prevent damage.

Notes

The GIANT GIRDLED LIZARD (Plate 19) could be South Africa's national lizard. It is an impressive species, the largest in family Cordylidae. Another common name, Sungazer, refers to its habit of basking while facing the sun. The body is protected with very large spines, particularly on the mace-like tail. This lizard is terrestrial, which is unique for a girdled lizard, and digs long burrows in deep soil. Females may live with their young for some time. If a predator follows into their burrow, these lizards move backwards and lash their spiky tails from side to side, forming a formidable barrier.

Status

The range of the Giant Girdled Lizard falls within the "Maize Triangle" of the Free State and Gauteng that is extensively ploughed for corn. The few surviving populations are threatened by illegal collecting for the pet trade. EASTWOOD'S SEPS is a snake-like plated lizard that lived in montane grassland along the Mpumalanga escarpment. The area is now covered in pine plantations, and this lizard has not been seen for more than 50 years; it is likely the first African lizard to become extinct in modern times.

Profiles

Cape Grass Lizard, *Chamaesaura anguina*, Plate 19a
Black Girdled Lizard, *Cordylus nigra*, Plate 19b
Giant Girdled Lizard, *Cordylus giganteus*, Plate 19c
Cape Crag Lizard, *Pseudocordylus microlepidotus*, Plate 19d
Broadley's Flat Lizard, *Platysaurus broadleyi*, Plate 19e
Dwarf Plated Lizard, *Cordylosaurus subtessellatus*, Plate 20a
Giant Plated Lizard, *Gerrhosaurus validus*, Plate 20b

10. Monitor Lizards

Monitors (family Varanidae) are the world's largest lizards, and include the fabulous KOMODO DRAGON from Indonesia. There are five African monitors, or *leguaans*, as they are locally known, of which only two live on the subcontinent. Leguaan is an English corruption of the Afrikaans "likkerwaan," itself derived from the Portuguese "l'iguana," which in turn derives from an Amerindian word for lizard. Known for their great size, monitors' bodies are covered in small, bead-like scales, and they are the only lizards with a snake-like, prehensile, forked tongue. All have muscular bodies and powerful feet with sharp claws. The tail is often used like a whip in defense and cannot be shed or regenerated. The WATER MONITOR

(Plate 20) regularly reaches 2 m (6.5 ft) long. Most of this is tail, which is strong, tapering, and has a dorsal crest to aid swimming. This species is restricted to the vicinity of water and is therefore absent from the western arid regions and the temperate southern Cape. The tail of the thickset SAVANNAH MONITOR (Plate 20) is as long as the body and lacks a raised dorsal crest. Exceptional adults may exceed 1.5 m (5 ft), and males grow bigger than females. They can be ugly lizards, with a body sullied with unshed skin and numerous ticks.

Natural History

Ecology and Behavior

The life of the Savannah Monitor has been studied in Etosha Game Reserve in northern Namibia. They have large home ranges (6 sq km, 2.3 sq mi, for females, and 7 sq km, 2.7 sq mi, for males). However, the full territory is used only during the four-month wet season (January to April). At other times, they stay in or near a favored retreat, usually a burrow at the base of a fallen tree. They spend 3- to 7-day periods foraging for invertebrates such as insects, snails, and millipedes. Lizards, snakes, and tortoises are also eaten. Less is known about the lives of Water Monitors. Much of their day is spent searching riverbanks and reedbeds for food. Adults eat mainly freshwater crabs but also take frogs, bird eggs, and fledglings. They also scavenge dead fish.

Breeding

During the mating period (August to mid-September) the female Savannah Monitor lies at the entrance to her burrow and waits for males to find her. She will mate with more than one. As she basks, body fat accumulated during the previous summer is converted to eggs. She also releases a pheromone, the smell of which attracts males. Copulation is frequent; males may travel 8 to 10 km (5 to 6 mi) per round trip, visiting receptive females and mating with them daily. Up to 50 eggs are laid in an old ground-squirrel burrow or in accumulated leaf litter. They take from 120 to 150 days to hatch. Mating and egg-laying at the end of the dry winter is important: It allows the hatchlings to emerge during the warm wet season, when food is plentiful, and they can lay down food reserves to last during their first winter. They grow slowly and mature in 4 to 6 years. To protect her large eggs, the Water Monitor lays them within a live termite nest. After early summer rains, she leaves the river valleys and climbs to adjacent grasslands that are covered in termite nests. She scrapes a hole in the side of a living nest and lays 20 to 60 eggs. The termites repair the damage, and during the next 10 to 12 months the eggs develop in warm, air conditioned safety. The following summer the brightly colored young dig out of the rain-softened termite nest.

Ecological Interactions

In suitable habitats monitors can reach very high populations. It is calculated that nearly 6,500 Savannah Monitors occur in Etosha Game Reserve. This translates into a monitor *biomass* (total amount of living tissue) of a staggering 45,000 kg (99,000 lb)! This exceeds that of all the more visible carnivores, including Lions, Leopards, Cheetahs, hyenas, and even jackals. Why are they so successful, and yet so inconspicuous? First, they are easily overlooked because they are secretive and retreat to cover when disturbed. They are also food generalists, eating a wide variety of food. Being ectotherms ("cold-blooded"), they do not waste energy maintaining body temperature during cool weather. During the cool dry season they live off their fat reserves, and may lose up to 50% of their body weight. At this time they rarely move from their retreats; one male spent 73 days in the same tree. Water Monitors reach even higher densities in the great inland floodplains, such as the Okavango Swamp and Lake Chad. They can exploit infrequent food surpluses, such as fish trapped in drying water bodies.

Notes

When unable to flee, monitors hiss and stand their ground. The long tail may be used as a painful whip, and they bite with a bulldog's tenacity. If these threats fail, they fall limp and play dead. The skin and body fat is prized in tribal medicine. The flesh is reputed to taste like chicken. Ancient Egyptians revered the Water Monitor, embalming its body and portraying it in their rock carvings.

Status

Many monitors are endangered; vast numbers are killed in Asia and West Africa. Over half a million Water Monitor skins enter the international skin trade each year, many from Lake Chad. Their skins are turned into fashion accessories such as watchbands, belts, and shoes. Thousands of West African DWARF SAVANNAH MONITORS are also captured for the international pet trade. Fortunately, monitors are protected in all southern African countries.

Profiles

Water Monitor, *Varanus niloticus*, Plate 20c
Savannah Monitor, *Varanus albigularis*, Plate 20d

11. Crocodiles

Until their mass extinction, dinosaurs ruled the world. Only two close relatives of these ruling reptiles now survive: crocodiles and birds. Crocodiles differ from other living reptiles in many features. Their hearts have four chambers, allowing more efficient blood oxygenation, and an extra eyelid, the *nictitating membrane*, sweeps dirt from the eyeball. Although three other crocodiles occur in Africa, only the NILE CROCODILE (Plate 20) occurs in southern Africa. Young crocodiles cannot be confused with Water Monitors. They are greenish in color with irregular black markings, unlike the black and yellow coloration of Water Monitors. A crocodile's tail also has two raised dorsal keels, not one as in monitors.

Natural History

Ecology and Behavior

The Nile Crocodile inhabits larger rivers, lakes, and swamps, and also estuaries and mangrove swamps. They swim effortlessly, using the broad, flattened tail for propulsion. The webbed hind feet are not used for swimming. The valved nostrils and throat flap at the back of the mouth enable them to feed underwater. Young crocodiles dig a burrow (sometimes communally) up to 3 m (10 ft) long. It is their shelter for their first 4 or 5 years. They spend a lot of time out of water hunting small prey such as frogs and grasshoppers. Most adults feed on fish, particularly catfish. Large adults also ambush game coming to drink. Attacks on domestic animals and people are still relatively common. A few human fatalities occur yearly in southern Africa. Large prey is grasped with a fast, sideways swipe of the head. Large food items are softened with strong bites before being swallowed. Prey too large to engulf is torn to bits. Chunks of flesh from large prey such as zebra and buffalo may be torn off as the crocodile spins. Smaller antelope are thrashed to bits at the surface. Carrion is readily taken. These crocs live for up to 60 years in captivity; very large wild specimens may be up to 100 years old.

Breeding

Crocodiles are attentive parents that build nests and care for the young. Sexual maturity is reached in 12 to 15 years, when the crocodile is about 2 to 3 m (6 to 10 ft) in length and 70 to 100 kg (150 to 220 lb) in weight. At the start of the breeding season (May), males display and fight to achieve dominance. Courtship is elaborate, and mating takes place in the water in July/August. The female selects a suitable sunny sandbank above the floodwater level, with good drainage and cover nearby. She will use it, unless disturbed, for the rest of her life. At night, usually in November, she digs a hole and lays 16 to 80 white, hard-shelled eggs. The nest site is defended against predators and other crocodiles. During this period the female does not eat, but may drink. The male remains in the vicinity but is not allowed near the nest mound. After 84 to 90 days the hatchlings, while still in the egg, give a high pitched cheeping noise that is audible 20 m (65 ft) away. The female carefully opens the nest and takes the young into her mouth. The hatchlings are taken to the water, washed, and released. They remain in a crèche for 6 to 8 weeks. The sex of hatchlings is determined by egg incubation temperature; females are produced at lower temperatures (26 to 30°C, 79 to 86°F) than males are (31 to 34°C, 87 to 93°F).

Ecological Interactions

Nile Crocodiles and Water Monitors have an uneasy relationship. They share the same habitat but feed mainly on different prey. Monitors forage in wetlands, shallows, and bankside vegetation. When disturbed, they may plunge into deep water to escape, but they do not swim with impunity in water. Large crocodiles eat any monitors they catch. Open water is the crocodile's realm, but the tables are turned when crocodiles come ashore to breed. Female crocodiles stay alongside their egg-mounds, but if their vigilance drops, monitors quickly dig up and eat the eggs. During her breeding life a female crocodile may lay more than 1,000 eggs, but few of these survive to become adults due to monitor predation of nests and hatchlings. The monitor lizards, therefore, help to control crocodile numbers.

Notes

Crocodiles basking on sandbanks often lie with a gaping mouth. This is a form of thermoregulation, as heat is lost by evaporation from the moist mouth lining. In East Africa, crocodiles share the sandbanks with Egyptian Plovers. Folklore says that these elegant birds, like ox-peckers on antelope, pick ticks and other debris from the crocodile's open jaws. It is a story that dates back to the Greeks, but no modern observations have confirmed such a relationship.

Status

The Nile Crocodile was once widespread throughout Africa, and even swam in the Mediterranean. Left-over, "relict" populations still survive in Madagascar. However, after years of persecution and hunting for the skin trade, viable populations are now restricted to game reserves, and the species is considered vulnerable (South African Red Data Book).

Profile

Nile Crocodile, *Crocodylus niloticus*, Plate 20e

Chapter 8

BIRDS

by Warwick Tarboton

- *Introduction*
- *General Characteristics of Birds*
- *Classification of Birds*
- *Features of Southern Africa's Birds*
- *Seeing Birds in Southern Africa*
- *Family Profiles*
    1. *Large Terrestrial Birds (Ostrich, Cranes, Bustards)*
    2. *Swimming Waterbirds*
    3. *Seabirds, Including Penguins and Pelicans*
    4. *Large Wading Birds*
    5. *Birds of Prey*
    6. *Game Birds*
    7. *Marsh Birds*
    8. *Shorebirds*
    9. *Gulls and Terns*
    10. *Pigeons and Doves*
    11. *Parrots, Turacos (Louries), and Cuckoos*
    12. *Owls and Nightjars*
    13. *Swifts and Swallows*
    14. *Mousebirds and Trogons*
    15. *Kingfishers, Bee-eaters, and Rollers*
    16. *Hornbills and Hoopoes*
    17. *Woodpeckers, Barbets, and Honeyguides*

18. *Larks, Pipits, Wagtails, and Longclaws*
19. *Crows, Drongos, Orioles, and Tits*
20. *Bulbuls and Babblers*
21. *Thrushes, Chats, and Robin-Chats*
22. *Warblers*
23. *African Flycatchers*
24. *Shrikes*
25. *Starlings and Oxpeckers*
26. *Sunbirds, Sugarbirds, and White-eyes*
27. *Sparrows, Weavers, Bishops, and Widowbirds*
28. *Waxbills and Whydahs*
29. *Canaries and Buntings*

Introduction

The ecotraveller to southern Africa will probably be primed for seeing the "Big Five" mammals, for watching whales, or for enjoying the spectacle of a savannah landscape teeming with antelope. The truth, however, is that the first form of wildlife usually encountered on such a trip, in this region or anywhere else, will probably be a bird. And it is usually birds, rather than some other animal, that one can rely on to always be around and to provide interest and entertainment during one's travels. There are good reasons for this, of course; birds mostly outnumber other vertebrates in abundance and diversity. They are, in most instances, visually conspicuous, often noisy, and with a few exceptions, active during the day just as we are, and so are more likely to be encountered than any night-living creature. Much of this is a consequence of the simple fact that birds can fly, and this supreme capability of theirs to take flight and escape from predators enables birds to behave in ways that so many flightless land vertebrates, ever mindful of the prospect of becoming another meal for somebody higher up the food chain, can never do. So while snakes, amphibians, rats, mice, and a host of other creatures resort to nocturnal lifestyles or develop cryptic colors and stealthy ways, many bird species flaunt their presence, endure being scrutinized, and may even tolerate being closely approached. For visitors unfamiliar with watching, identifying, and enjoying birds, there lies a pleasurable experience ahead, and because birds are ubiquitous, this pleasure can be indulged anywhere and anytime.

General Characteristics of Birds

Birds have been on the planet far, far longer than people. The first bird to appear in the fossil record, a pigeon-sized creature named *Archaeopteryx*, is dated as having lived about 140 million years ago—in contrast to people's brief 3 or 4 million year history on Earth. *Archaeopteryx* was feathered, could fly, and had clawed hind legs like those of a modern bird. It also had a lizard-like toothed jaw, and it is thought to have descended from a lizard-like reptile that lived in trees during the Jurassic Period of the Mesozoic Era. The great diversification in birds that we find today commenced much later than this, about 50 million years ago, when many of the present-day bird families, including penguins, pelicans, cranes, and owls, first came on the scene. They have certainly proliferated, and although there have been innumerable extinctions along the way, there are currently nearly 10,000 bird species living in the world today. They range in size from the huge (2.5 m, 8 ft, tall) Ostrich that weighs 135 kg (300 lb) to the insect-like hummingbirds that, in some species, weigh a mere 3 g (0.1 oz), and they come in all shapes, with long or short wings, long or short legs, and very variably sized bills. The ability to fly is the common feature that birds share with each other and, despite their diversity, birds are remarkably uniform in their structure and biology. Mechanical flight requires strength and lightness and these are the features that birds have in common. Their bones are lighter than those of other vertebrates as a result of being mainly hollow or latticed with fine cross-strutting. Their coating of feathers provides a lightweight, waterproof, streamlined, and well-insulated covering to the body and, in the wings and tail, a strong but light surface area that is used for obtaining lift. A bird's strength to fly resides in its exceptionally well-developed pectoral (breast) muscles, and these are attached to the breast-bone (sternum) which, in birds, is also exceptionally large. Bats, the flying mammals, are the only other creatures to share these traits.

A number of birds have lost the ability to fly. These are often species that occur on isolated, predator-free islands where the need to be able to fly in order to survive has disappeared, or, in the case of the ostrich, the birds have developed powerful legs and can escape predation by running away. With back legs that have developed for the purpose of running or perching, and forelimbs that have become wings, birds lack "hands" with which to gather and eat food. For this purpose the bill has come into its own as a foraging tool and the many shapes that birds' bills take all reflect the feeding habits of the species involved. Long, thin bills, for example, belong to species that probe for their food, hooked bills good for tearing flesh are found in meat-eating birds, and seed-eaters have blunt conical bills that are capable of dehusking seeds.

Classification of Birds

Bird classification is about grouping like species together and arranging them in a hierarchy that reflects the relationships between groups. It is an area of science that is continually undergoing revision as new techniques are developed and new information becomes available. A few years ago the number of bird species in the world was thought to be a little over 8,000; now, with increasingly sophisticated

DNA techniques being used, this number has increased to over 9,700. In southern Africa, for example, a common and widespread lark (the Long-billed Lark) has recently been proved to be comprised of no fewer than 5 species. At the lowest level of hierarchical grouping, two or more similar, closely related species may be grouped into the same genus, and there are about 2,000 genera currently recognized that embrace all the world's birds. The genera, in turn, are grouped into about 150 families. For example, there are 15 living species of cranes in the world and these are grouped into two, three, or four genera (depending on whose classification is used); they, in turn, all belong to a well-defined family, the cranes, or Gruidae. Families, in turn, are grouped into orders, and here again the number of orders into which the world's birds are allocated varies according to one's source of reference, lying anywhere between 22 and 30. Cranes, for instance, are placed in the relatively small order (comprising fewer than 200 species) known as the Gruiformes, sharing it with, among others, the bustard and crake families. More than half the world's birds belong to a single very large order, the Passeriformes, and these species are usually referred to as *passerines*. Passerines are characterized by having specialized perching feet (three fore-toes and one hind-toe) and they comprise most of the small land birds with which we are familiar—swallows, sparrows, robins, tits, warblers, and a host of others. All other orders of birds, from penguins to woodpeckers, are known as *non-passerines*.

Features of Southern Africa's Birds

The southern African bird fauna reflects the make-up of its natural regions. A large proportion of the subcontinent is savannah, semi-arid shrubland, or grassland, and so families of ground-living birds—francolins and spurfowl, bustards, plovers/lapwings, sandgrouse, coursers, larks, pipits, chats, and others—are especially well represented in the region. There are no fewer than 31 species of larks, 20 different game bird species, and 11 of the world's 25 bustards found here, and many of the species in these families are endemic to the region. Birds of prey are also very well represented, with no fewer than 70 different species of diurnal raptors occurring here and 12 species of owls. Eagles feature strongly, with 17 different species; so do vultures, with 8 species present. One of the more remarkable raptors in the region is the long-legged Secretarybird (Plate 21), a terrestrial eagle that is commonly seen striding about briskly in areas of open grassland or savannah; the head and raised wings of this bird form the centerpiece in the new South African coat of arms. The waterbird community is also well served in the region, especially the heron and crake families and the shorebird (Scolopacidae) family. All told, between 170 and 200 species of birds are dependent on southern Africa's wetland habitats, which extend from the lagoons and estuaries along the coast to the inland swamps (such as the Okavango Delta) and vast ephemeral pans (such as Makgadikgadi and Etosha). Because evergreen forest is the most restricted of the major habitat types found in southern Africa, the forest bird fauna of the region is not exceptional. For example, there is only one forest parrot to be found here (the endemic Cape Parrot) and only one species of trogon; hummingbirds are entirely absent, not only in southern Africa, but in Africa as a whole. The hummingbird's place is taken by the sunbird family, 21 species of which occur in the region. Sunbirds and hummingbirds are unrelated but they resemble each other by having colorful, metallic plumages and by living on nectar, both having long thin bills to extract it from flowers. Southern Africa has just two bird families that are endemic to the region, the sugarbirds (which somewhat resemble sunbirds by subsisting largely on nectar and having long, curved bills that they use in the same way that sunbirds do) and the rockjumpers (which, as their name implies, live on rocky slopes and behave in much the same way as rock thrushes and chats).

Southern Africa is visited in the summer months by a considerable number of migratory bird species. Some of these originate from the Palearctic region (Europe and Asia, excluding India and Southeast Asia) where they breed, and some come from other parts of Africa; very few originate from North America, and those that have been recorded (for example, the Hudsonian Godwit) represent instances of birds that have strayed from their normal winter migration to South America. More than 100 species visit the region from the Palearctic, and although none of them breed in southern Africa, many of them (Willow Warbler, Plate 62, and Red-backed Shrike, Plate 69, for instance) are so abundant that they outnumber any of the local resident species in the areas where they are present. Whereas most land birds visit southern Africa during its summer months, many of the pelagic birds that inhabit the offshore waters come here in winter, driven northwards from the Antarctic by the harsh conditions that prevail there during this time.

Seeing Birds in Southern Africa

About a third of the bird species occurring in southern Africa have been selected for illustration in the color plates (21 to 84) and, with a few provisos, these are generally the region's most frequently seen birds. To see them all, though, one would need to travel fairly widely in southern Africa and visit each of the major natural regions, and one would need to be in the right place at the right time, since some of the selected species are seasonal in their occurrence. It is likely that some species not illustrated here will also be encountered, so a dedicated regional bird field guide (of which there are several available for southern Africa) may be useful. Bird-watching, or "birding," as it is usually termed, requires little by way of equipment besides binoculars. Binoculars are almost indispensable, though, as close-up views of plumage detail are often needed in order to clinch identification; also, it is one of birding's great pleasures to look at your subject really close up. It is also invaluable to tune in to the sounds of birds in the field. Even if one is unable to identify the songster from its call, one is alerted to its presence and is given a direction in which to look. Most of the species selected for the plates in this book are birds that either perch conspicuously along roadsides or are easily visible in the landscape. A few are real skulkers but they are included here because of their abundance, and should one become familiar with the calls made by these species, they are likely to be detected on this basis almost everywhere. Birding is usually most productive in the early morning, when the majority of species are most active and most vocal. So this is the time to get into the field, whereas in the heat of the day one should take a cue from the birds and take it easy.

There is no doubt that birding in some habitats is easier than in others. Wetlands, for example, are great places to begin birding, as many waterbird species are large and conspicuous and they remain in one place sufficiently long to give good views and allow comparision with guide book illustrations. Many wetlands, especially those in game parks and nature reserves, have bird-watching blinds built at ideal vantage points. Coastal birding is also easy, given the open terrain, although many of the shorebirds that frequent such areas seldom allow a close approach; the use of a telescope is often invaluable in such situations. To see *pelagic* birds (such as albatrosses and petrels) that rarely venture within sight of land, one needs to take a boat trip out to sea. This is becoming an increasingly popular aspect of birding, and dedicated boat trips to see pelagic birds are regularly conducted from Cape Town and Durban. Details of these trips can be obtained by contacting the museums or bird clubs in these cities, but remember that a strong stomach is needed should bad weather be encountered on such a trip. Birding becomes increasingly more difficult as one ventures from wetlands and the coast into grasslands, shrublands, savannahs, and forests, and one becomes progressively more reliant on using bird sounds to detect and identify the less conspicuous species in these environments.

One may imagine that birding in open grasslands is easy because the visibility there is good. It is easy for some species; cranes and bustards, for example, are large and conspicuous, although they rarely allow a close approach, and the colorful bishops and widows that are so common in this environment are easily located. Many of the chat and wheatear species that live in grasslands are also conspicuous, favoring prominent perches such as roadside fences. But there are many more elusive grassland species than there are conspicuous ones, and the cryptically marked larks, pipits, and cisticolas in particular, which are such a feature of these environments, provide a special challenge when it comes to their identification. Forest birding is, however, where most novices have the greatest difficulty. This is because many forest species, although very vocal, take great pains not to show themselves, and many of them live in the leafy canopy high above the ground, where spotting them and trying to see detail against the light is difficult. A good technique for seeing birds in forests is to simply sit quietly and wait at one spot, instead of blundering about and crashing through the undergrowth. It may take 20 or 30 minutes, but eventually one becomes accepted as part of the landscape and, with luck, even the most elusive forest birds may show themselves. Pausing for a while at one place to watch and listen also has merit when birding in savannah habitats. In the large national game parks in the savannah region (such as Kruger, Etosha, and Hwange), where it is not permitted to leave one's vehicle except in rest camps and demarcated areas, it is often very productive simply to park alongside a waterhole and watch for birds from the car, a very effective blind. Birding on foot inside the rest camps of such parks is always rewarding because the birds there are habituated to the presence of people and often allow a close approach.

Family Profiles

1. Large Terrestrial Birds (Ostrich, Cranes, Bustards)

The open grasslands and shrublands of southern Africa are inhabited by a number of large, long-legged birds that, although unrelated, are brought together here for convenience.

The largest, and probably best known, since it ranks as the world's largest and heaviest living bird, is the OSTRICH (Plate 21). It is flightless, and an adult male stands 2.1 to 2.75 m (6.7 to 8.9 ft) tall, while the female is a little smaller (1.7 to 1.9 m, 5.6 to 6.1 ft). Commercially bred Ostriches, widely farmed for their meat, feathers and skin, may be encountered almost anywhere in the world, whereas naturally occurring Ostriches are restricted to the African continent. Those found in southern Africa belong to the race *australis* and they are largely confined to the semi-desert regions of Namibia and Botswana. Ostriches also occur widely outside these more arid parts of southern Africa on farmlands where they have been introduced or bred for commercial purposes, but these are invariably semi-domesticated birds, commonly referred to as "Oudtshoorn Ostriches" (named after the area where they were first farmed). They are the offspring of hybrids bred specifically for plume and meat production, and they are smaller and differently structured than the natural *australis* race Ostriches.

Male Ostriches are not only larger than females, but are more strikingly colored, with contrasting black body feathers and white wings and tails. Females are brownish, with dull white wings and tail plumes. Young Ostriches initially have a spiky, hedgehog-like body covering that is gradually replaced by female-like brown plumage. It takes 12 months from hatching to attain adult height. Being flightless, Ostriches move about on foot, and they are capable of trotting steadily at a speed of about 30 kph (19 mph); they can, however, attain speeds of up to 70 kph (44 mph) in short bursts.

Not remotely related to ostriches, but sharing their terrestrial habit and love of open landscapes are *cranes*. These are long-legged, long-necked birds with large wingspans and loud, bugle-like calls. The sexes are alike, they are omnivorous in their diet, and they obtain all their food and live and nest on the ground. Cranes are commonly regarded as birds of wetlands: this is largely true for two of the southern African species, but the third, the BLUE CRANE (Plate 21), is almost as much a dry land bird as the Ostrich. This species frequents open grasslands and shrublands, and it is also commonly encountered in grain-growing areas. It is virtually endemic to South Africa and is the national bird of the country. Less colorful than other cranes, it is a uniform bluish-gray, but it has a graceful elegance imparted by its long, curved neck and the sweep of its long "tail" (formed by the elongated inner-wing feathers that lie on top of the tail), which nearly reaches the ground. Its bugle-like call is an evocative sound of the empty spaces of the karoo shrublands and Highveld grasslands.

A second widespread species is the more flamboyant GRAY CROWNED CRANE (Plate 21). Its plumage is a patchwork of black, white, maroon, and gold, and it has an extraordinary black-and-white painted face, with a vivid red gular sac and a head-tuft of spiky yellow feathers. It has many other un-crane-like features: its call is different, a booming note rather than a bugle; it lays unmarked white eggs (whereas other cranes lay cryptically marked brownish eggs); and it commonly perches in trees, often roosting in them at night and occasionally even nesting on top of them. It breeds in wetlands, but at other times of the year it often wanders far from water, sometimes mingling with Blue Cranes, especially where grain has recently been harvested on farmlands. The third southern African crane is the very rare Wattled Crane, a tall, mainly black, gray, and white species which is the most wetland-dependent of the trio; the only area where it is encountered with relative ease is in the Okavango Swamp.

Bustards are classified as belonging to the same order as Cranes (Gruiformes) and, although most of the species are much smaller than cranes, they share their long-legged, long-necked build. The African continent is home to 18 of the world's 25 bustard species, and 11 of these are found in southern Africa alone, six of them being endemic to this region. They are strictly terrestrial birds, although they fly strongly when the need arises. They never perch in trees and they are omnivorous in their diets. They share the attachment that Ostriches and cranes have for open landscapes, often in semi-arid regions. Without exception, they are cautious and unapproachable, either keeping their distance or avoiding detection by lying flat on the ground. The smaller species are locally known as "korhaans" ("crowing hens") while the term "bustard" is restricted to the three largest species. Some of the species have croaking, far-carrying calls (for example, the BLUE KORHAAN, Plate 34), some make a raucous clattering noise (for example, the NORTHERN BLACK KORHAAN, Plate 34), while the largest species, the KORI BUSTARD (Plate 21), makes a deep, booming sound, rather like the sound made by a male Ostrich. A few species, though, are largely silent.

Natural History

Ecology and Behavior

Ostriches often share the open terrain in which they live with herds of antelope (especially Springbok in southern Africa), and like their ungulate companions on the plains, they are primarily grazers and browsers of plant material. Vigilant while foraging, feeding ostriches often pause, raise their heads to full height, and scan the surroundings. Ostriches are usually encountered in groups or flocks that, especially in the vicinity of waterholes where they drink, may reach hundreds of birds. Flocking probably has advantages for the Ostrich in the form of enhancing overall vigilance: it has been shown that individuals feeding among other Ostriches spend less time with heads raised (and more time feeding) than do birds that feed solitarily. Ostriches are day-active, and at night they usually roost in groups of individuals squatting on the ground near each other, usually holding their heads high.

Cranes are also gregarious birds, and on some continents they gather in great flocks when they've completed their breeding cycle to undertake long-distance migrations between their breeding grounds and wintering areas. In southern Africa, the Blue Crane and Gray Crowned Crane also commonly gather in flocks during winter, and although they don't migrate in the sense of commuting seasonally betwen one area and another, they do wander widely in response to food availability. They are particularly attracted to grain-growing areas during and after harvesting, feeding on grain spillage in the fields.

Most bustard species are sedentary. They lead relatively solitary lives, or remain year-round in pairs or small family groups. The only species that is gregarious to any extent is the Denham's Bustard, in which, outside the breeding season, flocks of up to 20 to 25 birds may be encountered. The other large bustard, Ludwig's, which is an arid-country species, is the only one to undertake significant movements (across the Karoo and Namib) in response to rainfall events.

Breeding

Ostriches, cranes, and bustards all nest on the ground (or, in the case of cranes, nests are often in marshes), but their mating systems and nesting habits show great variability. Ostriches are opportunistic nesters, laying when the right environmental conditions present themselves rather than having a fixed breeding season. They usually breed in polygamous groups of one male and 2 to 5 females, and the females lay their enormous white eggs at 2-day intervals in a single communal nest. With each female laying 3 to 8 eggs, nests commonly contain 15 to 20 eggs and sometimes twice this number. The nest is a wide, shallow scrape in the ground, often at a site used previously. The incubation is shared by the male (mainly at night) and the dominant female (mainly during the day). She is apparently capable of recognizing her own eggs and pushes those laid by subordinates to the edges of the nest where they are less efficiently incubated, more vulnerable to predation and consequently less likely to hatch. The incubation lasts 42 to 46 days and, like cranes and bustards, the chicks leave the nest scrape permanently within a few hours of hatching.

Cranes are monogamous; the same partners often remain together as breeding pairs for many successive years, returning annually to the same nesting area. Blue Cranes typically lay their two-egg clutch on bare ground, usually where they have a clear view in all directions, while Wattled Cranes and Gray Crowned Cranes build substantial nest mounds of sedges and grass placed over water, often in the depths of a large marsh. Wattled Cranes typically lay 1 or 2 eggs while Gray Crowned Cranes lay 2 to 3 eggs. Incubation periods vary between 30 to 35 days according to species, and fledging periods between 2 to 4 months.

Monogamy is the exception rather than the rule for bustards and korhaans; the majority of species are polygamous. The males of these birds display or call loudly (or both) during the breeding period to attract mates; females, once they've mated, undertake all parental care without further male involvement. In bustards, males display in dispersed leks, at sites that are regularly re-used each year. Several korhaan species (including the Blue Korhaan, Plate 34) are apparently monogamous rather than polygamous and remain in pairs throughout the year, often accompanied by one or more offspring from a previous year. Although only females incubate, both sexes care for the chick (or chicks) as they grow up. These species live in permanently defended territories, and they advertise their presence by frequent calling, especially in the early morning, their deep, frog-like croaking calls carrying over long distances.

The displays of some of the polygamous species are spectacular. Males of the three bustards grow elongated chest plumes that are puffed out during display, briefly turning an ordinary-looking bird into a giant mushroom. The RED-CRESTED KORHAAN (Plate 34) male's method of drawing attention to himself is to utter a series of increasingly loud whistles, interspersed with tongue clicks, then concluding the show by launching himself vertically into the air to a height of perhaps 15 to 20 m (50 to 60 ft), closing his wings, and dropping back to the ground like a stone. None of the species in this family construct any sort of nest but instead lay their clutch of 1 or 2 eggs (rarely 3) on bare ground. For species that incubate, periods range between 20 to 25 days, and young first fly when 4 to 5 weeks of age.

Notes

Ostriches have featured strongly in human cultures since Stone Age times: their hollowed eggshells were used then, and are still used today by the San (or bushmen) in the Kalahari, for storing water; eggshell fragments were, and are, used for making decorative beads, bracelets, and necklaces. Ostrich feathers have been used for decorative and other purposes for the past 5,000 years. Today, their meat is highly valued as a source of low-fat protein and their skin for making fine-leather products.

Status

The crane species in southern Africa, like their counterparts elsewhere in the world, have undergone severe declines both in numbers and ranges, largely a consequence of a variety of people-related impacts. The Blue Crane, for example, has declined in numbers by 90% in large parts of its South African breeding range. Loss of breeding habitat has been one factor, excessive mortality as a result of agrochemical poisoning, another. All three species that occur in southern Africa are included in Red Data listings as endangered, vulnerable, or near-threatened.

Profiles

Gray Crowned Crane, *Balearica regulorum*, Plate 21a
Blue Crane, *Anthropoides paradiseus*, Plate 21c
Ostrich, *Struthio camelus*, Plate 21d
Kori Bustard, *Ardeotis kori*, Plate 21e
Blue Korhaan, *Eupodotis caerulescens*, Plate 34c
Northern Black Korhaan, *Eupodotis afraoides*, Plate 34d
Red-crested Korhaan, *Eupodotis ruficrista*, Plate 34e

2. Swimming Waterbirds

Five unrelated families of water-associated birds spend much of their time swimming, and they are here lumped together under the rather vague heading of "swimming waterbirds." Grebes, cormorants, and especially ducks are unlikely to be missed by a visitor anywhere in southern Africa who encounters a freshwater wetland.

Grebes are a worldwide family numbering 22 species, 3 of which occur in southern Africa. They are duck-like to the extent that they swim on open water, are short-tailed, and long-necked, but they differ by having sharp-tipped bills (dagger-like in some species) and lobed, not webbed toes. Only one species, the LITTLE GREBE (also known as Dabchick, Plate 27) is profiled here, the most frequently encountered grebe in the region. It is found on almost any sizeable, open, freshwater wetland and is immediately recognizable by its small size, its fluffy rear end that has a tail-less look about it, and during summer, by its rusty-brown head coloration. They are rather frustrating to watch, however, as no sooner does one have them in the binoculars than they dive underwater!

Cormorants are also widely distributed in the world and are perhaps best known for the ancient eastern custom of training them to use for catching fish. These birds are exclusively fish-hunters and they have long, sharply hooked bills for this purpose. They dive and swim underwater in search of prey and have powerful feet with webbed toes, set well back on the body so as to propel them rapidly through the water. There are 39 species in all, 5 of which occur in southern Africa. One of these, the WHITE-BREASTED CORMORANT (Plate 24), occurs widely around the world; elsewhere in its range it is an entirely black bird and known as the Great Cormorant, but the southern African race has striking white underparts, hence the local name. The cold sea off the West Coast, swept by the Benguela Current, is one of the world's premier fishing grounds and is home to no fewer than 4 cormorant species, one of which, the CAPE CORMORANT (Plate 24), is profiled here. These highly gregarious birds live in vast colonies, most on offshore islands, and they deposit here thousands of tons of guano (bird droppings) annually, a resource which is commercially harvested for fertilizer. By contrast, the small, long-tailed REED CORMORANT (Plate 24) is a bird of inland waters. One is likely to encounter it, usually solitary and often perched with wings spread to dry, on most river edges or along the margins of a dam or lake.

Darters (or *anhingas*) closely resemble cormorants and differ mainly in their bill structure (it is dagger-like rather than hooked). The species found in southern Africa, the AFRICAN DARTER (Plate 24), is a long-necked, long-billed black bird that at a glance could be mistaken for a large cormorant. Often regarded as a race of the darter found in Asia and Australia, it is restricted to the larger freshwater wetlands of the region. *Finfoots* are another group in this "swimming waterbird" category, but they have not been profiled here because they are extremely secretive and elusive birds; they live along rivers bordered by dense vegetation and they take cover at the slightest hint of danger. They are cormorant-like in many respects but don't dive, instead gleaning insects from the fringing vegetation. Their bright orange legs and toes are the best distinguishing feature.

Ducks are universally recognizable by the shape of their bills, their webbed toes, and their aquatic disposition. They are an abundant, diverse group (the families Anatidae and Dendrocygnidae) that includes about 150 species, 20 of which occur in southern Africa. Nine of these are profiled here, all species that are likely to be encountered at almost any wetland. Perhaps the two species most likely to be seen are the YELLOW-BILLED DUCK (Plate 27) and the EGYPTIAN GOOSE (Plate 28). The Yellow-billed Duck is the only duck in the region with a bright yellow bill; it is very common, sometimes found in flocks numbering in the hundreds (but only rarely in the thousands), and is easily recognized. Apart from its colorful bill, it is an undistinguished grayish-brown bird, its plumage much resembling that of several other ducks, including the RED-BILLED TEAL (Plate 27), CAPE SHOVELER (Plate 27), and CAPE TEAL (Plate 27). The Egyptian Goose (misnamed, really a shelduck) is also a very common species, often found in parks and on golf courses as well as in more natural habitats. It is closely related to the SOUTH AFRICAN SHELDUCK (Plate 28), which is similar in size but more ruddy-colored; this bird is endemic to southern Africa and found mainly in the semi-arid west. The largest African duck is the SPUR-WINGED GOOSE (Plate 28). It too has been misnamed; it belongs to the so-called perching ducks, a group which includes such well-known species as the Muscovy Duck, American Wood Duck, and Mandarin Duck. It is a very large, glossy black bird with a red bill and frontal shield and some white patches on its head, shoulders, and underparts.

Natural History

Ecology and Behavior

All but a few of the swimming species described derive their food from the waterbodies they inhabit. Grebes, cormorants, and darters all swim underwater in pursuit of fish and other prey. Some duck species dive for food as well, but most of the southern African species are *dabblers*, eating aquatic plants and small invertebrates such as fly larvae, which they obtain by dabbling at or just below the surface of the water, sometimes upending to reach deeper sources of food. All the species grouped here have their legs set well back on the body, and their toes are large and either webbed (ducks, darters, cormorants) or lobed (grebes, finfoots) to facilitate their propulsion through water.

Some of the species, notably the Cape Cormorant and other coastal cormorants, are extremely gregarious and live year-round in large flocks, foraging together and roosting and nesting in dense colonies. Ducks and grebes are also often gregarious, but many of these become territorial during the breeding season, dispersing as pairs during this time and excluding others of their kind from their nesting areas. Egyptian Geese, for example, become extremely aggressive then, noisily driving and pursuing other geese from their territories, whereas outside the breeding period they may gather in large flocks. This species differs from most of the swimming waterbirds by being primarily herbivorous, much attracted to short, grassy places (such as golf courses!) where it grazes off the emerging sprouts. Agricultural lands that have been harvested recently are also a great attraction to them and large flocks may gather at such sites, sometimes feeding alongside flocks of cranes, Spur-winged Geese, and other birds.

With the exception of the coastal cormorants and the finfoots, many of the ducks, grebes, and inland cormorants are nomadic, and although they do not undertake any formal migration, they move widely about southern Africa in response to changing conditions. They quickly find and colonize ephemeral wetlands when these receive sufficient water to flood, but equally quickly vacate them and move on elsewhere when conditions deteriorate.

Breeding

Cormorants and darters breed colonially, and they often join in with other colonial-nesters such as ibises, herons, and egrets to form enormous, noisy, smelly nestling factories that are often termed "rookeries" or "heronries." In some cases the colonies involve tens of thousands of birds—these are remarkable ornithological spectacles, with birds arriving and departing, nestlings clamoring for food whenever a parent alights, neighbors squabbling constantly for space or nesting material, and among all this noisy activity, innumerable birds sitting quietly, incubating their eggs. Along the coast most of these breeding colonies are on offshore islands; inland, however, dense reedbeds or submerged trees over water provide the most popular sites.

Cormorants and darters are monogamous breeders that share parental care; grebes and finfoots are the same, whereas ducks have more variable nesting behavior, some being monogamous (for example, Egyptian Goose, WHITE-FACED DUCK, Plate 28), others polygamous (for example, Spur-winged Goose). Ducks, grebes, and finfoots tend to nest solitarily. Their nests are widely spaced and invariably well hidden, far less conspicuous than those of the colonial breeders. Grebes build a floating nest that is made of soggy plant stems that they collect in the water and pile up to form a platform, adding to it whenever it threatens to sink; if the level of the water rises, the nest rides up with it. They lay white eggs (4 to 7 per clutch) that are deliberately covered by the parent with nest material whenever the nest is left unattended. Duck nests are usually well concealed, either in thick grass at the water's edge or in sedges and reeds over water. They lay large clutches (usually 8 to 15 eggs), and in most species (for example, Yellow-billed Duck, Red-billed Teal) the female incubates without male assistance, leaving the eggs at intervals to go and feed, during which time she covers them with down feathers. The eggs of grebes and ducks hatch after an incubation period ranging between 20 to 30 days, and in all cases the young are highly precocial, leaving the nest immediately and soon learning how to feed themselves.

Notes

Cormorants derive their odd-sounding name from the latinization of the name originally given to them by European mariners: "sea raven" (Corvus marinus, or cor-mor-ant). Darters are often known as *snake-birds*, which comes from their habit of swimming with body submerged and only head and neck extended, snake-like, above the water. Ducks have centuries-old associations with man, ranging from their early domestication to become an important agricultural resource to being hunted for meat and for sport. Duck-hunting has a small following in southern Africa, but it is insignificant compared with the following it has in some Northern Hemisphere countries.

Status

None of the species profiled are threatened; on the contrary, many of them are very common, widely distributed birds.

Profiles

White-breasted Cormorant, *Phalacrocorax carbo*, Plate 24a
Cape Cormorant, *Phalacrocorax capensis*, Plate 24b
Reed Cormorant, *Phalacrocorax africanus*, Plate 24c
African Darter, *Anhinga rufa*, Plate 24d
Little Grebe, *Tachybaptus ruficollis*, Plate 27a
Yellow-billed Duck, *Anas undulata*, Plate 27b
Cape Teal, *Anas capensis*, Plate 27c
Red-billed Teal, *Anas erythrorhyncha*, Plate 27d
Cape Shoveler, *Anas smithii*, Plate 27e
White-faced Duck, *Dendrocygna viduata*, Plate 28a
Egyptian Goose, *Alopochen aegypticus*, Plate 28b
South African Shelduck, *Tadorna cana*, Plate 28c
Spur-winged Goose, *Plectropterus gambensis*, Plate 28d
Southern Pochard, *Netta erythropthalma*, Plate 28e

3. Seabirds, Including Penguins and Pelicans

A remarkable diversity of *pelagic* (open ocean) birds inhabits the food-rich marine waters off southern Africa's coastline; they include *albatrosses, petrels, shearwaters, prions, storm petrels,* and *gannets*, many of which rarely range within sight of the mainland. Of these, only the CAPE GANNET (Plate 23) breeds in the region, using the offshore islands along the Namibian and South African coastlines. The others are non-breeding seasonal visitors that either move into the region's seas from the south during winter, coming from the sub-Antarctic oceans (where they breed in summer); or they are North Atlantic breeding species that move into the southern oceans during the (northern) winter. The result is that the seas around southern Africa have a seasonally changing array of ocean-dwelling birds that can be witnessed in all their glory and at close quarters—if one can stomach a boat trip out to the trawling grounds where these birds congregate in the thousands.

Apart from the gannets, which belong to a different family, the species described here (belonging to the family Procellariidae) are often referred to as *tubenoses*, a name given to them because of the prominent tubular nostrils that lie at the top of their longish, strongly hooked bills. They are among relatively few birds that have a well-developed sense of smell, thought to assist them in locating food at sea. Variations in bill structure distinguish the various groups of tube-noses; albatrosses, for example, have two separate nostrils on either side of the upper mandible, whereas petrels and shearwaters have a single fused nostril, and prions have a row of fine, comb-like lamellae in the bill that enable them to sift plankton from the sea.

Some of the commonest tube-noses off the southern African coast are profiled here. The most numerous visitor from the north is CORY'S SHEARWATER (Plate 22), a pale brown-and-white bird that, unusual for the group, often ventures within sight of the shore. Another abundant shearwater, uniformly sooty-black in color, is the SOOTY SHEARWATER (Plate 22), most numerous in spring when it moves up the west coast from the Antarctic, heading for the northern seas. The largest of the common species is the NORTHERN GIANT PETREL (Plate 22), another visitor from the southern oceans, a dull gray bird with a 2 m (6 ft) wingspan that approaches the size of a small species of albatross. It is primarily a scavenger and often visits seal colonies off the west coast for this purpose. In winter, three other southern ocean species also arrive by the thousand in the region: the brown-plumaged WHITE-CHINNED PETREL (Plate 22), PINTADO PETREL (Plate 22), with its checkered black-and-white plumage, and WILSON'S STORM PETREL (Plate 22), the latter often quoted as being the world's single most numerous bird species.

Penguins, which are restricted to the Southern Hemisphere, number 17 species. One of these, the AFRICAN PENGUIN (Plate 23), also known as the Jackass Penguin because of its unearthly braying call, is endemic to the southern African coast; four others occasionally occur here, but they are rare vagrants from the Antarctic. Penguins are highly specialized, flightless marine birds, streamlined for swimming, with sturdy flippers in place of wings to propel themselves through the water. They hunt in groups, pursuing shoals of fish underwater.

Two *pelican* species may be encountered in southern Africa, the one profiled here being the GREAT WHITE PELICAN (Plate 23), the more numerous and widespread of the two. Its range extends across Africa into Eastern Europe and Asia. It is not really a marine bird, although some of its nesting sites are located on offshore islands. Pelicans are among the heaviest of all flying birds, weighing up to 13 kg (29 lb) and having wingspans up to 3.4 m (11 ft); their enormous wings enable them to soar effortlessly and commute over large distances, sometimes undertaking lengthy daily round trips between their nesting areas and feeding grounds. The pelican's pouch, which hangs from its lower mandible and is used as a scoop for catching fish (while the upper mandible acts as a lid), is probably the best-known—and most caricaturized—feature of any bird.

Natural History

Ecology and Behavior

Some tube-nose species feed primarily on fish, others on crustaceans or plankton. They are all masterful fliers, with the ability to remain on the wing for long periods. Many species make use of land only during the months when they are nesting and otherwise remain constantly out at sea; when conditions prevent them from flying, they simply settle on the water. The huge albatrosses, which are largely restricted to the trade wind belt in the southern oceans, are famed for their phenomenal ability to use wave and wind action to keep aloft. Shearwaters fly with a rapid, stiff-winged action interspersed with bouts of gliding, and skim the sea's surface along the troughs between the swells. The much smaller storm petrels forage by hovering close to the water; they face the wind, legs extended and feet trailing in the water to anchor themselves, dipping their bills to scoop up food items from the surface. Most of the species are attracted to fishing trawlers, where they feed on discarded entrails and offal from the boats; regrettably, many fall victim to hooks used in long-line fishing or get caught up in gill nets.

Flocks of Cape Gannets also follow the fishing trawlers, but normally they hunt fish from high on the wing, making spectacular plunging dives into the sea when prey is sighted; their torpedo-shaped bodies, long bills, and long tails are well adapted for this. For the five-month breeding cycle, they are tied to seas that are within a reachable range of their nesting islands, but for the rest of the year they wander widely up the east and west coasts.

The Great White Pelican is a gregarious species that fishes in freshwater wetlands rather than at sea. Groups of these birds often fish cooperatively, swimming in a half-circle behind shoals of fish that they herd into shallow water, where they then lunge at them, using their huge pouches to scoop up the trapped fish. When not fishing, pelicans spend long periods loafing on dry land, often squatting low on the ground, head and neck well drawn back so that their bill can rest on their chest.

Breeding

Tube-noses, gannets, and pelicans all breed colonially, often in very large, densely packed aggregations. For example, the Cape Gannets that breed annually on Bird Island in Algoa Bay number about 65,000 pairs, while Dassen Island in the Western Cape is occupied annually by about 90,000 nesting pairs of African Penguin. This strong tendency towards colonial breeding is probably partly the result of few safe breeding sites, highly gregarious natures, and their foraging behavior, which often involves searching for and hunting prey cooperatively. Most or all the species so far studied have prolonged nesting cycles and are monogamous, with both parents sharing duties at the nest.

Only one tube-nose species is known to breed around the southern African coast: in 1995, the first nesting pair of Leach's Storm Petrel was discovered (nesting in a hole in a wall) on a small offshore island along the southern Cape coast. African Penguins, which nest at a few dozen sites around the coastline, normally dig a burrow for a nest, but on some islands the penguins often lay their clutch (of two eggs) in an exposed place; these birds invariably suffer higher egg mortality than the burrow nesters. Cape Gannets build a nest mound by scraping guano together, and they incubate by holding their webbed feet on top of the egg. Their nests are particularly closely packed, usually only 0.5 m (1.5 ft) apart; a bird nesting in the center of such a colony has to thread its way past all the neighboring nests to the edge, where it can make a run in order to take off. Such birds signal their non-aggressive intent to the neighbors by pointing the bill upwards. Returning birds don't run this gauntlet of territorial neighbors, but rather drop straight out of the sky onto their own nest. An outstanding place to witness breeding gannets and penguins is at Lambert's Bay, up the west coast from Cape Town, where a blind with one-way glass, reached via a tunnel, has been constructed in the midst of the nesting birds.

Great White Pelicans are also monogamous breeders and nest colonially on islands, each pair building a rudimentary platform on the ground using sticks and plant debris collected from nearby. They usually lay a clutch of two eggs, but rarely raise more than a single chick as a result of "inter-sibling cainism" (the first-hatched killing the second-hatched; or siblicide). Their incubation and nestling periods are about 38 and 75 days respectively, while those of the Cape Gannet are 42 and 97 days and those of the African Penguin are 37 and 72 days.

Notes

The unusual name of "penguin" is derived from Latin's pinguis (meaning "fat"), a name originally used for the Great Auk, a North Atlantic species that became extinct in 1844 as a result of over-exploitation for its fat; penguins look like auks and the misused name has become entrenched.

Status

The African Penguin and Cape Gannet are both regionally listed (in South Africa) as Red Data species (vulnerable) on the basis of their restricted breeding ranges, their declining numbers, and their vulnerability to offshore oil spillages and other factors.

Profiles

Northern Giant Petrel, *Macronectes halli*, Plate 22a
Pintado Petrel, *Daption capense*, Plate 22b
White-chinned Petrel, *Procellaria aequinoctialis*, Plate 22c
Sooty Shearwater, *Puffinus griseus*, Plate 22d
Wilson's Storm Petrel, *Oceanites oceanicus*, Plate 22e
Cory's Shearwater, *Calonectris diomedea*, Plate 22f
Great White Pelican, *Pelecanus onocrotalus*, Plate 23a
African Penguin, *Spheniscus demersus*, Plate 23b
Cape Gannet, *Morus capensis*, Plate 23d

4. Large Wading Birds

Herons (and *egrets*, their more elaborately plumed counterparts), storks, ibises, spoonbills, and flamingos are all distinctive, long-legged birds that prey mainly on fish, amphibians, and other water-dwelling creatures by hunting them in shallow water. The most diverse family in the group is the heron-egret clan (Family Ardeidae), which numbers about 60 species worldwide and 20 in southern Africa. Many species in this family have very extensive global ranges; the GRAY HERON (Plate 25) for example, extends across Africa, Europe, and Asia. Herons are easily distinguished by their long, dagger-like bills and their sinuous, rather snake-like necks that they retract in flight, giving them a distinctive head-against-body silhouette when seen flying. Leg length in the various heron species varies greatly and dictates the depths to which each wades while fishing; short-legged species are confined to the shallows while the longest-legged herons are capable of hunting in water around 0.7 m (2.3 ft) deep. Some heron species are gregarious and commonly fish together, but others (including the Gray Heron) hunt solitarily. A few species, of which the BLACK-HEADED HERON (Plate 25) and CATTLE EGRET (Plate 25) are examples, have forsaken the aquatic habitats so favored by the family to become dry land hunters, preying mostly on grasshoppers.

Storks (family Ciconiidae) also have long, dagger-like bills used for impaling their prey, but they do not retract their heads as herons do, instead flying with their long necks extended. Although most are aquatic birds, there are also a few stork species that prefer feeding in dry land habitats. Best known of these is the WHITE STORK (Plate 26), a gregarious and migratory species that breeds in Europe and overwinters in Africa. It is the commonest of the 8 stork species found in southern Africa and one of 19 species found in the world. Flocks of these large black-and-white birds range widely while they are in their African winter grounds in pursuit of concentrations of grasshoppers and outbreaks of locusts. None of the aquatic storks have been profiled here because they tend to be uncommon and localized in the region. A very unusual stork-like bird that is wholly restricted to the African continent is the brown-plumaged, crested HAMERKOP ("hammer head," Plate 26). It has no other close avian relatives and comprises a one-bird family, the Scopidae. It inhabits the fringes of ponds and streams and specializes in eating frogs. It can sometimes also be found working its way along the muddy edges of a roadside puddle.

Ibises and *spoonbills* (family Threskiornithidae) are distinguished from other large wading birds by the shape of their bills. Ibises have bills that are long and sickle-shaped, while those of spoonbills have broad, flat, spatula-like tips. Ibises forage by probing in mud or water, their down-curved bill adapted perfectly for this. Spoonbills feed by sweeping their bill, held slightly open, from side to side in front of them while slowly wading in shallow water. The family is represented by 5 species in southern Africa (4 ibises, 1 spoonbill) and by 32 species worldwide.

Flamingos are the most specialized of the large wading birds. They are quite unmistakable, with pink plumage; exceptionally long, slender legs and necks; webbed feet (not shared by the others dealt with here); and large, banana-shaped bills. They are extremely gregarious, and flocks of hundreds, thousands, or even millions of birds may gather to feed in food-rich wetlands. The GREATER FLAMINGO (Plate 23) is one of two southern African species (and of five in the world); the two local species are most easily distinguished by their different bill color (pink in Greater Flamingo, dark red in LESSER FLAMINGO).

Natural History

Ecology and Behavior

The basic technique used by the large wading birds to secure food is to stand or walk slowly in shallow water searching for prey, then lunge at it when it is detected. Many species have developed subtle variations on this, and a few, as mentioned, have forsaken water altogether as a foraging medium. Some species of heron remain rooted to one spot for long periods waiting for a suitably sized fish to pass; others, including the LITTLE EGRET (Plate 25), which has bright yellow toes, shuffle their feet below the water, apparently to lure fish. At least one species has developed the technique of luring fish by dropping bait into the water; and still another uses its wings to form an umbrella over the water, either to see into the water more clearly or to draw small fish into the "safety" of the shade offered. Cattle Egrets have very successfully formed a profitable association with grazing herbivores (from elephants and buffalo to antelope and cattle), walking alongside these animals and pouncing on grasshoppers and other insects that are flushed. Their range and numbers have increased dramatically in southern Africa, largely in response to the growth of cattle and dairy farming in the region, and they have expanded their range in recent times into many new areas elsewhere in the world.

Flamingos feed on small to microscopic-sized organisms with a specialized bill structure that facilitates this. The shape of their bills is such that, when held slightly open, it leaves a gap of similar width between the mandibles along its whole length. The inner edges of these mandibles are lined with fine *lamellae* (thin plates) which, when the bill is almost closed, form a filter. Flamingos feed with their heads submerged and held upside down and, using their tongue as a piston, they first draw water into the bill, then force it out through the filters, trapping small organisms against the lamellae in the process. The Greater

Flamingo often rotates slowly about one point while doing this, rhythmically treading with its feet to stir up organisms in the water; when it moves on it often leaves behind a circular depression that marks the place where it stood.

Breeding

Monogamy, in which each member of the pair shares the incubation and care of the nestlings, is the rule in this group of large wading birds. Some of the species breed colonially, others solitarily. Flamingos invariably nest colonially, and in southern Africa they breed very erratically, in very large concentrations, and at very few sites. Pairs construct their turret-like mud nests close together in shallow water or on low islands, and these colonies are usually situated in very inaccessible parts of large, shallow-water saline pans. Other species in this large wading bird category—herons, storks, ibises, and spoonbills—construct nest-platforms of sticks or reed stems, in some cases nesting in trees, in others nesting in reedbeds. The colonial breeders commonly share the nesting site with several, and sometimes a dozen or more, species.

Hamerkops build a remarkable nest that is uniquely different from that built by any other species in this group. It is an enormous domed structure made of sticks, grass, mud, and debris that encloses a central mud-lined inner chamber, reached from the outside via a narrow tunnel. Nests are typically 1 to 1.5 m (3.2 to 4.8 ft) high and about 1 m (3.2 ft) wide, with an entrance situated low on one side that leads upward via the tunnel to the inner chamber, which is about 0.3 m (1 ft) wide and high. A nest typically takes a pair of Hamerkops 4 to 6 weeks to construct and they are usually built in trees, less often on cliff ledges. A nest is usually used for a single breeding attempt by the Hamerkops, but a variety of other bird species, especially owls, geese, and raptors, also make use of their nests, sometimes usurping the Hamerkops to do so.

The number of eggs laid per clutch varies between 1 and 5 according to species; flamingos invariably lay single-egg clutches, whereas ibises and spoonbills usually lay 2 or 3 eggs and storks, herons, and hamerkops lay 3 to 5 eggs. The incubation and nestling periods are also variable, the former ranging between about 18 to 35 days according to species and the latter between about 20 to 100 days. The young in all species are *altricial* (born helpless) but nestling herons develop rapidly and usually leave the nest well before they can fly.

Notes

The White Stork, which builds its nests on roofs and chimneys and has a close association with people in Europe, is entrenched in European folklore as a symbol of reliability and good luck. It does not, however, have such symbolism in its non-breeding range in Africa. The Hamerkop, on the other hand, is the subject of much superstition among tribal Africans—it is regarded as a bird of great wisdom, of ill omen, and of having magical powers.

Status

Three of the large wading birds of the region—the SLATY EGRET, SOUTHERN BALD IBIS, and Lesser Flamingo—are ranked as globally threatened (vulnerable) on account of their restricted breeding ranges. In South Africa, two others—the WHITE-BACKED NIGHT HERON and EURASIAN BITTERN—are also ranked as vulnerable on a regional scale due to their declining numbers and ranges.

Profiles

Gray Heron, *Ardea cinerea*, Plate 25a

Black-headed Heron, *Ardea melanocephala*, Plate 25b
Cattle Egret, *Bubulcus ibis*, Plate 25c
Little Egret, *Egretta garzetta*, Plate 25d
Great Egret, *Casmerodius albus*, Plate 25e
Hamerkop, *Scopus umbretta*, Plate 26a
White Stork, *Ciconia ciconia*, Plate 26b
Hadeda Ibis, *Bostrychia hagedash*, Plate 26c
Sacred Ibis, *Threskiornis aethiopicus*, Plate 26d
African Spoonbill, *Platalea alba*, Plate 26e
Greater Flamingo, *Phoenicopterus ruber*, Plate 23c

5. Birds of Prey

Birds of prey, or *raptors*, as they are commonly called, are a very diverse group of birds found widely on all continents. They number about 280 species worldwide, 71 of which are represented in southern Africa. They are broadly divided (at family level) into "falcons" (family Falconidae) and "non-falcons" (family Accipitridae), with a few other single-species families, including the SECRETARYBIRD (family Sagittariidae; Plate 21), added in. Below family level there are numerous distinctive groups of raptors in the assemblage: *vultures, eagles, kites, buzzards, sparrowhawks, harriers, falcons,* and *kestrels* feature prominently in southern Africa. They are so diverse that it is really only their powerful, hooked bills and sharp claws that set raptors apart from other birds; the variation in sizes, for example, is enormous, with the largest species reaching about 1.1 m (3.6 ft) in length and the smallest a mere 20 cm (8 in). Their shape, wing and tail proportions, and the ways in which they hunt prey are just as variable. Their coloration is also very variable, both between species and, in some cases, between the different age-classes within a species. These can present considerable challenges in correct identification!

Vultures and eagles are the largest and most imposing species: they have large to very large wingspans (up to 2.6 m, 8.4 ft) and are often seen soaring at great heights above the ground. Both groups are well represented in southern Africa (9 vultures, 16 eagles) and they are a conspicuous part of the fauna in all the larger game parks in the region. Vultures are scavengers, and some species, including the CAPE VULTURE (Plate 29) and WHITE-BACKED VULTURE (Plate 29), are extremely gregarious, often seen soaring together and descending in large numbers to feed on a carcass. Eagles, on the other hand, tend to live solitary lives or hunt in pairs. Some species specialize in hunting a particular prey type (for example, the *snake eagles*, which live mainly on snakes, and the AFRICAN FISH EAGLE (Plate 29), which preys mainly on fish), while others are more opportunistic in their prey selection. The unusual Secretarybird is generally regarded as being derived from eagle ancestry because it soars like an eagle and much of its breeding behavior is eagle-like. It is, however, a terrestrial bird that preys on rodents, insects, and small reptiles. Buzzards also soar like eagles, but they have smaller wingspans and hunt smaller prey. Harriers, a distinctive raptor group, are more commonly seen on the wing than perched; they live in open country and hunt by flying slowly and buoyantly a few meters (yards) above the ground while watching for movement below. By contrast, sparrowhawks live in woodlands or forests; they have long tails and short, rounded wings that provide the agility and maneuverability needed to pursue other small birds—which form their main prey—in flight.

Because of their hunting technique and their speed, sparrowhawks are widely used in falconry. They are often termed "short-wings" in falconry parlance, whereas falcons, the other raptor group so popular with falconers, are termed "long-wings." Falcons indeed have long, pointed wings and bullet-shaped bodies, and also hunt by hot pursuit, but their particular technique is to dive ("stoop") at great speed from a height onto flying birds. A branch of the falcon family in which these rapacious hunting methods are less developed is the kestrels. These small falcons have developed the ability to hover in wind in order to hunt, doing this more effectively than almost any other raptor.

Natural History

Ecology and Behavior

With the exception of the species that scavenge, most raptors hunt and kill their prey—whether it be a fish, a snake, another bird, or an insect—with its feet and sharply pointed claws. The size of prey taken is related to the size of the predator: the largest and most rapacious species of eagles are capable of killing monkeys and small antelope, while insects and termites often form the main prey of the smaller species. Many species specialize in hunting a single prey type and have adaptations designed for this. BAT HAWKS, for example, live mainly on bats, and they catch these in flight at dawn and dusk, often hunting on the wing, close to places where bats roost or concentrate. They have unusually large eyes, presumably to enhance their vision in poor light. VERREAUX'S EAGLES (Plate 29) prey almost exclusively on Rock Hyraxes ("dassies"), and they are restricted to rocky and mountainous habitats where their prey is most abundant. They commonly hunt in pairs and snatch basking hyraxes from rocks while on the wing. Two snake eagle species prey on snakes, which they hunt rather leisurely by watching the ground from a high vantage point or while cruising slowly in the sky. They often catch highly venomous snakes and are protected from bites, at least to some extent, by dense plumage and the thick scales coating their legs and feet.

Among the more rapacious birds of prey there is a noticeable size difference between the sexes, females being much larger than males, in a phenomenon often referred to as *reversed sexual size dimorphism*. This dimorphism ("two forms") is most pronounced in falcons and sparrowhawks, non-existent in vultures, and developed to a greater or lesser extent in other groups according to their rapaciousness. There has been some debate as to why it exists. In the most dimorphic species, the larger females often take larger prey than the males, so one explanation offered is that dimorphism helps reduce competition for prey between the members of a pair. Another explanation relates to the roles of the sexes in the nesting cycle: while nesting, there is a conflicting need to remain agile and swift in order to hunt successfully for the brood, but also to put on fat reserves in order to continue incubating and brooding nestlings even if food becomes scarce. It has been suggested that the reversed dimorphism has evolved to satisfy these two conflicting requirements by having each partner undertake one of the roles; thus, females do all the nest-related duties while males do all the hunting. In non-rapacious species such as vultures, there is no need to remain lean and agile in order to hunt successfully, so both sexes share parental care and no dimorphism is found.

Many of the smaller raptors that live on grasshoppers or small rodents have lifestyles that are much affected by the availability of their preferred prey. Some of the kestrel species, AMUR FALCONS (Plate 31) and LESSER KESTRELS (Plate 31) for example, prey mainly on grasshoppers and thus are migratory, leaving southern Africa in winter when grasshopper numbers plummet. The BLACK-SHOULDERED KITE (Plate 30) is a specialized rodent hunter, but rodents are prone to cyclic irruptions and slumps. The kite's response has been to adopt a nomadic lifestyle, staying in one place for as long as the food supply is good, then moving elsewhere when it declines. Consequently, in Black-shouldered Kites, breeding seasons are ill-defined, pairs bond for only a single nesting attempt, sometimes splitting up even before the nesting cycle is over, and places that support many kites in one year may become deserted by these birds in another. They also have the habit, shared by the migratory kestrels, of gathering at night to roost in flocks. This behavior likely provides the means whereby nomadic birds like these are quickly able to assess hunting conditions in an area (lots of well-fed birds coming to roost means lots of prey about) and can respond appropriately by staying or moving on.

Breeding

Monogamy is the rule in all but a few raptors; a low incidence of polyandry (one female has more than one male partner) is found in the SOUTHERN PALE CHANTING GOSHAWK (Plate 30) and Black-shouldered Kite, and harrier species are sometimes polygynous (one male has more than one female partner). Few raptor species are colonial nesters (as are the Cape Vulture and White-backed Vulture); most nest as widely spaced pairs. As mentioned earlier, parental roles while nesting vary from shared duties in the least rapacious species, to each partner assuming one role (hunting or nest attendance) in the more rapacious species. Apart from falcons and kestrels (which do not build nests), birds of prey construct a nest for themselves in which they lay their eggs. The largest species (vultures, most eagles, buzzards, and others) generally build large nests—open-topped platforms of sticks that are often refurbished for re-use in successive years. Verreaux's Eagle nests, almost invariably built on ledges of cliffs, may become very large, even reaching a height of 4.1 m (13 ft), and successive generations of eagles may occupy such sites. The nests of the smaller species, of course, are much smaller, but they invariably follow the formula of making an open platform or saucer using sticks, twigs, weeds stems, or similar materials. Cliff-nesting is less common than tree-nesting, and while a few species such as the JACKAL BUZZARD (Plate 30) are equally at home building their nest in a tree or on a cliff ledge, others use one site or the other but not both. Harriers are unusual in building their nest in thick cover on the ground or in a marsh. Falcons and kestrels do not build nests; they either take over old nests of other raptors (or other birds), or they lay in a hole or on a cliff ledge. The tiny PYGMY FALCON is unusual in using a nest chamber in a Sociable Weaver colony for this purpose.

The number of eggs per clutch laid by birds of prey varies between 1–5 eggs. The majority of species lay small clutches, with vultures and some eagles laying a single egg; many intermediate-sized, and several smaller species, usually lay two eggs, and a few species including some sparrowhawks and the Black-shouldered Kite lay clutches of 3 to 5 eggs. Incubation and nestling periods are highly variable and dependent on the size of the species concerned.

Notes

Curiously, birds of prey have not featured prominently in tribal African customs or lore, whereas eagles and falcons have been important symbols in Western cultures, their usage dating from ancient Greek/Roman and early Anglo-Saxon times to the present. Falconry, the art of training hawks to hunt, has been practiced for thousands of years and has a strong following in southern Africa.

Status

A number of southern African birds of prey are considered threatened at a national level (in South Africa, five vultures, three eagles, a harrier, and a kestrel are Red Data-listed). Five southern African species are ranked internationally, one (TAITA FALCON) regarded as vulnerable and four as near-threatened.

Profiles

Secretarybird, *Sagittarius serpentarius*, Plate 21b
Cape Vulture, *Gyps coprotheres*, Plate 29a
White-backed Vulture, *Gyps africanus*, Plate 29b
Verreaux's Eagle, *Aquila verreauxii*, Plate 29c
Bateleur, *Terathopius ecaudatus*, Plate 29d
African Fish Eagle, *Haliaeetus vocifer*, Plate 29e
Yellow-billed Kite, *Milvus aegyptius*, Plate 30a
Black-shouldered Kite, *Elanus caeruleus*, Plate 30b
Jackal Buzzard, *Buteo rufofuscus*, Plate 30c
Steppe Buzzard, *Buteo buteo*, Plate 30d
Gabar Goshawk, *Micronisus gabar*, Plate 30e
Southern Pale Chanting Goshawk, *Melierax canorus*, Plate 30f
Lanner Falcon, *Falco biarmicus*, Plate 31a
Amur Falcon, *Falco amurensis*, Plate 31b
Rock Kestrel, *Falco tinnunculus*, Plate 31c
Greater Kestrel, *Falco rupicoloides*, Plate 31d
Lesser Kestrel, *Falco naumanni*, Plate 31e

6. Game Birds

Game bird is one of those general catchall terms (like waterfowl or wader) that includes several unrelated bird families that share common features; in this particular case it includes several families of birds that live on the ground, are edible, and are traditionally hunted. Depending on how far the word is stretched, it extends to between 250 and 300 species, which include such familiar birds as *grouse, turkeys, partridges, quail, guineafowl,* and *sandgrouse*; the domestic fowl is another very familiar member. All the species involved are chicken-like birds varying in size from very small to large, some brilliantly colored with extravagant plumages (pheasants and peafowl), others dull-colored and cryptic (francolins, sandgrouse). They are all heavy-bodied birds with strong but rather short legs and strong, arched bills designed particularly for grubbing in soil.

Game birds are represented in southern Africa by 25 species, the most prolific of which, with 12 species found in the region, are a group of partridge-like birds known as *francolins* and *spurfowl* (Family Phasianidae). There are also several species of quail (Family Phasianidae), guineafowl (Family Numididae), and sandgrouse (Family Pteroclidae) found here, as well as two species of the tiny, quail-like *button-quails* (Family Turnicidae), a group with uncertain taxonomic affinities. A visitor to the region is unlikely to miss seeing the very common and widespread HELMETED GUINEAFOWL (Plate 34) and one or more francolin species, and if the visit extended into the arid west, one or two sandgrouse species would certainly also be added to the list. The Helmeted Guineafowl is widely distributed across the savannah regions of Africa, and although it and others in its family are endemic to the African continent, it now has a worldwide distribution in the form of both feral populations and captive stock as a result of introduction and domestication. In their natural range, Helmeted Guineafowl live for much of the year in flocks, dividing into pairs for the midsummer nesting period. They are not shy birds and quickly become bold if they are not bothered, and they are very commonly found on farmlands, scratching and digging for spilled grain or running after insects. Although reluctant to take to the wing in most situations, they invariably fly up into the branches of trees to sleep at night, and flocks often gather in the evening to roost at regular sites. They are especially vocal when gathering in this way.

Francolins and spurfowl are generally dull brown birds, some having barring or streaking on their bodies and distinctive facial or throat patterns, others having areas of bare red facial skin. In all species the males are distinguishable from the females by having prominent spurs (hard, horn-like growths) projecting from the back of their lower legs; females lack the spurs. Like guineafowl, they spend virtually all their time on the ground and similarly, they are far from silent birds, calling with gusto especially at dawn and dusk. In some species (for example, SWAINSON'S SPURFOWL, Plate 32) the call is a raucous crowing, in others it is much more melodious or lilting, and it is often these calls that alert one to their presence in an area. The habitats occupied by francolins and spurfowl are very variable. Some of the species have adapted remarkably well to the transformation of their natural habitats to farmland or suburbia; the Swainson's Spurfowl, for example, has expanded its range and increased its numbers dramatically as a result of the transformation of natural habitats into agricultural land, while the CAPE SPURFOWL (Plate 32) has adapted remarkably well to suburban environments in much of its range in the South-Western Cape, often being seen on the sides of busy roads. Other species, though (e.g. CRESTED FRANCOLIN, Plate 32; GRAY-WINGED FRANCOLIN, Plate 32), are restricted to natural habitats and their survival is dependent on these.

Whereas guineafowl, francolin, and spurfowl are remarkably sedentary birds, quail are not, and their often spectacular migrations have been known since biblical times. They are smaller than francolins and much more secretive, so their presence is usually given away only when they call. One of the three southern African species, the Common Quail, has a vast range that extends across Africa into Europe and Asia; those that occur in southern Africa range seasonally between the southern and central parts of the continent. Button-quails are tiny versions of quail, and like them they range widely in the region, but with far less predictable movements.

The African continent is the home of sandgrouse, since 12 of the world's 16 species occur here. Four are found in southern Africa, one occurring widely in the savannah areas while three are restricted to semi-arid country. One of these, the NAMAQUA SANDGROUSE (Plate 39), is one of the region's most familiar desert birds. Apart from their terrestrial lifestyle and popularity for hunting, sandgrouse have little in common with the francolin-quail-guineafowl suite, and they belong to a quite different family (Pteroclidae). They look like pigeons rather than chickens; their legs are very short and they have a shuffling walk, with the body held close to the ground. They are also powerful fliers and are often seen on the wing, commuting between drinking sites and feeding areas. The daily flight that sandgrouse make to and from water, sometimes involving a round trip of more than

100 km (60 mi), is probably the single most characteristic feature of these birds—because they feed entirely on dry seeds and derive no moisture from these, access to drinking water is crucial for their survival.

Natural History

Ecology and Behavior

Game birds are day-active birds that live on the ground—they derive all their food at ground level, they nest on the ground, and in most species, they spend their nights sleeping on the ground. With the exception of sandgrouse, which are strictly seed-eaters, they have mixed diets, often eating seeds, but also taking insects when available, fruits, and digging for bulbs and tubers (an especially important source of food in francolin species such as the GRAYWING). The usual response on being approached varies from species to species; guineafowl typically keep their distance and retreat on foot, whereas many of the francolin and spurfowl, and particularly quail and button-quail, freeze and can be virtually walked on before they fly away in a flurry. This behavior has led to their reputation as ideal birds for sport shooting, which uses trained dogs to locate the birds and "point" them. Francolins are gregarious when not nesting and characteristically form "coveys" that, depending on the species, may number 5 to 20 birds. Coveys are usually well spaced, each occupying a home range that doesn't overlap with those of neighboring groups. A few francolins, however, are much less gregarious. Species such as the Crested Francolin remain in pairs throughout the year, with their offspring remaining with them for a period after the breeding season. Least gregarious are the button-quail, which may migrate in flocks but live solitarily once settled, males and females only coming together briefly prior to nesting.

Sandgrouse are particularly sociable birds, and in some situations will gather in thousands at their favored drinking sites. The trips to drink are well synchronized within each species (but quite variable between species), and one does not find individual birds simply making random visits to water at any time of the day. Namaqua Sandgrouse drink in early- to mid-morning, whereas DOUBLE-BANDED SANDGROUSE (Plate 39) gather to drink at dusk. While gathering at the water's edge there is a great deal of calling, posturing, and other social interaction among individuals, and it is clear that these gatherings serve purposes other than simply to take up water. In desert areas the sandgrouse often run the gauntlet of predatory birds, especially falcons, which take up positions around waterholes in anticipation of their arrival. After drinking, groups of birds fly off in different directions, some to forage while others, during the breeding season, return to nests to relieve their mates.

Breeding

Ground-nesting is the rule in game birds; in all cases a shallow scrape is made in the ground and sparsely lined with pieces of grass or other vegetation before the clutch of eggs is laid. Guineafowl, francolins, and quail lay a clutch that usually numbers at least 7 to 8 eggs (and up to 41 recorded in guineafowl), whereas sandgrouse and button-quail lay clutches of only 2 to 4. Guineafowl and francolin eggs are an unmarked dull white or beige and are extremely hard-shelled, whereas those of button-quails and sandgrouse are not thick-shelled and are buff in color, attractively marked with brown. Incubation is usually undertaken by the female without male assistance; she leaves the nest briefly from time to time to feed. In sandgrouse the incubation is shared, the male taking the night shift and the female the day shift. Button-quail are unusual in being polyandrous (one female has more than one male partner) and males undertake all parental care. All young game birds are *precocial* and leave the nest within hours of hatching. In many of the species, the chicks' wings develop rapidly so that they can fly long before they are fully grown. Sandgrouse have evolved the unusual behavior of carrying water to their chicks before they can fly: the water is absorbed into the belly feathers (which are modified to maximize their ability to absorb and retain water) while the parents are drinking (a behavior known as "belly-wetting"), and on the return of the parent to the brood, the young know instinctively to sip water from these feathers. The water-carrying habit is best developed in male birds.

Notes

The striking spotted plumage of the Helmeted (and some other) Guineafowl gave rise to this species' name, *meleagris*. Meleager was a Greek hero whose death was so grieved by his sisters that they turned into birds, and the droplets from all the tears they shed formed white spots on their dark mourning clothes.

Status

One game bird, the BLACK-RUMPED BUTTON-QUAIL, is Red Data-listed at a national level (in South Africa) as endangered, but none have received international Red Data status.

Profiles

Crested Francolin, *Francolinus sephaena*, Plate 32a
Gray-winged Francolin, *Francolinus africanus*, Plate 32b
Swainson's Spurfowl, *Pternistis swainsonii*, Plate 32c
Red-billed Spurfowl, *Pternistis adspersus*, Plate 32d
Cape Spurfowl, *Pternistis capensis*, Plate 32e
Helmeted Guineafowl, *Numida meleagris*, Plate 34a
Crested Guineafowl, *Guttera pucherani*, Plate 34b
Namaqua Sandgrouse, *Pterocles namaqua*, Plate 39d
Double-banded Sandgrouse, *Pterocles bicinctus*, Plate 39e

7. Marsh Birds

The particular marsh birds brought together here represent three families—*rails, jacanas*, and *painted snipe*—and they share the features of being small- to medium-sized, of having long toes and being heavy-bodied, with short tails and rounded wings. They live in a variety of marshy habitats, some species frequenting open-water areas while others live in dense, marshy vegetation where they are rarely seen; a few species of rails are terrestrial and live in forests or grasslands. The rails (family Rallidae) are the most diverse and widespread marsh bird family, and 143 species are currently recognized, 18 of which occur in southern Africa. Although all are lumped under the collective name of "rail," there is less ambiguity if these birds are collectively referred to as *rallids*; this is because within the family there are both rails in the narrow sense of the term and several other distinctive groups, including *crakes, flufftails, moorhens, gallinules,* and *coots*. These different groups of rallids are separated on the basis of size, bill length, and plumage differences; for example, many crakes and rails are small, brown- or gray-colored and have barred underparts, whereas moorhens and coots are larger and have mainly black plumage. Rails, crakes, and flufftails are notoriously secretive birds, and the habits and life histories of many are poorly known. Flufftails in particular live like mice in thick marshy undergrowth, seldom showing themselves, only giving away their presence with their eerie hooting calls. By contrast, coots are invariably conspicuous and unlikely to be overlooked; the particular species found in southern Africa, the RED-KNOBBED COOT (Plate 33), is one of the most widespread and abundant wetland birds in the region. Coots, gallinules, and moorhens differ from other rallids by having a "frontal shield" (area of bare skin on the forehead) that varies in color according to species. In coots, for instance, it is white, whereas in some gallinules (such as the PURPLE SWAMPHEN or GALLINULE, Plate 33) it is red, and in others it is blue or green.

Jacanas (family Jacanidae) are easily recognized by their enormously long toes (and equally long toenails), which, in proportion to the size of their bodies, are longer than those of any other bird. Two of the world's 8 jacana species are found in southern Africa and one of these, the AFRICAN JACANA (Plate 35), is found widely in the more tropical parts of the region. This species has rich warm brown plumage with a white chest and bright blue frontal shield. It lives in wetlands where open water is covered by floating aquatic plants, especially water-lilies; their preference for such areas has led to jacanas often being referred to as "lily-trotters" or "lotus-birds." Their long toes give these birds a unique advantage in being able to walk and feed in places otherwise only reached by birds that can swim. Painted snipe (family Rostratulidae) are a family of only 2 species, and the southern African representative (the Greater Painted Snipe) is not profiled because it is not commonly encountered. It prefers muddy, vegetated edges of pans and swamps.

Natural History

Ecology and Behavior

Whereas coots, gallinules, and moorhens are largely vegetarian, rails, crakes, flufftails, jacanas, and painted snipe are mainly insectivorous. Red-knobbed Coots are highly gregarious and feed on submerged aquatic plants, simply pulling these up and consuming them as they swim about. Large rafts of these birds may gather where there are concentrations of submerged plants such as pond-weed and parrot's feather. COMMON MOORHENS (Plate 33) resemble miniature coots in many ways, often found in groups and commonly seen feeding while swimming in the way that coots do or probing for food along the muddy edges of marshes; they are, however, more secretive than coots and keep in or close to cover. Purple Swamphens, also gregarious, use their powerful bills to break off and chew open the stems of rushes and sedges, and they are often seen gnawing at such tasty items while grasping them between the toes of one foot. With the exception of one or two species, seeing a rail, crake, or flufftail is usually a matter of luck, as they remain inside cover and, at best, give only fleeting glimpses of themselves when they are forced to cross an open space. Several species are migratory and commute widely across the African continent, while a few species migrate annually to southern Africa from Europe. A number of rail species, mostly confined to isolated islands, are flightless. The BLACK CRAKE (Plate 33) is less of a skulker than most other crakes and is relatively easily seen, although it never ventures too far from cover and dashes back in when threatened. Its striking coloration (red legs and yellow bill contrasting sharply with its all-black plumage) is also unusual for a crake. Rails, crakes, and flufftails are less gregarious than coots, moorhens, and gallinules, and many of these species lead solitary lives, only pairing up to breed. In the case of the Black Crake, family groups, comprising the parent birds and young from previous broods, often remain together for extended periods and the offspring assist the parents in raising later broods.

The African Jacana is primarily insectivorous. It gleans small prey items such as flies, dragonflies, and beetles from emergent plants and from the surface of the water, stalking these slowly and deliberately, neck stretched low and far forward, each step taken cautiously as its weight is redistributed on its long, outstretched toes. Where conditions are ideal, many jacanas may live in close proximity to each other, promoting endless chasing, squabbling, and shrill calling between birds. Females are considerably heavier than males, but not proportionately longer-toed, and as a result they often sink on floating vegetation where males can walk with impunity. They particularly favor ephemeral wetlands and often have to move in response to the flooding and drying out of such habitats; as a result African Jacanas occasionally turn up in very unusual places, sometimes far from the nearest wetland.

Breeding

Marsh birds are very diverse in their nesting habits. Most species are probably monogamous, but some are polygynous and a few are polyandrous; none breed colonially. All the species involved construct a nest of sorts; in some species (such as the Red-knobbed Coot) the nest is a large, conspicuous mound of plant material surrounded by water, whereas many other species build a well-hidden, cup-shaped nest set deep inside marshy vegetation, above but close to the water's surface. The African Jacana's nest ranks as one of the most feeble nests built by any bird—it is little more that a few stems of aquatic plants pulled together on floating vegetation, and it rocks with every movement of the water beneath it, with the eggs sometimes rolling off the nest when there is strong wave action. Jacanas' eggs have a highly glossed surface that serves to waterproof them, a useful adaptation given the precarious nature of the nest. Provided the eggs don't sink (which a freshly laid egg will do), the parent jacana usually retrieves any eggs that roll out, using its bill or chest to nudge them back onto the nest platform. Clutch sizes are variable, typically ranging between 4 and 7 in most rallids (except flufftails, which lay 3 to 5), while the African Jacana almost invariably lays a clutch of 4 eggs. Flufftails lay plain white eggs, whereas other rallids typically lay eggs that are buff- or brown-colored, variably covered with darker markings, and jacanas lay chestnut-colored eggs richly marked with thick black scrolls. Parental care is shared by the sexes in most, and perhaps all, the monogamous species, but in the African Jacana, which is polyandrous, males do all incubation and nestling care without female assistance. In this species females lay successive clutches of eggs for different males (up to 7 males in a season), and because a female mates with several males, when a male commences incubating a clutch he has little guarantee of paternity of the eggs. Incubation periods are shortest (about 14 to 16 days) in the rails, crakes, and flufftails and longer (22 to 25 days) in coots, gallinules, and jacanas. In all the species the young are highly precocial, leaving the nest within hours of hatching. In the case of jacanas, the chicks learn to find their own food within a day of hatching and they are not fed by the parent at any stage.

Notes

The name "jacana" is derived from a native Brazilian name for the species found in South America; although its Portuguese pronunciation is "hah-san-nah," normal English pronunciation is "ja-ka-na."

Status

For one reason or another, the populations of many rallid species in the world are under threat, and three of the species occurring in southern Africa are currently Red Data-listed. The White-winged Flufftail is ranked as globally endangered, the Corncrake as globally vulnerable, and the Striped Flufftail is ranked as vulnerable in South Africa. Loss of breeding habitat is thought to be the primary threat to these species.

Profiles

Black Crake, *Amaurornis flavirostris*, Plate 33a
Common Moorhen, *Gallinula chloropus*, Plate 33b
Red-knobbed Coot, *Fulica cristata*, Plate 33c
Purple Swamphen, *Porphyrio porphyrio*, Plate 33d
African Jacana, *Actophilornis africanus*, Plate 35a

8. Shorebirds

Almost any stretch of shoreline, be it along the coast, on a tidal mudflat, on the edges of a freshwater pond or lake, or along the edges of a saline pan, is likely to be frequented by one or more species of *shorebird*. These are birds that vary in size from very small to large, have longish legs, and probe and glean small prey items from the ground or from shallow water. Although very variable in shape, they tend to be long-winged and short-tailed, and in most species, to have necks disproportionately thick and heads too broad for their bodies. Most shorebird species belong to two large families, either the *plovers* and *lapwings* (family Charadriidae) or the *sandpipers* (family Scolopacidae), but there are several smaller families also represented in the group, including *oystercatchers* (family Haematopodidae), *avocets* and *stilts* (family Recurvirostridae), *dikkops* or *thick-knees* (family Burhinidae), and the *coursers* and *pratincoles* (family Glareolidae). Despite their collective name, not all shorebirds live alongside water; many plovers and coursers are dry land birds, some living in very arid environments.

Shorebirds are well represented in southern Africa; 70 of the world's approximately 200 species are found here. The majority, however, are non-breeding visitors (or vagrants) that use southern Africa as a wintering area, migrating here from their Northern Hemisphere breeding grounds. Foremost among these migrants are the Scolopacidae (or *scolopacids*, as they are commonly labeled); there is only a single one of these that is resident in southern Africa, and the rest, some 31 species that include *greenshanks, stints, sandpipers, godwits,* and others, are non-breeding visitors, each of which undertakes a remarkable twice-a-year migration between its summer and winter quarters. The RUFF (Plate 37), for instance, makes a flight of at least 10,000 km (6,300 mi) in spring and again in autumn. Scolopacids are dull-colored birds in their winter quarters, streaky brown above and paler below, but many acquire bright plumages in their breeding grounds. The different species are very variable in size and shape, and a typical cross-section of these is shown in the species profiled, from the very small LITTLE STINT (Plate 36) to the larger, long-billed COMMON GREENSHANK (Plate 37). This migratory habit is shared by 8 species of plovers, and when these Northern Hemisphere breeders move south into their wintering grounds they nearly double the number of plover species in southern Africa. Plovers have a distinctive bill shape—it is relatively short (never exceeding the bird's head in length) and it swells out near the tip—which is one of the features distinguishing this family from scolopacids. Plovers are rather variable in size, and the larger species are nowadays termed "lapwings," with the smaller species sometimes being known as "sandplovers." Of the two most widespread and abundant species, one (BLACKSMITH LAPWING, Plate 35) is a bird of freshwater wetlands while the other (CROWNED LAPWING, Plate 35) is a dry land bird.

Oystercatchers are a family of shorebirds that are widely represented in the world, and the southern African coastline is populated by a very distinctive member in the form of the AFRICAN BLACK OYSTERCATCHER (Plate 35), a striking black bird with a red bill and red legs. It is endemic to the region and is found mostly along the southern and western coasts. Stilts and avocets live along the margins of freshwater wetlands. They have boldly contrasting black-and-white plumages and are longer-legged and longer-billed than most shorebirds; the 2 species that are resident in southern Africa, the PIED AVOCET (Plate 37) and BLACK-WINGED STILT (Plate 37), both have ranges that extend across several continents. Dikkops and coursers are more nocturnal than others in the group, and as one would expect, they have unusually large eyes. With the exception of the WATER DIKKOP (Plate 39), which lives along the edges of rivers and estuaries, these two groups comprise species that frequent dry land habitats.

Natural History

Ecology and Behavior

The assemblages of migratory shorebirds that often gather on favored coastal or inland wetlands are among the most spectacular avian sights on offer—at the right time and place one may find tens of thousands of CURLEW SANDPIPERS (Plate 36), Little Stints (Plate 36), and others packed together, feeding rapidly, running this way and that in the shallow water, then without warning taking flight in a tight formation, the flock wheeling and moving in a remarkably well-coordinated way before, just as suddenly, they re-alight elsewhere. Such flocking behavior is a feature at many west coast lagoons, particularly in the month or two prior to migration.

Shorebirds feed primarily on molluscs, crustaceans, worms, and aquatic and non-aquatic invertebrates. Different species secure their prey in different ways and the techniques they use are dictated by their morphology, especially the length and shape of their bills. Long-billed species (such as snipe) tend to probe deep into the substrate for prey, while short-billed birds (stints, plovers) mostly glean prey from its surface. In some species prey is mainly located using tactile clues, whereas in others it is located visually. Oystercatchers have long, powerful bills that are laterally flattened and chisel-shaped at the end, and they use these to scrape mussels off rocks and pry them open. Avocets such as the Pied Avocet forage by wading briskly in shallow water, sweeping their up-curved bill from side to side in front of them. Pratincoles are an exception in the group as mainly aerial feeders; they are short-legged, fork-tailed, swift-flying birds that are very maneuverable on the wing, and they have short, down-curved bills that, when opened wide, have a very large gape. They pursue and secure their prey (mainly aerial insects) in flight, foraging much like large swallows.

Breeding

Shorebirds characteristically nest on the ground, preferring open country where they have an unimpeded view of their surroundings. Some species lay their clutch on bare ground without making any pretext of a nest, but the majority, if nesting on dry ground, lay their clutch in a shallow scrape, or, if the nest is located over water, construct a rudimentary saucer-shaped nest of plant material. The eggs laid by all the species involved are buff to brownish in color, marked with darker streaks and spots and designed to blend into their surroundings; in some species, this is achieved very effectively. A few plover species (e.g., WHITE-FRONTED PLOVER, Plate 35) bury their eggs when they are left unattended, and in one courser species, the eggs are cemented firmly into the soil for the duration of the incubation period. In a few of the southern African breeding species there is a tendency towards nesting in small colonies (for example, Pied Avocet and Black-winged Stilt), and in one species, the RED-WINGED PRATINCOLE, breeding invariably takes place in colonies, these sometimes numbering hundreds or even thousands of pairs. The majority of species, however, breed solitarily. Most, and perhaps all, of the shorebird species breeding in southern Africa are monogamous and the incubation and care of the young is shared equally by the sexes. By contrast, many of the Northern Hemisphere breeders that spend their winters in southern Africa practise polygyny (for instance, the Ruff and Little Stint) or polyandry (phalaropes). Clutch size is rather variable: a few species (for example, DOUBLE-BANDED COURSER, Plate 39) consistently lay a single egg per clutch and several (e.g. THREE-BANDED PLOVER, Plate 35; African Black Oystercatcher) consistently lay two-egg clutches, but the majority normally lay a clutch of 3 or 4 eggs. Incubation periods range between 24 and 27 days for most species, with only the African Black Oystercatcher having a somewhat longer duration (32 days). Young are precocial, and depending on species, the time taken from hatching to flying lasts 4 to 7 weeks.

Status

The African Black Oystercatcher has a limited breeding range, restricted to the southern and western coasts of southern Africa. Although locally abundant, its overall population is small (about 5,000 birds) and its breeding success on many of the mainland beaches is poor as a result of human disturbance. As a result it has been designated as a Red Data species and is classified as "near-threatened."

Profiles

African Black Oystercatcher, *Haematopus moquini*, Plate 35b
White-fronted Plover, *Charadrius marginatus*, Plate 35c
Three-banded Plover, *Charadrius tricollaris*, Plate 35d
Crowned Lapwing, *Vanellus coronatus*, Plate 35e
Blacksmith Lapwing, *Vanellus armatus*, Plate 35f
Common Sandpiper, *Tringa hypoleucos*, Plate 36a
Wood Sandpiper, *Tringa glareola*, Plate 36b
Curlew Sandpiper, *Calidris ferruginea*, Plate 36c
Little Stint, *Calidris minuta*, Plate 36d
Common Greenshank, *Tringa nebularia*, Plate 37a
Ruff, *Philomachus pugnax*, Plate 37b
Black-winged Stilt, *Himantopus himantopus*, Plate 37c
Pied Avocet, *Recurvirostra avosetta*, Plate 37d
Spotted Dikkop, *Burhinus capensis*, Plate 39a
Water Dikkop, *Burhinus vermiculatus*, Plate 39b
Double-banded Courser, *Smutsornis africanus*, Plate 39c

9. Gulls and Terns

Coastlines, estuaries, and harbors around the world are populated by *gulls* and *terns*, birds that are typically medium-sized, gregarious, have crisp white plumages, are often noisy, and are unlikely to go unnoticed. Some authorities group gulls and terns together into a single family, Laridae, but more often today they are separated into two families. The world's 44 tern species (family Sternidae) are narrowly outnumbered by the world's 50 gull species (family Laridae). There are two other closely related gull- or tern-like families: the *skuas* (or *jaegers*, as they are called in North America; family Stercorariidae), and the *skimmers* (family Rynchopidae), and about 36 species of this quite diverse array are to be found in southern African waters.

Gulls need little introduction because they are such a common feature of the world's seashores. Most species are medium-sized birds. They are all quite uniform in shape, with heavy bodies; long, rather broad wings; square tails; longish legs with webbed feet; and sturdy bills with a hooked tip. The sexes are alike, but juvenile plumages differ markedly from those of adults, being motley brown instead of white. Only 3 gulls are resident in southern Africa, the KELP GULL, GRAY-HEADED GULL and HARTLAUB'S GULL (all on Plate 38), but the coastal waters are visited from time to time by at least 6 Northern Hemisphere species. The Kelp Gull, the largest of the residents, has a black back and black upperwing surfaces. These birds occur along the coasts of all the continents in the Southern Hemisphere, and in southern Africa they are most abundant along the south and west coasts. The smaller Hartlaub's Gull is more restricted to the west coast than the Kelp Gull and it is endemic to this region; it is white except for a light gray back and upperwings, and its wing-tips are black. The Gray-headed Gull also ranges along the coast, but it is more common in inland wetlands; it is much like Hartlaub's Gull in size and appearance but, in breeding plumage, has a distinctive gray head.

With a few exceptions, terns are smaller than gulls and have more slender, elongated bodies; shorter legs; longer, narrower wings; deeply forked tails; and longish, slim bills. These features impart an elegance to terns that the more robustly built gulls lack, and their form gives terns the edge when it comes to flying. They spend much of their time hunting on the wing, gracefully hovering as they work their way upwind, poised several meters (yards) above the water; when prey is sighted they swoop down, plunging headfirst into the water to snatch up the victim with their bills. In most species their plumage is rather gull-like, mainly white with pale gray upperparts; many species have a black head-cap while breeding, but this is reduced or absent in non-breeding plumage. Their bills and legs are red in some species, but yellow or black in others, a useful distinguishing feature among some of the similar-looking species. At least 20 tern species have been recorded in southern Africa, but only 5 of these nest in the region and the others are seasonal or erratic visitors. The COMMON TERN (Plate 38) is by far the most abundant species when it is present, which is mostly between November and March; flocks of these graceful birds are likely to be seen in summer along almost any stretch of coastline. They are non-breeding visitors from the Northern Hemisphere that use the southern African coast as a wintering area; many other tern species do the same thing, but in lesser numbers. While most species come from the north, a few originate elsewhere; the ANTARCTIC TERN, for instance, is an off-season visitor from its Antarctic breeding grounds, while the SOOTY TERN, a species that lives in the tropical oceans, is brought in to the region from time to time by cyclones.

There is a sub-group within the tern family that frequents freshwater wetlands rather than the seashore, and these are collectively known as *marsh terns*. Three species occur in southern Africa, the most plentiful of which is the WHITE-WINGED TERN (Plate 38), a species that brings grace and charm to many inland waters. It migrates south from its breeding range in the Northern Hemisphere and is present between October and March; it may be seen in flocks on many of the interior's seasonal pans and wetlands and, in farmlands, following in the wake of a plough. Lastly, there is another freshwater species in this group, the AFRICAN SKIMMER, a tern-like bird that is restricted to large, tropical rivers such as the Zambezi or Kavango. It is black above and white below, and it has a long red bill, the lower mandible of which is longer than the upper mandible. Its unusual name derives from its technique of fishing by flying slowly just above the water with its bill open and lower mandible trailing in the water.

Natural History

Ecology and Behavior

The birds discussed here—terns, gulls, skuas, and skimmers—are, almost without exception, gregarious in all stages of their daily life, and they are seldom seen solitarily. They nest colonially, roost colonially, and usually forage in groups or flocks. Despite this common theme, the different families have distinctly different foraging habits and food preferences. Terns mainly prey on small fish, using the hunting technique described above, and tend to prefer fishing over calm rather than choppy water, often using inshore bays, estuaries, and lagoons for this; it is also not uncommon for several tern species to fish in the company of each other. Gulls feed mostly on marine invertebrates, and the intertidal zone is where they secure much of their food. They are great scavengers, as many fishermen who have lost their bait to a gull will know, and this trait has led to their frequent presence at rubbish dumps and sewage outlets. The inland-living populations of the Gray-headed Gull have colonized many towns as a result of this dump-scavenging habit. Skuas are also scavenging birds, but their speciality is piracy, and they obtain much of their food by robbing other seabirds of their catches. The five skua species that visit southern African offshore waters seldom come close to land, spending their time at sea and often associating with the trawling fleets operating off the west coast.

Breeding

With few exceptions, gulls and terns breed colonially. Many of the southern African breeding species nest on offshore islands, laying their eggs on the ground either in a shallow scrape or in a rudimentary saucer-shaped nest made of plant material. Most species are monogamous, and the incubation and care of young is shared by both parents. Kelp Gulls, Hartlaub's Gulls, and SWIFT TERNS (Plate 38) breed in large numbers at a few offshore island and coastal sites. Their colonies sometimes consist of thousands of closely spaced nests, and if these are approached or threatened, the birds at the colony rise *en masse* to attack the intruder. Gray-headed Gulls and CASPIAN TERNS are also colonial, but they nest at much lower densities and their colonies sometimes adjoin colonies of breeding pelicans, cormorants, or ibises. The endemic DAMARA TERN is the least sociable of the southern African nesters; some breeding occurs in small colonies, but it is more usual for nesting pairs to be well spaced, scattered widely across the gravelly washes they so favor, set well back from the beaches along the Namibian and southern Cape coasts. The WHISKERED TERN, which is the only member of the marsh tern group that nests in southern Africa, builds a floating nest of plant stems, often situated over deep water. It nests in small colonies, in numbers usually in the order of 5 to 15 pairs. African Skimmers breed in similar small colonies, using sandbanks in rivers that are temporarily exposed during low-flow periods, laying their eggs in a deep scrape in the sand. Gulls and terns lay small clutches in which the number of eggs varies between 1 and 3 (rarely 4); Damara Terns and Swift Terns invariably lay single-egg clutches whereas other southern African gulls and terns usually lay 2 or 3 eggs. Incubation periods range between 19 to 27 days, the variation being more or less related to size (19 days in Damara Tern, 27 in Kelp Gull), and the chicks first fly when 5 to 7 weeks old.

Status

Although there is a high potential for disturbance and persecution of the birds and their eggs and young at breeding colonies, most of the islands used by the coastal-breeding gulls and terns are well protected. The African Skimmer is a threatened species in the region because the number of safe breeding sites is steadily diminishing as a result of increasing human disturbance and changed river flow patterns that reduce sandbank availability. The Damara Tern, because of its restricted range and the fragmented nature of its breeding population, is listed as near-threatened in the most recent world Red Data rankings.

Profiles

Kelp Gull, *Larus dominicanus*, Plate 38a
Gray-headed Gull, *Larus cirrocephalus*, Plate 38b
Hartlaub's Gull, *Larus hartlaubii*, Plate 38c
Common Tern, *Sterna hirundo*, Plate 38d
Swift Tern, *Sterna bergii*, Plate 38e
White-winged Tern, *Chlidonias leucopterus*, Plate 38f

10. Pigeons and Doves

The *pigeon* family is one of the world's most widespread and successful groups of birds. Pigeons and doves are familiar thanks to their close association with humans, their domestication, and the abundance of feral populations of certain species in many of the world's towns and cities. The family is represented, often in large numbers, on all continents except in Antarctica, and is otherwise absent from only the coldest regions of the Arctic and from some isolated oceanic islands. They inhabit almost all kinds of habitats, from high rainforests to the edges of deserts, and they range considerably in size, from very small (sparrow-sized) to fairly large (chicken-sized). The terms "pigeon" and "dove" are often used interchangeably, although "pigeon" is usually reserved for the larger species and "dove" for the smaller—both belong to the same family, Columbidae. They are characterized by having a generally plump body, a short, rather weak bill, short legs, a thin neck and a small head, with the eye encircled by a small area of bare flesh. They are strong-winged birds and powerful fliers. A few species have long tails. A little over 300 species of pigeons and doves are currently recognized in the world, and the family is best represented in the Australasian region. In southern Africa there are 13 indigenous species, with two additions to this, if the feral populations of the introduced ROCK DOVE (town and city pigeons), and a handful of unusual sightings of the EUROPEAN TURTLE-DOVE from the region are included.

The characteristic profile of a pigeon or dove is of a gray-, buff-, or brown-colored bird that feeds on seeds on the ground and otherwise sits in a tree where it makes cooing sounds. This fits many of the species, but not all members of the family are *granivorous*, and there is a distinctive group which, instead of feeding off seed on the ground, eats fruit that is sought in the canopies of trees. These fruit-eaters tend to be forest-dwellers; they are often more gaudily-colored than typical doves, they do not descend to the ground, and in many instances their calls—whistling and quacking noises—sound like anything but those made by pigeons and doves. The fruit-eating species are often gregarious, gathering in flocks where trees are in fruit, and they are subject to local movements in response to seasonal patterns of fruit availability. By contrast, many of the seed-eating species are sedentary, living in the same places throughout the year. None of the southern African pigeons and doves are migratory, although one species, the NAMAQUA DOVE (Plate 40), which lives in semi-arid regions, is nomadic over much of its range. It is also the only member of the family in this region in which the sexes are dissimilar; males have a black face and throat and a yellow bill, whereas females have uniformly pale gray heads and dull flesh-colored bills.

Natural History

Ecology and Behavior

Two of southern Africa's doves, the CAPE TURTLE-DOVE and LAUGHING DOVE (both Plate 40), rank among the commonest and most widespread of all birds in the region. They live in all the towns and cities and are found almost as widely in all rural regions, avoiding only areas of continuous evergreen forest or desert. Both are seed-eaters and they have benefited enormously from the changes that agriculture has made to the landscape, which has provided both an abundant food source (in the form of spilled grain and the seeds produced by weeds) and trees, mostly planted around farm homesteads, that offer nesting and roosting sites. Seed-eating doves need to drink water, and in arid regions, the gathering of doves around water sources is a striking feature, matching the gatherings of sandgrouse in some places. Pigeons and doves have weak bills and whatever they eat is swallowed whole, with the *gizzard*, a muscular portion of the stomach, breaking the seed or fruit into more digestible fragments. These birds often swallow small pebbles that assist the gizzard in performing this grinding action.

Although most pigeons and doves rely on trees (or shrubs in arid areas) to provide shelter in the form of nesting and roosting sites, one local species, the SPECKLED PIGEON (alternatively named Rock Pigeon; Plate 40), roosts and nests on cliffs, making daily foraging trips from such places into areas where it can find seed. It has adapted its cliff-dependence in South Africa to using buildings for this purpose and in this country (but curiously not in the adjacent country of Zimbabwe) it has become a common town and city bird; flights of these pigeons from city centers to outlying farmlands are a daily sight.

Breeding

Pigeons and doves are monogamous breeders. Elsewhere in the world there are a few that nest colonially, but in southern Africa all the species are solitary breeders. Parental care, from building the nest to incubating the eggs and tending the young, is shared by the sexes. All species build a rather similar nest that varies only in size and construction materials: it is a flimsy, saucer-shaped platform, often see-through, and it is usually made of dry twigs and placed on a tree branch. Some species nest high up in forest canopies, others close to the ground. Eggs are plain white and, in most cases, number 1, 2, or 3 in a clutch. Incubation periods vary between 11 and 28 days (mostly about 14 or 15 days in the southern African species) and nestling periods are similarly variable. Nestlings are fed with a milk (often called *pigeon milk*) produced in the pigeon's *crop* (esophagus), which they receive from the parent by inserting their bills into its open bill. As the nestlings become older, this regurgitated liquid increases in its seed and solid food content. A feature of pigeon and dove breeding is that relatively few of the species in the region adhere to well-defined breeding seasons, and in some cases, pairs continue laying successive clutches of eggs throughout the year.

Notes

The continued ecological success of doves and pigeons as a family is surprising and not well understood, given that they are largely defenseless creatures and highly edible, featuring prominently in the diets of many predators, human beings included. One explanation offered is that because of the low "investment" they make in nesting (simple nest, small clutch, unpigmented eggs, seed diet), they are better able than other, more specialized bird species to re-lay after nesting failures and to breed more than once in a year. However, not all the world's pigeons and doves have fared well. North America's PASSENGER PIGEON, which became extinct in the early 1900s, was once a widespread and prolific bird on that continent. Its demise is thought to be the result of over-exploitation (over-hunting). The famous DODO that once lived on the island of Mauritius became extinct in the 17th century, also the result of being hunted, both by passing seafarers and by animals introduced to the island by people. The Dodo, weighing about 20 kg (44 lb), was vastly bigger than any of today's pigeons (the largest of which weighs about 2 kg, 4 lb) and it was flightless. Otherwise, though, it shared many of the physical attributes found in the species that have survived to the present time.

Pigeons have long been known for their homing ability and this trait no doubt contributed to their domestication—to their use as carriers of messages in the past, as well as for racing, an activity which continues today to be a popular hobby. The mechanics of their ability to return home have been the subject of considerable research and experimentation, and findings indicate that pigeons use the sun as their primary means of orientation. In its absence (that is, when hidden by cloud cover) they find their way by responding to the Earth's magnetic field. Pigeons apparently have fine magnetic material spread uniformly throughout the skull and in the neck muscles, and the responses of these to the Earth's magnetic fields serve to trigger reflexes in the flying bird.

Status

None of southern Africa's pigeons and doves are under threat, although one, the EASTERN BRONZE-NAPED (or Delegeorgue's) PIGEON, a fruit-eating, forest-dwelling species with a restricted range, is ranked in South Africa as "near-threatened."

Profiles

Speckled Pigeon, *Columba guinea*, Plate 40a
Red-eyed Dove, *Streptopelia semitorquata*, Plate 40b

Cape Turtle-Dove, *Streptopelia capicola*, Plate 40c
Laughing Dove, *Streptopelia senegalensis*, Plate 40d
Namaqua Dove, *Oena capensis*, Plate 40e
Emerald-spotted Wood Dove, *Turtur chalcospilos*, Plate 40f

11. Parrots, Turacos (Louries), and Cuckoos

Parrots, turacos (*louries*), and *cuckoos* are three bird families, each quite distinctive, that are brought together here because they are (distantly) related. Parrots (family Psittacidae, the "P" being silent) are by far the largest and most diverse family, with well over 300 species worldwide, and they are the best known, given their centuries-old association with people as their pets. Louries, on the other hand, are an exclusively African bird family that numbers about 23 species, and these birds are parrot-like only to the extent that many of them live in forest canopies. Cuckoos are better known, mostly as a result of the human connotations (e.g., "cuckolded") attached to the behavior of some species in "parasitizing" other birds in the form of having them rear their young. They are a diverse family (Cuculidae) and number about 140 species in the world, of which about 50, belonging to the subfamily known as the "Old World Cuckoos," are parasitic. Old World Cuckoos are well represented in southern Africa, and a visitor to the region in spring cannot fail to hear the calls of one or more of them heralding the arrival of the breeding season. In Europe, spring is also announced by a parasitic cuckoo; in this instance it is the Common Cuckoo, with its familiar cuckoo-clock "cu, koo" call that is spring's ambassador. *Coucals* are another subfamily of the cuckoos, and 5 species of these occur in southern Africa. Their most notable feature is the deep, bubbling call they utter, a sound that suddenly becomes commonplace at the start of the rainy season, and is the reason for their nickname "rainbirds."

Parrots are a diverse group, and *macaws, parakeets, lovebirds, conures,* and *amazons* reflect just some of this variety. Although they differ considerably in size and shape, parrots are characterized by particular foot and bill structures; they are also short-legged and have large heads and short, thick necks. Their feet have two forward-facing and two backward-facing toes and their bills are short but strong, broadest at the base with the top mandible curving sharply downwards over the smaller lower mandible, an arrangement that provides the bird with both a powerful cutting tool and a versatile instrument—used, for instance, as a third leg when clambering through branches. In contrast to the Neotropics (Central and South America) and Australia, Africa has little parrot variety. There are only 18 species on the continent, none vividly colored, and 8 of these extend into southern Africa. This is not the case with the turacos, which are confined to Africa, and many are brightly colored. The name is derived from pigments (turacin and turacoverdin) that are unique to turacos and impart the rich green body plumage and brilliant red wings found in many of the forest-living species. These are copper-based pigments, and it is thought that the copper comes from particular fruits in their diet. Other turaco features are a long tail and long crest, and many have bare, brightly colored skin surrounding their eyes. Some of the species live outside of forest, and these are dull-colored, gray birds. One of them, the GRAY LOURIE (Plate 41), is a very common bird of the bush with a loud, unmistakable cry—"g,way"—that gives rise to its alternative name of "Go-away-bird." Forest turacos make harsh barking calls, which are among the most familiar of all forest sounds. Parrots and turacos tend to be very sedentary, whereas the cuckoos in southern Africa visit the region as migrants, arriving in early summer and departing in autumn. Two of the commonest and most widespread, the RED-CHESTED CUCKOO (Plate 42), and DIEDERIK CUCKOO (Plate 42) are gray colored and glossy green respectively, and their monotonous calling lends much to the summer ambience.

Natural History

Ecology and Behavior

Parrots and turacos are *frugivorous*, that is, they live on fruit. They inhabit forested or well-wooded country, living in the canopies of trees and moving with great agility through the branches. When they remain silent, blending closely with the foliage, they are easily overlooked; however, neither parrots, with their shrill screeches, nor the forest louries with their hoarse barking calls, seem capable of remaining quiet for long, and it is this that gives them away. The forest turacos, such as the KNYSNA TURACO (Plate 41) and LIVINGSTONE'S TURACO (Plate 41), are reluctant fliers, preferring to hop and run from branch to branch, and when they do, their vivid crimson wings are suddenly revealed. The Gray Lourie much resembles a forest species in its food habits, but it provides a contrast by being one of the more conspicuous savannah birds, as it often perches on the very tops of trees. It is also much less reluctant to fly, and single birds and groups routinely commute, with a rather labored flight, between trees and bush clumps and from one area to another. Parrots have the ability to open up hard seedpods with their powerful bills, and they are often found foraging in the upper branches of an acacia or albizzia tree, working through the seedpods and discarding the unconsumed shells in a steady rain to the ground. Turacos lack such bills and tend to eat softer or smaller fruits in addition to foliage and buds. Cuckoos are *insectivorous,* and the southern African species have a predilection for eating caterpillars, the more noxious and hairy the better. During the courtship period, males present their prospective mates with food items, in most instances a large, hairy caterpillar.

Breeding

The nesting habits of southern Africa's parrots, turacos, and cuckoos have little in common. Monogamous turacos build, from twigs, a dove-like, flimsy platform, placed inside dense foliage; they lay 2 or 3 white, almost spherical eggs and share parental care. Parrots, too, are monogamous and share parental care. They lay their clutch of 2 to 4 white eggs in a cavity in a tree, although the ROSY-FACED LOVEBIRD (Plate 42) usually nests in a cavity in a rock face or uses a nest chamber inside the communal nest of a Sociable or Red-billed Buffalo Weaver. These lovebirds have the unusual habit (for a parrot) of lining the nest chamber, and an even less usual habit of carrying the nest material to the site, not in their bills as most birds do, but tucked into their rump feathers. The parasitic habits of the cuckoos are both complex and intriguing. Some species are monogamous whereas others are polygamous; some parasitize a single host species whereas others lay their eggs in the nests of a range of host species. Some species remove a host egg when they lay in the nest; others don't. In some species the nestlings of both host and parasite are raised together, whereas in others, such as the Red-chested Cuckoo, the cuckoo chick has evolved the behavior, as soon as it hatches, of pushing its siblings or the remaining eggs out of the nest. Those cuckoos that specialize in parasitizing just one or two host species have evolved eggs that closely match the color and markings of those of their hosts; their hosts, in turn, have developed a keen ability to distinguish any eggs in the nest not laid by themselves, and to evict these. In the case of the Diederik Cuckoo, there are strains of females (termed "gentes") that lay eggs of a specific type (appearance), and these females seek out nests of hosts whose eggs are a match for their particular strain. Red Bishops, for example, lay plain blue eggs and they are commonly parasitized by the Diederik Cuckoo strain that lays plain blue eggs; similarly, another Diederik Cuckoo strain, laying mottled brown eggs, parasitizes sparrows that lay mottled brown eggs, and so on.

Notes

The name "parrot" is derived from the French word "pierrot," or "talking companion." The ability of captive parrots, particularly the AFRICAN GRAY PARROT, to mimic the human voice is unmatched by any other group of birds; some captive parrots develop strong bonds with their human custodians and are responsive to certain words and gestures. Because of their popularity as pets and as collectable items, trade in parrots has grown into a large, profitable industry, and tens of thousands of birds flow annually, both legally and illegally, from Third World to First World countries despite all attempts to legislate or control the flow. A number of species have been brought close to extinction because of this.

Status

The CAPE PARROT is endemic to South Africa, where it is restricted to scattered blocks of higher-elevation forest; its preferred habitat has diminished or been altered, its numbers are steadily declining, and as a result it is listed as endangered in that country.

Profiles

Knysna Turaco, *Tauraco corythaix*, Plate 41a
Livingstone's Turaco, *Tauraco livingstonii*, Plate 41b
Purple-crested Turaco, *Tauraco porphyreolophus*, Plate 41c
Gray Lourie, *Corythaixoides concolor*, Plate 41d
Red-chested Cuckoo, *Cuculus solitarius*, Plate 42a
Rosy-faced Lovebird, *Agapornis roseicollis*, Plate 42b
Diederik Cuckoo, *Chrysococcyx caprius*, Plate 42c
Burchell's Coucal, *Centropus burchellii*, Plate 42d

12. Owls and Nightjars

Owls and *nightjars* are nocturnal, and because of this they are much overlooked by people and usually only encountered by chance. Yet they are common and widespread, and if one is aware of what to look for, and more especially, what to listen for, these birds can be found almost anywhere, from within the boundaries of towns and cities to the remotest rural areas. Owls and nightjars are more closely related to each other than to any other birds but, beyond their nocturnal habits, large eyes, and soft, cryptically marked plumage, they do not have much in common. All owls, from the largest *eagle owl* to the tiniest *pygmy owl*, are keen predators that hunt prey much as diurnal raptors do, armed for this purpose with powerful feet, sharp claws, and hooked bills. While they may function as the nocturnal equivalents of day-active birds of prey, owls and hawks are not closely related. The adaptations that make owls successful in hunting at night include their very large eyes (in proportion to their bodies), so their night-vision is superior to that of any day-living bird; secondly, they have acute hearing ability. This is enhanced by the owl's unique "facial disc"—a rim of stiff feathers that encircles the eyes and serves to amplify and reflect incoming sounds directly to the ear entrances, which lie right behind each eye. Thirdly, they have soft plumage and their flight feathers are edged with down, so flight, in all but a few species, is almost soundless. Owls are among the least colorful of birds, and their plumages, with few exceptions, are dominated by grays and browns that provide them with camouflage during the daylight hours when they rest in a concealed place; if they were conspicuous then, they'd be harassed and mobbed incessantly by small birds. There are about 200 owl species in the world and they range from the size of a shrike, weighing 40 g (1.4 oz), to the size of a large eagle, weighing 4 kg (9 lb). One of the world's most widely distributed birds is an owl (the BARN OWL, Plate 43), and its eerie screech is a familiar sound around many a southern African farmstead; it is one of the 12 owls found in the region.

Nightjars (family Caprimulgidae) are uniformly small birds, long-winged but with very short legs and weakly developed feet. They bed down low on the ground for much their time, their large eyes closed to narrow slits so as to avoid revealing their presence from eye-glint, and they choose a site where their plumage most effectively blends with the surroundings. Some species, for instance, select a thick bed of leaf litter for this, others lie up among fire-blackened debris, and others use lichen-covered rocks. At dusk and dawn, and on moonlit nights, they leave these hideaways and spend a few hours hawking insects in the air. This is when one usually sees the birds, flitting like ghosts between the trees and across open ground. To find one resting during the day is sheer chance. There are about 90 nightjar species found worldwide, 7 of which occur in southern Africa. All the species have cryptic buff, gray, brown, and chestnut plumage and they are not easily distinguished, except by their calls. Like owls, they are often very vocal at night, and during certain times of the year they call endlessly from dusk to dawn. One of southern Africa's commonest species, the FIERY-NECKED NIGHTJAR (Plate 43), is often referred to as the "litany bird," and its melodious, whistled "Good Lord, deliver us" is one of the region's characteristic night sounds.

Natural History

Ecology and Behavior

The feeding habits of owls are often better known than any other aspect of their biology as a consequence of their unusual habit of regularly leaving pellets containing the indigestible parts of their most recent meal. These pellets, which are usually produced once a day and regurgitated from the bird's crop, often accumulate below a regular sleeping site, and if collected systematically and analysed, they reveal exactly what prey is being taken by the particular owl involved. Many of the smaller species, such as the AFRICAN SCOPS-OWL (Plate 43), are insectivorous and hunt moths and other nocturnal insects, whereas larger species usually hunt larger prey. The Barn Owl is a specialist rodent catcher, and it uses its acute hearing, rather than its eyes, to locate prey. It is thus able to hunt even on the darkest of nights, by detecting small rodents from the rustling sounds they make in the grass, swooping onto its victims, and snatching them up in its sharp claws. The tiny PEARL-SPOTTED OWLET (Plate 43) is partly diurnal, and small birds make up a significant proportion of its diet. It has an unusual plumage feature, shared by many of the other species of pygmy owls (the group of which it is a member): it has a pair of "false eyes"—large black spots—on the back of its head so that at a glance you can never be sure whether it is facing toward you or away. The function of these "false eyes" is, apparently, to put off a would-be predator approaching from behind, duping it into believing that its approach is being watched.

Nightjars are insectivorous and they hunt aerial insects, from mosquitoes to moths and beetles, snatching these from the air in their bills. Some species make sallies into the air from the ground, whereas others hawk on the wing, hence their alternative name of "nighthawk" (the name "nightjar" refers to the jarring calls made by many species). Although their bills are tiny, nightjars have an enormous gape that, when opened, reveals a cavernous mouth, and prey items are simply gulped in and swallowed whole while the bird is in flight. Nightjars are one of the few groups of birds that have reflective eyes, much like those of a cat. Because of this, and because they often sit on the verges of rural roads at night, nightjars can often be detected from their glowing red eyes reflecting in the headlights of a car.

Breeding

Neither owls nor nightjars construct nests of their own. Nightjars lay their eggs, usually only 1 or 2 per clutch, on the ground, where they select the same kinds of places that they use to rest/sleep during the day. In most nightjars, incubation and nestling care is shared by the sexes, and the eggs and young are rarely left unattended. In owls, the number of eggs per clutch is much more variable, and while many species lay only 2 or 3 per clutch, some lay much larger numbers of eggs, with as many as 18 per clutch being recorded in the Barn Owl. Owls select a variety of sites for nesting purposes; some are specific in their selection, for example, always laying in a hole in a tree, or using an old nest platform built by some other bird, or nesting in thick grass. Others are less selective and may lay on the ground, in tree-cavities, among rocks, and so on. As its name suggests, the Barn Owl has a long association with nesting in farm outbuildings, but it also commonly occupies the huge nests built by Hamerkops. Although most owls are monogamous, it is a general rule that females undertake all the incubation while males hunt and provide their mates with prey.

Notes

Owls, with their wide heads and front-facing eyes, have rather human-like faces and this, linked with their nocturnal habits and often eerie calls, have spawned a wealth of myths, legends, and contradictory beliefs about these birds that probably date back to the beginning of humans. On the one hand, they are held up as symbols of wisdom, on the other, as messengers of death or linked to witchcraft and magic; even the scientific name for one of the very common owl genera, *Strix*, is the Greek word for witch. The belief that owls are harbingers of death is commonplace in African tribal cultures, and when such people encounter owls or their young, the birds are often stoned to death.

Status

Many owl species are widespread and abundant, but two southern African species, the GRASS OWL and PEL'S FISHING OWL, have small, fragmented populations in South Africa, where they are currently ranked as vulnerable.

Profiles

African Scops-Owl, *Otus senegalensis*, Plate 43a
Barn Owl, *Tyto alba*, Plate 43b
Pearl-spotted Owlet, *Glaucidium perlatum*, Plate 43c

Spotted Eagle-Owl, *Bubo africanus*, Plate 43d
Fiery-necked Nightjar, *Caprimulgus pectoralis*, Plate 43e

13. Swifts and Swallows

Swifts and *swallows*, although not closely related, are remarkably similar in appearance and habit. Both have a slender, streamlined build and wings that are long and pointed; both also hunt small, airborne insects (often referred to as "aerial plankton") in flight, often mingling together in mixed flocks in places where such food concentrations are found. The two families, swallows (family Hirundinidae) and swifts (family Apodidae), each number about 80 species, and both are well represented in southern Africa, with no less that 21 swallow species and 13 swifts found here. The majority of these species, however, are summer visitors to the region and when cold weather sets in during winter, diminishing the availability of insects, they head north, some to Europe and others to warmer parts of Africa.

Most of the southern African swallows have glossy blue upperparts whereas their underparts are variable, both in coloration and markings; identification of the different species is usually based on this underpart coloration, whether or not it is streaked, and whether or not the species has a dark collar below its throat. One group of swallows, known as *martins*, are mainly brown-plumaged birds, and another, the *sawwing swallows*, are completely black. Swallows fly with alternate bouts of flapping and gliding, nimbly twisting and turning in pursuit of prey. Between foraging spells they rest, perching on twigs, fences, or telephone lines. Sometimes thousands of BARN SWALLOWS (Plate 53) gather in this way, perched like countless clothespins on a wash-line, the wires of roadside telephone lines often sagging under their weight. This perching habit is one of the major differences between swallows and swifts: the latter never perch on lines or twigs, and in many species, it is probable that they remain continuously on the wing—day and night—until they return to their nesting sites for the next breeding season. Swifts have tiny feet with strong claws, and when alighting, they settle against a vertical surface onto which they cling; if stranded on flat ground, swifts are often incapable of becoming airborne.

The secret to swifts being able to live on the wing without resting lies with their aerodynamic design. They have the lowest energetic cost of flying of any bird measured, and most of their time on the wing is spent gliding (an energy-free activity) rather than flapping; when they flap, they do it briefly and their wingbeats are shallow. Swifts have very narrow wings, being almost the same width at their base as near their tips, and it is this sickle-shaped wing silhouette—compared with the swallow's broad-based, sharp-tipped wings—that distinguishes the swifts from the swallows in a flying mixed flock. The southern African swift species are mostly dark-colored birds, black or dark brown, some having white rumps, others white throats or bellies. In both families the sexes are alike, although male swallows have more elongated outer tail feathers than females.

Natural History

Ecology and Behavior

Swifts and swallows represent the pinnacle of flying prowess, spending much of their time on the wing, circling back and forth low over water or grassland or flying in erratic patterns overhead in their pursuit of aerial insects. Swifts derive their family name Apodidae ("without feet") from the perception long ago that they were incapable of landing—they even perform such delicate operations as copulating, as well as collecting nesting material, while on the wing. They are aptly named, as several swift species have been timed flying at speeds of 100 to 150 kph (60 to 90 mph). Swallows are not capable of such feats; their flight is altogether gentler, and it involves less high-speed gliding and more flapping. While breeding, pairs of swallows do not range far from their nests, and much of their foraging then is done solitarily, unless other swallows are in the vicinity, in which case, of course, they will mingle. The ranges of many species of swallows have been greatly increased as a result of countless manmade structures, especially road bridges, becoming ever more available and providing them with ideal nest sites in areas where these were previously absent or in short supply. Following in their wake are those swift species, especially the WHITE-RUMPED SWIFT (Plate 44), that habitually appropriate swallow nests for their own use.

Breeding

Both swifts and swallows are monogamous breeders, and in both families parental care is shared by the sexes. Both colonial-nesting species and solitary-nesting species are represented in the two families. The endemic SOUTH AFRICAN CLIFF SWALLOW (Plate 53), for instance, always nests in large numbers and in tightly packed colonies, as does the LITTLE SWIFT (Plate 44), whereas the WHITE-THROATED SWALLOW (Plate 53) and White-rumped Swift (Plate 44) are two species that invariably nest solitarily. The majority of swallow species build nests from wet mud, collecting this material, one pellet at a time, from the edges of ponds and rain puddles. Usually both parents build, and a nest may take 2 or 3 weeks to complete; once the mud dries, the nests have a strong, durable structure that may last for years and they may be re-used for successive broods in successive years. Different species have distinctively different architectures, some constructing a simple half-cup attached to a vertical surface, whereas other species build an enclosed bowl, and some species add a long entrance tunnel. Although bridges and buildings have provided an abundance of nesting sites for many swallow species, there are several species that have not taken advantage of these and continue to nest only in the sites they have used historically. southern Africa's endangered BLUE SWALLOW is an example of a species still much dependent on the excavations of Aardvarks to provide it with subterranean cavities in which it likes to build its mud nest. Martins and sawwing swallows differ from typical swallows in their nesting habits by digging a tunnel in an earth bank and laying their eggs at the end of this.

The nests of swifts are quite different from those of swallows. Their main distinction is that they use saliva to glue their nests together, which dries to produce a strong, rigid structure. The nests are typically attached to a vertical wall (especially a rock face), usually concealed in a crack and shaped like a bracket with a shallow open cup on top. Material for the nest, mostly feathers and pieces of dry grass, is collected in flight. Some species differ in their nest architecture; the Little Swift, for instance, builds an enclosed bowl with a narrow entrance hole on one side. Another species uses a tunnel in an earth bank, usually one dug by a martin or bee-eater, and the White-rumped Swift routinely takes over tunneled swallow nests. The AFRICAN PALM-SWIFT'S (Plate 44) nest is unusual in being secured to the underside of a palm tree leaf; these birds glue their eggs to the nest with saliva to secure them to this rather precarious site. Swifts lay plain white eggs and they are characteristically long and thin, presumably so that while still being carried inside the female they do not compromise the bird's aerodynamic ability. Swallow's eggs are a typical egg-shape (ovate), and in many species, they are colorfully speckled. In southern Africa, swifts and swallows lay small clutches, usually only 2 or 3 eggs per clutch. Swallows have more rapid nestling cycles than swifts, with incubation and nestling periods averaging about 16 days and 23 days respectively, whereas in swifts, these average about 24 days and 40 days respectively. As a result, swallows commonly raise two or more broods in a summer, whereas swifts tend to be single-brooded.

Notes

The famous "bird's nest soup," a Chinese delicacy with a centuries-old tradition, uses the saliva nests built by a swift, the Edible-nest Swiftlet, that occurs widely in Asia. This species breeds in caves in enormous colonies, and the nests are collected on a vast scale, supporting an industry valued at billions of dollars. For example, in a single year, 1989, an estimated 25 million nests were reportedly consumed in Hong Kong alone, at prices around US$3 to $12 per nest. There is much international concern at the uncontrolled and unsustainable way this resource is being harvested.

Status

No species of swifts are under threat in southern Africa. One of the region's swallows, however, is ranked as endangered in South Africa and as "vulnerable" elsewhere in its African range. This species, the Blue Swallow, is closely tied to a habitat type, mist-belt grassland, that has almost disappeared as a result of commercial deforestation, and the South African population is now restricted to a few small, scattered sites where fragments of its original habitat survive.

Profiles

African Black Swift, *Apus barbatus*, Plate 44a
Little Swift, *Apus affinis*, Plate 44b
Alpine Swift, *Apus melba*, Plate 44c
African Palm-Swift, *Cypsiurus parvus*, Plate 44d
White-rumped Swift, *Apus caffer*, Plate 44e
Barn Swallow, *Hirundo rustica*, Plate 53a
White-throated Swallow, *Hirundo albigularis*, Plate 53b
Wire-tailed Swallow, *Hirundo smithii*, Plate 53c
South African Cliff Swallow, *Hirundo spilodera*, Plate 53d
Greater Striped Swallow, *Hirundo cucullata*, Plate 54a
Lesser Striped Swallow, *Hirundo abyssinica*, Plate 54b
Rock Martin, *Hirundo fuligula*, Plate 54c
Brown-throated Martin, *Riparia paludicola*, Plate 54d

14. Mousebirds and Trogons

The *mousebirds*, sometimes referred to as *colies*, are a uniquely African group of birds; in fact they comprise the only order (Coliiformes) of birds that is endemic to the continent. The order consists of the single family Coliidae, of which there are six species, all remarkably alike in shape and appearance. They are small birds, although their small size is offset by their long, stiff-feathered tails. They have short, rounded wings, their bills are short and somewhat parrot-like, and their heads have a pronounced crest. All the species have sleek but dull-colored plumage that is either gray, brown, or buff according to species. Several have bare skin forming a mask around the eyes, and in two species (including the RED-FACED MOUSEBIRD, Plate 45) this is colored red, whereas in the others it is black or gray. All the species have red or reddish legs and feet. Their feet are unusually structured, with all four toes facing forwards and none backwards, so instead of perching like other birds, mousebirds usually hang from branches. The sexes are alike. Mousebirds derive their name partly from their mouse-like appearance (dull colors and long tails) and partly from their behavior of scuttling through the branches of trees, of living in groups, and of commonly huddling together.

Three species of mousebirds are found in southern Africa and they are common and conspicuous birds, with one or more species likely to be found wherever you happen to be. They live in wooded or bushy country, one (WHITE-BACKED MOUSEBIRD, Plate 45) being found mainly in the semi-arid western regions, another (SPECKLED MOUSEBIRD, Plate 45) in the less arid southern and eastern districts, and the third, the Red-faced Mousebird, found everywhere. Wherever encountered, mousebirds are likely to be found in groups, often numbering between 5 and 8 birds, but when certain fruiting trees are bearing prolifically, dozens and perhaps as many as a hundred birds may gather to feed on the harvest. Groups move about locally as food availability changes, but they do not undertake any extensive migrations.

Trogons, *broadbills*, and *pittas* are three bird families that are best represented in the tropics, but a single species of each occurs in southern Africa. The NARINA TROGON (Plate 45; the only member of these groups detailed here) is the most striking of these, a vividly colored bird that lives in the canopies of evergreen forests and gives away its presence with its hoarse hooting call. It lives on large arboreal insects that it catches in the foliage of trees.

Natural History

Ecology and Behavior

Mousebirds are mainly arboreal birds and they live exclusively on plant material, eating both fruits and the foliage, buds, flowers, and stems of plants. Their vegetarian diets have not endeared them to gardeners, as a flock of mousebirds is capable of inflicting extensive damage to crops of soft fruits such as figs, grapes, peaches, and plums. Vegetable farmers do not like mousebirds either, as these birds find ground crops such as lettuces and tomatoes utterly irresistible. For those not affected, however, mousebirds are charming birds and a source of much pleasure to watch. They commonly come to food trays where fruit is made available and pack tightly against each other without any visible aggression, as each wolfs down the food on offer. Mousebirds are very agile in trees and may even dangle from one foot while trying to reach a fruit at the end of a stem. They are also highly sociable, seemingly lacking any desire for individual space; they often groom each other, and at night they sleep together in a tight huddle. On cold, wintery days mousebirds often clamber up into the topmost branches of trees and settle themselves in positions where they can bask in the sun, mostly hanging from twigs with legs spread wide, feet up at shoulder level, underparts exposed to catch the warmth; one can almost read the contentment in their faces as they languidly soak up the early morning sun. This behavior, together with their habit of sleeping at night in a huddle, suggests (although it has not been proved) that mousebirds have more difficulty than other birds in maintaining body temperature. Their plumage is less waterproof than that of most birds, and mousebirds easily become drenched in heavy rains, which, if accompanied by cold weather, can lead to significant mortality.

Breeding

The sociable habits of mousebirds persist throughout the year, although while breeding, pairs tend to split off from the flock and raise their broods without the group's involvement. However, two or more pairs may build nests near each other, and there are cases of more than one female laying in a nest, and of more than two parents attending a brood of young. Monogamy is thus probably the usual, but not invariable, matrimonial arrangement. Mousebird nests are invariably placed in a shrub or tree, usually well hidden among thick foliage. The nest in each species is a simple open cup made of grass, twigs, or weed stems. Clutches number 2 to 4 eggs; when more than this are found in a nest, laying by more than one female is indicated. Both sexes build the nest and share parental care. Eggs take about 13 days to hatch, and nestlings take about 17 to 20 days to fly; they can, however, clamber about in the branches well before this.

Status

Mousebirds are common and widespread birds and none are threatened anywhere in their range.

Profiles

Red-faced Mousebird, *Urocolius indicus*, Plate 45a
White-backed Mousebird, *Colius colius*, Plate 45b
Narina Trogon, *Apaloderma narina*, Plate 45c
Speckled Mousebird, *Colius striatus*, Plate 45d

15. Kingfishers, Bee-eaters, and Rollers

Although the species that comprise each of the families brought together here are distinctly different, they clearly have much in common: they are brightly colored (and in some cases brilliantly colored); the sexes are alike; they have a particularly upright perching stance; and they have thickset heads, short necks, strong bills, and short legs. The *kingfishers, bee-eaters,* and *rollers* are related, albeit distantly, and together they make up the majority of species in the order Coraciiformes, although each belongs to a family of its own. Kingfishers (family Alcedinidae) are the most diverse and widely distributed group, with 86 species found around the world. They range considerably in size, from tiny to large, but are always recognizable by their long, dagger-like bills. In addition, most species have at least some blue in their plumage and all the African species have short tails. Their name is something of a misnomer as the majority of the world's kingfishers do not fish, but instead hunt over dry land, subsisting on insects and other terrestrial prey; in southern Africa, for instance, only 4 of the 10 kingfisher species found in the region take fish. Bee-eaters (family Meropidae) are also easily recognized, as they are always colorful and have long, down-curved bills. In their case the name is apt, for they prey extensively on bees and have evolved a particular technique with which to deal with the stings and venoms of these. The African continent is home to two-thirds of the world's 26 bee-eater species, and 9 of these occur in southern Africa.

Lastly, there are the colorful rollers (family Coraciidae). These are medium-sized, chunky-looking birds with a robust, slightly hooked bill. They are not as diverse a family as the kingfishers and bee-eaters, but they are particularly well-represented in southern Africa, with 5 of the world's 12 species found here. Rollers earn their name from the rolling display flight that most of the species make. In the case of the LILAC-BREASTED ROLLER (Plate 47), the courting bird flies high into the air, then swoops downwards, accelerating with wing-flaps; it then levels out and rocks wildly and seemingly uncontrolled, from one side to the other, before climbing again and repeating the performance. This acrobatic display is accompanied by a cacophony of harsh screams. In other respects rollers are very sedate and solitary birds that spend most of their time sitting quietly for long periods on a perch that enables them to watch their surroundings for prey. They are masters of the "sit-and-wait" hunting technique and their dependence on suitable perches spaced at suitable intervals means they are confined to wooded country. Several species are familiar roadside birds that commonly hunt from telephone wires.

Natural History

Ecology and Behavior

Kingfishers, bee-eaters, and rollers are all essentially "sit-and-wait" hunters. With few exceptions kingfishers and rollers hunt solitarily and rather lethargically, moving at intervals from one perch to another if no prey materializes. In the case of the terrestrial kingfishers (for example, the BROWN-HOODED KINGFISHER, Plate 46) and rollers, insects of all kinds are taken (especially grasshoppers and beetles), as are lizards and other small reptiles, spiders, and scorpions. When such items are sighted, the bird gently swoops onto it, takes it in the bill and returns to a perch where it proceeds to dispatch the victim, beating it vigorously against the perch before swallowing it whole. The aquatic kingfishers mostly do the same thing, only differing in that their target is fish. Most of these species hunt along the edges of rivers, ponds, and lakes, using overhanging branches or reed stems as perches. Although many live together in pairs, their hunting is usually done solitarily. They are also territorial, and a pair of large kingfishers (such as the GIANT KINGFISHER, Plate 46) require the exclusive use of several kilometers of riverfront to sustain themselves. PIED KINGFISHERS (Plate 46) are unusual fish-hunters: they have evolved the technique of hovering over the water and searching for fish while on the wing. Although this requires far more energy than is used in perch-hunting, it permits these birds to fish in places that are out of range for any perch-hunter, and the benefits of this presumably outweigh the high energy cost involved.

Bee-eaters are altogether much more active than kingfishers and rollers in the way they go about securing prey, and they are always a delight to watch. Firstly, all their prey is caught on the wing, which often involves a lively aerial pursuit. Secondly, many bee-eater species wheel and circle about in the air rather like swallows, hunting in this way and showing much agility when chasing prey. Thirdly, even when bee-eaters hunt using the "sit-and-wait" technique, they are always active, alertly watching their surroundings, twisting their head this way or that, cocking an eye skyward, leaning forward in anticipation of a chase, and seldom staying still for more than a moment. And lastly, bee-eaters are gregarious, and their sociability is accompanied by frequent calling between birds, these vocalizations being infinitely more melodious and pleasing to the ear than the harsh sounds made by rollers and kingfishers. Bee-eaters make no attempt to pick up insects on the ground, but the moment such animals become airborne, they become potential victims. Bees and wasps are commonly taken and bee-eaters handle these carefully, usually rubbing the insect's hind parts against a branch to discharge its venom and body fluids before swallowing it. Some species, such as the EUROPEAN BEE-EATER (Plate 47), specialize in hunting bees, whereas others hunt dragonflies or some other particular aerial insect. Flocks of the stunning-looking SOUTHERN CARMINE BEE-EATER (Plate 47) often gather at bush fires to feast on the insects driven up by the flames, and they have also cultivated the habit of using mammals, or even large birds such as Ostriches and Kori Bustards, as "beaters," even riding on their backs while waiting for prey to be driven up. Because insect availability changes dramatically through the year, many bee-eater species are migratory, and about half of those found regularly in southern Africa leave the subcontinent in winter.

Breeding

The Coraciiformes are, without exception, hole-nesters. Bee-eaters and some kingfisher species excavate tunnels in the ground in which they nest, whereas certain other kingfishers, together with the rollers, nest in tree cavities. Many bee-eaters breed colonially, and Southern Carmine Bee-eaters, which nest in the northern parts of Botswana and Zimbabwe, often breed in huge colonies that may number thousands of birds. They dig their nest tunnels in high riverbanks that gradually become honeycombed after many successive years of use. Banks, however, eventually succumb to the forces of erosion and slide into the rivers that created them, causing the birds to seek another site further upstream or downstream. Studies done on the colonial-nesting WHITE-FRONTED BEE-EATER (Plate 47) have revealed that they live in a complex society in which different clans share a breeding site but each controls its own exclusive feeding territory in the surrounding bush. Solitary breeders such as the LITTLE BEE-EATER (Plate 47) very commonly excavate their nest tunnels in the roofs of Aardvark holes. The nest tunnels of bee-eaters and kingfishers can become foul-smelling, messy homes as the nestlings grow and discharge their feces against the nest chamber's walls. Some kingfisher nests even end up having mucky liquid oozing from the entrance, which necessitates the parent birds having to take a bath after every nest visit! The species that breed in tree cavities do not face this sanitation problem—the young soon learn to squirt their feces out of the entrance hole. All Coraciiformes lay unmarked white eggs, and clutch sizes range between about 3 and 7. The incubation periods range between 15 days in the smallest species to 27 days in the largest. The fledgling periods are similarly variable, from 18 to 37 days. All but a few kingfishers, bee-eaters, and rollers are monogamous and parental care is shared by the sexes.

Notes

Kingfishers are the subject of a particularly rich mythology as a result of their conspicuousness and their association with water. In parts of the world they are associated with the biblical Great Flood, and in this instance the kingfisher's orange-colored underparts are reputed to have come about as a result of the bird being burnt while it was stealing fire from the gods to bring to other survivors of the flood. Many of the terrestrial kingfishers have the scientific name Halcyon, and this has its origins in Greek mythology. Halcyon (sometimes spelled Alcyone), the wife of a sailor, had power over the wind and waves. The god Zeus, jealous of this power, killed her husband by destroying his ship with lightning. In her grief, Halcyon threw herself into the sea to join her dead husband and both of them turned into kingfishers ("halcyon birds"). Halcyon's power was transferred to these birds and this enabled them to calm the sea and bring out a blue sky during the period when they nested. "Halcyon days" refers to this calm time when the kingfishers nest.

Status

Kingfishers, bee-eaters, and rollers tend to be common, wide-ranging birds, but there is one species in South Africa, the MANGROVE KINGFISHER, that has a severely restricted breeding range and is listed as vulnerable in that country.

Profiles

Pied Kingfisher, *Ceryle rudis*, Plate 46a
Giant Kingfisher, *Ceryle maxima*, Plate 46b
Malachite Kingfisher, *Alcedo cristata*, Plate 46c
Brown-hooded Kingfisher, *Halcyon albiventris*, Plate 46d
Woodland Kingfisher, *Halcyon senegalensis*, Plate 46e
European Bee-eater, *Merops apiaster*, Plate 47a
Southern Carmine Bee-eater, *Merops nubicoides*, Plate 47b
Little Bee-eater, *Merops pusillus*, Plate 47c
Swallow-tailed Bee-eater, *Merops hirundineus*, Plate 47d
White-fronted Bee-eater, *Merops bullockoides*, Plate 47e
Lilac-breasted Roller, *Coracias caudata*, Plate 47f

16. Hornbills and Hoopoes

Hornbills are medium- to large-sized birds that are best known for two things: they have enormous bills that, in some species, are capped by an even larger casque, and they have the unique habit, while nesting, of sealing the female into the nest hole for the duration of the incubation. Hornbills are a family (Bucerotidae) of about 60 species equally distributed in Asia and Africa, but absent from elsewhere in the world. Their ecological equivalents in Central and South America are the colorful toucans, a family of equally large-billed birds, and first-time visitors to Africa often think they're seeing a toucan when they spot their first hornbill. Hornbills, though, are not very colorful birds and most species are mainly black, gray, or brown with patches of white somewhere in the plumage. With the exception of the unusual SOUTHERN GROUND-HORNBILL (Plate 21), they have long tails, short but sturdy legs, rather gangly-looking bodies, and very rounded wings; their flight alternates between bouts of flapping and gliding; and they have extraordinarily long eyelashes. The Southern Ground-Hornbill is a turkey-sized bird, considerably larger than any other hornbill, and it is thickset, with a proportionately shorter tail but longer legs than other species in the family. It is largely terrestrial and it has an unusual gait from walking on tiptoe rather than on its soles. Most of the southern African hornbills (of which there are 9 species) belong to the genus *Tockus* and these are all similar in size and shape, differing only in plumage details and in bill coloration. Some, such as the SOUTHERN YELLOW-BILLED HORNBILL and RED-BILLED HORNBILL (both Plate 48), are common birds throughout the savannah areas; they are often seen on the roadside in this type of country and become tame and confiding in the rest camps of game parks. On the other hand, CROWNED HORNBILLS and TRUMPETER HORNBILLS (both Plate 48) are more restricted to forested habitats and they are much less approachable.

Related but not very similar in appearance to hornbills are the families of *hoopoes* (Upupidae) and *wood-hoopoes* (Phoeniculidae). These are smaller than hornbills and they have long, slender, down-curved bills. Wood-hoopoes are long-tailed and have iridescent purplish-black plumage, whereas hoopoes are short-tailed and cinnamon-colored, with black-and-white wings and tail and a large, striking crest that can be raised like a fan or retracted. There is just one member of the hoopoe family and it occurs throughout Africa (where it is known as the AFRICAN HOOPOE, Plate 50), Asia, and the Palearctic, whereas the wood-hoopoe family, consisting of 8 species (3 in southern Africa) is endemic to the African continent. The GREEN WOOD-HOOPOE (sometimes called Red-billed Wood-Hoopoe; Plate 50) is the most widespread member of the family, with a range that stretches across Africa.

Natural History

Ecology and Behavior

Hornbills exhibit much variability between species in their diets and feeding habits, with forest-living species being mainly frugivorous, savannah-living species being omnivorous, and the Southern Ground-Hornbill being largely carnivorous. Most species forage in trees but some feed on the ground at certain times of the year, and the Southern Ground Hornbill obtains all its prey on the ground. This species is unusual in many other respects; it lives in family groups, usually comprising 3 to 5 birds, in which there is a single dominant female that breeds, and the groups maintain very large, permanently defended territories. These groups routinely call each morning at first light, making a deep booming noise that can be heard 3 to 4 km (2 to 3 mi) away, and thereafter they set off on foot in search of food, covering perhaps 10 km (6 mi) before returning to their roost at night. They catch snakes, lizards, insects, rodents, nestling birds—in fact, anything they can overpower. Other hornbills tend to be territorial only while nesting, and at other times of the year they may congregate, especially the frugivorous species when a fruiting tree, a fig for example, has a large crop.

Wood-hoopoes are insectivorous, and they obtain much of their food rather in the manner of a woodpecker, clambering about on the stems and trunks of trees. Instead of excavating, though, they probe their long bills into crevices and beneath the bark in search of beetles and insect larvae. The Green Wood-Hoopoe lives in family groups, having a mating system akin to that of the Southern Ground Hornbill, and these birds also defend permanent territories against neighboring groups. They are noisy birds, and their hysterical cackling has led to the name "Nhlekabafazi" ("laughter of women") in Zulu. African Hoopoes feed on the ground, and although they live in pairs while breeding, one tends to encounter them solitarily, walking about with a waddling gait, pausing here and there to probe their long bill into the soil. On taking to flight they are suddenly conspicuous with their striking black-and-white checkered wings. It is their gentle call "hoop-hoop-poo" that gives its sound to the name of the two families.

Breeding

Monogamy is the rule in hornbills and hoopoes, but in some species (Southern Ground-Hornbill, Green Wood-Hoopoe) that live in extended family groups, nesting is a cooperative effort with helpers assisting the breeding pair. All the species in these families nest in cavities, usually located in the trunks of large trees; such sites are often re-used by the same birds year after year. The second trait these families have in common is that the female undertakes the incubation solo, and while doing this she is provisioned by her partner (with helpers assisting in the group-living species). Hornbills take this a stage further. In their case the female plasters the hole closed once she enters the nest cavity, leaving a narrow slit just wide enough to receive the delivery of food parcels that the male brings at intervals during the day. She uses her feces and debris from the nest floor, and in some cases mud brought in by the male, to do this. The seal soon sets rock-hard and for a month or more (depending on the species) she remains thus incarcerated, entirely dependent on her mate for food. During the time inside she sheds and regrows her wing and tail feathers; if she were to emerge before this was completed, she would be incapable of flight. The incubation period lasts at least 25 days (40 days in the Southern Ground Hornbill) and, some time after the young have hatched, the female breaks out. The nestlings seal the entrance closed again after her departure and thereafter the female assists the male in feeding the brood. In the case of Southern Ground Hornbills, although the female remains in the nest for the duration of the incubation, the hole is not sealed, perhaps because of its large size and the difficulty in achieving this. Hornbills lay plain white eggs that number between 1 and 5 to a clutch, and the nestling periods of the various species range between 44 and 86 days.

Hoopoes and wood-hoopoes lack the nest-sealing characteristic of the hornbills but are otherwise quite similar in their nesting behavior. In these species clutch sizes range between 3 and 7 eggs, incubation periods between 14 and 18 days, and nestling periods between 23 and 29 days. These two families share a very effective defense mechanism that is often used if the nest is disturbed or if the birds are handled: they discharge a foul-smelling fluid from a gland on their rump.

Notes

The hoopoe has had a long history of featuring in human art and culture, one that dates back as early as ancient Egyptian times, when this bird was used as a hieroglyph. Hornbills also have a long tradition of human association, especially in Asia, where their tail feathers are used in headdresses among tribesmen and the casques of the largest species are used for carvings.

Status

The range of the Southern Ground-Hornbill in South Africa has diminished as a result of changing land-use patterns, and because of this and its large spatial requirements, it is ranked as vulnerable in that country. All the other hornbills, together with the hoopoe and wood-hoopoes, are common and widespread.

Profiles

Southern Ground-Hornbill, *Bucorvus leadbeateri*, Plate 21f
African Gray Hornbill, *Tockus nasutus*, Plate 48a
Trumpeter Hornbill, *Bycanistes bucinator*, Plate 48b
Red-billed Hornbill, *Tockus erythrorhynchus*, Plate 48c
Southern Yellow-billed Hornbill, *Tockus leucomelas*, Plate 48d
Crowned Hornbill, *Tockus alboterminatus*, Plate 48e
African Hoopoe, *Upupa africana*, Plate 50a
Green Wood-Hoopoe, *Phoeniculus purpureus*, Plate 50b

17. Woodpeckers, Barbets, and Honeyguides

Woodpeckers are birds that are known to most people, at least in name—an attribute that can perhaps be credited to the once-famous cartoon character "Woody Woodpecker." On the other hand, anyone who has watched a woodpecker at work would be captivated by its remarkable ability to excavate into the heart of a hardwood tree in a way that a human could match only by using power tools. They excavate by rapidly striking the wood with their bills, and this capability is the result of three features that are unique to woodpeckers: a powerful chisel-shaped bill, a skull structure that cushions each blow and makes their heads "shock-proof," and strong, stiff tail feathers that provide a pivot, or "third leg" that props them up as they hammer away at a tree stem. Because of their "third leg," woodpeckers seldom perch in the way that conventional birds do, but instead cling against the side of upright branches, even when not at work. Woodpeckers excavate into wood both to make nest chambers and to secure food. Their feeding method reveals another unusual feature—they have extraordinarily long tongues, capable of being extended several centimeters (inches) beyond the tip of the bill. The tongues of some species have barbed tips, and these species extend their tongues deep into cavities in the wood and harpoon insects with them; in other woodpeckers the tongue is coated with a sticky secretion used to mop up surface insects. When not extended, the tongue is retracted under and behind the bird's skull, reeled in like a cable being wound onto a drum. Except for Australia, where they are absent, woodpeckers (family Picidae) occur widely in the world, and although they are well represented in Africa (with about 30 species), South America and Asia are the real home of this family of 210 species. There is a great deal of variation to be found in their size (from tiny to large), coloration, and plumage, but common features most woodpeckers share are that most species have some red on the head (usually on the crown), and in most species the sexes look different. The African woodpeckers, and especially the 10 species found in southern Africa, are uniformly rather small and the plumage differences between them are slight.

Barbets (family Lybiidae) and *honeyguides* (family Indicatoridae) are the closest relatives that woodpeckers have in the bird world, but their similarities are not all that apparent. There are about 80 barbet species in the world, half of these found in Africa, and they vary in size from tiny (the *tinker barbets*) to medium-sized. They are chunky-looking birds with thick necks, large heads, short tails and legs, and, in most species, large, toothed bills. Many are also strikingly colored; the CRESTED BARBET (Plate 49) looks like a painter's palette on which much testing and mixing of colors has been done. Many of the species are gregarious, they have loud, distinctive calls, and they are uniformly frugivorous. The honeyguides comprise a quite extraordinary bird family that is almost entirely restricted to Africa: 2 of the world's 18 species occur in Asia and the remainder are African, with 6 occurring in southern Africa. Their name is derived from the habit, found in just two species, of guiding humans to beehives. These and other honeyguide species visit beehives routinely and they eat bees' wax, having particular enzymes that are capable of digesting this unlikely source of food. Honeyguides have a third trait—of being parasitic and laying their eggs in the nests of other birds—and this adds to their unusual nature.

Natural History

Ecology and Behavior

Woodpeckers often give their presence away by the sound of their tapping on wood. They do this as they shuffle up and down branches, pausing here and there to work more intently at one spot, at intervals excavating into the wood in a great flurry until the larvae of a woodborer beetle is triumphantly extracted. Dead wood is usually targeted since it is where woodborers are most active, but different woodpecker species have different techniques and specialize in different foods. Many species are primarily ant-eaters and they glean these from the surface as often as they dig for them; some woodpeckers even tap into a tree's sap and consume this. One southern African species, the GROUND WOODPECKER (Plate 50) is almost unique in the world for being a terrestrial woodpecker; it is endemic to South Africa and lives in pairs and family parties in mountainous grassland, foraging on the ground and subsisting entirely on ants. Woodpeckers generally have loud, distinctive calls and some species supplement these by making a mechanical sound known as "drumming." These birds use drumming as much as they use their calls, to advertise their presence. The sound is produced by rapidly tapping their bill on a branch, and drumming sites are usually on dead limbs at sites selected for their resonance.

Woodpeckers are generally territorial and live year-round in pairs in the same areas, having a few favored roosting places to which they return each night. Barbets, on the other hand, share the habit common in frugivorous birds of being mobile and coming and going according to fruit availability. BLACK-COLLARED BARBETS (Plate 49) typically do this, and are often found in family groups that forage together during the day and sleep together at night, with 7 or 8 birds sometimes to be found all squeezing into the same hole! Barbets are undoubtedly important agents in dispersing the seeds of fruiting trees in forests and savannahs. In this respect the YELLOW-FRONTED TINKERBIRD (Plate 49) has a special relationship with a variety of mistletoe species. These mistletoes are parasitic plants that grow on the stems of other trees. They have brightly colored fruits, with soft flesh encasing a hard, sticky seed. The tinker barbets commonly feed on these fruits but regurgitate the seeds; because these are sticky, the barbets have to wipe them from their bills, and they do this against tree branches onto which the seeds become attached and later take root.

Breeding

Woodpeckers and barbets both nest in holes in trees, and both excavate a neatly finished bowl inside a tree stem that is reached via a small, circular entrance that leads in from one side. Barbets, because of their less well-adapted bills and skulls, invariably select soft, decaying wood for their nests, which seldom last long, whereas many woodpecker species dig their nest holes in hard wood, often taking a month or more to complete it, but producing a hole that may last for many years. Holes like this are often used by a succession of hole-nesting birds (owls, starlings, parrots, rollers, and others) and the original nest-maker may never be successful in reclaiming it. Woodpeckers and barbets are monogamous, and both parents share in excavating the nest hole and in all other nesting duties. Some barbet species have cooperative breeding systems whereby the extended family members assist as "nest-helpers" in raising the young. Woodpeckers and barbets lay plain white eggs numbering 3 to 6 per clutch. The incubation and nestling periods are variable depending on the species, ranging between 11 and 18 days and 20 and 35 days, respectively.

Honeyguides are polygamous. The male honeyguide establishes a call-site, usually in the upper branches of a tree, and he calls from this throughout the breeding season to attract mates. Such call-sites are often used in successive years, and there are instances known in which particular trees have been used by GREATER HONEYGUIDES (Plate 50) for as long as 20 successive years. After visiting such a male and mating, the female honeyguide seeks out a host nest in which to lay her eggs. Like those of woodpeckers and barbets, honeyguide eggs are plain white, and they often go undetected in the host's clutch when such birds are parasitized. Woodpeckers and barbets are commonly targeted, especially by the LESSER HONEYGUIDE, but a variety of other species, including swallows, starlings, bee-eaters, cisticolas, and white-eyes, also play host to the various honeyguide species. It is usual for a single egg to be laid per host nest and for the nestling honeyguide to kill its "siblings." It does this within the first few days of hatching, equipped at birth with sharp hooks on its bill that it uses to bite its siblings to death. The dead young are then removed by the parent birds from the nest, and the hooks fall off the honeyguide chick once the grisly deed is complete.

Notes

The woodpecker's family name, Picidae, comes from Picus, a figure in Roman mythology who was the son of Saturn. Picus was god of the forests before he was turned into a woodpecker by a sorceress, Circe, whose advances he rather unwisely spurned.

The Greater Honeyguide is the honeyguide best known for the habit of guiding people to beehives. In much of the bird's range this guiding behavior is diminishing or has disappeared, but in undeveloped rural areas where local people still harvest honey, these honeyguides commonly perform their guiding routine. The bird has a distinctive guiding call, a sound rather like that made by shaking a matchbox, and it attempts to catch one's attention by making the sound in a nearby tree. If one approaches the bird, it flies to the next tree, and continues calling there, and so on. If it isn't followed, it returns to the person it has targeted and calls more insistently. The route followed to the hive is seldom direct, and it may be a kilometer (0.6 mi) or more away. One knows the journey is over when the bird finally remains calling in one tree—the prize will be in a hole somewhere close by. Rural people who know the birds well often whistle to the bird as they follow it, and they always leave part of the comb behind for the bird.

Status

With the exception of two range-restricted species, all the woodpecker, barbet, and honeyguide species found in southern Africa are widespread and common. The KNYSNA WOODPECKER is endemic to the southern and eastern Cape and has a limited range, while the only occurrence of the GREEN BARBET in southern Africa is in a single patch of forest (known as Ngoye) in northern KwaZulu-Natal.

Profiles

Black-collared Barbet, *Lybius torquatus*, Plate 49a
Acacia Pied Barbet, *Lybius leucomelas*, Plate 49b
Red-fronted Tinkerbird, *Pogoniulus pusillus*, Plate 49c
Yellow-fronted Tinkerbird, *Pogoniulus chrysoconus*, Plate 49d
Crested Barbet, *Trachyphonus vaillantii*, Plate 49e
Greater Honeyguide, *Indicator indicator*, Plate 50c
Ground Woodpecker, *Geocolaptes olivaceus*, Plate 50d
Cardinal Woodpecker, *Dendropicos fuscescens*, Plate 50e
Golden-tailed Woodpecker, *Campethera abingoni*, Plate 50f

18. Larks, Pipits, Wagtails, and Longclaws

There are few other bird families as notorious for the identification problems they pose as *larks* and *pipits* are; they epitomize the "LBJs" ("little brown jobs")—the birds that newcomers to the birding game despair of ever being able to identify. Larks and pipits are uniformly dull-colored and nondescript, they live on the ground where they often cannot be seen easily, and when not displaying, they give very little of themselves away. Furthermore, they are birds that taxonomists, geneticists, and nomenclaturists dream about, as they provide endless opportunities for prising new species from the established lineup, rearranging which species should be grouped with which, and generally tinkering with their taxonomies. In short, larks and pipits provide good reason for bird field guides to be revised at regular intervals.

The identification difficulties start right up at family level—how does one distinguish a lark from a pipit? The two families (larks, family Alaudidae, and pipits, family Motacillidae), though not at all closely related, both comprise small, ground-living birds that are mainly tawny-colored and marked with darker streaking. Their underparts are generally paler than their upperparts, their tails and legs are moderate in length, and their bills vary from being slender to heavy. In general, pipits are slimmer-looking birds than larks, longer in the tail and leg and with longer, more delicate bills. Within the pipit family there are, fortunately, two easily identified groups, *wagtails* and *longclaws*, that provide a gentle entry into the minefield. Longclaws are restricted to Africa, but they have an ecological counterpart in North America in the form of *meadowlarks*. Longclaws have brightly colored underparts that offset their dull, cryptically marked backs. YELLOW-THROATED LONGCLAWS and CAPE (or ORANGE-THROATED) LONGCLAWS (both Plate 68), for instance, have yellow and orange fronts respectively, and each has a black necklace just as meadowlarks do. Wagtails are also quite distinctive, with half of the world's 11 species found in Africa. They are long-tailed versions of the typical pipit, and they have gray or black-and-white plumage, with some species having variable amounts of yellow on them. Their name comes from the habit of bobbing their tails up and down as they walk, such an entrenched mannerism that the birds probably only stop doing it when asleep at night. The remaining "true" pipits, which number perhaps 40 species, are a rather homogenous group, with one or two abundant, ubiquitous species (for example, the AFRICAN [or GRASSVELD] PIPIT, Plate 68), and others that have restricted ranges or very specific habitat preferences. In most cases the best clues to their identification are the differences in their calls and displays.

Larks are mainly African birds, with no less than 72 species (of the world's 96) on the continent. Southern Africa has a good share of these, of which 16 are endemic to this area, and it is finding these endemics that often draws birdwatchers to the region. Many of the larks have restricted ranges and are very specific in their habitat requirements, but others, such as the RED-CAPPED LARK (Plate 52) for instance, are widespread and common. Many have distinctive songs and several have distinctive aerial displays that immediately give away their identity. The EASTERN CLAPPER LARK and FLAPPET LARK (both Plate 51) are two that perform wonderfully in the air; they make a rattling or clapping noise with their wings as part of this. Another impressive performer is the common RUFOUS-NAPED LARK (Plate 51), which now and then flies up high and circles about, imitating brief snatches of the calls of other birds in a melody of great variety. With few exceptions, the larks are birds of open country and they extend across the savannah, the grasslands, and shrublands, right into the driest desert areas in the west. Their similar appearances belie a great diversity in lifestyles.

Natural History

Ecology and Behavior

Most species of larks and pipits (including their sister groups, wagtails and longclaws) are insectivorous, a trait that is reflected in the shape of their bills, which are somewhat long and slender and provide ideal tools for handling small insects. Several larks, however, feed mainly on grass seeds and they have differently shaped bills—thicker and blunter—that are designed for picking up and rolling the casings off of small seeds. The GRAY-BACKED SPARROWLARK (Plate 52) is one of these, and its bill is finch-like in shape. It is a bird of semi-arid areas, and it lives here in flocks that are highly nomadic and move about widely in response to erratic and unpredictable rainfall. Many arid-zone larks live this way, whereas the lark species occurring in more predictable environments tend to be more sedentary and to live in pairs in permanent territories. Of all the species in the two families, the one most familiar to most people is undoubtedly the CAPE WAGTAIL (Plate 68). It occurs widely and is common, typically living along the marshy edges of streams, rivers, lakes, and wetlands. But it has also moved into towns and cities where it is a tame and confiding bird, and a familiar sight in parks, gardens, around housing estates, and wherever there are well-watered lawns and open ground. Pairs often nest in gardens, perhaps using a hanging flower pot or a creeper against a wall for a nest site, and often become part of the household as they raise successive broods each year from the same nest.

Breeding

The nesting habits of larks, pipits, wagtails, and longclaws are all remarkably similar. They are monogamous breeders; they all build cup-shaped nests which, except for wagtails, are invariably placed on the ground, hidden beneath a grass tuft or low shrub; they all lay small clutches (usually 2 to 4 eggs); and in most cases the sexes share incubation and care of the nestlings. In larks, incubation periods vary between 11 and 17 days and their nestlings usually leave the nest before they can fly, when about 9 to 12 days old. Pipits, wagtails, and longclaws have incubations lasting about 13 to 14 days and nestling periods of about 13 to 16 days. Wagtails are commonly parasitized by the RED-CHESTED CUCKOO (Plate 42).

Notes

The SKYLARK, and particularly its song, has been woven into European culture and literature for centuries. In reference to their song, the family name, Alaudidae, comes from the Latin word "laudare" (to praise).

Status

Given the very specific habitats used by some of the larks and pipits, and the restricted ranges they occupy, it is not surprising that several species have become threatened as a result of changing patterns of land use. One of South Africa's endemic larks (RUDD'S LARK) is ranked as critically endangered, another (BOTHA'S LARK) is endangered, and several more are ranked as vulnerable.

Profiles

Rufous-naped Lark, *Mirafra africana*, Plate 51a
Eastern Clapper Lark, *Mirafra fasciolataa*, Plate 51b
Flappet Lark, *Mirafra rufocinnamomea*, Plate 51c
Sabota Lark, *Mirafra sabota*, Plate 51d

Stark's Lark, *Spizocorys starki*, Plate 51e
Spike-heeled Lark, *Chersomanes albofasciata*, Plate 52a
Red-capped Lark, *Calandrella cinerea*, Plate 52b
Large-billed Lark, *Galerida magnirostris*, Plate 52c
Gray-backed Sparrowlark, *Eremopterix verticalis*, Plate 52d
African Pied Wagtail, *Motacilla aguimp*, Plate 68a
Cape Wagtail, *Motacilla capensis*, Plate 68b
African Pipit, *Anthus cinnamomeus*, Plate 68c
Long-billed Pipit, *Anthus similis*, Plate 68d
Cape Longclaw, *Macronyx capensis*, Plate 68e
Yellow-throated Longclaw, *Macronyx croceus*, Plate 68f

19. Crows, Drongos, Orioles, and Tits

Crows need no introduction to most people as they are one of those cosmopolitan groups of birds, like ducks, eagles, storks, or robins, that become part of one's vocabulary during childhood; few people would not be able to say that crows are rather large black birds, that they are intelligent, and that they make a loud, awful cawing noise. There are about 40 crow species in the world and they belong to a larger family (the Corvidae, numbering 119 species) that includes *jays, magpies, choughs, ravens,* and others. Three are indigenous to southern Africa and a fourth, the HOUSE CROW, has established itself in a few coastal cities as a result of unwitting introductions. These species all match the typical crow mold of being medium-sized birds (but they are the largest birds in the entire Passerine order) that are mainly or entirely black, with long, robust bills and sturdy legs and feet. The WHITE-NECKED RAVEN (Plate 55) has a particularly powerful bill that goes with its habit of scavenging off carcasses. It lives in mountainous areas, whereas the PIED CROW and CAPE CROW (both on Plate 55) are found more commonly on the plains.

Drongos, orioles, and *tits* are brought together with crows because they belong to families that have a common ancestry with the Corvidae. Drongos (family Dicruridae) are a mainly Asian family of birds, but 7 species occur in Africa and 2 of these are found in southern Africa. The FORK-TAILED DRONGO (Plate 56) is a very typical member of this family, being entirely black, with a hooked bill, a spray of stiff hairs (*rictal bristles*) protruding from around the base of its bill, and a pugnacious disposition. Some of the Asian drongos have ornate head plumes and/or elaborate tail structures, but in this species only the tail, which is deeply forked, diverges from the normal. Fork-tailed Drongos are never demure; they perch conspicuously; they have discordant raspy calls; they pirate food from other birds; and they are always the first bird to tackle any bird of prey that may venture into their area. They are also gifted mimics and impersonate the calls of many birds of prey—why they should do this, though, is uncertain. The orioles (family Oriolidae) that occur in Africa are known as the "Old World Orioles" and are unrelated to a group of birds found in the Americas, confusingly also known as orioles ("New World Orioles;" family Icteridae). African oriole males are brilliant yellow birds with black in the wings, or in the case of the BLACK-HEADED ORIOLE (Plate 56), with a black head. Although this species is an exception, females are generally duller colored than males. Some species are migratory whereas others are resident. Lastly, there are two families of birds that go by the name of "tit" (abbreviated from its original name "tit-mouse"). The first of these is the family Paridae, a well-represented group in the Northern Hemisphere that includes several species—GREAT TITS and chickadees, for example—that are familiar birds to residents of cities in Europe and North America. The second closely related family, Remizidae, consists of about a dozen species of tiny birds, most occurring in Africa, that are known as penduline tits. The species in both of these families are tree-living insectivores.

Natural History

Ecology and Behavior

The species that make up the families outlined here live their lives in a fairly similar way: during the breeding season they tend to be dispersed as scattered pairs, whereas outside of this period they are, in most cases, more gregarious. Crows are the most sociable, and flocks of dozens and occasionally hundreds may congregate where there is a good food supply. Their diets are catholic, and this extends to eating carrion, insects, fruit, grain, bird's eggs, nestlings, and many other things; PIED CROWS, for instance, regularly patrol busy highways on the lookout for roadkill. In short, crows are opportunistic and very adaptable when it comes to food.

Drongos are insectivorous birds that catch most of what they eat on the wing, and the Fork-tailed Drongo, thanks to its forked tail, is extremely agile in the air. These birds often gather in numbers at bush fires to catch grasshoppers fleeing from the flames, or they perch around beehives and swoop on the incoming and outgoing bees. Orioles are omnivorous, and in addition to taking insects, they eat berries, other fruit, and nectar, which they sip from flowering plants. They are relatively unsociable birds once nesting is over, and are usually encountered solitarily outside the breeding season. Tits give the impression of always being on the move, forever active in their search for small caterpillars and other insects in the foliage of trees. The SOUTHERN BLACK TIT (Plate 56) is the commonest of the tits in southern Africa, and it lives in pairs or family groups that move about in cohesive units, each bird maintaining contact with the group by regularly uttering its conversational *churring* call. Other species of insectivorous birds often associate with tit families, and these "mixed species bird parties" as they are known, are a common feature in woodlands and savannahs, especially during the winter months when insect availability is at a low ebb. Many insectivorous birds, including drongos, orioles, penduline tits, woodpeckers, and shrikes, spend their days foraging together during the dry season, and birdwatching in such areas at this time of the year is often an all-or-nothing experience, depending on whether or not one encounters a bird party.

Breeding

Tits nest in cavities in trees (or in holes in rocks in the case of the arid-country species) and they line the nest hole with soft, warm material before laying. The other species covered here all build nests in the branches of trees. Crows build a large, open-cupped stick nest in the topmost branches of the largest tree they can find, hence the term "crow's nest" used in sailing ships in the past. The tall electricity transmission towers that crisscross parts of southern Africa provide crows with ideal substitutes for trees, and their nests are commonly seen in the topmost crossbars of these towers. Drongos and orioles build a hammock-like nest that is slung between the horizontal twigs of an outer branch, and the nests of the penduline tits are enclosed balls made of cobweb and finely felted plant down with a narrow spout entrance leading in near the top of one side. Drongos and orioles usually lay a clutch of 3 eggs, whereas crows and tits typically lay 4 or 5 eggs. Incubation and nestling periods are rather variable, being longest in crows (18 and 38 days respectively) and shortest in orioles (15 and 16 days respectively). All the species are monogamous breeders.

Notes

Crows and ravens featured prominently in the folklore of earlier European cultures. It was, no doubt, their all-black plumage and habit of eating carrion that branded them as birds of ill-omen and harbingers of death. Orioles derive their common name from the Latin word "aureolus," meaning "gold."

Status

Several tit species are endemic to southern Africa but none of these are under threat; nor are any local species of crows, drongos, or orioles.

Profiles

Cape Crow, *Corvus capensis*, Plate 55a
Pied Crow, *Corvus albus*, Plate 55b
White-necked Raven, *Corvus albicollis,* Plate 55c
Fork-tailed Drongo, *Dicrurus adsimilis*, Plate 56a
Black-headed Oriole, *Oriolus larvatus*, Plate 56b
Southern Black Tit, *Parus niger*, Plate 56c

20. Bulbuls and Babblers

First-time visitors to southern Africa from North or South America will be encountering two entirely foreign bird families when they come into contact with *bulbuls* and *babblers*, two large and diverse groups of birds that are entirely confined to the "Old World"; on the other hand, visitors from Asia will probably be very familiar with them in one form or another, as these families make up a significant proportion of the Asian avifauna. There are about 130 bulbul species (family Pycnonotidae) in the world and they are evenly divided between Africa and Eurasia. The African bulbuls are rather small, uniformly drab-colored birds; many of them are known by their alternative names of *brownbul* and *greenbul* and this gives an indication of the nature of their plumage. In addition to being sombre-colored, the brownbuls and greenbuls are skulking, forest-dwelling birds that don't easily show themselves and are often overlooked. Several species, however, are somewhat more conspicuous and striking in their appearance, with prominent crests and more colorful undertail coverts. They are collectively known as *crested bulbuls* and three, the DARK-CAPPED (or Black-eyed), AFRICAN RED-EYED, and CAPE BULBULS (all Plate 57) are common birds in southern Africa, often coming into gardens and familiarly known in many places as "toppies." They are likely to be encountered anywhere in their respective ranges, the Cape Bulbul being restricted to the southern Cape region, the African Red-eyed Bulbul to the semi-arid western areas, and the Dark-capped Bulbul being found pretty much everywhere else, its range extending northward across Africa and into the Middle East. The three resemble each other closely and vary mainly in the color of their eye-rings. They are closely related, and where they come in contact with each other, some hybridization takes place. Although easily overlooked, the greenbuls and brownbuls are among the commonest birds that live in the forested parts of southern Africa. One of these, the SOMBER GREENBUL (Plate 57), gives its presence away by its cheerful singing, this usually emanating from dense cover and punctuated at intervals with the vigorously uttered note "willie"; not surprisingly, the bird is known to many people simply as "Willie."

The babbler family (Timaliidae) is an even larger, mainly Asian group of birds, of which about 35 species live on the African continent, with 5 found in southern Africa; Asia supports over 220 species. There is no general consensus as to where babblers belong in the bird kingdom. From external appearances they would seem to be most like thrushes, but certain structural and genetic features align them more closely with either warblers or flycatchers. The 5 southern African species, of which the ARROW-MARKED BABBLER and SOUTHERN PIED BABBLER (both Plate 56) are two common examples, bear scant resemblance to any warbler or flycatcher in the region—they are robustly built, noisy and garrulous, and they live at ground level. The most noticeable thing about these babblers is that they are always found in groups, typically about 6 to 9 birds together, and they share a territory in which they live as a close-knit family. They spend much of their time grubbing about in the leaf litter beneath trees and under thickets, never straying far from each other, and punctuating the silences with frequent choruses in which the whole group participates, producing a cacophony of "chow-chow-chow...." cackling. The Southern Pied Babbler is a quite unmistakable, striking-looking white bird with black wings and tail, whereas the Arrow-marked Babbler is brown-colored and looks much like the three other babblers in the region, distinguished only by the whitish flecks ("arrow marks") on its head and chest. The sexes are alike in both the babbler and bulbul families, and they do not have distinctively different juvenile plumages.

Natural History

Ecology and Behavior

Southern Africa's bulbuls and babblers prefer wooded habitats, some living in forests, but the majority being found in savannah country. Babblers like bushy thickets and they are mainly insectivorous, foraging for insects on the ground and in the undergrowth, using their bills to turn over the leaf litter and bounding from one spot to the next in large hops. When one bird in the group flies, the others usually follow suit. Between spells of foraging the members of the group often perch huddled against each other, and they may preen each other elaborately while doing this. They are remarkably sedentary birds that live year-round in the same restricted area, a territory that is defended against invasions by other babblers by all members of the group. Bulbuls are mainly frugivorous, although some forest species, such as the TERRESTRIAL BROWNBUL (Plate 57) for instance, are insectivorous. The fruit-eating bulbuls, like those that share this diet in other bird families, are often gregarious and gather in numbers where the pickings are good, and they come and go in any given area in response to the changing availability of fruit. Particularly abundant in much of its range, the Dark-capped Bulbul is an important dispersal agent for the seeds of many fruiting trees and shrubs.

Breeding

Bulbuls and babblers are monogamous breeders that nest during the summer months when their respective food supplies are at a maximum. Bulbuls nest in scattered pairs, building a small open-cupped structure that is well hidden in the thin twigs and foliage of a tree or shrub. They lay a clutch of 2 or 3 speckled eggs; incubation and nestling periods are about 11 to 16 days and 13 to 16 days respectively. Babblers are *cooperative breeders,* and although they live together in groups, only one male and one female in the group mates and produces a clutch of eggs. Others in the group are subordinate to this dominant pair and they perform the function of being "nest helpers," sharing in the nest-building, incubation, and nestling care, but not breeding themselves. Cooperative breeding, as practiced by babblers, occurs widely in a variety of unrelated bird families and it is the subject of much ongoing research. The explanation usually offered for the behavior is that it occurs in sedentary, long-lived species in which immature birds, once independent, are faced with two options, neither of which provides any prospect of breeding in the near future. They can disperse into surrounding habitat that is inferior to that which is occupied by their parents, or they can stay in the family and share the group territory but remain subordinate. The latter option offers the best prospect for immediate survival, and in the long term it provides the chance that they may become dominant and so secure the breeding position. The southern African babblers lay uniformly dark blue eggs, 2 to 4 in a clutch, and in some species, the eggs have a very rough, noduled shell texture. Incubation and nestling periods are about 16 and 20 days respectively. Bulbuls and babblers are both common hosts to two cuckoo species. Bulbuls, especially the Somber Greenbul and Dark-capped Bulbul, are frequently parasitized by the Jacobin Cuckoo, whereas the Arrow-marked Babbler (and several other babblers) are parasitized by the Jacobin Cuckoo's look-alike, the Levaillant's Cuckoo. What is oddly different in these two parasite-host associations is that the Jacobin Cuckoo lays a plain white egg in its host's nest that, although very obviously different from the speckled eggs of its host, is not rejected by the bulbuls. The Levaillant's Cuckoo, on the other hand, lays a dark blue egg that closely matches those of its hosts, and if there is any mismatch it is detected by the babblers and the cuckoo egg is ejected.

Status

Although a few species have restricted ranges, there are no bulbuls or babblers in southern Africa that are ranked as threatened. Several of them are endemic to southern Africa.

Profiles

Arrow-marked Babbler, *Turdoides jardineii*, Plate 56d
Southern Pied Babbler, *Turdoides bicolor*, Plate 56e
African Red-eyed Bulbul, *Pycnonotus nigricans*, Plate 57a
Cape Bulbul, *Pycnonotus capensis*, Plate 57b
Dark-capped (Black-eyed) Bulbul, *Pycnonotus tricolor*, Plate 57c
Somber Greenbul, *Andropadus importunus*, Plate 57d
Terrestrial Brownbul, *Phyllastrephus terrestris*, Plate 57e

21. Thrushes, Chats, and Robin-Chats

Virtually every terrestrial habitat in southern Africa, from extreme desert to humid lowland forest, is inhabited by one or more species of *thrush*, *robin-chat*, or *chat*. These birds, together with several other groups not represented in southern Africa, make up the large, diverse family previously known as the Turdidae, but recently brought under the umbrella of the family Muscicapidae. They constitute an important group of birds both in global terms, where about 330 different species are known, and in a southern African context, where 46 species occur, many of them endemic to the region. The distinction between a thrush, a chat, and a robin-chat (often referred to simply as robins) is vague, and what is called a robin in one country may be called a chat or thrush in another. Some species are colorful, others are very drably colored; in some, the sexes are similar, in others they are quite different; some are noisy and conspicuous, others are subdued and skulking. If any generalizations are possible about the Turdidae, it is that they are small, but not tiny in size, plumpish, with rather slender bills and robust, longish legs; they are largely solitary or in pairs, mainly insectivorous, and they forage on the ground.

The thrushes in the family include a distinctive group known as *rock-thrushes*, 5 different species of which occur in southern Africa. The CAPE ROCK-THRUSH (Plate 58) is a typical example of a rock thrush: males have blue heads and russet bodies, whereas females are mottled brown. As their name implies, they live in rocky habitats. Another group might be called "typical" thrushes, and in these the sexes are alike. The KURRICHANE THRUSH and OLIVE THRUSH (both Plate 58) are examples—two similar-looking birds, both mainly olive- and buff-colored, one living in savannah, the other in forest. The Olive Thrush, which is the forest bird, has a sister species, the recently split KAROO THRUSH, which frequents drier country and has extended its range into cities and towns wherever exotic trees have become established; it is also common in many parks and gardens. The GROUNDSCRAPER THRUSH (Plate 58), although different in appearance from the first two, having a white chest boldly spotted with black, is another example of a typical thrush. Chats differ from thrushes in their open, treeless habitats, some species preferring open grasslands, others shrublands and desert areas. They probably derive their odd name from the conversational nature of their calls. Many chats are conspicuous birds, partly because of the open landscapes they inhabit and partly because it is their custom to perch on prominent rocks, on tops of bushes, or on roadside fence posts. Some chats, such as the MOUNTAIN WHEATEAR (Plate 59) for instance, are strikingly marked black-and-white birds, whereas others, such as the SICKLE-WINGED CHAT (Plate 59), are dull-colored and easily confused with other similar-looking chats that share their habitats.

The African robin-chat—until recently simply called robin—is taxonomically unrelated to the European Robin, although many species, such as the CHORISTER ROBIN-CHAT, WHITE-BROWED ROBIN-CHAT and RED-CAPPED ROBIN-CHAT (all Plate 60) for instance, have bright orange-colored heads and underparts, and so resemble the European Robin. In addition to having orange fronts, these robin-chats also have orange-colored tails, a useful feature for identifying one as it flits out of view into dense undergrowth. Most of the African robin-chats are forest-dwelling, and it is not uncommon to find several different species sharing the same forest patch. Another related group are the *scrub-robins*, duller-colored (mainly gray or light brown), mostly non-forest species; the KAROO SCRUB-ROBIN (Plate 61), for instance, is a common inhabitant of the semi-arid shrublands of the Karoo, and the KALAHARI SCRUB-ROBIN (Plate 61), as its name indicates, is a bird of the semi-arid Kalahari region. Robin-chats and scrub-robins are all fine songsters, are territorial, and live in pairs.

Another unusual group in the Turdidae family lineup are the *palm thrushes*. They are unusual in that they are restricted to the vicinity of tall palm trees, and the two species in southern Africa are restricted to low-lying areas in the north and east where this type of habitat occurs. These birds often build their mud nests in the crowns of palm trees, but their dependence on such trees does not seem to extend beyond this use.

Rockjumpers are another unusual group that, in appearance and behavior, have much in common with robin-chats and scrub-robins. But recent studies indicate that they comprise a family of their own, the Chaetopidae, one of only two families of birds endemic to South Africa and comprising just two species. One of these is restricted to the southern Cape and the other, the DRAKENSBERG ROCKJUMPER (Plate 61), to the high-lying parts of the Drakensberg Mountains. They are long-legged, colorful birds that live on boulder-strewn slopes, and they bound from rock to rock with great agility, only flying as a last resort.

Natural History

Ecology and Behavior

Berries and other small fruits feature in the diets of many thrushes, but these birds, together with the chats and robin-chats, are primarily insectivorous. With few exceptions they forage at ground level, those living in forests (such as many robin-chats) searching the damp leaf litter on the forest floor for food, those in grasslands (rockjumpers and chats) hunting among and between the grass tufts for insects, and the desert-living species seeking their food among low shrubs and rocks. Thrushes often adopt a comical pose while foraging—they stand erect and cock their head to one side, apparently listening for the movement of an earthworm or insect beneath the litter. Thrushes, chats, and robin-chats are, almost without exception, territorial while breeding. They live in pairs, and in some, the pair remains together year-round in the same territory, but in others the breeding area is vacated during winter when the occupants move to lower (and warmer) ground. This is a common occurrence in the species that nest in higher-elevation forests, which become cold in winter. These birds then move to coastal forests. Similarly, chats that breed in the bleak uplands of the Drakensberg Mountains move to lower altitudes in winter. The forest robin-chats are among the finest songsters of all African birds, and in spring when the territorial urge peaks, many forests come alive with the sweet, mellow refrains of species such as the Red-capped Robin-Chat, Chorister Robin-Chat, and WHITE-STARRED ROBIN-CHAT. The Red-capped Robin-Chat and Chorister Robin-Chat are accomplished mimics and much of their repertoire is made up of mimicked phrases taken from other birds' calls, it often being impossible to distinguish whether or not such calls are the real thing.

Breeding

Thrushes, chats, and robin-chats build open-cupped nests, and these, in many species, are placed at ground level; some species, though, build their nests in a crevice in a tree trunk or rock face or in a forked branch. Palm thrushes are unusual in using mud to construct their nest; the structure is then attached to a vertical surface in the manner of some swallow nests. One species, the MOCKING CLIFF-CHAT, commandeers the mud nests of Greater Striped and Lesser Striped Swallows (both Plate 54) and it builds its nest inside these. The typical clutch size varies between 2 and 4 eggs, and the eggs of the different species are very variable in color and markings. Incubation and nestling periods vary from species to species, but range between 12 to 15 days and 11 to 20 days, respectively. With few exceptions, the species in this family are monogamous. A few, the ANT-EATING CHAT (Plate 59), for instance, are cooperative nesters in which the breeding pair has one or more "nest helpers."

Notes

During Britain's colonial era almost every red- or orange-fronted bird encountered in the colonies became known as a "robin," and these names have become entrenched despite their nostalgic rather than taxonomic origins. Thus Africa and India both live with chats that are called "robins," North America has a thrush that is called a "robin," Australia lives with flycatchers and others that are called "robins," and an Asian babbler is known as the "Pekin Robin."

Status

One local member of the Turdidae is threatened: the SPOTTED GROUND-THRUSH is restricted to coastal and lowland forests, and because of its fragmented distribution and low numbers, it is currently ranked as endangered throughout its African range.

Profiles

Kurrichane Thrush, *Turdus libonyana*, Plate 58a
Olive Thrush, *Turdus olivaceus*, Plate 58b
Groundscraper Thrush, *Turdus litsitsirupa*, Plate 58c
Cape Rock-Thrush, *Monticola rupestris*, Plate 58d
Mountain Wheatear, *Oenanthe monticola*, Plate 59a
Capped Wheatear, *Oenanthe pileata*, Plate 59b
Familiar Chat, *Cercomela familiaris*, Plate 59c
Sickle-winged Chat, *Cercomela sinuata*, Plate 59d
Ant-eating Chat, *Myrmecocichla formicivora*, Plate 59e
African Stonechat, *Saxicola torquata*, Plate 59f
Chorister Robin-Chat, *Cossypha dichroa*, Plate 60a
White-browed Robin-Chat, *Cossypha heuglini*, Plate 60b
Red-capped Robin-Chat, *Cossypha natalensis*, Plate 60c
Cape Robin-Chat, *Cossypha caffra*, Plate 60d
Drakensberg (Orange-breasted) Rockjumper, *Chaetops aurantius*, Plate 61a
White-browed Scrub-Robin, *Erythropygia leucophrys*, Plate 61b
Karoo Scrub-Robin, *Erythropygia coryphaeus*, Plate 61c
Kalahari Scrub-Robin, *Erythropygia paena*, Plate 61d

22. Warblers

The name *warbler*, stemming from the sweet warbling songs uttered by some of its species, is applied to a large number of small to tiny birds that are found widely in the world. In North America, the name is applied to *parulids* (finch-related birds), whereas in Australia a group of birds aligned with *honey-eaters* are known as warblers. The warblers in Africa (family Sylviidae) are not related to either of these, although they do share many features, especially their small size; to distinguish them they are often known as "Old World Warblers." This family extends across Africa, Europe, and Asia, and its best-known members are the small, sweet-singing warblers of Europe, of which the WILLOW WARBLER (Plate 62) is a typical example. Many of these spend summers in Europe and migrate south into Africa during winters, here joining a great array of warblers that are resident on the continent—at least 150 endemic species—that go by such unusual names as *eremomela, crombec, camaroptera, hyliota,* and *apalis*, all members of this same large Sylviidae family. They are consistently small to tiny insectivorous birds, slim-bodied and slender-billed. Most are short- rather than long-tailed, and with few exceptions, the sexes do not differ in plumage. Otherwise they are infinitely variable in their shape, plumage, behavior, and song, and they inhabit every type of country, from dense evergreen forest to savannahs, grasslands, shrublands, and desert. Many species are bewilderingly similar and some are only identifiable in the field during the breeding season, when they sing and their voices enable them to be distinguished. More than 70 species occur in southern Africa and many of these will be encountered by even the most casual observer visiting the region. One can dismiss them all as unidentifiable "LBJs" ("little brown jobs"), although a little bit of preparation will go a long way to sorting out the identity of many of the species one meets along the way.

Cisticolas and *prinias* belong to a related family, the Cisticolidae. They are among Africa's most notoriously unidentifiable warbler groups, and with 18 species found in southern Africa, they are likely to be encountered everywhere. They are small or tiny, buff-colored, streaky birds that live in grasslands, shrublands, and savannah, and in any one place 3 or 4 species are often present. Habitat choice is the first key to their identification, length of tail the second, and voice the third. LEVAILLANT'S CISTICOLA (Plate 65), for instance, is long-tailed and restricted to places where tall grass or sedges are found; because of this, it is usually found, often abundantly, in wetlands. The WING-SNAPPING (or AYRES') CISTICOLA (Plate 64), a short-tailed species, favors shortly cropped, upland grasslands, and it too is often the most abundant bird in such habitats. A third very common cisticola, found everywhere in savannah country, is the longish-tailed RATTLING CISTICOLA (Plate 65), easily identifiable (at least in summer when it sings!) by the throaty rattle it uses to conclude its chirping call. Thus, each cisticola has a combination of characteristics that gives away its identity.

Prinias are long-tailed versions of cisticolas, and they are easily identified as a group by this feature and by their behavior of cocking their tails vertically as they hop about in the shrubbery. The crombecs, of which the LONG-BILLED CROMBEC (Plate 62) is a common example, are also easily identified warblers because they have absurdly short tails, and in flight they appear tailless. Reedbeds and marshes are favorite warbler habitats and at least a dozen species frequent such places. Many of these are real skulkers, and in their case, voice is the key to finding and identifying them. Forest and tall woodland canopies are inhabited by a particular group of warblers known as *apalises*; they are quite distinctive, having a crisp chest collar (as, for example, the BAR-THROATED APALIS, Plate 63), yellow plumage, or some other similar feature.

Natural History

Ecology and Behavior

The majority of southern Africa's warblers are sedentary and territorial, and they live in pairs that remain around the year in the same places. In summer, when they breed, the males often call and display with great vigor, whereas in winter they become largely silent and are much less detectable. Many cisticolas perform aerial display flights that make them particularly conspicuous; male Wing-snapping Cisticolas, for example, cruise about, way up in the sky, uttering a squeaky song, and when they descend to the ground they plummet down, making loud wing-snaps as they drop. In summer, the hilltops where they live often reverberate with the sound of displaying birds, in stark contrast to their behavior in winter, when they become silent and furtive and leave the ground with great reluctance. The migration performed by Europe's warblers to Africa is a remarkable feat by any standards. How does a little bird such as the Willow Warbler, weighing a mere 9 g (0.3 oz), make a journey of 8,000 km (5,000 mi) twice a year, without the benefit of being able to soar or use prevailing winds, faithfully returning each year to its natal area in Europe and its wintering area in Africa? Vast numbers of such birds pour into Africa as the weather in Europe turns cold, and the numbers of Willow Warblers, just one of the many migrants entering Africa, has been estimated at a thousand million birds. These birds put on body fat to fuel the migration and they fly at night, settling in woodland along the way during the day to fuel up for the next night's leg. For such birds the benefit of living in summer climates year-round, with continuously high insect availability, outweighs the high cost of migrating.

Breeding

Not unexpectedly, southern Africa's warblers have very diverse nesting habits. Most are monogamous breeders, although some cisticolas are known to be polygamous. The types of nests built by the various species range from open-cupped structures to enclosed balls; some are placed on the ground or inside grass tufts or thick clusters of leaves, others are suspended from trailing branches. Prinias make an enclosed purse-shaped nest woven from thin strands of green grass, using similar techniques to those used by true weaver-birds. Several species, for example the very similar GRAY-BACKED and GREEN-BACKED CAMAROPTERAS (or BLEATING WARBLERS, both Plate 63), are locally known as "tailor-birds" on account of their nests, which are enclosed by the broad leaves of a tree or shrub, these being sewn together using strands of cobweb threaded through tiny holes in the leaves. Without exception, the nests of warblers are well concealed and difficult to find. Most species lay between 2 and 4 eggs per clutch and parental care is rather variable; in many, the female incubates without male assistance, but feeding of the nestlings is almost invariably shared by both parents. Incubation and nestling periods vary among species and lie in the range of 12 to 21 days and 12 to 19 days, respectively.

Notes

Many warbler species are commonly parasitized by cuckoos, honeyguides, and by a parasitic weaver known as the Cuckoo Finch, in relationships that are complex and highly evolved. Apalises and crombecs, for example, are commonly parasitized by the Klaas's Cuckoo, which lays a variety of egg types in order to match those of its hosts. The GREEN-BACKED CAMAROPTERA is host to another closely related cuckoo, the Emerald Cuckoo, which, in southern Africa, specializes in parasitizing just this warbler, laying a similar-colored egg to that of its host. Curiously, the very similar GRAY-BACKED CAMAROPTERA is not parasitized by this or any other cuckoo. Many cisticolas and prinias are parasitized by the Cuckoo Finch and the Brown-backed Honeybird, and it is not uncommon for these hosts to have more than one parasite egg laid in their nests and to hatch and rear them successfully. Cisticolas and prinias lay eggs that are very variably colored and marked, and it is often suggested that this behavior has evolved in these hosts to enable them to better detect any parasite's eggs laid in their nests, since such *polychromatism* decreases the parasite's chances of laying a closely matched egg.

Status

None of the southern African warblers are threatened, although a few species, the VICTORIN'S WARBLER (Plate 62) being one, are confined to very specific habitats and narrowly restricted ranges.

Profiles

Chestnut-vented Tit-Babbler, *Parisoma subcaeruleum*, Plate 62a
Lesser Swamp-Warbler, *Acrocephalus gracilirostris*, Plate 62b
Little Rush-Warbler, *Bradypterus baboecala*, Plate 62c

Victorin's Warbler, *Bradypterus victorini*, Plate 62d
Willow Warbler, *Phylloscopus trochilus*, Plate 62e
Long-billed Crombec, *Sylvietta rufescens*, Plate 62f
Bar-throated Apalis, *Apalis thoracica*, Plate 63a
Yellow-bellied Eremomela, *Eremomela icteropygialis*, Plate 63b
Cape Grassbird, *Sphenoeacus afer*, Plate 63c
Green-backed Camaroptera, *Cameroptera brachyura*, Plate 63d
Gray-backed Camaroptera, *Cameroptera brevicaudata*, Plate 63e
Zitting Cisticola, *Cisticola juncidis*, Plate 64a
Wing-snapping Cisticola, *Cisticola ayresii*, Plate 64b
Gray-backed Cisticola, *Cisticola subruficapilla*, Plate 64c
Wailing Cisticola, *Cisticola lais*, Plate 64d
Neddicky, *Cisticola fulvicapilla*, Plate 64e
Rattling Cisticola, *Cisticola chiniana*, Plate 65a
Levaillant's Cisticola, *Cisticola tinniens*, Plate 65b
Tawny-flanked Prinia, *Prinia subflava*, Plate 65c
Black-chested Prinia, *Prinia flavicans*, Plate 65d
Spotted Prinia, *Prinia maculosa*, Plate 65e

23. African Flycatchers

Aerial insects, especially flies, provide a vast food resource for insectivorous birds, and in different parts of the world different bird families have evolved to exploit this type of prey. These fly-catching birds are typically small and agile on the wing, and they hunt mostly from perches, from which they make short sallying flights to pursue passing aerial insects. A common feature in these birds is a short bill that is broad at its base and usually surrounded by a well-developed fringe of bristles (*rictal bristles*) that assist the bird in grabbing flying insects. The *African flycatchers* do not belong to a single homogeneous family but rather to three groups that are probably genetically unrelated, and even less closely related to the flycatchers found on other continents. One group consists of birds that have crests (*crested flycatchers*) and among them is the delightful little AFRICAN PARADISE-FLYCATCHER (Plate 67), a warm orange-brown bird with a greenish head and, in males, greatly elongated tail streamers. A second group consists of very small, short-tailed birds with mainly black-and-white plumage that are known as *batises* (and in some species, as *wattle-eyes*). The third group consists of the "Old World Flycatchers," which are the original birds to be named "flycatcher" and which belong to the family Muscicapidae (from Latin; *musci* = flies, *capa*, from *captus* = to catch). The three groups together comprise about 70 species found in Africa as a whole, and 22 in southern Africa. Athough they are not so conspicuous as some birds, they are nonetheless commonly encountered when travelling through the subcontinent.

Natural History

Ecology and Behavior

The African flycatchers are found in most wooded or bushy habitats in southern Africa, and they are represented by species in humid lowland forests, in higher-elevation forests, in savannahs, in shrublands, and even along the fringes of deserts. But, because flycatchers are dependent on perches from which to hunt, they are not found unless trees or shrubs are present, so the grasslands of South Africa are devoid of these birds. The "Old World" flycatchers use a "perch-and-watch" hunting technique. They hunt mostly from a perch within a meter or two (3 to 6 ft) of the ground, and from this they fly out after prey, catch it, and return to the perch to eat it. The SPOTTED FLYCATCHER (Plate 66)—when it is present—is the most widespread and abundant of these. It is a seasonal visitor to Africa from Europe, arriving in November and departing in March. It snaps up most of its prey on the wing, but it also alights on the ground and catches insects there, especially in rainy weather when flying insects are temporarily grounded. There are several species in this group, for instance the resident MARICO FLYCATCHER and the locally migratory FISCAL FLYCATCHER (both Plate 66), that almost always take their prey from the ground rather than catching it in flight. They hunt from perches in the same way, but methodically scan the ground below rather than the surrounding airspace. At intervals while hunting, or when no prey is forthcoming, they move on to another perch.

Batises and wattle-eyes are arboreal birds that forage in the canopies and interiors of trees. The hunting technique that these species share is to move at intervals through a tree, pausing at each stop to scan the surroundings, usually slowly revolving their heads, in a way reminiscent of the eye movements of a chameleon. When a prey item is detected, the bird flits up to catch it, often collecting it with an audible bill-snap. These birds are common members of "mixed species bird parties"—groups of insectivorous birds that, especially in winter, move around together in search of food. In southern Africa, the individual batis species each occupy a distinctly different habitat, so that their respective ranges hardly overlap; the CAPE BATIS (Plate 67), for instance, lives in higher-elevation forests, the CHINSPOT BATIS (Plate 67) lives in savannah, and the PRIRIT BATIS (Plate 67) is largely restricted to arid shrublands. Batises are non-migratory, and once established, live as pairs in permanently occupied territories. The "crested flycatchers" are mostly forest-dwelling birds and they hunt in much the same way as batises. Some of these species, while moving from perch to perch, have the habit of fanning their tails, apparently to scare or lure insects into flight. The African Paradise-Flycatcher, which is a summer migrant to the region, favors shady glades in forests and tall woodland, and it has become a common visitor to well-wooded parks and gardens.

Breeding

The African flycatchers are monogamous breeders but the roles of the sexes in the nesting cycle are rather variable. In some species (batises , for example) the female builds the nest and undertakes the incubation without male assistance, whereas in others these activities are shared. In batises, and in some of the other flycatchers, the male of the pair brings food to his partner as she incubates. In all known cases both parents assist in feeding the nestlings. The nests and nest sites also exhibit much variability, although they are always open-cupped structures. In some (for instance, AFRICAN DUSKY FLYCATCHER, Plate 66) the nest is an untidy wad of material built into a cavity in a tree or rock; in other species (for instance, African Paradise-Flycatcher) it is delicately made, shaped like a wine glass and built into a thin forked branch that is suspended above a clearing or over a stream. The incubation and nestling periods in these birds range between 13 to 19 days and 11 to 18 days, respectively.

Status

Most of the southern African flycatchers have extensive ranges and are common. WOODWARD'S BATIS is restricted to coastal and lowland forests, and although not considered threatened, it is the most range-restricted member of the group.

Profiles

Spotted Flycatcher, *Muscicapa striata*, Plate 66a
African Dusky Flycatcher, *Muscicapa adusta*, Plate 66b
Marico Flycatcher, *Melaenornis mariquensis*, Plate 66c
Fiscal Flycatcher, *Sigelus silens*, Plate 66d
Cape Batis, *Batis capensis*, Plate 67a
Chinspot Batis, *Batis molitor*, Plate 67b
Pririt Batis, *Batis pririt*, Plate 67c
African Paradise-Flycatcher, *Terpsiphone viridis*, Plate 67d

24. Shrikes

The *shrikes* constitute one of the most characteristic groups of birds found in sub-Saharan Africa. They are mostly conspicuous, striking-looking or colorful, and they are always interesting. There are very few places that one might travel through in Africa where one or more species of shrikes won't be present, and many habitats support 10 or 12; in fact, 64 of the world's 78 shrike species occur on the continent, and 26 of these are found in southern Africa. Shrikes are uniformly small birds (mostly about 20 to 25 cm, 8 to 10 in long) and their most distinctive feature is a strongly hooked bill. They are rather short-legged, and with a few exceptions (most notably the MAGPIE SHRIKE, Plate 70), they have tails that are shorter in length than their bodies. Their plumages are distinctive, and the identification of the various species seldom poses any difficulty. Many species have striking black-and-white plumage (usually with white underparts and black upperparts); some are colored mainly green and yellow (some *bush-shrikes*), and some have rich chestnut-colored wings (*tchagras*). An unusual group, known as the *helmet-shrikes*, have a puff of bristle-like feathers that protrude from their foreheads over their bills, and the males of another group, the *puffbacks*, have long, fluffy rump feathers that can be raised during courtship displays. The taxonomic relationship between these different types of shrikes has been debated over the years, and current thinking is that they comprise two unrelated families, the "true shrikes" (family Laniidae), and the remainder (bush-shrikes, tchagras, helmet-shrikes, and so on) that make up the family Malaconotidae.

Outside of the breeding period, "true shrikes" are mainly solitary; species such as the COMMON FISCAL, RED-BACKED SHRIKE, and LESSER GRAY SHRIKE (all Plate 69) are typical in this respect. These shrikes perch conspicuously and are easily seen. The Magpie Shrike, another conspicuous "true shrike," is exceptional in being gregarious throughout the year; one can often see 4 or 5 of these birds perched together on a treetop. The majority of the other shrikes, however, do not perch in the open, and some of them are real skulkers. But what they lack in visibility, they make up in voice and, once heard, the calls of some of these are not likely to be forgotten. The BOKMAKIERIE (Plate 70), for example, derives its odd-sounding name from its fluty whistling notes "bok, mak, irie." Another species, the GORGEOUS BUSH-SHRIKE, utters a penetrating whistle that sounds like "kong, kong, kooit" and, although always very difficult to see, its call is a familiar sound of the dense bush thickets in areas where it occurs. Some bush-shrikes call in duet, the female responding to the male's notes with split-second precision so that the call seems to come from one bird. Bokmakieries commonly duet like this, but the best-known duetters are the group of shrikes known as *boubous* (for instance, the SOUTHERN BOUBOU and TROPICAL BOUBOU, both Plate 69), and in these it is rare to hear the male calling without hearing a responding duet from its mate. These are species that live year-round in pairs in permanently defended territories, and their duetting behavior apparently serves to maintain the pair-bond and to advertise occupation of the territory. The CRIMSON-BREASTED SHRIKE (Plate 69) is another duetter that belongs to this boubou group, but instead of having white underparts like the rest of the clan, its are a startlingly vivid red, and one's first glimpse of this elusive thornveld bird usually has the effect of taking one's breath away.

Natural History

Ecology and Behavior

Shrikes are found in most terrestrial habitats in southern Africa, from the leafy canopies of dense evergreen forests to the edges of desert. The richest shrike habitats, though, lie in the savannah region, and a mosaic of wooded habitats here often supports up to a dozen species. Some of these species live in the leafy canopy of the trees and feed on caterpillars and other foliage insects; some perch-hunt from vantage points overlooking open ground, and others forage on the ground beneath shrubbery or under cover of other vegetation. All shrikes are insectivorous, although some of the large species are also accomplished predators of rodents and small reptiles and birds. Several, especially the boubous, commonly rob other bird's nests of eggs and young. The Common Fiscal is one of the more predatory species, and it also has the habit of storing surplus items of food by hanging them on thorns or on the barbs of barbed-wire fences, a behavior that has earned it nicknames such as "Butcher-bird" and "Jacky Hangman." This is one of the common roadside birds in much of South Africa, as it uses fences and telephone lines from which to hunt. In summer it often shares its habitat with two migratory species, the Red-backed Shrike and Lesser Gray Shrike, both of which breed in Europe and spend the non-breeding season in southern Africa. All three are typical "perch-and-hunt" shrikes.

Most African shrikes are territorial and live in pairs, but there are several species that live year-round in family groups, and all the members of these groups cooperate in territory defense and in the breeding cycle. These cooperative breeders include the Magpie Shrike and SOUTHERN WHITE-CROWNED SHRIKE, but the best-known exponents of the system are the helmet-shrikes. WHITE-CRESTED HELMET-SHRIKES (Plate 70), which are common and very typical of the helmet-shrikes, live in parties of between 3 and 12 birds that share a common territory. One pair of birds in the group dominates the others and reduces their roles to that of helpers; although all members participate in the chores, only the dominant pair gets to breed. *Cooperative breeding* is particularly strongly developed in bird families found in Africa, and helmet-shrikes, together with babblers (where the subject is discussed further) and wood-hoopoes, provide the best examples of this behavior to be seen in the bird world.

Breeding

Shrikes build their open-cupped nests in trees, creepers, shrubs, and matted undergrowth. The "true shrikes" tend to build a rather bulky, poorly concealed nest, whereas many of the other shrikes build cunningly concealed nests, in some cases blending the nest with its surroundings by covering it with lichen or cobwebs. There is much variation among species in the pattern of parental attendance at the nest. Nest building is done by just the female in some species and by both sexes in others. Similarly, the incubation is done only by the female in some, but is shared in others. The "true shrikes" have a system resembling that found in many birds of prey whereby the female, who does the incubation without male assistance, is fed by the male during this period. Once the nestlings hatch, it is usual in all shrikes for the nestlings to be fed by both parents, assisted by helpers in those species that breed cooperatively. Shrikes lay clutches numbering between 2 and 4 eggs and their incubation and nestling periods range from 14 to 18 days and 14 to 22 days, respectively.

Notes

Cuckoos often target shrikes as hosts for their eggs, and there are three cuckoo species that specialize in parasitizing these birds. The Thick-billed Cuckoo is dependent on just one host, the RETZ'S (RED-BILLED) HELMET-SHRIKE, for its survival, and its eggs are indistinguishable from those of its host. The Black Cuckoo specializes in parasitizing various boubou shrikes, and it too lays eggs that are a close match to those of its hosts. Such close matching suggests that the host-parasite association has been a long-standing one, in which hosts have developed the ability to distinguish and eject foreign eggs, only to have this matched by the parasite evolving the ability to lay eggs that match those of the host and thus they cannot be easily distinguished; it has been aptly described as an "evolutionary arms race." The third cuckoo-shrike association is apparently recent in origin as it has not yet evolved to this level of sophistication: Jacobin Cuckoos commonly parasitize the Common Fiscal (among a variety of other host species), laying a large, plain white egg in the nest alongside the shrike's heavily mottled greenish-gray eggs. Despite the mismatch, these particular shrikes do not evict the cuckoo's egg and, when it hatches, they raise the cuckoo chick. These cuckoos use many host species, sometimes getting away with it, sometimes not.

Status

As a group, the shrikes in southern Africa have not fared badly in the face of many land transformations and none of the species are threatened.

Profiles

Common Fiscal, *Lanius collaris*, Plate 69a
Lesser Gray Shrike, *Lanius minor*, Plate 69b
Red-backed Shrike, *Lanius collurio*, Plate 69c
Southern Boubou, *Laniarius ferrugineus*, Plate 69d
Tropical Boubou, *Laniarius aethiopicus*, Plate 69e
Crimson-breasted Shrike, *Laniarius atrococcineus*, Plate 69f
Magpie Shrike, *Corvinella melanoleuca*, Plate 70a
Black-backed Puffback, *Dryoscopus cubla*, Plate 70b
Brown-crowned Tchagra, *Tchagra australis*, Plate 70c
Black-crowned Tchagra, *Tchagra senegala*, Plate 70d
White-crested Helmet-Shrike, *Prionops plumatus*, Plate 70e
Bokmakierie, *Telophorus zeylonus*, Plate 70f

25. Starlings and Oxpeckers

Starlings (family Sturnidae) are an Old World bird family found mainly in Asia and Africa, but they have close kin in the New World in the form of mockingbirds and thrashers. North America also has a starling, though many inhabitants probably wish it was not there—the COMMON (or EUROPEAN) STARLING, an extremely successful bird that was introduced more than a century ago and is now firmly established across the continent. The Common Starling provides the mold for this quite diverse family: these are all small to medium-sized, stockily built birds (about 16 to 45 cm, 6 to 18 in, long) with well-developed legs and feet and moderately long, sharp-pointed bills; they are gregarious by nature, omnivorous, and they forage mostly on the ground, walking with purposeful strides. About 50 of the world's 110 species are found in Africa and 14 of these occur naturally in southern Africa, plus two more which have been introduced (one of which is the Common Starling).

About half the starling species in Africa, birds known collectively as *glossy starlings*, have iridescent dark blue plumage and these species all resemble each other quite closely, differing mainly in size, tail length, eye color, or some minor plumage feature. Many of the glossy starling species become tame and confiding around sources of food, for example at picnic sites and rest camps in game parks; and their antics at such places often provide as much entertainment for visitors as do the lions and elephants. The species most addicted to eating the remains of sandwiches and discarded food under picnic tables in southern Africa are the CAPE GLOSSY STARLING and GREATER BLUE-EARED STARLING (both Plate 72). The blue coloration in these birds is not derived from a pigment, but is created by a particular microstructure in the feathers that refracts light. The iridescence and changing tints in the bird's plumage is dependent on the intensity of the incoming light and the changing angle from which the bird is viewed. Although the VIOLET-BACKED (or PLUM-COLORED) STARLING (Plate 72) is not one of the glossy starlings, it too has brilliantly iridescent plumage; in this instance it is only the male bird's upperparts, head, and neck that are a glossy violet color. Most starlings are *monomorphic* (the sexes are alike) and this is one of the few exceptions, the female being a streaky brown-and-white bird that is barely recognizable as a starling. Another unusual feature of the Violet-backed Starling is that it is migratory. Although many starlings are nomadic, this is the only southern African species to undergo a regular seasonal movement, in this case from southern Africa, where it breeds in summer, to tropical Africa, where it spends the winter.

The *non-glossy starlings* in the region vary a great deal. One species, the WATTLED STARLING, is a mainly white to grayish-white bird with black wings and tail; at the onset of breeding, males grow floppy, loose-skinned black wattles that hang from their heads. Two others, the RED-WINGED STARLING (Plate 71) and its sister species, the PALE-WINGED STARLING, are black birds with wings that are chestnut-colored and buff-colored respectively. *Oxpeckers*, often classified as a subfamily of starlings, are unusually dependent on large mammals for their survival. They forage on ticks and other parasites that they find on the skin of animals such as giraffe, buffalo, rhinos, and other game, obtaining these by clambering about on the body of the host animal. There are 2 oxpecker species, easily distinguishable by their differently colored bills, and both have sharply hooked claws that give them purchase on the mammals' skin. The most widespread of the two is the RED-BILLED OXPECKER (Plate 71). These, like all the other starlings of the region, are gregarious birds, and hundreds may be found where large herds of game, especially buffalo, are gathered. In the case of the Wattled Starling, flocks may number tens of thousands of birds. Even those starling species that live year-round in pairs, such as the BURCHELL'S STARLING (Plate 72), often gather with other starlings to sleep in communal roosts at night.

Natural History

Ecology and Behavior

In general, starlings are *omnivorous* birds, but some species specialize in either a particular spectrum of food or a particular way of foraging. The Violet-backed Starling is a fruit-eating specialist and it rarely descends to the ground when foraging, whereas a species such as the PIED STARLING (Plate 71) is mainly a terrestrial bird that only forages on the ground. Wattled Starlings are specialists in locating and preying on locust swarms. When these are not available Wattled Starlings take fruit and other foods, but their breeding is dependent on and closely geared to locust invasions—as a result the birds are often known as "locust birds." Huge flocks of these birds gather at locust outbreaks, where males rapidly acquire their strange-looking breeding plumage and nesting quickly gets underway. They are extremely nomadic birds, found mainly in the semi-arid savannahs and living a "here-today-gone-tomorrow" existence. Oxpeckers are even more specialized in their food habits. The Red-billed Oxpecker is the less specialized of the two species, foraging on a wider spectrum of host animals from giraffe, buffalo, and rhinos to small antelope and even warthogs. Its preference, though, is for hosts that are not flighty or too quick in their movements, that aggregate together, and that remain in relatively open terrain. The Red-billed Oxpecker locates ticks by a bill action known as "scissoring," in which it half-opens the bill and runs it sideways through the hair on the mammal's skin, snapping up any parasites it encounters.

Symbiosis with mammals is a prevalent feature in other starling species' behavior too. Red-winged Starlings sometimes ride on the backs of antelope and Pied Starlings often forage among the feet of grazing animals, commonly gathering in numbers around herds of dairy cattle, flocks of sheep, and so on, just as the glossy starlings flock around picnic sites. The two foreign starling species introduced to South Africa a century ago, the Common Starling in Cape Town and the COMMON (or INDIAN) MYNA (Plate 71) in Durban, have both extended their ranges for more than 1,000 km (600 mi) inland as a result of their ability to live alongside humans and exploit manmade habitats for their own benefit. These birds live in cities and towns across large parts of South Africa, feeding on lawns, around trash dumps and sewage works, and generally wherever food is available, and they use holes in buildings for nest sites.

Breeding

Monogamy is the usual breeding system of starlings, with several species, especially oxpeckers, being cooperative breeders. In most species nest-building, incubation, and nestling care is shared by the sexes. Starlings typically nest in holes, which may be in buildings (Common Myna, Common Starling), in trees (oxpeckers and most species of glossy starlings), in rock faces (Red-winged and Pale-winged Starlings) and in earth banks (Pied Starling). The exception to the rule is the Wattled Starling, which constructs a large, enclosed, ball-shaped nest of twigs. It and the Pied Starling are colonial breeders; the latter species is also unusual in that it excavates a long tunnel into an earth bank, much as kingfishers and bee-eaters do when nesting, and the nest is placed at the end of this. Other hole-nesters also build bulky, open-cupped nests in the cavities they occupy. Typically 3 or 4 eggs are laid per clutch, and with few exceptions, starlings lay bright blue eggs, in some cases spotted with red-brown. Their incubation and nestling periods are somewhat variable, ranging between 11 and 18 days and 18 to 30 days, respectively.

Status

Oxpeckers are the most threatened group in the starling family in southern Africa. Once widespread across the region, these birds have become fragmented and restricted in their ranges as a result of the use of toxic chemicals to control ticks and other parasites on commercially farmed cattle. Tick control involves the periodic dipping or spraying of cattle with an insecticide that remains on the animal's skin as a tick repellent—even arsenic was used for this purpose in the past. The result of this, for oxpeckers, was their total extinction from all commercial cattle-farming areas where dipping was practiced. The YELLOW-BILLED OXPECKER became extinct in South Africa in about 1950 and the Red-billed Oxpecker shrank from most of its range in the 1950s and 1960s, remaining common only in large game parks such as Kruger National Park. In the past decade, bird-safe dips have been introduced and oxpeckers are now slowly making a comeback. Although commercial cattle herds may not carry ticks on which the birds can feed, at least it is safe for them to settle on these animals, and provided there are indigenous ungulates in the area, oxpeckers can survive in these farming areas. The birds have been successfully assisted by numerous translocations of flocks from residual populations into areas where they became extinct, and the Yellow-billed Oxpecker is now back in South Africa; although still rated as vulnerable in the country, its tenure is now more assured.

Profiles

Common Starling, *Sturnus vulgaris*, Plate 71a
Common Myna, *Acridotheres tristis*, Plate 71b
Pied Starling, *Spreo bicolor*, Plate 71d
Red-winged Starling, *Onychognathus morio*, Plate 71e
Violet-backed Starling, *Cinnyricinclus leucogaster*, Plate 72a
Burchell's Starling, *Lamprotornis australis*, Plate 72b
Cape Glossy Starling, *Lamprotornis nitens*, Plate 72c
Greater Blue-eared Starling, *Lamprotornis chalybeus*, Plate 72d
Black-bellied Starling, *Lamprotornis corruscus*, Plate 72e
Red-billed Oxpecker, *Buphagus erythrorhynchus*, Plate 71c

26. Sunbirds, Sugarbirds, and White-eyes

What hummingbirds are to the New World, *sunbirds* are to the Old World; these two nectar-feeding families of hyperactive little birds have so much in common, yet they are not remotely related to one another. Sunbirds (family Nectariniidae) are small to tiny birds and they have long, thin, down-curved bills, short but strong legs, and in the males of most species, brightly colored, iridescent plumages. Some of the larger species have elongated central tail feathers, but in others the tail is usually short. Sunbirds and hummingbirds both subsist on nectar and they both have a similar tongue structure that enables them to suck this liquid from the flowers that produce it. Their tongues are basically long, thin, extendible tubes, with a pump at the throat and a hole at the tip; the tip is dipped into the nectar and this is sucked into the bird's throat in an action lasting a few seconds. The most obvious difference between the two groups is that "hummers" suck nectar while hovering in front of the plant, whereas sunbirds perch on the plant as they feed.

There are about 120 sunbird species in the world (compared with over 300 hummingbird species) and Africa is home to the majority of these (about 80), followed closely by Asia; nowhere in the world do the two families meet or overlap. Southern Africa has a good cross-section of sunbirds, and the 21 species found here include some of the largest (for example, the MALACHITE SUNBIRD, Plate 73), and some of the tiniest (COLLARED SUNBIRD, Plate 74, for instance). Apart from size, bill length, and plumage differences, however, sunbirds are a remarkably uniform bird family, diverging very little in morphology, behavior, or ecology. The greatest diversity of sunbirds in this region occurs along the warm, wet, eastern seaboard, where a mosaic of coastal forest, lowland forest, and savannah provides a rich mix of habitats, and it is not uncommon here to find 5 or 6 species foraging in a single flowering tree. But as one moves westwards into drier areas, this diversity diminishes so that by Namaqualand and southern Namibia only one, the desert-living DUSKY SUNBIRD (Plate 75), is to be found, despite the flowering aloes that are sometimes present in this arid region. In all except two species in southern Africa, male sunbirds are brightly colored and females are drab, and whereas males are easily identified by their coloration, females of the different species can be easily mistaken for one another.

Sugarbirds belong to an entirely unrelated bird family (Promeropidae), and it is simply convergence that has led both sugarbirds and sunbirds to their nectar-dependence, to having similar morphologies (forms), and to being commonly found alongside each other. The sugarbirds comprise a family of just 2 species, the CAPE SUGARBIRD and the GURNEY'S SUGARBIRD (both Plate 73), and the two have complementary ranges, the first being restricted to the southern Cape and the second to the escarpment mountains that run northwards from Eastern Cape to Zimbabwe. They are both thus endemic to southern Africa, and this bird family is the only one that is endemic to the region. The two sugarbird species are much alike, dull brownish birds with long, thin, curved bills and long tails. Their tongue structures differ from those of sunbirds (although they serve the same purpose of sucking in nectar) and their plumages lack the metallic sheen found in male sunbirds.

The *white-eye* family is often treated as an extension to the sunbird clan, but they are unrelated and instead have their closest taxonomic links with warblers. The connection with sunbirds is that they also feed, at least to some extent, on nectar, despite their having shorter bills and tongues that lack a sucking mechanism. White-eyes (family Zosteropidae) have a very distinctive appearance due to the white ring of fine feathers that encircles each eye; otherwise they are small to tiny warbler-like birds that are, in most species, mainly green-colored. Like sunbirds, they are an Old World family, and they consist of about 85 species spread across Africa, Asia, Australia, and many of the Indian Ocean islands. There are 2 species in southern Africa, of which the CAPE WHITE-EYE (Plate 74) is a very typical family member.

Natural History

Ecology and Behavior

Sunbirds inhabit virtually the entire spectrum of non-aquatic habitats in southern Africa, some species (GRAY SUNBIRD, Plate 75, for example) living in the interiors of evergreen forests, some living in savannah country (MARICO SUNBIRD and WHITE-BELLIED SUNBIRD, both Plate 75), some in shrublands (including the ORANGE-BREASTED SUNBIRD, Plate 74, a species that is restricted to the protea plant communities in the southern Cape), at least one species lives in grassland (Malachite Sunbird), and one (Dusky Sunbird) lives on the edges of deserts. Everywhere, though, sunbirds are dependent on flowers that produce nectar, and the range of plants used by the birds is enormous. Aloes are much favored, as are mistletoes, coral-trees, tobacco-bush, tecomarias, kniphofias, and hallerias. A tree in full flower or a patch of flowering aloes holds a magnetic attraction for these birds, and dozens of them may gather to harvest such nectar sources with much jostling, flitting between flowers, twittering song, and general activity taking place around the food source. When the flower crop comes to an end, the sunbirds move elsewhere, and although they don't migrate as such, they do move about widely in response to the ever-changing availability of flowers. Sugarbirds do much the same thing, although they are particularly dependent on proteas for nectar and their breeding is timed to coincide with the flowering periods of their preferred protea species. The birds are territorial at this time, but once the proteas have finished flowering, like sunbirds, sugarbirds move around according to nectar availability and are often gregarious.

White-eyes spend most of their time foraging in the leafy canopies of trees. They occur in abundance in evergreen forests and very commonly in broad-leafed woodlands and wooded parks and gardens. In spring, when their song is most prolific, their wispy, rambling notes are a familiar sound in such habitats. In addition to taking nectar, they eat small berries, other fruit, and small insects, such as aphids, gleaned from leaf buds. They are gregarious, except when nesting, and flocks of a dozen or more birds are commonly encountered.

Breeding

The nests and nesting habits of sunbirds, sugarbirds, and white-eyes differ greatly, showing just how unrelated these three families are. Sunbirds of all species build consistently similar nests—they are small and oval-shaped, suspended at the roof from a twig or creeper, and they have a ragged appearance, being built with rough, dry plant material, a tail of which often trails below the nest, bound together with cobweb. Different species build their nests with different materials, and the identity of a nest's owner can usually be told from this, with some species building their nests mainly from dead leaves, others using lichen, and so on. The entrance to the nest is near the top of one side and, in many species, it has a roof protruding over it. White-eyes and sugarbirds build open-cupped nests, those of white-eyes resembling the nests of many warblers: small, neatly finished, and slung between leafy twigs of a tree or bush. Sugarbird nests are bulky, untidy bowls much like the nests built by thrushes, and they are hidden inside a leafy protea bush. As far as is known, the species in each family are monogamous. In white-eyes, though, both parents build the nest and share the incubation and nestling care, whereas in sugarbirds and sunbirds, nest-building and incubation is done by the female alone; males assist to varying degrees in feeding the nestlings, the trait occurance itself varying according to species. Between 1 and 3 eggs per clutch are laid (sunbirds and sugarbirds usually lay 2, white-eyes 3) and incubation and nestling periods range between 11 and 17 days and 13 and 23 days, respectively.

Notes

Mounted sunbirds were popular collectables during Victorian times; they were displayed in glass cabinets in drawing rooms, with male birds of the most colorful and iridescent species being especially popular. A proverb in the Xhosa language uses the phrase "the person has a sunbird's tongue," implying that the person cannot be trusted with a secret, as he or she does just what the sunbird does, going from one flower to the other, whispering in their "ears."

Status

A few species of sunbirds in southern Africa have restricted ranges but none are at risk; nor are any of the white-eyes or sugarbirds in the region. Elsewhere in their range, though, several island-living and forest-dependent species of white-eyes in East and West Africa are ranked as critically endangered.

Profiles

Cape Sugarbird, *Promerops cafer*, Plate 73a
Gurney's Sugarbird, *Promerops gurneyi*, Plate 73b
Malachite Sunbird, *Nectarinia famosa*, Plate 73c
Orange-breasted Sunbird, *Nectarinia violacea*, Plate 74a
Greater Double-collared Sunbird, *Nectarinia afer*, Plate 74b
Southern Double-collared Sunbird, *Nectarinia chalybea*, Plate 74c
Collared Sunbird, *Anthreptes collaris*, Plate 74d
Cape White-eye, *Zosterops pallidus*, Plate 74e
Marico Sunbird, *Nectarinia mariquensis*, Plate 75a
White-bellied Sunbird, *Nectarinia talatala*, Plate 75b
Dusky Sunbird, *Nectarinia fusca*, Plate 75c
Gray Sunbird, *Nectarinia veroxii*, Plate 75d
Scarlet-chested Sunbird, *Nectarinia senegalensis*, Plate 75e
Amethyst Sunbird, *Nectarinia amethystina*, Plate 75f

27. Sparrows, Weavers, Bishops, and Widowbirds

Sparrows need no introduction to most people because they are probably the single most familiar group of birds to be found anywhere in the world. There are about 20 species of "true sparrows," and these are mostly African birds; the global familiarity with sparrows is not based on these, however, but on a single species, the HOUSE SPARROW (Plate 76), that has undergone a remarkable world expansion in its range in the past century. It has spread in this time from Europe to the Americas, Africa, Asia, and Australia and New Zealand, as well as many oceanic islands; as we speak, there is probably a group of these irrepressible little birds somewhere in the world settling in at a place where they never occurred previously. House Sparrows were introduced to South Africa in the late 1800s and today they are encountered wherever one travels in southern Africa, from cities to rural villages. The physical appearance of the House Sparrow is very typical of the sparrow family as a whole: these are small birds with mainly brown and gray plumage and, in the males, a black bib. The CAPE SPARROW (Plate 76), a very common species in the drier parts of southern Africa, is the most handsome member of the family, males having, instead of a black bib, a black head with a broad white crescent behind the eye.

Sparrows belong to the family Passeridae and they are closely related to the weavers and widowbirds (family Ploceidae); all of these birds are often collectively referred to as *finches*. About 150 species make up these mainly African bird families and there are several distinctive groups represented in them, especially *sparrow-weavers, weavers, bishops, widowbirds,* and *queleas*. Between them they provide some of Africa's most interesting ornithological spectacles—from colorful plumages and extravagant behaviors to remarkable nests, polygamous mating systems, and flocks numbering millions of birds. They are characterized by being rather uniformly small, slimly built, and having a stout, conical bill that is typical of all seed-eating birds. Sparrows are linked to weavers by a group of birds that share characteristics of both, and the WHITE-BROWED SPARROW-WEAVER (Plate 76) is an example of these, a brown-and-white bird that builds a nest that is somewhere between that of a weaver and a sparrow. The weavers—so-named for the remarkable, finely crafted, kidney-shaped nests that they weave—are mostly bright yellow birds with brown or black throats, masks, or heads. Three species are plentiful in their respective ranges in southern Africa (the SOUTHERN MASKED-WEAVER, CAPE WEAVER, and VILLAGE [or SPOTTED-BACKED] WEAVER, all Plate 78), and their nesting colonies can be seen along the roadsides in many places, suspended from the outer branches of trees, especially where they overhang the water. The sizes of these colonies vary from about a dozen nests in the first two to several hundred in the Village Weaver. Weavers are *sexually dimorphic* (male and female look different), and in most species, males are more brightly colored and more strikingly marked than females; this is only during the breeding season, however, and once breeding is completed, males molt into female-like plumage. For bishops and widows, this sexual dimorphism is even more manifest: here breeding males are commonly black with variable amounts of red or yellow in the plumage, and several species (the LONG-TAILED WIDOWBIRD, Plate 80, for instance) have elongated tail feathers. By contrast, the females have streaky brown plumage and the males revert to this same plumage once breeding is over. Unlike the weavers, most widows and bishops do not nest colonially, and their nests lack both the craftmanship and the conspicuousness of those built by weavers. The SOUTHERN RED BISHOP (Plate 79) is one exception, as it nests colonially and its nest is also finely woven.

The RED-BILLED QUELEA (Plate 79) is the most prolific of Africa's three quelea species, and it is claimed in some quarters to be the most numerous land bird in the world. Flocks numbering millions of birds are a common occurrence, and when feeding on grain on the ground, such flocks rise and fall like great waves as the flock rolls forward, rear birds leapfrogging over the leading birds. Like weavers and widows, queleas are also sexually dimorphic, breeding males acquiring a black mask rimmed with pink or yellow.

Natural History

Ecology and Behavior

With few exceptions, finches are seed-eating birds. Many species feed on grass seed, others on the seeds and fruits of sedges, shrubs, and trees. A few species (RED-HEADED WEAVER, Plate 77, for instance) are mainly insectivorous, and the diets of such species are reflected in their thinner and more pointed bill structures. Most species inhabit open or lightly wooded country, and in the grassland and savannah regions of southern Africa 10 to 15 species in this family often breed alongside each other, each occupying its own particular niche. The rather similar-looking FAN-TAILED WIDOWBIRD, RED-COLLARED WIDOWBIRD, and Long-tailed Widowbird (all Plate 80), for example, may be found in the same general area, but each has a different preference for grass height and either wet or dry ground. In winter, when breeding is over and males have reverted to non-breeding plumage, the different species often form mixed-species flocks. The Red-billed Quelea has developed a liking for small-grained crops, especially manna, millet, and sorghum, and across most of Africa this bird has become a serious crop pest that is feared and hated by grain-growers, irrespective of whether they are subsistence farmers or large commercial operations. An individual quelea eats about 18 g (0.6 oz) of grain a day and at the same time it spills at least the same amount. Given the birds' numbers, the damage to a grain crop can thus be enormous: a smallish flock of, say, a million queleas can consume and damage a crop of sorghum at a rate of 30 to 40 tons per day. Although large sums of money continue to be spent on quelea research and control, no long-term solutions have come to light, and the problem of effective control is compounded by the nomadic behavior and unpredictable movements of queleas and their habit of moving between different countries at different times of the year.

Breeding

The Ploceidae exhibit an immense variability in their breeding habits. Species with the most highly developed sexually dimorphic plumages are generally *polygamous* (or, more specifically, *polygynous*, in which one male has several mates) but several groups—sparrows and queleas, for instance—are monogamous breeders, despite their dimorphism. In the polygynous species the roles of the sexes are clearly divided and females undertake most or all parental care without male assistance. The male's activity is restricted to building nests, displaying to potential mates, and mating with them. Once a female has accepted a nest and commenced laying, his attentions turn elsewhere. The polygynous weavers are particularly prolific nest builders: one male may construct 30 to 50 nests in a single breeding season, tearing down those that don't attract mates and replacing them with fresh structures. The various weaver species all construct broadly similar nests that have an entrance hole that leads into an enclosed nest chamber from below. The nests of the different species vary in detail, though, with some using coarse material to build, others using fine material, some adding long nest tunnels, others lacking this addition, and so on. The nests built by widows and bishops are simpler structures made of coarse grass, and they differ from weaver nests by having side entrances. In some widows, especially the Long-tailed Widowbird, males display in a repeatedly used arena which may be far removed from the nesting area. Red-billed Queleas nest in vast colonies that sometimes stretch over as much as 80 ha (195 ac). Their nests are usually densely packed inside thorn-trees; the males weave these and while the nest is still being built, the female commences laying. These finches are unusual in that they share the incubation and nestling care and they have a remarkably rapid nesting cycle: within 35 to 40 days of the first nests being initiated in a colony, the last chicks fledge and the site is abandoned by the birds.

The claim to nesting fame, however, lies with the SOCIABLE WEAVER (Plate 76), another gregarious species that lives in the arid savannah and along the edges of the Namib Desert. These finches live in flocks of up to 300 birds, and such groups construct and maintain what ranks as the largest nest structure built by any bird in the world. It is a huge dome made of dry grass, usually placed in the branches of a camelthorn tree, with a sloping roof above and a maze of entrance holes that lead into nest chambers below. Such nests can attain a width of 7 m (23 ft) and a height of 4 m (13 ft). Each chamber is occupied by a monogamous breeding pair but all individuals participate in maintaining the nest—which may last for decades—and in repelling predators from it. Very substantial nests are also built by the RED-BILLED BUFFALO-WEAVER (Plate 76), but in their case 2 or 3 males share in the building of a multi-apartment conglomerate, constructed with thorny twigs in the outer branches of a large tree or in the crossbars of an electricity transmission tower. The finches in this family typically lay clutches of 2 or 3 eggs and they have incubation and nestling periods of 11 to 15 days and 17 to 23 days, respectively. Weavers are commonly parasitized by the Diederik Cuckoo, while there is a single weaver species, the CUCKOO FINCH, that is itself parasitic, using small warblers as hosts.

Notes

The reasons for "widowbird" and "bishop" being named thusly relate to their colors, male widowbirds being mainly black birds (a color associated with a bereavement) and male bishops being red and black or gold and black. It is probable that the name "quelea" came from quail, and it has been suggested that references to enormous flocks of quail in the Bible may actually refer to queleas. "Sparrow" owes its origin to an old English word "speerwa," or "little flutterer."

Status

None of the finches (families Passeridae and Ploceidae) in southern Africa is under threat.

Profiles

Red-billed Buffalo-Weaver, *Bubalornis niger*, Plate 76a
White-browed Sparrow-Weaver, *Plocepasser mahali*, Plate 76b
Sociable Weaver, *Philetarius socius*, Plate 76c
House Sparrow, *Passer domesticus*, Plate 76d
Cape Sparrow, *Passer melanurus*, Plate 76e
Southern Gray-headed Sparrow, *Passer diffusus*, Plate 76f
Scaly-feathered Finch, *Sporopipes squamifrons*, Plate 77a
Thick-billed Weaver, *Amblyospiza albifrons*, Plate 77b
Chestnut Weaver, *Ploceus rubiginosus*, Plate 77c
Red-headed Weaver, *Anaplectes rubriceps*, Plate 77d
Cape Weaver, *Ploceus capensis*, Plate 78a
Village Weaver, *Ploceus cucullatus*, Plate 78b
Southern Masked-Weaver, *Ploceus velatus*, Plate 78c
Yellow Weaver, *Ploceus subaureus*, Plate 78d
Southern Red Bishop, *Euplectes orix*, Plate 79a
Red-billed Quelea, *Quelea quelea*, Plate 79b
Yellow-crowned Bishop, *Euplectes afer*, Plate 79c
Yellow Bishop, *Euplectes capensis*, Plate 79d
Long-tailed Widowbird, *Euplectes progne*, Plate 80a
Fan-tailed Widowbird, *Euplectes axillaris*, Plate 80b
Red-collared Widowbird, *Euplectes ardens*, Plate 80c

28. Waxbills and Whydahs

Waxbills (family Estrildidae) and their parasitic counterparts, *whydahs* and *indigo birds* (also called widow-finches, family Vidua), have much in common with the sparrow-weaver-widow clan, and like them, they are commonly referred to collectively as "finches." To distinguish these groups, each one's scientific family name is often added to the word "finch," so that the sparrows, weavers, and widows are commonly referred to as "ploceid-finches," the waxbills as "estrildid-finches," and the whydahs and indigobirds as "vidua-finches." The estrildid-finches are a mainly

African bird family, but some species are found in Asia and Australia; together they number about 125 species worldwide, 28 of which occur in southern Africa. These are small to tiny seed-eating birds, short-legged, slimly built, with short- to medium-length tails and short, conical ("seed-eater") bills. Many are brightly colored, which, coupled with their seed-eating habits, has led to their popularity as caged birds, second only to parrots in this regard. Although the name "waxbill" is often used collectively for all the estrildid-finches, there are several distinctive groups in the family, of which waxbills are only one. There are, for example, *firefinches* (mainly pink and red-colored birds), *pytilias* (green and red birds with barred underparts), *twinspots* (vivid red or green with spotted underparts), *mannikins* (black, white, and chestnut-colored birds) and *cordon-bleus* (blue-colored birds). Males are more colorful than females in some species, but in most instances they are alike. In contrast to weavers, widows, and bishops, the summer and winter plumages of the estrildid-finches do not differ. Some estrildids (mannikins, for instance) are gregarious throughout the year, whereas others live in pairs while nesting and in flocks outside of the breeding season.

The vidua-finches are, like estrildids, small to tiny seed-eaters. They differ by being very markedly sexually dimorphic, with the males having distinctly different breeding and non-breeding plumages. The females of the various viduas are short-tailed, streaky brown birds that look much like one another. Outside of the breeding season males resemble females, but in summer males acquire striking plumages. Male whydahs grow long tails and become boldly patterned, and male indigobirds become glossy black. They are brood parasites, and with few exceptions, each species of whydah and indigobird uses a single species of estrildid-finch as a host for its eggs. Thus the LONG-TAILED PARADISE-WHYDAH (Plate 82) parasitizes the GREEN-WINGED PYTILIA (or MELBA FINCH, Plate 81), and the VILLAGE INDIGOBIRD (or STEELBLUE WIDOWFINCH, Plate 82) parasitizes the RED-BILLED FIREFINCH (Plate 81). During the breeding season, vidua-finch males call and display from regularly used sites to attract mates; some simply sing from these sites, whereas others perform aerial displays too. In contrast to the females of each species, males are noisy and conspicuous at this time of the year, and they often perch on roadside telephone lines. The male songs of the different species include mimicked snatches of the song of each one's host; thus male Village Indigobirds mimic the tinkling song of the Red-billed Firefinch, PURPLE INDIGOBIRDS parasitize and mimic the song of JAMESON'S FIREFINCH (Plate 81), and so on. Some of the indigobird species are closely similar in appearance, and the males of these are readily identifiable only by determining the identity of the host species' song that is being mimicked: if the notes in its song are, for example, those of the Red-billed Firefinch, then one can be certain that the singing bird is a Village Indigobird.

Natural History

Ecology and Behavior

Small grass seeds constitute the main diet of the estrildid- and vidua-finches, and these are either picked up off the ground where they have fallen (this is typical of firefinches), or they are consumed directly off of the flowering heads of grasses. VIOLET-EARED WAXBILLS (Plate 81) commonly feed in the latter manner, often settling on a grass stem that has ripening seeds and letting their weight pull it to the ground, where they hold it down with their feet and pick off the seeds. Each seed is quickly rolled in the bill so as to de-husk it, the casing is shed, and the contents are then swallowed. Small insects, especially termites, are taken by many waxbills in summer, and they derive moisture both from these and from the moisture that is available in ripening seeds. But as winter draws in, their source of food is increasingly restricted to dry, fallen seeds, and to get moisture during this period the birds need to drink. In semi-arid areas where access to water is restricted, large mixed flocks of estrildid-finches often gather around leaking pumps and at watering points used for cattle and goats. Estrildid-finches in one form or another inhabit every type of non-aquatic habitat found in southern Africa, from the edges of desert to evergreen forest, and in savannah habitats, up to 10 species may occur alongside each other. The forest species (which are mainly twinspots and *crimson-wings*) are secretive and easily overlooked, whereas some of the savannah-dwelling species are conspicuous. The BLUE WAXBILL (Plate 81), for instance, is often one of the first birds to be encountered if one visits any acacia savannah.

Breeding

Estrildid-finches build roughly finished nests of dry grass that are shaped rather like a milk bottle lying on its side; some species have a lengthy tunnel leading into the nest, whereas others' are more ball-shaped and the entrance hole leads directly into the enclosed nest chamber. Different species place their nests in different positions: COMMON WAXBILLS (Plate 81), for example, usually hide their nest in thick grass on the ground, whereas Green-winged Pytillas (Melba Finches), Blue Waxbills, and Violet-eared Waxbills nest in the branches of a tree or bush. A few species make use of old weaver or widowbird nests on occasion, and the RED-HEADED FINCH (Plate 82) invariably does this, either using an abandoned weaver or sparrow nest or, occasionally, occupying the mud nest chamber of a swallow. At least two waxbill species commonly build their nests alongside active wasp nests, presumably using these belligerent creatures as a deterrent against would-be nest predators. The courtship displays engaged in by some estrildid-finches are a comedy to watch: the male selects a stem of grass, and holding it triumphantly in his bill, he waves it like a flag from side to side in front of the female; if she flies off, he pursues her with his grass and tries again. In all these species it is typical for both sexes to build the nest, to share the incubation, and to feed and care for the nestlings. Estrildids commonly lay clutches of 4 to 6 unmarked white eggs and their incubation and nestling periods last between 12 and 17 days and between 14 and 22 days, respectively.

In contrast to estrildid-finches, which are monogamous, the vidua-finches are *polygynous* (one male mates with several females) and their sexually dimorphic plumages in the breeding season are a reflection of this, males having ornate breeding plumages that are designed to attract the opposite sex and females remaining cryptically colored all year. The vidua-finches neither build their own nests nor rear their own young, but instead parasitize various members of their sister family, the estrildid-finches. Their mating system has minimal male involvement: females are attracted to males at display sites, mate with them, and seek out appropriate host nests on their own to parasitize. The vidua-finches lay plain white eggs similar to those of their hosts, usually 1 or 2 per nest, and these hatch and are raised alongside the host's own brood. The nestlings of the different estrildid species are recognizable by the species-specific patterns of spots found inside their mouths, which, it is thought, act as a feeding stimulus to the parents; vidua-finch nestlings have evolved mouth patterns that exactly match those of their respective hosts. This remarkable mimicry goes further: the parasite nestling learns the calls of its host during its host-dependency period and this is later manifested in males by their mimicking the host's song at their display-sites and in females by their responding to the appropriate singing male on the basis of the host-call he is mimicking. It is one of the most unusual host-parasite associations found in the bird world.

Status

None of the estrildid-finches or vidua-finches found in southern Africa is threatened.

Profiles

Green-winged Pytilia, *Pytilia melba*, Plate 81a
Red-billed Firefinch, *Lagonosticta senegala*, Plate 81b
Jameson's Firefinch, *Lagonosticta rhodopareia*, Plate 81c
Blue Waxbill, *Uraeginthus angolensis*, Plate 81d
Common Waxbill, *Estrilda astrild*, Plate 81e
Violet-eared Waxbill, *Uraeginthus granatinus*, Plate 81f
Bronze Mannikin, *Spermestes cucullatus*, Plate 82a
Shaft-tailed Whydah, *Vidua regia*, Plate 82b
Long-tailed Paradise-Whydah, *Vidua paradisaea*, Plate 82c
Pin-tailed Whydah, *Vidua macroura*, Plate 82d
Red-headed Finch, *Amadina erythrocephala*, Plate 82e
Village Indigobird, *Vidua chalybeata*, Plate 82f

29. Canaries and Buntings

With nearly 1,000 species included in it, the bird family known as the Fringillidae is one of the world's larger and more diverse bird families. *Canaries* and *buntings* are just two of many Fringillidae tribes, and visitors from other parts of the world who are familiar with *linnets, chaffinches, crossbills, grosbeaks, juncos, longspurs,* or *cardinals* will recognize the similarities that these species share with the canaries and buntings that they encounter in southern Africa. The family is well represented in the region, with 20 canary species and 5 buntings present, and several of these are common, widespread birds that are often encountered in roadside flocks. The canaries and buntings in southern Africa are uniformly small, sparrow-like birds with shortish tails and robust, conical-shaped, seed-eating bills; the canaries in this region tend to have yellow, green, or grayish-brown plumages, whereas the buntings are shades of warm brown and some species have bright yellow underparts, while most have striped heads. Their bills are also slighter and more pointed than those of canaries. In some species in these two groups the sexes are indistinguishable, whereas in others females are less intensely colored than males, or lack the male's specific facial features. Canaries are mainly arboreal birds, although many species do feed frequently on the ground; buntings are mainly terrestrial birds. The extent to which canaries and buntings are gregarious varies from species to species; some (the GOLDEN-BREASTED BUNTING, Plate 84, for instance) live year-round in pairs, but the majority tend to gather in parties or flocks outside of the breeding season, and nomadic species such as the LARK-LIKE BUNTING (Plate 84) may move around in flocks numbering hundreds or even thousands of birds.

Canaries are renowned for their singing ability and most of the southern African species share this aptitude. The species from which the domestic canary was originally derived, the Canary Island's Canary, closely resembles the CAPE CANARY (Plate 83) both in looks and vocal ability; this fine songster is a common bird in many parts of the region. YELLOW-FRONTED and BLACK-THROATED CANARIES (both Plate 83) also sing well, although most of their singing is performed during the early part of their breeding cycle, while at other times of the year they are silent. Buntings are no match for canaries at singing, and their vocal talent is restricted to monotonously repeating a short jingle.

Natural History

Ecology and Behavior

Most of southern Africa's canaries and buntings are found in the savannah regions and in the semi-arid shrublands of the karoo, and species such as the Yellow-fronted Canary (in savannah) and WHITE-THROATED CANARY (Plate 83, in karoo shrublands) are often among the commonest birds occurring in their respective environments. There are, however, several species that are tied to specific habitats and consequently have restricted ranges. Finding these endemics is one of the big challenges enjoyed by birders visiting southern Africa. The PROTEA SEED-EATER is one such species, an easily-overlooked, large, dull brownish-gray canary that is restricted to isolated, protea-clad hillsides in the southern Cape, where it subsists on the dry seeds of proteas and other fynbos vegetation. Another sought-after southern Cape endemic, the CAPE SISKIN (Plate 84), lives on the steep slopes of Table Mountain and other western Cape mountains. Then, in the eastern lowlands of Mozambique and northern kwaZulu-Natal, there is the LEMON-BREASTED CANARY, which is one of the most recently discovered birds in southern Africa—first described in 1960—and is restricted here to groves of ilala palms. Canaries and buntings are primarily seed-eaters, but the types of seed taken and where the birds forage vary enormously among species. Many species feed on fallen seeds of grasses and weeds, and the terrestrial-living CAPE BUNTING, CINNAMON-BREASTED BUNTING, and Lark-like Bunting (all Plate 84) all feed on these by walking about and searching for them. Other species pick seeds directly off the plants bearing them; depending on species, they may forage in low shrubbery close to ground level (as the Cape Siskin does) or right up to the tops of tall forest trees (as the FOREST CANARY often does). Emerging leaf and flower buds provide canaries with another common food resource, and in several species, small insects feature prominently in the diet. As expected with seed-eating birds, most canaries and buntings require access to drinking water at certain times of the year, and they are frequent winter visitors to birdbaths in gardens.

Breeding

The southern African canaries and buntings have rather uneventful breeding cycles. They are monogamous and, except for the CAPE CANARY, which sometimes nests colonially (up to a dozen pairs together), nesting pairs are usually widely spaced. All the species build a warmly lined, open-cupped nest that is either placed on the ground (as with, for example, the Lark-like Bunting or Cinnamon-breasted Bunting), in a low shrub (Cape Bunting, BLACK-HEADED CANARY), in the branches of a tree (Yellow-fronted Canary), or in a hole on a cliff face (Cape Siskin). Females build the nest and are accompanied by the male while doing so, his contribution not usually extending beyond some lusty singing while she is at work. Females do all the incubation too, but males assist them in feeding the young. In some species the male feeds his mate on the nest while she incubates. The usual clutch size in canaries and buntings is 3 eggs (2 or 4 in a few species), and the incubation and nestling periods range between 12 and 15 days and between 12 and 21 days, respectively. In contrast to the related seed-eating weavers and bishops, which are commonly parasitized by cuckoos, canaries and buntings are rarely selected by cuckoos as hosts.

Notes

The COMMON CHAFFINCH, which is a common and colorful member of this family in Europe, was one of several bird species that was introduced to Cape Town by Cecil John Rhodes in the late 1800s. Unlike the Song Thrush, which died out, and the European Starling, which has become enormously successful in its new range, the Chaffinch has done little more than maintain a small foothold in the immediate vicinity of where it was introduced, living here in the alien vegetation—groves of oak and pine trees—that was also introduced to the area.

Status

Several of the range-restricted species of canaries and buntings in southern Africa (Protea Seed-eater, Cape Siskin, and others) have been ranked as near-threatened in some Red Data assessments on account of their small population sizes. There is no evidence, though, that these populations are declining or under threat.

Profiles

Yellow-fronted Canary, *Serinus mozambicus*, Plate 83a
Black-throated Canary, *Serinus atrogularis*, Plate 83b
Cape Canary, *Serinus canicollis*, Plate 83c
Yellow Canary, *Serinus flaviventris*, Plate 83d
White-throated Canary, *Serinus albogularis*, Plate 83e
Cape Siskin, *Serinus totta*, Plate 84a
Golden-breasted Bunting, *Emberiza flaviventris*, Plate 84b
Cape Bunting, *Emberiza capensis*, Plate 84c
Cinnamon-breasted Bunting, *Emberiza tahapisi*, Plate 84d
Lark-like Bunting, *Emberiza impetuani*, Plate 84e

Chapter 9

MAMMALS

by Chris and Tilde Stuart

- *Introduction*
- *General Characteristics of Mammals*
- *Classification of Mammals*
- *Family Profiles*
    1. *Insectivores—Shrews, Golden Moles, Hedgehogs, and Elephant-shrews*
    2. *Bats*
    3. *Primates*
    4. *Aardvark and Pangolin*
    5. *Hares, Rabbits, and Hyrax*
    6. *Rodents*
    7. *Carnivores*
    8. *Seals*
    9. *Zebras and Rhinoceroses*
    10. *Giraffe, Antelope, Buffalo, Pigs, and Hippopotamus*
    11. *Elephant*

Introduction

There are more than 4,000 living species of mammal worldwide, of which about 1,100 occur on the African continent. Why do we say "more than" and "about" and not give fixed numbers? In the recent past, there have been several new species collected, classified, and identified. These are not just tiny bats, shrews, and mice—several primate species have joined the checklist. As our knowledge of genetics and molecular biology has improved, scientists have discovered several species that had been "overlooked." Those primitive primates the *bushbabies*, or *galagos*, have recently seen their number of species more than double. This is mainly because increased study has shown that species of bushbaby that are visibly very similar actually have very different calls and do not interbreed. At last count there were 343 mammal species living in the area covered by this book. Some of these are known from very few (and in three cases, single) records. Many very common but small mammals, such as bats, shrews, and golden moles, are difficult to see, and should you be lucky enough to glimpse one, even harder to identify the species. Fortunately, Africa has a great diversity of "visible" mammals in its many national parks, nature reserves, and game ranches, and some even on farmland. Southern Africa is not an exception and offers the possibility of good viewing and sightings to the ecotraveller—who usually does not need to travel far to start adding to his or her mammal "life-list." Obviously, many visitors wish to see the "Big Five," the Lion, Leopard, Buffalo, Elephant, and Hook-lipped (Black) Rhinoceros, and all can be found here. But the many species of antelope, smaller carnivores, hyraxes, rodents, and others can frequently offer many fascinating viewing hours. See the "big and the cuddly" certainly, but spend time on your safari with some of the smaller beasties—you will not regret it!

General Characteristics of Mammals

What makes a mammal a mammal? As a group, the mammals had their origins some 245 million years ago in what is known as the late Triassic Period. The mammals have a number of common characteristics that set them apart from the other vertebrates. The vast majority are covered in *hair* that provides insulation against cold, heat, and other environmental influences; they give birth to *live young*, as opposed to laying eggs, allowing females greater mobility and safety than if they had to sit on eggs for several weeks and therefore be more vulnerable to predators; females produce *milk* in special glands, freeing them from the need to search for specific foods to feed the young; and they have *advanced* brains, with obvious survival advantages.

Classification of Mammals

Mammals are very variable in size and appearance, and over time, through evolution, have become adapted to a wide range of different habitats and lifestyles. In fact there are few places on earth where mammals have not prospered. Monkeys have conquered the trees, bats dominate the night skies, and whales and dolphins have become specialized to survive in an aquatic environment. Mammals range in size from some of the shrews that weigh 3 g (0.1 oz) and less, to what is probably the largest animal that has ever lived, the Blue Whale, which can tip the scale at more than 100,000 kg (220,000 lb).

Mammals are divided into three distinct groups, mainly on the basis of their reproductive strategies. The *monotremes* are a very ancient group of mammals that includes only three species, the platypus and two spiny anteaters, which are restricted to Australia and Papua New Guinea. They are unique in the mammal world because they lay eggs—you see that there are always exceptions! The second group are the *marsupials*, found in Australia, New Guinea, and the Neotropics, with a single species extending to North America. In this group the young are born at an early stage of development, and they crawl across the mother's fur into her pouch. To make this difficult journey a little easier the mother usually licks her fur, smoothing the way. Once in the pouch the youngster finds a nipple and attaches itself to this milk supply. There are about 240 species of marsupials, including the *kangaroos, wombats, koalas, bandicoots,* and *opossums*. The third mammal group is the largest—the placental mammals, or eutherians. These include, among others, elephants, giraffe, lions, pygmy mice, and humans. The placenta connects the mother to her babies inside her body, providing two great advantages: the embryos can develop to an advanced state in a safe environment, and the mother is able to travel and forage right up to giving birth.

Family Profiles

1. Insectivores—Shrews, Golden Moles, Hedgehogs, and Elephant-shrews

The order Insectivora is represented by three families in southern Africa, the Chrysochloridae (*golden moles*), Erinaceidae (*hedgehogs*) and the Soricidae (*shrews*). Until recently, *elephant-shrews* were included in this order, but scientific wisdom has now placed them in a separate order, Macroscelidea, more closely related to rabbits and rodents. During the 18th century scientists lumped the insectivores together with the rodents. It was only in the early 19th century that a separate order, Insectivora, was recognized. Insectivores are considered to be the most primitive of placental mammals. Golden moles and elephant-shrews are African endemics; that is, they occur only on this continent, and the majority of species occur within southern Africa. With the exception of a few species of elephant-shrews, none of the insectivores are easy to see. The main common denominator linking the different families is that insects and other invertebrates make up the bulk of their food. All have teeth highly suited to killing, tearing, and crushing their prey.

Shrews. Without doubt, shrews are the most numerous species of insectivores in Africa, though many species are known from just a few specimens and often from very limited areas. Within southern Africa there are 17 species, and all are small to very small, with the GIANT MUSK-SHREW weighing some 35 g (1.2 oz) and the LEAST DWARF SHREW, just 3.5 g (0.1 oz). They all have short legs, long, narrow and wedge-shaped snouts, and the tail is usually less than half the total length. Fur is short, soft, and silky, and in most species it is dark gray to brown. Shrews are very secretive and are seldom seen by the casual ecotraveller, so we have excluded them from the species profiles.

Golden moles. If shrews are difficult to locate, golden moles are even more elusive. Their mainly subterranean lifestyle makes them difficult subjects for study, hence our limited knowledge of these elusive creatures. Of the 21 species known, 18 occur in southern Africa. Often, the only evidence of their presence are the characteristic domed feeding tunnels that lie just below the soil surface. All golden moles are small, ranging from 16 g (0.6 oz) to 538 g (19 oz) in weight, and have no visible tail, eyes, or ears. The head is wedge-shaped, with a horny pad at the tip of the snout that serves as a "shovel" when burrowing. The legs are very short, and each of the front feet is equipped with a stout claw that is used for digging. With the exception of the two largest species, all have smooth, dense, and glossy coats. Should you be lucky enough to see one of these interesting insectivores, it is unlikely you will mistake it for any other mammal group. (Other small, underground dwellers, molerats, do not have glossy coats, their tail is short but visible, and they have small eyes and two pairs of large incisor teeth.) The golden moles have been called "animated powder-puffs."

Hedgehogs. Of the 14 species of hedgehogs, all from the Old World, only 4 occur in Africa and only 1 in this region. There is a lot of controversy as to how many hedgehog species there actually are, and differences are often based on small issues such as tooth structure and the minutiae of the skull. All hedgehogs are relatively small, rarely weighing more than 1 kg (2.2 lb), and have a coat of stiff banded spines that cover the back and sides. The snout is pointed and the nose seems to be constantly twitching. When hedgehogs are resting or are threatened, they roll into a tight ball, with their spines protecting the vulnerable belly.

Elephant-shrews. Small insect-eating mammals, elephant-shrews, or sengis, have been around for a long time. The first elephant-shrew fossils were collected in Egypt and are estimated to be as much as 35 million years old, with specimens from the Namib Desert dated at 22 million years old. Of the 15 species, all restricted to Africa, 8 occur in the covered region. Although they range from just 30 g (1.1 oz) to almost 500 g (17.6 oz), all are instantly recognizable as elephant-shrews because they all have an elongated, trunk-like snout with nostrils at the tip. The hind feet and legs are much longer than the front, and when moving rapidly they do so in a series of hops. In all except the ROUND-EARED ELEPHANT-SHREW (Plate 85), the ears are noticeably long, thin, and mobile. Unlike other insectivores, elephant-shrews are mainly active during the day and can be quite easy to observe. They are also found in a wide range of habitats, from flatlands (SHORT-SNOUTED ELEPHANT-SHREW, Plate 85) to rocky areas (EASTERN ROCK ELEPHANT-SHREW, Plate 85). Most elephant-shrews in the region weigh less than 65 g (2.3 oz). Their tail lengths are about half of the total length or marginally longer. Unlike shrews, with their tiny eyes, elephant-shrews have large eyes.

Natural History

Ecology and Behavior

Shrews. Shrews have been described as eating machines that rival the large carnivores as ferocious predators. Because of their very high metabolism, they need to eat frequently and in quantity. Studies have shown that they need to eat between one-third and two-thirds of their body weight every 24 hours. Although insects, sometimes as large as themselves, make up most of their diet, they also kill other invertebrates, small reptiles, and even mice if the opportunity presents itself. Many species are active both during the day and night in a series of intensive feeding forays. The few shrew species that have been studied in the region will actively and aggressively defend a territory. Both sexes have scent glands on their sides, between the front and back legs. The musky secretions from these glands serve to mark territories and inform males of the sexual state of females. The secretions are obviously distasteful to dogs and cats, because although they often kill shrews, they very rarely eat them. However, this does not prevent birds of prey such as the Barn Owl from consuming large numbers of these tiny mammals. Most, if not all, shrews dig burrows that are normally shallow "bolt-holes" below their nests. Nests are usually among dense vegetation and, depending on the species, can be cup-shaped or domed. They are made from grass and other fine plant material and are extremely difficult to find. Apparently, few individuals live longer than one year in the wild.

Golden moles. Although golden moles spend most of their lives below ground in networks of self-excavated burrows, an amazing number are caught and eaten by owls. Some may be caught when moving just below the soil surface but they do occasionally forage above ground. One study found that individuals hunting on the surface at night could cover as much as 4.8 km (3 mi) in one nocturnal feeding session. Obviously this was not in a straight line but was restricted to relatively small areas. It is possible that other species are active on the surface but this hasn't been documented. All of the golden moles are insectivorous but they also take earthworms and at least some eat legless lizards and worm snakes that share their underground homes. The HOTTENTOT GOLDEN MOLE (Plate 85) is able to excavate tunnels at up to an estimated 1.5 m (4.9 ft) per hour. All golden moles are especially active after rain. Like shrews, golden moles have high metabolic rates that require frequent bursts of feeding activity, which are interspersed with short resting periods.

Hedgehogs. Hedgehogs, small, prickly mammals, are almost entirely nocturnal. SOUTH AFRICAN HEDGEHOGS (Plate 85) spend the daylight hours curled into a ball among vegetation tangles, under plant debris, and occasionally in shallow burrows dug by other species. Except in the case of a female with small young, these hedgehogs usually rest up in a different location each day. Although the South African Hedgehog does not hibernate to the same extent as its counterparts in colder climes, it does hole up during cold periods, but this seldom lasts for more than six weeks. During the warm, wet months, when food is abundant, these hedgehogs accumulate substantial fat deposits to carry them through the lean times. When the warm weather returns in October, they have just about used up their fat reserves. The period of greatest activity lies between August and April. Most of their food consists of insects, millipedes, earthworms, and snails, but they will eat lizards, frogs, mice, and young birds if the opportunity presents itself. They are also partial to certain fungi and some fruits and berries. When they roll into their defensive ball they are protected from most mammalian predators, but their main enemies are Giant Eagle Owls; the owls' long, curved talons easily penetrate the defensive quills. Unfortunately, hedgehogs have no defense against motor vehicles and many are killed on roads.

Elephant-shrews. All elephant-shrews, to varying degrees, seem to be both nocturnal and diurnal. The different species have successfully occupied most of the major habitats in the region, from desert (Round-eared Elephant-shrew and Short-snouted Elephant-shrew), to rocky terrain (Eastern Rock Elephant-shrew), to riverine and evergreen forest (FOUR-TOED ELEPHANT-SHREW). All species can move at great speed when alarmed, and for their size they must be among the fastest of mammals. When they feel threatened or become alarmed, they drum rapidly with their hind feet. In the case of species that live in relatively open sandy areas, networks of pathways can be seen radiating from their dens. Most species are solitary or live in pairs. In suitable areas populations may reach high densities, thus giving the impression that they are colonial. Some species live among dense vegetation, others in deep rock crevices, and a few dig shallow burrows at the bases of bushes or rocks. On hot days they will lie in deep shade, rushing out to snatch an insect foolish enough to wander close by. In the covered region all of the elephant-shrews are exclusively insect-eaters, with ants and termites often taken in quantity. It is suspected that some may take a little plant food.

Breeding

Shrews. Most shrews in the region breed during the warmer summer months, with litter sizes ranging from 2 to 6. Young are born in small nests made from fine vegetation. The young are naked and helpless at birth, and are dropped after a pregnancy lasting from 18 to 22 days. At least some, if not all, species may produce two or more litters in a season.

Golden moles. Our knowledge of breeding in golden moles is minimal at best. The Hottentot Golden Mole normally has two young at a time (but some species have only one). Most, if not all, golden moles have their litters during the wet summer months. At this time, soil is often easier to work and their insect food more abundant. Young Hottentots are born in a domed grass nest located in an enlarged side tunnel. They are born naked and helpless and weigh just 4.5 g (0.2 oz).

Hedgehogs. The South African Hedgehog is a seasonal breeder, bearing litters in the warm, wet months. The young, ranging from 1 to 11, are born after pregnancies of about 35 days. Leaf nests may be among dense vegetation or in holes. Weighing less than 10 g (0.4 oz), the young are naked and helpless at birth and only start to accompany the mother when they are between 4 and 6 weeks old, by which time they have grown the sharp adult spines that will protect them from predators. By five weeks of age they no longer suckle from the mother and she may mate again during the season.

Elephant-shrews. In contrast to the other insectivores in this section, elephant-shrew females produce just 1 or 2 young per litter. They are covered in hair and active shortly after birth. Most litters are produced during the warm, wet summer months. The Eastern Rock Elephant-shrew has a pregnancy of about 56 days. Depending on the habitat favored by a particular species, litters are born in rock crevices, in shallow burrows, or under rocks. Because the young are active so shortly after birth, there is little or no attempt to build a nest. When searching for lizards and snakes in the Namib Desert, we have located young Round-eared Elephant-shrews in slight hollows below flat blocks of hardened soil.

Notes

Except for the South African Hedgehog and a few of the elephant-shrews, we know very little about these small insect-eating mammals. Most are difficult to observe, with the exception of some elephant-shrews. In Matobo National Park in western Zimbabwe, the ROCK ELEPHANT-SHREW can be most obliging. Should you visit this park, go to the area known as World's End, in the vicinity of Cecil John Rhodes's grave, settle down in the shade of a boulder, and presently these fascinating animals will show themselves.

Although South Africa is the best zoologically explored country on the continent, a new shrew species, the LONG-TAILED FOREST SHREW, was discovered in 1978 near the coastal town of Knysna. What makes this discovery even more amazing is that the area lies in one of the country's busiest tourist destinations and has seen a steady stream of mammalogists and collectors.

A puzzle for mammalogists interested in the "animated powder-puffs" is how GRANT'S GOLDEN MOLE is able to breathe under the soft sands of the Namib Desert. These sands are so soft and dry that tunnels cannot be formed.

Status

No southern African insectivore or elephant-shrew is considered to be threatened or endangered, but the lack of knowledge of the biology of many species means that we cannot put forward an informed opinion. Species that are only known to occur in very small areas, or in specialized habitats, may be threatened in the longer term. The GIANT GOLDEN MOLE is only known to occur in a few small, isolated forests in the extreme southeast of South Africa. Should these forests be destroyed, this largest of golden moles would disappear. But where they occur now they are still quite common. DE WINTON'S GOLDEN MOLE, restricted to coastal sand dunes just to the south of the Orange River, may be threatened by strip-mining activities. The South African Hedgehog is considered at risk because it is eaten by people in parts of its range. Many are also killed on roads at night. There appear to be fluctuations in the number of hedgehogs in some areas, and this may be an influence of drought periods and the use of pesticides and insecticides in agriculture.

Profiles

Eastern Rock Elephant-shrew, *Elephantulus myurus*, Plate 85a
Round-eared Elephant-shrew, *Macroscelides proboscideus*, Plate 85b
Short-snouted Elephant-shrew, *Elephantulus brachyrhynchus*, Plate 85c
Hottentot Golden Mole, *Amblysomus hottentotus*, Plate 85d
South African Hedgehog, *Atelerix frontalis*, Plate 85e

2. Bats

Bats are the masters of the night, the only true flying mammals! These aerial specialists, comprising the order Chiroptera, are divided into two suborders: the Megachiroptera, which are fruit- and nectar-eating bats, and the Microchiroptera, which are predominantly insect-eaters. As their scientific names indicate, the "megas" are mostly larger than the "micros," but there are exceptions. At last count there were 986 species of bat belonging to 18 different families. The bats are second in diversity among mammals only to the rodents. In southern Africa, 7 species of fruit-eating bats and some 65 insect-eating bats have been recorded (out of an African total of 27 fruit-eaters and 183 insect-eaters).

What makes bats special is that they have the power of sustained flight. Although several other mammals are said to "fly," such as the flying squirrels, they in fact can only glide over short distances. Bats' forelimbs, with greatly elongated fingers, have evolved into wings. The skin of the upper and lower surfaces have fused to form a very thin and elastic wing membrane. This membrane extends along the bats' sides and is attached to the ankles. The order name, Chiroptera, refers to the wings and translates as hand (*chiro*) and wing (*ptera*). In many species of insect-eating bats the tail supports a thin membrane (*interfemoral*) that extends to the ankles and assists in flight maneuverability. In a few species, the tail membrane is used as a "net" to hook flying insects, which are then drawn to the mouth. The Old World fruit-eating bats have a short tail and a very narrow membrane. When at rest most bats hang head-down, holding on by the claws on the short hind feet. Some species hang totally suspended, while others cling to the surface on which they are roosting. Some bats roost in dense clusters, sometimes numbering in the tens of thousands, but others prefer to hang singly and keep a distance from neighbors. Some are solitary roosters, or roost at most in groups of two to six individuals. Most insect-eating bats fold their wings against their sides, whereas the majority of fruit-eating bats and the *horseshoe bats* envelope the body with the wings.

In the covered region, all of the insect-eating bats and the EGYPTIAN FRUIT-BAT (Plate 86) rely on *echolocation* to move around safely in the dark, and in most cases to locate their prey. When flying, these bats emit high-frequency sound-waves through the mouth or the nostrils. The clicks and beeps are reflected by objects in the immediate vicinity of the bat and picked up on the rebound by the bat's ears. This provides the information the bats need to avoid obstacles and locate potential prey. The time from the call being "released" to the bat's reaction to the sound's echo may be as little as 1/100 of a second. In the case of the Egyptian Fruit-bat, the clicks are made by the tongue and emitted through the corners of the mouth. These calls are of a much lower frequency than those of the insect-eating bats and are easily picked up by the human ear. Although many species of insectivorous bat, and all fruit-eating bats in the region, have plain mouse- or fox-like faces, an equal number have facial flaps and structures that act as an aid to echolocation.

In southern Africa, the smallest bat species is the RUSTY BAT, with an average weight of 3.5 g (0.1 oz), and the largest is a vagrant from the tropics, the STRAW-COLORED FRUIT-BAT, at some 300 g (10.6 oz). This fruit-bat also has the largest wingspan, at 75 cm (29.5 in). The species that we have profiled range in size from the CAPE SEROTINE BAT (Plate 86), with an average weight of 6.5 g (0.2 oz) and a wingspan of 24 cm (9.5 in), to the Egyptian Fruit-bat (Plate 86), which averages 130 g (4.6 oz) and has a wingspan of about 60 cm (23.6 in). Males and females of nearly all southern African bat species are similar in size.

Natural History

Ecology and Behavior

All bats, whether insectivorous (insect-eaters) or frugivorous (fruit-eaters), are largely restricted to feeding on nutritionally concentrated and easily absorbed food items. The digestive tracts of most species are short and digestion is rapid. Fruit-eating bats rarely spend much time at fruiting trees or bushes; they fly in, grasp the fruit in the mouth, and take it to a *night-roost* tree. Where the fruits are too large to carry away in the mouth, the benefits of a large quantity of food at one site have to be weighed against the bats' increased vulnerability to predators. Several years ago we lived in northern South Africa and frequently observed WAHLBERG'S EPAULETTED FRUIT-BATS (Plate 86) nibbling neat holes in the large ripe fruits of the pawpaw. A partially folded wing was then inserted in the hole and used in much the same way as an ice-cream scoop. The soft pulp was withdrawn and then licked from the wing. However, it is the insect-eating bats that have perfected foraging and hunting techniques to a point where they have few equals in the vertebrate world. Reflected calls are picked up by the bats' highly sensitive ears, and if they signal potential prey, the bat goes into "attack mode." Different species of insect-hunting bats have evolved specialization in such aspects as wing and tail structure and hunting area. Some have long, slender, pointed wings that enable fast, higher-level flight. Others have broad, rounded wings that allow for rapid, easy flight between thickets and trees. Species such as the LARGE-EARED FREE-TAILED BAT hunt at altitudes of 200 m (656 ft) and more. The EGYPTIAN SLIT-FACED BAT (Plate 86) takes most of its prey just 2 to 4 m (6.6 to 13 ft) above the ground. In most cases prey items are snatched in flight in the mouth and held securely by the needle-sharp teeth. Some species may also use the tail membrane, and even the wings, for plucking their prey from the air. There are several bat species that are not averse to snatching prey from the ground, usually in flight. We have watched EGYPTIAN FREE-TAILED BATS (Plate 86) on the ground around holes from which termites were emerging. This is unusual feeding behavior, but it shows how versatile these small mammals are. Some potential prey species fight back: Certain moth species can detect the ultrasonic sounds of predatory bats and take immediate evasive action. This may involve erratic flight or diving into cover that bats cannot penetrate. There are even moths that beat the bats at their own game, by emitting their own clicking sounds that are believed to confuse the bats.

Not only have bats conquered the night skies, but they spend the daylight hours in virtually all possible shelters. Nearly all of Africa's fruit-eating bats roost in trees, including Wahlberg's Epauletted Fruit-bat. Some species roost in small clusters, others in vast, noisy, smelly aggregations. The Straw-colored Fruit-bat falls into the latter group, sometimes gathering in roosts that number in the hundreds of thousands. There are a few fruit-eaters that roost in caves, such as the Egyptian Fruit-bat; its roosts vary from a few dozen bats to several thousand. In some places it is believed that these "ancestral" cave-roosts have been in use for hundreds of years. Insect-eating bats, depending on the species, roost in caves, rock crevices, tree hollows, and holes, under tree bark, and/or in covered irrigation canals and other manmade structures. A few species, such as the BUTTERFLY BAT, roost in trees among the leaves, or on the trunks of trees such as the Baobab. Then there is the tiny BANANA BAT, which lives in groups of just 2 to 6 animals, often in the curled leaves of banana and strelitzia plants. To move up and down these slippery vertical tubes, they have developed "non-slip pads" on the leading edge of the wings.

Below are details of the natural history of the bats we profile; each is typical of a group of similar species.

Egyptian Fruit-bat. The Egyptian Fruit-bat is the largest resident bat in southern Africa. Unlike most fruit-bats, it spends the daylight hours in caves and has developed primitive echolocation abilities. Entering a cave-roost where thousands of these bats are present provides an enormous sensation of sounds, smells, and textures. You ask, why the latter? All bats produce copious quantities of droppings, and fruit-bat droppings are very sloppy! In a cave situation this "porridge" is concentrated and can reach 1 m (3 ft) and more deep. Once these bats locate a suitable food tree, fruit may be taken in the mouth while the bat briefly hovers, or as frequently happens, a bat may land on a branch and then shuffle about seeking suitable fruit. Throughout their southern African range this species has a broad breeding season. Most females give birth to a single young but occasionally twins are born. Pregnancy averages 105 days, and from birth to about six weeks of age the young clings to the mother, even when she forages at night. At this point it is left in the cave, where the mother brings it food, until it begins to fly at 9 to 10 weeks of age.

Wahlberg's Epauletted Fruit-bat. The male Wahlberg's Epauletted Fruit-bat (Plate 86) has glandular pouches on the shoulders that are covered with long white hairs (forming "epaulets"). When opened they resemble white rosettes. As with many species of fruit-bats, Wahlberg's travels frequently, its movements dictated by the availability of suitable fruit. Unlike the Egyptian Fruit-bat, Wahlberg's Fruit-bat roosts in quite small numbers among the foliage of trees. At night at the feeding trees they can be very noisy; a friend of ours has likened the noise to a pack of demented chihuahuas. Very little is known about their breeding behavior, other than that it is probably a year-round activity, and a single young is usual.

Egyptian Slit-faced Bat. Sometimes called the Common Slit-faced Bat, the Egyptian Slit-faced Bat (Plate 86) has a wide range and occurs throughout southern Africa, much of the rest of Africa, and in western Arabia. In southern Africa it occurs from sea level to about 1,500 m (4,900 ft), and from near desert to areas receiving up to 1,400 mm (55 in) of rain yearly. It roosts in many different places and in small groups of up to several hundred. Much of its prey, including grasshoppers, beetles, and scorpions, is snatched off the ground and carried to an established feeding site. As with many bat species, pairs mate in flight and a single young is born after about a five-month pregnancy.

Cape Serotine Bat. The CAPE SEROTINE BAT (Plate 86) is one of the most widespread of all sub-Saharan bats and also one of the smallest. Females are slightly larger than males. We have a small population of these bats sharing the roof space of our house with a much larger number of Egyptian Free-tailed Bats. Serotines roost in small numbers, often tucking themselves away in narrow crevices and cracks. They seldom fly higher than 15 m (50 ft) above the ground, and they commonly hawk for insects around lights at night. At least in parts of their range, they breed in the summer months, with females giving birth to 1 to 3 naked and helpless young.

Butterfly Bat. The attractive Butterfly Bat (Plate 86) derives its name from the pattern of dark lines on the wings that resemble the veins in the wings of butterflies. It is sometimes called the Leaf-winged Bat. It is a high but slow flier and commonly hunts in the late afternoon, particularly on overcast days. Its small roosts (usually just 2 or 3 individuals) are often located among leaves in trees. Nothing is known of its breeding and, other than it hunts during the day, little of its behavior.

Egyptian Free-tailed Bat. Also called Bulldog Bat or Wrinkle-lipped Bat, the Egyptian Free-tailed Bat (Plate 86) is called "free-tailed" because its tail is only partly enclosed by the interfemoral membrane. It lives in colonies that may number in the hundreds, and individuals are often tightly packed together. Unlike most species of bat, it can scuttle around rapidly on the ground, using both feet and folded wings. As with a number of bat species, the Egyptian females form maternity and nursery colonies during the summer birthing months, with males roosting elsewhere. A single young appears to be the rule.

Ecological Interactions

Fruit-eating bats, which often also eat nectar and pollen, are essential to the well-being, and even the survival, of tropical and subtropical forests. Many trees, including species of economic importance to people, have fruit-bats as their most important pollinators. Most people living in temperate zone areas associate pollination with bees and birds, but in many parts of Africa it is the bats that are the principal transferers of pollen. This is promoted by the fact that many of the tree flowers open at night, and most are white to aid visibility. As the bat touches the flower to extract nectar, pollen sticks to its head and body, and, when it flies to the next flower, some of the pollen is brushed off, thus achieving cross-pollination. That venerable savannah giant, the Baobab tree, is almost entirely "bat controlled." Without fruit-bats feeding on its nectar and cross-pollinating in return, these majestic giants would eventually slip into extinction, as would many other organisms that depend on bats. Apart from being pollinators, the fruit-bats are also supreme seed-dispersers. This aspect is little understood in southern Africa, but in the African tropics several commercially important timber trees would almost certainly become extinct without the feeding attentions of bats. Unfortunately, in commercial fruit-growing areas, fruit-bats are not very popular. Although bat damage to fruit trees is generally held to be minimal, and fruit taken is often over-ripe for marketing, many fruit-bats are killed. However, in Africa this is not considered to be a serious threat to their survival.

The insect-eating bats are essential in controlling the populations of many insects that are a threat to people, livestock, and crops. Some years ago, on a visit to the Augrabies Falls National Park in South Africa, we attempted to estimate the number of insectivorous bats that were emerging from their daytime roosts in the caves and rock crevices. Most were Egyptian Free-tailed and Cape Serotine Bats, and over a 20 m (65 ft) area during a 10-minute period, we estimated that 6,000 bats flew past us. This number of bats amounts to 90 kg (200 lb) of animated "insecticide" moving through that flight path. Most insect-eating bats devour at least 25% of their body weight each night, and therefore the bats we saw that evening could consume some 23 kg (50 lb) of flying insects each night.

Bats in their turn appear on the menus of a wide range of predators. In Africa, one bird of prey, the Bat Hawk, has evolved as a specialist predator of these flying mammals. Early-flying bats are taken by Rock Kestrels and even crows. Genets are not averse to snacking on bats, and neither are snakes, when opportunities present themselves.

Notes

Unfortunately, bats are widely feared, and false but horrific tales have been woven about them. Contrary to popular folklore, bats do not get tangled in human hair! One of our favorite verses, written by T. S. Eliot in *The Waste Land* (1922), at least puts hair and bats in a positive context—"A woman drew her long black hair out tight/ and fiddled whisper music on those strings/ and bats with baby faces in the violet light/ whistled..." Bats feature widely in literature but, sadly, are often the victims of bad press. Their secretive lifestyles, nocturnal activity, and the association with witches and vampires (of the human type) do nothing to improve their image. They have come to be feared, or regarded with superstitious awe by many people and communities. Vampire bats are found only in the Americas and are in fact the only mammals that feed solely on blood.

Status

Because of their nocturnal behavior and often difficult-to-access roosting sites, we know very little about the status of the vast majority of African bat species. It is unlikely that any southern African bat species are seriously threatened or endangered. On occasion, fruit-bats are killed in areas where commercial soft-fruit crops are grown. The use of pesticides and insecticides in the region may harm insect-eating bat populations.

Many African bat species are known from just a few dusty museum specimens, and often from widely scattered localities. This does not necessarily mean they are rare; in some cases it may just indicate how few researchers have studied bats in Africa. HAYMAN'S EPAULETTED FRUIT-BAT is known from only four museum specimens collected in a narrow belt close to the border of Angola and the Congo. However, there are great expanses of suitable forest habitat to the north of its known range. This is a hostile environment for people and the area is virtually unexplored, so this bat is almost certainly more abundant than the records indicate. The TWILIGHT BAT, which occurs from Gambia in West Africa to Malawi, in the southeast of the continent, is known only from 11 museum specimens. WOERMANN'S LONG-TONGUED FRUIT-BAT occurs in the tropical forest belt and for many years was believed to be very rare. However, further research within its range showed that it was in fact common. The point is that we know very little about bats and their ecology and conservation statuses.

Profiles

Egyptian Fruit-bat, *Rousettus aegyptiacus*, Plate 86a
Wahlberg's Epauletted Fruit-bat, *Epomophorus wahlbergi*, Plate 86b
Cape Serotine Bat, *Neoromicia capensis*, Plate 86c
Butterfly Bat, *Glauconycteris variegatus*,Plate 86d
Egyptian Slit-faced Bat, *Nycteris thebaica*, Plate 86e
Egyptian Free-tailed Bat, *Tadarida aegyptiaca*, Plate 86f

3. Primates

On a visit to a zoo, one cannot help but notice the large crowds of people that congregate around the primate enclosures. Warthogs and antelope are given passing glances, but the gorillas, chimps, and monkeys are guaranteed sustained attention. What evokes this interest and fascination is their similarity to us and, in some of them, their "quasi-humanness." Although some people try to deny this similarity, it cannot be escaped—we are also primates. Human primates are distributed pretty much worldwide, while the greatest diversity of nonhuman primates is found in the tropics of South and Central America, Africa, and Asia. As one moves to the subtropics of these areas, primates are present but in much less diversity. In Africa there are approximately 65 species of primates, out of a world total of more than 240 species.

Because of their relationship and similarities to people, nonhuman primates have been intensively studied. They are distinguished by a number of anatomical and ecological traits. The vast majority are arboreal, spending most of their time in trees, although several in Africa spend a considerable amount of time on the ground. They have well-developed brains, complex social lives, and their fingers and toes are highly dexterous. Their eyes are in the front of the skull and forward-facing. This allows for binocular vision and good perception of depth, without which there would be a lot of monkeys falling out of trees!

Primates are divided into four distinct groups:

1. *Prosimians* include several families of primitive primates, and with the exception of a few, all are small and nocturnal. This group includes the lemurs (almost entirely restricted to Madagascar), the bushbabies (galagos), pottos, and angwantibos of Africa, and the lorises and tarsiers of Asia.

2. *New World monkeys* are those primates that live in South and Central America. They include the marmosets, squirrel monkeys, douroucoulis, titi monkeys, howlers, sakis, uakaris, capuchins, and woolly and spider monkeys. New World monkeys have wide-open nostrils located far apart.

3. *Old World monkeys* are found in Africa, Arabia, and Asia. In Africa these include baboons, mandrills, Barbary Macaques, patas, and a wide range of "true monkeys," which incorporate the guenons, colobus, and mangabeys. In

contrast to the New World monkeys, Old World monkeys have nostrils that are narrow, close together and point downward.

4. *Hominoidea* include what are considered the "more advanced" primates—gibbons, orangutans, chimpanzees, bonobos, gorillas, and people.

Although the African tropics are rich in primate species, only 5 species occur within the region covered by this book. They include 2 strictly night-active prosimians and 3 day-active Old World monkeys.

The prosimian species are the THICK-TAILED BUSHBABY and the LESSER BUSHBABY (both Plate 87). The name *galago* is sometimes used in preference to bushbaby. The Lesser Bushbaby is found only in the extreme north and northeast of the covered region, but in most places it is common. It is the smallest primate in the area, weighing only between 120 and 210 g (4.2 and 7.4 oz). Lesser Bushbabies have long, powerful hind legs that are used to leap between trees and branches; the tail aids in balance. The Thick-tailed Bushbaby is considerably bigger, weighing up to 1.5 kg (3.3 lb), and males are about 20% larger than females. Unlike its smaller cousin, it often forages on the ground, where it moves in somewhat cat-like fashion. The race of the SAVANNAH BABOON (Plate 87) in southern Africa is called the CHACMA BABOON. It is by far the largest regional wild primate, the fourth largest in Africa, and occurs widely across the region. There is a considerable difference in the size of males (25 to 45 kg, 55 to 99 lb) and females (12 to 28 kg, 26 to 62 lb). VERVET MONKEYS (Plate 87) weigh between 3.5 and 8 kg (7.7 and 18 lb), and males are larger than females. Their tails make up more than half their total length. This monkey occurs widely through sub-Saharan Africa and it is common in the covered region. The SYKES' MONKEY (Plate 87) is often also called Samango Monkey in the region, where it has a limited and patchy distribution in the extreme east. It has a typical monkey appearance, but with a relatively long, coarse coat and long facial whiskers. Males weigh from 8 to 10 kg (18 to 22 lb) and females 4 to 5 kg (9 to 11 lb).

Natural History

Ecology and Behavior

Thick-tailed Bushbaby. The bushbabies get their common name from the calls of some species, which to some sound like the cries of human babies. These rather hair-raising calls are particularly well developed in this species. Calling intensifies during the breeding season. Thick-tailed Bushbabies occupy areas of coastal and montane forest, but prefer fairly dense savannah woodland in the northeast of the region. Resin, or gum, particularly from acacia trees, makes up as much as 62% of their diet in some areas. This is supplemented with wild fruits and an occasional insect or gecko. They are strictly nocturnal and sleep away the daylight hours in self-constructed leaf nests or among dense vegetation tangles. Although they are solitary foragers, they frequently rest together in groups of 2 to 6 individuals. Each group has an established home range that is usually 7 to 10 ha (17 to 25 ac), and densities as high as 125 animals in a single sq km (0.4 sq mi) have been recorded. The home range of a male overlaps those of several females, and the females and young form the stable social grouping. Home ranges are marked by rubbing secretions from a chest gland on branches. Unlike the Lesser Bushbaby, the Thick-tailed spends some time foraging on the ground.

Lesser Bushbaby. Lesser Bushbabies have a strong preference for acacia and other savannah woodland but are found on the fringes of some forest patches. They are strictly night-active and nearly all of their foraging is in the trees and bushes; seldom do they move around on the ground. During the day they sleep in tree holes, leaf nests, or among dense plant tangles. When they move around at night they do so alone, but members of a group keep in continuous contact with a range of squeaks, grunts, and chittering. A male territory (in one study measured at 11 ha, 27 ac) may overlap the home ranges of up to 5 females. Females in small groups occupy home ranges that vary greatly in size depending on the quantity and quality of the available food. In optimal habitat, up to 400 Lesser Bushbabies may live in each sq km (0.4 sq mi) of habitat. Territories and home ranges are marked with urine. The bushbabies urinate on their hand and then rub it on the foot on the same side, and in this way their scent is evenly spread. Dominant males are larger, do a lot of calling, and give off a strong smell, whereas subordinate males are smaller, less vocal, and do not give off a distinctive smell. Apart from tree gum, these bushbabies also eat many insects, other invertebrates, tree frogs, and geckos that are caught with their hands.

Savannah Baboon. Baboons occupy a wide range of habitats, from semi-desert to high rainfall montane areas. Two factors dictate where they will live: there must be access to permanent drinking water and tall trees or cliffs for sleeping at night out of reach of predators. These large primates do most of their foraging on the ground, using their hands to pluck vegetation, turn stones, and dig. They have a broad diet that includes many different plant parts, insects, other invertebrates, reptiles, and birds. If the opportunity presents itself, they will actively hunt, taking young antelope, other primates, and anything that they can easily catch and overpower. In some areas they do considerable damage to crops. They are highly social animals, living in troops that normally number from 15 to 50 individuals, but in food-rich areas troops may number 100 or more. Home range size varies from area to area, from 210 to 3,367 ha (520 to 8,300 ac). Within a troop, all adult males (at least 5 years old) are dominant over the females. There is a strict ranking, or pecking order, and only dominant males mate with receptive females. Subordinate males do mate with non-receptive and young females. It is the dominant male that determines when the troop will move, and females and youngsters try to keep close to him. Non-breeding females associate with subordinate males that are often referred to as lieutenants. The young and subadult troop members circulate around the edges of the troop. If threatened by a predator, the dominant male and his lieutenants will not hesitate to attack, especially if a young animal has been taken. With their long canine teeth, longer than those of the Leopard, and powerful grasping hands and feet, they can be formidable foes.

Vervet Monkey. Vervet Monkeys are highly adaptable, inhabiting savannah woodland but also penetrating dry areas along tree-fringed watercourses. They forage both in trees and on the ground. Particularly in the east of the covered region, the Vervet is the most commonly seen primate, and in some areas it has become a nuisance. Leave something unattended on your picnic table in their presence and invariably they will help themselves. They are omnivores; plant parts, especially resin, flowers, and fruits, make up the bulk of their diet, but insects are readily taken. When the opportunity presents itself they catch lizards and young birds from nests. The normal troop size is 15 to 20, but it may rarely be as low as 5 individuals, with up to 76 on record. The home range varies according to such factors as food abundance and availability of water. Average ranges are about 40 ha (99 ac), but they vary from 18 to 96 ha (44 to 237 ac). Each troop is dominated by an adult male who has mating rights with all receptive females. There is a strict social ranking, or pecking order, within the troop, and any individual stepping out of line is severely chastised. Vervets react noisily, with harsh barks and chattering, to the presence of carnivores, people, and large birds of prey. At night they roost in trees.

Sykes' Monkey. Sykes' Monkeys are the only truly forest-dwelling primates in the region. More than 50% of their food consists of green tree leaves, and about 20% is made up of resin and gum. The remainder consists of other plant parts and, taken opportunistically, birds and reptiles. As with the other monkeys of the region, Sykes' Monkeys are strictly day-active and seldom descend to the ground except to cross forest clearings or to drink. They live in troops numbering from 12 to 70 individuals, made up of a dominant adult male, numerous females, and young of different ages. The male has a distinctive barking call that carries a considerable distance over the forest. Troops move over a home range of 23 to 50 ha (57 to 124 ac), and ranges seldom overlap. Although troops tend to be secretive, in some conservation areas, such as Cape Vidal in the Greater St. Lucia Wetland Park, they have become used to people and allow you to approach quite closely.

Breeding

Female Vervet and Sykes' Monkeys and Savannah Baboons produce a single, helpless young, that is able to do little more in the first few weeks of life than cling to the mother's belly and suckle. In all three species young may be born at any time of the year, but there are birth peaks during the wet, productive summer months. In the case of the baboon, the female exhibits vastly swollen tissue around the anal and vulval region when she is ready to mate. This state often causes people to think that they are diseased, but in fact it is normal and healthy tissue. A single young, with a pink face and large ears, is born after a pregnancy of about 180 days. As the youngster gains strength it starts to ride jockey-style on the mother's back, using her tail to hold on. Females usually give birth to their first young in their fifth year and there are at least 15 months between subsequent births. Young are weaned at about 6 months of age. Vervet Monkey gestation averages 210 days, and the single young weighs between 300 and 400 g (11 and 14 oz). In the case of the Sykes' Monkey, the newly born young weighs about 400 g (14 oz) and is dropped after a pregnancy of 220 to 230 days. Thick-tailed Bushbaby young are born in October and November, and a litter consists usually of 2, but occasionally 3 babies. Lesser Bushbabies are born after a pregnancy of about 120 days, and each of the 1 or 2 young weighs just 9 g (0.3 oz). When the mother goes out to feed, she carries the young and then leaves them clinging to a branch near to her foraging area.

Ecological Interactions

In southern Africa, primates are the targets of a wide range of predators. Both bushbaby species in the region have been recorded in the diet of Genets, Leopards, Giant Eagle Owls, and Rock Pythons. Because it spends more time on the ground, the Thick-tailed Bushbaby is vulnerable to motor traffic when crossing roads. Vervet and Sykes' Monkeys are occasionally taken by mammalian carnivores, but they are particularly vulnerable to large birds of prey. These include the Crowned and Martial Eagles, and Vervets are occasionally taken by Tawny Eagles. Both are targeted in some areas by people, principally for the damage they cause in gardens, commercial orchards, and plantations. Savannah Baboons, especially young animals, are occasionally killed by Leopards, but not as frequently as is often believed. There are several records of Leopards having been seriously wounded by baboons.

Primates in the tropics are major seed dispersal agents, but in Africa, this important aspect is not well studied. Certainly many plant seeds pass unharmed through the gut and the monkey droppings provide an ideal growing medium when they drop to the ground. Feeding monkeys are often accompanied by other species that feed on items dropped or discarded by the primates. We have observed or heard about several such associations. In Botswana and northern South Africa we have watched Savannah Baboons feeding on the prolific blossoms of the Winterthorn and Knobthorn trees. Many blossoms were dropped or dislodged and then gobbled up by waiting Impalas and Bushbucks. On the island of Unguja (Zanzibar), a troop of endangered ZANZIBAR RED COLOBUS monkeys were feeding on berries about 4 m (13 ft) above the ground. Busily eating below, and overlooking our approach, was a flock of Crested Guineafowl and a single Ader's Duiker, also an endangered species. Sykes' Monkeys are often accompanied in the forest by mixed flocks of insect-eating birds that snatch up disturbed flies, moths, and beetles.

Notes

Savannah Baboons and Vervet and Sykes' Monkeys have large cheek pouches that are often rapidly stuffed full so that the primates, even when danger threatens, can retreat to places of relative safety and enjoy their meal. It also pays younger animals to stuff in as much as possible before an older monkey or baboon monopolizes a good source of food. The back of a hand is used to press against the cheek and move food into the mouth for chewing.

Ecotravellers should take precautions in localities where Savannah Baboons and Vervet Monkeys have lost their fear of people. Never try to touch a small youngster, as you then have an excellent chance of being severely bitten by an adult. In such situations, never leave food or snatchable valuables unattended. Should an animal succeed in getting something from you, do not contest the issue. If it is food you have lost it; if it is something inedible, keep the "thief" within sight if at all possible and eventually it will abandon it. Wait until the baboon or Vervet moves away before retrieving the item.

Status

None of the five primates in southern Africa is considered to be endangered or threatened. A few populations may be locally threatened by direct persecution by people, but overall all is well with the region's primates. Sykes' Monkeys may in the long term face threats because of their more restricted habitat requirements, coupled with loss of some of their isolated forest pockets. Both bushbaby species are generally common where they occur. Savannah Baboons and Vervet Monkeys are frequently used in medical and other research, but this trade is strictly controlled and appears to hold little threat for their future.

Profiles

Thick-tailed Bushbaby, *Otolemur crassicaudatus*, Plate 87a
Lesser Bushbaby, *Galago moholi*, Plate 87b
Sykes' Monkey, *Cercopithecus (mitis) albogularis*, Plate 87c
Savannah Baboon, *Papio (ursinus) cynocephalus*, Plate 87d
Vervet Monkey, *Chlorocebus aethiops*, Plate 87e

4. Aardvark and Pangolin

The AARDVARK (Plate 95) and PANGOLIN (Plate 88) are two of Africa's strangest mammals. They both feed mainly on ants and termites, but beyond this similarity they are not related. The Aardvark is the only species in order Tubilidentata, and it is entirely restricted to sub-Saharan Africa. The order's name is taken from the numerous tubular structures that make up the Aardvark's peg-like teeth, which lack enamel and grow continuously. The Pangolin shares its order, Pholidota, with several similar looking animals; 4 of these species occur in Africa and the remaining 3 in Asia. Pholidota simply means "scaled animals," a reference to the many large scales, or plates, that cover much of these animals' bodies. Both the Aardvark, and to a lesser extent, the Pangolin, are night-active and are not commonly seen, although the former is occasionally spotted on game-viewing drives.

The Aardvark is one species that, even if you are a beginner ecotraveller, you will be able to identify without difficulty. It resembles no other African mammal, with its long, pig-like snout; elongated, tubular, and somewhat mule-like ears; heavily muscled and kangaroo-like tail; and powerful, stout legs. The toes are armed with strong, spade-like nails. The body is sparsely covered with coarse, bristly hairs. Overall coloration is gray-fawn, with darker colored legs, but because of their prodigious digging habits, Aardvarks frequently take on the color of the local soil. We have seen ocher-red Aardvarks, almost black individuals, and some off-white. These are large beasts of the night, weighing in at between 40 and 70 kg (88 and 154 lb) and standing on average 80 cm (31.5 in) at the highest point of the back (Aardvarks walk with the back distinctly arched). The name Aardvark is a Dutch/Afrikaans word which translates as "earth pig."

Of the 4 pangolin species in Africa, two are confirmed ground-dwellers and 2 spend their time in the trees of the equatorial forest belt. The largest of the pangolins, appropriately named GIANT GROUND PANGOLIN, weighs a respectable 30 to 35 kg (66 to 77 lb) and lives in the tropics. Only the Pangolin, sometimes called Temminck's Ground Pangolin, occurs in southern Africa. The word pangolin comes from the Malay *peng-goling*, which means "the roller." Pangolin underparts are not covered with scales, and when alarmed these animals roll into a tight ball to protect the vulnerable belly. Not even a lion can penetrate this armor! Pangolins have been referred to as animated pine-cones, a description that is not far off the mark. They have tiny, pointed heads and powerful hind legs and tails. The smaller front legs are seldom used for walking but are their main digging tools. Pangolins weigh between 5 and 18 kg (11 and 40 lb) and their tail length is slightly less than half of their total length. Both Aardvarks and Pangolins have extremely long, sticky tongues for extracting ants, termites, and their larvae from their nests.

Natural History

Ecology and Behavior

Aardvarks are limited to areas where there is an abundance of their ant and termite prey. To catch sufficient food, they cover considerable distances, often ranging from 10 to 30 km (6 to 19 mi) each night. Of course, this is not a straight line measurement; it follows a zigzag course between ant, and especially termite, colonies. The nightly feeding forays are not undertaken in random directions, but follow a set pattern that is repeated each week or so. The powerful spade-like nails on the front feet are used to tear into ant and termite nests. Even the hardest soils yield to the sheer power of these mammals. Certain species of termites, especially the harvesters, move on the surface in columns when gathering plant material to be transported to their underground nests. The 30 cm (12 in) long tongue of an Aardvark is flicked along these columns and the termites are drawn into its mouth to be ground between the teeth. In similar fashion, the tongue penetrates along tunnels in exposed nests, moving in much the same way as a snake. Aardvarks are mainly solitary animals, except when a male consorts with a female, or a mother and young forage together. During the day, Aardvarks rest in extensive burrow systems. Females are generally more bound to a specific area than males, the latter tending to go on more extensive journeys. Aardvarks are almost entirely nocturnal but will sun themselves at their burrow entrances, especially after a cold night. During severe droughts, when their prey is greatly reduced or deep underground, these strange animals forage during the day. On one memorable occasion in northern Namibia we had three Aardvarks within sight at about mid-morning. We were able to follow them around at a distance of some 15 m (50 ft) while they dug for termites. Although Aardvarks prefer areas of open woodland, semi-arid scrub, and open grassland, they occur in just about any habitat where their prey is common.

Pangolins are mainly active at night, but they will also frequently forage on cool, overcast days. When resting during the day, they may do so in burrows they have dug themselves, but more commonly they use burrows of other species or seek cover among dense plant growth. When occupying a tunnel, they often block the entrance from the inside. They are solitary animals, only coming together to mate or when a female is accompanied by its single young. They inhabit dry woodland savannah, sometimes extending into quite arid areas such as the Kalahari. They use the long front claws to dig for their mainly ant and termite prey, and the tail is used as a brace. Unlike the Aardvark, the Pangolin has no teeth; instead, the thick, muscular, rough walls of its stomach and the tiny pebbles it contains have taken over the food-crushing role.

Breeding

The Pangolin has a single young that weighs between 330 and 450 g (11.5 and 16 oz) at birth, following a pregnancy that has been recorded to last 139 days. However, there are very few records of newborn Pangolins. The young rides on the mother's tail or back when she is out foraging, but if they are threatened, she curls the young securely against her belly, protecting it with her scales. Aardvarks appear to be seasonal breeders in the region and probably elsewhere. In some areas births are linked to the warm, wet summer months, and in others to the cooler, dry season. After a pregnancy of 7 months, a single 2 kg (4.4 lb) youngster is born, remaining in a chamber in the tunnel until it is about 2 weeks old. From this age it begins to follow the mother on her nightly searches for termites and ants. It is only at 6 months of age that it is able to start digging for itself.

Ecological Interactions

The prodigious digging activities of the Aardvark have not been studied, but we do know that these animals turn a great deal of soil. In the process, they eat large numbers of termites that are often destructive to crops and pastureland. Unfortunately, they also undermine earthen dam walls and dig holes in roads and under fences. As a result, they are often killed illegally by landowners. The burrows of the Aardvark serve as breeding and retreat locations for a great number of other animal species. For instance, within its limited range, the South African Shelduck relies heavily on abandoned Aardvark burrows for nesting. The Ant-eating Chat is another bird that nests in these burrows, and Rock Python females have been recorded laying their eggs in them.

Status

The Aardvark is CITES Appendix II listed because it has seen considerable losses of range and numbers in parts of its distribution. This is at least in part because of conflict with farming interests, direct hunting for its meat, and possibly the influence of pesticides and insecticides. Within southern Africa it is widespread, and with a few localized exceptions, we feel that by and large it still occurs at its maximum possible density. Certainly on the central Karoo plain of South Africa, where we live, we have not observed any obvious decline in numbers even though we know some are killed illegally each year. Unfortunately, the Pangolin is another story. It is CITES Appendix I listed and is generally considered to be endangered in parts of its range. Within the covered region and elsewhere, Pangolin scales are a sought-after item for sale in the traditional medicine trade.

Profiles

Pangolin, *Manis temminckii*, Plate 88a
Aardvark, *Orycteropus afer*, Plate 95a

5. Hares, Rabbits, and Hyrax

The *hares* and *rabbits*, along with the *pikas*, belong to order Lagomorpha, and of the 69 species worldwide, 6 occur in southern Africa. These are made up of 3 *red rock rabbits*, the seriously endangered RIVERINE RABBIT, and 2 hares. New genetic research is beginning to show that the SCRUB HARE (Plate 88) will in time probably be divided into three distinct species within the region. *Lagomorphs* are widely distributed, absent only from southern South America, Madagascar, and the islands of the West Indies and most of those in Southeast Asia. Lagomorphs were once lumped together with rodents and some still believe that is where they belong. Others believe they show affinities to the hoofed mammals, others to the elephant-shrews; if you are confused, so are we!

Unlike the rodents, which have just two pairs of incisors at the front of the mouth, the hares and rabbits have three pairs. On the top jaw there is a pair of prominent cutting incisors and directly behind them a smaller pair that is not used in feeding. As with the rodents, the incisor teeth continue to grow throughout life. All lagomorphs in the region have longer and more developed hind legs than front legs; this is especially obvious in the Scrub Hare and the CAPE HARE (Plate 88). The two hares also have very long ears and short, fluffy black-and-white tails. Although the Riverine Rabbit of the South African central Karoo more closely resembles a hare, genetically it is in fact a rabbit. Other factors separate hares from rabbits: Rabbits dig burrows in which to live and hares rest above ground. Young rabbits are born naked and helpless in burrows, but the young of hares, perhaps because of their increased exposure to predators, are born with fur, with eyes open, and able to move about within minutes of birth. In nearly all lagomorphs, the females are larger than males, unusual in the mammalian world.

The Scrub Hare is larger than the Cape Hare over much of southern Africa, but in some parts they are similar in size. Cape Hares prefer drier and open areas, even desert, but the Scrub Hare occupies areas of woodland or good bushland, as long as there is grass to eat. The hare that you see in cultivated land and in rural gardens is nearly always the Scrub Hare. SMITH'S RED ROCK RABBIT (Plate 88) is one of three rabbit species occupying hill and mountain country in the region. They have fairly long ears and a short, fluffy, reddish tail, usually with a black tip.

We have included the ROCK HYRAX (Plate 88) with the rabbits and hares, not because it is related to them—it is not—but because it is of similar size; it is often misleadingly called a "rock rabbit." In fact, hyraxes, order Hyracoidea, are considered to be primitive ungulates, or hoofed mammals, with distant relationships to the Elephant and Dugong! Hyraxes are widespread in Africa and extend into Arabia. They can be broadly divided into two groups, the tree-dwellers and the rock-dwellers. Confusingly, the tree-dwellers sometimes take to living among rocks and the rock-dwellers readily climb trees. Hyraxes are small (2 to 5 kg, 4.4 to 11 lb), stockily built, and have no tail. The ears are small and rounded, and overall coat color is variable but usually gray-brown to dark brown.

Natural History

Ecology and Behavior

The Cape and Scrub Hares, as well as Smith's Red Rock Rabbit, are principally nocturnal, but on cool, overcast days they may come out of cover to feed. Just behind our village home in the South African Karoo there is a low, rocky outcrop that is occupied by a population of red rock rabbits. We often see them basking in the sun, particularly after a cold night. Both hare species are encountered mainly in flat to undulating country, with the Scrub Hare favoring those areas with more cover. The red rock rabbit occupies rocky hill and mountain country, even on relatively small and isolated outcrops that are surrounded by open plains. Both hare species spend the daylight hours resting in what are known as *forms*. These are areas of flattened vegetation that neatly outline the impression left by the body of the hare. Red rock rabbits rest in rock crevices, among boulder tumbles, or in dense vegetation.

These three species are mainly solitary, but where there is an abundance of food they may be present in substantial numbers. This may give the observer the false impression that they live in colonies. Grass makes up much of their diet but they readily eat other plants, and red rock rabbits frequently eat from herbs and low-growing bushes. Hares deposit their droppings at random throughout their range but red rock rabbits make use of midden sites, where these rabbits go specifically to defecate. These accumulations can cover an area of up to 2 sq m (21 sq ft). Hares rely on their speed to escape predators, but red rock rabbits dive rapidly for cover.

Rock Hyraxes are diurnal. They occupy mountain and hill ranges, as well as isolated rock outcrops. They live in colonies of 4 to 8 individuals, but densities may be very high. Rock Hyraxes sunbathe in the early morning hours for long periods before they move off to feed. During the basking period an adult will keep watch from a prominent point for birds of prey and other predators, especially the Verreaux's Eagle. Should a predator be sighted, the animal on watch will utter a sharp cry and all hyraxes in the vicinity will dive for cover. Each colony has a strict "pecking order," with a dominant male and female. Most feeding takes place in two intensive periods, in the morning and again in the late afternoon. When feeding, hyraxes rarely move more than a few hundred meters (yards) from their rocky retreats. They eat a wide range of plants and include leaves, flowers, and fruits in their diet.

Breeding

The two hares breed throughout the year in the region, each female producing up to four litters in a year. In the case of the Cape Hare, a female that is ready to mate may be pursued by several males, each hoping to impregnate her. Males may fight viciously over a female, kicking with their powerful hind legs. Much fur can fly in such encounters, although serious injury seems to be rare. The females of both hare species give birth to a litter of between 1 and 3 young, which are known as *leverets*. The length of pregnancy in the two hares averages 42 days. As we have already mentioned, the young hares are well developed at birth but the rabbits are naked and helpless. The female red rock rabbit makes a neat nest of fine vegetation and then lines this with her own fine belly fur, which she plucks out with her front teeth.

The Rock Hyrax female has a long pregnancy for such a small mammal, some 210 days. The 1 to 3 (rarely 4 or 5) hairy young move around shortly after birth. Male young are heavier than females, a situation that reverses as they mature. Birth weights vary from 150 to 300 g (5.3 to 10.6 oz). Hyraxes in the region are seasonal breeders, but the timing varies from area to area.

Ecological Interactions

The hares, Red Rock Rabbit, and the Rock Hyrax frequently feature in the diet of a wide range of mammalian predators, birds of prey, and large snakes. In the case of the hyrax, its principal predator is Verreaux's Eagle (also called Black Eagle); in fact, more than 90% of the diet of this magnificent bird consists of these small mammals. In some parts of the South African range of the Rock Hyrax, farmers have killed off the eagle and now complain bitterly about hyraxes competing with their sheep for food. We have done extensive studies of the diet of mammalian predators in the region, and hares, Red Rock Rabbits, and Rock Hyraxes appear frequently in our records. Two studies found that Rock Hyraxes make up more than 60% of the prey items of Leopards. This was interesting for two reasons: it indicated that the Leopards were hunting mainly during the day, and also that hyraxes seemed to be favored over abundant antelope. Hares, rabbits, and hyraxes are commonly hunted by people, but this does not seem to pose any threat to their populations.

Notes

Interestingly, the upper pair of incisors of the adult Rock Hyrax continues to grow throughout its life, in much the same way as an elephant's tusks, but the four lower incisors do not. Another anatomical feature worth mentioning is that the soles of hyrax feet are naked and are kept moist by glandular secretions. Muscles in the foot are able to retract the middle of the sole so that the moist foot acts like a suction cup, an important aid to climbing.

Status

Of the lagomorphs, only the Riverine Rabbit gives cause for concern within the region and it is now considered endangered (IUCN Red List). It occurs only in a narrow belt of scrub along a few normally dry watercourses in the central Karoo of South Africa. Much of its habitat has been cleared for agriculture, and it is extensively hunted by domestic dogs and farm workers. Several habitat fragments on private land have been set aside as conservancies but this may not be enough to save it. It is believed that its total population may be less than 1,000 individuals. The hares, red rock rabbits, and Rock Hyraxes are common to abundant. Periodic population crashes of the Rock Hyrax result from overcrowding, vegetation depletion, and disease, but numbers soon build up again.

Profiles

Rock Hyrax, *Procavia capensis*, Plate 88b
Smith's Red Rock Rabbit, *Pronolagus rupestris*, Plate 88c
Cape Hare, *Lepus capensis*, Plate 88d
Scrub Hare, *Lepus saxatilis*, Plate 88e

6. Rodents

Rodents are a very successful group of mammals, so much so that a few species have become major nuisances to people and their crops, and are common vectors of disease. However, this involves only a handful of species and most rodents are harmless and even beneficial. Although the order, Rodentia, is by far the most diverse of all mammal orders, many rodent species are nocturnal and secretive and do not make for easy viewing. Almost 1,750 different species have been described, no less than 43% of all known mammalian species. With the exception of the Antarctic and a few small oceanic islands, rodents occur just about everywhere. No other mammalian order shows such a wide range of adaptations for colonizing and inhabiting virtually any type of habitat. Some species are habitat-specific, others are generalists and can live in many different types of habitats, including those created by people. The rodents include, among others, the *mice, rats, gerbils, squirrels, molerats, porcupines, beavers,* and *Springhares.*

The reader might well ask why rodents as a group are so successful. One characteristic that contributes to their success is their teeth. All rodents have two pairs of *incisors.* They sit at the front of the mouth, one pair of long, slightly curved, chisel-like incisors in each jaw. Not only are these teeth in a constant state of sharpness, but they continue to grow throughout the animal's life. The incisors are separated by a long gap from the grinding teeth, or *cheek teeth,* which are set well back on the jaws. The incisors are used to gnaw (the order name, Rodentia, comes from the Latin verb *rodere,* to gnaw), cut, and slice food, with the cheek-teeth then reducing it to sizes suitable for swallowing. In some burrowing species the incisors are also put to work as excavating tools. With this combination of specialized teeth and the associated strong jaw muscles, the rodents are well set to be successful.

The vast majority of the world's rodents are small mouse-like or rat-like mammals, most weighing less than 1 kg (2.2 lb); in fact, a great number weigh less than 100 g (3.5 oz). In southern Africa they range in size from the 6 g (0.2 oz) PYGMY MOUSE to the 20 kg (44 lb) SOUTHERN PORCUPINE (Plate 90). At the last count there were 83 rodent species known to occur within the region. Only a few of these species are likely to be seen by the ecotraveller and we have detailed these here, as well as some nocturnal species that you may see on night game-viewing drives. Both the Southern Porcupine and the kangaroo-like SPRINGHARE (Plate 90) are common, widespread, and are often seen in the lights of vehicles at night. The Southern Porcupine has a formidable body covering of long, black-and-white banded, very sharp quills. Contrary to popular opinion, porcupines cannot "shoot" their quills and impale their enemies. However, quills are loosely attached to the skin and they detach easily. This is a powerfully built rodent, with short and stocky legs. Springhares, weighing in at up to 3.8 kg (8.4 lb), with their very long hind legs, tiny front legs used only for digging, and hopping gait, should not be mistaken for any other mammal in southern Africa. Two other large species, the GREATER CANERAT and the GIANT RAT (both Plate 90), stand out because of their size, but unfortunately they are seldom seen. The Greater Canerat can weigh up to 5 kg (11 lb) and bears a passing resemblance to an overgrown guinea pig, but with a short tail. The Giant Rat, weighing between 1 and 3 kg (2.2 and 6.6 lb), is the largest "rat-like" rodent in the region and to some it is a terrifying sight.

Several of the smaller species are day-active and sometimes easy to observe. In fact one can often get as much enjoyment out of watching these smaller animals as the larger ones. Of the 7 species of squirrel occurring in the region, out of a world total of some 350 (family Sciuridae), 2 are commonly seen. The SOUTHERN GROUND SQUIRREL and TREE SQUIRREL (both Plate 89) occupy totally different habitats. Southern Ground Squirrels live in self-excavated burrow systems in the west and central areas that are arid and have mainly sparse plant cover. The tail of this squirrel is often raised over the back and used as a "sunshade" on warm days. The much smaller Tree Squirrel occupies dry woodland in the north and northeast of the region. Although a tree-dwelling squirrel, it spends a lot of time seeking food on the ground. The DASSIE RAT (Plate 90), which has a somewhat squirrel-like appearance, occurs in dry, rocky hills in the west. Another "squirrel-like" rodent in the region is the WOODLAND DORMOUSE (Plate 89). There are four species of dormouse in southern Africa but the Woodland Dormouse is the most widespread and usually quite common. Weighing just 30 g (1.06 oz), it is one of the smallest of the local dormice.

Molerats, which live underground, have soft fur, short, flattened tails, large rounded heads, and prominent incisor teeth. Their ears and eyes are tiny and barely visible, and the snout is flattened, naked, and pig-like. The COMMON MOLERAT (Plate 89), as its name implies, is abundant, but it is very rarely seen. Signs of its passing, in the form of numerous earth heaps, are commonly seen throughout its wide range. It is the smallest of the five molerat species in the region, weighing an average of 150 g (53 oz). In contrast, the largest species, the CAPE DUNE MOLERAT, may tip the scales at a respectable 750 g (26.5 oz). There are three day-active mouse/rat types that are commonly seen if one exercises a little patience. These are the FOUR-STRIPED GRASS MOUSE, BRANT'S WHISTLING RAT, and the BUSH KAROO RAT (all Plate 91). We have also included three nocturnal mice, not because they are particularly easy to see but because they are firm favorites of ours. The POUCHED MOUSE (Plate 89) is very hamster-like and has soft fur and a short tail. A characteristic of this mouse and the Giant Rat is that they have the ability to carry large quantities of food in cheek pouches. The ACACIA RAT (Plate 91), which weighs about 100 g (3.5 oz), spends virtually its entire life aloft in the trees; its tail, more than half of the total length of its body, provides balance. There are in fact two species, but to the non-specialist they are impossible to distinguish in the field. BUSHVELD GERBILS (Plate 91), the smallest of their genus at 70 g (2.5 oz), have bright, silky, reddish-brown fur with white underparts.

Natural History

Ecology and Behavior

Southern Ground Squirrels are day-active and occupy dry areas with sparse vegetation cover. They are social squirrels that live in colonies numbering from 5 to 30 animals. Colony members excavate extensive burrow systems, usually in sandy soils. Females and their young remain close to the colony, but the adult males move between different colonies. The burrow networks are often shared with two small carnivore species, the Yellow Mongoose (Plate 94) and Suricate (Plate 93)—all apparently living in harmony. The squirrels rarely move more than a few hundred meters (yards) from a colony when feeding. They eat a wide variety of roots, leaves, seeds, flowers, and bulbs, and whenever the opportunity presents itself they will eat insects, especially termites. Food items are often held in the front paws while the animal sits erect. This not only makes handling and eating food easier, but when erect they are better able to detect predators. Tree Squirrels are usually solitary foragers, but several animals may be seen together. They are quite quarrelsome creatures and when annoyed, when a predator is in the area, or when proclaiming their right to their piece of turf, they chatter harshly and flick their tails. Despite their name, they spend a lot of time foraging on the ground; at the first hint of danger, however, they return to the trees. At night they take shelter in tree hollows that are lined with dry grass and leaves. Pods, seeds, and berries make up much of their diet, but they are not averse to snacking on flowers and insects. In one study, they ate parts of 38 different plant species.

The Woodland Doormouse spends the day sleeping in holes and hollows in trees and large bushes, where they build substantial domed nests. They also make use of closed birds' nests, such as those of the weavers. If left in peace, they will move into buildings, constructing nests in roofs or walls. They are apparently territorial, and vicious fights may occur between rivals. They are equally at home seeking food in trees or on the ground. Woodland Dormice are omnivores; seeds and other plant parts are eaten, but they also take substantial quantities of insects, millipedes, and the occasional gecko. In some areas they are known to make their nests in beehives, where they feed on dead bees, honey, and wax. Because of their *fossorial* (living underground) lifestyle, not a great deal is known about the Common Molerat. They dig extensive burrow systems. Soil is loosened by the large incisor teeth and then pushed away by the feet. Surplus soil is pushed to the surface, where it lies in small mounds. Without continuous growth of the incisor teeth, the corrosive action of the soil would soon wear them away. At night they often move around above ground, particularly after rain. They live in small colonies, with several animals sharing the same burrow system. Roots, bulbs, and tubers make up much of their diet.

Southern Porcupines dig large burrows that may be occupied by a single animal but commonly by several. In very rocky ground they make use of caves and holes among boulder tumbles. Foraging is usually a solitary activity. These porcupines are strictly nocturnal, although we have seen them basking in the sun at the entrance to their burrows. The entrances to many of these shelters are littered with gnawed bones. These bones provide the porcupines with the minerals they need for growing their armory—the quills—as well as for sharpening the continuously growing incisors. Much of their food consists of roots, bulbs, and tubers, which are dug out of the ground with the front paws. They also favor the bark of certain trees, which sometimes results in severe bark damage. Unfortunately, their taste for potatoes and pumpkins brings them into conflict with farmers and gardeners.

Springhares occur in sandy areas. They live in loose colonies and can reach very high densities, but each burrow is occupied by only one animal, or a female and its single young. Each burrow has two separate entrances, a sloping one for normal use and a vertical escape-burrow. The tiny forefeet are used to dig out grass and roots to eat. They are apparently not territorial, and there appears to be little conflict between individuals. The Greater Canerat is known in some parts of its range as the "Grass-cutter," and it forms an important part of human diets in some areas. Its meat has a flavor something like a chicken/pork mix. The preferred habitat is dense reedbeds and vegetation tangles, always near water. Canerats create networks of pathways and tunnels and live in loosely associated groups. Although mainly night-active, we have seen them during the day, but they do not like the hotter hours. Their feeding areas are easily identified by small piles of cut grass or reed segments, which make up much of their diet. They are disliked in areas where sugarcane is grown, as they can do considerable damage to young cane. Giant Rats are mainly active at night but, where not disturbed, are happy to forage in the cooler daylight hours. They often dig their own burrows but also take shelter among rocks and dense plant growth. Entrances to burrows are often closed when a rat is in residence. Feeding mainly on fruits, seeds, and roots, they also occasionally eat insects.

The rock-dwelling Dassie Rat is the only rodent in Africa that chews cud in the same way as a cow or antelope. They live in rock crevices in pairs or small family parties, and are active during early morning and early evening. They are fond of basking in the sun, particularly after a cold night. A great variety of plant food is eaten, but they prefer leaves and flowers. These are harvested and then taken back to the rock crevices, where they can eat out of sight of predators. Pouched Mice seem to prefer a life of solitude, although in favored areas loose colonies may become established. Unlike most small rodents, they are quite slow-moving and we have caught several by hand at night. They often dig their own burrows but are not averse to taking over those dug by other species, or making themselves comfortable among a pile of rocks. We have caught them living in debris deposited on riverbanks after floods. Seeds and small fruits are favored foods but they do take the occasional insect. Four-striped Grass Mice can reach near-plague proportions after a good season. They often become used to people and their activities, and they are very inquisitive. They seem to be able to adapt to most habitats where some grass grows. Frequently seen during the day, these mice are also active at night, depending on temperature and the level of disturbance. Numerous paths radiate from their burrows. Grass seeds make up much of their diet, but they take plant parts and insects as well. The almost entirely arboreal Acacia Rat emerges only at night from its tree hole or domed stick nest. These nests are often decorated with a formidable array of "harvested" thorny twigs. Acacia Rats live in family groups and small parties of adults, and they can provide an amusing time if you choose to camp under an occupied tree. Green leaves, seed pods, and seeds, with the occasional insect, constitute their menu. Little is known about their behavior but it would certainly make an interesting study subject. Bushveld Gerbils are night-active, live in loosely knit colonies in burrow networks, and feed mainly on grass seeds. Brant's Whistling Rats are diurnal and usually live in colonies, although some individuals seem to prefer a solitary existence. They dig extensive burrow systems in sandy soils. Although a variety of plant food is eaten, they prefer green leaves, especially from succulents. These are harvested and usually carried back to the burrow entrance, where the rat sits on its haunches, leaving the front feet free for handling the food. In some parts of their range, particularly the Kalahari, many colonies lie adjacent to each other. Bush Karoo Rats are "master builders," constructing above-ground nests of twigs and other plant debris. Some of these nests may reach almost 1 m (3.3 ft) in height and 2 m (6.6 ft) across. Each nest is occupied by a family group, and harvested green plant food is eaten, or stored, at the nest. Generally believed to forage only on the ground, we have watched them climb several meters into bushes to collect leaves and the occasional berry.

Breeding

Southern Ground Squirrels are known to breed throughout the year, but the number of births peaks during the summer rains. The helpless young, usually numbering 1 to 3 in each litter, are born in a nest chamber that is lined with dry grass. It is only when they are about 6 weeks old that the pups make their first visit to the outside world. Females may have more than one litter during the course of the year. The Tree Squirrel, as with many arboreal squirrels, indulges in vigorous sex chases in which a receptive female may be chased by several males. Once the female is ready to mate, the "chosen" male first grooms her rump and then mounts. More litters are born during the summer months but births have been recorded throughout the year. Pregnancy is about 55 days, with 1 to 3 young being born in a tree hole lined with leaves and grass. Woodland Doormice litters are mainly born in the summer months after a pregnancy of about 24 days. The naked, helpless young weigh just 3.5 g (0.1 oz) at birth. By contrast, the young of the Dassie Rat are well developed at birth, with a full coat of hair. Litters are small, usually with only 1 or 2 young, and they are born in a vegetation-lined nest deep in a rock crevice. The breeding behavior of these interesting rodents is largely unknown. In the region, most Greater Canerat litters are born between August and December. The average number of young in each litter is 4, but as many as 8 have been recorded. They are fully covered with hair and the eyes are open at birth. The female builds a shallow nest among dense vegetation and lines it with grass and shredded reeds. When she leaves the nest she covers the young with a thin layer of the same material. The pups soon accompany the mother along the network of pathways to the feeding sites. Giant Rat females produce litters of 2 to 4 *altricial* (helpless) young after a pregnancy of about 28 days.

Southern Porcupines are monogamous, and sexual interaction between the male and female takes place throughout the year. Despite this, a female usually has only one litter, of 1 to 4 young, each year. The young are well developed at birth, *precocial*, with eyes open and a covering of short quills. It takes them more than a year to reach their full adult weight. Litters are born in deep burrows, or among rock tumbles. The single young of the Springhare is also well developed at birth, but it remains in the burrow for the first 6 or 7 weeks of its life. When it emerges it is almost the same size as the adults—this is why one never sees young Springhares. Births take place at any time of the year. The sex life of the Common Molerat is very much a mystery, but we do know that there may be as many as 5 pups (usually 1 to 3) in a litter and that they are helpless at birth. The length of pregnancy, about 98 days, is very long for such a small rodent. Studies in captivity show that young are weaned at about 105 days old. In the case of the smaller mice, litter sizes are often quite high. A Pouched Mouse female has between 2 and 10 hairy young in a litter, the Bushveld Gerbil from 2 to 9 naked young, and the Four-striped Grass Mouse also 2 to 9. These smaller species mostly have their young during the wet summer months, and often more than one litter per season. Acacia Rats have smaller litters, 2 to 5, which are born in their thorn-bedecked tree holes and nests. The young of the Brant's Whistling Rat and the Bush Karoo Rat are known as "nipple-clingers." When mother goes foraging, the young remain attached to the nipples, and they get dragged along for a bumpy ride. For obvious reasons, litter sizes are small, just 1 to 3 young in each species.

Ecological Interactions

Rodents are particularly important because of their great abundance. This is significant because some species become a nuisance and even a threat to people, but rodents are also an important source of food for carnivores, birds of prey, and some reptiles. In the Kalahari, several prides of Lion include large numbers of porcupines in their diet. Certain individuals have learned how to flip these sharp-quilled rodents onto their backs, exposing their vulnerable bellies. Some rodents, such as the Greater Canerat, are regarded as delicacies by some people, and attempts have been made to farm them for their tasty flesh. Some species are destructive to crops and stored foodstuffs, and as a result, they are often the targets of mass-poisoning campaigns. Many of the poisons used are also harmful to the predators that hunt these rodents. Several rodents, especially the smaller colony dwellers, are occasionally implicated in the spread of diseases that are harmful, and on occasion deadly, to people. Rodents are useful soil "tillers and turners," important in aerating and loosening topsoil, often on a grand scale. In the region, the master rodent soil-turner must be the Southern Porcupine. Apart from their great burrow systems, they are constantly making shallow excavations as they forage at night for roots and bulbs. Molerats move vast quantities of soil as they extend and enlarge their burrow systems. Many a person has ended up knee-deep in soil where molerats have been active, and these areas are avoided by wise horse riders.

Notes

Although most rodent species keep their distance from people, a few, such as the House Mouse, House Rat, and the Brown or Norwegian Rat, have found a comfortable lifestyle with people. They have spread throughout much of the world, including southern Africa, and people surely wish they had not. Even in the arid interior of the region, the House Rat and House Mouse have established themselves in small settlements and on farmsteads. Once established, they are destructive and extremely difficult to eradicate.

Status

All of the rodents in this section are common to very common throughout the region. Some concern has been expressed that localized extinctions may befall the Acacia Rat because in some areas its favored tree, the camel thorn, is being chopped out. However, this does not pose a threat to the species as a whole. Some species, such as the Southern Porcupine, Greater Canerat, and Springhare, are heavily hunted for their meat, but this seems to have little effect on populations. A few species, including the SUN SQUIRREL, STRIPED TREE SQUIRREL, and RUDD'S MOUSE, are at the southern limits of their range in southern Africa, and in the long term may face threats through habitat loss. Farther to the north they are quite common. There are also a number of species that are endemic to the region and have restricted ranges or habitat needs, but none are now considered threatened or endangered, and most occur in substantial numbers. The DUNE HAIRY-FOOTED GERBIL is only known to live in a small area of sand dunes in the Namib Desert, and the harsh and isolated nature of its habitat is its best protection.

Profiles

Southern Ground Squirrel, *Xerus inauris*, Plate 89a
Tree Squirrel, *Paraxerus cepapi*, Plate 89b
Woodland Dormouse, *Graphiurus murinus*, Plate 89c
Pouched Mouse, *Saccostomus campestris*, Plate 89d
Common Molerat, *Cryptomys hottentotus*, Plate 89e
Giant Rat, *Cricetomys gambianus*, Plate 90a
Dassie Rat, *Petromus typicus*, Plate 90b
Springhare, *Pedetes capensis*, Plate 90c
Greater Canerat, *Thryonomys swinderianus*, Plate 90d
Southern Porcupine, *Hystrix africaeaustralis*, Plate 90e
Four-striped Grass Mouse, *Rhabdomys pumilio*, Plate 91a
Acacia Rat, *Thallomys paedulcus*, Plate 91b

Bushveld Gerbil, *Tatera leucogaster*, Plate 91c
Brant's Whistling Rat, *Parotomys brantsii*, Plate 91d
Bush Karoo Rat, *Otomys unisulcatus*, Plate 91e

7. Carnivores

The *carnivores* are the predators, the hunters, and they include some of the mammals most eagerly sought by the ecotraveller. Most folk visiting the region want to see LIONS, CHEETAHS, and LEOPARDS, and so they should, but no fewer than 36 carnivore species call southern Africa home. In addition to the fierce, wild predators, order Carnivora also includes dogs and house cats. Within the order there are 7 families, with approximately 240 species occurring worldwide (with the exception of Australia, Antarctica, and a number of oceanic islands). (Australia has the Dingo, but this dog descended from domesticated animals brought there by prehistoric people.) In southern Africa, there are representatives of 5 families. These are *canids* (dogs), *felids* (cats), *mustelids* (weasels, badgers, otters), *viverrids* and *herpestids* (genets, civets, mongooses) and *hyaenids* (hyenas). Some species are common and frequently seen but many are night-active and secretive.

The name Carnivora is taken from the Latin *caro,* for flesh, and *voro,* to eat. Carnivores are all, to a greater or lesser extent, predators. As more research has been done on this group, it has become clear that although a good number of species are mainly flesh-eaters, a fair proportion are insect-eaters, and some include large quantities of plant food in their diet. The carnivores have teeth designed to seize, puncture, and tear flesh. All have 2 pairs of long, sharp-pointed and conical-shaped *canine teeth,* and back teeth designed for cutting or crushing, depending on the species and prey type. The SPOTTED HYENA (Plate 95) has massive teeth that are designed to slice and break up tough food. Powerful jaw muscles aid this process. By way of contrast, the BAT-EARED FOX (Plate 92) eats mainly insects, and its numerous back teeth are ideal for crushing grasshoppers and termites.

All of the cats are similar in general appearance, and all but the Cheetah (Plate 97) have fully retractile claws. This means that the claws can be drawn back into a protective sheath so they can retain their sharpness for grasping prey and climbing trees. Seven of the world's 37 species of cat occur in the covered region, of which 4 have spotted coats and 3 are more uniform in color. The cats are best adapted to meat-eating, with large canines for grasping and killing and back teeth that function almost like scissors to cut muscle. The largest African cat by far is the Lion (Plate 97), with males weighing between 150 and 225 kg (330 and 495 lb) and females from 110 to 152 kg (242 to 334 lb). The Lion is usually uniformly tawny in color, but in cubs and occasionally adults there is some faint spotting on the belly. Adult males develop a *mane* of long hair, blond, dark brown, or black, that extends from the sides of the face to the neck, chest, and shoulders. CARACALS (Plate 97) have uniform reddish-fawn coats and a short tail of similar color. Should you be lucky enough to see one, you will observe that the ears are quite long and pointed, with a tuft of black hair at the tip. Adults weigh between 7 and 19 kg (15 and 42 lb). AFRICAN WILD CATS (Plate 96) look very similar to domestic cats, with which they readily interbreed, but they have longer legs and the backs of their ears are always rich reddish-brown. They range from pale sandy brown in drier areas to light or dark gray in locations with higher rainfall. Weights range from 2.5 to 6 kg (5.5 to 13 lb). The smallest of the region's spotted felids is the SMALL SPOTTED CAT (Plate 96), weighing between 1 and 2 kg (2.2 and 4.4 lb). Overall coloration is reddish-fawn to almost pale cream. The SERVAL (Plate 96) is a long-legged, short-tailed, spotted cat that weighs between 8 and 13 kg (18 and 29 lb). The swiftest of all cats, the Cheetah, has a grayhound-like build, a long tail, and a dark line that runs from the inner corner of each eye to the mouth. Unlike the Leopard (Plate 97), the spots are solid and do not form rosettes. Adults weigh between 40 and 60 kg (88 and 132 lb). The largest and most powerfully built of the spotted cats in the region, with usually a heavier build than the Cheetah, is the Leopard. Males weigh from 20 to 90 kg (44 to 198 lb) and females 17 to 60 kg (37 to 132 lb). Much of the body has a dense scattering of rosette-like spots.

Of the 36 dog species (family Canidae) worldwide, 12 occur in Africa, 5 in southern Africa; all can be readily identified as dogs. Only one true fox occurs in the region, the CAPE FOX (Plate 92), also called Silver Fox because silvery gray is the dominant coat color. This is a small dog weighing between 2.5 and 4 kg (5.5 and 9 lb). The Bat-eared Fox (Plate 92) has large ears and a bushy, silvery gray coat, with the legs and most of the tail much darker, often black. It weighs between 3 and 5 kg (6.6 to 11 lb). The 2 jackal species, the BLACK-BACKED (Plate 92) and the SIDE-STRIPED (Plate 92) JACKALS, are similar in build and size, 6 to 12 kg (13 to 26 lb), although the latter averages slightly larger. At between 20 and 30 kg (44 and 66 lb), the WILD DOG (Plate 92) is Africa's largest canid. It has long legs, large rounded ears, and very variable color patterns. The coat is heavily blotched with black, white, and yellow-brown, and the tail is usually white tipped.

Family Mustelidae has about 70 species worldwide, with just 5 in southern Africa. Members of the family are small to medium-sized carnivores and diverse in terms of appearance, behavior, and choice of habitat. Two species are mainly aquatic, the SPOTTED-NECKED OTTER and CAPE CLAWLESS OTTER (Plate 93). The first is very localized and rare, but the Cape Clawless Otter is widely distributed. The latter takes its name from the fact that it does not have claws at the toe-tips but nails very similar to ours. The Cape Clawless is a large otter, weighing 10 to 18 kg (22 to 40 lb), and it has a short, dense, and very soft coat. The legs are short and stout, and the long, broad tail serves as a rudder in the water. The HONEY BADGER (Plate 93) is a stocky, short-legged, and powerfully built mustelid, with silvery gray upperparts and black underparts. The short, hairy tail is often held erect when walking. It weighs from 8 to 14 kg (18 to 31 lb). The STRIPED POLECAT (Plate 93) is by far the most commonly seen mustelid in the region, unfortunately usually squashed on the road! It weighs 600 g to 1.4 kg (1.3 to 3 lb) and is overall black, with 4 broad white stripes running from the base of the tail and meeting on top of the head.

Viverrids (family Viverridae) are a very diverse group in Africa, including all of the *mongooses, genets,* and *civets*. Some of the mongooses have been placed in a separate family, the Herpestidae. Of the 16 viverrids in the region, we have profiled 7, those that you as an ecotraveller have the best chance of seeing. The largest is the AFRICAN CIVET (Plate 96), which weighs from 9 to 15 kg (20 to 33 lb) and has a gray coat that is liberally marked with black spots, blotches, and irregular stripes. When it walks, the back is distinctly arched and the head held close to the ground. A similarly marked species is the SMALL-SPOTTED GENET (Plate 96), but it has a longer tail, shorter legs, and weighs just 1.5 to 2.6 kg (3.3 to 5.7 lb). The other species in the region, the LARGE-SPOTTED GENET, usually has a black-tipped tail.

Two of the most highly social mongooses are the SURICATE (Plate 93) and the BANDED MONGOOSE (Plate 94). Both are superficially similar but they can be separated by their distribution. They both have black to dark brown stripes across the backs, but those of the Suricate are irregular. The background color of the fur is pale fawn in the Suricate and gray to gray-brown in the Banded. Tail hairs are shorter in the Suricate and there is a black tip. Both species commonly stand on the hind legs, using the tail as a prop. When running away, the tail of the Suricate is held erect, that of the Banded parallel to the ground. Suricates weigh from 620 to 960 g (1.4 to 2.1 lb), and the Banded Mongoose 1 to 1.6 kg (2.2 to 3.5 lb). The smallest viverrid in the region, the DWARF MONGOOSE (Plate 94), weighs up to 350 g (12.3 oz) and has a glossy, uniformly dark brown coat. Another social viverrid is the YELLOW MONGOOSE (Plate 94), weighing 450 to 900 g (1 to 2 lb). Over much of its range it has reddish-yellow fur, with a white throat and tip of the tail. Three solitary mongooses are commonly seen, 2 during daylight and one on night drives. The largest of the 3 is the WHITE-TAILED MONGOOSE (Plate 94), which weighs up to 5.2 kg (11.4 oz). It has a dark-colored body and legs, a distinctive white, bushy tail, and, when walking, the back is arched and the head held close to the ground. SMALL GRAY MONGOOSES (Plate 94) are colored as their name implies, without any distinctive markings. Large specimens may reach just 1 kg (2.2 lb), and the tail is long and bushy. The SLENDER MONGOOSE (Plate 94), is very slender and has short legs. Color varies from yellow-brown or gray to rich red-brown, and the tail has a distinctive black tip. When running, the tail is held vertically and curves over the back. Males may weigh up to 800 g (1.8 lb); females are about 30% lighter.

Of the 4 species of *hyena*, Family Hyaenidae, 3 occur in southern Africa. The backs of all species slope downwards from the shoulders to the rump. The head and chest are large but the hindquarters are more weakly developed. Both the BROWN HYENA (Plate 95) and the Spotted Hyena (Plate 95) have massively developed teeth and jaw muscles, but those of the AARDWOLF (Plate 95) are weak and the teeth peg-like. The largest of the 3 is the Spotted, which weighs between 60 and 80 kg (132 and 176 lb), and has a short, fawnish-yellow coat with numerous dark spots and blotches. The ears are rounded and the tail short and bushy. Brown Hyenas weigh about 45 kg (100 lb) and have shaggy, dark-colored coats, but are much paler on the neck and shoulders. The ears are long and pointed. The Aardwolf, at a maximum weight of 11 kg (24 lb), is the smallest member of the family. The gray-brown coarse coat is marked with dark, vertical body stripes and there are black bands on the upper parts of the legs. A long, narrow mane of hair runs from the neck and onto the back. This is raised when the animal is frightened or threatened, and along with impressive barking roars, is usually enough to chase off an aggressor.

Natural History

Ecology and Behavior

Felids. All of the cats are highly adapted for hunting and killing vertebrate prey. Cats are very adept at carefully approaching their intended prey, often using minimal cover, and then either pouncing on it or chasing it over a short distance. Whether it be the tiny Small Spotted Cat or the majestic Lion, killing techniques are very similar. Prey is usually bitten on the neck, throat, or head, and death is usually rapid. With the exception of the Lion, and to a lesser extent the Cheetah, the cats in the region are solitary animals. Lions live in groups known as *prides*, and the size of a pride is largely dictated by how much food is available in the area. Each pride consists of a stable group of related females and their dependent cubs. There is usually a "coalition" of 2 or more adult males that spend part of their time with the pride and the rest circulating through their territory. Both male and female pride members vigorously defend their territory. The size of home ranges depends on the habitat and prey; studies have shown that they vary between 26 sq km (10 sq mi) and 2,000 sq km (773 sq mi). Most males are able to hold a pride for only 2 or 3 years, and are then driven off by younger and stronger males. When this happens, all young cubs may be killed by the new males, bringing the females quickly into breeding condition. Most hunting is carried out by the females, but if males are in the vicinity, they generally eat first. Lions hunt a wide range of large to medium-sized mammals, usually at night. Lions will tackle anything they can overpower, from young Elephants and Hippopotamuses to Plains Zebras, Warthogs, and Buffalo, but antelope make up the bulk of their diet. The "king of beasts" is also a master scavenger, often chasing other predators away from their kills.

Cheetahs usually live alone, except when a female is accompanied by cubs or when related males form bachelor groups. Females establish and hold territories that they defend against other females, but males are wanderers and do not lay down territorial roots. Females sometimes range over areas larger than those of the males. In a Namibian study, females occupied areas averaging 1,500 sq km (580 sq mi) and males 800 sq km (310 sq mi). In Kruger National Park, both sexes range over about 175 sq km (68 sq mi). They do most of their hunting during the cooler daylight hours, taking mostly small and medium-sized antelope. In the covered region, they hunt mainly Impalas, Springboks, and the young of larger antelope. Cheetahs are the fastest of all terrestrial predators, with verified speeds of 70 to 100 kph (44 to 62 mph) over short distances.

Leopards take a wide range of prey, varying in size from small rodents to large antelope, but medium-sized antelope are the most common prey. In areas where they have to compete with other carnivores, Leopards often haul prey into trees, out of reach of prowling Lions and Spotted Hyenas. Most of the hunting by these solitary cats is done at night, but where they are not disturbed, they will hunt during the day, especially where hyraxes form an important part of their diet. The Leopard is the most widespread and common of the region's big cats, but it is secretive and seldom seen. The Caracal, despite its relatively small size, readily hunts antelope weighing up to 40 kg (88 lb), although rodents, hyraxes, and hares are important. The Serval is a specialist rodent hunter but is not averse to snacking on birds or reptiles. It hunts during the night and day, and as with the Caracal, both sexes hold and defend territories. African Wild Cats have a very catholic diet, but it is dominated by small rodents and insectivores. Occupying most habitats, from desert to high-rainfall woodland, they may reach high densities. Until recently, little was known about that southern African endemic, the Small Spotted Cat. A nocturnal hunter, small rodents make up most of its diet, but it readily takes hares and birds that may be heavier than itself.

Canids. The most social of Africa's canids is the Wild Dog, which lives in close-knit packs that average 10 to 15 adults and subadults. Wild Dogs hunt as a pack, and a chosen prey animal may be chased for several kilometers. They are the most successful of the large predators on hunts, with 70% of chases resulting in a kill. They range over vast areas but do not establish territories. Medium-sized hoofed mammals, especially antelope, make up most of the Wild Dog diet. Both the Black-backed and Side-striped Jackals live in mated pairs, each couple defending a territory against other jackals. The Black-backed occurs virtually throughout the region, but the range of the other is limited to the northeast. Black-backed Jackals will eat virtually anything, ranging from berries to insects and young antelope to rodents. Unfortunately, they are also adept at catching sheep and are therefore targeted by farmers. The call of this jackal is, in our opinion, one of the finest in Africa, but then, we do not have any sheep. Side-striped Jackals are also omnivores but seldom take prey as large as those occasionally hunted by the Black-backed. Bat-eared Foxes forage during both night and day, resting in burrows when not on the hunt. They are social, living in small family parties, and occupy small home ranges, seldom bigger than 3 sq km (1.2 sq mi). Insects, especially termites, make up most of their food. Cape Foxes live in mated pairs within a small home range, but they forage and hunt alone. Small rodents and insects are important in their diet, but young hares and birds are also often taken. These foxes are strictly night-active but may bask in the sun at the entrance to their burrows.

Mustelids. The mustelids are, by and large, strongly carnivorous and efficient hunters, but most include a wide range of foods in their diet. The Cape Clawless Otter, unlike most otters, does not eat many fish. As it often hunts in dirty or silt-laden water, where hunting by sight is difficult, it uses its fingers to probe in mud and under rocks. Crabs are taken in quantity, as are freshwater mussels and frogs. The otters frequently forage away from water and hunt small mammals, birds, and insects. Although mainly solitary, pairs may live and hunt together. Spotted-necked Otters hunt almost exclusively in water and take more fish than Cape Clawless Otters. We have to admit to having a soft spot for Honey Badgers. They are tough and rarely back down for anything. Pairs occupy a home range and are active mainly at night, but they will also forage on cool, overcast days. They feed on a wide range of prey, which they catch on the ground or dig out with their powerful claws. Also, not uncommonly, they will climb into trees to prey on nestlings and snakes. As their name implies, they have a strong love for honey, and vigorously dig into underground hives. Their thick skin protects them against bee stings. Despite the fact that they are very common, little is known about Striped Polecats. As with other polecats and skunks, they can spray a foul-smelling fluid from the *anal glands* when threatened. They live in burrows, among rock and wood piles, and often take advantage of buildings. Hunting is a night-time activity, and a wide range of invertebrates and small rodents are taken, most dug out of the soil with the long front claws.

Viverrids and Herpestids. African Civets are nocturnal and solitary foragers, feeding on invertebrates and small vertebrates. They also eat a lot of wild fruits, especially wild dates where they occur. The copious secretions of the anal glands (used in the perfume industry) are used to mark their home ranges and the droppings are deposited in a few core sites. These dropping accumulations are called *civetries.* Strictly terrestrial, the civet's smaller relatives, the genets, are agile climbers as well as ground hunters. This is aided by retractile claws, similar to those of cats. Small-spotted Genets occupy nearly all habitats, and are common in most areas. They are strictly nocturnal, resting under dense cover during the day. Insects and small rodents are their main prey but reptiles, amphibians, and birds are also eaten. The 4 social mongooses, the Dwarf, Banded, Yellow, and the Suricate, live in colonies and all are strictly day-active. Insects, other invertebrates, rodents, and reptiles make up most of their food. With the exception of the Yellow Mongoose, which lives in groups but forages alone, the other 3 move about and forage in groups. Troop members are constantly calling, ensuring that none wander too far away and become more vulnerable to predators. The Suricate and Yellow Mongoose dig their own warrens of burrows but the other 2 species usually live in large termite mounds. Small Gray and Slender Mongooses prefer the solitary life and both are only active during the day. When they are foraging, they explore under every bush, nosing under rocks and plant debris. Both take a wide range of prey but small rodents and insects are the most important. These mongooses spend most of their time on the ground but they will scramble into bushes if there is a hint of food there. The White-tailed Mongoose is strictly nocturnal and most of their hunting is a solitary affair. In one study they occupied home ranges averaging 8 sq km (3 sq mi). They will take prey up to the size of hares and canerats, but small rodents, invertebrates, and wild fruits are also important.

Hyaenids. Spotted Hyenas are highly social, living in clans numbering from 3 to 15 or more individuals. Each clan has a clearly defined territory that is defended against intruding clans or individuals. The clan is dominated by an adult female that leads hunting forays. Far from being the skulking scavengers that they are often portrayed as, hyenas are highly efficient hunters, although they will also chase other predators from their kills. Hunting is a team effort, with the Buffalo, Plains Zebra, and antelope making up the bulk of their food. Most hunting is undertaken at night or in the cooler daylight hours. Their howling, whooping, and cackling calls are typical of the African night. The Brown Hyena is mainly night-active. Although several related individuals share a territory, foraging is a solitary activity. Nomadic males wander between different groups, mating with receptive females. Brown Hyenas scavenge and hunt a variety of small mammals, including Springhares and, on the coast, young fur seals. Wild fruits, especially Kalahari melons and cucumbers, are also eaten. The Aardwolf is mainly nocturnal, and several individuals usually share a home range. During the day they rest in burrows, sometimes dug themselves but usually excavated by other species. Termites, especially the harvesters, make up most of their food. All 3 hyena species mark their territories and home ranges with secretions from anal glands.

Breeding

Felids. With the exception of the Lion, the male and female of the other southern African cats usually come together only to mate. Males then move away and the females raise the young alone. Cubs are born under dense cover, such as in thickets or rock tumbles, or in caves. Lion cubs only join the pride when they are old enough to compete for suckling space. As the lionesses in a pride usually give birth at about the same time, cubs have several "milk bars" to choose from. Lion, Leopard, and Cheetah litter sizes vary from 1 to 5, with 2 to 4 average. Lion cubs weigh an average 1.5 kg (3.3 lb) at birth, Leopard cubs 500 g (1.1 lb) and Cheetah, 300 g (10 oz). Pregnancy in the large cats averages 100 days. The 3 big cats in the region have no fixed breeding season, but the smaller cats do. African Wild Cat females have between 1 and 5 kittens, after a pregnancy lasting between 56 and 65 days. Most births are geared to the warm, wet summer months. Small Spotted Cat females have 1 to 3 kittens following a pregnancy of up to 68 days. Serval females have a similar length of pregnancy and number of kittens, which are usually born in a flattened area among tall grass or reeds. In the case of the Caracal, births have been recorded throughout the year, but most are in the spring and summer. Kittens, normally 1 to 3, weigh about 250 g (8.8 oz) at birth, following a 79-day pregnancy.

Canids. Wild Dog pups, usually carried by a pack's dominant female, are mainly born in the dry months, when grass is short and hunting conditions for the adults are at their best. Between 2 and (a staggering) 19 pups per litter is the norm. Pups remain at the den, usually a burrow, for about 3 months before joining their first hunt as observers. Southern African canids are born after pregnancies of 60 to 70 days, although that of the Cape Fox is a bit shorter. The 2 jackals have distinct breeding seasons, and 2 to 4 pups per litter is usual. In the case of the Black-backed Jackal, young from the previous season, known as "helpers," will bring food to the new pups. The Bat-eared Fox is also a seasonal breeder; births coincide with the beginning of the rains, when insects are most common. If more than one female has given birth in a group, the pups can suckle from any of them. Pups of all species are usually born in burrows located among boulders or dense vegetation.

Mustelids. Mustelid litters are dropped in burrows, among boulders, or under dense vegetation cover. Cape Clawless Otter females have 1 to 3 cubs, following about 65 days of pregnancy. Litter sizes are similar for the other southern African mustelids. In areas such as the Kalahari, female Honey Badgers seldom successfully raise more than 1 cub. Pregnancy in the Striped Polecat is just 36 days.

Viverrids and Herpestids. Most of the region's viverrids and herpestids have litter sizes that range from 1 to 5, but Slender and Small Gray Mongoose females have 1 to 3 young (usually 2). Average length of pregnancy runs from 45 to 70 days in the different species. As with all carnivores in the region, young are born helpless and with eyes closed. Some species, such as the Small-spotted Genet, are seasonal breeders, but others, including the Banded Mongoose, are not. Those that are non-seasonal breeders do, however, see an increase in the number of litters during the rainy season.

Hyaenids. Spotted Hyenas breed at any time of year, and the 1 or 2 cubs are born after a pregnancy of about 110 days. More than one female may den down in the same burrow, giving the impression that litters are larger. Cubs weigh about 1.5 kg (3.3 lb), and are uniformly dark brown at birth. The pregnancy of the Brown Hyena is just 90 days, and 2 to 3 cubs is usual. Aardwolf pregnancy lasts 60 days. Litters usually number 1 to 4 pups, each weighing an average 500 g (1.1 lb). Several females may drop their pups in the same burrow. The hyaenids normally have their young in burrows but occasionally they make use of caves in mountainous areas.

Ecological Interactions

Both the Lion and Spotted Hyena are *communal hunters* of the African savannahs. They hunt similar prey and not infrequently steal each other's kills. Solitary male Lions are usually able to intimidate and drive groups of Spotted Hyenas from their kills, but lionesses, even in groups, often give way to Hyenas. Leopards are the only large carnivores in the region that are capable of carrying their prey high into trees and out of reach of other predators and scavengers. The cat that suffers most from kill-raiding is the Cheetah. In some areas, Cheetahs lose more than 50% of all their kills to Lions, Leopards, and Spotted Hyenas. This is why Cheetahs never occur in large numbers where other large predators are common.

An interesting *niche separation* can be found between the Yellow and Small Gray Mongooses. On our farm in the Karoo, both species occur but there is little or no competition between them. They are both day-active, and both feed on similar food, so how can they coexist? We can sit and watch both foraging within a few meters (yards) of each other, but the Small Gray seldom moves far from cover, whereas the Yellow is bolder, often moving into open areas. Therefore, their foraging behaviors are sufficiently different to minimize competition for food between them. A similar situation arises with the highly social Dwarf and Banded Mongooses, as they occur in the same areas and have a similar diet. The Dwarfs forage closer to cover but the Banded troop will range onto more open terrain. Should the Bandeds be attacked, they run in close formation, weaving and turning to confuse whatever animal is threatening.

Notes

Incidents of Lions eating people in several parts of Africa still occur from time to time. Historically, the most infamous man-eaters were probably those of Tsavo, in Kenya, during the building of the Mombasa-Uganda Railway; other major incidents occurred in Zambia, northern Mozambique, and southern Tanzania. More recently, there were attacks on refugees fleeing across South Africa's Kruger National Park from Mozambique. With these attacks, it was feared that the Lions might cast their eyes in the direction of the hundreds of thousands of ecotravellers that visit Kruger each year. Why do Lions occasionally prey on humans? Contrary to popular opinion, it is not always old and infirm animals that attack people, but often healthy animals in their prime taking advantage of an easy meal. As you are unlikely to be walking alone in lion country, you have little to fear. Periodically in other parts of Africa, rogue Spotted Hyenas and Leopards attack humans, but we know of few such records in southern Africa. In general, large predators will leave you alone if you leave them alone and don't approach them too closely.

The Wild Dog has a reputation as a wanton, bloodthirsty predator, but nothing could be further from the truth. Sadly, this false reputation has caused it to be ruthlessly hunted. Although the Wild Dog's image has improved as scientists have studied them, and we have come to realize that they are highly efficient hunters that only kill for their immediate needs, still, some are killed. Not too long ago an entire pack was shot by a farmer adjacent to Kruger National Park. Despite their endangered status, the farmer argued that they posed a threat to his stock and he was right to have shot them. The law was on his side!

Status

The large carnivores of southern Africa are now mainly confined to large national parks and game reserves. The exception is the Leopard, which has managed to survive, even within a few kilometers of a major city such as Cape Town. In fact, Leopards are reappearing in some areas where they have not been seen for decades. Because of their secretive ways, it is impossible to establish their population size, but they are the true survivors of the big cat world. The Cheetah is considered vulnerable, and less than 5,000 survive in southern Africa, the vast majority in Namibia and Botswana. The approximately 3,000 Cheetahs in Namibia comprise the largest national population in Africa, and no less than 95% of them occur on farm and ranchland. This is mainly because here they do not have to compete with Lions and Spotted Hyenas. In South Africa, less than 500 Cheetahs survive in the wild, half of which are in Kruger National Park. In the long term, the future for the Cheetah looks gloomy. Both Cheetahs and Leopards are CITES Appendix I listed. Lions number less than 6,000 in the covered region, with about one third of these living in Kruger and a large percentage of the remainder in Botswana and Zimbabwe. Current Lion estimates for Namibia are less than 350, a major shrinkage over just ten years. Lions used to occur over the entire region, from Cape Town to the Zambezi, but no longer. In general, the smaller cats all manage to hold their ground, although the Serval has disappeared from a few areas. The Caracal, as a predator of sheep and goats, is heavily targeted by farmers, yet remains widespread and successful. Small Spotted Cats are generally quite rare, but do not seem to be threatened. Surprisingly, it is the common and widespread African Wild Cat that may be pushing itself to extinction, breeding and hybridizing with the domestic cat. Spotted Hyenas are now mainly restricted to large conservation areas. The Brown Hyena (CITES Appendix II listed) is classified as vulnerable, but it is also very much a survivor. We have found it well established on large ranches where even the owners were not aware of its presence. The other carnivores we have profiled can be considered secure, with the exception of the Wild Dog, one of Africa's most endangered species. In southern Africa there are known to be no more than 1,000 of these magnificent painted dogs, with a quarter of these in Kruger and much of the remainder in Botswana.

Profiles

Cape Fox, *Vulpes chama*, Plate 92a
Bat-eared Fox, *Otocyon megalotis*, Plate 92b
Side-striped Jackal, *Canis adustus*, Plate 92c
Black-backed Jackal, *Canis mesomelas*, Plate 92d
Wild Dog, *Lycaon pictus*, Plate 92e
Cape Clawless Otter, *Aonyx capensis*, Plate 93a
Honey Badger, *Mellivora capensis*, Plate 93b
Striped Polecat, *Ictonyx striatus*, Plate 93c
Suricate, *Suricata suricatta*, Plate 93d
Slender Mongoose, *Galerella sanguinea*, Plate 94a
Dwarf Mongoose, *Helogale parvula*, Plate 94b
Banded Mongoose, *Mungos mungo*, Plate 94c
Small Gray Mongoose, *Galerella pulverulenta*, Plate 94d
Yellow Mongoose, *Cynictis penicillata*, Plate 94e
White-tailed Mongoose, *Ichneumia albicauda*, Plate 94f
Aardwolf, *Proteles cristatus*, Plate 95b
Brown Hyena, *Parahyaena brunnea*, Plate 95c
Spotted Hyena, *Crocuta crocuta*, Plate 95d
Small-spotted Genet, *Genetta genetta*, Plate 96a
African Civet, *Civettictis civetta*, Plate 96b
Small Spotted Cat, *Felis nigripes*, Plate 96c
African Wild Cat, *Felis sylvestris libyca*, Plate 96d
Serval, *Leptailurus serval*, Plate 96e
Caracal, *Caracal caracal*, Plate 97a
Lion, *Panthera leo*, Plate 97b
Leopard, *Panthera pardus*, Plate 97c
Cheetah, *Acinonyx jubatus*, Plate 97d

8. Seals

Only one species of seal occurs in southern Africa, the CAPE FUR SEAL (Plate 105). Several other seal species arrive on southern Africa's shores as very rare vagrants from the Antarctic and the Southern Ocean islands, but ecotravellers are unlikely to see them. Seals belong to order Pinnipedia, and they are primarily marine mammals that hunt in the oceans and seas. To breed and rest they come ashore (*haul-out*) to ancestral sites, called *rookeries*, that often have been in use for hundreds, if not thousands, of years. In the past, the *fur seals* were heavily hunted, and most populations were at the brink of extinction by the middle of the 19th century. They were mainly exploited for their skins—unfortunately for the fur seals, they have a dense coat of soft and attractive hair that has considerable commercial value—and to a lesser extent for the oils that were rendered from their fat, or *blubber*. The Cape Fur Seal belongs to family Otariidae, the *eared seals*, those that have small but visible ears. The other seal family, Phocidae, the so-called *true seals*, have no external ears. The Cape Fur Seal is restricted to the oceans around South Africa and Namibia, with the majority to be found in the cold waters of the Atlantic Ocean. The Benguela Current that sweeps these shores is rich in plankton and in vast shoals of pelagic fish, which provide an abundance of food for Cape Fur Seals. There are 23 colonies, most of which are on islands, but a few are very accessible to the ecotraveller. The largest mainland colony, with more than 100,000 animals, is located at Cape Cross on the Skeleton Coast of Namibia.

Male, or bull, Cape Fur Seals are much larger than cows. A mature bull at the beginning of the breeding season is in peak condition and can weigh as much as 300 kg (660 lb). The average weight through the rest of the year is 190 kg (418 lb). Cows average just 75 kg (165 lb), and are of a much more slender build. On dry land the hind flippers (modified feet and legs) are brought forward to support some of the body and the front flippers bend outwards and slightly backwards.

Natural History

Ecology, Behavior, and Breeding

Cape Fur Seals spend much of their lives at sea, often resting by floating on their backs on the surface. They frequently haul-out on islands and the mainland if they have been hunting close inshore. Very little is known about their behavior at sea. In mid-October mature bulls arrive at the traditional breeding sites to establish territories. These are vigorously defended against rival bulls, and the territory-holders are known as *beach-masters*. Several weeks later the cows arrive to give birth to a single calf that weighs between 4.6 and 7 kg (10 and 15 lb). Nearly all calves are born between late November and early December. During this time a beach-master will control the cows within his territory, and within 5 to 6 days of giving birth they are receptive to mating again. During this time the bulls hold their territories and vicious fighting with other males takes place, sometimes resulting in serious injuries. Territorial bulls will mate with between 7 and 66 cows during the short season. Cows also defend their area within a bull's territory, often no less vigorously than the bulls. The calves suckle for almost a year before becoming fully independent of their mothers.

Notes

Cape Fur Seals have been exploited for their pelts, blubber, and meat for about 400 years by Europeans, and by local peoples probably for much longer. Fur seal bones have been found in cave deposits and middens dating back thousands of years. It is likely that prehistoric people relied mainly on dead seals washing onto beaches, and had little or no impact on populations. Commercial sealers, however, nearly drove this and other fur seal species to extinction by the end of the 19th century. A Dutch expedition between March and October of 1610 killed 45,000 Cape Fur Seals. Small numbers of fur seal pups and bulls are culled each year under a carefully controlled quota system—the pups for their fine skins and the bulls for their penises, which are sold in the Far East for their supposed medicinal value.

Status

Some commercial fishermen dislike fur seals because they believe the seals compete with them for fish and damage their nets. However, in contrast to the quantities of fish taken by people, fish losses to fur seals are very small. Because of strict controls on culling, numbers of Cape Fur Seals today have risen sharply, and there are now well over one million individuals.

Profiles

Cape Fur Seal, *Arctocephalus pusillus*, Plate 105e

Ungulates

Ungulates are mammals that have hoofs instead of claws. They are divided into 2 orders, the Perissodactyla and the Artiodactyla. Modern scientific thinking is that these 2 groups of mammals diverged from a common hoofed ancestor about 60 million years ago. All ungulates have thickened, hard-edged hoofs and, as they stand, are actually balancing on the tips of their toes. Most of these animals can move with great speed and with high endurance, particularly the horses and antelope. The Artiodactyls, or *even-toed ungulates*, such as the antelope and giraffe, bear their weight on 2 toes, or, like the Hippopotamus, on 4. Perissodactyls, the *odd-toed ungulates*, "balance" on one or 3 toes, for example, zebras on one and rhinos on 3. All ungulates lead a terrestrial lifestyle and the vast majority are fleet of foot. With very few exceptions, they are exclusively herbivores, grazing and/or browsing. Africa has more species of ungulates than any other continent, as well as the greatest numbers and density of hoofed mammals. Most are quite big, none weighs less than 1 kg (2.2 lb), and a great number weigh 50 kg (110 lb) and more. Our most important commercial animals are ungulates—cattle, sheep, goats, pigs, camels, and horses.

9. Zebras and Rhinoceroses

The *zebras* and the *rhinoceroses* belong to the order Perissodactyla, the group of hoofed mammals having an odd number of toes. Within this group are the familiar horse, pony, and donkey; people have yet to get around to domesticating the rhinos! Two of the 3 families in the order have representatives in southern Africa; the third encompasses the 4 species of *tapirs*, which occur only in South/Central America and Southeast Asia. Members of the horse family run on a single toe at the tip of each leg, and the rhinos on 3. Within the covered region there are 2 species of zebra, the MOUNTAIN ZEBRA and PLAINS ZEBRA (both Plate 100), and both African rhino species, the SQUARE-LIPPED (WHITE) RHINOCEROS (Plate 98) and HOOK-LIPPED (BLACK) RHINOCEROS (Plate 98); 3 other rhino species occur in Asia.

There are 4 wild members of the horse family in Africa, the 2 zebras mentioned above, the GREVY'S ZEBRA of East Africa, and the AFRICAN WILD ASS. The Plains Zebra is the most widespread and common of Africa's wild horses. Apart from occurring in most of the major savannah parks of the region, it has been widely introduced on game farms and smaller conservation areas. This species inhabits grassy savannah and open woodland, from sea level to 4,000 m (13,100 ft) altitude. It is stoutly built and very pony-like in appearance, but the mane is erect and much of the body and legs are covered in black and white stripes. The white stripes usually have an overlaid brownish stripe, especially towards the rump, known as a shadow stripe (some populations in East Africa lack shadow stripes). Within any one population the striping is variable and no 2 individuals are exactly the same. They weigh from 290 to 340 kg (638 to 748 lb). The

Mountain Zebra, of Namibia and mountainous country in southern South Africa, is also black and white striped, but it lacks shadow stripes. This species inhabits rugged mountains and adjacent flatland. Mountain and Plains Zebras occur together only in the extreme west of Etosha National Park.

Both of the African rhino species have 2 horns on the face, one behind the other, and the one on the nose is usually the longest. It is these horns, made up of a substance similar to hair, that have caused rhinos to be hunted to the verge of extinction. The Square-lipped Rhinoceros, sometimes called White Rhino or Grass Rhino, is second in weight among terrestrial mammals only to the Elephant. The word white in the name is misleading because the animal is gray, but its hairless skin takes on the color of the local soil. It is clearly larger than the Hook-lipped Rhinoceros, has a distinctive hump on the neck, and the large head is carried just a few centimeters above the ground. It takes its name from the broad, squared-off muzzle that is adapted for grazing. When running, the tail tip is often curled towards its base, something like that of a domestic pig. These rhinos may reach a total length of 4.8 m (15.7 ft) and a shoulder height of 1.8 m (5.9 ft). Bulls are heavier than cows, reaching between 2,000 and 2,300 kg (4,400 and 5,060 lb), with the females a "dainty" 1,400 to 1,600 kg (3,080 to 3,520 lb). Apart from their general appearance and massive size, they differ from the Hook-lipped Rhinoceros (also called Black Rhino) in their choice of habitat. They occupy areas of short-grass savannah, with some thick bush to provide shade and cover. The Hook-lipped Rhinoceros is mainly found in moderate to very dense bush and woodland. Its name is derived from the pointed, triangular-shaped prehensile upper lip that is used to grasp twigs and leaves and pull them into its mouth. Because of its diet it is sometimes referred to as the Browse Rhinoceros. It lacks a raised hump on the neck and the head is smaller (not small!) than in the Square-lipped Rhino and carried quite high off the ground. It has a shoulder height averaging 1.6 m (5.25 ft) and weighs from 800 to 1,100 kg (1,760 to 2,420 lb). Bulls are larger than the cows. The front horn of both species can reach impressive lengths, with the record for the Hook-lipped being 1.2 m (3.9 ft) and the Square-lipped, 1.6 m (5.2 ft).

Natural History

Ecology and Behavior

Plains Zebras form small family herds (4 to 6) that include an adult stallion, mares, and their dependent foals. You might question this when you see what appear to be herds hundreds strong! These large aggregations are generally temporary groupings, and each family herd keeps closely together. Stallions will fight viciously to keep other males away from their mares. Some populations stay in an area throughout the year, but others follow annual migration routes to better grazing and water, as they need to drink every day. They are often seen in the company of antelope such as Blue Wildebeests. Mountain Zebras form small stallion-led herds, usually with 4 or 5 mares and their foals. Stallions without harems form bachelor groups. Although stallions are not territorial, they will fight with any potential competition; however, if an intruding stallion is submissive, he is usually tolerated.

The Square-lipped (White) Rhino is more social than the Hook-lipped, with groups sharing a common home range. Each group is made up of a territorial bull, subordinate bulls, and cows and their dependent young. Territorial bulls leave their areas only if they do not have access to water. If they have to pass through the territories of other bulls to reach water, as long as they make no threatening moves, they are generally allowed to pass. Bull territories are quite small, with one study finding sizes that averaged just 3 sq km (1.2 sq mi). Cows occupy ranges from 6 to 20 sq km (2.3 to 7.7 sq mi), and these might overlap several bull territories. Territories and ranges are marked with mounds of dung that are thoroughly kicked around with the hind feet. These rhinos feed mainly at night and during the cooler daylight hours, and in the warm hours they rest in shade. They prefer to eat short grasses but will take a wider range during the dry season. Mud wallowing and bathing is very important, both as cooling agents and also to reduce attacks by a host of biting insects.

Hook-lipped (Black) Rhinos are solitary, except when a bull links up with a cow for mating. They occupy home ranges but bulls do not establish true territories. Within a population, bulls establish a dominance hierarchy, or "pecking order," which is put to use when encountering each other. The pecking order is established, maintained, and changed by posturing and by impressive and occasionally fatal fights. The size of home ranges varies greatly according to food and water availability, from 0.5 to 500 sq km (0.2 to 190 sq mi). These rhinos are browsers, taking leaves and nipping off twigs. It is easy to tell which rhino species you are dealing with from their cannonball-like droppings; that is, if you are do not mind breaking them apart. Those of the Square-lipped are made of fine material, and those of the Hook-lipped are course and fibrous. Both species have poor eyesight, but their hearing and sense of smell are very acute.

Breeding

Mountain Zebra mares have a 1-year pregnancy. They produce their first foal when they are 4 or 5 years old and may continue to breed into their 20s. The single foal of the Plains Zebra weighs from 30 to 35 kg (66 to 77 lb) and is born after about a 375-day pregnancy. Although Mountain Zebras may breed at any time of the year, Plains Zebras see most births at the onset of the rainy season, when grass is abundant.

The calves of both rhino species weigh an average 40 kg (88 lb) at birth, which comes after a pregnancy lasting 450 to 480 days. Calves stay with the mother for 2 or 3 years. If you see a rhino walking or running with a small calf just in front, it is a Square-lipped; if at the side or behind, it is a Hook-lipped. Calves are able to walk and suckle within 3 to 4 hours after birth. Close encounters with cows and small calves should be avoided, as cows can become very aggressive and, despite their bulk, can reach speeds of 40 kph (25 mph).

Ecological Interactions

Plains Zebras commonly associate with other antelope species. This is because there is little competition for food because they favor different grasses, or different grass growth stages, and in part because more pairs of eyes mean greater alertness for predators. Plains Zebras and Blue Wildebeests commonly feed together, and both zebra species will associate with Ostriches.

Oxpeckers, two bird species that specialize in eating external parasites such as ticks, associate with many different game species, but they seem to favor rhinos where they occur. The rhinos benefit from this "cleaning service" and also by the birds acting as early-warning systems, for they often detect danger before their hosts.

Notes

Two different races (subspecies) of the Mountain Zebra are recognized, the Cape from South Africa and the Hartmann's from Namibia. There are some very slight differences, but probably as little as 100 to 150 years ago these populations were not separate or different. Massive hunting pressure in the past caused populations to fragment and become widely separated, and now evolution is causing variation. More than 500,000 Plains Zebras take part in the great annual migration in the Serengeti of East Africa, but this is often overshadowed by the 1.5 million Blue Wildebeests that make the same circuit. The largest migration in southern Africa occurs in north-central Botswana and involves tens of thousands of zebras.

Status

Plains Zebras number an estimated 700,000 across their Southern, Central, and East Africa range. The main populations today are found in national parks and game reserves. Mountain Zebras are under much greater pressure, with the Cape race numbering just over 1,000 animals and the Hartmann's, fewer than 7,000. The Cape race was reduced to perhaps as few as 50 individuals in the 1930s and Mountain Zebra National Park was established with the aim of saving it from extinction. Today, Cape Mountain Zebras occur in several national parks and nature reserves. Hartmann's was estimated to number 16,400 in 1972, with most herds occurring on ranchland fringing the Namib Desert. The largest fully protected population is now located in the Namib-Naukluft Park. Farmers dislike them because they break fences and compete with domestic stock for sparse grazing. East Africa's GREVY'S ZEBRA is endangered (CITES Appendix I listed).

The Hook-lipped (Black) Rhino has seen catastrophic declines in numbers and range. It has become extinct in many countries during the past 30 years and its last remaining strongholds are in South Africa and Namibia. It has been estimated that at the start of the 20th century there were as many as a million of these magnificent beasts; by 1984, there were fewer than 9,000, and today, perhaps 2,500! This species, along with the Square-lipped (White) Rhino, lost some ground to development and habitat loss, but the vast majority were killed for their fibrous horns. Although some were taken for their alleged medicinal value in the Far East, many horns ended up in the Arabic countries of Yemen and Oman. There they were carved into traditional dagger handles for tribesmen. There are 2 races of the Square-lipped (White) Rhino: the northern race, with just 10 to 15 survivors confined to northeastern Democratic Republic of Congo (formerly Zaire) in 2006; and the southern race, with over 8,000 individuals, mostly in South Africa. At one point early in the 20th century, the southern race was reduced to probably less than 50 (some say as few as 30) wild survivors, located in thicket country in KwaZulu-Natal province of South Africa. Fortunately, a few far-sighted conservationists realized how serious the situation was and set about protecting them in game reserves. Square-lipped Rhinos are now doing so well in South Africa that there is difficulty finding enough protected space in which to release them. Many now live on game ranches and some have been sent to several other African countries, such as Kenya and Namibia. Populations released into Botswana and Zimbabwe have been wiped out by poachers. Both the Hook-lipped (Black) Rhino and the northern race of the Square-lipped (White) Rhino are considered endangered (CITES Appendix I listed).

Profiles

Hook-lipped (Black) Rhinoceros, *Diceros bicornis*, Plate 98b
Square-lipped (White) Rhinoceros, *Ceratotherium simum*, Plate 98c
Plains Zebra, *Equus quagga*, Plate 100d
Mountain Zebra, *Equus zebra*, Plate 100e

10. Giraffe, Antelope, Buffalo, Pigs, and Hippopotamus

The HIPPOPOTAMUS (Plate 98), GIRAFFE (Plate 100), AFRICAN BUFFALO (hereafter called Buffalo; Plate 100), pig, and antelope are those ungulates (hoofed mammals) that have an even number of toes on each foot and belong to order Artiodactyla. The *artiodactyls* can be divided into 2 suborders, the *Suina*, which encompasses the pigs and hippopotamuses, and the *Ruminantia*, which includes those that chew cud, such as Giraffe, Buffalo, cattle, antelope, sheep, and goats. The *ruminants* in southern Africa fall into families Giraffidae and Bovidae. With the exception of pigs and Hippopotamuses, artiodactyls do not have upper incisor teeth. All are principally herbivorous, although the BUSHPIG (Plate 99) is more correctly placed as an omnivore (eats both plant and animals), and duiker occasionally eat animals. Artiodactyl diversity in southern Africa is great, with one species of Giraffe, one Hippopotamus, two species of pig, the Bushpig and COMMON WARTHOG (Plate 99), the Buffalo, and no less than 32 different antelope.

The Giraffe should need little description, being by far the tallest of all mammals. Although as many as 8 subspecies are recognized, only one occurs in the covered region. Bulls measure from 3.9 to 5.2 m (12.8 to 17 ft) from the ground to the top of the head, with cows reaching a maximum of 4.7 m (15 ft). Bulls weigh from 970 to 1,400 kg (2,130 to 3,080 lb) and cows 700 to 950 kg (1,540 to 2,090 lb). They are always associated with dry savannah woodland but may cross open areas between feeding grounds. The Hippopotamus ranges from 1,000 to 2,000 kg (2,200 to 4,400 lb), with females always smaller than the males. The body is barrel-shaped, the legs short and stout, and the head massive, broad-snouted, and held close to the ground when on land. The grayish black, pink-tinged skin is hairless. Most of its day is spent submerged in water with just the top of its head in view, but it also basks on sandbanks. The Bushpig, a denizen of bush, thicket, and forest, weighs from 46 to 115 kg (100 to 250 lb), with boars always larger than sows. It is a typical pig in appearance, but the body is covered in coarse, bristle-like hair that ranges from reddish brown to gray-brown. Warthogs have typical pig form, with sparse hair cover except for a long mane on the neck and shoulders and, in younger animals, tufts of white hair on the cheeks. There are 2 pairs of large wart-like lumps on the face, and the boars especially grow long, curved tusks. Because warthogs live in open grassland and wooded savannahs, and are day-active, they are much more commonly seen than Bushpigs.

Southern Africa's 32 antelope species are divided into 8 sub-families, and we have profiled several examples from each:

1. *Bovinae/Tragelaphinae.* In this group we find the Buffalo and the "spiral-horned" antelope—COMMON ELAND (Plate 100), GREATER KUDU (Plate 99), NYALA (Plate 99), and BUSHBUCK (Plate 99). The Buffalo is obviously cow-like, with bulls weighing on average 700 kg (1,540 lb) and cows about 550 kg (1,210 lb). They are heavily built, with fairly short, stocky legs and massive horns, especially those of the bulls. This is Africa's only wild cattle species. The "spiral-horned" antelope range in size from Africa's largest, the Common Eland, with bulls tipping the scales at more than 900 kg (1,980 lb), to the 30 to 40 kg (66 to 88 lb) Bushbuck. The males of all species have horns that are spiraled to a greater or lesser extent, this being most pronounced in the Greater Kudu bull. The only species in which the female also has horns is

the Common Eland. Most species have variable numbers of narrow white stripes on the body, this being particularly evident in the Greater Kudu and the Nyala and least developed in the Common Eland. Overall body coloration is similar in both sexes, with the exception of the Nyala. All of the species we have profiled are commonly associated with woodlands and will penetrate dry areas along wooded rivers and riverbeds.

2. In the *Hippotraginae* we find the SOUTHERN ORYX, ROAN ANTELOPE, and SABLE ANTELOPE (all Plate 101). These are all large antelope weighing in the range of 180 to 300 kg (396 to 660 lb), with bulls heavier on average than cows. In this group both sexes have similar horns, but those of the cows are less robust. Horns of the Oryx are straight and rapier-like, those of the other 2 are heavily ringed and back-curving. Coats of these mammals are short, manes erect, and ears fairly long. All 3 species have distinctive black-and-white markings on the face. The Sable and Roan species inhabit open woodland with abundant grass, while the Oryx prefers dry, open grassland and scrubland.

3. The *Reduncinae* is a group of antelope usually associated with watery habitats. In this group we find the WATERBUCK (Plate 101), RED LECHWE (Plate 102), MOUNTAIN REEDBUCK (Plate 102), and SOUTHERN REEDBUCK (Plate 102). The largest of the group is the 250 to 270 kg (550 to 594 lb) Waterbuck, and the lightest is the Mountain Reedbuck, which averages just 30 kg (65 lb). All species have longish coats, and in the case of the Waterbuck, this trait yields a somewhat shaggy appearance. Overall coloration is gray-brown to reddish brown, with pale to white underparts in all except the Waterbuck. Only the males carry the forward-swept, heavily ringed horns. Those of the Waterbuck average 75 cm (29.5 in) in length, and of the Mountain Reedbuck, just 14 cm (5.5 in). The 2 reedbucks have short, hairy tails that are raised vertically when they are running away, clearly showing their white undersides. All species of this group are found near water—rivers, lakes, or marshes. The Mountain Reedbuck prefers grassy hill and mountain slopes but the others favor flood-plains, reedbeds, and areas of long grass. The Waterbuck will also occupy woodland close to water.

4. The *Peleinae* has only one member, the GRAY RHEBOK (Plate 102), which is endemic to South Africa and a few other adjacent areas. It inhabits hill and mountain country, from desert fringe to high rainfall montane grasslands. Weighing only 20 kg (44 lb), it has a woolly gray coat. Only the male carries the thin, vertical, sharp-pointed horns.

5. The *Alcelaphinae* includes some of Africa's most abundant antelope species. We have profiled the BLACK WILDEBEEST, BLUE WILDEBEEST, RED HARTEBEEST, BLESBOK/BONTEBOK, and TSESSEBE (all Plate 103). This subfamily includes some of the fastest animals in the antelope world. All have long heads/faces and their backs slope down from shoulder to rump. The largest in the group is the Blue Wildebeest, which averages 250 kg (550 lb), and the smallest is the Blesbok/Bontebok, at 62 to 70 kg (136 to 154 lb). The others fall between 100 and 180 kg (220 and 400 lb), and in all cases males are larger than females. Both sexes have horns but those of females are always more slender. The wildebeest species are superficially buffalo-like, especially in horn structure. The Bontebok and Blesbok are races, or subspecies, of one species,

and are very similar in shape and form. All the species profiled live in savannah and lightly wooded grassland.

6. Another one-member subfamily is the *Aepycerotinae*, containing only the IMPALA (Plate 102). This is the only antelope with a black tuft on the rear face of the back leg, just above the hoof. Only male Impalas carry the fairly long "U"-shaped horns. It inhabits open or light savannah woodland.

7. Then there is a group known as subfamily *Antilopinae*, a rather unusual mix of gazelles and the so-called "dwarf antelope," such as dik-diks and grysboks. One has the impression that the taxonomists did not know what to do with this rather mixed bag and cast them all together on a whim. Here are the KIRK'S DIK-DIK (Plate 104), KLIPSPRINGER (Plate 104), STEENBOK (Plate 104), CAPE GRYSBOK (Plate 104), SHARPE'S GRYSBOK (Plate 104), ORIBI (Plate 105), and the SPRINGBOK (Plate 104). These antelope range from the 5 kg (11 lb) Kirk's Dik-dik to the 26 to 41 kg (57 to 90 lb) Springbok. The others range from averages of 7.5 kg (16 lb) in the Sharpe's Grysbok to 14 to 20 kg (31 to 44 lb) in the Oribi. With the exception of the Oribi, which is a grazer, they are all mixed feeders and browsers.

8. Although 16 members of subfamily Cephalophinae, the duiker, occur in Africa, only 3 are found in the covered region. These are the RED DUIKER, BLUE DUIKER, and COMMON DUIKER (all Plate 105). The largest, at 18 to 21 kg (40 to 46 lb), is the Common, the only duiker that occurs away from forest or dense woodland. It can be found in relatively open country, as long as there are areas of bush and thicket. It is also the only duiker that walks with a straight, not arched, back. Both Red and Blue Duiker are found only in a narrow strip in the east of the region. Weighing just 3 to 6 kg (6.6 to 13 lb), the Blue, along with Kirk's Dik-dik, is our smallest antelope.

Natural History

Ecology and Behavior

The 2 pigs, the Common Warthog and the Bushpig, contrast in that the first is mainly diurnal and the latter nocturnal. Warthogs spend the night in self-dug burrows, or those of other mammals such as Aardvarks and porcupines. Both pigs are social, living in groups known as *sounders*. Warthog sounders consist of 1 to 3 sows and their young. Warthog boars move off to form bachelor groups at the age of 2 years, or often move around on their own as adults. Sexually active boars move from sounder to sounder, not forming territories but sometimes fighting over breeding rights. In one study, sounder home ranges varied from 64 to 374 ha (158 to 924 ac). Warthogs are heavily preyed upon by the larger carnivores. Bushpig sounders range from 1 to 15 animals, each with sows with young and a dominant boar. Bachelor groups may form for short periods and adult boars will also wander alone. In one area sounders moved an average of 3 km (2 mi) per night, with an average home range of 7.2 sq km (2.8 sq mi). It is thought the dominant boar and sow defend a resource territory against other sounders. Warthogs feed mainly on grasses (both above- and below-ground parts), but Bushpigs eat a wide range of animals and plants.

The semi-aquatic Hippopotamus lives in herds known as *schools*. Each school of cows and their young stays within the territory of a dominant bull, which vigorously chases or fights with intruding bulls. Although a warning and threat are usually enough to prevent aggressive interactions, vicious fights sometimes take place. When the animals move out to the grazing grounds (called *hippo lawns*) at night, there is no defense of exclusive territories. Early each morning, schools return to the same area of water, whether in a river, lake, or pond. The average school size is 10 to 15, but in some areas it may reach 30 or more. Adults can remain underwater for as long as 6 minutes and can run rapidly on the bottom of a river or lake. The Hippo is considered by many to be the most dangerous mammal in Africa. Without doubt, getting between a hippo and its watery retreat is a potentially fatal situation. Because of their size and impressive array of large teeth, encounters usually result in death—so steer clear! Hippos are selective grazers and can eat up to 40 kg (88 lb) per night.

Giraffe do not establish territories but remain within home ranges of 20 to 120+ sq km (7.7 to 46+ sq mi). They live in relatively loose herds of 4 to 30 animals, but there is much movement of individuals between herds. Only the cow with a dependent calf is a stable unit; adult bulls live mainly alone and circulate looking for cows ready to breed. Bulls establish a dominance hierarchy that results in little conflict, and dominant bulls do most of the mating. Giraffe feed at night and during the day, their height giving them a great feeding advantage over other browsers. Pods, leaves, and flowers are stripped from twigs by the 45 cm (18 in) long tongue and the lips. Despite their size, Giraffe can reach a galloping speed of 60 kph (37 mph).

The Buffalo is a herd animal, sometimes gathering in the thousands, although solitary bulls and small parties of bulls are common. Herds contain cows, calves, and bulls, with the latter maintaining a dominance hierarchy among themselves. Cows likewise establish a "pecking order" that gives them ranking in the herd. Most grazing takes place at night, with herds resting in shade during the hottest hours.

Most of the "spiral-horned" antelope lead social lives, although the Bushbuck tends to be more solitary. In suitable areas this species may reach very high numbers; one study found densities of 26 per sq km (0.4 sq mi)! There is a great deal of overlapping of home ranges, but each adult seems to have its own exclusive rest area. No territories are established but males have a dominance hierarchy. They are mainly active at night and in the cooler day hours. As with the majority of antelope in this group, they are browsers. Nyala rams establish their dominance by dramatic stiff-legged displays, and fighting is rare. Nyala may be seen in ewe/fawn groups, bachelor herds, or as solitary rams. Herds are unstable, with much individual movement between them. Home ranges are usually smaller than 5 sq km (1.9 sq mi). Nyala are mainly browsers but rams especially take some grass. The Greater Kudu lives in herds numbering between 3 and 10 animals, with larger herds often being temporary. Herds are mainly made up of cows and their young, with bulls coming and going, usually only sticking to herds during the rutting periods. Nursery herds occupy home ranges of 1 to 25 sq km (0.4 to 9.6 sq mi, and bulls, up to 50 sq km (19 sq mi). Feeding occurs both night and day, but in areas where they are hunted, Kudu stick to dense bush in daylight. They are mainly browsers but because of their amazing jumping skills (able to leap more than 2 m, 6.6 ft), they are a nuisance in some farming areas, especially where alfalfa is grown. Common Elands normally live in herds of 25 to 60 animals, but in some areas they may number in the hundreds. Unlike the other antelope in this group, the Eland is highly nomadic, particularly in dry areas. Bulls do not form territories but establish hierarchies that determine breeding rights, and cows have a "pecking order" among themselves. Elands are mainly browsers and will use their horns to break branches that are beyond easy feeding distance.

The 3 *Hippotragines* in the region, the Southern Oryx, and Roan and Sable Antelopes, are social, herding antelope. Herd size in the Oryx may number up to 30, with groups made up of cows, bulls, and young, or only cows and young. Solitary bulls are commonly seen; they attempt to hold cow/calf herds within their territories, and when they do, have sole mating rights with cows in breeding condition. Recorded territory sizes range from 7.6 to 25.7 sq km (2.9 to 9.9 sq mi) and herd home ranges average almost 1,500 sq km (580 sq mi). Roan herd size varies from 5 to 12, occasionally larger, and each herd is accompanied by an adult bull, although a dominant cow decides on feeding and resting sites. Young bulls form bachelor herds until they can contest with breeding bulls. Sables form herds usually numbering from 10 to 30, and several cow/calf (*nursery*) herds may overlap the territory of a dominant bull. The nursery herds are stable and generally occupy much smaller ranges than the other 2 profiled species. Bulls try to hold nursery herds within their territories during the *rut* (mating season). As with the Roan, a Sable cow establishes dominance over her herd and determines its movements. All 3 species are mainly grass-eaters but, particularly during the dry season, some browsing takes place.

The members of the subfamily *Reduncinae*, the Waterbuck, RED LECHWE, MOUNTAIN REEDBUCK, and SOUTHERN REEDBUCK, are all social animals to a greater or lesser extent. Waterbucks usually live in nursery herds 5 to 10 strong, with bulls establishing territories through which the herds move. During the rut, bulls try to hold nursery herds to mate with cows ready for breeding. Bull territories are very stable and may be held for several years. Red Lechwe have a similar system, but herds commonly number 30 or more, and rams have elaborate territorial displays that often serve to prevent serious fighting. Common Reedbucks live in pairs, within a territory defended by the ram, or in small family groups. The ram Mountain Reedbuck holds a territory, usually 10 to 28 ha (25 to 69 ac), on a year-round basis, through which small groups of ewes and their young pass. Females occupy home ranges about 3 times this size. All species are predominantly grass-eaters but will eat other vegetation as well.

The Gray Rhebok lives throughout the year in small family parties of ewes, lambs, and a single ram. The ram is very territorial and determinedly drives away any challenge to its position. Nearly all activity apparently takes place during the day.

The Impala rutting season is one of the most exciting and noisy of any of the antelope. Nursery herds of ewes and lambs spend much of the year apart from the rams, which roam in bachelor herds. With the onset of the rut, rams establish territories in which they "hold" harems of 15 to 20 ewes and their lambs of the previous season. Rams are very vocal during this time, growling, roaring and snorting, and chasing intruders. To the uninitiated ecotraveller it can be an unnerving experience. At the end of the rut the ewes rejoin into larger herds and the rams return to bachelor life. The Impala is a mixed feeder, taking grass and browse.

Alcelaphines, that is, the Blue and Black Wildebeest, Red Hartebeest, Tsessebe, and Bontebok/Blesbok, are all herding antelope. Blue Wildebeests form fairly stable herds of up to 30 individuals, and during the breeding season bulls hold territories in which they try to keep the nursery herds. These may be fixed seasonal territories, or those in which cows are held for a short period for mating when herds are migrating. Many such herds may come together at certain times and form into groups of tens and even hundreds of thousands. Outside the breeding season, maternity groups are not "herded" by the dominant bulls. The herding system of the Black Wildebeest is similar to that of the Blue. Red Hartebeests live in herds averaging 20 animals, although much larger temporary groups may be seen. Bulls establish territories, and maternity herds (cows and young) stay temporarily within these areas. These territories usually encompass the best grazing, so there is double motivation for cows to stick around. In the case of the Tsessebe, a bull establishes a permanent territory with up to 5 or 6 cows and calves. The Bontebok and Blesbok are mainly active during the day and both are grass-eaters, but these subspecies have very different social patterns. Bontebok rams establish territories and hold and defend them on a continuous basis. Nursery herds, usually 6 to 10 strong, wander at will through these territories, with the ram trying to keep them within his area only during the January to March mating season. Blesbok live in harem herds of 2 to 25 ewes, each accompanied by a territorial ram. During the dry winter months, many such mixed herds come together.

Now we come to the so-called "dwarf antelope," Kirk's Dik-dik, Klipspringer, Steenbok, Sharpe's and Cape Grysbok, and the Oribi. All tend to live in pairs with the single young of the season within a defended territory. In some cases both male and female defend the jointly occupied territory. Oribi may live in pairs but it is not unusual, in good habitat, for one ram to be accompanied by as many as 4 ewes. In the Steenbok, the 2 grysboks, and the dik-dik, male and female tend to feed in different areas of the home range. In the case of the Klipspringers and Oribi, the pairs tend to keep close to each other. All except the Steenbok, which is the only antelope that buries its droppings, have midden (dung piles) sites located within their home ranges. Another means of marking territories and home ranges is employed by all these species. Each has a gland in front of the eye that secretes an oily substance, which is rubbed onto twigs, grass stalks, and sometimes rocks. All species occupy small home ranges; for example, those of some Cape Grysboks have been recorded as smaller than 1 ha (2.5 ac), and some Klipspringers have ranges up to perhaps 50 ha (123 ac). Home range size is largely dependent on food availability. None need to drink (their water comes from their food), although some will when water is available. The other member of this subfamily, the Springbok, is a herding animal of the deserts and semi-deserts of southern Africa. Outside the rut they live in separate nursery and bachelor herds and also mixed groups, which usually number 20 to 40; when moving to new feeding grounds, they may form temporary groupings in the thousands. During the 19th century, Springboks formed into vast herds that moved among various grazing grounds. During the rut, rams hold territories in which they try to hold the nursery herds and mate with the ewes. Springboks are mixed feeders, taking graze and browse, as well as digging out roots and bulbs with the front hooves.

Duiker live a mainly solitary existence, although pairs may live in loose association. The 3 duiker in the region are strongly territorial, with rams being extremely intolerant of each other. Females will also drive other females away from the shared home ranges. All the duiker have large glands in front of the eyes from which a oily, tar-like substance is smeared on twigs and grass stalks to mark territories. Home range sizes are very variable, those of the Blue Duiker averaging 2 to 4 ha (5 to 10 ac), and Common Duiker, from 4 to 27 ha (10 to 67 ac). The duiker are unique in the antelope world, as not only do they eat a wide range of plants, but they also eat other animals. They can open their mouths considerably wider than most other antelope. Insects, snails, small mammals, frogs, lizards, and even scavenged fish are on record as being diet items. Duiker will also actively hunt birds up to the size of domestic chickens! The name duiker is the Dutch word for "diver," given to these antelope because of their habit of plunging into dense cover when they are disturbed.

Breeding

The Impala, Sprinkbok, and the smaller antelope species have pregnancies of 167 to 210 days. Most other antelope have 220- to 280-day pregnancies. A single lamb or calf is usual, but in rare situations some species have twins. As one would expect, birth weights vary according to the species; for example, lambs of Blue Duiker weigh just 400 g (14 oz), Kirk's Dik-diks, 600 g (21 oz). The heaviest calves are those of the Common Eland, at 22 to 36 kg (48 to 79 lb), and the Blue Wildebeest at an average 22 kg (48 lb). In several species the newborn calf or fawn stays put for a few days, even weeks or months, before accompanying the mother. The female returns to suckle her young once or twice during the day. In other species, especially those of the open grasslands, young are able to walk and run less than an hour after birth. Although several species have no fixed breeding season, most coincide birthings with the onset of the southern Africa rainy season. Buffalo also have most young during the summer rains, when food is abundant. The single calf, weighing on average 40 kg (88 lb), is dropped after about a 340-day pregnancy. Within a few hours, the calf can keep up with the herd. The Giraffe calf, at about 100 kg (220 lb), is born after a pregnancy that averages 450 days. Giraffe cows nearly always drop the young at traditional birthing grounds. Able to walk within an hour after birth, young Giraffe are kept isolated for up to 3 weeks, when they join in "creches" of similar-aged calves. Common Warthog sows have litters of 1 to 8 piglets, weighing from 480 to 850 g (17 to 30 oz). They spend the first days of their lives in a grass-lined chamber in a tunnel. Bushpig sows have litters of between 2 to 4 piglets, rarely more. After a 120-day pregnancy, young are born that weigh about 750 g (26 oz). Most births in the region take place from September to November. Surprisingly, the single newborn Hippopotamus calf is proportionally a "lightweight," at an average of 30 kg (66 lb). Length of pregnancy varies from 225 to 257 days, and the calf joins the school with the mother only after several weeks.

Status

Although several artiodactyl species have seen declines in numbers and range, only a few are of conservation concern in the region. Extensive development of game ranching in southern Africa has aided considerably in boosting the numbers of many of these species, for sport and meat hunting as well as for ecotourism. Some species, such as the Hippopotamus, Buffalo, Giraffe, and several antelope, are almost entirely restricted to national parks, nature reserves, and game ranches. A few species have very restricted ranges, such as the Nyala; but where it occurs it is common. Another is the Red Lechwe, which lies at the very southern limit of its range in northern Botswana and the Caprivi Strip of Namibia. In the latter country it has seen catastrophic declines because of uncontrolled poaching during the late 1980s. A success story among the larger antelope is the Greater Kudu. It has expanded its range quite dramatically over much of the region, to the point where it has become a problem in some agricultural areas. During the 19th century, the Bontebok was brought to the brink of extinction within its limited South African range. The actions of a group of farmers, long before conservation was considered important, saved the species. Today, more than 2,000 Bontebok are found in a national park, several nature reserves, and game farms through their traditional range. Another antelope that was almost lost to us was the Black Wildebeest. Herds numbering in the hundreds of thousands roamed the interior plains of South Africa in the 19th century. Hunting for their hides and meat reduced them to just a few dozen. However, under strict protection, they have started to recover; today there are about 5,000 in reserves and on farms. The Oribi is of major concern in southern Africa, where it has lost vast areas of its traditional range to agriculture and deforestation. Very few suitable areas of its favored grasslands survive, and only small numbers occur in protected areas.

Profiles

Hippopotamus, *Hippopotamus amphibius*, Plate 98a
Bushbuck, *Tragelaphus scriptus*, Plate 99a
Nyala, *Tragelaphus angasii*, Plate 99b
Greater Kudu, *Tragelaphus strepsiceros*, Plate 99c
Bushpig, *Potamochoerus larvatus*, Plate 99d
Common Warthog, *Phacochoerus africanus*, Plate 99e
African Buffalo, *Syncerus caffer*, Plate 100a
Common Eland, *Tragelaphus oryx*, Plate 100b
Giraffe, *Giraffa camelopardalis*, Plate 100c
Roan Antelope, *Hippotragus equinus*, Plate 101a
Sable Antelope, *Hippotragus niger*, Plate 101b
Southern Oryx, *Oryx gazella*, Plate 101c
Waterbuck, *Kobus ellipsiprymnus*, Plate 101d
Mountain Reedbuck, *Redunca fulvorufula*, Plate 102a
Gray Rhebok, *Pelea capreolus*, Plate 102b
Impala, *Aepyceros melampus*, Plate 102c
Red Lechwe, *Kobus leche*, Plate 102d
Southern Reedbuck, *Redunca arundinum*, Plate 102e
Tsessebe, *Damaliscus lunatus*, Plate 103a
Red Hartebeest, *Alcelaphus buselaphus*, Plate 103b
Blesbok/Bontebok, *Damaliscus pygargus*, Plate 103c
Black Wildebeest, *Connochaetes gnou*, Plate 103d
Blue Wildebeest, *Connochaetes taurinus*, Plate 103e
Kirk's Dik-dik, *Madoqua kirkii*, Plate 104a
Cape Grysbok, *Raphicerus melanotis*, Plate 104b
Sharpe's Grysbok, *Raphicerus sharpei*, Plate 104c
Klipspringer, *Oreotragus oreotragus*, Plate 104d
Steenbok, *Raphicerus campestris*, Plate 104e
Springbok, *Antidorcas marsupialis*, Plate 104f
Blue Duiker, *Cephalophus (Philantomba) monticola*, Plate 105a
Red Duiker, *Cephalophus natalensis*, Plate 105b
Common Duiker, *Sylvicapra grimmia*, Plate 105c
Oribi, *Ourebia ourebi*, Plate 105d

11. Elephant

There can be few people who do not recognize an *elephant* when they see one. Through millions of years there have been many different species of elephant, but today there are only 2, the ASIATIC ELEPHANT and the AFRICAN ELEPHANT (hereafter called Elephant; Plate 98), the sole living members of order Proboscidea. The African Elephant has 2 subspecies, the smaller tropical forest form and the one you will see as an ecotraveller, the large savannah form. Elephants in Africa occur in virtually all habitats, except those from which they have been driven out by people. In northern Namibia, Elephants occupy desert country; in other areas they live in woodland, mountain forest, and swamps. The main requirements for Elephants are drinking water, sufficient food, and shade.

The African Elephant is the largest living land mammal, with adult bulls reaching weights of 5 to 6.3 tons, and cows 2.8 to 3.5 tons. Shoulder heights range from 2.5 to 5 m (8.2 to 16.4 ft). It has a very long and highly mobile trunk, very large and rounded ears, and in most individuals, a pair of tusks that grow from the upper jaw. The largest tusks ever recorded came from an animal shot in Kenya, and weighed a staggering 200 kg (440 lb) combined. In several populations some, or most, cows do not develop tusks. Elephant tusks grow throughout the animal's life, but because of wear and breakage they never reach the maximum possible length. The tusks serve as picks, shovels, and probes. The gray-brown "wrinkled" skin is virtually hairless, and because Elephants are fond of mud bathing, it often takes on the color of the local soil.

Natural History

Ecology and Behavior

Elephants are active both day and night. They are highly social and intelligent animals, living in small family herds made up of an older cow (often called the *matriarch*), related cows, and their calves of all ages. Adult bulls move freely among these cow/calf herds, constantly on the alert for any cow that may be ready to mate. Although young cows usually remain with the group into which they were born, bulls reaching puberty leave or are driven away by the cows. Several young bulls may move around together, sometimes joining up with an older, mature bull. It was fairly recently discovered that Elephants have very complex acoustic communication, even over quite long distances. Some of these sounds cannot be heard by people but may be picked up by other Elephants several kilometers away. Adult Elephants have no enemies other than people, but youngsters are sometimes killed by Lions and Spotted Hyenas. In some populations, up to 50% of all young die before they reach the age of 15, from predators, disease, and accidents. Elephants have a similar life expectancy as that of humans. They feed on a very wide range of plants, including grass and browse. The tusks are used to strip bark from trees, and the feet may be used to kick smaller plants loose from the soil. Some particular tree species are eagerly sought out when they are bearing fruit, and Elephants may travel considerable distances to enjoy these delicacies. Elephants are very important distributors of seeds, which pass through their guts unharmed and drop to the ground surrounded by the perfect fertilizer.

Breeding

A single calf that weighs about 120 kg (264 lb) is born after a pregnancy that lasts 22 months. Mature cows give birth normally every 3 to 4 years, but this varies.

Newborn calves are protected by the mother and the other herd members and woe betide anything or anyone that dares to approach too closely. A calf that misbehaves is given a "spanking" with the mother's trunk.

Ecological Interactions

The Elephant is what is known as a *keystone species*. This means that it is critical to the welfare of many habitats and species, both plant and animal. Elephants keep dense woodland open for other species that require grassland areas with some cover, they are super seed-dispersers, and their mud-wallowing opens up waterholes that hold drinking water well into the dry season. A benefit to people from Elephants in the past was the paths they created through the mountain ranges of South Africa. Many of the passes people use today in part follow the ancient pathways made by these gentle gray giants.

Notes

An adult Elephant eats between 150 and 300 kg (330 and 660 lb) of plant material every day, and drinks between 100 and 220 liters (22 and 48 gallons) of water. It never ceases to amaze us how quietly, almost silently, these massive beasts can move through the bush. If undisturbed, they often make rumbling sounds, and they make considerable noise when feeding. Should they hear your approach, they become absolutely quiet and then seem to drift away. In all situations, you should never approach Elephants on foot unless you are with an experienced tracker or guide.

Status

Although not known with certainty, it has been estimated that between 5 and 10 million Elephants wandered sub-Saharan Africa as recently as 1930. By 1992 this number had dwindled to no more than 600,000, with recent estimates bringing this total down even further. During the 1970s and into the 1980s the poaching of Elephants for their valuable ivory tusks spiraled out of control all across the continent, with the exception of southern Africa. Only a ban on the trade in ivory and, in some countries, a shoot-to-kill policy when poachers were encountered, slowed the slaughter. To those humanitarians among us, this policy may sound rather drastic, but one has to remember that poaching gangs were often better armed than the wardens and rangers that faced them. If you did not shoot the poacher, he would almost certainly kill you. On January 18, 1990, the Elephant was moved from CITES Appendix II to Appendix I, listing the species as endangered, and, in effect, banning the trade in ivory—an act perhaps akin to closing the stable door after the horse has bolted! Sadly, the main threat to Elephants today is the loss of habitat to people, their infrastructures, and agriculture. Many traditional Elephant areas are now lost to these mighty beasts forever. Today there are about 130,000 Elephants in southern Africa, with about 65% of these in Botswana.

Profile

African Elephant, *Loxodonta africana*, Plate 98d

REFERENCES AND ADDITIONAL READING

Branch, W. R. 1998. *Field Guide to the Snakes and Other Reptiles of Southern Africa*, 3rd ed. Cape Town, South Africa: Struik Publishers.

Boycott, R. C., and O. Bourquin. 2000. *The Southern African Tortoise Book: A Guide to Southern African Tortoises, Terrapins and Turtles*, 2nd ed. Hilton, South Africa: Privately published.

Fry, C. H., S. Keith, and E. K. Urban, eds. 2000. *The Birds of Africa*, vols. 1–6. London and San Diego: Academic Press.

Maclean, G. L. 1993. *Robert's Birds of Southern Africa*, 6th ed. Cape Town, South Africa: John Voelcker Bird Book Fund.

Passmore, N. I., and V. C. Carruthers. 1995. *South African Frogs: A Complete Guide.* Johannesburg, South Africa: Wits. University Press.

Sinclair, I., P. Hockey, and W. Tarboton. 1997. *Birds of Southern Africa*, 2nd ed. Cape Town, South Africa: Struik Publishers.

Skinner, J., and R. H. N. Smithers. 1990. *The Mammals of the Southern African Subregion.* Pretoria, South Africa: University of Pretoria Press.

Stuart, C., and T. Stuart. 1995. *Field Guide to the Mammals of Southern Africa.* New Holland, Cape Town, and London: Struik Publishers.

———. 1995. *Southern, Central and East African Mammals.* New Holland, Cape Town, and London: Struik Publishers.

———. Stuart. 1996. *Africa's Vanishing Wildlife.* Halfway House, London: Southern/Smithsonian.

———. Stuart. 1997. *Field Guide to the Larger Mammals of Africa.* New Holland, Cape Town, and London: Struik Publishers.

———. 1997. *Guide to Southern African Game and Nature Reserves.* New Holland, Cape Town, and London: Struik Publishers.

———. 1998. *Africa's Great Wild Places.* Halfway House, London: Southern.

HABITAT PHOTOS

1. Evergreen forest. The Woodbush Forest in Magoebaskloof, on the eastern escarpment. Climbers, ferns, and shrubs are common in the understory. © W R Branch

2. Evergreen forest. Fishing with thrown baskets in small stream in the Zambezi River floodplain (Mozambique). © W R Branch

3. Coastal evergreen forest along the south coast mountains of Western Cape Province, South Africa. © Chris & Tilde Stuart

4. Arid savannah. Ostriches forage among sparse Acacia savannah and shiny quartzitic plains in the Kaokoveld of northern Namibia. © W R Branch

5. Mopane woodland. Some deciduous woodland in northern and eastern areas of southern Africa are mostly made up of mopane trees (here in Botswana). © Chris & Tilde Stuart

6. Arid savannah. A giant Baobab tree in mixed Acacia and broad-leaved arid savannah south of Opuwo, northern Namibia. © W R Branch

7. Mixed broad-leaved moist savannah and granite outcrops in Matopos National Park, Zimbabwe. © W R Branch

8. Palm savannah in the Zambezi River floodplain, dominated by the palm *Hyphaene natalensis* and tussock grassland. © W R Branch

9. Dense, thorny, moist thicket habitat (also called valley bushveld) covers slopes in the Great Fish River Conservation Area, Eastern Cape Province. © Chris & Tilde Stuart

10. Fynbos. Admiring a Geometric Tortoise in the Elandsberg Private Nature Reserve. This is the largest piece of Coastal Renosterveld that remains. © W R Branch

11. Fynbos. The impressive flowers of *Protea exima* in the Great Swartberg, north of Oudtshoorn. © W R Branch

12. Mountain fynbos in the Cedarberg Wilderness Area, Western Cape Province. Larger gray-green bushes in the background are Waboom, or Wagon-tree Protea, *Protea nitidia*. © Chris & Tilde Stuart

13. Karoo. The cliffs of the Nuweveldberg form the edge of the Great Escarpment and overlook the scrub-covered plains of Karoo National Park. © W R Branch

14. Karoo. A *Brunsvigia* sp. (Amaryllidaceae) blooms in the rocky plains of the Great Karoo near Beaufort West. © W R Branch

15. Walking in the valley of the Little Karoo, looking south to the cloud-capped Langeberg. Succulent Karoo plants cover the quarzitic plains, with karooid mountain fynbos on the slopes. © W R Branch

16. A carpet of flowering mesems (Mesembryanthemaceae) cover the valley bottom in the Goegab Nature Reserve near Springbok in Namaqualand. © W R Branch

17. The giant "halfmens" (*Pachypodium namaquensis*) is restricted to the Richtersveld National Park, Namaqualand, South Africa. The head of the plant always faces north. Nama legend believes the plants are men, frozen in place when they looked back at God. © W R Branch

18. An oasis of succulent vegetation covers the upper slopes of the Aurusberg in the southern Namib Desert. The plants survive on advective fogs from the cold Atlantic waters. An endangered Hedgehog aloe (*Aloe erinae*) flowers in the foreground. © W R Branch

19. A lone ostrich walks the gravel plains of the Namib Desert inland from Luderitz, Namibia. © W R Branch

20. The large tattered leaves of the bizarre Welwitchia (*Welwitchia mirabilis*) hug the gravel plains of the Namib Desert, with the crest of the Brandberg in the distance. © Chris & Tilde Stuart

21. Beneath the world's highest sand dunes, and looking more dead than alive, a large Camel thorn (*Acacia erioloba*) awaits the return of water to Sussosvlei. © W R Branch

22. Mountain grassland with granite "koppies" on the edge of the Escarpment east of Pietersburg, with Candelabra tree (*Euphorbia ingens*, background) and *Aloe marlothii* (foreground). © W R Branch

23. Alpine grasslands cover the rocky slopes beside the crest of the Sani Pass climbing the Drakensberg to Lesotho. Severe frosts and snowfall can occur in any month. © W R Branch

24. Secondary grassland in the Transkei resulting from overgrazing. © W R Branch

25. The Okavango Swamp is the largest wetland in southern Africa. © W R Branch

26. Baobabs cling to the steep walls of Epupa Falls in northern Namibia, with palms and acacia trees fringing the Cunene River. © W R Branch

27. There are few natural lakes in southern Africa, but an irrigation dam in the Little Karoo forms suitable habitat for Sacred Ibis and other waterbirds. © W R Branch

28. The distant peaks of the Cape Fold Mountains overlook the picturesque estuarine lagoon of the Keerbooms River at Plettenberg Bay. © W R Branch

29. The Eastern Cape coast near Bosbokstrand near East London. It forms the southern region of the East Coast Littoral, a mosaic of coastal grasslands, dunefields, and patches of coastal forest. © W R Branch

30. Typical rocky shoreline along the South African coast. © Chris & Tilde Stuart

NATIONAL PARK PHOTOS

1. River-associated evergreen forest dominated by large Sycamore Fig Trees, Kruger National Park, South Africa. © Chris & Tilde Stuart

2. The Oliphants River, one of several major natural waterways that penetrate Kruger National Park, South Africa. © Chris & Tilde Stuart

3. Marsh and swampland on the western flank of Greater St. Lucia Wetland Park in KwaZulu-Natal Province, South Africa. © Chris & Tilde Stuart

4. Nsumo Pan in the Mkuzi Game Reserve, KwaZulu-Natal Province, South Africa. © Chris & Tilde Stuart

5. Evergreen forest dominated by fig trees and Yellow-barked Acacias in the Mkuzi Game Reserve, KwaZulu-Natal Province, South Africa. © Chris & Tilde Stuart

6. River-associated evergreen forest in the Hluhluwe-Umfolozi Park complex, KwaZulu-Natal Province, South Africa. © Chris & Tilde Stuart

7. A mountain stream in Drakensberg Park, KwaZulu-Natal Province, South Africa. © Chris & Tilde Stuart

8. Kalahari thornveld habitat (small trees often in sandy soils with sparse grass cover) in Kgalagadi Transfrontier Park; the antelope species in the foreground is the Common Eland. © Chris & Tilde Stuart

9. Kalahari thornveld habitat in Kgalagadi Transfrontier Park, characterized here by a scattering of larger acacia tree species and smaller, bush-like thorn trees.
© Chris & Tilde Stuart

10. The large Etosha Pan in northern Namibia (Etosha National Park) was once part of a great lake, but today, even during exceptionally heavy rains, only relatively small sections hold water, and then only for a limited time. © Chris & Tilde Stuart

11. Extensive gravel plains dominate the northern sector of Namib-Naukluft Park, Namibia.
© Chris & Tilde Stuart

12. River-associated evergreen forest on the Chobe River, Chobe National Park, Botswana.
© Chris & Tilde Stuart

13. Papyrus beds dominate large areas of the Okavango Delta in northern Botswana. © Chris & Tilde Stuart

14. A section of the floodplain of the Okavango River with a small herd of Red Lechwe in the foreground, northern Botswana. © Chris & Tilde Stuart

15. Mixed tree and grass savannah in Hwange National Park, western Zimbabwe, during the rainy season. © Chris & Tilde Stuart

16. Flame Lily, here photographed in Hwange National Park, western Zimbabwe, is one of the most attractive savannah woodland flowers. © Chris & Tilde Stuart

IDENTIFICATION PLATES

The species pictured on any one plate are not necessarily to scale.

Abbreviations are as follows: M, male; F, female; IM, immature; B, breeding; N, non-breeding.

Explanation of habitat symbols (see Chapter 2 for some definitions):

= Evergreen forest (includes coastal, river-associated, and higher elevation evergreen forests).

= Deciduous woodland and savannah (includes all non-forest woodland types such as miombo, thornveld, mopane, and Kalahari sandveld).

= Shrubland (includes fynbos and both karoo types).

= Grassland (includes natural grasslands and agricultural lands such as pastures).

= Desert and near-desert.

= Inland wetlands (includes rivers, marshes, lakes, pans, estuaries, floodplains, impoundments).

= Marine (includes ocean beaches, intertidal zone and open sea).

Regions (see Map 2, p. 22–23):

EC = Eastern Cape Province
FS = Free State
KZN = KwaZulu-Natal Province, Lesotho, Swaziland
MPG = Mpumalanga and Gauteng
NC = Northern Cape Province
LNW = Limpopo and North-West Provinces
WC = Western Cape Province
NAM = Namibia
BOT = Botswana
ZIM = Zimbabwe

Plate 1a

Shovel-footed Squeaker
(also called Common Squeaker)
Arthroleptis stenodactylus

ID: A small, squat frog with a wide head; back mottled brown, usually with diamond pattern; cream belly; sides of head darker; third finger elongated; fingers and toes lack webbing; to 4.2 cm (1.7 in); call a brief, high-pitched chirp.

HABITAT: Varied; eastern moist evergreen forest, miombo woodland, and thickets in open savannah; shelters in leaf litter and under dead logs; eggs laid in ground; no free-swimming tadpole stage; burrows backwards into ground and moves in short hops.

REGIONS: KZN, LNW, ZIM

Plate 1b

Bushveld Rain Frog
Breviceps adspersus

ID: A small, rotund, flat-faced frog with short legs and toes that lack webbing; heel with "spade" for digging; back mottled brown and belly cream; broad, black eye-stripe; throat mottled black, heavily in males; to 5 cm (2 in); call a series of short, burred whistles.

HABITAT: Varied; northern and eastern savannah and deciduous woodland, and coastal grassland and thicket; only found above ground following rains, looking for mates, or feeding on termites; eggs laid in ground; no free-swimming tadpole stage; burrows backwards into ground and moves in a waddling run.

REGIONS: KZN, MPG, LNW, NAM, BOT, ZIM

Plate 1c

Cape Rain Frog
Breviceps gibbosus

ID: A sad-faced "dumpling" of a frog, with very short legs and toes that lack webbing; heel with "spade" for digging; rough-skinned back is mottled brown and granular belly is darkly speckled; to 7 cm (2.8 in); call an intermittent, burred squawk.

HABITAT: Southwestern Cape flats with short fynbos vegetation; adapts well to gardens; found above ground only following rains; eggs laid in ground; no free-swimming tadpole stage; burrows back-wards into ground and moves in a waddling run.

REGIONS: WC

Note: Considered vulnerable, South African Red Data Book.

Plate 1d

Red-banded Rubber Frog
Phrynomantis bifasciatus

ID: A round-nosed, small-eyed frog with smooth skin; toes lack webbing; flat, black body with two bright red lateral bands (that bleach pink in daylight) and red-spotted legs; gray belly is heavily speckled with white; to 7 cm (2.8 in); call a loud trill sustained for 1 to 2 seconds.

HABITAT: Varied; northern and eastern savannah and deciduous woodland, and coastal grassland and thicket; usually inhabits termitaria (termite nests) and is rarely found above ground; breeds in shallow pans of flooded grassland; runs quickly.

REGIONS: KZN, MPG, LNW, NAM, BOT, ZIM

Plate 1e

Marbled Snout-burrower
(also called Marbled Shovel-snouted Frog)
Hemisus marmoratus

ID: A small, pig-nosed frog with a squat, smooth-skinned body; transverse fold across top of head; toes slightly webbed; body mottled brown with a pinkish white belly; males have dark throats; to 3.8 cm (1.5 in); call an incessant buzzing from a mud bank.

HABITAT: Varied; central and eastern savannah and deciduous woodland, and coastal grassland and thicket; prefers damp soils and burrows nose-first into the ground; eggs laid in damp soil next to water; moves in short hops.

REGIONS: FS, KZN, MPG, LNW, BOT, ZIM

a Shovel-footed Squeaker

b Bushveld Rain Frog

c Cape Rain Frog

d Red-banded Rubber Frog

e Marbled Snout-burrower

Plate 2a

Common Platanna

Xenopus laevis

ID: A small, slimy, pear-shaped frog with tiny eyes perched on a flat head; hindlimbs very large, fully webbed, and with large claws on three toes; forelimbs small with soft, tapering fingers; mottled gray-brown above, with a grayish belly; to 11.5 cm (4.5 in); call an almost inaudible buzzing given underwater.

HABITAT: Widespread where there is still or slow-moving, permanent water; fully aquatic, only crossing land during heavy rains; surfaces infrequently to gulp air; hops poorly on land.

REGIONS: EC, FS, KZN, MPG, NC, LNW, WC, NAM, BOT, ZIM

Plate 2b

Guttural Toad

Bufo gutturalis

ID: A large, rough-skinned toad with prominent, bean-shaped glands on either side of neck; toes of fat hindlimbs lack webbing; back mottled brown with paired dark patches; top of head with paired dark blotches separated by a pale cross shape on the crown; thighs with red inner surfaces; belly granular, off-white in color; to 9.8 cm (3.9 in); call a regular, loud snore.

HABITAT: Varied; widespread in moist savannah but entering grassland and adapting to gardens; shelters in burrows, rock cracks, termitaria (termite nests), etc., emerging at night to feed; takes short hops.

REGIONS: EC, FS, KZN, MPG, NC, LNW, NAM, BOT, ZIM

Plate 2c

Raucous Toad

(also called Ranger's Toad)

Bufo rangeri

ID: A large, rough-skinned toad with prominent, bean-shaped glands on either side of neck; toes of fat hindlimbs have small webbing; back mottled brown with paired dark patches that may fuse in midline; top of head has only small, irregular dark blotches; belly granular, off-white in color; to 11.5 cm (4.5 in); call a regular, loud, rasping quack.

HABITAT: Varied; southern and eastern regions in fynbos, grassland, coastal thicket, and moist savannah; adapts well to gardens; shelters during day under cover, emerging at night to feed on insects, worms, slugs, etc; takes short hops.

REGIONS: EC, FS, KZN, MPG, LNW, WC

Plate 2d

Southern Pygmy Toad

Bufo vertebralis

ID: A very small toad without prominent glands on sides of neck; toes of hindlimbs unwebbed; back mottled brown, cream, and red, usually with a pale spot between shoulders; belly granular, white with scattered black spots; to 3.6 cm (1.4 in); call a continuous, cricket-like rasping.

HABITAT: Central grasslands and scrubland; breeds in temporary pools in rocky areas; moves in short hops.

REGIONS: EC, FS, NC

Plate 2e

Red Toad

Schismaderma carens

ID: A large, rough-skinned toad with prominent glandular ridge on either side of body; toes of fat hindlimbs have webbed margins; back rusty brown with a pair of dark spots near the rear; top of head unblotched; belly granular, white with gray flecks; to 9.2 cm (3.6 in); call a regular, deep, muffled booming.

HABITAT: Varied; northern savannah, grassland, and coastal thicket; shelters under cover, emerging at night to feed; often enters caves; breeds in deep water; takes short hops.

REGIONS: KZN, MPG, LNW, NAM, BOT, ZIM

a Common Platanna

b Guttural Toad

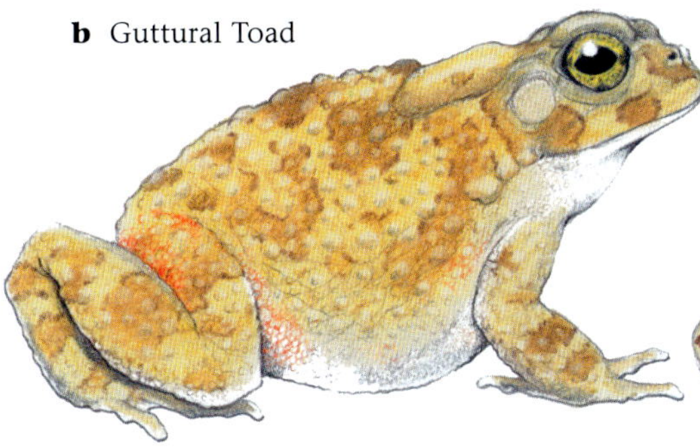

c Raucous Toad

d Southern Pygmy Toad

e Red Toad

Plate 3a

Foam Nest Frog
(also called Gray Tree Frog)
Chiromantis xerampelina

ID: A large, sticky-skinned frog with large eyes that have horizontal pupils; toes of long hindlimbs webbed, with large adhesive pads; marbled gray and tan, bleaching to cream in sunlight; belly granular and pinkish; throat usually speckled; to 8.5 cm (3.4 in); call a subdued, irregular, discordant, chirping croak.

HABITAT: Varied; northern moist savannah, deciduous woodland, coastal thicket; huddles in a compact ball on exposed branches, often in full sun; eggs laid in foam nest suspended in branches overhanging water; often shelters in buildings during dry season; takes gangly leaps.

REGIONS: KZN, MPG, LNW, NAM, BOT, ZIM

Plate 3b

Brown-backed Tree Frog
(also called Mozambique Tree Frog)
Leptopelis mossambicus

ID: A mid-sized, fat-bodied tree frog with large eyes that have vertical pupils; digits with adhesive pads; toes with little webbing; body tan with dark brown horseshoe-shape on back (juveniles plain green); belly granular and fawn-colored with darker stippling on the throat; to 6.3 cm (2.5 in); call a loud yack-yack, usually made from a perch, often far from water.

HABITAT: Eastern wooded savannah and coastal forest; shelters in hollow trees during day; agile leaper.

REGIONS: KZN, MPG, LNW, ZIM

Plate 3c

Painted Reed Frog
(also called Marbled Reed Frog)
Hyperolius marmoratus

ID: A small reed frog with large eyes and horizontal pupils; digits with large adhesive pads; toes webbed; color varied, males in north boldly striped in yellow, black, and orange, males in Cape to Zululand have purple-brown backs with cream spots; juveniles and many males brown and tan with vague stripes; smooth belly whitish, pink under limbs; to 4.3 cm (1.7 in); call a short, loud whistle, about once per second.

HABITAT: Varied; eastern coastal thicket and grasslands, and moist savannah; absent from thick forest; sleeps huddled during the day on reed stem, bleaching to ivory color; moves in agile leaps.

REGIONS: EC, KZN, MPG, LNW, WC, ZIM

Plate 3d

Long Reed Frog
Hyperolius acuticeps

ID: A tiny, elongate reed frog with a sharp nose; eyes with horizontal pupils; limbs thin, translucent; digits with large adhesive pads and toes webbed; back usually leaf green, sometimes brown, with a white stripe on each side (sometimes absent); smooth belly silvery white; males have a yellow throat; to 2.4 cm (0.9 in); call a harsh, acute chirp given every second.

HABITAT: Eastern open savannah and grassland; males call from grass or reed stems high above water; moves in agile leaps.

REGIONS: EC, KZN, BOT, ZIM

Plate 3e

Greater Leaf-folding Frog
(also called Fornasini's Spiny Reed Frog)
Afrixalus fornasinii

ID: The largest leaf-folder, with a flat head and bulging eyes with vertical pupils; long, thin limbs with long digits and adhesive pads; back covered with small spines; body brownish with a broad white band on each side and on upper surfaces of hindlimbs; belly granular and creamy white; males with yellow throats; to 4 cm (1.6 in); call a rapid, loud series of knocking clicks.

HABITAT: Eastern swamps and wetlands in grassland and moist savannah; climbs well, and shelters in tree holes or leaf junctions, particularly in banana plants; eggs laid in folded leaves above water; moves in agile leaps.

REGIONS: KZN, ZIM

a Foam Nest Frog

b Brown-backed Tree Frog

c Painted Reed Frog

d Long Reed Frog

e Greater Leaf-folding Frog

Plate 4a

Bubbling Kassina
(also called Senegal Kassina)
Kassina senegalensis

ID: A plump, smooth-skinned, short-legged, round-headed frog, with bulging eyes that have vertical pupils; toes almost webless; feet and hands white; back yellowish with bold, dark stripes; belly white, rough towards rear; to 5 cm (2 in); call a single, explosive, cork-popping quoip.

HABITAT: Varied; northern and eastern moist savannah, grassland, coastal thicket, and forest edge; shelters underground in termitaria (termite nests) or animal burrows; runs rather than hops.

REGIONS: EC, FS, KZN, MPG, LNW, NAM, BOT, ZIM

Plate 4b

Lightfoot's Moss Frog
(also called Cape Chirping Frog)
Arthroleptella lightfooti

ID: A minute frog with bent back and medium-sized hindlimbs; digits thin and without webbing; back purplish black to golden brown, prominent black eye stripe; belly varied from plain white to black, or heavily speckled; to 2.2 cm (0.9 in); call a rapid, insect-like chirp given irregularly.

HABITAT: Southwestern Cape, seepage areas in fynbos; shelters in grass tufts; eggs laid in damp soil, develop directly without free-swimming tadpole stage.

REGIONS: WC

Note: Considered near-threatened, South African Red Data Book.

Plate 4c

Common Caco
(also called Boettger's Dainty Frog)
Cacosternum boettgeri

ID: A minute frog with a flat back and small hindlimbs; digits thin and without webbing; back smooth with scattered small, soft lumps; color highly varied, from bright green to orange-brown, often with a lighter stripe down backbone; always a black eye-stripe and white lip; belly with large, vague, dark spots; throat orangish in males; to 2.3 cm (0.9 in); call a fast series of clicks, like castanets.

HABITAT: Widespread; favors marshes and drainage areas in savannah and grassland, but enters clearings in thickets, forests, and mesic habitats in near-desert; shelters in mud cracks and rodent tunnels; moves in short, quick hops; breeds all year.

REGIONS: EC, FS, KZN, MPG, NC, LNW, WC, NAM, BOT, ZIM

Plate 4d

Snoring Puddle Frog
Phrynobatrachus natalensis

ID: A small, squat frog with sharp nose and warty skin; toes webbed but without expanded tips; back mottled brown, often with a light orange line along backbone; belly whitish, throat gray in males; to 3.5 cm (1.4 in); call a loud and rapid snoring.

HABITAT: Eastern grassland, deciduous woodland and savannah, entering coastal thicket, but absent from Mozambique coastal plain; shelters in mud cracks and under logs; moves in fast hops; breeds in summer in pools or marshes.

REGIONS: EC, FS, KZN, MPG, LNW, BOT, ZIM

Plate 4e

Clicking Stream Frog
(also called Gray's Stream Frog)
Strongylopus grayii

ID: Common, small, "typical" frog, with roundish nose and large eyes; hindlimbs large with long toes that lack webbing; skin smooth but with scattered ridges; color highly varied; usually mottled brown and cream, sometimes plain orange-rust, often with orange band along backbone; black spot behind eye; lower leg usually barred; belly smooth and white; to 6.4 cm (2.5 in); call a monotonous, wooden tapping.

HABITAT: Southern and eastern regions; scrubland, grassland and edges of thick and forest; leaps well, shelters in thick grass; breeds any time after rain and lays a small clump of eggs in wet vegetation at water's edge; good leaper.

REGIONS: EC, KZN, MPG, LNW, WC

a Bubbling Kassina

b Lightfoot's Moss Frog

c Common Caco

d Snoring Puddle Frog

e Clicking Stream Frog

Plate 5a

Tremolo Sand Frog
(also called Cryptic Sand Frog)
Tomopterna cryptotis

ID: Dumpy body with short, wide head and bulging eyes; stocky hind legs are well webbed and have a large tubercular "spade" on outer edge; back lumpy and mottled brown, tan, and cream; often a thin, pale stripe along backbone and pale patch on top of head; belly smooth and white, with gray around lower jaw in breeding males; to 5 cm (2 in); call a train of short, high-pitched, monotonous notes.

HABITAT: Widespread; deciduous woodland, savannah, grassland and coastal thicket; burrows backwards into damp, sandy soil, emerging after heavy rains to feed and breed; moves in rapid hops.

REGIONS: EC, FS, KZN, MPG, NC, LNW, NAM, BOT, ZIM

Plate 5b

Giant Bullfrog
Pyxicephalus adspersus

ID: Largest frog in region; an obese blob with a wide mouth and two large peg-like teeth in lower jaw; the fat hindlimbs have short webbed toes and a tubercular "spade" for digging; the back has long skin folds and is olive green with scattered white ridges and spots; the belly is white with orange infusions in the armpits; juveniles are bright green with blackish markings, often with a yellow stripe down the backbone; to 20 cm (7.9 in) (males much larger than females); call a deep, low-pitched whoop, but gives open-mouthed bray if abused.

HABITAT: Northern and central regions; near desert, scrubland, and grassland; lives underground, emerging after rain to feed and in summer to breed in shallow, temporary pans; preys on anything that will fit in its massive mouth; moves in labored leaps.

REGIONS: EC, FS, KZN, MPG, LNW, NAM, BOT, ZIM

Note: Considered near-threatened, South African Red Data Book.

Plate 5c

Sharp-nosed Grass Frog
(also called Sharp-nosed Ridged Frog)
Ptychadena oxyrhynchus

ID: A medium-sized frog with a long, pointed snout and massive, muscular hindlimbs; eyes large and bulging; toes long and extensively webbed; back with prominent skin folds; body mottled brown, tan, and black; top of snout has pale triangular patch; back of thighs mottled; belly smooth and white; to 6.3 cm (2.5 in); call a high-pitched, intense trill.

HABITAT: Eastern deciduous woodland, savannah, and coastal thicket; rarely far from water; moves in massive leaps; feeds mainly on grasshoppers.

REGIONS: EC, KZN, MPG, LNW, NAM, BOT, ZIM

Plate 5d

Common River Frog
(also called Angola River Frog)
Afrana angolensis

ID: A large frog with a pointed snout and massive, muscular hindlimbs; eyes large and bulging; toes long and webbed; back has numerous, thin skin folds; body green to brown with numerous dark spots and often a green line along the backbone extending onto the snout; belly smooth and white; to 9 cm (3.5 in); two calls, one a short croak, the other a sharp rattle lasting 1 to 2 seconds.

HABITAT: Widespread; needs permanent water in savannah, grassland, or at forest edge; prefers slow-flowing rivers; shelters in thick bank vegetation, active during day and night; escapes into water with great leaps.

REGIONS: EC, FS, KZN, MPG, NC, LNW, NAM, BOT, ZIM

Plate 5e

Natal Ghost Frog
Heleophryne natalensis

ID: A medium-sized, rarely seen frog with a wide mouth and bulging eyes with vertical pupils; toes blunt-tipped and webbed; back mainly smooth, purplish brown with yellow blotches; belly white, pinkish under limbs; to 6.5 cm (2.6 in); call a gentle, clear note given a few times per second.

HABITAT: Permanent tumbling streams in eastern escarpment forests; very secretive, sheltering in rock cracks on mossy waterfalls; eggs laid under stones in small pools in mountain torrents; adhesive toe-pads cling to wet rocks; short movements by a waddling crawl interspersed with long leaps.

REGIONS: EC, KZN, MPG

a Tremolo Sand Frog

b Giant Bullfrog

c Sharp-nosed Grass Frog

d Common River Frog

e Natal Ghost Frog

Plate 6a

Serrated Hinged Terrapin

Pelusios sinuatus

ID: The domed, hard shell is hinged beneath the head, which is withdrawn into the shell sideways; shell is keeled along the backbone and has a serrated rear margin (particularly in juveniles); uniform black above, whitish with a dark, geometric edge below; shell to 47 cm (18.5 in).

HABITAT: Eastern slow-flowing rivers, swamps, and pans; passes the dry season in torpor, buried in soft mud; feeds on soft water weeds, aquatic and drowned insects, shells, and even frogs; lays soft-shelled eggs in sand bank.

REGIONS: KZN, MPG, LNW, ZIM

Plate 6b

Marsh Terrapin

Pelomedusa subrufa

ID: The very flat, hard shell is not hinged; extended neck is very long and head is withdrawn sideways beneath shell; two small soft tentacles on chin; olive to dark-brown above (usually sullied with mud and algae) and either dark below or with symmetrical, pale-centered pattern; shell to 33 cm (13 in).

HABITAT: Widespread; freshwater swamps and pans, and slow sections of southern rivers even in semi-desert; leaves water in dry season to bury in soft mud to await rains; feeds on water weeds, insects, and even birds coming to drink; lays soft-shelled eggs.

REGIONS: EC, FS, KZN, MPG, NC, LNW, WC, NAM, BOT, ZIM

Plate 6c

Loggerhead Sea Turtle

Caretta caretta

ID: A large turtle; shell smooth in adults, heavily keeled in juveniles, elongate and tapering at rear; head large and cannot be withdrawn; each limb has only 2 claws; shell dark brown above with pale margins, yellowish below; shell to 1 m (3.3 ft).

HABITAT: Marine; east coast tropical and subtropical waters; nests locally only on northern Zululand beaches; feeds mainly on large, hard-shelled coral reefs, invertebrates.

REGIONS: EC, KZN

Note: This species is endangered, South African Red List and CITES Appendix I listed.

Plate 6d

Leatherback Sea Turtle

Dermochelys coriacea

ID: Largest sea turtle; soft shell is like rubber and has 12 prominent ridges; flippers very long and without claws; juveniles covered in small, hexagonal scales; head massive, cannot be withdrawn, and with strong bicuspid jaws; body black above (blue-black in hatchlings) with scattered white spots, below is white suffused with pink and gray; shell to 1.7 m (5.6 ft).

HABITAT: Marine; all waters; nests locally only on northern Zululand beaches; basks in surface waters but can dive to 1,000 m; feeds almost exclusively on jellyfish.

REGIONS: EC, KZN, NC, WC, NAM

Note: This species is endangered, South African Red List and CITES Appendix I listed.

a Serrated Hinged Terrapin

b Marsh Terrapin

c Loggerhead Sea Turtle

d Leatherback Sea Turtle

Plate 7a

Parrot-beaked Tortoise
Homopus areolatus

ID: A very small tortoise with a flat, sculptured shell; shell scutes have deeply grooved margins and indented centers; no hinge; head is withdrawn straight back; breeding males have an orange nose; shell is greenish with black (female) or orange (male) margins; belly is yellowish with a brown center; shell to 12 cm (4.7 in).

HABITAT: Southern fynbos and coastal thicket; shelters in small holes or in grass clumps; lays 2 to 4 small, hard-shelled eggs in summer; active in early morning and on cool days.

REGIONS: EC, WC

Plate 7b

Angulate Tortoise
Chersina angulata

ID: Medium-sized with domed shell without raised scutes; no hinge; in breeding males the shell extends well forward beneath the head; black and yellow above, with pale-centered central scutes and radiating marks on the margins; belly (particularly in WC) often reddish; shell to 30 cm (11.8 in).

HABITAT: Southern coastal fynbos, scrubland, and coastal thicket; shelters in grass clumps and under scrub; males fight using the enlarged gular plate (the front part of bottom shell) to overturn opponents; females lay a single hard-shelled egg every 5 to 8 weeks.

REGIONS: EC, NC, WC, NAM

Plate 7c

Leopard Tortoise
Stigmochelys pardalis

ID: Largest tortoise in region; shell very domed, lacks a hinge, and has no small scute (horny plate at head end of top shell) above neck; horn-colored, heavily blotched and streaked in black (almost uniform gray in large adults); juveniles bright black and yellow, each scute having 1 or 2 black spots; shell to 75 cm (30 in).

HABITAT: Widespread; absent only from mountain fynbos and extreme desert; females lay 6 to 15 hard-shelled eggs 3 to 5 times per year; floats well and is often in water on hot days.

REGIONS: EC, FS, KZN, MPG, NC, LNW, WC, NAM, BOT, ZIM

Plate 7d

Karoo Tent Tortoise
Psammobates tentorius

ID: Small with a domed shell that lacks a hinge but has a small scute (nuchal) above neck; scutes in Karoo population prominently raised ("knoppies"); yellow to reddish, each scute boldly marked with radiating black bands; a large tubercular scale usually on each thigh (reduced or absent in west); shell to 15 cm (5.9 in).

HABITAT: Karoo scrubland and near desert; very shy and rarely seen; shelters beneath low bushes; active in early morning or on cloudy days; females lay 4 to 6 small, hard-shelled eggs and grow much larger than males.

REGIONS: EC, NC, WC, NAM

Plate 7e

Spek's Hingeback Tortoise
Kinixys spekii

ID: Medium-sized with flat-topped, rounded shell with a rear hinge that closes to protect the hind legs (only develops in adults); small scute (nuchal) above neck; yellow, each scute boldly marked with wide, irregular, radiating black bands; yellowish below (blackish in juveniles, except for yellow band); shell to 21 cm (8.3 in).

HABITAT: Eastern deciduous woodland and coastal thicket; shelters beneath low bushes; eats vegetation, snails, and millipedes; lays 4 to 6 hard-shelled eggs in summer.

REGIONS: KZN, ZIM

a Parrot-beaked Tortoise

b Angulate Tortoise

c Leopard Tortoise

d Karoo Tent Tortoise

e Spek's Hingeback Tortoise

Plate 8a

Cape Spade-snouted Worm Lizard
Monopeltis capensis

ID: Body worm-like, segmented, and without limbs; eyes reduced to minute black spots; top of head covered in horny "thumbnail"; two pores in front of vent; pink above and below; to 34 cm (13.5 in).

HABITAT: Central deciduous woodland and grassland; burrows underground using "thumbnail" to scrape through hard soils; feeds on insect larvae and termites; up to 3 young born in late summer.

REGIONS: FS, LNW, BOT

Plate 8b

Schlegel's Giant Blind Snake
Rhinotyphlops schlegelii

ID: A large, fat-bodied, blunt-headed snake with horizontal edge on snout; eyes reduced to black spots; tail minute, ending in spine; scales highly polished and same size and shape on back and belly; blue-gray with scattered black blotches when freshly shed, tanning to rust-brown with age; to 95 cm (37 in).

HABITAT: Northern deciduous woodland and savannah; burrows underground and feeds on ant larvae; found above ground only following summer rains; lays 12 to 40 soft-shelled eggs.

REGIONS: KZN, MPG, LNW

Plate 8c

Western Thread Snake
Leptotyphlops occidentalis

ID: Minute and very slender; eyes reduced to black spots; scales highly polished and same size and shape on back and belly; light gray-brown to purple-brown above, lighter below; pale-edged scales give checkered effect; to 28 cm (11 in).

HABITAT: Western savannah and near desert; burrows in sandy soils; feeds on termites, ant eggs and larvae; lays 2 to 4 rice-shaped eggs joined like sausages.

REGIONS: NC, NAM

Plate 8d

Southern African Python
Python natalensis

ID: Largest snake in region; heavy, muscular body; neck narrow, head with small scales on crown; heat pits on lips; small spurs on either side of vent; ventral scales small, not as wide as body; olive with dark blotches; dark spearhead mark on head; to 5.6 m (18 ft) in region.

HABITAT: Widespread in north and east; deciduous woodland, savannah, coastal thicket, and near desert; kills mammals by constriction; female lays and protects up to 60 orange-sized eggs in nest; attacks on humans extremely rare.

REGIONS: EC, KZN, MPG, NC, LNW, NAM, BOT, ZIM

Note: This species is threatened, CITES Appendix II listed.

Plate 8e

Angolan Dwarf Python
Python anchietae

ID: Medium-sized, muscular snake; head broad, covered with tubercular scales; 5 heat pits on upper lip; small spurs on either side of vent; ventral scales small, narrower than body; body red-brown with black-edged white spots and bands; triangular red-brown mark on top of head; belly yellowish, spots on sides; to 1.8 m (5.9 ft).

HABITAT: Northwest deciduous woodland and near desert; kills mammals and birds by constriction; coils into defensive ball when molested; female lays and protects 5 or 6 large eggs in retreat.

REGIONS: NAM

Note: This species is threatened, CITES Appendix II listed.

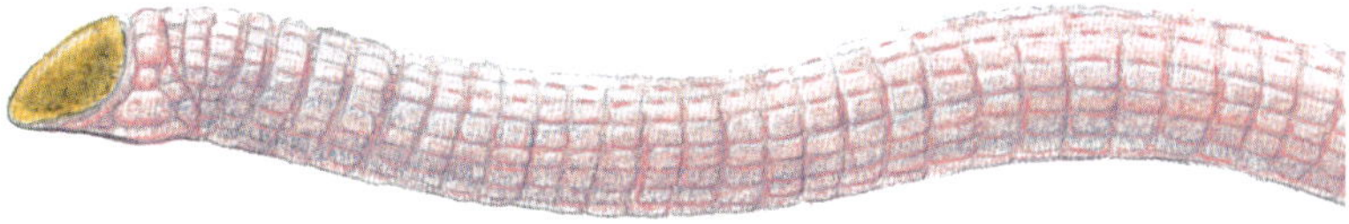

a Cape Spade-snouted Worm Lizard

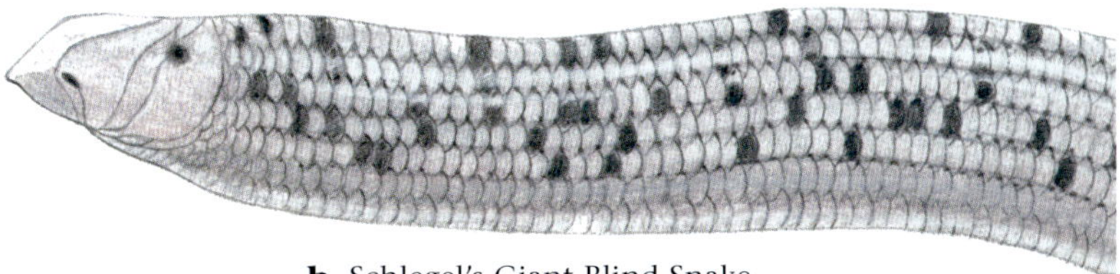

b Schlegel's Giant Blind Snake

c Western Thread Snake

d Southern African Python

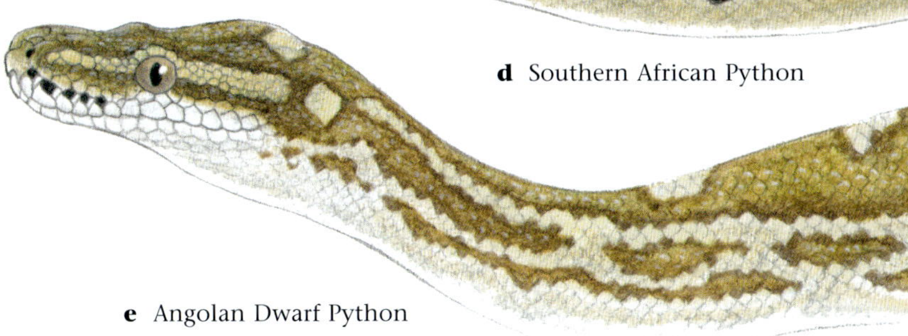

e Angolan Dwarf Python

Plate 9a

Southern Brown House Snake

Lamprophis capensis

ID: Medium-sized with muscular body, obvious head and small body scales; body rust brown with a pale yellow stripe on each side, extending from snout through eye to neck; paler below; to 1.5 m (4.9 ft).

HABITAT: Widespread, absent only from extreme desert and high mountains; common snake in region; terrestrial and nocturnal; kills by constriction.

REGIONS: EC, FS, KZN, MPG, NC, LNW, WC, NAM, BOT, ZIM

Plate 9b

Cape Wolf Snake

Lycophidion capense

ID: A small snake with flat, obvious head and small eyes with vertical pupils; body scales shiny; blue-gray (brownish in Cape), usually with white-tipped scales; cream to dark gray below; to 64 cm (25 in).

HABITAT: Northern and eastern regions with relicts in Cape; rare in scrubland and absent from desert and mountain grassland; nocturnal and terrestrial; kills sleeping lizards by constriction.

REGIONS: EC, FS, KZN, MPG, NC, LNW, WC, NAM, BOT, ZIM

Plate 9c

Cape File Snake

Mehelya capensis

ID: An unusual large snake with flat, blunt head; body triangular with hard, enlarged, keeled scales along backbone; body scales conical and separated by pink skin; gray-brown with creamy pink belly and flanks; to 1.65 m (5.4 ft).

HABITAT: Varied; northern moist savannah and coastal thicket; terrestrial and nocturnal; feeds on other snakes, which it kills by constriction.

REGIONS: KZN, MPG, LNW, NAM, BOT, ZIM

Plate 9d

Southern Slug-eating Snake

Duberria lutrix

ID: A small snake with a short head; neck indistinct; scales smooth; back red-brown to pale brown, sometimes with broken black line along backbone; flanks paler and belly cream, edged with a dark, dotted line; to 43 cm (17 in).

HABITAT: Moist eastern regions; fynbos, coastal thicket, and mountain grasslands; nocturnal and terrestrial; eats only slugs; protects head by rolling into tight coils when threatened; gives birth to 6 to 12 babies in late summer.

REGIONS: EC, FS, KZN, MPG, LNW, WC, ZIM

Plate 9e

Mole Snake

Pseudaspis cana

ID: Large, muscular snake with a slightly hooked snout; body scales smooth (keeled in WC); neck indistinct; adults uniform red-brown to pale brown (black in WC); juveniles light brown with four rows of dark, pale-edged spots; to 2.1 m (6.9 ft).

HABITAT: Widespread, absent only from extreme desert; terrestrial; constricts rodents in their burrows; up to 95 small babies born in late summer.

REGIONS: EC, FS, KZN, MPG, NC, LNW, WC, NAM, BOT, ZIM

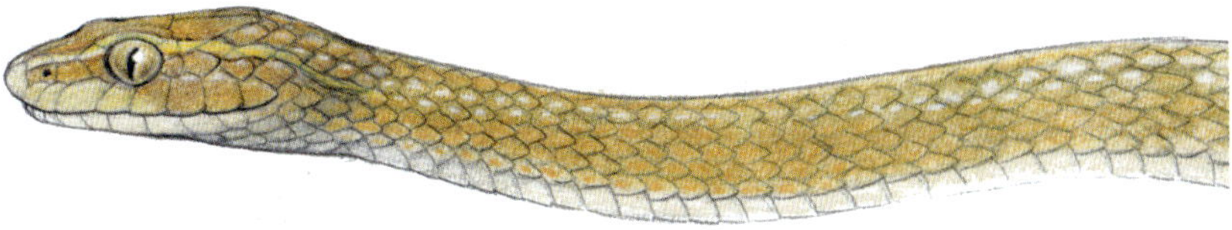

a Southern Brown House Snake

b Cape Wolf Snake

c Cape File Snake

d Southern Slug-eating Snake

e Mole Snake

Plate 10a

Sundevall's Shovel-snouted Snake
Prosymna sundevallii

ID: Small; snout shovel-shaped and upturned; eyes small with round pupils; scales smooth; tail short with spiny tip; body dark brown with paired dark spots; belly white; to 36 cm (14 in).

HABITAT: South and central regions; scrubland, grassland, and open savannah; terrestrial and nocturnal; eats only reptile eggs; rolls into tight coils when handled.

REGIONS: EC, FS, MPG, NC, WC

Plate 10b

Western Keeled Snake
Pythonodipsas carinata

ID: Thin with very flat head and obvious neck; nostrils raised; eyes large with vertical pupils; head scales small and fragmented; females much bigger than males; back yellow-olive, pale buff, or gray-brown, with double row of dark-edged blotches that may form zigzag pattern; belly white, sometimes spotted on sides; to 77 cm (30 in).

HABITAT: Western rock desert and scrubland; terrestrial and nocturnal; constricts small lizards and rodents; rare, gentle snake.

REGIONS: NAM

Plate 10c

Bicolored Quill-snouted Snake
Xenocalamus bicolor

ID: Body very thin with a short tail; head elongate with quill-like snout, minute eyes, and under-slung mouth; scales smooth; color varied, body yellow and black, striped or spotted (or all black); to 71 cm (28 in).

HABITAT: Scattered and widespread, in open savannah, deciduous woodland, coastal grasslands; burrows in deep sands; feeds only on worm lizards; lays 3 or 4 elongate eggs.

REGIONS: FS, KZN, MPG, NC, LNW, NAM, BOT, ZIM

Plate 10d

Cape Centipede-eater
Aparallactus capensis

ID: A small, slender snake with rounded snout and small eyes with round pupils; scales smooth; gray-buff to reddish brown body with prominent black head and collar; belly cream; to 41 cm (16 in).

HABITAT: Eastern regions in grassland, deciduous woodland, and coastal thicket; lives in burrows and termite nests; feeds only on centipedes, which it kills with venom; lays 2 to 4 elongate eggs.

REGIONS: EC, FS, KZN, MPG, LNW, BOT, ZIM

Plate 10e

Common Egg-eating Snake
Dasypeltis scabra

ID: A thin snake with rough scales; head small with rounded snout and prominent black "V" mark; long tail; back creamy gray with numerous dark blotches; mouth black inside; belly white, sometimes flecked; to 1.16 m (3.8 ft) .

HABITAT: Widespread and absent only from high mountains and barren desert; terrestrial and nocturnal; feeds only on bird eggs; in defence, coils tightly and makes hissing noise by rubbing scales together; lays up to 12 eggs in summer.

REGIONS: EC, FS, KZN, MPG, NC, LNW, WC, NAM, BOT, ZIM

a Sundevall's Shovel-snouted Snake

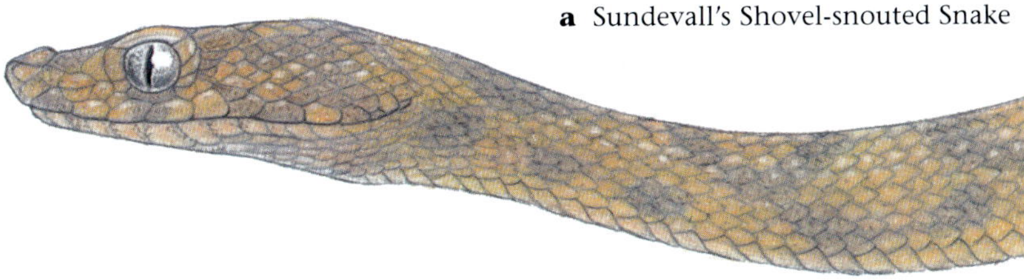

b Western Keeled Snake

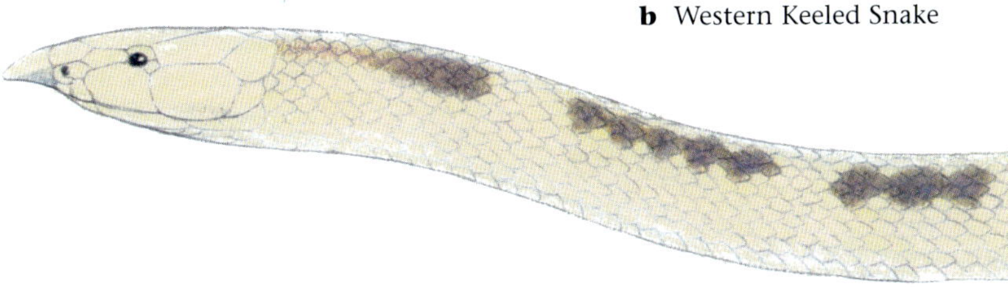

c Bicolored Quill-snouted Snake

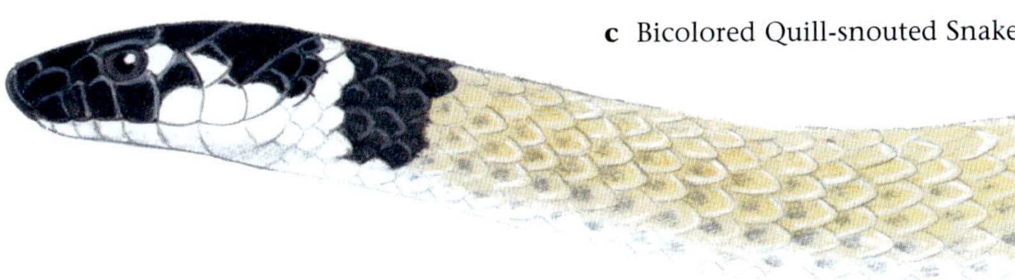

d Cape Centipede-eater

e Common Egg-eating Snake

Plate 11a

Spotted Skaapstekker

Psammophylax rhombeatus

ID: Medium-sized with a rounded snout and longish tail; scales smooth; back yellowish to pale olive, boldly marked with 3 or 4 rows of dark blotches that may form a zigzag or vague stripes; belly yellowish with dark flecks; to 1.46 m (4.8 ft).

HABITAT: Southeast regions, with rare scattered records in west; fynbos, moist grassland, and open savannah; terrestrial, chasing small lizards, frogs, and mice during day; may bite, but harmless; lays up to 30 eggs.

REGIONS: EC, FS, KZN, MPG, NC, LNW, WC, NAM

Plate 11b

Stripe-bellied Sand Snake

Psammophis subtaeniatus

ID: Elongate and graceful; head lance-shaped with large eyes; long tail; back light gray-brown with broad, dark band along backbone; belly with bright yellow, black-edged stripe; to 1.37 m (4.5 ft).

HABITAT: Northern dry savannahs; fast-moving daytime hunter of lizards and mice; lays 4 to 10 eggs in summer.

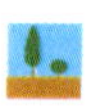

REGIONS: MPG, LNW, NAM, BOT, ZIM

Plate 11c

Dwarf Beaked Snake

Dipsina multimaculata

ID: Small and slender; head distinct with V-shaped mark and hooked snout; short tail; back buff to pink-brown, with 3 to 5 rows of darker blotches that may form vague bands; belly whitish with dark lateral spots; to 45 cm (17.5 in).

HABITAT: Western deserts and scrubland; catches small lizards by ambush; shelters in grass clumps or under stones; lays 2 to 4 small eggs.

REGIONS: NC, WC, NAM, BOT

Plate 11d

Beaked Snake

Rhamphiophis rostratus

ID: Large, muscular snake; head distinct, with dark stripe on side and prominent hooked snout; back yellow- to red-brown, scales sometimes pale-centered; belly whitish; to 1.57 m (5.1 ft).

HABITAT: Northeastern moist savannah; hunts small rodents in burrows; kills by constriction; lays 8 to 17 large eggs in summer.

REGIONS: MPG, LNW, BOT, ZIM

Plate 11e

Bark Snake

Hemirhagerrhis nototaenia

ID: Small, elongate snake with flat, distinct head and large eyes; long tail; back gray to gray-brown with a dark stripe along backbone, bordered by rows of dark blotches that may fuse to form crossbars or a zigzag; to 43 cm (17 in).

HABITAT: Deciduous woodland; secretive, sheltering under loose bark and hunting small day geckos and frogs; prey swallowed as snake hangs head-down; lays 2 to 8 elongate eggs.

REGIONS: MPG, LNW, BOT, ZIM

a Spotted Skaapstekker

b Stripe-bellied Sand Snake

c Dwarf Beaked Snake

d Beaked Snake

e Bark Snake

Plate 12a

Red-lipped Snake
Crotaphopeltis hotamboeia

ID: A small to mid-sized, relatively slender snake with wide head; tail short and body scales smooth; olive green body with scattered small white flecks; head black with bright red lip (pale in far north); belly white; to 81 cm (32 in).

HABITAT: Southern and eastern regions, in moist fynbos, grassland, coastal thicket, and woodland; terrestrial and nocturnal, feeding mostly on frogs; threatens with flat head to show red lips; bites readily, but harmless; lays 6 to 19 eggs.

REGIONS: EC, FS, KZN, MPG, LNW, WC, BOT, ZIM

Plate 12b

Tiger Snake
Telescopus semiannulatus

ID: A mid-sized, very slender snake with a distinct neck, flat head, and large eyes; long tail; dull orange back with 22–50 black bars that are larger on forebody; belly orangish yellow; to 1.05 m (3.4 ft).

HABITAT: Northern and eastern savannahs and western scrublands; arboreal, sheltering in hollow trees; nocturnal, catches lizards and sleeping bats and birds; lays 6 to 20 elongate eggs.

REGIONS: KZN, MPG, NC, LNW, NAM, BOT, ZIM

Plate 12c

Spotted Bush Snake
Philothamnus semivariegatus

ID: A mid-sized, slender snake with obvious head and large, reddish eyes; long tail; belly scales flat with lateral edge to aid climbing; body green at front merging to gray-bronze on tail, with black blotches on forebody; skin between scales blue; belly pale green; to 1.26 m (4.1 ft).

HABITAT: Mainly in north and east, in open woodland; arboreal excellent, speedy climber catching small lizards and reed frogs; lays 3 to 12 eggs.

REGIONS: EC, FS, KZN, MPG, NC, LNW, NAM, BOT, ZIM

Plate 12d

Twig Snake
Thelotornis capensis

ID: A mid-sized, very slender snake with lance-shaped head and large eyes with keyhole pupils; long tail; body twig-colored with a series of diagonal pale blotches; top of head blue-green, heavily speckled with dark spots; belly pink-gray with many gray blotches; to 1.5 m (4.9 ft).

HABITAT: Northeast woodlands and open savannah; ambushes small vertebrates from low branches; perfectly camouflaged; kills with venom and eats hanging downward; lays 4 to 18 elongate eggs; swells neck in threat; very shy but bite can be fatal.

REGIONS: KZN, MPG, LNW, NAM, BOT, ZIM

Plate 12e

Boomslang
Dispholidus typus

ID: A large snake with rounded head and large eyes; body scales keeled and squarish; long tail; juveniles with twig-colored bodies, emerald eyes, and chocolate-brown heads above, cream below; females turn olive-green with white to brown bellies; male color varied, may be plain leaf green, powder blue, or rusty red, with lighter belly, or bright green or yellow with black-edged scales and black-spotted heads; to 2.0 m (6.6 ft).

HABITAT: Widespread, wherever there are bushes and trees; active, arboreal hunter of birds and chameleons; lays up to 24 elongate eggs; kills with venom; swells neck in threat; very shy but bite can be fatal.

REGIONS: EC, FS, KZN, MPG, LNW, WC, NAM, BOT, ZIM

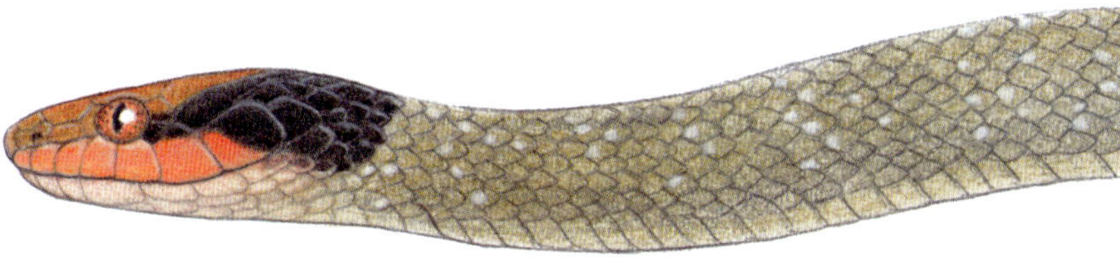

a Red-lipped Snake

b Tiger Snake

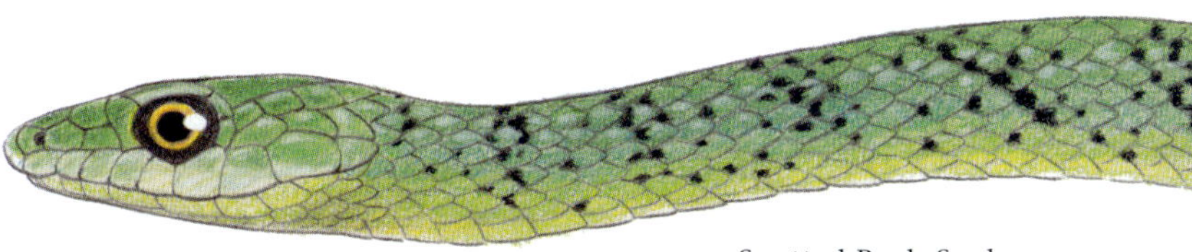

c Spotted Bush Snake

d Twig Snake

e Boomslang

Plate 13a

Spotted Harlequin Snake
Homoroselaps lacteus

ID: A small snake with elongate body, short tail, rounded head and small eyes; scales shiny; brightly colored; from East London north, shiny black, each scale with yellow spot giving a speckled appearance; from Port Elizabeth west, body yellow with black blotches and bright red-orange line along backbone; in EC any color combination of above; to 63 cm (25 in).

HABITAT: Eastern regions, in scrubland, grassland, and thicket; burrows in sandy soils, hunting small snakes and legless lizards; lays up to 13 elongate eggs; rarely bites, but mildly venomous.

REGIONS: EC, FS, KZN, MPG, NC, LNW, WC

Plate 13b

Coral Snake
Aspidelaps lubricus

ID: A small, stocky snake with rounded head, smallish eyes, and bulldozer-like nose with enlarged front scale; scales smooth and shiny; tail short; body orange to coral red, with numerous black bands that extend onto belly and are narrower toward the tail; head reddish with black crossbar between eyes, arrow-mark on crown and collar on neck; belly yellowish between crossbars; to 80 cm (32 in).

HABITAT: Western deserts and scrublands; terrestrial, sheltering in burrows and under rocks, emerging at night to hunt small vertebrates; lays up to 11 eggs; in threat huffs, rears forebody, and spreads narrow hood; venomous but rarely fatal.

REGIONS: EC, NC, WC, NAM

Plate 13c

Rinkhals
Hemachatus haemachatus

ID: A mid-size, stocky snake with a large, blunt head; body scales are rough; juveniles with about 40 black and tan bands; these persist in adults from Cape, Kwazulu-Natal, and Zimbabwe, but fade in adults from central grasslands; belly dark with 1 or 2 white bands on throat; to 1.5 m (4.9 ft).

HABITAT: Scattered populations in temperate grasslands and coastal fynbos; terrestrial and nocturnal in summer; hunts toads and rodents; up to 63 babies born in late summer; may play dead or display by raising forebody and spreading hood; can spit venom; bites rare, but can be fatal.

REGIONS: EC, FS, KZN, MPG, WC, ZIM

Plate 13d

Cape Cobra
Naja nivea

ID: Large, slender cobra with a broad head; shiny scales; juveniles dirty yellow with black throat band; adults dark brown to butter yellow, plain or speckled; to 1.7 m (5.6 ft).

HABITAT: Western scrublands; active daytime hunter of rodents, frogs, snakes, and lizards; shelters in burrows; lays up to 20 large eggs; cannot spit venom; rears and spreads hood; usually avoids people; bites very dangerous.

REGIONS: EC, FS, NC, WC, NAM, BOT

Plate 13e

Black Mamba
Dendroaspis polylepis

ID: Large, slender, muscular snake; head elongate and flat-sided; scales smooth but dull; tail long; body dirty gray, sometimes olive; belly paler, usually with dark flecks; mouth black inside; to 4.3 m (14 ft).

HABITAT: Terrestrial, daytime hunter of small vertebrates, including ground birds, squirrels, and hyraxes; lays up to 20 large eggs; in threat rears forebody, flattens neck, and gapes mouth (heed the warning!); bites rapidly and often; untreated bites usually fatal.

REGIONS: EC, KZN, MPG, LNW, NAM, BOT, ZIM

a Spotted Harlequin Snake

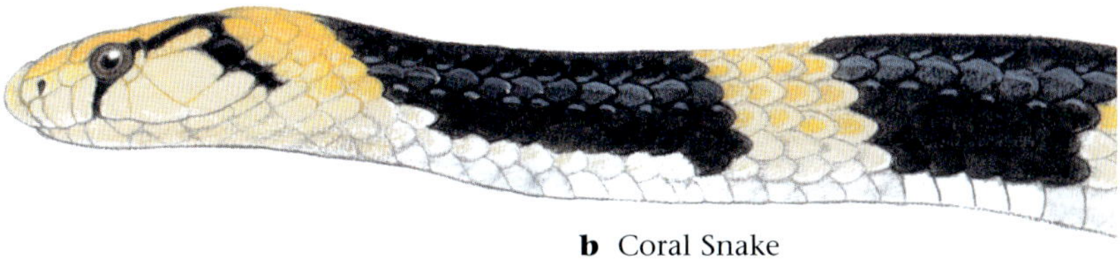

b Coral Snake

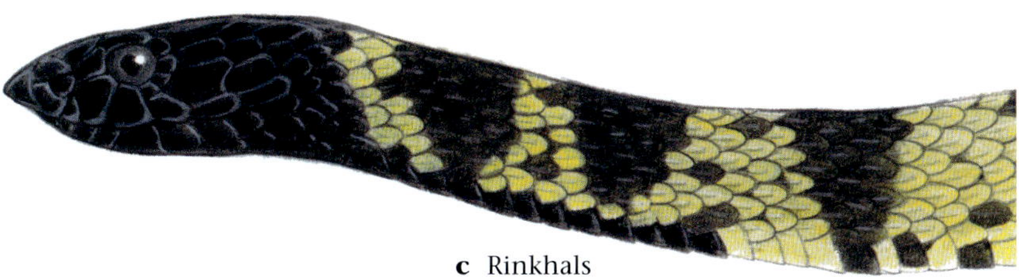

c Rinkhals

d Cape Cobra

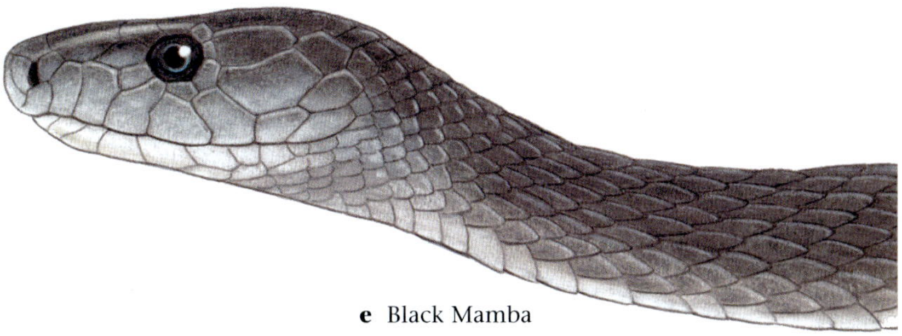

e Black Mamba

Plate 14a

Common Night Adder

Causus rhombeatus

ID: Short, stocky snake with blunt head; scales soft; tail short; body gray-pink with numerous dark, pale-edged blotches (faded in north); head with dark "V" shape; to 1 m (3.3 ft).

HABITAT: Moist eastern woodlands; terrestrial, nocturnal, feeds mainly on frogs; lays up to 26 eggs; hisses and strikes readily; bites rarely fatal.

REGIONS: EC, KZN, MPG, LNW, WC, BOT, ZIM

Plate 14b

Puff Adder

Bitis arietans

ID: Large, verging on obese; head broad and covered in small scales; scales rough; tail very short; body tan to brown (yellow in Cape males) with numerous dark, pale-edged chevrons; belly pale with scattered blotches; to 1.2 m (3.9 ft).

HABITAT: Widespread, absent only from extreme desert and high mountains; terrestrial and sluggish, except when striking; eats mainly rodents; up to 40 babies born in late summer; in threat gives deep hiss; bite very painful, often fatal.

REGIONS: EC, FS, KZN, MPG, NC, LNW, WC, NAM, BOT, ZIM

Plate 14c

Horned Adder

Bitis caudalis

ID: Small and stout; wide, flat head with single horn above each eye; tail very short; color varies from light tan to red-brown with dark blotches; top of head with dark "V" shape; belly plain cream; to 51 cm (20 in).

HABITAT: Western scrublands and northern dry savannah; terrestrial, active in twilight; ambushes lizards and small mice; up to 18 small babies born in summer; puffs and strikes in threat; venom mild, rarely dangerous.

REGIONS: EC, NC, NNW, WC, NAM, BOT, ZIM

Plate 14d

Peringuey's Side-winding Adder

Bitis peringueyi

ID: Tiny, slender adder; eyes perched on top of flat, wide head; tail very short, often black-tipped; body sand-colored with faint, paired dark spots; to 29 cm (11.5 in).

HABITAT: Namib Desert shifting dunes; shuffles into sand; lures lizards within reach using tail tip; sidewinds in loose sand; up to 10 tiny babies born in summer; venom not dangerous.

REGIONS: NAM

Plate 14e

Southern Burrowing Asp

Atractaspis bibronii

ID: Slender, shiny black snake; head small and bluntly pointed; eyes tiny; short tail with spiny tip; black above; belly dark gray to cream; to 63 cm (25 in).

HABITAT: Savannah and grassland; burrows, shelters under rocks and in termite nests; eats other reptiles and baby rodents; lays up to 7 eggs; cannot be held safely; bite very painful but not fatal.

REGIONS: KZN, MPG, NC, LNW, NAM, BOT, ZIM

a Common Night Adder

b Puff Adder

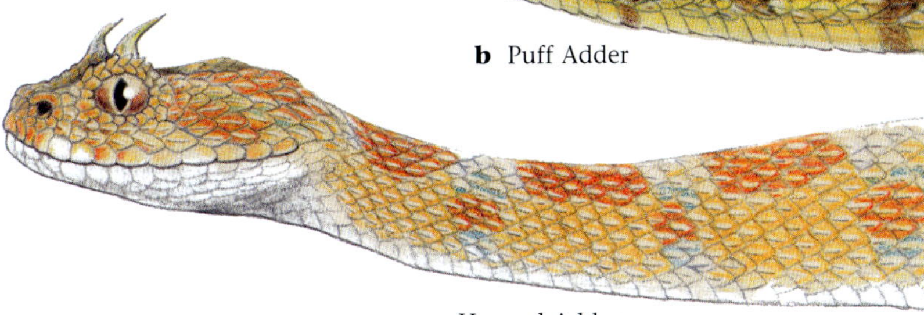

c Horned Adder

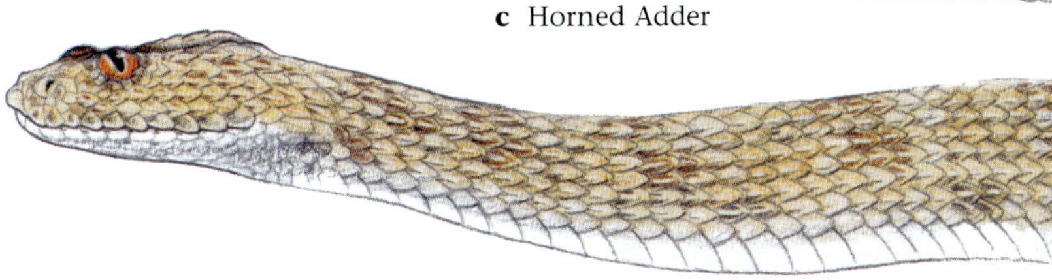

d Peringuey's Side-winding Adder

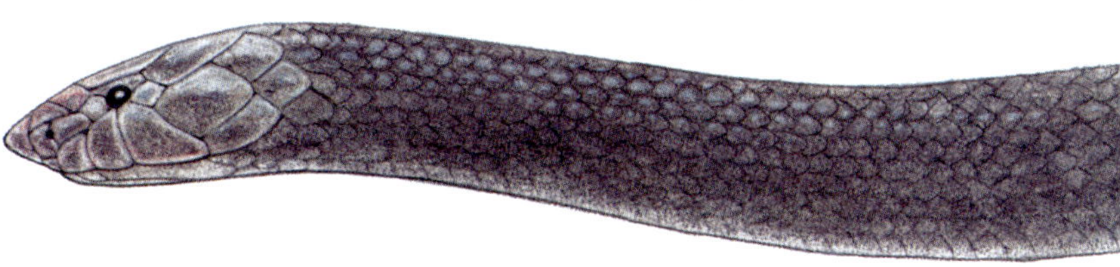

e Southern Burrowing Asp

Plate 15a

Tropical House Gecko
Hemidactylus mabouia

ID: Small, flattened lizard; eyes large with vertical pupils; neck distinct; toe tips flared with paired adhesive pads and a claw; body with granular scales and rows of large conical scales; tail cylindrical with rings of spiny scales; blotchy gray and cream, bleaching white in light; to 17 cm (6.7 in).

HABITAT: Eastern moist savannah and thicket; nocturnal and arboreal, shelters under bark; common on houses around lights.

REGIONS: EC, KZN, MPG, LNW, BOT, ZIM

Plate 15b

Common Barking Gecko
Ptenopus garrulus

ID: Tiny, plump gecko; head rounded with bulging eyes; clawed toes strongly fringed; body round; tail short; mottled reddish brown; belly cream; male throat yellow; to 10 cm (4 in).

HABITAT: Western deserts and scrublands; nocturnal and terrestrial; digs deep, branching tunnel; male calls (ceek, ceek, ceek...) at burrow mouth at sunset.

REGIONS: EC, NC, LNW, NAM, BOT, ZIM

Plate 15c

Web-footed Gecko
Pachydactylus rangei

ID: Small, slender, semi-transparent body; head flat with swollen nostrils, bulging jewel-like eyes; delicate skin; limbs thin, toes webbed; tail smooth, tapering; flesh-pink with dark reticulations; belly chalk white; to 14 cm (5.5 in).

HABITAT: Shifting dunes of Namib Desert; nocturnal, terrestrial; digs deep tunnels; active late at night, feeds on crickets.

REGIONS: NC, NAM

Plate 15d

Turner's Thick-toed Gecko
Chondrodactylus turneri

ID: Stocky build, broad head, powerful jaws; eyes large; body with rough scales; tail with whorls of spiny scales; toes broad with single pad and no claw; mottled gray with large white spots and 4 or 5 vague crossbands; belly white; to 17 cm (6.7 in).

HABITAT: Widespread, in desert, scrubland, and deciduous woodland; lives mostly in rock cracks, but also in trees, houses, and rock piles; nocturnal; bites readily and painfully.

REGIONS: KZN, MPG, NC, LNW, NAM, BOT, ZIM

Plate 15e

Common Namib Day Gecko
Rhoptropus afer

ID: Small and long-legged; head flat, nostrils swollen, eyes large; skin smooth with small, granular scales; tail cylindrical; limbs thin with 4 long toes (inner toe minute); dappled gray; lower surfaces of limbs, tail, and throat lemon yellow; to 11 cm (4.3 in).

HABITAT: Flat rocks in Namib Desert; active in day, sitting in shade of rocks and ambushing insects; territorial, males flash yellow of tail in display.

REGIONS: NAM

a Tropical House Gecko

b Common Barking Gecko

c Web-footed Gecko

d Turner's Thick-toed Gecko

e Common Namib Day Gecko

Plate 16a

Southern Rock Agama

Agama atra

ID: Body plump with narrow neck and rounded head; mouth wide; body scales small and spiny; tail long, tapering with crest; toes thin and clawed; mottled gray-brown with vague bands on tail; pale line along backbone; bright blue head and forelimbs in breeding males; to 32 cm (12.5 in).

HABITAT: Cape scrubland and central grasslands; forms colonies on rock outcrops; basks on prominent rocks; displays by bobbing bright head; eats ants and other insects; shy, retreats into rock cracks.

REGIONS: EC, FS, KZN, NC, LNW, WC, NAM

Plate 16b

Etosha Ground Agama

Agama etoshae

ID: Squat body, muscular limbs, broad head with rounded snout and wide mouth; body scales small and spiny; tail tapering, about as long as body; toes thin and clawed; back yellowish to rust-red, with four dark, pale-ringed blotches; two dark bars between eyes; breeding males with yellow throat with black spot; belly cream; tail vaguely barred; to 16 cm (6.3 in).

HABITAT: Sand and calcrete flats in open savannah; terrestrial; shelters at night in burrow; eats beetles and termites; avoids sun and danger by shuffling into loose sand.

REGIONS: NAM

Plate 16c

Tree Agama

Acanthocercus atricollis

ID: Large and stocky, with big head and large earhole; tail long, barred and tapering; jaws powerful; body scales very rough with scattered spines; body mottled gray-brown to olive with black spot above each shoulder; juveniles with dark "X" shapes on back, surrounded by white blotches; breeding males with ultramarine heads; to 39 cm (15.5 in).

HABITAT: In northeast in open Brachystegia or Acacia savannah; arboreal, running on vertical trunk and main branches; descends to ground to lay eggs and feed on termites and other insects; males display by bobbing bright head.

REGIONS: KZN, MPG, LNW, NAM, BOT, ZIM

Plate 16d

Flap-necked Chameleon

Chamaeleo dilepis

ID: Body flattened; head with turreted eyes and large flaps on neck; crest of small spines along backbone and center of belly; tail long and prehensile; feet clasping, with clawed toes; green to pale yellow or brown, sometimes speckled or with white band along side; mouth bright orange; to 35 cm (14 in).

HABITAT: Widespread in northern woodlands and savannah; arboreal; moves slowly; catches insects with projectile tongue; lays up to 65 eggs in hole in ground.

REGIONS: KZN, MPG, NC, LNW, NAM, BOT, ZIM

Plate 16e

Cape Dwarf Chameleon

Bradypodion pumilum

ID: Small, leaf-shaped body and long prehensile tail; eyes large and turreted; head extends back in pointed, helmet-like "casque"; crest of spines along back and on throat; bright green, paler on belly, and often with bright orange stripe along side; to 18 cm (7.1 in).

HABITAT: Southwest Cape, in fynbos and riverine bushes; adapts well to gardens; catches insects with projectile tongue; 2 or 3 broods of 6 to 8 live babies born each summer.

REGIONS: WC

a Southern Rock Agama

b Etosha Ground Agama

c Tree Agama

d Flap-necked Chameleon

e Cape Dwarf Chameleon

Plate 17a

Giant Legless Skink

Acontias plumbeus

ID: Very large legless lizard; body muscular with short tail; broad head bluntly rounded with lidded eyes; uniform black to brown, paler below; to 55 cm (22 in).

HABITAT: Moist eastern coastal forests; burrows in leaf litter and humic soil; eats grubs and worms; 2 to 14 babies born in late summer.

REGIONS: EC, KZN, MPG, LNW, ZIM

Plate 17b

Lowveld Dwarf Burrowing Skink

Scelotes bidigittatus

ID: Very small and slender; no forelimbs; hindlimbs minute, two-toed; tail as long as body; dark brown with broad yellowish stripe on each side, extending onto sides of head; tail often bluish; to 16 cm (6.3 in).

HABITAT: Woodlands along eastern escarpment; wriggles among dead leaves and in loose soil beneath dead logs; 1 or 2 large babies born in late summer.

REGIONS: LNW

Plate 17c

Sundevall's Writhing Skink

Lygosoma sundevallii

ID: Small and stocky, with fat tail and flattened snout; no neck; spiny tail tip; scales smooth and shiny; limbs small but five-toed; bronze body with dark spot on each scale; belly cream; to 19 cm (7.5 in).

HABITAT: Widespread in northern savannahs and woodlands; terrestrial, burrowing in loose sand; feeds on termites; lays a few eggs in summer.

REGIONS: MPG, LNW, NAM, BOT, ZIM

Plate 17d

Wahlberg's Snake-eyed skink

Panaspis wahlbergii

ID: A small skink with small but well-developed limbs; eyes snake-like, without eyelids; scales smooth and shiny; females and non-breeding males olive-bronze to dark brown back with a black lateral stripe, sometimes with a pale upper edge; belly grayish; breeding males with pink to vermillion flush; to 10-12 cm.

HABITAT: Varied; grassland, open savannah, and woodlands; secretive, diurnal, terrestrial, squirming among leaf litter and grass tussocks; feeds on small insects; lays 2–6 eggs.

REGIONS: KZN, MPG, LNW, BOT, NAM, ZIM

Plate 17e

Striped Skink

Trachylepis striata

ID: Mid-sized, stocky skink with well-developed limbs, smooth and shiny scales; body black with a wide, white stripe on each flank; belly grayish; to 23 cm (9.1 in).

HABITAT: Eastern regions in woodlands and rocky regions; adapts well to houses; crawls on trees and walls and on ground searching for insects; 3 to 9 babies born live in late summer.

REGIONS: KZN, MPG, LNW, ZIM

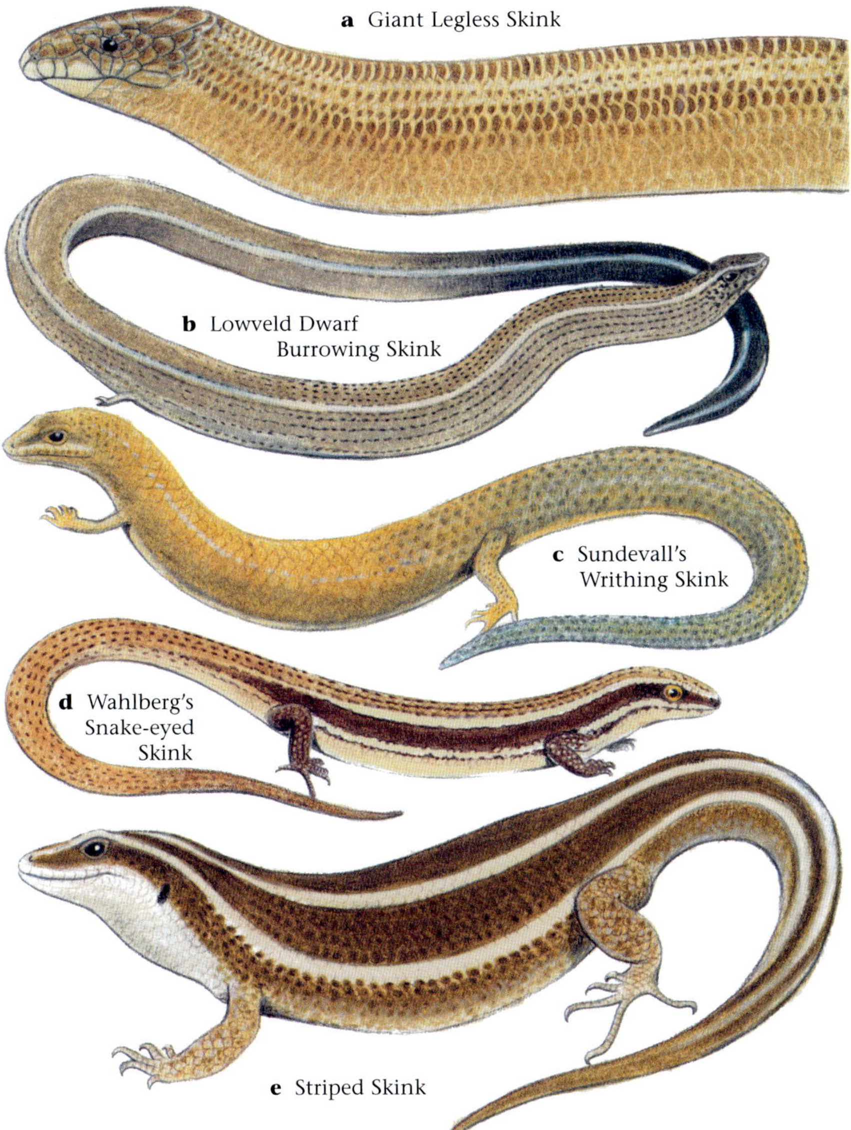
a Giant Legless Skink
b Lowveld Dwarf Burrowing Skink
c Sundevall's Writhing Skink
d Wahlberg's Snake-eyed Skink
e Striped Skink

Plate 18a

Spotted Desert Lizard
Meroles suborbitalis

ID: Slender, with tail as long as body; snout rounded; scales small and granular; small fringe on hind toes; collar on throat; juveniles tan with bold stripes and reddish tail; adults mottled brown (blue-gray in rocky Namib), sometimes with faint stripes; to 21 cm (8.3 in).

HABITAT: Western deserts and scrubland; terrestrial, sprints from shelter of bush to catch insects; lays 3 to 6 eggs.

REGIONS: EC, NC, NAM

Plate 18b

Bushveld Lizard
Heliobolus lugubris

ID: Cylindrical body; large hindlimbs; well-developed collar; tail slightly longer than body; scales small and keeled; hatchlings jet black with 3 yellow-white broken stripes; adults gray-tan to red-brown with faint crossbars and pale stripes; white spots on hindlimbs; to 22 cm (8.7 in).

HABITAT: Sandy flats in northern savannahs; terrestrial, darts between bushes catching small insects; shelters in tunnel at base of bush; lays 4 to 6 eggs in summer.

REGIONS: MPG, NC, LNW, NAM, BOT, ZIM

Plate 18c

Common Rough-scaled Lizard
Ichnotropis squamulosa

ID: Small head, stocky body covered in spiny, overlapping scales; tail slightly longer than body; buff-brown with dark crossbands or blotches and rows of pale spots; to 23 cm (9.1 in).

HABITAT: Vegetated flats in northern savannahs; terrestrial; darts between bushes catching small insects; shelters in tunnel at base of bush, lays 4 to 6 eggs; grows to maturity in 6 to 8 months and dies after breeding once.

REGIONS: KZN, MPG, NC, LNW, NAM, BOT, ZIM

Plate 18d

Western Sandveld Lizard
Nucras tessellata

ID: Elegant, slender body with very long tail; head short and snout rounded; body scales granular; body bright, with coral-red hind body and tail; front of body and head black with fine white bars on sides, and fine stripes down backbone; to 31 cm (12 in).

HABITAT: Rocky flats in western scrublands; terrestrial, sheltering in burrow or under stone; stalks slowly looking for scorpion burrows and beetles; lays 3 or 4 eggs.

REGIONS: NC, WC, NAM, BOT

Plate 18e

Namaqua Sand Lizard
Pedioplanis namaquensis

ID: Small and slender, with tail longer than body; scales granular; distinct collar; head small and pointed; juveniles brightly striped in black and tan with pinkish tail; adults mottled brown, sometimes with vague stripes; to 18 cm (7.1 in).

HABITAT: Widespread in western deserts, scrublands, and open savannah; very fast, dashing between low bushes to catch insects; shelters in hole at base of bush; lays 3 to 5 eggs.

REGIONS: EC, FS, NC, WC, NAM, BOT

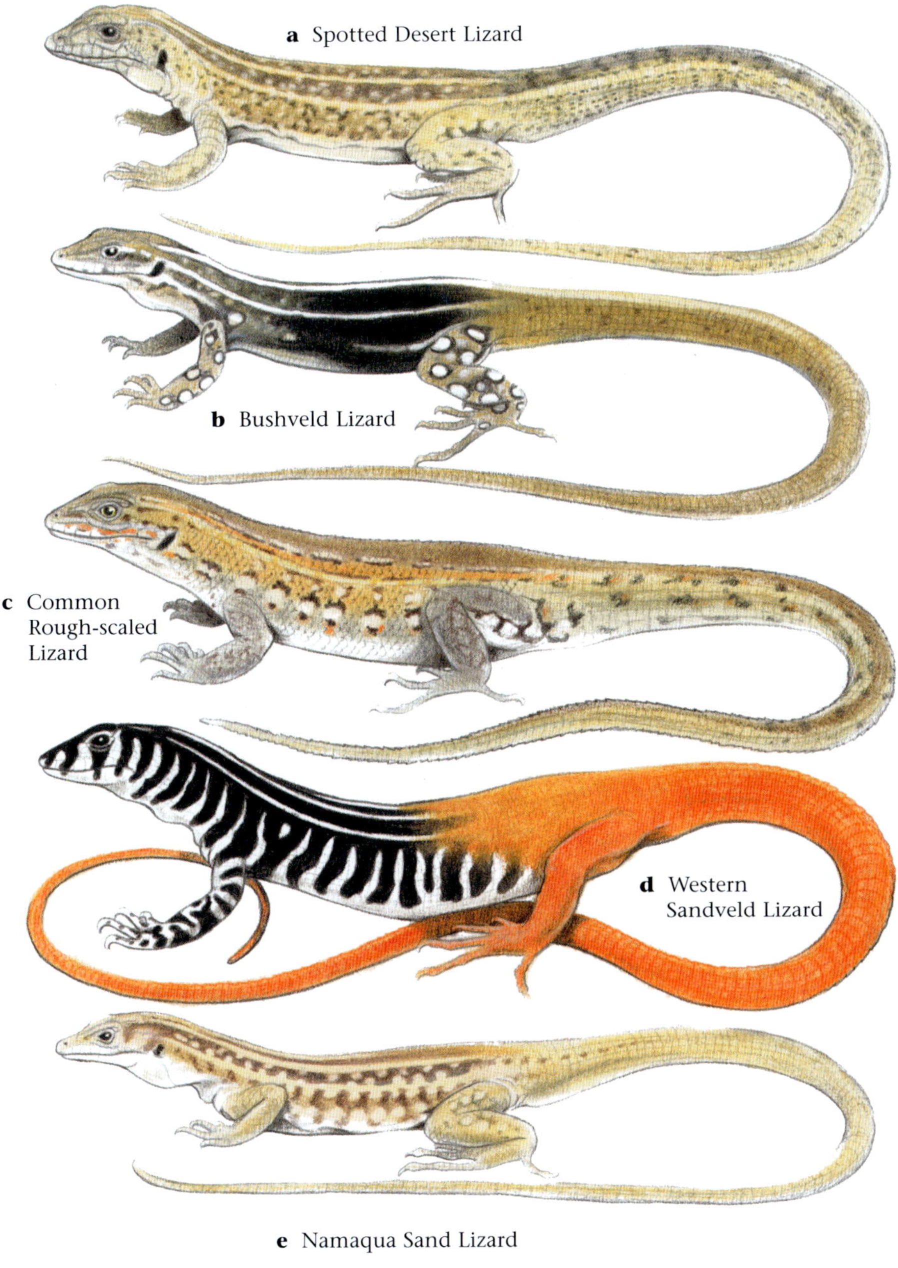
a Spotted Desert Lizard
b Bushveld Lizard
c Common Rough-scaled Lizard
d Western Sandveld Lizard
e Namaqua Sand Lizard

Plate 19a

Cape Grass Lizard
Chamaesaura anguina

ID: Elongate; very slender tail is three times the body length; limbs are vestigial spikes with only 1 or 2 claws; scales very spiny and overlapping; drab brown and tan stripes, with broader pale stripe along backbone; to 49 cm (19 in).

HABITAT: Coastal and mountain grasslands and scrublands; terrestrial, "swimming" snake-like through long grass, hunting grasshoppers and other insects; gives birth to 6 to 9 babies in late summer.

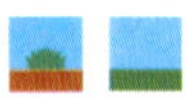

REGIONS: EC, KZN, MPG, LNW, WC

Plate 19b

Black Girdled Lizard
Cordylus niger

ID: Small, with broad, flat head; spiny scales girdle body; tail as long as body with whorls of thorny spines; body jet black, slightly paler below; to 20 cm (7.9 in).

HABITAT: Rocky outcrops in fynbos on Cape Peninsula and around Saldanha Bay; terrestrial, sheltering in rock cracks, making short dashes to catch grasshoppers and beetles; gives birth to 2 to 4 babies in late summer.

REGIONS: WC

Plate 19c

Giant Girdled Lizard
Cordylus giganteus

ID: Large, plump body; broad head fringed behind with four large spines; body and tail scales very spiny; tail as long as body; plain brown with yellow-brown belly; to 40 cm (16 in).

HABITAT: Central grasslands; terrestrial, living in deep burrows; basks on termite nests, looking into sun; eats large grasshoppers and beetles; gives birth to 2 or 3 babies every 2 or 3 years.

REGIONS: FS, KZN, MPG

Plate 19d

Cape Crag Lizard
Pseudocordylus microlepidotus

ID: Flat, muscular body with very broad head; powerful jaws; body scales flat and granular on sides; tail spiny, as long as body; body brown above, yellow (orange in EC) on flanks with vague crossbars; irregular, dark mark on throat; to 35 cm (14 in).

HABITAT: Rock outcrops in southern mountains, in fynbos and grassland; lives in deep rock cracks; basks on boulders, making dashes to catch grasshoppers, beetles, and even other lizards; gives birth to 2 to 5 babies in late summer.

REGIONS: EC, WC

Plate 19e

Broadley's Flat Lizard
Platysaurus broadleyi

ID: Very flat with broad head; spiny tail longer than body; males brightly colored, head deep blue, flanks blue-green, forelimbs yellow, groin and sides of tail red-brown, chest black, lower belly orange; females and juveniles dark brown above with three broad cream stripes, belly whitish suffused with orange near tail; to 22 cm (8.7 in).

HABITAT: Granite walls of lower Orange River in arid savannah; lives under thin rock flakes; very agile, catching small insects by running across vertical rock walls.

REGIONS: NC

a Cape Grass Lizard
b Black Girdled Lizard
c Giant Girdled Lizard
d Cape Crag Lizard
e Broadley's Flat Lizard

Plate 20a

Dwarf Plated Lizard
Cordylosaurus subtessellatus

ID: Small, elegant, flattened lizard with prominent fold on side of body; head pointed and tail long and bright blue; back dark brown to black with two broad cream stripes on upper flanks; to 17 cm (6.7 in).

HABITAT: Rocky, succulent scrubland and near desert; wriggles among rocks and plants catching small insects; alert, hides quickly.

REGIONS: NC, WC, NAM

Plate 20b

Giant Plated Lizard
Gerrhosaurus validus

ID: A very large, flattened lizard with a prominent fold on each side of the body; adults dark brown to purple-black, speckled with a yellow spot on most scales; breeding males with pink-purple throat and neck; juveniles more heavily spotted and barred in yellow; to 69 cm (27 in).

HABITAT: Rock outcrops in savannah, basking on large rock slabs and retreating to shelter in cracks and overhangs.

REGIONS: KZN, MPG, LNW, NAM, BOT, ZIM

Plate 20c

Water Monitor
Varanus niloticus

ID: A very large lizard, with long head, stout body, powerful limbs, and strong claws; tail longer than body and flattened with dorsal crest; skin covered in bead-like scales; adults grayish olive with scattered darker blotches and 6 to 11 broken yellow bands (that may fade) on body and 10 to 18 on tail; belly white with black bars; juveniles much more boldly patterned in yellow; to 2.5 m (8.2 ft).

HABITAT: Rivers, pans, large lakes, and large swamps; may wander far from water, particularly in droughts and when females look for nesting sites.

REGIONS: EC, FS, KZN, MPG, NC, LNW, NAM, BOT, ZIM

Plate 20d

Savannah Monitor
Varanus albigularis

ID: A very large lizard, with bulbous head, stout body, powerful limbs, and strong claws; tail only as long as body and rounded; body covered in bead-like scales and often dead skin; adults gray-brown with 5 or 6 pale yellow, dark-edged blotches; limbs spotted and tail banded, belly dirty cream with scattered dark spots; juveniles much more boldly patterned with blackish throats; to 1.8 m (5.9 ft).

HABITAT: Savannah and scrublands, sheltering in rock cracks, hollow trees, or old burrows; may wander far, particularly males in the breeding season.

REGIONS: EC, FS, KZN, MPG, LNW, WC, NAM, BOT, ZIM

Plate 20e

Nile Crocodile
Crocodylus niloticus

ID: Africa's largest reptile, growing to 5.9 m (19 ft). Head massive and bony, with teeth exposed and eyes and nostrils on top; skin covered in horny, geometric plates; tail shorter than body, rectangular in cross-section, and with 2 raised dorsal keels; hind feet webbed; adults uniform olive to gray with a yellowish belly; juveniles greenish with irregular black markings.

HABITAT: Large rivers, lakes, and swamps, entering estuaries and mangroves.

REGIONS: KZN, MPG, LNW, NAM, BOT, ZIM

Note: Rare out of protected areas, but not currently endangered.

a Dwarf Plated Lizard

b Giant Plated Lizard

c Water Monitor

d Savannah Monitor

e Nile Crocodile

Plate 21a

Gray Crowned Crane
(also called Southern Crowned Crane)
Balearica regulorum

ID: Very large terrestrial bird; mainly gray with maroon-brown back, white panels in the wings, yellow back plumes, and spiky yellow crest; in pairs while nesting but flocks in winter; utters a booming, two-syllabled call ("ma, hem," which gives rise to its locally used name); to 1.05 m (3.4 ft).

HABITAT: Nests in extensive marshlands; forages on marsh edges, grassland, and agricultural fields.

REGIONS: EC, FS, KZN, MPG, LNW, NAM, BOT, ZIM

Plate 21b

Secretarybird
Sagittarius serpentarius

ID: Very large; long-legged, long-tailed predatory bird, usually seen striding purposefully through the grass; mainly gray, with black tail, black outer wings, and a spray of black feathers projecting from nape; solitary or in pairs; to 1.3 m (4.3 ft); wingspan to 2.1 m (7 ft).

HABITAT: Open, flat, or gently undulating grassland and savannah (avoids mountains); hunts on the ground, roosts and nests in treetops.

REGIONS: EC, FS, KZN, MPG, NC, LNW, WC, NAM, BOT, ZIM

Plate 21c

Blue Crane
Anthropoides paradiseus

ID: Very large, terrestrial; uniform bluish gray with elongated tertiary wing feathers that extend gracefully beyond tail; in pairs while nesting but flocks in winter; call a far-carrying, guttural croak; to 1.05 m (3.4 ft).

HABITAT: Open grassland, shrubland, and farmland, often near water; roosts in shallow water.

REGIONS: EC, FS, KZN, MPG, NC, LNW, WC, NAM

Plate 21d

Ostrich
Struthio camelus

ID: Unmistakable; huge, long-necked, long-legged, flightless; female smaller and browner than male; found solitarily, in groups, or in flocks; capable of running at speeds of up to 60 km per hour (37 mph); to 2.2 m, 7 ft, tall.

HABITAT: Ancestrally restricted to semi-arid shrubland, savannah, and desert, but has been introduced widely to more mesic (wet, humid) habitats.

REGIONS: EC, FS, KZN, MPG, NC, LNW, WC, NAM, BOT, ZIM

Plate 21e

Kori Bustard
Ardeotis kori

ID: Very large, thickset; terrestrial; head, neck, chest vermiculated gray, shoulders and back brown, underparts white; short crest on nape; solitary or in small groups; male makes a deep booming call during breeding period; male larger than female; to 1.35 m (4.4 ft).

HABITAT: Savannah and shrubland, mostly in semi-arid areas.

REGIONS: EC, FS, MPG, NC, LNW, WC, NAM, BOT, ZIM

Plate 21f

Southern Ground-Hornbill
Bucorvus leadbeateri

ID: Large, heavily built, and long-billed; terrestrial; black except for white outerwings (only visible in flight) and red facial skin and throat sack; female only has blue patch on throat sack; in family groups, occasionally solitary; to 95 cm (35 in).

HABITAT: Woodland, savannah, and forest-grassland mosaics; forages on the ground, but roosts and nests in trees.

REGIONS: EC, KZN, MPG, LNW, NAM, BOT, ZIM

a Gray Crowned Crane
b Secretarybird
c Blue Crane
d Ostrich
e Kori Bustard
f Southern Ground-Hornbill

Plate 22a

Northern Giant Petrel

Macronectes halli

ID: Large marine bird; long-winged, short-tailed, with heavy, flesh-colored bill; plumage variable (especially on head) but typically dark gray-brown; solitary or in flocks; to 85 cm (34 in); wingspan to 1.9 m (6.1 ft).

HABITAT: Open ocean, especially off West Coast, rarely inshore (at harbors); often follows fishing trawlers; mainly in winter.

REGIONS: EC, KZN, NC, WC, NAM

Plate 22b

Pintado Petrel

Daption capense

ID: Medium-sized marine bird; checkered black-and-white plumage diagnostic; usually in flocks; to 40 cm (16 in); wingspan to 90 cm (35 in).

HABITAT: Open ocean, especially along West Coast; often follows fishing trawlers; an abundant winter visitor offshore.

REGIONS: EC, KZN, NC, WC, NAM

Plate 22c

White-chinned Petrel

Procellaria aequinoctialis

ID: Medium-sized to large marine bird; uniform dark brown except for white chin (not always visible); pale bill diagnostic; usually in flocks; to 55 cm (22 in); wingspan to 1.4 m (4.8 ft).

HABITAT: Open ocean; often follows fishing trawlers; all year, but commonest in winter.

REGIONS: EC, KZN, NC, WC, NAM

Plate 22d

Sooty Shearwater

Puffinus griseus

ID: Medium-sized marine bird with long, narrow wings; dark sooty brown except for silvery underwing; usually in flocks; to 43 cm (17 in); wingspan to 107 cm (3.4 ft).

HABITAT: Open ocean; often follows fishing trawlers; mainly in spring.

REGIONS: EC, KZN, NC, WC, NAM

Plate 22e

Wilson's Storm Petrel

Oceanites oceanicus

ID: Small marine bird; black, with conspicuous white rump and sides of undertail; has characteristic foraging method of hovering close to ocean surface, trailing feet in the water; usually in flocks; to 18 cm (7 in); wingspan to 40 cm (16 in).

HABITAT: Open ocean; often follows fishing trawlers; mainly in winter.

REGIONS: EC, KZN, NC, WC, NAM

Plate 22f

Cory's Shearwater

Calonectris diomedea

ID: Medium-sized marine bird; upperparts uniformly sooty brown, underparts white; bill yellow; solitary or in flocks; to 50 cm (20 in); wingspan to 1.1 m (3.6 ft).

HABITAT: Open ocean, but sometimes visible from land; often follows fishing trawlers; mainly in summer.

REGIONS: EC, KZN, NC, WC, NAM

a Northern Giant Petrel

b Pintado Petrel

c White-chinned Petrel

d Sooty Shearwater

e Wilson's Storm Petrel

f Cory's Shearwater

Plate 23a

Great White Pelican
(also called Eastern White Pelican)
Pelecanus onocrotalus

ID: Very large; thickset bird with long, yellow bill that has a distendible pouch; mainly white, with contrasting black outerwings; juvenile brown-colored; soars to great heights when commuting between wetlands; usually in flocks; to 1.4 m (4.8 ft); wingspan to 2.7 m (8.4 ft).

HABITAT: Large freshwater lakes and pans and coastal lagoons; hunts in packs that swim in formation, herding and trapping fish shoals in shallow water; nests colonially on islands.

REGIONS: KZN, LNW, WC, NAM, BOT, ZIM

Plate 23b

African Penguin
(also called Jackass Penguin)
Spheniscus demersus

ID: Large, flightless marine bird with upright, straight-backed gait on land; swims horizontally, with head upright; legs short; has long, leathery flippers; black and white plumage and diagnostic elliptical black band around white front ; in flocks; to 60 cm (2 ft).

HABITAT: Roosts and nests on offshore islands (and at a few mainland beaches), but forages underwater at sea, fishing up to 12 km offshore.

REGIONS: EC, NC, WC, NAM

Plate 23c

Greater Flamingo
Phoenicopterus ruber

ID: Very large; tall, slimly built, long-legged and long-necked waterbird; bill large and curved downwards; the more ubiquitous of the two flamingos in the region; mainly white, with red legs and red wings (most conspicuous in flight) and a pink, black-tipped bill; juvenile mottled white and brown; to 1.4 m (4.8 ft).

HABITAT: Coastal lagoons and shallow, inland pans and other wetlands usually devoid of vegetation; in flocks, rarely solitarily; feeds by wading with head inverted and immersed below the water.

REGIONS: EC, FS, KZN, MPG, NC, LNW, WC, NAM, BOT, ZIM

Plate 23d

Cape Gannet
Morus capensis

ID: Large; sleek, long-winged, long- and sharp-tailed marine bird; all-white, except for black flight feathers and tail, black facial markings, a yellowish wash on head and a blue eye ring; highly gregarious; to 90 cm (35 in); wingspan to 1.8 m (6 ft).

HABITAT: Roosts and nests in colonies on offshore islands; fishes in flocks at sea, often following trawlers, plunging from the air into the sea after fish.

REGIONS: EC, KZN, NC, WC, NAM

a Great White Pelican

b African Penguin

c Greater Flamingo

d Cape Gannet

Plate 24a

White-breasted Cormorant

(African race of Great Cormorant)

Phalacrocorax carbo

ID: Large; mainly black waterbird with white chest, throat, and face; bill longish and sharply hooked; solitary or in flocks; to 90 cm (35 in).

HABITAT: Lives both along the coast and on inland wetlands; especially common on large impoundments; usually fishes solitarily but roosts and nests in colonies; nomadic.

REGIONS: EC, FS, KZN, MPG, NC, LNW, WC, NAM, BOT, ZIM

Plate 24b

Cape Cormorant

Phalacrocorax capensis

ID: Large; a marine bird, entirely black, except for orange skin at base of bill; bill longish, thin, and hooked; in flocks, sometimes numbering thousands; to 63 cm (25 in).

HABITAT: Inshore coastal waters (always within 10 km of land); highly gregarious when foraging, roosting, and nesting; often seen flying over the sea in long, single-file lines.

REGIONS: EC, KZN, NC, WC, NAM

Plate 24c

Reed Cormorant

Phalacrocorax africanus

ID: Medium-sized; a mainly black waterbird with spangled silver-and-black markings on wings and a dull yellow bill (which is hooked) and area between bill and eye; when breeding, grows a short crest and eyes become red; juvenile is browner and has dull white underparts; solitary, in groups, or in flocks; to 55 cm (22 in).

HABITAT: Lakes, dams, pans, rivers, and other freshwater wetlands; often perches with spread wings after swimming; nests colonially.

REGIONS: EC, FS, KZN, MPG, NC, LNW, WC, NAM, BOT, ZIM

Plate 24d

African Darter

Anhinga rufa

ID: Large; a mainly black waterbird with long neck, long tail, and long, dagger-like bill; mainly black with white streaks on wings and a chestnut throat; juvenile initially white, becoming buff before assuming adult plumage; solitary, in groups, or in flocks; to 80 cm (32 in).

HABITAT: Large, deep, inland freshwater wetlands, especially lakes and floodplains; nomadic; often perches with spread wings after swimming.

REGIONS: EC, FS, KZN, MPG, NC, LNW, WC, NAM, BOT, ZIM

a White-breasted Cormorant

b Cape Cormorant

c Reed Cormorant

d African Darter

Plate 25a

Gray Heron
Ardea cinerea

ID: Large; mainly gray-colored heron with a white head and neck, black crest and line along belly, and yellow bill; in flight distinguished from next species by its uniform gray underwing; usually hunts solitarily but nests in colonies; to 90 cm (35 in); wingspan to 1.7 m (5.6 ft).

HABITAT: Shallow edges of coastal and inland wetlands.

REGIONS: EC, FS, KZN, MPG, NC, LNW, WC, NAM, BOT, ZIM

Plate 25b

Black-headed Heron
Ardea melanocephala

ID: Large; mainly gray-colored heron with a black head and hind-neck and a white throat; bill black in adult, yellowish in juvenile; in flight distinguished from Gray Heron by its contrasting black and white underwing; solitary or in small flocks; nests colonially; to 90 cm (35 in); wingspan to 1.7 m (5.6 ft).

HABITAT: Hunts mostly in dry land situations, especially at grass fires or on farmlands.

REGIONS: EC, FS, KZN, MPG, NC, LNW, WC, NAM, BOT, ZIM

Plate 25c

Cattle Egret
Bubulcus ibis

ID: Medium-sized; an all white-plumaged heron except during breeding, when it grows buff-colored plumes on chest, back, and crown; stockier and shorter-legged than other white herons in the region, and not restricted to wetland habitats; to 55 cm (22 in); wingspan to 95 cm (37 in).

HABITAT: Grassland, savannah, and farmlands where usually associated with cattle or other large herbivores; in flocks; in summer only.

REGIONS: EC, FS, KZN, MPG, NC, LNW, WC, NAM, BOT, ZIM

Plate 25d

Little Egret
Egretta garzetta

ID: Medium-sized to large; an all white-plumaged heron; has black legs and yellow feet (diagnostic) and black bill; has 2 elongated head plumes, but not always present; usually solitary, occasionally in flocks; to 60 cm (24 in); wingspan to 90 cm (35 in)

HABITAT: Shallow edges of coastal and inland wetlands; often hunts by stirring water with foot to disturb fish.

REGIONS: EC, FS, KZN, MPG, NC, LNW, WC, NAM, BOT, ZIM

Plate 25e

Great Egret
(also called Great White Egret)
Casmerodius albus

ID: Large; all white-plumaged heron, with long all-black legs and feet and a bill that is either black (while breeding) or yellow (non-breeding); assumes long, white chest and back plumes while nesting; solitary or in flocks; to 95 cm (38 in); wingspan to 1.6 m (5.2 ft).

HABITAT: Shallow inland wetlands, especially seasonally flooded pans and floodplains; nomadic.

REGIONS: EC, FS, KZN, MPG, NC, LNW, WC, NAM, BOT, ZIM

a Gray Heron
b Black-headed Heron
IM
IM
c Cattle Egret
B
e Great Egret
N
d Little Egret

Plate 26a

Hamerkop

Scopus umbretta

ID: Medium-sized wading waterbird; all-brown, with diagnostic crest ("hammerhead") at back of head, present from juvenile stage onwards; solitary or in pairs, rarely in groups; to 55 cm (22 in); wingspan to 90 cm (3 ft).

HABITAT: Freshwater wetlands, especially streams and ponds with muddy edges; enormous, domed stick nest in tree or on rock is easily recognizable, even in absence of birds.

REGIONS: EC, FS, KZN, MPG, NC, LNW, WC, NAM, BOT, ZIM

Plate 26b

White Stork

Ciconia ciconia

ID: Very large; mainly white, with black outerwings, long red legs, and a long red bill; usually in flocks; to 1.1 m (3.6 ft); wingspan to 1.6 m (5.2 ft).

HABITAT: Grassland, shrubland, and farmlands, especially fields under irrigation; gregarious, sometimes in hundreds at locust outbreaks; soar to great heights when migrating; in summer only.

REGIONS: EC, FS, KZN, MPG, NC, LNW, WC, NAM, BOT, ZIM

Plate 26c

Hadeda Ibis

Bostrychia hagedash

ID: Large; grayish brown, iridescent on shoulders; long sickle-shaped bill blackish below and red above; solitary or in pairs, but flocks at nighttime roosts; raucous cry ("ha, ha, hadeda," hence name) given whenever it flies off; to 80 cm (32 in).

HABITAT: Moist ground, especially in grasslands and farmland; increasingly found in suburban gardens.

REGIONS: EC, FS, KZN, MPG, NC, LNW, WC, NAM, BOT, ZIM

Plate 26d

Sacred Ibis

Threskiornis aethiopicus

ID: Large; mainly white with bare black head and neck, long, sickle-shaped black bill, a black margin to the wings (seen in flight), and black plumes that spray out from the rump; when breeding, underparts become yellowish, and develops a red line under the wing; in flocks; commonly flies in "V"-formation; to 85 cm (34 in); wingspan to 1.2 m (3.8 ft).

HABITAT: Diverse—usually associated with freshwater and coastal wetlands, but also feeds at refuse tips, in plowed fields, and around livestock pens; nests in large colonies.

REGIONS: EC, FS, KZN, MPG, NC, LNW, WC, NAM, BOT, ZIM

Plate 26e

African Spoonbill

Platalea alba

ID: Large, white wading bird; legs, bill, and bare facial skin pinkish red; long, spoon-shaped bill diagnostic, present from juvenile stage; solitary or in flocks; to 90 cm (35 in); wingspan to 1.2 m (3.8 ft).

HABITAT: Edges of shallow lakes, pans, dams, lagoons, and floodplains; forages while wading, sweeping bill from side to side in water; nests colonially in reedbeds or trees.

REGIONS: EC, FS, KZN, MPG, NC, LNW, WC, NAM, BOT, ZIM

a Hamerkop
b White Stork
c Hadeda Ibis
d Sacred Ibis
e African Spoonbill

Plate 27a

Little Grebe
(also called Dabchick)
Tachybaptus ruficollis

ID: Small to medium-sized waterbird; appears tailless; plump-bodied, with short, pointed bill; cheeks chestnut only while breeding, at other times dull brown; usually seen bobbing about on the water, often diving and re-emerging; seldom seen out of the water; solitary, in pairs, or in flocks; makes a loud trilling call during breeding season; to 25 cm (10 in).

HABITAT: Open and sparsely vegetated freshwater dams, lakes, pans, and floodplains; feeds by diving below surface for prey.

REGIONS: EC, FS, KZN, MPG, NC, LNW, WC, NAM, BOT, ZIM

Plate 27b

Yellow-billed Duck
Anas undulata

ID: Medium-sized duck; dappled grayish brown, feathers edged with white to give a scaled appearance; bright yellow bill (diagnostic); solitary, in pairs, or in flocks; to 55 cm (22 in).

HABITAT: Lakes, dams, pans, and marshy ground, especially in grasslands.

REGIONS: EC, FS, KZN, MPG, NC, LNW, WC, NAM, BOT, ZIM

Plate 27c

Cape Teal
Anas capensis

ID: Medium-sized duck; uniformly pale gray with paler edging to the body feathers, giving it a scaled appearance; bill pink; solitary, in pairs, or in flocks; to 45 cm (18 in).

HABITAT: Frequents both coastal and inland wetlands, favoring saline and nutrient-rich pans and lakes; commonest in the drier west.

REGIONS: EC, FS, KZN, MPG, NC, LNW, WC, NAM, BOT, ZIM

Plate 27d

Red-billed Teal
Anas erythrorhyncha

ID: Medium-sized duck; brown-colored, with underparts paler than upperparts; cheeks buff-colored; paler edges to body feathers give plumage a scaled appearance; brown cap and red bill diagnostic; in pairs, groups or flocks; to 45 cm (18 in).

HABITAT: Inland wetlands, especially seasonally flooded grassy pans and floodplains.

REGIONS: EC, FS, KZN, MPG, NC, LNW, WC, NAM, BOT, ZIM

Plate 27e

Cape Shoveler
Anas smithii

ID: Medium-sized duck; pale grayish brown with long, spatula-like bill, orange legs and feet; male is larger, has a lighter-colored head than female, and has yellow, not brown eyes; in flight shows distinctive blue shoulders; in pairs while nesting, otherwise in flocks; to 53 cm (21 in).

HABITAT: Open, shallow-water wetlands, especially seasonal pans.

REGIONS: EC, FS, KZN, MPG, NC, LNW, WC, NAM, BOT, ZIM

a Little Grebe

b Yellow-billed Duck

c Cape Teal

d Red-billed Teal

e Cape Shoveler

Plate 28a

White-faced Duck

Dendrocygna viduata

ID: Medium-sized duck; head pattern (white face and throat, black nape, and chestnut-colored neck) diagnostic; juvenile has buff-colored face; in pairs while nesting, otherwise in flocks; has very distinctive call, a three-syllabled whistle; to 45 cm (18 in).

HABITAT: Inland freshwater wetlands, especially grassy, seasonally flooded areas; often seen loafing in flocks at water's edge.

REGIONS: FS, KZN, MPG, NC, LNW, NAM, BOT, ZIM

Plate 28b

Egyptian Goose

Alopochen aegypticus

ID: Large duck; upperparts chestnut, underparts buff grading to gray, with diagnostic chestnut patch around eye; in flight, striking white shoulders contrast with dark green to black flight feathers; in pairs or flocks; noisy and aggressive, with loud honking call (female) or hiss (male); to 68 cm (27 in).

HABITAT: Likely to occur on any inland lake, dam, pan, or river that has fringe of short grassy vegetation; often feeds on agricultural lands.

REGIONS: EC, FS, KZN, MPG, NC, LNW, WC, NAM, BOT, ZIM

Plate 28c

South African Shelduck

Tadorna cana

ID: Large duck; mainly chestnut-colored with gray (male) or white (female) head; in flight shows striking white shoulders and dark green/black flight feathers; in pairs while breeding, flocking during the winter; to 62 cm (24 in).

HABITAT: Freshwater and saline pans and dams, mainly in semi-arid regions.

REGIONS: EC, FS, KZN, MPG, NC, LNW, WC, NAM, BOT

Plate 28d

Spur-winged Goose

Plectropterus gambensis

ID: Large to very large duck (male 20% larger than female); mainly black, with bluish iridescence and a variable amount of white on belly, shoulders, and on the face; bill, legs, and fleshy forehead pink; usually in flocks; to 1 m (3.3 ft).

HABITAT: Grassy floodplains and marshes; molts on large open lakes; often feeds on agricultural lands.

REGIONS: EC, FS, KZN, MPG, NC, LNW, WC, NAM, BOT, ZIM

Plate 28e

Southern Pochard

Netta erythropthalma

ID: Medium-sized duck; sexes differ, male a uniform glossy purplish black, female sooty brown with an indistinct white, crescent-shaped mark around back of eye; in flight appears all dark except for white wing-bar; fast-flying; usually in flocks; to 51 cm (20 in).

HABITAT: Inland freshwater wetlands, especially those with deep water and sheltered edges; often dives.

REGIONS: EC, FS, KZN, MPG, NC, LNW, WC, NAM, BOT, ZIM

a White-faced Duck
b Egyptian Goose
c South African Shelduck
F
M
d Spur-winged Goose
M
F
e Southern Pochard

Plate 29a

Cape Vulture
Gyps coprotheres

ID: Very large bird of prey; upperparts and underparts cream in adult, streaky brown in juvenile, with bluish neck and head; in flight underwing of adult shows slightly contrasting (darker brown) flight feathers (diagnostic); usually in flocks; to 1.1 m (3.6 ft); wingspan to 2.5 m (8.1 ft).

HABITAT: Savannah, grassland, and shrublands; gregarious when breeding and foraging; nests colonially on inaccessible ledges on high cliffs.

REGIONS: EC, FS, KZN, MPG, NC, LNW, WC, NAM, BOT, ZIM

Plate 29b

White-backed Vulture
Gyps africanus

ID: Large bird of prey; upperparts and underparts light brown (streaked with lighter brown in juvenile); adult has white lower back; neck and head black-skinned with whitish covering of woolly feathers; in flocks; to 94 cm (37 in); wingspan to 2.2 m (7.1 ft).

HABITAT: Savannah, especially tall thornveld; gregarious when breeding and foraging; nests colonially on treetops.

REGIONS: FS, KZN, MPG, NC, LNW, NAM, BOT, ZIM

Plate 29c

Verreaux's Eagle
(also called Black Eagle)
Aquila verreauxii

ID: Large bird of prey; all-black except for white panels in outerwings (only visible in flight) and white rump and back, which forms a "V" on upper back; legs and cere (fleshy covering of part of upper bill) bright yellow; juvenile mottled and streaked brown and buff; flight silhouette distinctive (wings narrowest close to body); usually in pairs; to 84 cm (33 in); wingspan to 2 m (6.5 ft);

HABITAT: Restricted to mountains and ravines where cliffs provide nest sites and dassies (hyraxes) provide prey.

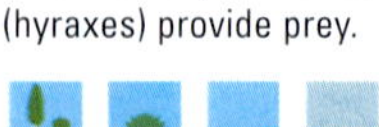

REGIONS: EC, FS, KZN, MPG, NC, LNW, WC, NAM, BOT, ZIM

Plate 29d

Bateleur
Terathopius ecaudatus

ID: Large bird of prey; rich coloring of adult unmistakable, but all-brown juvenile less easily identified; long, tapering wings and very short tail diagnostic; in adult, sexes of flying birds distinguished by width of black edging to underwing (narrow in female, wide in male); solitary or in pairs; to 62 cm (24 in); wingspan to 1.8 m (6 ft).

HABITAT: Savannah; spends much of the day hunting on the wing, cruising back and forth across the plains in a fast gliding flight.

REGIONS: KZN, MPG, NC, LNW, NAM, BOT, ZIM

Plate 29e

African Fish Eagle
Haliaeetus vocifer

ID: Large bird of prey; coloring of adult unmistakable (white tail, head, and chest diagnostic); juvenile less easily distinguished, being streaked shades of brown and white (association with wetland habitat the best clue); solitary or in pairs; has loud, ringing call, "kyow, kow-kow-kow"; to 68 cm (27 cm); wingspan to 2 m (6.5 ft).

HABITAT: Lakes, estuaries, lagoons, large rivers fringed by trees.

REGIONS: EC, FS, KZN, MPG, NC, LNW, WC, NAM, BOT, ZIM

b White-backed Vulture
a Cape Vulture
c Verreaux's Eagle
M
d Bateleur
F
e African Fish Eagle

Plate 30a

Yellow-billed Kite

Milvus aegyptius

ID: Medium-sized bird of prey; all-brown, with deeply forked tail, yellow legs and bill; solitary, in pairs, or in flocks; to 55 cm (22 in), wingspan to 1.4 m (4.8 ft).

HABITAT: Diverse—woodland, savannah, shrubland, grassland, edges of forests; often found around rural settlements; usually seen in slow, wheeling flight; in summer only.

REGIONS: EC, FS, KZN, MPG, NC, LNW, WC, NAM, BOT, ZIM

Plate 30b

Black-shouldered Kite

Elanus caeruleus

ID: Medium-sized bird of prey; white head and underparts, gray upperparts, and black shoulders diagnostic; juvenile browner above, with buff edging to wing feathers; solitary or in pairs, but flocks at nighttime roosts; to 30 cm (12 in); wingspan to 84 cm (33 in).

HABITAT: Diverse—savannah, grassland, shrubland, and desert; nomadic; regularly hunts by hovering; often perched on roadside poles (usually the commonest roadside hawk in the region).

REGIONS: EC, FS, KZN, MPG, NC, LNW, WC, NAM, BOT, ZIM

Plate 30c

Jackal Buzzard

Buteo rufofuscus

ID: Medium-sized bird of prey; upperparts and head black, tail and chest bar reddish brown; throat and belly blackish mottled and barred with white; juvenile has cinnamon underparts and darker brown upperparts; solitary or in pairs; to 50 cm (20 in); wingspan to 1.3 m (4.3 ft).

HABITAT: Grassland and shrubland, especially in hilly or mountainous country; often seen perched on roadside telephone poles.

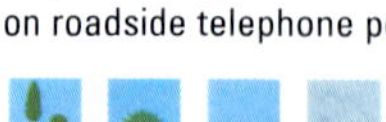

REGIONS: EC, FS, KZN, MPG, NC, LNW, WC, NAM

Plate 30d

Steppe Buzzard

(also called Common Buzzard)

Buteo buteo

ID: Medium-sized bird of prey; upperparts brown, underparts streaked brown and white with distinctive white chest bar; solitary but migrates in flocks; to 47 cm (19 in); wingspan to 1.1 m (3.6 ft).

HABITAT: Grassland, shrubland, and savannah; in summer only; often seen perched on roadside telephone poles.

REGIONS: EC, FS, KZN, MPG, NC, LNW, WC, NAM

Plate 30e

Gabar Goshawk

Micronisus gabar

ID: Small bird of prey; diagnostic features are white rump (conspicuous in flight), white and gray barred underparts, and red legs, feet, and cere (fleshy covering of part of upper bill); juvenile is streaky brown; solitary or in pairs; to 25 cm (10 in).

HABITAT: Savannah, especially thornveld.

REGIONS: EC, FS, KZN, MPG, NC, LNW, WC, NAM, BOT, ZIM

Plate 30f

Southern Pale Chanting Goshawk

Melierax canorus

ID: Medium-sized bird of prey; mainly gray, with long red legs, feet, and bill; shows white rump and conspicuous white wing panels in flight; juvenile streaked with shades of brown; solitary or in pairs; to 50 cm (20 in); wingspan to 1.1 m (3.6 ft).

HABITAT: Arid grasslands, shrublands, and savannah; often seen perched on roadside poles.

REGIONS: EC, FS, NC, LNW, WC, NAM, BOT, ZIM

a Yellow-billed Kite

b Black-shouldered Kite

d Steppe Buzzard

c Jackal Buzzard

e Gabar Goshawk

f Southern Pale Chanting Goshawk

Plate 31a

Lanner Falcon
Falco biarmicus

ID: Medium-sized, long-winged, fast-flying bird of prey; upperparts gray, underparts buff, with chestnut crown and conspicuous black moustache stripes; juvenile streaked with dark brown on underparts; solitary or in pairs; to 38 cm (15 in); wingspan to 1 m (3.3 ft).

HABITAT: Diverse—open grassland, shrublands, savannah, and desert; often in vicinity of cliffs.

REGIONS: EC, FS, KZN, MPG, NC, LNW, WC, NAM, BOT, ZIM

Plate 31b

Amur Falcon
(also called Eastern Red-footed Kestrel)
Falco amurensis

ID: Medium-sized, slim, and long-winged bird of prey; sexes differ, male uniform dark gray with reddish brown vent and conspicuous white areas in underwing (visible in flight), female dark gray above, white below streaked with black; in flocks, often with other migratory kestrel species; to 30 cm (12 in); wingspan to 70 cm (28 in).

HABITAT: Open grasslands; commonly hunts from perches on roadside telephone lines or by hovering; in summer only.

REGIONS: EC, FS, KZN, MPG, LNW, NAM, BOT, ZIM

Plate 31c

Rock Kestrel
(also called Eurasian Kestrel)
Falco tinnunculus

ID: Medium-sized bird of prey; mainly reddish brown-colored with gray head and tail (tail unbarred in male, barred with black in female); solitary or in pairs; to 32 cm (12.5 in); wingspan to 73 cm (29 in).

HABITAT: Grassland, shrubland, and savannah, especially in vicinity of cliffs; often hunts by hovering.

REGIONS: EC, FS, KZN, MPG, NC, LNW, WC, NAM, BOT, ZIM

Plate 31d

Greater Kestrel
Falco rupicoloides

ID: Medium-sized bird of prey; pale reddish brown in color, upperparts barred with black, underparts streaked with black; tail barred gray and white; solitary or in pairs; adult has diagnostic pale yellow eye (brown in juvenile); to 36 cm (14.5 in); wingspan to 84 cm (33 in).

HABITAT: Grassland, shrubland, and desert (commonest in semi-arid regions); often seen perched on roadside poles; often hunts by hovering.

REGIONS: EC, FS, KZN, MPG, NC, LNW, WC, NAM, BOT, ZIM

Plate 31e

Lesser Kestrel
Falco naumanni

ID: Medium-sized bird of prey; sexes differ, male has chestnut back and shoulders, gray head, wings, and tail, and buff underparts; female brown above, barred with black; buff below, streaked with black; in flocks, often with other migratory kestrel species; to 31 cm (12 in).

HABITAT: Open grassland and shrubland, especially in agricultural areas; commonly hunts from perches on roadside telephone lines, or by hovering; in summer only.

REGIONS: EC, FS, KZN, MPG, NC, LNW, WC, NAM, BOT, ZIM

a Lanner Falcon
b Amur Falcon
F
M
c Rock Kestrel
M
F
e Lesser Kestrel
d Greater Kestrel

Plate 32a

Crested Francolin

Francolinus sephaena

ID: Medium-sized, chicken-like bird; upperparts brown or reddish brown, underparts grayish brown, streaked above and below with white; head and neck reddish brown with white streaks and a distinctive white eyebrow; legs and feet pinkish red; often walks with tail cocked; crest is raised in alarm; in pairs while nesting, otherwise in family groups; makes a lilting call, often in duet ("tina-turner, tina-turner..."); to 33 cm (13 in).

HABITAT: Woodland and savannah, especially thornveld.

REGIONS: KZN, MPG, LNW, NAM, BOT, ZIM

Plate 32b

Gray-winged Francolin

Francolinus africanus

ID: Medium-sized, chicken-like bird; mainly gray, with finely barred underparts and streaked upperparts; throat gray spotted with black and fringed by a reddish brown neck band; in flight shows gray and reddish brown in wing; in pairs while nesting, otherwise in flocks; utters a ringing whistled call; to 32 cm (12.5 in).

HABITAT: Grassland or low shrubland.

REGIONS: EC, FS, KZN, MPG, NC, WC

Plate 32c

Swainson's Spurfowl

(also called Swainson's Francolin)

Pternistis swainsonii

ID: Medium-sized, chicken-like bird; uniformly dark brown with black streaking, especially on belly; legs and feet black, facial area of bare skin and bill red; solitary or in groups; males make a harsh crowing call; to 38 cm (15 in).

HABITAT: Savannah and agricultural lands.

REGIONS: FS, KZN, MPG, NC, LNW, NAM, BOT, ZIM

Plate 32d

Red-billed Spurfowl

(also called Red-billed Francolin)

Pternistis adspersus

ID: Medium-sized chicken-like bird; dark brown, underparts finely barred and vermiculated with white; legs and bill red, with diagnostic bare yellow skin around the eye; solitary, in pairs, or in family groups; makes a raucous screeching call; to 38 cm (15 in).

HABITAT: Arid savannah, especially thornveld; often along dry watercourses.

REGIONS: NC, LNW, NAM, BOT, ZIM

Plate 32e

Cape Spurfowl

(also called Cape Francolin)

Pternistis capensis

ID: Medium-sized, chicken-like bird; dark grayish brown with diffuse buff and pale gray streaking on underparts; bill and legs dull reddish; in pairs or family groups; to 41 cm (16 in).

HABITAT: Fynbos shrubland and bushy areas along rivers, in agricultural lands, and in suburban areas.

REGIONS: EC, NC, WC, NAM

a Crested Francolin

b Gray-winged Francolin

c Swainson's Spurfowl

d Red-billed Spurfowl

e Cape Spurfowl

Plate 33a

Black Crake

Amaurornis flavirostris

ID: Small, long-toed marsh bird; all-black with yellow bill, red legs, feet, and eye; juvenile sooty black and lacks bright coloration in bill and legs; skulking, but more easily seen than most other crakes, running for cover if alarmed; in pairs or family groups; call an unusual jumble of clucking, bubbling, and growling notes; to 21 cm (8.5 in).

HABITAT: Marshy ground alongside open water.

REGIONS: EC, FS, KZN, MPG, NC, LNW, WC, NAM, BOT, ZIM

Plate 33b

Common Moorhen

Gallinula chloropus

ID: Medium-sized, chicken-like bird; sooty black, except for white undertail and white streaks along flanks; bill and frontal shield red with yellow tip to bill; legs yellow with red 'garter' above knee; juvenile a duller version of adult; usually seen swimming; call a sharp "krikk"; solitary, in pairs, or in flocks; to 33 cm (13 in).

HABITAT: Reeds or sedges over water; skulking and keeps to cover rather than swims in open water.

REGIONS: EC, FS, KZN, MPG, NC, LNW, WC, NAM, BOT, ZIM

Plate 33c

Red-knobbed Coot

Fulica cristata

ID: Medium-sized, chicken-like bird; all-black with white frontal shield and bill, red eye and two small red knobs on top of head; legs and feet gray; juvenile pale gray, without frontal shield or knobs; usually in flocks; to 43 cm (17 in).

HABITAT: Lakes, pans, dams, estuaries, and other open, freshwater wetlands; commonly in flocks and typically seen swimming on open water.

REGIONS: EC, FS, KZN, MPG, NC, LNW, WC, NAM, BOT, ZIM

Plate 33d

Purple Swamphen

(also called Purple Gallinule)

Porphyrio porphyrio

ID: Medium-sized, chicken-like bird; head and underparts iridescent purple, back and wings greenish bronze; bill, frontal shield, and legs red; juvenile dull grayish brown; solitary, in pairs, or in flocks; to 43 cm (17 in).

HABITAT: Reedbeds, bulrushes, and sedges over water.

REGIONS: EC, FS, KZN, MPG, NC, LNW, WC, NAM, BOT, ZIM

b Common Moorhen

a Black Crake

c Red-knobbed Coot

d Purple Swamphen

Plate 34a

Helmeted Guineafowl

Numida meleagris

ID: Medium-sized, chicken-like bird; dark gray, finely and densely spotted above and below with white; blue head unfeathered, with red crown and wattles, and protruding horny casque; brownish juvenile lacks casque and facial coloration; in pairs while nesting, otherwise in flocks; commonly heard calling, a far-carrying, oft-repeated "buck-wheat"; to 55 cm (22 in).

HABITAT: Grassland, savannah, farmlands (especially after harvest).

REGIONS: EC, FS, KZN, MPG, NC, LNW, WC, NAM, BOT, ZIM

Plate 34b

Crested Guineafowl

Guttera pucherani

ID: Medium-sized, chicken-like bird; grayish black, finely and densely spotted above and below with white; face unfeathered and crown ringed by short, curly, black feathers; makes a harsh grating call; in pairs or family groups; to 50 cm (20 in).

HABITAT: Lowland and coastal forests.

REGIONS: KZN, LNW, NAM, ZIM

Plate 34c

Blue Korhaan

Eupodotis caerulescens

ID: Medium-sized, long-legged, terrestrial bird; wings and back brown, throat black, neck and underparts grayish blue; sexes differ in face color, the male's white and the female's buff; in pairs or family groups; skulking, and more usually heard calling (a harsh, frog-like crowing, especially at sunrise) than seen; to 54 cm (21.5 cm).

HABITAT: Open grassland and low shrubland.

REGIONS: EC, FS, KZN, MPG, NC.

Plate 34d

Northern Black Korhaan

(also called White-quilled Korhaan)

Eupodotis afraoides

ID: Medium-sized, long-legged, terrestrial bird; sexes differ, the male being mainly black and white, with a brown back and extensive white patches in the wings; the female is mainly brown, finely barred and vermiculated with black, and has a black belly; both sexes have bright yellow legs and feet; males are noisy during breeding period, performing conspicuous aerial flights during which they crow raucously; to 52 cm (21 in).

HABITAT: Grassland, shrubland, and open scrubby savannah.

REGIONS: EC, FS, MPG, NC, LNW, NAM, BOT, ZIM

Plate 34e

Red-crested Korhaan

Eupodotis ruficrista

ID: Medium-sized, long-legged, terrestrial bird; upperparts brown marked with down-pointing black chevrons; underparts black; neck and head grayish buff; male has long, reddish brown plumes on nape that are not visible except in display; solitary; skulking, but calling of male often gives his position away: he makes a series of penetrating whistles interspersed with tongue-clicks and often follows this by flying vertically upwards above the canopy of the trees, then dropping, stone-like, with wings closed, back to the ground; to 50 cm (20 in).

HABITAT: Woodland and savannah.

REGIONS: FS, KZN, MPG, NC, LNW, NAM, BOT, ZIM

b Crested Guineafowl
a Helmeted Guineafowl
M
c Blue Korhaan
F
F
M
M
M
F
e Red-crested Korhaan
d Northern Black Korhaan

Plate 35a

African Jacana

Actophilornis africanus

ID: Medium-sized, long-toed waterbird; upperparts and underparts chestnut, with white throat and face, black nape and back of neck, and gold band on upper chest; bill and frontal shield bright blue; legs and feet gray; juvenile has entirely white underparts and lacks blue frontal shield; usually in flocks; noisy, quarrelsome, and conspicuous birds; to 28 cm (11 in).

HABITAT: Freshwater wetlands that are extensively covered with floating plants, especially waterlilies.

REGIONS: EC, FS, KZN, MPG, NC, LNW, WC, NAM, BOT, ZIM

Plate 35b

African Black Oystercatcher

Haematopus moquini

ID: Medium-sized, plump-bodied wading bird; all-black, with long red bill, red legs and feet, and orange eye ring; in pairs while nesting, otherwise often in flocks; to 41 cm (16 in).

HABITAT: Restricted to coast, found on both rocky and sandy shores.

REGIONS: EC, NAM, NC, WC

Plate 35c

White-fronted Plover

Charadrius marginatus

ID: Small wading bird; upperparts pale grayish brown, underparts white, with white forehead and white ring around back of neck; has thin black eye stripe; northern race has buffy underparts; solitary, in pairs, or in flocks; to 18 cm (7 in).

HABITAT: Sandy beaches, especially on coastline, but also along large, slow-flowing rivers.

REGIONS: EC, KZN, MPG, NC, LNW, WC, NAM, BOT, ZIM

Plate 35d

Three-banded Plover

Charadrius tricollaris

ID: Small wading bird; crown, back, wings, and tail brown; underparts white with two broad black chest bands; throat and cheeks gray; eyebrow white; legs dull red; bill and eye ring red; juvenile lacks chest bars and is duller than adult; solitary or in pairs; to 18 cm (7 in).

HABITAT: Sandy or pebbly margins of lakes, pans, rivers, or other freshwater wetlands.

REGIONS: EC, FS, KZN, MPG, NC, LNW, WC, NAM, BOT, ZIM

Plate 35e

Crowned Lapwing

(also called Crowned Plover)

Vanellus coronatus

ID: Medium-sized wading bird; upperparts, throat, and chest brown; underparts white, with thin black chest bar; top of head black with white ring forming crown; legs and bill red; in pairs while nesting, in flocks at other times; to 30 cm (12 in).

HABITAT: Open, flat, shortly cropped or burnt grassland; commonly on roadsides and playing fields.

REGIONS: EC, FS, KZN, MPG, NC, LNW, WC, NAM, BOT, ZIM

Plate 35f

Blacksmith Lapwing

(also called Blacksmith Plover)

Vanellus armatus

ID: Medium-sized wading bird; adult has striking black, white, and gray plumage; in juvenile black and gray replaced by dull brown; in pairs while nesting, flocking at other times; to 30 cm (12 in).

HABITAT: Damp marshy ground on edges of lakes, dams, pans, and other freshwater wetlands.

REGIONS: EC, FS, KZN, MPG, NC, LNW, WC, NAM, BOT, ZIM

a African Jacana

b African Black Oystercatcher

c White-fronted Plover

d Three-banded Plover

e Crowned Lapwing

f Blacksmith Lapwing

Plate 36a

Common Sandpiper

Tringa hypoleucos

ID: Small, short-legged shorebird; upperparts brown, underparts white, with diagnostic white crescent extending above shoulders; solitary; continuously bobs body up and down while feeding ; flies with a distinctive jerky flight; to 19 cm (7.5 in).

HABITAT: Edges of streams and rivers or rocky edges of lakes; in summer only.

REGIONS: EC, FS, KZN, MPG, NC, LNW, WC, NAM, BOT, ZIM

Plate 36b

Wood Sandpiper

Tringa glareola

ID: Small, long-legged shorebird; upperparts olive-brown, finely spotted with white; head and neck grayish brown; underparts white; white rump conspicuous in flight; bill long and straight; usually solitary; to 21 cm (8.5 in).

HABITAT: Margins and shallows of freshwater wetlands, even roadside puddles; in summer only.

REGIONS: EC, FS, KZN, MPG, NC, LNW, WC, NAM, BOT, ZIM

Plate 36c

Curlew Sandpiper

Calidris ferruginea

ID: Small, short-legged shorebird; down-curved bill diagnostic; upperparts pale gray with scalloped pattern from pale-edged feathers; underparts white; some birds attain cinnamon-colored breeding plumage before migration; in flocks; to 20 cm (8 in).

HABITAT: Shallow edges of coastal and inland wetlands; mainly in summer with small numbers overwintering.

REGIONS: EC, FS, KZN, MPG, NC, LNW, WC, NAM, BOT, ZIM

Plate 36d

Little Stint

Calidris minuta

ID: Small, short-legged, short-billed shorebird; upperparts grayish brown; underparts white; white eyebrow; some birds attain reddish brown breeding plumage before migration; in flocks; to 15 cm (6 in).

HABITAT: Shallow edges of most coastal and inland wetlands; mainly in summer, with small numbers overwintering.

REGIONS: EC, FS, KZN, MPG, NC, LNW, WC, NAM, BOT, ZIM

a Common Sandpiper

b Wood Sandpiper

c Curlew Sandpiper

d Little Stint

Plate 37a

Common Greenshank

Tringa nebularia

ID: Medium-sized, long-legged shorebird; upperparts gray with paler speckling and streaking; underparts white; legs greenish (hence name); bill long, slightly upcurved, and gray with black tip; usually solitary; to 34 cm (13 in).

HABITAT: Shallow edges of lakes, pans, estuaries, lagoons; in summer only.

REGIONS: EC, FS, KZN, MPG, NC, LNW, WC, NAM, BOT, ZIM

Plate 37b

Ruff

Philomachus pugnax

ID: Medium-sized, long-legged shorebird; upperparts gray to light brown with scalloped pattern from pale-edged feathers; underparts buffy white; legs usually orange, but variable; bill slightly down-curved, dark gray; males larger than females; in flocks; to 30 cm (12 in).

HABITAT: Inland and coastal shallow-water wetlands; in summer only.

REGIONS: EC, FS, KZN, MPG, NC, LNW, WC, NAM, BOT, ZIM

Plate 37c

Black-winged Stilt

Himantopus himantopus

ID: Medium-sized, long-legged shorebird; head, neck, tail, and underparts white; wings black; legs and long, needle-like bill red; solitary, in pairs, or in flocks; to 38 cm (15 in).

HABITAT: Shallow open wetlands with exposed edges.

REGIONS: EC, FS, KZN, MPG, NC, LNW, WC, NAM, BOT, ZIM

Plate 37d

Pied Avocet

Recurvirostra avosetta

ID: Medium-sized, long-legged shorebird; striking white and black plumage and long, up-curved bill diagnostic; juvenile washed with buff; solitary, in pairs, or in flocks; noisy birds, call an often-repeated, liquid "klooit"; to 45 cm (18 in).

HABITAT: Shallow wetlands with exposed muddy edges; often on saline and temporarily flooded pans.

REGIONS: EC, FS, KZN, MPG, NC, LNW, WC, NAM, BOT, ZIM

a Common Greenshank
F
M
b Ruff
c Black-winged Stint
d Pied Avocet

Plate 38a

Kelp Gull

Larus dominicanus

ID: Medium- to large-sized seabird; white with black back and wings; bill yellow with red spot near tip; legs and feet olive; juvenile mottled brown; in flocks; to 58 cm (23 in); wingspan to 102 cm (3.4 ft).

HABITAT: Seashore and offshore islands, most abundant along west coast.

REGIONS: EC, KZN, NC, WC, NAM

Plate 38b

Gray-headed Gull

Larus cirrocephalus

ID: Medium-sized seabird; wings and back pale gray; neck and underparts white; head gray while breeding, but color is reduced or absent at other times; legs, feet, and bill red; juvenile duller gray, rather mottled; in flocks; to 42 cm (16.5 in); wingspan to 102 cm (3.4 ft).

HABITAT: Frequents both inland wetlands and the seashore (especially east coast); inland birds often feed at refuse dumps.

REGIONS: EC, FS, KZN, MPG, NC, LNW, WC, NAM, BOT, ZIM

Plate 38c

Hartlaub's Gull

Larus hartlaubii

ID: Medium-sized seabird; white except for gray wings and back; legs, feet, and bill red; juvenile has buff wash; in flocks; to 40 cm (16 in); wingspan to 93 cm (37 in).

HABITAT: Coastline and estuaries, mainly along West Coast.

REGIONS: NAM, NC, WC

Plate 38d

Common Tern

Sterna hirundo

ID: Medium-sized seabird; resembles several other less common migrant tern species to region and best distinguished by bill length (long), bill color (black with red tip), and rump and tail color (grayish, not white); in flocks, often associated with other tern species; to 35 cm (14 in); wingspan to 80 cm (32 in).

HABITAT: Coastal waters and estuaries; in summer only.

REGIONS: EC, KZN, NC, WC, NAM

Plate 38e

Swift Tern

Sterna bergii

ID: Medium-sized seabird; wings, back, and tail (which is forked) pale gray; head, neck, and underparts white, with a black cap from behind eye to nape; bill yellow; juvenile is mottled in gray areas of plumage; in flocks, often associated with other tern species; to 45 cm (18 in); wingspan to 105 cm (3.4 ft).

HABITAT: Coastal waters and estuaries; nests on offshore islands.

REGIONS: EC, KZN, NC, WC, NAM

Plate 38f

White-winged Tern

Chlidonias leucopterus

ID: Small seabird of inland waters; back, wings, and tail pale gray; head, neck, and underparts white with a black smudge behind eye; bill black, legs and feet dull red; before migration some birds assume striking black-and-white breeding plumage; in flocks; to 23 cm (9 in); wingspan to 66 cm (26 in).

HABITAT: Inland wetlands, especially open-water pans; in summer only.

REGIONS: EC, FS, KZN, MPG, NC, LNW, WC, NAM, BOT, ZIM

a Kelp Gull

b Gray-headed Gull

c Hartlaub's Gull

d Common Tern

e Swift Tern

f White-winged Tern

Plate 39a

Spotted Dikkop
(also called Spotted Thick-knee)
Burhinus capensis

ID: Medium-sized, long-legged, terrestrial bird; large head, large eyes, and shortish bill distinctive; upperparts buff, spotted with brown; underparts buff, streaked with brown; legs, feet, eye, and base of bill yellow; nocturnal; in pairs or occasionally in flocks; makes a characteristic call at night, a series of piping whistles that increase in speed, then die away; to 43 cm (17 in).

HABITAT: Open, flat ground in grassland, savannah, shrubland, and farmland.

REGIONS: EC, FS, KZN, MPG, NC, LNW, WC, NAM, BOT, ZIM

Plate 39b

Water Dikkop
(also called Water Thick-knee)
Burhinus vermiculatus

ID: Medium-sized, long-legged, terrestrial bird; large head, large eyes, and shortish bill distinctive; buff-colored, streaked above and below with dark brown; has white belly and a broad pale gray wingbar; nocturnal; in pairs or occasionally in flocks; utters a piping whistle at night, more shrill than Spotted Dikkop; to 39 cm (15.5 in).

HABITAT: Edges of lakes, rivers, estuaries, pans; sometimes on sandy beaches at coast.

REGIONS: EC, KZN, MPG, LNW, WC, NAM, BOT, ZIM

Plate 39c

Double-banded Courser
Smutsornis africanus

ID: Small, long-legged, terrestrial bird; upperparts pale brownish gray, with scalloped pattern on wings from pale-edged feathers; chest and belly buff with two thin black chest bars; head and neck streaked light brown with broad white eyebrow; usually in pairs; reluctant to fly but when it does, reveals striking reddish brown secondary wing feathers; capable of running at high speed; to 24 cm (9.5 in).

HABITAT: Arid grassland, shrubland and desert, favoring bare, gravelly areas.

REGIONS: EC, FS, NC, LNW, WC, NAM, BOT, ZIM

Plate 39d

Namaqua Sandgrouse
Pterocles namaqua

ID: Medium-sized, terrestrial bird; pigeon-like in shape and posture with long, sharp-tipped tail; brown and buff-colored, female more cryptically marked than male; in pairs or flocks; often detected from calls of birds flying to drinking sites (a melodious "kelkiewyn"); to 27 cm (11 in).

HABITAT: Arid shrubland, dry grassland, and desert.

REGIONS: EC, FS, NC, LNW, WC, NAM, BOT, ZIM

Plate 39e

Double-banded Sandgrouse
Pterocles bicinctus

ID: Small to medium-sized, terrestrial bird; pigeon-like in shape and posture; yellowish brown colored, the female cryptically speckled and barred, the male plainer, with a black-and-white chest band and black and white spots on forehead; in pairs, but flocks at dusk at drinking sites; to 25 cm (10 in).

HABITAT: Woodland and savannah, especially mopane.

REGIONS: MPG, NC, LNW, NAM, BOT, ZIM

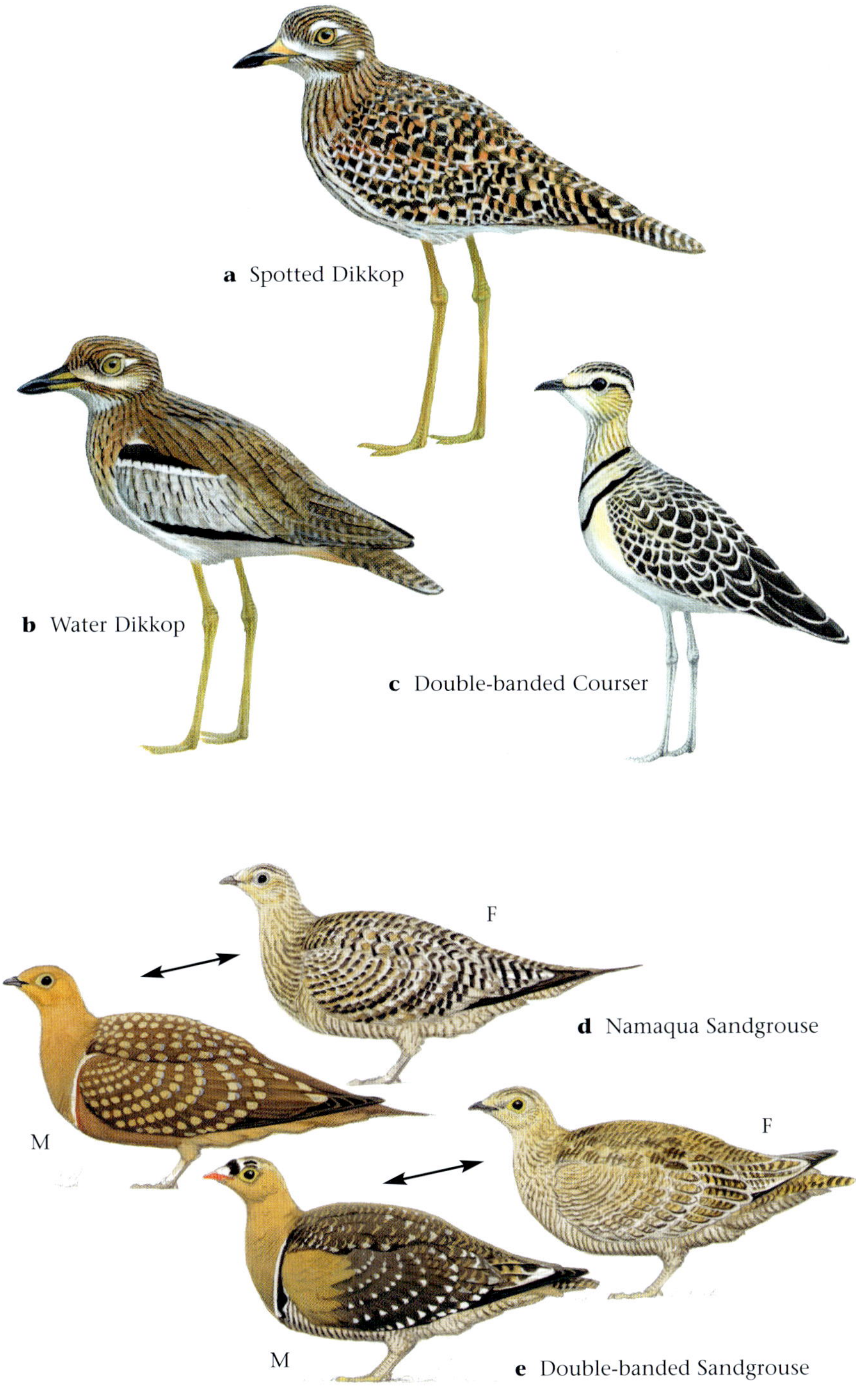
a Spotted Dikkop
b Water Dikkop
c Double-banded Courser
F
M
d Namaqua Sandgrouse
F
M
e Double-banded Sandgrouse

Plate 40a

Speckled Pigeon
(also called Rock Pigeon)
Columba guinea

ID: Medium-sized; upperparts and chest maroon-brown; underparts and head gray; wings spotted with white; has mask of red skin around eye; bill black, legs and feet dull red; usually in flocks; to 33 cm (13 in).

HABITAT: Roosts and nests on rock faces, in caves, and on ledges of buildings; feeds in agricultural lands.

REGIONS: EC, FS, KZN, MPG, NC, LNW, WC, NAM, BOT, ZIM

Plate 40b

Red-eyed Dove
Streptopelia semitorquata

ID: Medium-sized; head and underparts pink; wings, back, and tail brown; black ring on back of neck; eye red, ringed by dark red wattle; solitary or in pairs; call a hooting "you chew tobacco too"; to 34 cm (13 in).

HABITAT: Most types of tall, non-forest woodland; often in parks and gardens.

REGIONS: EC, FS, KZN, MPG, NC, LNW, WC, NAM, BOT, ZIM

Plate 40c

Cape Turtle-Dove
(also called Ring-necked Dove)
Streptopelia capicola

ID: Medium-sized; head and underparts pale gray; wings, back, and tail grayish buff; has black ring on back of neck; eye brown and lacks eye wattle; solitary, in pairs, or in flocks; call a characteristic repeated hooting "work har, der"; to 27 cm (11 in).

HABITAT: Woodland, savannah, and shrublands, often alongside human habitation.

REGIONS: EC, FS, KZN, MPG, NC, LNW, WC, NAM, BOT, ZIM

Plate 40d

Laughing Dove
Streptopelia senegalensis

ID: Small to medium-sized; mainly pinkish buff, with blue-gray wings and black speckles on chest; no neck collar; solitary, in pairs, or in flocks; call a mellow chuckle; to 25 cm (10 in).

HABITAT: Diverse—found commonly in most non-forest wooded country, including gardens and timber plantations.

REGIONS: EC, FS, KZN, MPG, NC, LNW, WC, NAM, BOT, ZIM

Plate 40e

Namaqua Dove
Oena capensis

ID: Small, but has diagnostic long tail; pale grayish brown; male has black face and throat, and red bill tipped with yellow; these absent in female; solitary or in pairs; to 25 cm (10 in).

HABITAT: Semi-arid shrubland and savannah.

REGIONS: EC, FS, KZN, MPG, NC, LNW, WC, NAM, BOT, ZIM

Plate 40f

Emerald-spotted Wood Dove
(also called Green-spotted Dove)
Turtur chalcospilos

ID: Small; upperparts grayish brown; underparts dull pink; has two black bands across back and two metallic green spots on each wing; usually solitary; presence often given away by its series of mellow hooting notes, which become faster before tailing off—a sound characteristic of many bushveld areas; to 20 cm (8 in).

HABITAT: Broad-leafed and mixed woodland; often seen flying up from roads.

REGIONS: EC, KZN, MPG, LNW, NAM, BOT, ZIM

a Speckled Pigeon
b Red-eyed Dove
c Cape Turtle-Dove
d Laughing Dove
F
e Namaqua Dove
M
f Emerald-spotted Wood Dove

Plate 41a

Knysna Turaco
(also called Knysna Lourie)
Tauraco corythaix

ID: Medium-sized, with long tail and pointed crest; head, back, and underparts apple-green, wings and tail dark bluish green; primary and secondary wing feathers red (usually only visible in flight); has white tips to crest and white line below eye; in pairs or groups; presence often given away by harsh croaking call; to 46 cm (18 in).

HABITAT: Forest, living in leafy canopy where not easily detected except in flight.

REGIONS: EC, KZN, MPG, LNW, WC

Plate 41b

Livingstone's Turaco
(also called Livingstone's Lourie)
Tauraco livingstonii

ID: Medium-sized, with long tail and long, pointed crest (longer than that of Knysna Lourie); head, back, and underparts apple-green; wings, back, and tail dark green; primary and secondary wing feathers red (usually only visible in flight); has white tips to crest and white line below eye; in pairs or groups; presence often given away by harsh croaking call; to 46 cm (18 in).

HABITAT: Coastal and riverine forest, living in leafy canopy.

REGIONS: KZN, NAM, ZIM

Plate 41c

Purple-crested Turaco
(also called Purple-crested Lourie)
Tauraco porphyreolophus

ID: Medium-sized, with long tail and crest; darker-colored than last two species, with purple crest, tail, back, and wings; neck and underparts green, washed with reddish brown on chest; flight feathers red (usually only visible in flight); in pairs or groups; presence often given away by croaking call; to 41 cm (16 in).

HABITAT: Woodland and edges of forest.

REGIONS: KZN, MPG, LNW, ZIM

Plate 41d

Gray Lourie
(also called Gray Go-away Bird)
Corythaixoides concolor

ID: Medium-sized; long tail, long crest, and wholly gray plumage diagnostic; usually in flocks; loud cry "go-way" unmistakable; to 48 cm (19 in).

HABITAT: Woodland and savannah, especially thornveld; becoming increasingly common in suburban areas.

REGIONS: KZN, MPG, LNW, NAM, BOT, ZIM

a Knysna Turaco

b Livingstone's Turaco

c Purple-crested Turaco

d Gray Lourie

Plate 42a

Red-chested Cuckoo

Cuculus solitarius

ID: Medium-sized; head and upperparts dark gray; chest reddish brown, belly buff, barred with dark brown; in juvenile reddish brown throat replaced by black; solitary or in pairs; skulking, often detected by its loud, distinctive whistled call "peet, may-frow"; to 29 cm (11.5 in).

HABITAT: Forest and tall woodland, including wooded parks and gardens; in summer only.

REGIONS: EC, FS, KZN, MPG, NC, LNW, WC, NAM, BOT, ZIM

Plate 42b

Rosy-faced Lovebird

Agapornis roseicollis

ID: Small; pale green parrot with pink face and throat and blue rump; in flocks; call a shrill screech; to 17 cm (6.5 in).

HABITAT: Arid savannah and edge of desert, especially in mountainous country.

REGIONS: NAM, NC

Plate 42c

Diederik Cuckoo

Chrysococcyx caprius

ID: Small; upperparts glossy bronze-green; underparts white; wings are spotted with white; eye and eye ring red; female duller than male, with buff-colored throat; solitary or in pairs; perches conspicuously and often detected by its monotonous whistling call "deee, dee, dee, deederik" (hence its name); to 19 cm (7.5 in).

HABITAT: Open woodland, shrubland, and grassland; common on farmland and in parks and gardens; in summer only.

REGIONS: EC, FS, KZN, MPG, NC, LNW, WC, NAM, BOT, ZIM

Plate 42d

Burchell's Coucal

Centropus burchellii

ID: Medium-sized, with long tail; wings and back reddish brown; tail, head, and nape black; underparts white; distinguished from other coucals in the region by finely barred upper tail and uniform black head; in pairs; often detected by its characteristic, loud, bubbling call which runs up and down the scales; to 41 cm (16 in).

HABITAT: Bushy thickets, reedbeds, and dense tangles in savannah.

REGIONS: EC, FS, KZN, MPG, NC, LNW, WC

a Red-chested Cuckoo

b Rosy-faced Lovebird

c Diederik Cuckoo

d Burchell's Coucal

Plate 43a

African Scops-Owl

Otus senegalensis

ID: Small; gray above and below, flecked and streaked with darker shades of gray and brown (a rare reddish brown form also occurs); nocturnal; roosts during the day pressed close against a tree trunk, with body feathers pulled in tight, eyes closed and ear tufts erect; solitary or in pairs; calls at night, a short frog-like "prrup," repeated at intervals; to 15 cm (6 in).

HABITAT: Woodland and savannah.

REGIONS: EC, KZN, MPG, NC, LNW, NAM, BOT, ZIM

Plate 43b

Barn Owl

Tyto alba

ID: Medium-sized; heart-shaped white face distinctive; upperparts pale gray with buff on wings, nape, and crown; underparts white, lightly spotted with black; lacks ear tufts found in many owls; solitary or in pairs; calls at night, an eerie, shrill screech; to 32 cm (12.5 in).

HABITAT: Diverse—found in savannah, shrubland, grassland, and desert; nocturnal, roosting during the day in the roofs of derelict buildings or in holes in trees or rock faces.

REGIONS: EC, FS, KZN, MPG, NC, LNW, WC, NAM, BOT, ZIM

Plate 43c

Pearl-spotted Owlet

Glaucidium perlatum

ID: Small; upperparts brown, speckled and spotted with white; underparts white, heavily streaked with dark brown; lacks ear tufts; has two large black spots ("false eyes") on nape; solitary or in pairs; partly diurnal, especially in winter; has a piercing whistling call; to 19 cm (7.5 in).

HABITAT: Woodland and savannah, especially areas with sparse ground cover.

REGIONS: KZN, MPG, NC, LNW, NAM, BOT, ZIM

Plate 43d

Spotted Eagle-Owl

Bubo africanus

ID: Medium-sized; head and upperparts brownish gray speckled and mottled with shades of gray; underparts light gray, finely barred with darker gray; has yellow eyes and prominent ear tufts; nocturnal; solitary or in pairs; often perches on roadside poles at night; call a mellow hooting; to 45 cm (18 in).

HABITAT: Diverse—found in woodland, savannah, grassland, shrubland, and desert; often in rocky places.

REGIONS: EC, FS, KZN, MPG, NC, LNW, WC, NAM, BOT, ZIM

Plate 43e

Fiery-necked Nightjar

Caprimulgus pectoralis

ID: Small; cryptically marked with shades of reddish brown, gray, brown, and buff, with spots of white (in male) or buff (in female) at end of the tail and wings that are conspicuous in flight; best distinguished from other nightjars by its mellow, whistled call ("good lord deliver us"); to 24 cm (9.5 in).

HABITAT: Woodland, savannah, and shrubland; nocturnal, resting during the day in leaf litter beneath trees; hunts on the wing at night.

REGIONS: EC, FS, KZN, MPG, NC, LNW, WC, NAM, BOT, ZIM

a African Scops-Owl

b Barn Owl

c Pearl-spotted Owlet

d Spotted Eagle-Owl

e Fiery-necked Nightjar

Plate 44a

African Black Swift

Apus barbatus

ID: Small; fast-flying, with long, thin wings, forked tail, and cigar-shaped body; brownish black with white throat and grayish black secondary wing feathers; in flocks; to 19 cm (7.5 in).

HABITAT: Hunts aerially and rarely seen except in flight; mostly confined to mountainous country, especially near cliffs.

REGIONS: EC, FS, KZN, MPG, NC, LNW, WC, BOT, ZIM

Plate 44b

Little Swift

Apus affinis

ID: Small; fast-flying, with long, thin wings, square tail, and cigar-shaped body; brownish black with white rump and white throat; usually in flocks; to 13 cm (5 in).

HABITAT: Hunts aerially over any terrain; flocks often seen wheeling above bridges and tall buildings, in which they nest and roost in closely packed colonies.

REGIONS: EC, FS, KZN, MPG, NC, LNW, WC, NAM, BOT, ZIM

Plate 44c

Alpine Swift

Apus melba

ID: Small; fast-flying, with long, thin wings, forked tail, and cigar-shaped body; upperparts grayish brown; underparts white with a broad dark brown chest band; solitary, in groups, or in flocks; to 22 cm (8.5 in).

HABITAT: Hunts aerially over any terrain; commonly seen around cliff faces, in which it nests and roosts.

REGIONS: EC, FS, KZN, MPG, NC, LNW, WC, NAM, BOT, ZIM

Plate 44d

African Palm-Swift

Cypsiurus parvus

ID: Small; fast-flying, with long, thin wings, deeply forked tail, and cigar-shaped body; uniform pale brownish gray; in flocks; to 16 cm (6.5 in).

HABITAT: Savannah; hunts aerially, usually seen in vicinity of long-stemmed palm trees, in which it nests and roosts.

REGIONS: FS, KZN, MPG, NC, LNW, NAM, BOT, ZIM

Plate 44e

White-rumped Swift

Apus caffer

ID: Small; fast-flying, with long, thin wings, deeply forked tail, and cigar-shaped body; glossy black, with white rump and white throat; solitary or in pairs; to 16 cm (6.5 in).

HABITAT: Hunts aerially over any terrain; often seen in vicinity of road bridges and buildings, in which pairs nest solitarily; in summer only.

REGIONS: EC, FS, KZN, MPG, NC, LNW, WC, NAM, BOT, ZIM

a African Black Swift

b Little Swift

c Alpine Swift

d African Palm-Swift

e White-rumped Swift

Plate 45a

Red-faced Mousebird

Urocolius indicus

ID: Small, but has long tail; head and upperparts bluish gray; underparts buff grading to pale gray below tail; has facial mask of unfeathered red skin; legs and feet red; in family groups; to 32 cm (12.5 in).

HABITAT: Woodland and savannah; common in gardens and orchards.

REGIONS: EC, FS, KZN, MPG, NC, LNW, WC, NAM, BOT, ZIM

Plate 45b

White-backed Mousebird

Colius colius

ID: Small, but has long tail; head, chest, and upperparts bluish gray, with two black lines, separated by white line, running down back; underparts buff; legs and feet red; has distinctive black-and-white patterned underwing (seen in flight); in family groups; to 31 cm (12 cm).

HABITAT: Semi-arid thornveld and shrubland; often in gardens and orchards.

REGIONS: EC, FS, MPG, NC, LNW, WC, NAM, BOT

Plate 45c

Narina Trogon

Apaloderma narina

ID: Medium-sized; thickset bird that perches with upright stance; sexes differ: in male, head and upperparts metallic green, underparts red with white undertail; female less colorful, with green upperparts, face and chest brown, and belly red; in both sexes, bill yellow and there are two areas of bare blue skin on face; solitary or in pairs; often detected by hearing its hollow-sounding, hooting call; to 32 cm (12.5 in).

HABITAT: Interiors of forest, living in mid-canopy.

REGIONS: EC, KZN, MPG, LNW, WC, NAM, BOT, ZIM

Plate 45d

Speckled Mousebird

Colius striatus

ID: Small, but has long tail; upperparts, including crest, brownish gray; underparts (including underwing) buff; face black; bill black above, white below; legs and feet dull red; in family groups or flocks; to 33 cm (13 cm).

HABITAT: Woodland, savannah, and second-growth on edges of forest; common in gardens and orchards.

REGIONS: EC, FS, KZN, MPG, NC, LNW, WC, BOT, ZIM

a Red-faced Mousebird
b White-backed Mousebird
F
M
c Narina Trogon
d Speckled Mousebird

Plate 46a

Pied Kingfisher

Ceryle rudis

ID: Medium-sized, with long, dagger-like bill; head and upperparts a checkerboard of black and white; underparts white, male with two black bands across chest, female with one; bill black; solitary, in pairs, or in family groups; to 27 cm (11 in).

HABITAT: Lakes, estuaries, lagoons, slow-flowing rivers; often fishes by hovering over open water.

REGIONS: EC, FS, KZN, MPG, NC, LNW, WC, NAM, BOT, ZIM

Plate 46b

Giant Kingfisher

Ceryle maxima

ID: Medium-sized, with long, dagger-like bill; the largest kingfisher in the region; head and upperparts black, densely and finely spotted with white; sexes differ in underpart coloration: male has reddish brown chest and white belly, female has reddish brown belly and black, speckled throat; bill black; solitary or in pairs; to 45 cm (18 in).

HABITAT: Fishes along rivers, lagoons, estuaries, and edges of lakes.

REGIONS: EC, FS, KZN, MPG, NC, LNW, WC, NAM, BOT, ZIM

Plate 46c

Malachite Kingfisher

Alcedo cristata

ID: Small, with long, dagger-like bill; upperparts purplish blue, with crown feathers tipped with black; underparts and cheeks reddish brown; throat and streak behind eye white; bill and feet red in adult, black in juvenile; solitary or in pairs; to 14 cm (5.5 in).

HABITAT: Fishes along edges of streams, ponds, and reed-lined dams and lakes.

REGIONS: EC, FS, KZN, MPG, NC, LNW, WC, NAM, BOT, ZIM

Plate 46d

Brown-hooded Kingfisher

Halcyon albiventris

ID: Small, with long, dagger-like bill; head brown; neck and underparts buff, streaked with brown; back and shoulders black (male) or brown (female); rump, tail, and most of wings blue; bill red; solitary or in pairs; to 23 cm (9 in).

HABITAT: Woodland, savannah, coastal bush, farmland; a terrestrial kingfisher that hunts insects and lizards from low perches.

REGIONS: EC, FS, KZN, MPG, NC, LNW, WC, NAM, BOT, ZIM

Plate 46e

Woodland Kingfisher

Halcyon senegalensis

ID: Small, with long, dagger-like bill; mainly azure-blue with black shoulders and white underparts; has black mask through eye; bill red above and black below; solitary or in pairs; to 23 cm (9 in).

HABITAT: Woodland and savannah; a terrestrial hunter, preying on insects and lizards; in summer only.

REGIONS: KZN, MPG, LNW, NAM, BOT, ZIM

a Pied Kingfisher
b Giant Kingfisher
M
F
c Malachite Kingfisher
F
d Brown-hooded Kingfisher
M
e Woodland Kingfisher

Plate 47a

European Bee-eater

Merops apiaster

ID: Medium-sized; bill long and down-curved, central tail feathers elongated; upperparts reddish brown with buff and bronze in wings; underparts blue, with yellow throat and black collar; in flocks; to 27 cm (11 in).

HABITAT: Savannah and shrublands, especially in semi-arid areas; often seen hawking from roadside telephone lines; in summer only.

REGIONS: EC, FS, KZN, MPG, NC, LNW, WC, NAM, BOT, ZIM

Plate 47b

Southern Carmine Bee-eater

Merops nubicoides

ID: Medium-sized; bill long and down-curved, central tail feathers elongated; vividly colored—upperparts carmine (reddish); crown, rump, and undertail blue; throat and chest pink; juvenile duller and shorter-tailed; in flocks; to 35 cm (14 in).

HABITAT: Woodland and savannah, especially along edges of rivers and floodplains; often hawking over bush fires; in summer only.

REGIONS: MPG, LNW, NAM, BOT, ZIM

Plate 47c

Little Bee-eater

Merops pusillus

ID: Small; tail slightly forked; crown, upperparts light green with outer tail reddish brown; underparts yellowish buff, with black collar and black line through eye; in pairs or family groups; to 18 cm (7 in).

HABITAT: Woodland and savannah.

REGIONS: KZN, MPG, LNW, NAM, BOT, ZIM

Plate 47d

Swallow-tailed Bee-eater

Merops hirundineus

ID: Small; deeply forked tail; crown, back, and wings green, tail and belly blue; throat yellow with black collar; chest green; solitary, in pairs or groups; to 21 cm (8.5 in).

HABITAT: Woodland, savannah, and shrubland; commonest in semi-arid areas; nomadic outside breeding season.

REGIONS: FS, MPG, NC, LNW, NAM, BOT, ZIM

Plate 47e

White-fronted Bee-eater

Merops bullockoides

ID: Small; bill long and down-curved; tail square; wings, back, and tail metallic green with blue rump; head and underparts (including underwing) dark buff; throat red, with white stripe below bill and eye; forehead white; black mask through eye; in flocks; to 23 cm (9 in).

HABITAT: Savannah, but seldom found far from rivers; hunts from a perch, often using roadside telephone lines.

REGIONS: FS, KZN, MPG, NC, LNW, NAM, BOT, ZIM

Plate 47f

Lilac-breasted Roller

Coracias caudata

ID: Medium-sized; outer tail feathers elongated; richly colored—crown and nape turquoise; back and shoulders brown; tail, wings, and belly shades of blue; chest lilac, streaked with white on throat; solitary or in pairs; has rolling flight during displays when it utters harsh screams; to 36 cm (14 in).

HABITAT: Savannah; perches conspicuously while hunting, often seen on roadside telephone wires and poles.

REGIONS: KZN, MPG, NC, LNW, NAM, BOT, ZIM

a European Bee-eater
b Southern Carmine Bee-eater
c Little Bee-eater
d Swallow-tailed Bee-eater
e White-fronted Bee-eater
f Lilac-breasted Roller

Plate 48a

African Gray Hornbill

Tockus nasutus

ID: Medium-sized; long-tailed; head, neck, and upperparts gray, with patterned wings caused by pale-edged feathers; chest and belly white; has a broad white eyebrow and tail tipped with white; sexes differ in bill size and color, the male's larger and casqued, the female's smaller and paler, with red tip; in pairs while breeding, but often flocking during winter; to 46 cm (18 in).

HABITAT: Broad-leafed woodland.

REGIONS: KZN, MPG, NC, LNW, NAM, BOT, ZIM

Plate 48b

Trumpeter Hornbill

Bycanistes bucinator

ID: Large; long-tailed with heavily casqued bill; head, chest, back, wings, and tail black, with white belly, rump, and trailing edges of wings; eye black, surrounded by bare red skin; in pairs or family groups while breeding, often in flocks during winter; makes a loud wailing call, very like a human baby crying; to 61 cm (2 ft).

HABITAT: Forest and tall woodland, especially along rivers.

REGIONS: EC, KZN, MPG, LNW, WC, NAM

Plate 48c

Red-billed Hornbill

Tockus erythrorhynchus

ID: Medium-sized; long-tailed; the smallest hornbill in the region; upperparts black, extensively speckled and spotted with white; underparts white, with red bill (female) or red and black bill (male); in pairs while breeding, but often in flocks during winter; to 44 cm (17.5 in).

HABITAT: Woodland and savannah, especially thornveld.

REGIONS: KZN, MPG, LNW, NAM, BOT, ZIM

Plate 48d

Southern Yellow-billed Hornbill

Tockus leucomelas

ID: Medium-sized; long-tailed with large yellow bill and bare red skin around eyes and below bill; upperparts black, extensively speckled and spotted with white; underparts white; solitary or in pairs; to 54 cm (21 in).

HABITAT: Woodland and savannah.

REGIONS: FS, KZN, MPG, NC, LNW, NAM, BOT, ZIM

Plate 48e

Crowned Hornbill

Tockus alboterminatus

ID: Medium-sized; long-tailed, with large red bill with thin yellow line at base; head, chest, and upperparts dark brown; belly white; eye yellow; in pairs while breeding, often in flocks outside breeding season; to 52 cm (20.5 in).

HABITAT: Tall woodland and coastal or riverine forest.

REGIONS: EC, KZN, MPG, LNW, WC, NAM

F
F
M
a African Gray Hornbill
b Trumpeter Hornbill
M
c Red-billed Hornbill
d Southern Yellow-billed Hornbill
e Crowned Hornbill

Plate 49a

Black-collared Barbet
Lybius torquatus

ID: Small, with heavy black bill; head, throat, and chest red, ringed by broad black collar and nape; back, tail, and wings brown, flight feathers edged with yellow; underparts pale yellow; rare form occurs with yellow, not red, head; in pairs or family groups; often detected by its ringing, duetting call (repeated "two-puddly"); to 20 cm (8 in).

HABITAT: Broad-leafed woodlands and edges of forest.

REGIONS: EC, FS, KZN, MPG, LNW, NAM, BOT, ZIM

Plate 49b

Acacia Pied Barbet
Lybius leucomelas

ID: Small, with heavy black bill; has distinctively patterned head, with red forehead, white sides of head with a black crown, nape, throat, and a broad black line through eye joining bill to nape; upperparts black, streaked with yellow and white, underparts white; solitary or in pairs; to 18 cm (7 in).

HABITAT: Savannah, especially thornveld; also in planted trees around farms in arid areas.

REGIONS: EC, FS, KZN, MPG, NC, LNW, WC, NAM, BOT, ZIM

Plate 49c

Red-fronted Tinkerbird
(also called Red-fronted Tinker Barbet)
Pogoniulus pusillus

ID: Small to tiny; forehead red; head strikingly patterned with black and white; upperparts mainly black, streaked with yellow; underparts pale yellow; solitary or in pairs; call is similar to Yellow-fronted Tinkerbird's; to 12 cm (4.5 in).

HABITAT: Coastal forest and mixed woodland.

REGIONS: EC, KZN, MPG.

Plate 49d

Yellow-fronted Tinkerbird
(also called Yellow-fronted Tinker Barbet)
Pogoniulus chrysoconus

ID: Small to tiny; bright yellow forehead (orange in some individuals); head strikingly patterned with black and white lines; upperparts black, streaked with white and pale yellow; underparts yellowish white; solitary or in pairs; its monotonous anvil-tapping call "tink, tink, tink..." often continues uninterrupted for long periods; to 12 cm (4.5 in).

HABITAT: Woodland and savannah, where much dependent on fruits of mistletoes.

REGIONS: KZN, MPG, LNW, NAM, BOT, ZIM

Plate 49e

Crested Barbet
Trachyphonus vaillantii

ID: Small to medium-sized; has a heavy yellow bill and crested head; head, throat, and underparts yellow, flecked and streaked with red, especially on face, with broad black speckled collar across chest; crest, nape, and upperparts glossy black, spotted and barred with white; makes a sustained, trilling, alarm clock-like call; to 24 cm (9.5 in).

HABITAT: Woodland and savannah; common in parks and gardens.

REGIONS: FS, KZN, MPG, NC, LNW, NAM, BOT, ZIM

a Black-collared Barbet

b Acacia Pied Barbet

c Red-fronted Tinkerbird

d Yellow-fronted Tinkerbird

e Crested Barbet

Plate 50a

African Hoopoe

Upupa africana

ID: Medium-sized; long, thin bill and prominent crest distinctive; mainly reddish brown with black and white wings and tail; crest feathers edged with black; crest usually lies flat and is raised fan-like when alarmed; solitary or in pairs; call a soft "hoop, hoop-hoop" (hence name); to 26 cm (10.5 in).

HABITAT: Diverse—found in grassland, shrubland, open savannah, parks, gardens, and farmlands.

REGIONS: EC, FS, KZN, MPG, NC, LNW, WC, NAM, BOT, ZIM

Plate 50b

Green Wood-Hoopoe

(also called Red-billed Wood-Hoopoe)

Phoeniculus purpureus

ID: Medium-sized; long-tailed, with long, down-curved, red bill; entire bird is iridescent purplish black with a green sheen on head, chest, and back; tail has white spots along edges and wings have white bar; in family groups; noisy birds, making a harsh cackling call; one bird calling usually triggers calling in whole group; to 33 cm (13 in).

HABITAT: Woodland and savannah.

REGIONS: EC, FS, KZN, MPG, NC, LNW, WC, NAM, BOT, ZIM

Plate 50c

Greater Honeyguide

Indicator indicator

ID: Small; upperparts grayish brown; underparts dull white; sexes differ in head markings—male has black throat and black eye mask, white cheeks, and a pink bill; female has a plain gray-brown head and a white throat; solitary; to 20 cm (8 in).

HABITAT: Woodland, savannah, timber plantations, orchards.

REGIONS: EC, FS, KZN, MPG, NC, LNW, WC, NAM, BOT, ZIM

Plate 50d

Ground Woodpecker

Geocolaptes olivaceus

ID: Medium-sized; the only terrestrial woodpecker in the region; head gray; back, wings, and tail olive brown, spotted with buff; underparts dull white, with chest and rump washed with pink; perches on rocks and boulders; in pairs or family groups; to 25 cm (10 in).

HABITAT: Rocky hillsides in hilly and mountainous country.

REGIONS: EC, FS, KZN, MPG, NC, WC

Plate 50e

Cardinal Woodpecker

Dendropicos fuscescens

ID: Small; upperparts blackish brown, barred with dull white; underparts white, streaked with black; both sexes have black moustachial stripe; nape is red in male, black in female; solitary or in pairs; to 15 cm (6 in).

HABITAT: Woodland, savannah, and wooded watercourses in arid shrubland.

REGIONS: EC, FS, KZN, MPG, NC, LNW, WC, NAM, BOT, ZIM

Plate 50f

Golden-tailed Woodpecker

Campethera abingoni

ID: Small; upperparts golden-brown, spotted and barred with pale yellow; underparts white, streaked with black; sexes differ in head markings—male has crown and nape red, female has nape red, crown and forehead black, speckled with white; red moustache stripe in male only; solitary or in pairs; to 21 cm (8.5 in).

HABITAT: Woodland and savannah.

REGIONS: FS, KZN, MPG, NC, LNW, NAM, BOT, ZIM

a African Hoopoe
b Green Wood-Hoopoe
c Greater Honeyguide
M
F
IM
d Ground Woodpecker
M
F
e Cardinal Woodpecker
M
F
f Golden-tailed Woodpecker

Plate 51a

Rufous-naped Lark

Mirafra africana

ID: Small; thickset, with heavy bill; distinguished from most other larks by combination of reddish brown crest and reddish brown wings; solitary or in pairs; males call all summer, singing a cheerful "tree, treeloo" from a low perch; to 17 cm (6.5 in).

HABITAT: Grassland and savannah.

REGIONS: EC, FS, KZN, MPG, LNW, NAM, BOT, ZIM

Plate 51b

Eastern Clapper Lark

Mirafra fasciolata

ID: Small; color variable across range (pale buff in west, cinnamon-colored in east) but all have reddish brown wings; solitary or in pairs; best identified by male's aerial display in which he flies up, then rapidly claps wings together, utters a drawn-out whistle, and glides back to the ground; to 15 cm (6 in).

HABITAT: Arid grasslands and low shrublands.

REGIONS: EC, FS, MPG, NC, LNW, WC, NAM, BOT

Plate 51c

Flappet Lark

Mirafra rufocinnamomea

ID: Small; a dark ruddy-colored lark, with reddish brown wings; usually detected, and best identified, when male performs aerial display: he flies up and cruises for a long period almost out of sight above the ground, at intervals making a distinctive, rapid clapping sound ("frrrrrrrrrp") with his wings; to 15 cm (6 in).

HABITAT: Broad-leafed woodland and savannah.

REGIONS: KZN, MPG, LNW, NAM, BOT, ZIM

Plate 51d

Sabota Lark

Mirafra sabota

ID: Small; upperparts light brown, streaked and speckled with shades of brown; underparts pale buff, lightly speckled with brown; has white throat and eyebrow; perches conspicuously and mimics calls of other birds; solitary or in pairs; to 15 cm (6 in).

HABITAT: Acacia savannah.

REGIONS: EC, FS, KZN, MPG, NC, LNW, WC, NAM, BOT, ZIM

Plate 51e

Stark's Lark

Spizocorys starki

ID: Small; a pale-colored lark (sand-colored above, white below) with a conspicuous pointed crest and black tail, edged with white; highly gregarious and nomadic in response to rainfall; when breeding, hundreds of males may display in same area, each hovering above the ground, uttering a short melodious note; to 14 cm; (5.5 in).

HABITAT: Arid shrublands and desert edge.

REGIONS: NAM, NC

b Eastern Clapper Lark
a Rufous-naped Lark
c Flappet Lark
d Sabota Lark
e Stark's Lark

Plate 52a

Spike-heeled Lark
Chersomanes albofasciata

ID: Small; a thickset, short-tailed lark with relatively long bill; color varies regionally (sandy-colored in west, cinnamon-colored in east); in pairs or family groups; to 15 cm (6 in).

HABITAT: Grassland and shrubland where ground-cover is low.

REGIONS: EC, FS, KZN, MPG, NC, LNW, WC, NAM, BOT

Plate 52b

Red-capped Lark
Calandrella cinerea

ID: Small and plain-colored; upperparts brown; underparts white, with distinctive reddish crest and reddish brown half-collar on chest; white eyebrow; in pairs while nesting, otherwise in flocks; to 16 cm (6.5 in).

HABITAT: Open areas where grass cover is very short; often seen on roadsides.

REGIONS: EC, FS, KZN, MPG, NC, LNW, WC, NAM, BOT, ZIM

Plate 52c

Large-billed Lark
(also called Southern Thick-billed Lark)
Galerida magnirostris

ID: Small (but the largest lark in the region); upperparts buffy-brown, streaked with darker brown; underparts dull white boldly streaked with black; white eye stripe; makes a call like the sound of a squeaky gate; solitary or in pairs; to 18 cm (7 in).

HABITAT: Grassland and low shrublands.

REGIONS: EC, FS, KZN, NC, WC

Plate 52d

Gray-backed Sparrowlark
(also called Gray-backed Finch-Lark)
Eremopterix verticalis

ID: Small; sexes quite different—male is blackish gray above and below with white ear patches that join on the nape and extend to shoulders; female has upperparts grayish buff and underparts dull white lightly streaked with brown; usually in flocks and nomadic in response to rainfall; to 13 cm (5 in).

HABITAT: Shrubland and scrub savannah in arid areas.

REGIONS: EC, FS, NC, LNW, WC, NAM, BOT, ZIM

a Spike-heeled Lark

b Red-capped Lark

c Large-billed Lark

d Gray-backed Sparrowlark

Plate 53a

Barn Swallow
(also called European Swallow)
Hirundo rustica

ID: Small; upperparts glossy blue-black; forehead and throat reddish brown, with black neck-collar; underparts white; in large flocks, and millions may gather at dusk at roost sites; commonly seen perched along roadside telephone lines; to 20 cm (8 in).

HABITAT: Very diverse—may be found hawking over virtually any area; in summer only.

REGIONS: EC, FS, KZN, MPG, NC, LNW, WC, NAM, BOT, ZIM

Plate 53b

White-throated Swallow
Hirundo albigularis

ID: Small; upperparts glossy blue-black; forehead reddish brown; throat and underparts white, cut by thin, bluish black chest band; in pairs; to 16 cm (6.5 in).

HABITAT: Any open country close to a river, lagoon, or lake; in summer only.

REGIONS: EC, FS, KZN, MPG, NC, LNW, WC, NAM, BOT, ZIM

Plate 53c

Wire-tailed Swallow
Hirundo smithii

ID: Small; upperparts glossy blue-black with bright reddish brown crown; throat and underparts white; in pairs; to 17 cm (6.5 in).

HABITAT: Savannah, usually close to rivers or lakes; resident.

REGIONS: KZN, MPG, LNW, NAM, BOT, ZIM

Plate 53d

South African Cliff Swallow
Hirundo spilodera

ID: Small; a drab-colored, square-tailed swallow with bluish black head and upperparts; underparts buff, streaked and mottled with brown; rump and undertail reddish brown; in flocks; to 15 cm (6 in).

HABITAT: Open grassland and shrubland, especially in vicinity of nest sites (road bridges, buildings, rock faces); in summer only.

REGIONS: EC, FS, KZN, MPG, NC, LNW, NAM, BOT, ZIM

b White-throated Swallow
a Barn Swallow
c Wire-tailed Swallow
d South African Cliff Swallow

Plate 54a

Greater Striped Swallow

Hirundo cucullata

ID: Small; upperparts glossy blue-black, except for crown, nape, and rump, which are pale orange; face and underparts are white, thinly streaked with black; in pairs or family groups; to 19 cm (7.5 in).

HABITAT: Open grassland and shrubland; in summer only.

REGIONS: EC, FS, KZN, MPG, NC, LNW, WC, NAM, BOT, ZIM

Plate 54b

Lesser Striped Swallow

Hirundo abyssinica

ID: Small; like the Greater Striped Swallow, but smaller, upperparts are more heavily streaked, and sides of head are orange, not white; in pairs or family groups; to 17 cm (6.5 in).

HABITAT: Grassland and open savannah, usually close to water; resident in parts of its range (mainly in east), but in most areas a summer visitor.

REGIONS: EC, KZN, MPG, LNW, NAM, BOT, ZIM

Plate 54c

Rock Martin

Hirundo fuligula

ID: Small; square-tailed; upperparts uniformly dark brown; underparts buffy brown, lightest on the throat; solitary or in pairs; to 13 cm (5 in).

HABITAT: Restricted to the vicinity of cliff faces; in places found around road bridges or buildings in villages.

REGIONS: EC, FS, KZN, MPG, NC, LNW, WC, NAM, BOT, ZIM

Plate 54d

Brown-throated Martin

(also called Plain Martin)

Riparia paludicola

ID: Small; tail slightly forked; uniformly grayish brown above and below except for a variable amount of white on chest, belly, and undertail—some individuals have no white on underparts, in others it is extensive; in flocks; to 13 cm (5 in).

HABITAT: Open grassland or shrubland close to water; a winter visitor to much of its range.

REGIONS: EC, FS, KZN, MPG, NC, LNW, WC, NAM, BOT, ZIM

b Lesser Striped Swallow

a Greater Striped Swallow

d Brown-throated Martin

c Rock Martin

Plate 55a

Cape Crow
(also called Black Crow)
Corvus capensis

ID: Medium-sized; uniformly glossy black; has broad wings and a rather slender bill; solitary, in pairs or in flocks; to 44 cm (17.5 in).

HABITAT: Open grassland and shrublands.

REGIONS: EC, FS, KZN, MPG, NC, LNW, WC, NAM, BOT, ZIM

Plate 55b

Pied Crow
Corvus albus

ID: Medium-sized; glossy black above and below, except for neck, which is white, linking to the chest, which is also white; solitary, in pairs, or in flocks; to 48 cm (19 in).

HABITAT: Open wooded country, farmlands, rural settlements.

REGIONS: EC, FS, KZN, MPG, NC, LNW, WC, NAM, BOT, ZIM

Plate 55c

White-necked Raven
Corvus albicollis

ID: Medium-sized; more thickly set than other crows in the region, with broad wings and a heavy bill; uniformly glossy black, except for a white crescent at the base of the neck; in pairs or flocks; to 55 cm (22 in).

HABITAT: Around cliffs in hilly and mountainous country.

REGIONS: EC, FS, KZN, MPG, NC, LNW, WC, ZIM

a Cape Crow

b Pied Crow

c White-necked Raven

Plate 56a

Fork-tailed Drongo
Dicrurus adsimilis

ID: Small to medium-sized; deeply forked tail distinguishes it from other all-black birds; entirely glossy black, except for red eyes; noisy and aggressive; often imitates calls of other birds, especially hawks and owls; solitary or in pairs, but flocks together to hunt at bush fires; to 25 cm (10 in).

HABITAT: Any deciduous woodland; also in eucalypt plantations, to feed on bees attracted there by nectar.

REGIONS: EC, FS, KZN, MPG, NC, LNW, WC, NAM, BOT, ZIM

Plate 56b

Black-headed Oriole
Oriolus larvatus

ID: Small to medium-sized; head, throat, and chest glossy black; upperparts greenish yellow, with black and white in wings; underparts vivid yellow; bill and eye red; solitary or in pairs; usually detected from its liquid "queop" call; to 25 cm (10 in).

HABITAT: Tall deciduous woodland, timber plantations, and edges of forest.

REGIONS: EC, KZN, MPG, LNW, WC, NAM, BOT, ZIM

Plate 56c

Southern Black Tit
Parus niger

ID: Small; head, chest, and upperparts glossy black, with white wingbar; belly gray; female duller than male; in pairs or family groups; often associated with mixed-species bird parties; to 16 cm (6.5 in).

HABITAT: Lives in the leafy canopy of tall, broad-leafed woodlands.

REGIONS: EC, KZN, MPG, LNW, NAM, BOT, ZIM

Plate 56d

Arrow-marked Babbler
Turdoides jardineii

ID: Small to medium-sized; upperparts dark brown; underparts paler brown, with chevron-shaped, whitish streaks on head, chest, and back; eye vivid orange in adult, brown in juvenile; in family groups; noisy birds, especially when whole group calls in unison; call a loud "chow-chow-chow..."; to 24 cm (9.5 in).

HABITAT: Bushy thickets in woodland and savannah.

REGIONS: KZN, MPG, LNW, NAM, BOT, ZIM

Plate 56e

Southern Pied Babbler
Turdoides bicolor

ID: Small to medium-sized; adults unmistakable with clean white head, back, rump, and underparts and black wings and tail; immature mottled white and brown; in family groups; noisy, calling like Arrow-marked Babbler, but notes more shrill; to 26 cm (10.5 in).

HABITAT: Arid savannah, especially thornveld.

REGIONS: NC, LNW, NAM, BOT, ZIM

a Fork-tailed Drongo
b Black-headed Oriole
d Arrow-marked Babbler
c Southern Black Tit
e Southern Pied Babbler
IM

Plate 57a

African Red-eyed Bulbul

Pycnonotus nigricans

ID: Small; blackish brown is head slightly crested; upperparts brown; underparts brown on chest grading to dull white on belly, with yellow under tail; eye is encircled by red wattle; solitary, in pairs, or in family groups; to 20 cm (8 in).

HABITAT: Dry woodlands, especially thornveld; much attracted to farms and gardens in dry areas.

REGIONS: EC, FS, MPG, NC, LNW, WC, NAM, BOT, ZIM

Plate 57b

Cape Bulbul

Pycnonotus capensis

ID: Small; head slightly crested; uniformly brown, except for paler brown belly, yellow under tail, and conspicuous white wattle encircling the eye; solitary, in pairs, or in family groups; to 20 cm (8 in).

HABITAT: Bush, tall fynbos and other shrubland, gardens, farmlands, orchards.

REGIONS: EC, NC, WC

Plate 57c

Dark-capped Bulbul

(also called Black-eyed Bulbul)

Pycnonotus tricolor

ID: Small; blackish brown head slightly crested; upperparts brown; underparts brown on chest grading to dull white on belly, with yellow under tail; eye and eye ring blackish brown; solitary, in pairs, or in family groups; to 21 cm (8.5 in).

HABITAT: Found wherever fruiting trees occur—from edges of forests to gardens, parks, woodland, and savannah.

REGIONS: EC, FS, KZN, MPG, LNW, NAM, BOT, ZIM

Plate 57d

Somber Greenbul

(also called Somber Bulbul)

Andropadus importunus

ID: Small; dull greenish olive above and below (underparts somewhat paler), its only contrasting feature being its conspicuous white eye; usually in pairs; although abundant in places, it is skulking, and its presence is usually given away by its cheery whistle ("willie") and jumbled song, coming from the depths of the undergrowth; to 22 cm (8.5 in).

HABITAT: Bushy thickets, especially fringing coastal forests.

REGIONS: EC, KZN, MPG, LNW, WC, ZIM

Plate 57e

Terrestrial Brownbul

(also called Terrestrial Bulbul)

Phyllastrephus terrestris

ID: Small; a uniformly dark brown bird except for white throat and whitish upper chest; skulking, living in pairs or family groups on the forest floor; its presence is usually given away by its scolding, chattering call; to 21 cm (8.5 in).

HABITAT: Undergrowth in forests and densely wooded stream beds.

REGIONS: EC, KZN, MPG, LNW, WC, NAM, BOT, ZIM

a African Red-eyed Bulbul
b Cape Bulbul
c Dark-capped Bulbul
d Somber Greenbul
e Terrestrial Brownbul

Plate 58a

Kurrichane Thrush

Turdus libonyana

ID: Small; head, chest, and upperparts grayish brown; chest grades to dull white on belly, washed with orange on the flanks; throat white with distinctive black moustache stripe; bill and eye ring orange; juvenile is browner and is speckled with buff; solitary or in pairs; to 22 cm (8.5 in).

HABITAT: Open woodland with tall trees.

REGIONS: KZN, MPG, LNW, NAM, BOT, ZIM

Plate 58b

Olive Thrush

Turdus olivaceus

ID: Small to medium-sized; head and upperparts dark olive-brown; throat whitish and speckled with dark brown; chest and belly overall yellow-orange or partly gray-brown; bill yellow; eye ring pale yellow-orange or blackish, depending on region; juvenile duller with buff speckling, especially on underparts; solitary or in pairs; male sings a sweet, fluty refrain during the breeding season; to 24 cm (9.5 in).

HABITAT: Forest, well-wooded parks and gardens, timber plantations.

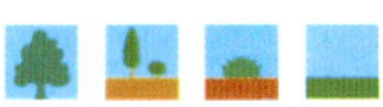

REGIONS: EC, FS, KZN, MPG, NC, LNW, WC, NAM, BOT, ZIM

Plate 58c

Groundscraper Thrush

Turdus litsitsirupa

ID: Small; crown and upperparts gray; face and underparts white, boldly marked with teardrop-shaped spots; eye has a vertical black line through it; in flight shows buff panels in wings; bill, legs, and feet yellow; in pairs; to 21 cm (8.5 in).

HABITAT: Any woodland or savannah where the ground cover is short and sparse.

REGIONS: FS, KZN, MPG, NC, LNW, NAM, BOT, ZIM

Plate 58d

Cape Rock-Thrush

Monticola rupestris

ID: Small; sexes dissimilar; male has dark blue head, brown upperparts, and reddish brown underparts; female has light brown head and upperparts, mottled with darker brown, and reddish brown underparts; juvenile like female but more mottled; in pairs; to 22 cm (8.5 in).

HABITAT: Rocky hillsides and boulder-strewn ravines.

REGIONS: EC, FS, KZN, MPG, LNW, WC

a Kurrichane Thrush
b Olive Thrush
c Groundscraper Thrush
M
F
d Cape Rock-Thrush

Plate 59a

Mountain Wheatear
(also called Mountain Chat)
Oenanthe monticola

ID: Small; males variable, some black, others gray, with white patches on shoulders, rump, and under tail; in some, crown and/or belly is white; female and juvenile are uniformly sooty brown apart from white rump; in pairs or family groups; to 18 cm (7.5 in).

HABITAT: Rocky hillsides or eroded riverbeds; often around farm buildings.

REGIONS: EC, FS, KZN, MPG, NC, LNW, WC, NAM

Plate 59b

Capped Wheatear
Oenanthe pileata

ID: Small; head and nape black with white eyebrow; throat white with broad black chestband; rest of underparts white; upperparts brown except for white rump; in juvenile black chestband is absent and bird is duller; solitary, in pairs, or in family groups; to 17 cm (6.5 in).

HABITAT: Open areas with stretches of bare ground in grassland and shrubland; perches conspicuously.

REGIONS: EC, FS, MPG, NC, LNW, WC, NAM, BOT, ZIM

Plate 59c

Familiar Chat
Cercomela familiaris

ID: Small; dull brownish gray with paler belly and reddish brown rump and outer tail feathers; juvenile with buff-colored speckles; solitary or in pairs; perches conspicuously; always gives a nervous wing twitch after alighting; to 15 cm (6 in).

HABITAT: Widespread but commonest in semi-arid, rocky, hilly country; often around farmsteads.

REGIONS: EC, FS, KZN, MPG, NC, LNW, WC, NAM, BOT, ZIM

Plate 59d

Sickle-winged Chat
Cercomela sinuata

ID: Small; upperparts pale brownish gray with wing feathers edged in reddish brown; underparts dull white; rump and outer tail feathers reddish brown; juvenile with buff-colored speckles; solitary or in pairs; perches on tops of bushes; to 15 cm (6 in).

HABITAT: Low shrubland, mainly in semi-arid country.

REGIONS: EC, FS, KZN, NC, WC, NAM

Plate 59e

Ant-eating Chat
Myrmecocichla formicivora

ID: Small; uniformly blackish brown except for a small white shoulder patch (in male) and whitish panels on outerwing, only visible in flight; usually in family groups that perch conspicuously, often on roadside fences; to 18 cm (7 in).

HABITAT: Open country, especially grassland or sparse shrubland.

REGIONS: EC, FS, KZN, MPG, NC, LNW, WC, NAM, BOT

Plate 59f

African Stonechat
Saxicola torquata

ID: Small; male brightly colored, female drab; male has black head, dark brown back, wings, and tail; reddish brown chest and white belly; female head and upperparts dull grayish brown; underparts buff; perches conspicuously, often along roadside fences; solitary or in pairs; to 14 cm (5.5 in).

HABITAT: Open country, especially in grassland, shrubland, or farmland, often close to water.

REGIONS: EC, FS, KZN, MPG, NC, LNW, WC, NAM, BOT, ZIM

a Mountain Wheatear
M
gray form
M
black form
F
b Capped
Wheatear
c Familiar Chat
d Sickle-winged Chat
e Ant-eating Chat
M
F
f African Stonechat

Plate 60a

Chorister Robin-Chat

(also called Chorister Robin)
Cossypha dichroa

ID: Small; head and upperparts brownish black; throat, underparts, and outer tail feathers warm orange; juvenile dark brown with buff-colored speckles; solitary or in pairs; a fine singer and excellent mimic of other birds' calls; to 20 cm (8 in).

HABITAT: Montane forest.

REGIONS: EC, FS, KZN, MPG, NC, LNW, WC

Plate 60b

White-browed Robin-Chat

(also called Heuglin's or White-browed Robin)
Cossypha heuglini

ID: Small; head black with white eyebrow; upperparts slaty-black; throat, underparts, and outer tail feathers warm orange; juvenile sooty brown with buff speckling; solitary or in pairs; a fine singer, heard especially at dawn and dusk; to 20 cm (8 in).

HABITAT: Low undergrowth in riverine forest, and creeper-tangled thickets in woodland.

REGIONS: KZN, MPG, LNW, NAM, BOT, ZIM

Plate 60c

Red-capped Robin-Chat

(also called Natal Robin)
Cossypha natalensis

ID: Small; head, throat, underparts, and outer tail feathers warm orange; back, wings, and central tail feathers bluish gray; juvenile dark brown with buff speckling; solitary or in pairs; a fine singer and outstanding mimic of other birds' calls; to 18 cm (7 in).

HABITAT: Undergrowth in lowland and coastal forest.

REGIONS: EC, KZN, MPG, LNW, NAM, ZIM

Plate 60d

Cape Robin-Chat

(also called Cape Robin)
Cossypha caffra

ID: Small; upperparts grayish brown, with white eyebrow; throat and upper chest light orange; rest of underparts light gray; juvenile dark brown with buff speckling; solitary or in pairs; to 17 cm (6.5 in).

HABITAT: Undergrowth at edges of forest; along wooded streams and dry watercourses; commonly in shrubby gardens.

REGIONS: EC, FS, KZN, MPG, NC, LNW, WC, NAM, ZIM

a Chorister Robin-Chat

b White-browed Robin-Chat

c Red-capped Robin-Chat

d Cape Robin-Chat

Plate 61a

Drakensberg Rockjumper
(also called Orange-breasted Rockjumper)
Chaetops aurantius

ID: Small; sexes dissimilar; in males, head and back gray, streaked with black; throat black with striking white moustachial stripe; rump reddish brown and tail black, tail-feathers with white tips; underparts buff; female has head, back, and throat dull white, streaked with gray, underparts pale yellow, rump reddish brown and tail black, feathers edged with white; in pairs or family groups; to 22 cm (8.5 in).

HABITAT: Open, rocky mountain slopes, mainly above 2,000 m (6,500 ft) elevation.

REGIONS: EC, FS, KZN.

Plate 61b

White-browed Scrub-Robin
Erythropygia leucophrys

ID: Small; head and upperparts light brown, with rump and upper part of tail reddish brown, grading to black towards end of tail, which has white tips; underparts white, lightly streaked with brown; in pairs; to 15 cm (6 in).

HABITAT: Bushy thickets in woodland and savannah.

REGIONS: EC, KZN, MPG, LNW, NAM, BOT, ZIM

Plate 61c

Karoo Scrub-Robin
(also called Karoo Robin)
Erythropygia coryphaeus

ID: Small; a uniformly dull brownish gray, darkest on wings and tail, with a white eyebrow, white throat, and white edges to tail tips; solitary or in pairs; usually seen on the ground; to 17 cm (6.5 in).

HABITAT: Arid woodland and karoo shrubland.

REGIONS: EC, FS, NC, LNW, WC

Plate 61d

Kalahari Scrub-Robin
(also called Kalahari Robin)
Erythropygia paena

ID: Small; head, back, and wings light brown, grading to reddish brown on rump and tail, with a broad black bar near end of tail, edged with white; throat and underparts white; white eyebrow; solitary or in pairs; to 17 cm (6.5 in).

HABITAT: Arid savannah, especially thornveld with extensive areas of bare ground beneath trees.

REGIONS: FS, MPG, NC, LNW, NAM, BOT, ZIM

a Drakensberg Rockjumper

b White-browed Scrub-Robin

c Karoo Scrub-Robin

d Kalahari Scrub-Robin

Plate 62a

Chestnut-vented Tit-Babbler

Parisoma subcaeruleum

ID: Small; all-gray; somewhat paler below, apart from throat, which has black speckles; chestnut under tail, and white tips on tail; in pairs; mimics calls of other birds; to 15 cm (6 in).

HABITAT: Bushy thickets in woodland and savannah.

REGIONS: EC, FS, KZN, MPG, NC, LNW, WC, NAM, BOT, ZIM

Plate 62b

Lesser Swamp-Warbler

(also called Cape Reed Warbler)

Acrocephalus gracilirostris

ID: Small; head and upperparts warm brown; underparts white, with white eyebrow; solitary or in pairs; male has sweet, warbling song, a characteristic sound of reedbed habitats; to 18 cm (7 in).

HABITAT: Reeds and bulrushes over water.

REGIONS: EC, FS, KZN, MPG, NC, LNW, WC, NAM, BOT, ZIM

Plate 62c

Little Rush-Warbler

(also called African Sedge Warbler)

Bradypterus baboecala

ID: Small; head and upperparts dark brown; underparts dull white, grading to buff under tail, and mottled with brown on throat; skulking, but presence often given away by call, a series of loud "tripp" notes that begin slowly, then speed up; to 17 cm (6.5 in).

HABITAT: Sedges, bulrushes, and reeds over water.

REGIONS: EC, FS, KZN, MPG, LNW, WC, NAM, BOT, ZIM

Plate 62d

Victorin's Warbler

Bradypterus victorini

ID: Small; head and upperparts brown; underparts warm orange, with grayish forehead and cheeks and orange eye; skulking, its presence given away by jingly song uttered from low perch; solitary or in pairs; to 16 cm (6.5 in).

HABITAT: Undergrowth of tall, thick fynbos on mountain slopes and in valleys.

REGIONS: EC, WC

Plate 62e

Willow Warbler

Phylloscopus trochilus

ID: Small; upperparts pale greenish gray; underparts dull white with pale yellow wash; has distinctive pale eyebrow; solitary; to 12 cm (4.5 in).

HABITAT: Lives in leafy canopy of forest, woodland, and savannah; also in timber plantations, parks, and gardens; in summer only.

REGIONS: EC, FS, KZN, MPG, NC, LNW, WC, NAM, BOT, ZIM

Plate 62f

Long-billed Crombec

Sylvietta rufescens

ID: Small; very short tail and long, rather down-curved bill are diagnostic; upperparts brownish gray; underparts buff, with buff eyebrow; in pairs; often in mixed species bird parties; to 11 cm (4.5 in).

HABITAT: Savannah, open woodland, and along watercourses in arid shrublands.

REGIONS: EC, FS, KZN, MPG, NC, LNW, WC, NAM, BOT, ZIM

a Chestnut-vented Tit-Babbler

b Lesser Swamp-Warbler

c Little Rush-Warbler

d Victorin's Warbler

e Willow Warbler

f Long-billed Crombec

Plate 63a

Bar-throated Apalis

Apalis thoracica

ID: Small; upperparts gray; underparts white (in northern races, washed with green above and yellow below); chest cut by thin black collar; eye white; in pairs; loud "pilli, pilli, pilli" call often gives its presence away; to 13 cm (5 in).

HABITAT: Leafy canopy of forest and dense woodlands.

REGIONS: EC, FS, KZN, MPG, LNW, WC, BOT, ZIM

Plate 63b

Yellow-bellied Eremomela

Eremomela icteropygialis

ID: Small; upperparts gray; throat and chest pale gray; belly lemon-yellow; in pairs or family groups; to 11 cm (4.5 in).

HABITAT: Scrubby woodland and shrublands, especially in semi-arid areas.

REGIONS: EC, FS, KZN, MPG, NC, LNW, WC, NAM, BOT, ZIM

Plate 63c

Cape Grassbird

Sphenoeacus afer

ID: Small; reminiscent of large, long-tailed cisticola; head, rump, and tail reddish brown; upperparts buff, streaked with brown; underparts buffy white, speckled with light brown; has thin black moustache line down side of face; in pairs; skulking, but gives its presence away by call, a loud, explosive, jingly song uttered from a low perch; to 20 cm (8 in).

HABITAT: Tall, dense grass or bracken or shrubbery along streams or on mountain slopes.

REGIONS: EC, FS, KZN, MPG, LNW, WC, ZIM

Plate 63d

Green-backed Camaroptera

(also called Green-backed Bleating Warbler)

Cameroptera brachyura

ID: Small; habit of cocking tail frequently is diagnostic; upperparts olive-green; underparts white; solitary or in pairs; male utters a loud song (a frequently repeated "tjip") while hidden in forest canopy; to 13 cm (5 in).

HABITAT: Interior and edges of forest.

REGIONS: EC, KZN, MPG, LNW, WC, ZIM

Plate 63e

Gray-backed Camaroptera

(also called Gray-backed Bleating Warbler)

Cameroptera brevicaudata

ID: Small; habit of cocking tail frequently is diagnostic; very similar to Green-backed Camaroptera but olive-green confined to wings while rest of upperparts are pale gray; underparts white; solitary or in pairs; male utters a loud song, similar to Green-backed's, while hidden in tree canopy; to 13 cm (5 in).

HABITAT: Bushy thickets in woodland and savannah.

REGIONS: MPG, LNW, NAM, BOT, ZIM

a Bar-throated Apalis

b Yellow-bellied Eremomela

c Cape Grassbird

d Green-backed Camaroptera

e Gray-backed Camaroptera

Plate 64a

Zitting Cisticola

(also called Fan-tailed Cisticola)
Cisticola juncidis

ID: Small to tiny; buff-colored, paler below, well marked with streaks of brown on wings, back, and tail; most readily distinguished from other small cisticolas by the male's display/song and by the preferred habitat; in pairs; male has an undulating display flight and makes a sharp "zit" note during each dip in the flight; to 11 cm (4.5 in).

HABITAT: Open grassland, especially in damp areas; also in pastures and between cultivated fields.

REGIONS: EC, FS, KZN, MPG, NC, LNW, WC, NAM, BOT, ZIM

Plate 64b

Wing-snapping Cisticola

(also called Ayres' Cisticola)
Cisticola ayresii

ID: Tiny; short-tailed; buff-colored, darker above and paler below, with well-patterned, brown-streaked upperparts; is most readily distinguished from other small cisticolas by the male's display/song and by the preferred habitat; throughout summer, males cruise high in the air uttering a high-pitched "soo, see-see-see," following this with a dive to ground, making a rapid clicking sound (from wings snapping) during the dive.

HABITAT: Open, short grassland; often the commonest bird in its habitat.

REGIONS: FS, KZN, MPG, LNW, ZIM

Plate 64c

Gray-backed Cisticola

Cisticola subruficapilla

ID: Small; long-tailed; head, wings, and tail buff, streaked with brown; back grayish; underparts pale buff-gray; birds in northwestern areas are less extensively gray; in pairs or family groups; male sings from a perch, a song very like that of the Wailing Cisticola; to 12 cm (4.5 in).

HABITAT: Karoo and fynbos shrublands.

REGIONS: EC, FS, NC, WC, NAM

Plate 64d

Wailing Cisticola

Cisticola lais

ID: Small; long-tailed; crown and tail light brown, streaked with darker brown; back and shoulders brownish gray streaked with black; underparts buff and unstreaked; in pairs; male sings from a rock or grass tuft, a series of piercing whistles; to 13 cm (5 in).

HABITAT: Grassy slopes of hills and mountains, usually among rocks.

REGIONS: EC, FS, KZN, MPG, LNW, ZIM

Plate 64e

Neddicky

Cisticola fulvicapilla

ID: Small to tiny; a relatively plain-colored cisticola (i.e., lacks spots or streaks); crown reddish brown, otherwise buff-colored, darker above and paler below; birds in southwestern areas are washed with gray; in pairs; male sings from a perch, a monotonous, repeated ticking note; to 11 cm (4.5 in).

HABITAT: Woodland, savannah, farmlands, edges of forest and planted timber.

REGIONS: EC, FS, KZN, MPG, NC, LNW, WC, NAM, BOT, ZIM

b Wing-snapping Cisticola
a Zitting Cisticola
c Gray-backed Cisticola
d Wailing Cisticola
e Neddicky

Plate 65a

Rattling Cisticola

Cisticola chiniana

ID: Small; a long-tailed cisticola; buff with upperparts darker than underparts; streaked with brown and black on wings; crown and tail reddish brown; in pairs; male sings from a perch, and his rattling song is distinctive; to 14 cm (6 in).

HABITAT: Savannah, especially where there is a good grass cover; often in thornveld, where it is frequently the commonest bird.

REGIONS: FS, KZN, MPG, LNW, NAM, BOT, ZIM

Plate 65b

Levaillant's Cisticola

Cisticola tinniens

ID: Small; a long-tailed cisticola; crown, nape, and tail reddish brown; back and shoulders black, streaked with gray; underparts buffy white; unmarked below; in pairs or family groups; males have a warbling song and sing from a high vantage point; to 14 cm (5.5 in).

HABITAT: Dense grass and weed growth, usually close to water.

REGIONS: EC, FS, KZN, MPG, NC, LNW, WC, ZIM

Plate 65c

Tawny-flanked Prinia

Prinia subflava

ID: Small; long-tailed, with tail often held cocked vertically; upperparts light brown; underparts white, with reddish brown flanks; distinctive white eyebrow; in pairs or family groups; to 12 cm (4.5 in).

HABITAT: Dense grass and weed growth in woodland or along streams.

REGIONS: EC, FS, KZN, MPG, LNW, NAM, BOT, ZIM

Plate 65d

Black-chested Prinia

Prinia flavicans

ID: Small; long-tailed, with tail often held cocked vertically; upperparts grayish brown; underparts white (washed with yellow in east of range), with broad black chestband in summer; in pairs or family groups; to 14 cm (5.5 in).

HABITAT: Thornveld, dense grass and weeds, farmlands, gardens.

REGIONS: EC, FS, MPG, NC, LNW, NAM, BOT, ZIM

Plate 65e

Spotted Prinia

Prinia maculosa

ID: Small; long-tailed, with tail often held cocked vertically; upperparts grayish brown; underparts dull white, streaked with black; in pairs or family groups; to 15 cm (6 in).

HABITAT: Fynbos and karoo shrubland, especially on mountain slopes.

REGIONS: EC, NC, LNW, WC

a Rattling Cisticola
b Levaillant's Cisticola
c Tawny-flanked Prinia
e Spotted Prinia
N
d Black-chested Prinia
B

Plate 66a

Spotted Flycatcher
Muscicapa striata

ID: Small; upperparts grayish brown, top of head finely streaked with dark brown; underparts white, with faint brown streaking on chest and sides of face; solitary; hawks insects from low perches; has a characteristic habit of briefly lifting its wings whenever it alights; to 14 cm (5.5 in).

HABITAT: Woodland and savannah, parks and gardens; in summer only.

REGIONS: EC, FS, KZN, MPG, NC, LNW, WC, NAM, BOT, ZIM

Plate 66b

African Dusky Flycatcher
Muscicapa adusta

ID: Small; very like Spotted Flycatcher but smaller and darker; upperparts brownish gray, underparts dull white, faintly streaked with darker gray on chest and flanks; solitary or in pairs; to 13 cm (5 in).

HABITAT: Forest, especially in open glades; also in timber plantations, wooded parks, and gardens.

REGIONS: EC, FS, KZN, MPG, LNW, WC, ZIM

Plate 66c

Marico Flycatcher
Melaenornis mariquensis

ID: Small; upperparts a uniform buffy brown; underparts white; juvenile has heavily streaked underparts, and is spotted with buff above; solitary or in family groups; birds perch conspicuously on edges of trees and bushes; to 18 cm (7 in).

HABITAT: Thornveld.

REGIONS: FS, MPG, NC, LNW, NAM, BOT, ZIM

Plate 66d

Fiscal Flycatcher
Sigelus silens

ID: Small; upperparts black, with white wingbar and white panels on sides of tail; underparts white; female is duller version of male; juvenile is streaked and spotted with buff; solitary or in pairs; to 19 cm (7.5 in).

HABITAT: Woodland, especially thornveld in drier areas; also in parks and gardens.

REGIONS: EC, FS, KZN, MPG, NC, LNW, WC, BOT

a Spotted Flycatcher

b African Dusky Flycatcher

c Marico Flycatcher

d Fiscal Flycatcher

Plate 67a

Cape Batis
Batis capensis

ID: Small, but has a large head for its size; crown gray, back olive-brown; tail black with white edges; wings russet and black; eye yellow with a broad black mask across it; underparts white with chestnut flanks, the male having a broad black chestband, the female a narrower chestnut collar and chestnut throat spot; juvenile spotted above with buff and black; in pairs; to 13 cm (5 in).

HABITAT: Lives in the mid-canopy of evergreen forests.

REGIONS: EC, FS, KZN, MPG, LNW, WC, ZIM

Plate 67b

Chinspot Batis
Batis molitor

ID: Small, but has a large head for its size; upperparts gray, with white wingbar and white edges to tail; eye yellow with a broad black mask across it; underparts white, the male having a broad black chestband, the female a narrower chestnut collar and chestnut throat spot; juvenile spotted above with buff and black; in pairs, often associated with mixed species bird parties; male's call (a three-syllabled, descending whistle rendered as "three blind mice") is a characteristic bushveld sound; to 13 cm (5 in).

HABITAT: Mixed woodland and thornveld.

REGIONS: EC, KZN, MPG, LNW, NAM, BOT, ZIM

Plate 67c

Pririt Batis
Batis pririt

ID: Small, but has a large head for its size; upperparts gray, with white wingbar and white edges to tail; eye yellow with a broad black mask across it; underparts white, the male having a broad black chestband, the female a lemon-yellow wash to her throat, cheeks, and chest; juvenile spotted above with buff and black; in pairs; to 12 cm (4.5 in).

HABITAT: Arid thornveld.

REGIONS: EC, FS, NC, LNW, WC, NAM, BOT

Plate 67d

African Paradise-Flycatcher
Terpsiphone viridis

ID: Small, but male has long tail (tail to 25 cm, 10 in, while breeding); head crested in both sexes; back, wings, and tail chestnut; head, throat, nape dark gray (greenish in southern race); chest pale gray, grading to white on belly; solitary or in pairs; to 18 cm (7 in).

HABITAT: Lives in small clearings in forest and tall mixed woodland; often in parks and gardens or along stream banks; in summer only.

REGIONS: EC, FS, KZN, MPG, NC, LNW, WC, NAM, BOT, ZIM

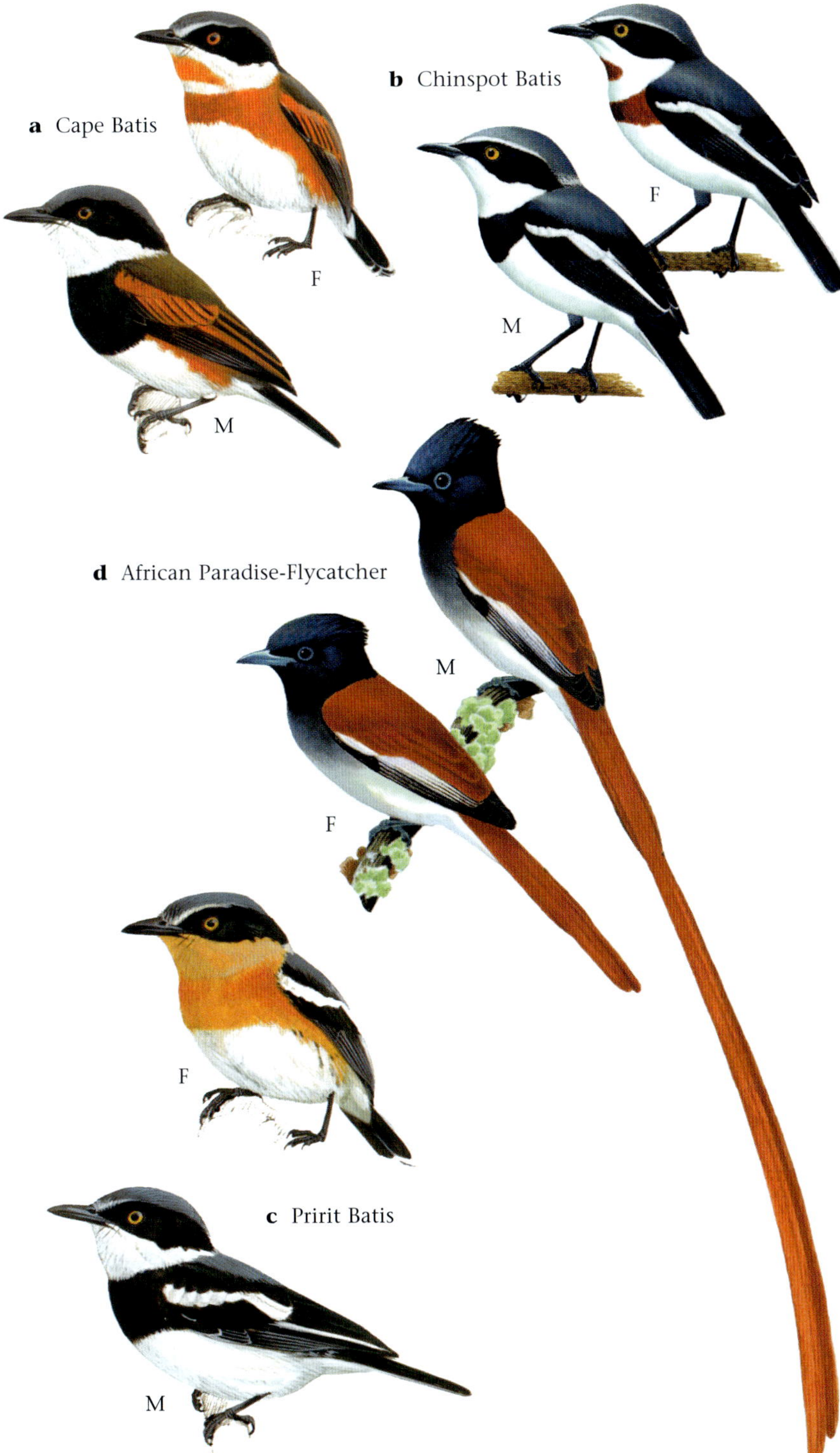
a Cape Batis
F
M
b Chinspot Batis
F
M
d African Paradise-Flycatcher
M
F
F
c Pririt Batis
M

Plate 68a

African Pied Wagtail

Motacilla aguimp

ID: Small; tail long, held horizontally, and often bobbed up and down; striking black-and-white plumage is unmistakable; juvenile has brown in place of black; solitary or in pairs; to 20 cm (8 in).

HABITAT: Edges of large rivers, lagoons, and other large, open water bodies.

REGIONS: EC, FS, KZN, MPG, NC, LNW, NAM, BOT, ZIM

Plate 68b

Cape Wagtail

Motacilla capensis

ID: Small; tail long, held horizontally, and often bobbed up and down; upperparts gray; tail has white edges; underparts white with thin gray chestband; white eyebrow; solitary or in pairs; flocks to nighttime roosts; to 19 cm (7.5 in).

HABITAT: Lives along edges of lakes, rivers, and streams; often on watered lawns in gardens and around farm buildings.

REGIONS: EC, FS, KZN, MPG, NC, LNW, WC, NAM, BOT, ZIM

Plate 68c

African Pipit

(also called Grassveld Pipit)

Anthus cinnamomeus

ID: Small; upperparts pale brown, indistinctly streaked with darker brown; tail has white edges; underparts white, buffy on belly, and finely streaked with pale brown on chest; solitary or in pairs; to 17 cm (6.5 in).

HABITAT: Any open grassy area—the ubiquitous pipit of the region.

REGIONS: EC, FS, KZN, MPG, NC, LNW, WC, NAM, BOT, ZIM

Plate 68d

Long-billed Pipit

Anthus similis

ID: Small; very like African Pipit, but slightly larger, darker, and with buff-colored (not white) edges to tail; it is also more habitat specific; in pairs; to 18 cm (7 in).

HABITAT: Rocky hillslopes in grassland or lightly bushed country.

REGIONS: EC, FS, KZN, MPG, NC, LNW, WC, NAM

Plate 68e

Cape Longclaw

(also called Orange-throated Longclaw)

Macronyx capensis

ID: Small, rather plump-bodied; upperparts grayish brown, with darker streaking on wings; underparts yellow, with orange throat and black chestband; juvenile lacks chestband and has dull yellow throat; in pairs or family groups; has distinctive cat-like mewing call; to 20 cm (8 in).

HABITAT: Open grassland, often in damp areas.

REGIONS: EC, FS, KZN, MPG, NC, LNW, WC, ZIM

Plate 68f

Yellow-throated Longclaw

Macronyx croceus

ID: Small; like Orange-throated Longclaw, but has bright yellow (not orange) throat and a broad yellow eyebrow; juvenile lacks chestband; in pairs or family groups; to 21 cm (8.5 in).

HABITAT: Grassy places with scattered trees and bushes.

REGIONS: EC, KZN, MPG, ZIM

a African Pied Wagtail
b Cape Wagtail
c African Pipit
d Long-billed Pipit
e Cape Longclaw
f Yellow-throated Longclaw

Plate 69a

Common Fiscal
(also called Fiscal Shrike)
Lanius collaris

ID: Small; upperparts black, with white wingbar and white edges to tail; underparts white; female differs from male by having a vertical chestnut line on flank (absent in male); western birds have broad white eyebrow; juvenile mottled with brown; perches conspicuously, often on roadside fences; solitary or in pairs; to 22 cm (8.5 in).

HABITAT: Any open country, provided perches are available.

REGIONS: EC, FS, KZN, MPG, NC, LNW, WC, NAM, BOT, ZIM

Plate 69b

Lesser Gray Shrike
Lanius minor

ID: Small; crown, back, and rump gray; wings and tail black, with white wingbar and white edges to tail; forehead black, extending as broad mask across eye; underparts white; solitary; perches conspicuously; to 21 cm (8.5 in).

HABITAT: Savannah, especially arid thornveld; often perches on tops of bushes; in summer only.

REGIONS: FS, KZN, MPG, NC, LNW, NAM, BOT, ZIM

Plate 69c

Red-backed Shrike
Lanius collurio

ID: Small; sexes differ—male has crown, nape, and rump gray; wings and back reddish brown; tail black with white edges; broad black mask through eye; underparts white, tinged pink; female has dull reddish brown upperparts and dull white underparts, indistinctly barred and mottled with gray-brown; perches conspicuously; solitary; to 18 cm (7 in).

HABITAT: Savannah, especially thornveld; in summer only.

REGIONS: EC, FS, KZN, MPG, NC, LNW, NAM, BOT, ZIM

Plate 69d

Southern Boubou
Laniarius ferrugineus

ID: Small; upperparts glossy black, with long white wingbar; underparts white to buff on belly; skulking; in pairs, which call in loud duets ("boo, boo," which gives rise to its name); to 22 cm (8.5 in).

HABITAT: Forest and bushy thickets in woodland, savannah, and shrublands; common in overgrown gardens.

REGIONS: EC, FS, KZN, MPG, LNW, WC

Plate 69e

Tropical Boubou
Laniarius aethiopicus

ID: Small; very like Southern Boubou, but underparts a cleaner white and calls differ; skulking; in pairs, which call in loud duets; to 24 cm (9.5 in).

HABITAT: Bushy thickets in woodland and savannah.

REGIONS: LNW, NAM, BOT, ZIM

Plate 69f

Crimson-breasted Shrike
Laniarius atrococcineus

ID: Small; upperparts glossy black, with long white wingbar; underparts crimson; a rare yellow-fronted form occurs; juvenile mottled grayish brown and white above and below; skulking; in pairs, which call in loud duets; to 23 cm (9 in).

HABITAT: Thornveld.

REGIONS: FS, MPG, NC, LNW, NAM, BOT, ZIM

a Common Fiscal

b Lesser Gray Shrike

c Red-backed Shrike

d Southern Boubou

e Tropical Boubou

f Crimson-breasted Shrike

Plate 70a

Magpie Shrike
(also called Long-tailed Shrike)
Corvinella melanoleuca

ID: Small, but long-tailed (tail 25 cm, 10 in); entirely black, except for white back and white panels on wing; juvenile browner with shorter tail; in pairs or family groups; perches conspicuously on tops of trees and bushes; to 45 cm (18 in) including tail.

HABITAT: Tall, open savannah.

REGIONS: FS, KZN, MPG, LNW, NAM, BOT, ZIM

Plate 70b

Black-backed Puffback
Dryoscopus cubla

ID: Small; head, mantle, wings, and tail black, with white streaking in wings, white edges to tail, and in males, silky white feathers on rump that can be raised (during display) to form a puff-ball; underparts white; eye red; female has white forehead and is duller than male; solitary or in pairs; to 18 cm (7 in).

HABITAT: Canopy of forest and tall woodland.

REGIONS: EC, KZN, MPG, LNW, NAM, BOT, ZIM

Plate 70c

Brown-crowned Tchagra
(also called Three-streaked Tchagra)
Tchagra australis

ID: Small; crown brown; back pale brown; wings reddish brown; tail black with white tips; underparts white; has a black mask through eye, a white eyebrow, and above this, a thin black line separating eyebrow from brown crown; in pairs; in summer males perform a noisy aerial display, flying up, then gliding to a perch, uttering a string of rolling notes that tail away; to 19 cm (7.5 in).

HABITAT: Shrub layer in savannah, especially thornveld.

REGIONS: FS, KZN, MPG, NC, LNW, NAM, BOT, ZIM

Plate 70d

Black-crowned Tchagra
Tchagra senegala

ID: Small; very like Brown-headed Tchagra but larger, with entirely black crown above a white eyebrow; its call, a lilting whistle, is also entirely different; solitary or in pairs; to 22 cm (8.5 in).

HABITAT: Shrub layer in broad-leafed woodland and savannah.

REGIONS: EC, KZN, MPG, LNW, NAM, BOT, ZIM

Plate 70e

White-crested Helmet-Shrike
(also called White Helmet-Shrike)
Prionops plumatus

ID: Small; strikingly marked—wings black with two white bars; tail black with white edges; head gray with a "helmet" of stiff, elongated feathers that extend above bill; eye yellow, ringed by conspicuous yellow wattle; juvenile duller, lacks eye wattle; in family groups; to 20 cm (8 in).

HABITAT: Broad-leafed woodland.

REGIONS: KZN, MPG, LNW, NAM, BOT, ZIM

Plate 70f

Bokmakierie
Telophorus zeylonus

ID: Small; crown and nape gray; back, wings, and tail olive-green, tail tipped with yellow; throat and underparts bright yellow, with a broad black chestband; has a black mask through eye and a narrow yellow eyebrow; in juvenile black chestband is absent; in pairs; call a series of loud, ringing whistles; pairs often sing in duet; to 23 cm (9 in).

HABITAT: Grassland and shrublands to desert-edge.

REGIONS: EC, FS, KZN, MPG, NC, LNW, WC, NAM, ZIM

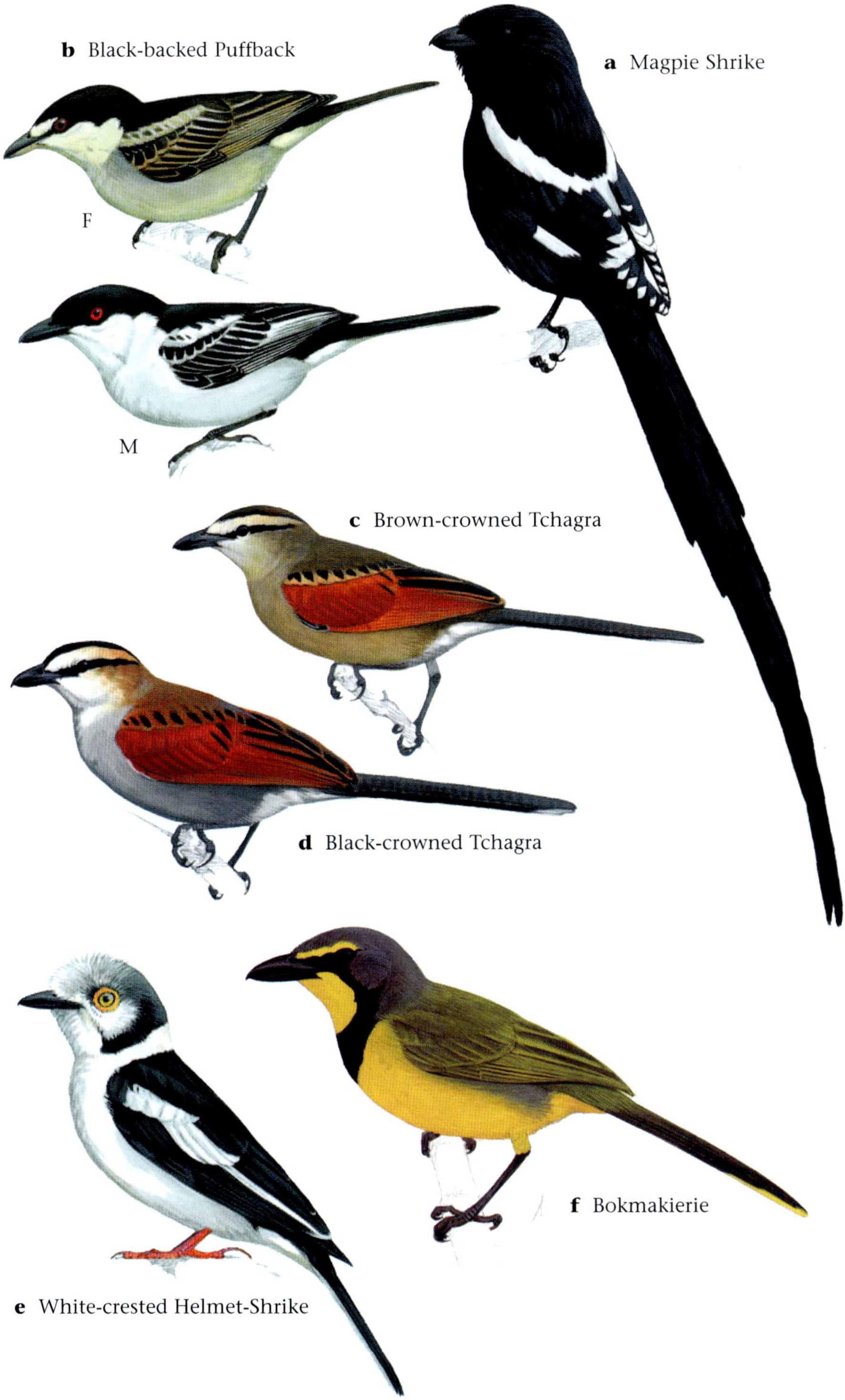
b Black-backed Puffback
F
M
a Magpie Shrike
c Brown-crowned Tchagra
d Black-crowned Tchagra
e White-crested Helmet-Shrike
f Bokmakierie

Plate 71a

Common Starling
(also called European Starling)
Sturnus vulgaris

ID: Small; iridescent purplish green above and below, faintly speckled with buff (but appears plain black from a distance); non-breeding season plumage is browner and less glossy; bill yellow; in pairs or flocks; to 21 cm (8.5 in).

HABITAT: An introduced species, restricted to areas close to human habitation—in cities, towns, villages, and around farms.

REGIONS: EC, FS, KZN, MPG, NC, WC

Plate 71b

Common Myna
(also called Indian Myna)
Acridotheres tristis

ID: Small; mainly dark brown with a glossy black head and chest; has white belly and a broad white panel in the wing (conspicuous in flight); bill, legs, feet, and bare skin surrounding eye is bright yellow; in groups or flocks; to 23 cm (9 in).

HABITAT: An introduced species, restricted to areas close to human habitation—in cities, towns, villages, and around farms.

REGIONS: EC, FS, KZN, MPG, LNW.

Plate 71c

Red-billed Oxpecker
Buphagus erythrorhynchus

ID: Small; head and upperparts dark brown; chest and belly buff; bill and eye red, eye ringed by yellow wattle; juvenile has brown bill and eye and lacks yellow eye ring; in family groups or flocks; to 21 cm (8.5 in).

HABITAT: Woodland or savannah wherever there are populations of large mammals to provide a food source.

REGIONS: EC, KZN, MPG, LNW, NAM, BOT, ZIM

Plate 71d

Pied Starling
Spreo bicolor

ID: Medium-sized; uniform glossy blackish brown, except for white belly and under tail; base of bill yellow; eye white in adult, brown in juvenile; in flocks; to 28 cm (11 in).

HABITAT: Any open grassy area; mainly terrestrial; often associated with cattle or sheep on farmlands.

REGIONS: EC, FS, KZN, MPG, NC, LNW, WC

Plate 71e

Red-winged Starling
Onychognathus morio

ID: Medium-sized; male is uniformly glossy blue-black with chestnut outer wings (usually only visible in flight); female similar, but head and chest dark gray, streaked with pale gray; in pairs or flocks; to 28 cm (11 in).

HABITAT: Mountainous grassland or shrubland; also in cities and around farms.

REGIONS: EC, FS, KZN, MPG, NC, LNW, WC, BOT, ZIM

a Common Starling
b Common Myna
c Red-billed Oxpecker
d Pied Starling
F
M
e Red-winged Starling

Plate 72a

Violet-backed Starling
(also called Plum-colored Starling)
Cinnyricinclus leucogaster

ID: Small; sexes dissimilar; male with head, chest, and upperparts iridescent bluish purple, and lower chest and belly white; female with brown upperparts streaked with dark brown, and white underparts streaked with blackish brown; juvenile like female; in pairs or flocks; to 17 cm (6.5 in).

HABITAT: Mixed woodland.

REGIONS: EC, KZN, MPG, LNW, NAM, BOT, ZIM

Plate 72b

Burchell's Starling
Lamprotornis australis

ID: Medium-sized (the largest starling in the region); uniformly iridescent bluish green, with dark cheeks and a purple sheen on wings, back, and tail; eye black; in pairs or flocks; to 33 cm (13 in).

HABITAT: Tall, open woodland and savannah, especially in areas of sparse grass cover.

REGIONS: KZN, MPG, LNW, NAM, BOT

Plate 72c

Cape Glossy Starling
(also called Red-shouldered Glossy Starling)
Lamprotornis nitens

ID: Small; iridescent bluish green; not as dark as Black-bellied Starling; lacks the blue "ear-patch" of the two Blue-eared Starling species; eye yellow; its call, a rolling "wreeu-wreeu," is also a good distinguishing feature; in pairs or flocks; to 23 cm (9 in).

HABITAT: Any woodland; often in parks and gardens.

REGIONS: EC, FS, KZN, MPG, NC, LNW, NAM, BOT, ZIM

Plate 72d

Greater Blue-eared Starling
Lamprotornis chalybeus

ID: Small; iridescent bluish green with distinctive blue "ear patch" and blue underparts; eye yellow; call a harsh, nasal "squeere"; in pairs or flocks; to 23 cm (9 in).

HABITAT: Deciduous woodland.

REGIONS: MPG, LNW, NAM, BOT, ZIM

Plate 72e

Black-bellied Starling
Lamprotornis corruscus

ID: Small; iridescent purplish green, darkest on the belly; eye orange; female duller than male; call a jumble of shrill and harsh notes; in pairs or flocks; to 21 cm (8.5 in).

HABITAT: Coastal forests.

REGIONS: EC, KZN, MPG, WC

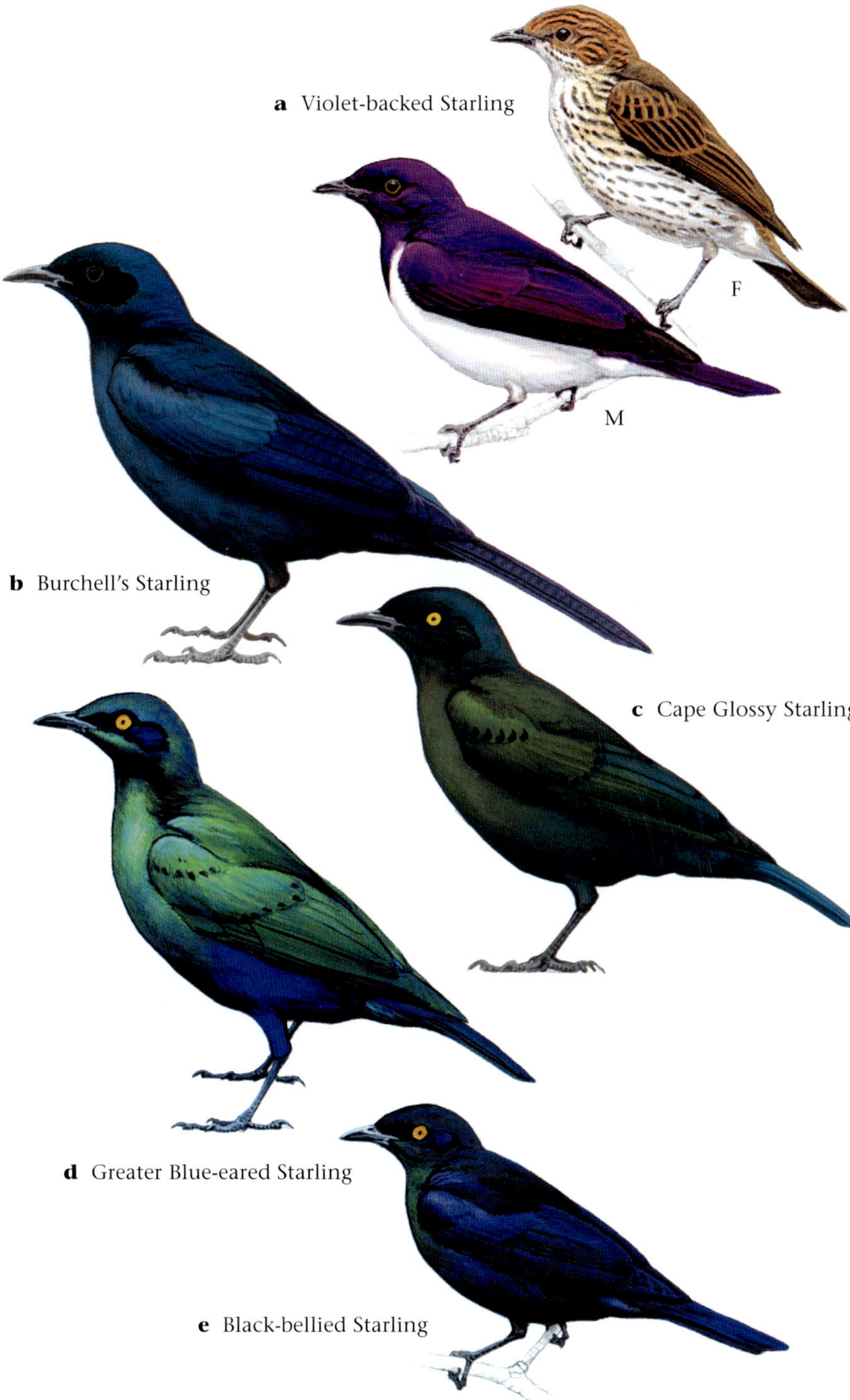
a Violet-backed Starling
F
M
b Burchell's Starling
c Cape Glossy Starling
d Greater Blue-eared Starling
e Black-bellied Starling

Plate 73a

Cape Sugarbird
Promerops cafer

ID: Medium-sized; long-tailed, with long, down-curved bill; head, chest, and upperparts brown; throat and belly white, flanks streaked with brown; yellow undertail; in pairs or flocks; male, including tail, to 44 cm (17.5 in); female (shorter-tailed) to 29 cm (12 in).

HABITAT: Tall fynbos shrubland, especially on mountain slopes.

REGIONS: EC, WC

Plate 73b

Gurney's Sugarbird
Promerops gurneyi

ID: Medium-sized; long-tailed, with long, down-curved bill; smaller and more colorful than Cape Sugarbird; crown and chest reddish brown, with nape, back, wings, and tail grayish brown; throat and belly white, flanks streaked with pale brown; yellow undertail; solitary, in pairs or flocks; male to 41 cm (16 in); female (shorter-tailed) to 23 cm (9 in).

HABITAT: Copses of tall Protea trees in mountainous grasslands; also in flowering gardens.

REGIONS: EC, FS, KZN, MPG, LNW, ZIM

Plate 73c

Malachite Sunbird
Nectarinia famosa

ID: Small; sexes dissimilar; breeding male is uniformly iridescent malachite-green with two center tail feathers elongated; male molts into another plumage outside the breeding season, and then resembles the female, but may retain the long tail and a few traces of green plumage; female has upperparts brown and underparts dull yellow; solitary or in pairs; male, including long tail, to 25 cm (10 in); female to 15 cm (6 in).

HABITAT: Grasslands and shrublands, especially in mountainous areas; also in parks and gardens.

REGIONS: EC, FS, KZN, MPG, NC, LNW, WC, ZIM

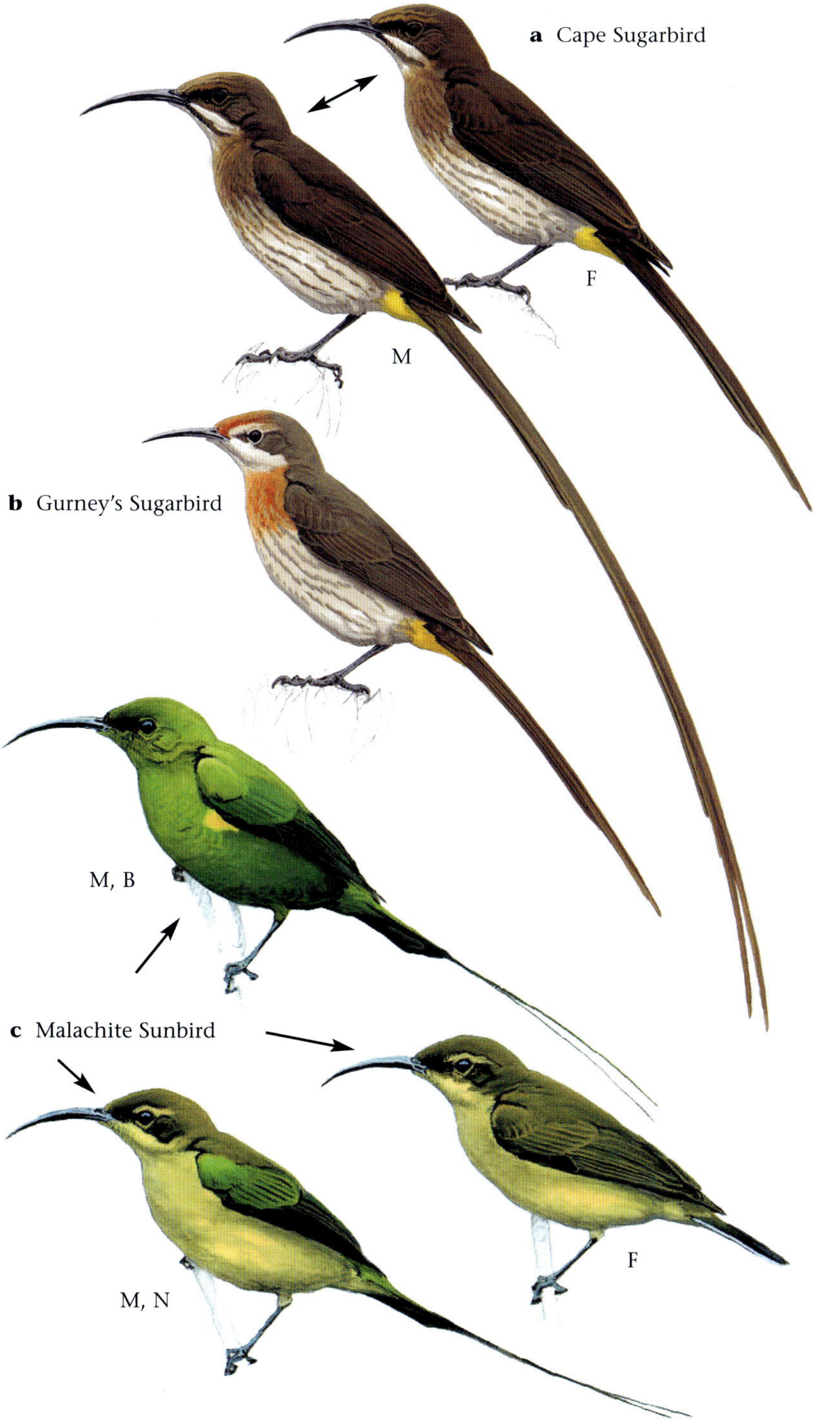
a Cape Sugarbird
F
M
b Gurney's Sugarbird
M, B
c Malachite Sunbird
F
M, N

Plate 74a

Orange-breasted Sunbird
Nectarinia violacea

ID: Small; sexes dissimilar; male has iridescent green head, throat, and back; wings and tail olive-green; lower chest and belly orange, with narrow purple chest collar; female has upperparts dull olive-gray, underparts dull yellow; solitary, in pairs; sometimes in flocks outside breeding season; male, including long tail, to 16 cm (6.5 in); female to 13 cm (5 in).

HABITAT: Fynbos shrublands.

REGIONS: EC, WC

Plate 74b

Greater Double-collared Sunbird
Nectarinia afer

ID: Small; sexes dissimilar; very like Lesser Double-collared Sunbird but larger, longer-billed, and red chestband is much wider (1.8 to 2.3 cm, 0.75 to 1 in); female has upperparts olive-gray, with darker wings and tail; underparts light olive-gray; solitary or in pairs; to 15 cm (6 in).

HABITAT: Forest edges, gardens and parks.

REGIONS: EC, FS, KZN, MPG, LNW, WC

Plate 74c

Southern Double-collared Sunbird
(also called Lesser Double-collared Sunbird)
Nectarinia chalybea

ID: Small; sexes dissimilar; male has head, back, and throat iridescent green; rump blue; wings and tail drab brownish black; has narrow (0.8 cm, 0.3 in) red chestband, separated by thin blue collar from green throat; lower chest and belly pale gray; female has upperparts grayish olive, underparts light grayish olive; non-breeding males molt into an eclipse plumage, then resembling females; solitary, in pairs or flocks; to 12 cm (4.5 in).

HABITAT: Fynbos and karoo shrublands in west, forest in east.

REGIONS: EC, FS, KZN, MPG, NC, LNW, WC

Plate 74d

Collared Sunbird
Anthreptes collaris

ID: Tiny; sexes dissimilar; in male, head, neck, upper chest and upperparts iridescent green; lower chest and belly bright yellow, with a narrow mauve collar separating green throat from yellow underparts; female has upperparts iridescent green, underparts, including throat, bright yellow; in pairs or flocks; to 10 cm (4 in).

HABITAT: Interior and edges of forest.

REGIONS: EC, KZN, MPG, LNW, NAM, BOT, ZIM

Plate 74e

Cape White-eye
(also called Pale White-eye)
Zosterops pallidus

ID: Small; warbler-like; mainly greenish yellow with a diagnostic broad white ring around eye; underparts variably colored according to region, being pale yellowish in the west; grayish in the southwest and greenish in the east; in pairs while nesting, otherwise in groups or flocks; to 12 cm (4.5 in).

HABITAT: Leafy canopy of forest and broad-leafed or mixed woodland; often in parks and gardens.

REGIONS: EC, FS, KZN, MPG, NC, LNW, WC, NAM, BOT

a Orange-breasted Sunbird
F
M
F
b Greater Double-collared Sunbird
F
M
c Southern Double-collared Sunbird
M
F
d Collared Sunbird
M
e Cape White-eye

Plate 75a

Marico Sunbird

Nectarinia mariquensis

ID: Small; sexes dissimilar; in male, head, neck, chest, back, and rump iridescent, dark bronze-green; wings, tail, and belly black; has a double chestband—a broad lower band of purplish red and a narrow upper band of blue; female upperparts olive-gray; underparts dull yellow, streaked with dark gray; solitary or in pairs; to 13 cm (5 in).

HABITAT: Thornveld.

REGIONS: KZN, MPG, NC, LNW, NAM, BOT, ZIM

Plate 75b

White-bellied Sunbird

Nectarinia talatala

ID: Small to tiny; sexes dissimilar; in male, head, throat, and upperparts iridescent green; chest and belly white, separated from green throat by purple collar; female has upperparts brownish gray; underparts dull white; solitary or in pairs; to 11 cm (4.5 in).

HABITAT: Any deciduous woodland.

REGIONS: FS, KZN, MPG, LNW, NAM, BOT, ZIM

Plate 75c

Dusky Sunbird

Nectarinia fusca

ID: Small to tiny; sexes dissimilar; in male head, throat, and upperparts sooty black; belly and undertail white; red shoulder tufts, usually only visible while displaying; female upperparts light brownish gray, underparts dull white; solitary, in pairs, or in flocks; to 11 cm (4.5 in).

HABITAT: Shrublands and thornveld in arid areas, often along watercourses or on rocky hills.

REGIONS: EC, FS, NC, LNW, WC, NAM, BOT

Plate 75d

Gray Sunbird

(also called Mouse-colored Sunbird)

Nectarinia veroxii

ID: Small; a dull-plumaged sunbird in which sexes are alike; upperparts gray with slight metallic sheen; underparts white to pale gray; male has red shoulder tufts, usually only visible while displaying; solitary or in pairs; to 15 cm (6 in).

HABITAT: Coastal and lowland forest.

REGIONS: EC, KZN.

Plate 75e

Scarlet-chested Sunbird

Nectarinia senegalensis

ID: Small; sexes dissimilar; male uniformly blackish brown except for iridescent green forehead, scarlet throat and chest; female upperparts dark olive-gray, underparts pale gray, heavily mottled with dark gray; solitary or in pairs; to 15 cm (6 in).

HABITAT: Mixed woodland, also in parks and gardens.

REGIONS: KZN, MPG, LNW, NAM, BOT, ZIM

Plate 75f

Amethyst Sunbird

(also called African Black Sunbird)

Nectarinia amethystina

ID: Small; sexes dissimilar; male uniformly brownish black except for iridescent patches of amethyst on throat and rump, green on forehead; female upperparts olive-gray, underparts pale gray, streaked with black; solitary or in pairs; to 14 cm (6 in).

HABITAT: Broad-leafed woodland, also in parks and gardens.

REGIONS: EC, FS, KZN, MPG, LNW, WC, NAM, BOT, ZIM

a Marico Sunbird
M
F
F
b White-bellied Sunbird
M
F
c Dusky Sunbird
M
d Gray Sunbird
F
e Scarlet-chested Sunbird
M
F
f Amethyst Sunbird
M

Plate 76a

Red-billed Buffalo-Weaver

Bubalornis niger

ID: Small; male entirely black, except for white wingbar (only visible in flight), and white-edged flank feathers; female drabber than male, underparts mottled with white below; in flocks; to 23 cm (9 in).

HABITAT: Tall open woodland.

REGIONS: KZN, MPG, LNW, NAM, BOT, ZIM

Plate 76b

White-browed Sparrow-Weaver

Plocepasser mahali

ID: Small; thickset; head and back pale brown, with broad white eyebrow and broad white rump; wings and tail blackish brown, feathers edged with white; throat and underparts white; sexes differ in bill color (black in male, horn-colored in female); in family groups; to 18 cm (7 in).

HABITAT: Open acacia savannah.

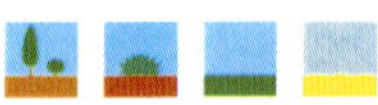

REGIONS: EC, FS, MPG, NC, LNW, NAM, BOT, ZIM

Plate 76c

Sociable Weaver

Philetarius socius

ID: Small; top of head and upperparts pale brown, marked on nape and wings with darker, scale-like edging to feathers; throat and area between bill and eye black; underparts white, with black crescent-shaped spots on flanks; juvenile lacks black on throat and face; in flocks, which remain in the vicinity of their gigantic nests year-round; to 14 cm (5.5 in).

HABITAT: Arid woodland, shrubland, or edges of desert.

REGIONS: FS, NC, LNW, NAM, BOT

Plate 76d

House Sparrow

Passer domesticus

ID: Small; sexes dissimilar; male has dark brown to reddish brown back and nape, streaked with black; crown and rump gray; cheeks, chest, and belly white; throat and face black; tail dark brown; female upperparts buffy brown, streaked with dark brown, underparts dull white and a faint buff eyebrow; in pairs or flocks; to 15 cm (6 in).

HABITAT: Cities, towns, villages, farmlands; always close to human habitation.

REGIONS: EC, FS, KZN, MPG, NC, LNW, WC, NAM, BOT, ZIM

Plate 76e

Cape Sparrow

Passer melanurus

ID: Small; sexes dissimilar; in male, head and chest black, with broad white crescent-shaped line behind eye; wings, back, and rump brown to reddish brown, tail dark brown; wings have black streaking and white wingbar; belly white; female like male, but has gray, not black head; in pairs or flocks; to 15 cm (6 in).

HABITAT: Grassland, shrublands; also in farmlands and gardens.

REGIONS: EC, FS, KZN, MPG, NC, LNW, WC, NAM, BOT

Plate 76f

Southern Gray-headed Sparrow

Passer diffusus

ID: Small; head plain gray; wings, back, shoulders brown to reddish brown; tail brown; wings have blackish streaking and a white wingbar; underparts dull white; bill black while breeding, otherwise yellowish; in pairs or flocks; to 15 cm (6 in).

HABITAT: Grassland, savannah, shrublands, farmlands.

REGIONS: EC, FS, KZN, MPG, NC, LNW, WC, NAM, BOT, ZIM

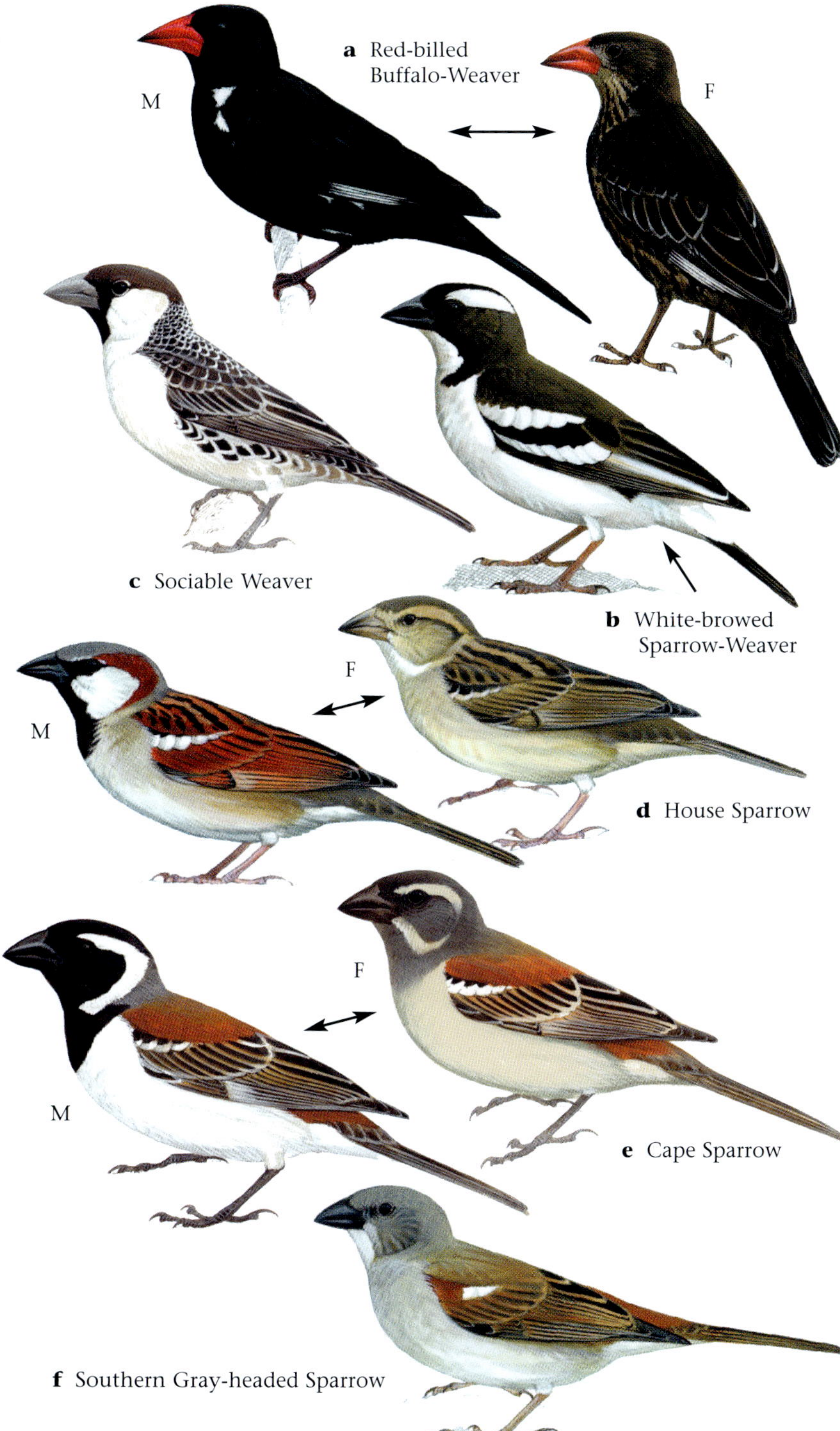
a Red-billed Buffalo-Weaver
M
F
c Sociable Weaver
b White-browed Sparrow-Weaver
F
M
d House Sparrow
F
M
e Cape Sparrow
f Southern Gray-headed Sparrow

Plate 77a

Scaly-feathered Finch
(also called Scaly Weaver)
Sporopipes squamifrons

ID: Small to tiny; plump-bodied; upperparts light brown; underparts whitish; bill pink; feathers on crown black, edged with white, giving top of head a scaly appearance; black area between bill and eye, separated from a black moustache stripe by white streak; wing and tail feathers have black-and-white edges; in flocks; to 11 cm (4.5 in).

HABITAT: Arid thornveld.

REGIONS: EC, FS, MPG, NC, LNW, WC, NAM, BOT, ZIM

Plate 77b

Thick-billed Weaver
(also called Grosbeak Weaver)
Amblyospiza albifrons

ID: Small; bill heavy, black in male, yellow in female; male uniformly chocolate-brown, except for white forehead and white wingbar; female has head and upperparts brown, streaked with dark brown; underparts white streaked with brown, especially on throat; in flocks; to 18 cm (7 in).

HABITAT: Nests along wetland edges; feeds in forest clearings; also gardens and farmlands.

REGIONS: EC, KZN, MPG, LNW, NAM, BOT, ZIM

Plate 77c

Chestnut Weaver
Ploceus rubiginosus

ID: Small; breeding male head and throat black; nape, back, rump, and underparts chestnut; wings and tail dark brown, edged with white; female and non-breeding male upperparts are pale brownish gray, flecked with black; underparts buff, chest washed with light brown; in flocks; to 16 cm (6.5 in).

HABITAT: Arid woodland; in summer only.

REGIONS: NAM, BOT

Plate 77d

Red-headed Weaver
Anaplectes rubriceps

ID: Small; breeding male head, throat, chest, and nape are red; back, wings, and tail grayish, wing feathers edged with yellow; underparts white; female and non-breeding male have yellow head, throat, chest, nape, otherwise like breeding male; in pairs or small groups; to 14 cm (5.5 in).

HABITAT: Broad-leafed woodland.

REGIONS: KZN, MPG, LNW, NAM, BOT, ZIM

a Scaly-feathered Finch
F
c Chestnut Weaver
F
M
M
b Thick-billed Weaver
F
d Red-headed Weaver
M

Plate 78a

Cape Weaver

Ploceus capensis

ID: Small; breeding male bright yellow above and below, with white eye, a reddish brown wash to forehead, face, and throat; wings and tail olive, feathers edged with dull yellow; female and non-breeding male upperparts are dull yellowish green, indistinctly streaked with dull yellow; underparts pale yellow; in flocks; to 17 cm (7.5 in).

HABITAT: Grassland, shrublands, farmlands; often near human habitation or water.

REGIONS: EC, FS, KZN, MPG, NC, LNW, WC

Plate 78b

Village Weaver

(also called Spotted-backed Weaver)

Ploceus cucullatus

ID: Small; breeding male has face and throat black; eye red; remainder of head (including forehead) and underparts bright yellow; wings and back yellow, mottled and spotted with black; tail greenish yellow; female and non-breeding male upperparts dull grayish green, underparts dull white; head and chest washed with yellow; in flocks; to 16 cm (6.5 in).

HABITAT: Bush and reeds, especially along rivers; nomadic.

REGIONS: EC, KZN, MPG, LNW, NAM, BOT, ZIM

Plate 78c

Southern Masked-Weaver

Ploceus velatus

ID: Small; breeding male has forehead, face, and throat black; eye red; remainder of head and underparts bright yellow; back, wings, and tail yellowish green, mottled with olive; female and non-breeding male upperparts dull yellowish green, underparts dull white; in flocks; to 14 cm (5.5 in).

HABITAT: Ubiquitous; in grassland, savannah, or shrublands; often near water.

REGIONS: EC, FS, KZN, MPG, NC, LNW, WC, NAM, BOT, ZIM

Plate 78d

Yellow Weaver

Ploceus subaureus

ID: Small; breeding male uniformly bright yellow above and below, with red eye and black bill; female and non-breeding male upperparts pale yellowish green, indistinctly mottled; underparts yellow; in flocks; to 14 cm (5.5 in).

HABITAT: Reeds and bush close to rivers.

REGIONS: EC, KZN.

M
a Cape Weaver
F
b Village Weaver
F
M
F
M
c Southern Masked-Weaver
d Yellow Weaver
F
M

Plate 79a

Southern Red Bishop
Euplectes orix

ID: Small; breeding male a striking red and black bird; crown, cheeks, throat, lower chest, and belly black; wings and tail brown; elsewhere red (including a broad red chestband); female and non-breeding male upperparts buff, streaked with dark brown; underparts dull white, faintly streaked with brown; in flocks; to 11 cm (4.5 in).

HABITAT: Nests in reeds and bulrushes over water; feeds in open land, especially in agricultural lands.

REGIONS: EC, FS, KZN, MPG, NC, LNW, WC, NAM, BOT, ZIM

Plate 79b

Red-billed Quelea
Quelea quelea

ID: Small; breeding male bill red, forehead, throat, and cheeks black, encircled by pink (or, rarely, with yellow) wash; nape, back, wings, tail grayish brown, streaked with black; underparts buff; female and non-breeding male head and upperparts gray-brown streaked with black; underparts buff; in large flocks, often numbering millions of birds; to 13 cm (5 in).

HABITAT: Nests in thornveld or reedbeds, forages in grass or croplands; nomadic.

REGIONS: EC, FS, KZN, MPG, NC, LNW, WC, NAM, BOT, ZIM

Plate 79c

Yellow-crowned Bishop
(also called Golden Bishop)
Euplectes afer

ID: Tiny; breeding male is a striking black and yellow bird; crown, nape, back, and rump are golden-yellow; throat, cheeks, and underparts black, with black collar extending behind neck; wing and tail black, feathers here edged with buff; female and non-breeding male upperparts buff, streaked with blackish brown; underparts pale buff, finely streaked with brown; in flocks; to 10 cm (4 in).

HABITAT: Long grass and weed growth, especially over shallow water.

REGIONS: EC, FS, KZN, MPG, NC, LNW, NAM, BOT, ZIM

Plate 79d

Yellow Bishop
(also called Yellow-rumped Widow)
Euplectes capensis

ID: Small; breeding male entirely black, except for bright yellow rump and shoulders; female upperparts buff, heavily streaked with black; underparts pale buff, streaked with black; non-breeding male similar to female, but retains yellow rump and shoulders; in flocks; to 15 cm (6 in).

HABITAT: Dense grassland and shrubland; often close to water.

REGIONS: EC, FS, KZN, MPG, NC, LNW, WC, ZIM

M
a Southern Red Bishop
F
M
b Red-billed Quelea
F
M
F
c Yellow-crowned Bishop
d Yellow Bishop
M
F

Plate 80a

Long-tailed Widowbird
Euplectes progne

ID: Small, but breeding male has long (40 cm, 16 in) tail; breeding male entirely black, except for orange-red and white shoulder patches and buff-edged wing feathers; bill bluish gray; female upperparts buff, heavily streaked with black; underparts dull white, indistinctly streaked on chest with buff; non-breeding male like female, but retains red and white shoulders through winter; in flocks; males, when displaying, are very conspicuous; breeding male, including tail, to 60 cm (24 in); female to 18 cm (7 in).

HABITAT: Open grassland, especially in vicinity of water.

REGIONS: EC, FS, KZN, MPG, NC, LNW, BOT

Plate 80b

Fan-tailed Widowbird
(also called Red-shouldered Widow)
Euplectes axillaris

ID: Small; breeding male entirely black, except for orange-red shoulders and buff-edged wing feathers; bill bluish gray; female upperparts buff, heavily streaked with black; underparts dull white, indistinctly streaked with buff on flanks; non-breeding male like female, but retains red shoulders through winter; in flocks; male to 17 cm (6.5 in); female to 14 cm (5.5 in).

HABITAT: Grassy edges of open wetlands.

REGIONS: EC, FS, KZN, MPG, NAM, BOT

Plate 80c

Red-collared Widowbird
Euplectes ardens

ID: Small, but breeding male has long (25 cm, 10 in) tail; breeding male entirely black, except for thin red collar on chest; female and non-breeding male upperparts buff, streaked with black; underparts unmarked pale buff; in flocks; breeding male, including tail, to 40 cm (16 in); female to 13 cm (5 in).

HABITAT: Dense grassy areas on hillsides and in valleys.

REGIONS: EC, FS, KZN, MPG, LNW, ZIM

a Long-tailed Widowbird
M, B
F
M, N
b Fan-tailed Widowbird
M
F
c Red-collared Widowbird
M
F

Plate 81a

Green-winged Pytilia
(also called Melba Finch)
Pytilia melba

ID: Small; head gray; back and wings olive-green; rump and tail dull red; chest and belly white, finely barred with black; bill red; male has red crown and throat and upper chest is washed with orange; in female, head is plain gray; in pairs or family groups; to 12 cm (4.5 in).

HABITAT: Thornveld.

REGIONS: FS, KZN, MPG, NC, LNW, NAM, BOT, ZIM

Plate 81b

Red-billed Firefinch
Lagonosticta senegala

ID: Tiny; like Jameson's Firefinch and distinguished by having pink (not blue) bill and the eye is encircled by a yellow ring; female duller and more buff-colored than male; in pairs or family groups; to 10 cm (4 in).

HABITAT: Any woodland; often in gardens.

REGIONS: EC, FS, KZN, MPG, NC, LNW, WC, NAM, BOT, ZIM

Plate 81c

Jameson's Firefinch
Lagonosticta rhodopareia

ID: Tiny; bill blue; male has nape, back, and wings brown; head, rump, tail, and underparts pinkish red; lower belly black; flanks lightly spotted with white; female duller than male and underparts buff-colored; in pairs or family groups; to 10 cm (4 in).

HABITAT: Undergrowth in thick woodland.

REGIONS: KZN, MPG, LNW, NAM, BOT, ZIM

Plate 81d

Blue Waxbill
(also called Blue-breasted Cordonbleu)
Uraeginthus angolensis

ID: Small; the only blue-colored waxbill in the region; upperparts light brown; rump, tail, throat, and underparts blue; sexes differ by male having blue extending to belly, whereas in female belly is white; in pairs or flocks; to 13 cm (5 in).

HABITAT: Any wooded area, but especially thornveld.

REGIONS: FS, KZN, MPG, NC, LNW, NAM, BOT, ZIM

Plate 81e

Common Waxbill
Estrilda astrild

ID: Small; upperparts grayish brown, finely barred with black; underparts white with fine black barring on flanks; belly red with black under tail; bill red, the red extending as a mask across the eye; in pairs or flocks; to 12 cm (4.5 in).

HABITAT: Dense vegetation (grass, bracken, shrubs); often near water.

REGIONS: EC, FS, KZN, MPG, NC, LNW, WC, NAM, BOT, ZIM

Plate 81f

Violet-eared Waxbill
Uraeginthus granatinus

ID: Small; sexes dissimilar; male has crown, nape, and underparts chestnut; wings and back brown; tail and throat black; forehead and rump deep blue; cheeks iridescent purple; eye encircled by red eye ring; female has blue forehead and rump; upperparts light brown; underparts buff, with mauve cheeks and black tail; in pairs or family groups; to 15 cm (6 in).

HABITAT: Open woodland and savannah.

REGIONS: FS, MPG, NC, LNW, NAM, BOT, ZIM

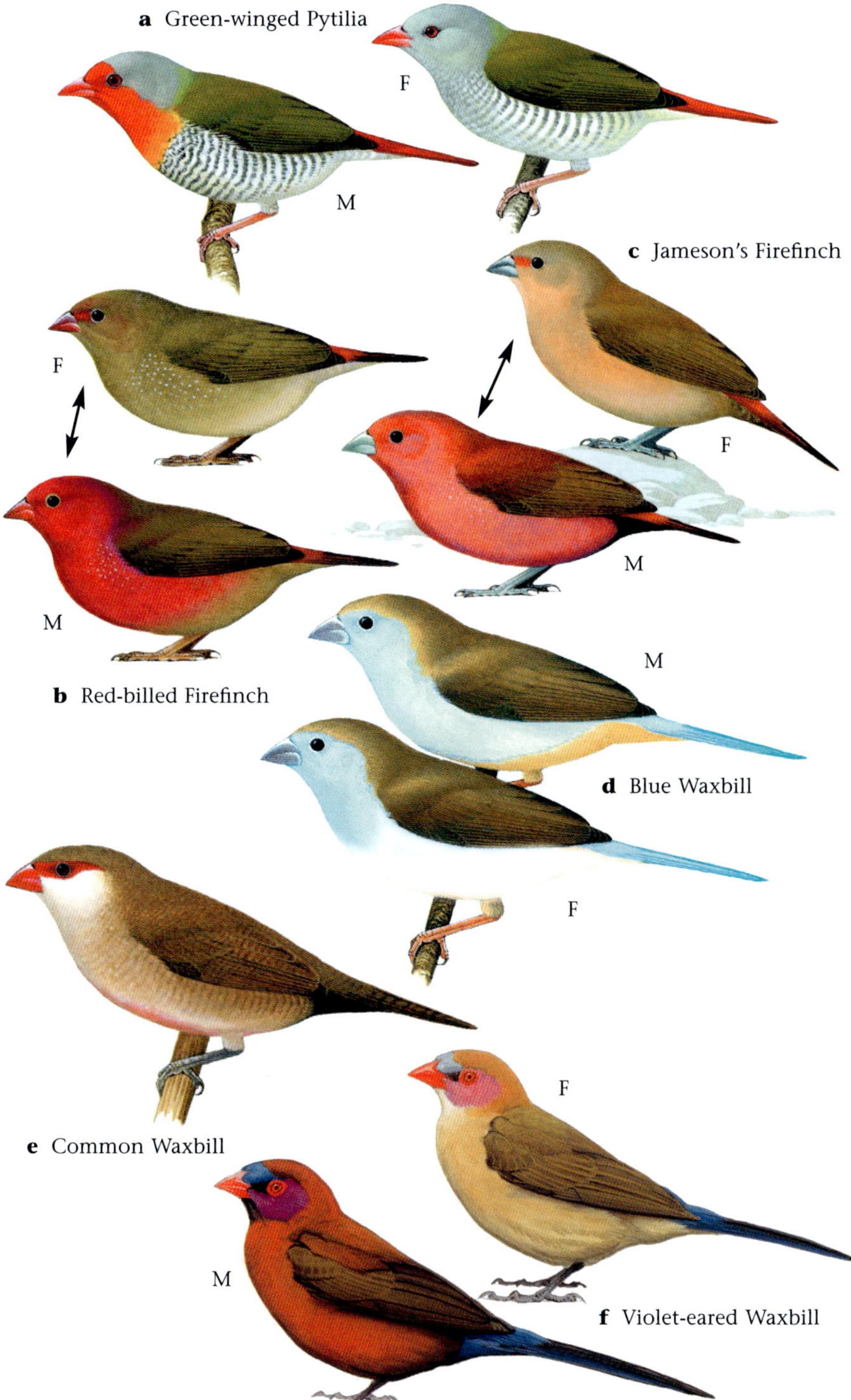
a Green-winged Pytilia
F
M
c Jameson's Firefinch
F
F
M
M
b Red-billed Firefinch
M
d Blue Waxbill
F
F
e Common Waxbill
M
f Violet-eared Waxbill

Plate 82a

Bronze Mannikin

Spermestes cucullatus

ID: Tiny; head and throat metallic black; back and wings grayish brown, with iridescent green spots on shoulders; rump finely barred, tail black; underparts white; juvenile buff-colored, paler on belly; in flocks; to 9 cm (3.5 in).

HABITAT: Dense vegetation (grass, bracken, shrubs); often in gardens and on edges of forest.

REGIONS: EC, FS, KZN, MPG, LNW, NAM, BOT, ZIM

Plate 82b

Shaft-tailed Whydah

Vidua regia

ID: Small, but male has long (22 cm, 8.5 in) tail; upperparts glossy blue-black; feathers of tail swell at base; underparts and nape buff-yellow; bill red; female and non-breeding male are buff, streaked above, unmarked below; streaked head; solitary or in flocks; breeding male, including tail, to 34 cm (13 in); female to 12 cm (4.5 in).

HABITAT: Dense thornveld. Displaying males occur solitarily; otherwise in flocks.

REGIONS: FS, NC, LNW, NAM, BOT, ZIM

Plate 82c

Long-tailed Paradise-Whydah

(also called Eastern Paradise-Whydah)

Vidua paradisaea

ID: Small, but male has long (23 cm, 9 in), distinctively shaped, black tail; head, throat, back, and wings black; nape orange; chest reddish brown; underparts buff; female buff-colored; streaked with brown above, unmarked below; head striped; non-breeding male like female, but retains some black on head; solitary or in flocks; breeding male, including tail, to 36 cm (14 in); female to 14 cm (5.5 in).

HABITAT: Open thornveld. Displaying males occur solitarily; otherwise in flocks.

REGIONS: FS, KZN, MPG, LNW, NAM, BOT, ZIM

Plate 82d

Pin-tailed Whydah

Vidua macroura

ID: Small, but breeding male has long (22 cm, 8.5 in) tail, upperparts glossy blue-black, white wingbar; underparts, rump, and nape white; bill red; female and non-breeding male are buff, upperparts streaked with brown; underparts unmarked; streaked head; solitary or in flocks; breeding male, including tail, to 34 cm (13 in); female to 12 cm (4.5 in).

HABITAT: Any open land, typically close to water.

REGIONS: EC, FS, KZN, MPG, NC, LNW, WC, NAM, BOT, ZIM

Plate 82e

Red-headed Finch

Amadina erythrocephala

ID: Small with heavy bill; upperparts grayish brown; underparts white, grading to buff on flanks, spotted on chest and belly; male has red head; female gray head; in pairs or flocks; to 13 cm (5 in).

HABITAT: Grassland with scattered trees, especially thornveld.

REGIONS: EC, FS, KZN, MPG, NC, LNW, WC, NAM, BOT, ZIM

Plate 82f

Village Indigobird

(also called Steelblue Widow-Finch)

Vidua chalybeata

ID: Small to tiny; breeding male glossy black with pink bill, legs, and feet; female and non-breeding male upperparts grayish brown, streaked with black; underparts off-white; solitary or in flocks; to 11 cm (4.5 in).

HABITAT: Any type of woodland.

REGIONS: EC, FS, KZN, MPG, NC, LNW, NAM, BOT, ZIM

a Bronze Mannikin
F
M
b Shaft-tailed Whydah
M
F
c Long-tailed Paradise-Whydah
d Pin-tailed Whydah
M
F
F
M
F
e Red-headed Finch
M
f Village Indigobird

Plate 83a

Yellow-fronted Canary
(also called Yellow-eyed Canary)
Serinus mozambicus

ID: Small; crown and nape dull gray; back and wings gray-green, streaked with olive; rump yellow; tail black, tipped with white; face distinctively patterned, with yellow eyebrow, black line across eye, yellow cheek, and black moustache stripe; throat and underparts yellow; in pairs or flocks; to 12 cm (4.5 in).

HABITAT: Broad-leafed woodland; often in second-growth bush and old fields.

REGIONS: EC, FS, KZN, MPG, LNW, NAM, BOT, ZIM

Plate 83b

Black-throated Canary
Serinus atrogularis

ID: Small to tiny; a drab-colored canary with upperparts grayish, streaked with brown; underparts dull white; throat has indistinct black patch; rump yellow; in pairs or flocks; to 11 cm (4.5 in).

HABITAT: Thornveld and shrubby grassland; often in old fields.

REGIONS: EC, FS, KZN, MPG, NC, LNW, WC, NAM, BOT, ZIM

Plate 83c

Cape Canary
Serinus canicollis

ID: Small; wings and tail yellow-green, streaked with olive; crown, cheeks, and throat golden-olive; nape gray; underparts yellow; juvenile dull yellow, streaked with olive; in flocks; has a fine song; to 13 cm (5 in).

HABITAT: Dense vegetation (grass, bracken, shrubs); often in old fields.

REGIONS: EC, FS, KZN, MPG, NC, LNW, WC, ZIM

Plate 83d

Yellow Canary
Serinus flaviventris

ID: Small; sexes dissimilar; male upperparts greenish yellow, streaked with olive; underparts bright yellow; face faintly marked with pale yellow eyebrow; female upperparts greenish-gray, streaked with brown-gray; underparts dull white, streaked with gray; rump yellow; in pairs or flocks; to 13 cm (5 in).

HABITAT: Thornveld, shrubby grassland, and karoo shrublands.

REGIONS: EC, FS, KZN, MPG, NC, LNW, WC, NAM, BOT

Plate 83e

White-throated Canary
Serinus albogularis

ID: Small, but largest canary in the region; bill heavy; drably colored, with upperparts grayish brown, except for yellow rump; underparts dull white, whitest on the throat; in pairs or flocks; to 15 cm (6 in).

HABITAT: Karoo shrublands, especially along dry watercourses.

REGIONS: EC, FS, NC, LNW, WC, NAM

a Yellow-fronted Canary

b Black-throated Canary

c Cape Canary

d Yellow Canary

e White-throated Canary

Plate 84a

Cape Siskin

Serinus totta

ID: Small; in male, upperparts dull yellowish brown, finely streaked with brown on head; rump yellowish green; tail black, tipped with white; underparts dull yellow; female similar but duller, and yellow restricted to belly; in pairs or flocks; to 13 cm (5 in).

HABITAT: Fynbos-covered hills and mountains, near rocks.

REGIONS: EC, WC

Plate 84b

Golden-breasted Bunting

Emberiza flaviventris

ID: Small; male has black head marked with three white stripes, one across top of head, one forming eyebrow, and one below eye; back reddish brown; wings dull brown with white wingbar; tail black with white edges; throat and chest orange-yellow; belly white; female similar but duller, and head brown, not black; in pairs; to 16 cm (6.5 in).

HABITAT: Any woodland or savannah.

REGIONS: EC, FS, KZN, MPG, NC, LNW, NAM, BOT, ZIM

Plate 84c

Cape Bunting

Emberiza capensis

ID: Small; upperparts gray with blackish streaking in back; wings reddish brown; tail black; head strongly patterned with alternating black and white stripes; throat white; underparts buff; in pairs; to 16 cm (6.5 in).

HABITAT: Rocky ground, especially in hills and mountains.

REGIONS: EC, FS, KZN, MPG, NC, LNW, WC, NAM, BOT, ZIM

Plate 84d

Cinnamon-breasted Bunting

(also called Cinnamon-breasted Rock Bunting)

Emberiza tahapisi

ID: Small; head, neck, and nape black (in male) or brown (in female), striped with white lines across crown and above and below the eye; wings, back, and tail brown, streaked with black; underparts chestnut; solitary, in pairs, or in flocks; to 15 cm (6 in).

HABITAT: Rocky ground; often in old quarries.

REGIONS: EC, FS, KZN, MPG, NC, LNW, WC, NAM, BOT, ZIM

Plate 84e

Lark-like Bunting

Emberiza impetuani

ID: Small; buff-colored above and below with grayish brown, streaked wings and tail; lacks facial pattern typical of other buntings; usually in flocks; nomadic, moving in response to rainfall; to 14 cm (5.5 in).

HABITAT: Sparsely vegetated, stony, semi-desert plains.

REGIONS: EC, FS, NC, LNW, WC, NAM, BOT, ZIM

a Cape Siskin

b Golden-breasted Bunting

c Cape Bunting

d Cinnamon-breasted Bunting

e Lark-like Bunting

Plate 85a

Eastern Rock Elephant-shrew
(also called Eastern Rock Sengi)
Elephantulus myurus

ID: Small size; elongated, trunk-like snout; long, rounded ears; large eyes narrowly ringed with white; soft, darkish gray-brown fur; pale belly; nearly hairless tail slightly longer than head and body; 12 cm (5 in).

HABITAT: Rocky outcrops; diurnal.

REGIONS: EC, FS, MPG, LNW, BOT, ZIM

Plate 85b

Round-eared Elephant-shrew
(also called Round-eared Sengi)
Macroscelides proboscideus

ID: Small size; elongated, constantly twitching, trunk-like snout; rounded, thin ears; large eyes; soft brownish gray fur; nearly naked, longish tail; lightning fast; 11 cm (4 in).

HABITAT: Open gravel plains with sparse vegetation; also flat sandy areas; diurnal.

REGIONS: EC, NC, WC, NAM,

Plate 85c

Short-snouted Elephant-shrew
(also called Short-snouted Sengi)
Elephantulus brachyrhynchus

ID: Small size; elongated, highly mobile snout; long, thin, rounded ears; soft, grayish brown fur, paler belly; white ring around eye; reddish spot at base of ear; 11 cm (4 in), plus tail about same length.

HABITAT: Sandy plains with vegetation cover; diurnal.

REGIONS: MPG, LNW, NAM, BOT, ZIM,

Plate 85d

Hottentot Golden Mole
Amblysomus hottentotus

ID: Looks like a powderpuff; lacks external tail; tiny eyes and ears not visible; hair soft, silky, and rich reddish brown; snout tipped with leathery pad; 13 cm (5 in).

HABITAT: Higher rainfall areas; mainly sandy soils but occasionally loamy and clay soils.

REGIONS: EC, FS, KZN, MPG, WC

Plate 85e

Southern African Hedgehog
Atelerix frontalis

ID: Small size; short, stiff, and banded spines cover the back and sides; pointed snout; band of white hair across forehead; tail not usually visible; curls up when threatened; 22 cm (9 in).

HABITAT: Avoids desert or areas of high annual rainfall (more than 800 mm, 31 in); nocturnal.

REGIONS: EC, FS, MPG, LNW, NAM, BOT, ZIM

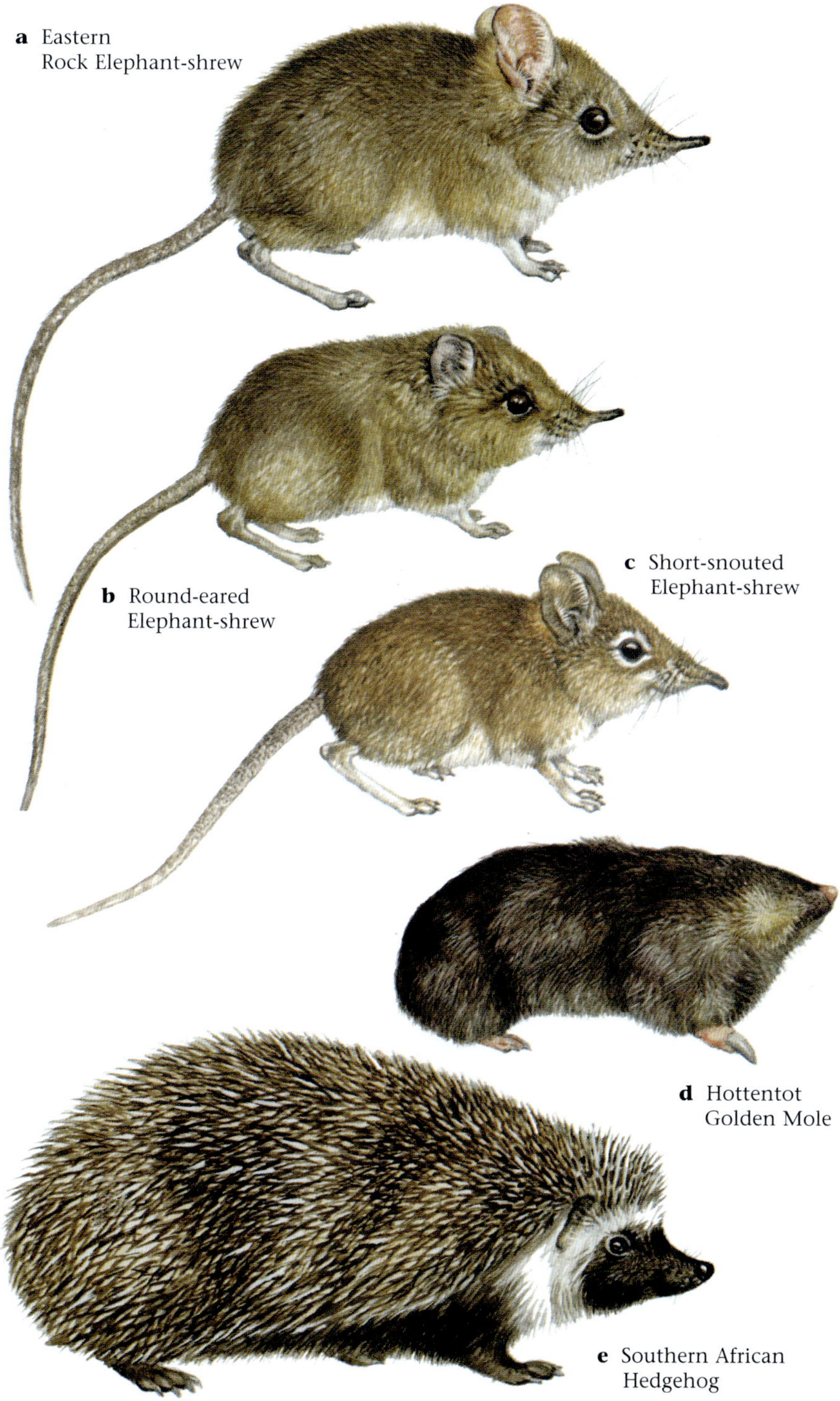
a Eastern Rock Elephant-shrew
b Round-eared Elephant-shrew
c Short-snouted Elephant-shrew
d Hottentot Golden Mole
e Southern African Hedgehog

Plate 86a

Egyptian Fruit-bat

Rousettus aegyptiacus

ID: A large bat; short fur, uniformly grayish brown to dark brown; very short, free tail; wings rounded and dark brown; 15 cm (6 in); wingspan 60 cm (24 in).

HABITAT: Forested areas; savannah woodland and river-associated woodland where tree fruits are plentiful; roosts in caves; nocturnal.

REGIONS: EC, KZN, MPG, WC, ZIM

Plate 86b

Wahlberg's Epauletted Fruit-bat

Epomophorus wahlbergi

ID: A large, buff-brown furred bat; very short tail; tufts of white hair at bases of ears; males have pouch ringed by white hair on each shoulder; 14 cm (5.5 in); wingspan 50 cm (20 in).

HABITAT: Forest and river-associated woodland; more open woodland in moist savannah areas.

REGIONS: EC, KZN, MPG, ZIM

Plate 86c

Cape Serotine Bat

Neoromicia capensis

ID: Small size; relatively short ears; tail entirely enclosed by membrane; straight head profile, no facial projections; soft fur varies from very pale gray-brown to dark brown; 8.5 cm (3.3 in); wingspan 24 cm (9.5 in).

HABITAT: All major habitats, from desert to high rainfall areas.

REGIONS: All

Plate 86d

Butterfly Bat

Glauconycteris variegatus

ID: Small size; overall pale yellow or fawn in color; yellow wing membranes with numerous black lines; smallish ears; no facial projections; 11 cm (4.3 in); wingspan 28 cm (11 in); starts hunting at dusk.

HABITAT: Dry woodland and open savannah bush country; roosts among leaves and thatch of abandoned huts.

REGIONS: KZN, MPG, NAM, BOT, ZIM

Plate 86e

Egyptian Slit-faced Bat

Nycteris thebaica

ID: Long, lobed slit runs down center of face; when slit is open, nose-leaves are visible; large, more or less straight—and parallel—sided ears; long ears almost one third of the animal's total length; wings broad and rounded at tips; forked tail tip; 10 cm (4 in); wingspan 24 cm (9.5 in).

HABITAT: Almost all major habitats, from desert to high rainfall areas; nocturnal.

REGIONS: All

Plate 86f

Egyptian Free-tailed Bat

Tadarida aegyptiaca

ID: Also called "wrinkled-lip" bats; only about half of tail enclosed by membrane, remainder projects beyond; ears large and about equal in length and breadth; hair short, lies close to body, usually dark brown; 11 cm (4.3 in); wingspan 30 cm (11.8 in); fast flier.

HABITAT: All types.

REGIONS: All

a Egyptian Fruit-bat

b Wahlberg's Epauletted Fruit-bat

c Cape Serotine Bat

d Butterfly Bat

e Egyptian Slit-faced Bat

f Egyptian Free-tailed Bat

Plate 87a

Thick-tailed Bushbaby
Otolemur crassicaudatus

ID: Superficially cat-like in movement on ground with tail held erect; fine, woolly, gray-brown fur; large forward-pointing eyes; large, thin mobile ears; unnerving screaming call at night; 34 to 40 cm (13.4 to 15.7 in) with well-haired bushy tail of equal length.

HABITAT: Forest, moist and dry woodland, wooded river margins; mainly in trees; nocturnal.

REGIONS: KZN, MPG, ZIM

Plate 87b

Lesser Bushbaby
Galago moholi

ID: Small size; long, fluffy tail; large, thin, rounded, highly mobile ears; large, forward-facing eyes; great jumping abilities in tree habitat; soft, woolly grayish to gray-brown hair; 10 to 15 cm (4 to 6 in); long, well-haired tail more than half its total body length.

HABITAT: Wooded savannah; particularly with Acacia trees and river-associated woodland.

REGIONS: MPG, LNW, NAM, BOT, ZIM

Plate 87c

Sykes' Monkey
(also called Samango Monkey)
Cercopithecus (mitis) albogularis

ID: Typical monkey; fairly long, grizzled coat, variable in color but usually grayish black to blue-gray; black on legs, shoulders, and much of tail; underparts paler, with white throat patch; black hands and feet; brown face with long hair on cheeks; lives in troops up to 30 strong; spends most of the time in trees; 50 to 60 cm (20 to 24 in), plus tail longer than head and body length.

HABITAT: High forest; river-associated forest and forest fringes.

REGIONS: EC, KZN, MPG, ZIM

Plate 87d

Savannah Baboon
(also called Chacma Baboon)
Papio (ursinus) cynocephalus

ID: Large primate; long, naked, dog-like snout in adults; walks on ground on all fours; mainly terrestrial; uniformly gray to gray-brown with coarse hair; "broken" tail appearance; nearly always seen in troops, rarely solitary; 50 to 75 cm (20 to 30 in), plus short-haired tail about the same length.

HABITAT: Mountain and hill country; river-associated woodland and wooded savannah; rocky cliffs and tall trees essential for sleeping.

REGIONS: All

Plate 87e

Vervet Monkey
Chlorocebus aethiops

ID: Typical monkey appearance; grizzled gray hair (sometimes with a brownish tinge), except underparts are white; black face rimmed by white hair; dark-colored hands and feet; adult males have a distinctive, powder-blue scrotum; lives in troops of 20 or more; 40 to 55 cm (16 to 22 in), plus short-haired tail longer than head and body.

HABITAT: Savannah woodland and river-associated woodland.

REGIONS: All

a Thick-tailed Bushbaby
b Lesser Bushbaby
c Sykes' Monkey
d Savannah Babboon
e Vervet Monkey

Plate 88a

Pangolin
(also called Scaly Anteater, Temminck's Pangolin)
Manis temminckii

ID: Covered in large, brown, overlapping scales; almost like an animate pinecone; heavy body and tail; small head; small forelegs often held off ground; rolls into a ball when threatened; 40 to 55 cm (16 to 22 in); tail heavy and slightly shorter than body.

HABITAT: Open grassland, woodland on flats and in hills; both in low and high rainfall areas; ground-dweller; solitary; nocturnal.

REGIONS: FS, KZN, MPG, NC, LNW, NAM, BOT, ZIM

Plate 88b

Rock Hyrax
(also called Rock Dassie)
Procavia capensis

ID: Small and stocky; no tail; small rounded ears; soft, dense yellow-fawn to dark brown coat; paler fur patches above each eye and at ear base; erectile black hair patch in center of back; 45 to 60 cm (17.5 to 23.5 in).

HABITAT: Rocky areas; mountain ranges to isolated rocky outcrops; dry to wet areas.

REGIONS: All

Plate 88c

Smith's Red Rock Rabbit
Pronolagus rupestris

ID: Typical rabbit; shortish back legs; ears shorter than those of hares; rump and back legs bright red-brown; overall pinkish gray soft fur; tail short and fluffy, dark to red-brown with black tip; 38 to 54 cm (15 to 21 in).

HABITAT: Rocky areas, isolated outcrops to mountain ranges; high and low rainfall areas.

REGIONS: EC, FS, KZN, MPG, NC, WC, NAM, ZIM

Plate 88d

Cape Hare
Lepus capensis

ID: Typical hare with hind legs much longer than front; very long ears; short, fluffy tail, white and black; body hair fine and soft; grizzled and often reddish on sides; often not complete white underparts; length 38 to 46 cm (16 to 18 in).

HABITAT: Preference for dry, open habitat such as grassland and sparse scrub; seldom in cultivated fields.

REGIONS: EC, FS, MPG, NC, LNW, WC, NAM, BOT, ZIM

Plate 88e

Scrub Hare
Lepus saxatilis

ID: Typical hare with hind legs much longer than front; very long ears; short, fluffy tail, white and black; body hair fine, soft, and grizzled, gray or gray-brown above, white below; moves by series of jumps; 38 to 48 cm (15 to 19 in).

HABITAT: Woodland and areas with closed scrub cover wherever grass is present; commonly in cultivated areas; rarely in very open country.

REGIONS: All

a Pangolin

b Rock Hyrax

c Smith's Red Rock Rabbit

d Cape Hare

e Scrub Hare

Plate 89a

Southern Ground Squirrel
Xerus inauris

ID: A terrestrial squirrel; long, bushy, black-and white-tail often used as sunshade; only active during day; short, coarse hair, cinnamon-brown above with thin white stripe along each side of body, shoulder to thigh; underparts paler; ears very short; often sits erect; 20 to 25 cm (8 to 10 in), plus tail same length as head and body.

HABITAT: Open, arid areas with sparse vegetation cover.

REGIONS: EC, FS, NC, LNW, NAM, BOT

Plate 89b

Tree Squirrel
(also called Bush Squirrel)
Paraxerus cepapi

ID: Typical squirrel; small size; body and tail uniformly grayish or yellow-brown; overall grizzled appearance; spends much time on ground but always retreats to trees; 19 cm (7.5 in), plus bushy tail that is slightly shorter than the body.

HABITAT: Variety of woodland; not true forest.

REGIONS: MPG, LNW, NAM, BOT, ZIM

Plate 89c

Woodland Dormouse
Graphiurus murinus

ID: Small, squirrel-like; bushy tail; prominent, rounded ears; fur soft and gray to silvery gray in color; cheeks, lips, and underparts white or grayish white; usually seen in trees or buildings; length 9 cm (3.5 in).

HABITAT: Wooded savannah and bush country.

REGIONS: EC, FS, KZN, MPG, LNW, WC, NAM, BOT, ZIM

Plate 89d

Pouched Mouse
Saccostomus campestris

ID: Rounded, fat, "hamster-like" mouse; soft, silky, gray or grayish brown fur; underparts white; large cheek pouches for food transport; 10 cm (4 in), plus tail that is a third of total length.

HABITAT: All except high mountains and true desert; preference for sandy areas.

REGIONS: All

Plate 89e

Common Molerat
Cryptomys hottentotus

ID: Cylindrical body shape; large rounded head with pig-like snout, tiny eyes, and minute ear openings; prominent front teeth; short, flattened tail; fur soft, plain grayish fawn to dark brown; 13 cm (5 in).

HABITAT: Mainly sandy soils, also clays and loams; desert to high rainfall areas; flats to mountains; dwells underground.

REGIONS: All

a Southern Ground Squirrel

b Tree Squirrel

c Woodland Dormouse

d Pouched Mouse

e Common Molerat

Plate 90a

Giant Rat

Cricetomys gambianus

ID: A truly "king-size" typical rat; long, whip-like, naked tail, white towards tip; large, thin ears; fur soft and gray to gray-brown, paler underparts; short hair around eyes forms dark ring; 38 cm (15 in).

HABITAT: Forest and dense woodland; also well-vegetated gardens; nocturnal.

REGIONS: KZN, ZIM

Plate 90b

Dassie Rat

Petromys typicus

ID: Superficial squirrel-like appearance; fairly long tail hairy but not bushy; overall color grizzled gray to gray-brown, becoming darker towards the rump; underparts paler; head fairly large and flattened; ears small and rounded; 16 cm (6.3 in); to 250 g (8.8 oz).

HABITAT: Rocky areas only, including isolated outcrops; diurnal.

REGIONS: NC, NAM

Plate 90c

Springhare

Pedetes capensis

ID: Kangaroo-like appearance; long, powerful hindlimbs; short forelimbs used for digging; long, well-haired tail with black tip; ears quite long and pointed; dark eyes large; soft, yellowish fawn fur, belly paler; 40 cm (16 in).

HABITAT: Short grassland and scrub with grass; sandy soils; nocturnal.

REGIONS: EC, FS, MPG, NC, LNW, NAM, BOT, ZIM

Plate 90d

Greater Canerat

Thryonomys swinderianus

ID: Large size; stocky appearance with coat of coarse, dark brown speckled hair very loosely attached to the skin; short legs; underparts paler; 28 to 42 cm (11 to 16.5 in), plus tail that is less than one third total length.

HABITAT: Reedbeds and other dense vegetation near water.

REGIONS: EC, KZN, MPG, NAM, BOT, ZIM

Plate 90e

Southern Porcupine

Hystrix aufricaeaustralis

ID: Body covered with long black-and-white banded quills; very large; long crest of hairlike quills on top of head and neck, raised when stressed; large head, small black eyes; short tail armed with hollow quills; 65 to 85 cm (25.5 to 33.5 in).

HABITAT: Almost everything but prefers rocky country; strictly nocturnal.

REGIONS: All

a Giant Rat

b Dassie Rat

c Springhare

d Greater Canerat

e Southern Porcupine

 (*See also:* Rodents, p. 204)

Plate 91a

Four-striped Grass Mouse

Rhabdomys pumilio

ID: Typical mouse appearance; four distinct dark stripes running down back from nape to tail root; overall color russet-brown to gray-white (paler animals usually live in arid country); backs of rounded ears and often the snout are russet or yellowish brown; diurnal; 10 cm (4 in), plus sparsely haired tail about same length.

HABITAT: Almost all habitats as long as grass is present; desert to high rainfall areas.

REGIONS: All

Plate 91b

Acacia Rat

Thallomys paedulcus

ID: Fairly large arboreal mouse; tail noticeably longer than head and body; long, rounded, thin ears; dark ring around eyes; soft, pale gray to fawnish yellow upperparts; white underparts; 13 cm (5 in).

HABITAT: Mainly acacia trees in savannah woodland; dry to moist areas; lives in tree holes and emerges at night.

REGIONS: KZN, MPG, NC, LNW, NAM, BOT, ZIM

Plate 91c

Bushveld Gerbil

Tatera leucogaster

ID: Typical large mouse; soft fur; upperparts reddish brown; underparts white; longish tail has darkish line above; large hindlimbs and feet; ears longer than wide; large dark eyes; 13 cm (5 in).

HABITAT: Sandy soils in grassland and open woodland; lives in burrows in scattered colonies; nocturnal.

REGIONS: FS, KZN, MPG, NC, LNW, NAM, BOT, ZIM

Plate 91d

Brant's Whistling Rat

Parotomys brantsii

ID: Stocky build, with lightly haired tail shorter than head and body length; soft, grayish yellow to grayish brown fur; paler underparts; gives sharp, short whistling call when alarmed; 15 cm (6 in).

HABITAT: Arid, sparsely vegetated, sandy areas; lives in burrows in colonies; diurnal.

REGIONS: EC, FS, NC, WC, NAM, BOT

Plate 91e

Bush Karoo Rat

Otomys unisulcatus

ID: Robust and stocky; short tail; rounded ears; soft brown to grayish brown fur; 15 cm (6 in).

HABITAT: Arid areas with low scrub; constructs large surface nests of sticks under bushes; diurnal.

REGIONS: EC, NC, WC

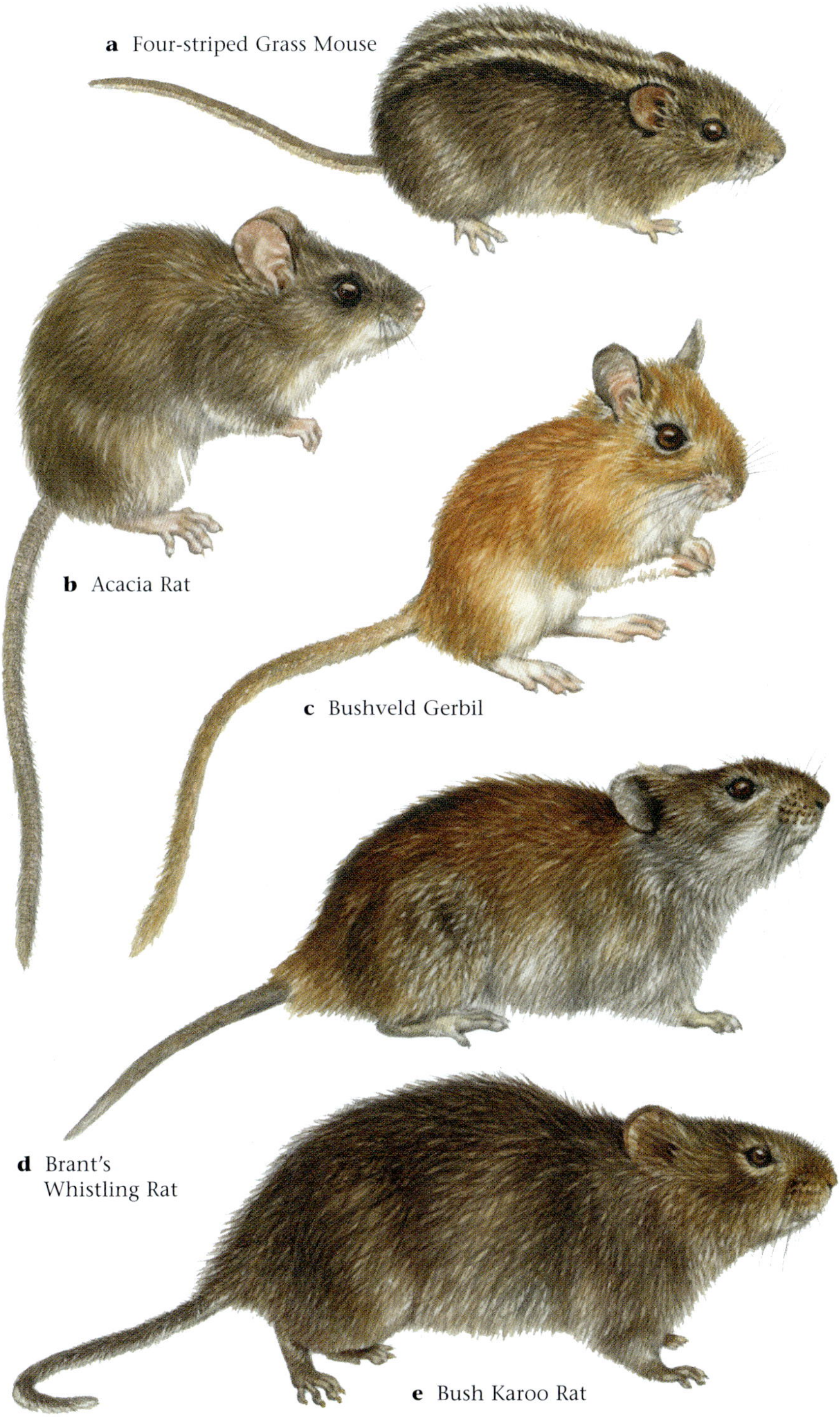
a Four-striped Grass Mouse
b Acacia Rat
c Bushveld Gerbil
d Brant's Whistling Rat
e Bush Karoo Rat

Plate 92a

Cape Fox
(also called Silver Fox)
Vulpes chama

ID: Fox-like appearance; long, bushy tail; silvery gray-grizzled upperparts; fawn-colored legs, face, and ears; long, pointed ears; 56 cm (22 in).

HABITAT: Open grassland and short, arid scrub areas; cultivated areas; seen alone or in pairs, always at night.

REGIONS: EC, FS, KZN, MPG, NC, LNW, WC, NAM, BOT

Plate 92b

Bat-eared Fox
Otocyon megalotis

ID: Fox-like appearance; very large ears; long, silvery gray coat; black legs; predominantly black, bushy tail; black and silvery facial mask; 52 to 56 cm (20.5 to 22 in).

HABITAT: Open, short scrub; open grassland and lightly wooded areas; lives in groups of 2 to 6; day- and night-active.

REGIONS: EC, FS, NC, LNW, WC, NAM, BOT, ZIM

Plate 92c

Side-striped Jackal
Canis adustus

ID: Dog-like appearance; the size of a Border collie; overall gray appearance; light and dark stripe on each side; tail with white tip, quite bushy; 66 to 80 cm (26 to 31.5 in).

HABITAT: Well-watered woodlands; solitary, occasionally in pairs.

REGIONS: KZN, MPG, NAM, BOT, ZIM

Plate 92d

Black-backed Jackal
Canis mesomelas

ID: Dog-like appearance; the size of a Border collie; overall reddish brown with dark, white-flecked saddle on back; mainly black tail that is about one-third of total length; 68 to 74 cm (27 to 29 in).

HABITAT: Avoids dense woodland and forest; high to low rainfall areas; seen singly or in pairs; mainly nocturnal.

REGIONS: All

Plate 92e

Wild Dog
Lycaon pictus

ID: Africa's largest member of the dog family; tall in leg; slender body; variably blotched black, white, and yellow-brown; large, dark, rounded ears; relatively short, bushy, and usually white-tipped tail; 75 to 110 cm (29.5 to 43 in).

HABITAT: Open country, grassy and lightly-treed savannah; always in packs.

REGIONS: KZN, MPG, LNW, NAM, BOT, ZIM

a Cape Fox
b Bat-eared Fox
c Side-striped Jackal
d Black-backed Jackal
e Wild Dog

Plate 93a

Cape Clawless Otter
Aonyx capensis

ID: Short, stout legs; finger-like toes; tail long and heavy at the base, tapering towards tip; short brown hair; looks black when wet; lips, chin, throat, and upper chest white; walks with back arched; 60 to 110 cm (23.5 to 43 in).

HABITAT: Most wetland types; penetrates dry areas along river beds.

REGIONS: All

Plate 93b

Honey Badger
(also called Ratel)
Mellivora capensis

ID: Typical badger form; stocky build; short and stout legs; short, hairy tail, black towards tip, often held erect when walking; silvery gray upperparts including top of head; black underparts, face, and legs; very small ears; 75 cm (29.5 in).

HABITAT: Almost all habitats but not commonly in forest; solitary or in pairs.

REGIONS: EC, KZN, MPG, NC, LNW, WC, NAM, BOT, ZIM

Plate 93c

Striped Polecat
(also called Zorilla)
Ictonyx striatus

ID: Small size; longish black-and-white hair; white hair in four stripes from top of head to base of tail; tail about half of total length, bushy and mainly white; white patch between eyes and one at base of each ear; short, rounded ears; 32 to 42 cm (12.5 to 16.5 in).

HABITAT: All habitats; usually solitary; nocturnal.

REGIONS: All

Plate 93d

Suricate
(also called Meerkat)
Suricata suricatta

ID: Small size; pale brown to gray-brown with several irregular, darker-colored bars across back; short-haired, reddish brown tail with black tip is slightly less than half total length; often stands on hind legs; 25 to 30 cm (10 to 12 in).

HABITAT: Open, dry, sparsely vegetated country; lives in groups; diurnal.

REGIONS: EC, FS, MPG, NC, LNW, WC, NAM, BOT

a Cape Clawless Otter

b Honey Badger

c Striped Polecat

d Suricate

Plate 94a

Slender Mongoose

Galerella sanguinea

ID: Small size; slender body, short legs; tail half total length, fairly bushy with black tip; tail often curved over back when running; fur gray, brown, or chestnut-orange; 27 to 35 cm (10.5 to 14 in).

HABITAT: Nearly all habitats, as long as there is adequate cover; solitary; diurnal.

REGIONS: FS, KZN, MPG, NC, LNW, NAM, BOT, ZIM

Plate 94b

Dwarf Mongoose

Helogale parvula

ID: Smallest mongoose in area; uniformly dark-brown, grizzled fur; at distance appears black; tail about half of total length; 20 cm (8 in).

HABITAT: Open woodland and grassland savannah; often in rocky areas; always seen in groups during the day.

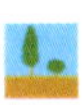

REGION: KZN, MPG, NAM, BOT, ZIM

Plate 94c

Banded Mongoose

Mungos mungo

ID: Small size; 10 to 12 dark brown or black transverse (across back) stripes on grayish to gray-brown background; tail fairly bushy and dark towards tip; ears short and rounded; 32 to 40 cm (12.5 to 15.5 in).

HABITAT: Different woodland types with good ground cover; lives in groups; diurnal.

REGIONS: KZN, MPG, LNW, NAM, BOT, ZIM

Plate 94d

Small Gray Mongoose

(also called Cape Gray Mongoose)

Galerella pulverulenta

ID: Small, grizzled gray mongoose; looks uniformly gray from a distance; feet black; 35 cm (14 in).

HABITAT: Forest to open scrub; requires some cover; solitary.

REGIONS: EC, FS, KZN, NC, WC, NAM

Plate 94e

Yellow Mongoose

Cynictis penicillata

ID: Small size; yellowish to grayish yellow fur; bushy tail has distinct white tip; chin, throat, and upper chest paler to white; eyes orange-brown; 22 to 35 cm (8.5 to 14 in)

HABITAT: Open grassland; semi-desert scrub; usually seen singly during the day.

REGIONS: EC, FS, KZN, NC, LNW, WC, NAM, BOT, ZIM

Plate 94f

White-tailed Mongoose

Ichneumia albicauda

ID: Large mongoose; white, bushy tail about one third the total length; coarse, shaggy, gray-brown coat; black legs; walks with rump higher than head; 55 to 100 cm (25 to 39 in).

HABITAT: Wooded savannah; solitary; nocturnal.

REGIONS: EC, FS, KZN, MPG, LNW, NAM, BOT, ZIM

a Slender Mongoose
b Dwarf Mongoose
c Banded Mongoose
d Small Gray Mongoose
e Yellow Mongoose
f White-tailed Mongoose

Plate 95a

Aardvark
(also called Antbear)
Orycteropus afer

ID: Large, stocky body; long pig-like snout; mule-like ears; powerful, tapering, kangaroo-like tail; walks with back arched; length 1 to 1.2 m (3.3 to 4 ft).

HABITAT: All habitats except true desert; strictly nocturnal.

REGIONS: All

Plate 95b

Aardwolf
Proteles cristatus

ID: Appearance of small hyena; shoulders higher than rump; pale buff background color with dark vertical stripes; black banding on upperparts of legs; feet, muzzle, and much of bushy tail black; long, pointed ears; long erectile mane on neck and back; 64 to 72 cm (25 to 28 in).

HABITAT: Most habitats, from arid to high rainfall areas; avoids forest.

REGIONS: All

Plate 95c

Brown Hyena
Parahyaena brunnea

ID: Large size; shoulders higher than rump; shaggy, dark brown coat; lighter colored on neck and shoulders; large head with long pointed ears; short, long-haired tail; 1.2 to 1.3 m (4 to 4.3 ft).

HABITAT: Desert and semi-desert, also open woodland and mountains.

REGIONS: FS, KZN, MPG, NC, LNW, NAM, BOT, ZIM

Plate 95d

Spotted Hyena
Crocuta crocuta

ID: Large size; shoulders stand higher than rump; short-haired, fawn-yellow to grayish coat with many dark brown spots and blotches; fairly large, rounded ears; short tail with coarse hair; 95 to 150 cm (3 to 5.1 ft).

HABITAT: Open country, also woodland and hilly areas; usually in groups.

REGIONS: KZN, MPG, NC, LNW, NAM, BOT, ZIM

a Aardvark

b Aardwolf

c Brown Hyena

d Spotted Hyena

Plate 96a

Small-spotted Genet

Genetta genetta

ID: Long, slender body and tail; short black legs; soft, off-white to grayish coat with numerous small dark brown to black spots and bars; tail black-ringed with white tip; black-and-white markings on face; 46 to 50 cm (18 to 20 in).

HABITAT: Desert fringes to high rainfall mountains; woodland, rocky hills; terrestrial and arboreal; nocturnal.

REGIONS: ALL

Plate 96b

African Civet

Civettictis civetta

ID: Large size; heavily built with long black legs; gray fur marked with black spots, blotches, and irregular stripes; bushy tail with white banding below and black tip; black, white, and gray facial markings; walks with back arched, head held low; 80 to 90 cm (31.5 to 35.5 in).

HABITAT: Open woodland, river-associated woodland; solitary; nocturnal.

REGIONS: KZN, MPG, LNW, NAM, BOT, ZIM

Plate 96c

Small Spotted Cat

(also called Black-footed Cat, Anthill Tiger)

Felis nigripes

ID: Small size; reddish fawn to yellow-gray with numerous dark brown and black spots and bars on body, head, and legs; fairly short, black-ringed, black-tipped tail; 34 to 47 cm (13.5 to 18.5 in).

HABITAT: Open and dry semi-desert areas with some cover; solitary; nocturnal.

REGIONS: EC, FS, NC, LNW, WC, NAM, BOT

Plate 96d

African Wild Cat

Felis sylvestris libyca

ID: Like domestic cat; fairly long legs; relatively long tail dark-ringed with black tip; sandy gray-brown to dark gray body marked with dark vertical stripes; legs ringed with black, brown, or gray; back of ears rich reddish brown; to 60 cm (23.5 in).

HABITAT: All habitats, wherever there is some cover; desert to high rainfall areas; solitary; nocturnal.

REGIONS: All

Plate 96e

Serval

Leptailurus serval

ID: Cheetah-like but smaller and much shorter, with black-banded and -tipped tail; large, rounded ears, the backs of which have black-and-white patches; yellowish fawn coat with many black spots and bars; 70 to 82 cm (27.5 to 32 in).

HABITAT: Near water in tall and mountain grassland, reedbeds, forest fringes.

REGIONS: KZN, MPG, LNW, NAM, BOT, ZIM

a Small-spotted Genet

b African Civet

c Small Spotted Cat

d African Wild Cat

e Serval

Plate 97a

Caracal

Caracal caracal

ID: Strongly built cat; tail less than one third total length; rump higher than shoulders; reddish fawn fur; long pointed ears, grizzled-black with black tuft at tip; black-and-white patches around eyes and mouth; 52 to 96 cm (20.5 to 40 in).

HABITAT: All major habitat types, high and low rainfall areas; solitary; nocturnal.

REGIONS: All

Plate 97b

Lion

Panthera leo

ID: Very large cat; short coat, reddish gray to pale tawny; adult males have long blonde or dark manes; tail less than half total length with black tip; males 1.5 to 2.3 m (4.9 to 7.5 ft), females 1.3 to 1.7 m (4.3 to 5.6 ft).

HABITAT: Desert fringe, open and wooded grassland, access always to shade and water; lives in groups.

REGIONS: KZN, MPG, NC, NAM, BOT, ZIM

Plate 97c

Leopard

Panthera pardus

ID: Large cat; gray-fawn to orange-russet coat, spotted on head, neck, and chest with rosettes, broken circles, and black spots; tail about half of total length, with rosette spots above and white tip; length 90 to 100 cm (35 to 39 in).

HABITAT: Desert fringe to dense forest; coastal plain to high mountains; solitary; mainly nocturnal.

REGIONS: EC, KZN, MPG, NC, LNW, WC, NAM, BOT, ZIM

Plate 97d

Cheetah

Acinonyx jubatus

ID: "Grayhound" of cat world; large size; slender with long legs; long, spotted and dark ringed, white-tipped tail; coat pale fawn to grayish brown, dotted with black, rounded spots; chin and throat white; black line ("tear mark") from inner corner of eye to corner of mouth; 1.2 to 1.4 m (4 to 4.6 ft).

HABITAT: Open grassland and woodland; mainly diurnal.

REGIONS: KZN, MPG, NC, LNW, NAM, BOT, ZIM

a Caracal

b Lion

c Leopard

d Cheetah

Plate 98a

Hippopotamus

Hippopotamus amphibius

ID: Large size; barrel-shaped body; massive, broad-muzzled head; short, stout legs; almost hairless skin, grayish black with some pink at skin folds; flattened tail; length 3 to 3.8 m (9.8 to 12.5 ft); shoulder 1.5 m (4.9 ft).

HABITAT: Permanent fresh water—rivers, lakes, swamps; adjacent grasslands.

REGIONS: EC, KZN, MPG, NAM, BOT, ZIM

Plate 98b

Hook-lipped Rhinoceros

(also called Black Rhinoceros)

Diceros bicornis

ID: Large size; short head held high when walking; short tail; two horns on face, longer one usually in front; large, pointed ears; almost naked, dark gray skin takes on soil color of area from mud bathing; length 2.8 to 3.6 m (9.2 to 11.8 ft); shoulder 1.6 m (5.3 ft).

HABITAT: Well-wooded country but not forest; some populations in semi-desert areas with bush stands.

REGIONS: EC, KZN, MPG, NC, NAM, BOT, ZIM

Note: This species is endangered, CITES Appendix I listed.

Plate 98c

Square-lipped Rhinoceros

(also called White Rhinoceros)

Ceratotherium simum

ID: Large size; massive head with broad, square muzzle; head held low; hump on neck; fairly large, pointed ears; two horns on face, front one longer; naked, gray skin; tail short; length 3.5 to 4 m (11.5 to 13.1 ft); shoulder 1.8 m (5.9 ft).

HABITAT: Short grass savannah, with some thick bush cover.

REGIONS: KZN, MPG, NAM, ZIM

Note: The northern race of this species is endangered, CITES Appendix I listed.

Plate 98d

African Elephant

Loxodonta africana

ID: Massive size; long trunk; huge, rounded ears; most animals carry tusks; almost hairless gray skin; tail fairly long with black tuft of hair at tip; length 3.1 to 5.8 m (10.2 to 19 ft); shoulder 2.5 to 4.0 m (8.2 to 13.1 ft).

HABITAT: Wherever there is sufficient water, food, and shade.

REGIONS: EC, KZN, MPG, NAM, BOT, ZIM

a Hippopotamus

b Hook-lipped (Black) Rhinoceros

c Square-lipped (White) Rhinoceros

d African Elephant

Plate 99a

Bushbuck

Tragelaphus scriptus

ID: Smallish; dark brown to bright chestnut with variable pattern of white spots on body; white patch on throat and lower neck; male has erectile mane down back; male has short, almost straight, sharp-pointed horns; length 1.16 to 1.4 m (3.8 to 4.6 ft); shoulder 70 to 80 cm (28 to 31 in).

HABITAT: River-associated woodland and bush close to water.

REGIONS: EC, KZN, MPG, LNW, WC, NAM, BOT, ZIM

Plate 99b

Nyala

Tragelaphus angasii

ID: Male slate-gray overall, lower legs yellow-brown; 8 to 14 vertical white stripes on sides; long mane of hair along back; long, shaggy fringe from throat to hind legs; bushy tail white below; narrow white line between eyes; shallowly spiraled horns; female's coat overall yellow-brown or bright chestnut, with up to 18 vertical white stripes on sides; male length 1.5 to 1.9 m (4.9 to 6.2 ft), female 1.3 to 1.5 m (4.3 to 4.9 ft); male shoulder 1.15 m (3.75 ft), female 97 cm (38 in).

HABITAT: Dry savannah woodland; lives in small groups, rams often solitary.

REGIONS: KZN, MPG, ZIM

Plate 99c

Greater Kudu

Tragelaphus strepsiceros

ID: Large and elegant; 6 to 10 vertical white stripes on the gray-brown sides; white band between eyes; ears large; male has long, spiraled horns; bushy tail brown above, white below; length 1.8 to 2.5 m (5.9 to 8.2 ft); shoulder 1.4 to 1.5 m (4.6 to 4.9 ft).

HABITAT: Woodland savannah; penetrates dry areas along wooded watercourses.

REGIONS: EC, FS, KZN, MPG, LNW, WC, NAM, BOT, ZIM

Plate 99d

Bushpig

Potamochoerus larvatus

ID: Pig-like; well-haired body gray-brown to reddish brown; head covered in shorter, grayish fawn hair; short tufts of hair at points of ears; thin tail always held down when running; length 92 cm to 130 cm (3 to 4.3 ft); shoulder 55 to 88 cm (22 to 35 in); piglets striped at birth (Warthog piglets are not).

HABITAT: Forest; dense bush; river-associated woodland; extensive stands of long grass and reedbeds; in small groups; mainly nocturnal.

REGIONS: EC, KZN, MPG, WC, NAM, BOT, ZIM

Plate 99e

Common Warthog

Phacochoerus africanus

ID: Pig-like appearance; light to dark gray, but because they wallow in mud, take on coloring of local soil; sparsely haired body; long-haired mane along back, raised when stressed; wart-like lumps on face; curved, upward-pointing tusks; thin, tufted-tipped tail held erect when running; length 75 cm to 130 cm (2.5 to 4.3 ft); shoulder 65 cm (26 in).

HABITAT: Savannah grass and lightly wooded country; strictly diurnal.

REGIONS: EC, KZN, MPG, NC, LNW, NAM, BOT, ZIM

F
a Bushbuck
M
d Bushpig
e Common Warthog
F
b Nyala
M
F
M
c Greater Kudu

Plate 100a

African Buffalo

Syncerus caffer

ID: Cow-like appearance; large, powerful build; short coat dark brown to reddish brown to black; massive "W"-shaped horns, especially so in bulls; large ears fringed with longish hair hang below horns; length 2.5 to 3.7 m (8.2 to 11.5 ft); shoulder 1.3 m (4.3 ft).

HABITAT: Open, well-grassed, woodland savannah.

REGIONS: EC, KZN, MPG, NAM, BOT, ZIM

Plate 100b

Common Eland

Ttragelaphus oryx

ID: Massive cow-like antelope; overall short, tawny-fawn coat; some gray on neck and face; tail with black tip; bulls have large neck flap (dewlap) and patch of longish, coarse hair on forehead; both sexes carry straight, tightly spiraled horns, those of male heavier; male length 2.4 to 3.6 m (7.9 to 11.8 ft), female 1.4 to 2.9 m (4.6 to 9.5 ft); shoulder 1.5 to 1.7 m (4.9 to 5.6 ft).

HABITAT: Semi-desert scrub to montane grasslands; prefers woodland savannah.

REGIONS: EC, KZN, MPG, NC, NAM, BOT, ZIM

Plate 100c

Giraffe

Giraffa camelopardalis

ID: World's tallest mammal; very long neck and legs; short-haired; lattice pattern of large, irregular, brown-shaded patches separated by paler bands; knob-like horns on top of head; longish tail with long brush at tip; length 3.6 to 4.5 m (11.8 to 14.8 ft); height 3.7 to 5.2 m (12.1 to 17.1 ft).

HABITAT: Dry savannah woodland.

REGIONS: KZN, MPG, NC, NAM, BOT, ZIM

Plate 100d

Plains Zebra

Equus quagga

ID: Stocky and horse-like; covered in black-and-white stripes; pale brown "shadow" stripes on white stripes; striping extends to underparts; length 1.8 to 2.5 m (5.9 to 8.2 ft); shoulder 1.3 m (4.3 ft).

HABITAT: Savannah grassland; open country; lives in herds.

REGIONS: KZN, MPG, LNW, NAM, BOT, ZIM

Plate 100e

Mountain Zebra

Equus zebra

ID: Horse-like; black-and-white stripes; lacks brownish "shadow stripes" on white stripes (like Plains Zebra has); striping to the hoofs; white belly; "gridiron" pattern on rump; throat with small skin flap (dewlap); in some regions, has broader white stripes on hindquarters; length 1.4 m (4.6 ft); shoulder 1.3 m (4.3 ft).

HABITAT: Mountainous areas and adjacent grass flats; lives in small groups.

REGIONS: EC, WC, NAM

a African Buffalo

b Common Eland

c Giraffe

d Plains Zebra

e Mountain Zebra

Plate 101a

Roan Antelope

Hippotragus equinus

ID: Large antelope with grayish brown coat (sexes similar in color and patterning); black-and-white facial markings; erect mane on neck, to shoulders; long, narrow ears with tuft at tip; both sexes with heavily ridged, back-curving horns; horns of female shorter and more slender; length 1.7 to 2.4 m (5.6 to 7.9 ft); shoulder 1.1 to 1.5 m (3.6 to 4.9 ft).

HABITAT: Open wooded grassland, with medium-length to tall grass.

REGIONS: MPG, NAM, BOT, ZIM

Plate 101b

Sable Antelope

Hippotragus niger

ID: Large antelope; strongly contrasting black (male) or reddish brown to chestnut (female) upperparts and legs, white belly and inner thighs; black-and-white facial markings; erect mane on neck and shoulders; long, ridged, back-curved horns, heavier and longer in male; length 1.8 to 2.1 m (5.9 to 6.9 ft); shoulder 1.1 to 1.5 m (3.6 to 4.9 ft).

HABITAT: Dry, open woodlands with medium-length to tall grass.

REGIONS: MPG, BOT, ZIM

Plate 101c

Southern Oryx

(also called Gemsbok)

Oryx gazella

ID: Heavily built with massive neck; distinct black-and-white facial markings; black markings on sides, legs, and rump; belly and inner thighs white; overall body color grayish fawn (sexes similar in color and patterning); long, black, horse-like tail; long, straight, rapier-like horns carried by male and female, those of latter longer but more slender; length 1.5 to 1.7 m (4.9 to 5.6 ft); shoulder 1.2 m (3.9 ft).

HABITAT: Open dry country, including open woodland, short-grassed plains, and sand dunes.

REGIONS: NC, LNW, NAM, BOT, ZIM

Plate 101d

Waterbuck

Kobus ellipsiprymnus

ID: Large, robust antelope; coarse, fairly shaggy, gray-brown coat; broad white ring around rump (in Zambia, subspecies *defassa* has a broad white patch on rump); white band runs from throat to base of ears; tail with black tuft at tip; male has long, heavily-ringed, forward-swept horns; length 1.7 to 2.4 m (5.6 to 7.9 ft); shoulder 1.2 m (3.9 ft).

HABITAT: Open dry country, including open woodland, short-grassed plains, and sand dunes.

REGIONS: NC, LNW, NAM, BOT, ZIM

a Roan Antelope
b Sable Antelope
M
F
c Southern Oryx
M
F
d Waterbuck

Plate 102a

Mountain Reedbuck

Redunca fulvorufula

ID: Smallest reedbuck; fairly long-haired, gray-fawn coat; white underparts; bushy tail with white underside that is visible when tail is held erect when running; male has short, ringed, forward-hooked horns; length 1.1 to 1.3 m (3.6 to 4.3 ft); shoulder 72 cm (28 in).

HABITAT: Mountains, rocky hill slopes, open grassy hillsides, all usually with scattered trees and bushes.

REGIONS: EC, KZN, MPG, NC, LNW

Plate 102b

Gray Rhebok

Pelea capreolus

ID: Medium-sized; thick, woolly, gray coat; white underparts, including short, bushy tail; white underside of tail is seen when running—often with tail held erect; ears long and narrow; nose somewhat bulbous; male has vertical, sharp-pointed horns; length 1 to 1.3 m (3.3 to 4.3 ft); shoulder 75 cm (29.5 in).

HABITAT: Open hill and mountain country.

REGIONS: EC, FS, KZN, MPG, NC, LNW, WC

Plate 102c

Impala

Aepyceros melampus

ID: Medium-sized, lightly built antelope; upperparts reddish fawn, paler on sides; white below; vertical black line on each buttock; black hair tuft above hoof on rear side of back leg; male has long, lyre-shaped, partly ringed horns (average 50 cm, 19 in, long); length 1.3 to 1.4 m (4.3 to 4.6 ft); shoulder 90 cm (35 in).

HABITAT: Open or light savannah woodland.

REGIONS: KZN, MPG, LNW, NAM, BOT, ZIM

Plate 102d

Red Lechwe

Kobus leche

ID: Medium-sized; rump higher than shoulders; coat chestnut above, white below; black lines on fronts of legs; male has long, strongly ridged, lyre-shaped horns; length 1.25 m (4.1 ft); shoulder 1 m (3.3 ft).

HABITAT: Floodplains and seasonal swamps; always close to water.

REGIONS: NAM, BOT

Plate 102e

Southern Reedbuck

Redunca arundinum

ID: Medium-sized; grayish fawn to brown coat, with white underparts; bushy tail white below; black line on surface of forelegs; only male has the forward-curved and ridged horns; length 1.2 to 1.55 m (3.9 to 5.1 ft); shoulder 80 to 95 cm (31.5 to 37.4 in).

HABITAT: Tall grass and reedbeds, usually close to water.

REGIONS: KZN, MPG, NAM, BOT, ZIM

a Mountain Reedbuck
M
F
b Gray Rhebok
c Impala
M
F
d Red Lechwe
M
F
e Southern Reedbuck
M
F

Plate 103a

Tsessebe

Damaliscus lunatus

ID: Much higher at shoulder than rump; much of body dark reddish brown with purplish sheen; lower legs yellowish brown; black facial blaze; both sexes have widely lyre-shaped and ridged horns; length 1.7 m (5.6 ft); shoulder 1.2 m (3.9 ft).

HABITAT: Open savannah woodland.

REGIONS: MPG, NAM, BOT, ZIM

Plate 103b

Red Hartebeest

Alcelaphus buselaphus

ID: Much higher at shoulder than rump; long, pointed head; very distinctive horns in both sexes resemble vertical, flat-handled bicycle handlebars; fawn to golden-brown coat with black on legs, face, and tail; pale fawn to almost white rump; length 1.8 m (5.9 ft); shoulder 1.3 to 1.5 m (4.3 to 4.9 ft).

HABITAT: Open savannah and open woodland.

REGIONS: NC, LNW, NAM, BOT, ZIM

Plate 103c

Blesbok and Bontebok

Damaliscus pygargus

ID: Medium-sized antelope with shoulders higher than rump. Two distinct subspecies: Bontebok is a glossy, rich dark brown, with white buttocks and lower legs and open, white facial blaze. Blesbok is reddish brown with no gloss, pale but not white buttocks, and white facial blaze usually broken between eyes by a narrow brown band. Both sexes in both subspecies have simple, ridged, lyre-shaped horns; length 1.4 m (4.6 ft); shoulder 90 to 95 cm (35 to 37 in).

HABITAT: Bontebok: scrub cover with grass. Blesbok: open grassland.

 (Bontebok)

 (Blesbok)

REGIONS: EC, FS, MPG, NC, WC

Plate 103d

Black Wildebeest

Connochaetes gnou

ID: Uniform dark brown coat, appears black at a distance; white, horse-like tail; white and black erect mane on neck to shoulders; large head; extensive patch of longish, coarse black hair on face; long hair on throat and chest; heavy "W"-shaped horns, those of female lighter; length 1.7 to 2.2 m (5.6 to 7.2 ft); shoulder 1.2 m (3.9 ft).

HABITAT: Open grassland and areas with low scrub cover.

REGIONS: EC, FS, KZN, MPG, NC

Plate 103e

Blue Wildebeest

(also called Brindled Gnu)

Connochaetes taurinus

ID: Shoulders higher than rump; coat overall dark gray with variable areas of brown; vertical darker stripes on neck and chest; erect mane, throat fringe, face and longish tail black (face brownish in youngsters); both sexes have shallow "W"-shaped horns, thicker at base; those of female lighter; length 2 to 2.3 m (6.6 to 7.5 ft); shoulder 1.3 to 1.5 m (4.3 to 4.9 ft).

HABITAT: Open savannah woodland, open short grassland.

REGIONS: KZN, MPG, NC, NAM, BOT, ZIM

a Tsessebe
b Red Hartebeest
c Blesbok
d Black Wildebeest
c Bontebok
e Blue Wildebeest

Plate 104a

Kirk's Dik-dik
(also called Damara Dik-dik)
Madoqua kirkii

ID: Very small; elongated, mobile nose; upperparts grayish yellow and grizzled; underparts paler; tuft of erectile hair on forehead; white ring around the eye; males have short, ridged, spike-like horns; length 59 to 71 cm (23 to 28 in); shoulder 38 cm (15 in).

HABITAT: Dense, dry woodland (with underbrush for hiding), often in association with rocky hills; solitary or in pairs.

REGIONS: NAM

Plate 104b

Cape Grysbok
Raphicerus melanotis

ID: Small, stout antelope; rufous-brown upperparts liberally sprinkled with white hairs; tail very short; large ears; ram has short, smooth, sharp-pointed horns (6 to 8 cm, 2.4 to 3.1 in, long); length 67 to 76 cm (26.5 to 30 in); shoulder 54 cm (21 in).

HABITAT: Thick scrub-bush sand dunes (Cape fynbos), hill and mountain slopes; fringes of agricultural land; solitary.

REGIONS: EC, WC

Plate 104c

Sharpe's Grysbok
Raphicerus sharpei

ID: Small, stoutly built; reddish brown upperparts liberally flecked with white hairs; underparts paler; male has short sharp, smooth horns (6 to 8 cm, 2.4 to 3.1 in, long); length 60 to 74 cm (23.5 to 29 in); shoulder 50 cm (20 in).

HABITAT: Low thicket and scrub, often adjacent to rocky hills and outcrops; solitary.

REGIONS: KZN, MPG, BOT, ZIM

Plate 104d

Klipspringer
Oreotragus oreotragus

ID: Small and stocky; coarse, dense, spiny hair; overall color yellow-brown to grayish yellow and grizzled; male has short, sharp-pointed, widely separated horns; walks on tips of hoofs; length 72 to 92 cm (28 to 36 in); shoulder 60 cm (23.5 in).

HABITAT: Rocky mountain and hill country, where they move easily over even the roughest slopes.

REGIONS: All

Plate 104e

Steenbok
Raphicerus campestris

ID: Small, elegant; general color reddish fawn, underparts white; very short tail same color as body; very large ears; male has short, sharp-pointed, vertical horns; length 70 to 85 cm (27.5 to 33.5 in); shoulder 50 cm (20 in).

HABITAT: Open grass, scrub, and lightly wooded areas, with some cover; mainly solitary.

REGIONS: EC, FS, KZN, MPG, NC, LNW, WC, NAM, ZIM

Plate 104f

Springbok
Antidorcas marsupialis

ID: Medium-sized; dark brown band separates fawn-brown upperparts from white underparts; white head with thin brown stripe from eye to mouth corner; both sexes have short, lyre-shaped, ridged horns, those of male much heavier; when jumping, reveals long white hairs on rump; length 85 cm to 1 m (33.5 to 39 in); shoulder 75 cm (29.5 in); the only gazelles in the region.

HABITAT: Open, arid, and semi-arid plains.

REGIONS: EC, FS, NC, LNW, WC, NAM, BOT

a Kirk's Dik-dik
b Cape Grysbok
d Klipspringer
c Sharpe's Grysbok
e Steenbok
f Springbok

Plate 105a

Blue Duiker

Cephalophus (Philantomba) monticola

ID: Very small; slate-gray to gray-brown to dark bluish brown coat, often with glossy sheen; short, bushy, black-and-white tail; very short horns in both sexes but often hidden in forehead crest; walks with arched back; length 52 to 70 cm (20.5 to 27.5 in); shoulder 35 cm (14 in).

HABITAT: Forests and dense stands of bush.

REGIONS: EC, KZN, WC, ZIM

Plate 105b

Red Duiker

Cephalophus natalensis

ID: Small size; uniformly glossy, rich reddish brown coat; very short black-and-white tipped tail; prominent crest of hair on top of head; both sexes have short, sharp-pointed horns, sloping backwards on plane of face; walks with arched back; length 70 to 98 cm (27.5 to 38.5 in); shoulder 43 cm (17 in).

HABITAT: Forest and dense woodland.

REGIONS: KZN, MPG

Plate 105c

Common Duiker

Sylvicapra grimmia

ID: Quite small, walks with straight back; uniform gray-brown to reddish yellow body color; pale to white underparts; narrow snout; short tail, black above, white below; crest of long hair on forehead; male has well-ringed, sharp-pointed horns; length 80 to 112 cm (31.5 to 44 in); shoulder 50 cm (20 in).

HABITAT: Scrub and bush-covered country; often close to human habitation; solitary.

REGIONS: All

Plate 105d

Oribi

Ourebia ourebi

ID: Largest of the "small" antelopes; hair on upperparts curly and overall rufous-yellow-orange; white underparts; short, black-tufted tail; male has erect, sharp-pointed horns; length 95 cm (37.5 in); shoulder 60 cm (23.5 in).

HABITAT: Open, short grassland with taller grass patches for cover.

REGIONS: EC, KZN, MPG, NAM, BOT, ZIM

Plate 105e

Cape Fur Seal

Arctocephalus pusillus

ID: Only resident, common seal in area; large size; back flippers under body on land, front flippers bent outwards from body; dark brown, grayish brown, or golden-brown short-haired coat; appears black when wet; young pups have black velvety coat; male to 2.2 m (7.2 ft), female to 1.6 m (5.3 ft).

HABITAT: Sea and shoreline.

REGIONS: NC, WC, NAM

a Blue Duiker

b Red Duiker

c Common Duiker

d Oribi

e Cape Fur Seal

SPECIES INDEX

Note: References to plate numbers are in **bold** type.

GENERAL INDEX

Explanation of habitat symbols (see Chapter 2 for some definitions):

 = Evergreen forest (includes coastal, river-associated, and higher elevation evergreen forests).

 = Deciduous woodland and savannah (includes all non-forest woodland types such as miombo, thornveld, mopane, and Kalahari sandveld).

 = Shrubland (includes fynbos and both karoo types).

 = Grassland (includes natural grasslands and agricultural lands such as pastures).

 = Desert and near-desert.

 = Inland wetlands (includes rivers, marshes, lakes, pans, estuaries, floodplains, impoundments).

 = Marine (includes ocean beaches, intertidal zone and open sea).

Regions (see Map 2, p. 22–23):

EC = Eastern Cape Province
FS = Free State
KZN = KwaZulu-Natal Province, Lesotho, Swaziland
MPG = Mpumalanga and Gauteng
NC = Northern Cape Province
LNW = Limpopo and North-West Provinces
WC = Western Cape Province
NAM = Namibia
BOT = Botswana
ZIM = Zimbabwe